The Grammar of Future Expressions in English

THE GRAMMAR OF
FUTURE EXPRESSIONS
IN ENGLISH

Naoaki Wada

KAITAKUSHA

Kaitakusha Co., Ltd.
5-2, Mukogaoka 1-chome
Bunkyo-ku, Tokyo 113-0023
Japan

The Grammar of Future Expressions in English

Published in Japan
by Kaitakusha Co., Ltd., Tokyo

Copyright © 2019
by Naoaki Wada

All rights reserved. No part of this publication may be reproduced, stored in a retrieval system, or transmitted, in any form or by any means, electronic, mechanical, photocopying, recording, or otherwise, without the prior permission of the copyright owner.

First published 2019

Printed and bound in Japan
by Hinode Printing Co., Ltd.

Cover design by Shihoko Nakamura

Preface

About two decades after the publication of my dissertation under the title *Interpreting English Tenses: A Compositional Approach*, I am still working on tense. It is something like a Möbius loop for me and I feel like I always gravitate to the "tense" fate. Included in it are "futures". In the year 2013, when I first encountered a new model of language use about the relation between grammar and pragmatics proposed by Yukio Hirose, I decided on my "future" project.

Since then, I have tried to develop the theory of tense proposed in that publication into a more comprehensive model which can cover a variety of phenomena concerning the future, i.e. a convergence area of tense and modality/mental attitudes/speech acts, drawing on the aforementioned model of language use as well as an advanced version of the theory about modality and speaker's mental attitudes adopted in my previous studies. I have been helped and supported by many people, including teachers, colleagues, friends, and students, without whom this book could not have been published. Some deserve special mention.

First of all, I would like to thank Yukio Hirose not only for providing insightful comments on and invaluable suggestions for this book, but also for discussing with me many linguistic topics as a colleague and giving me sound advice and heartfelt encouragement as a mentor. The developed model owes much to his latest theory, called *the Three-Tier Model of Language Use*, without which many of the phenomena taken up in this book would not have been considered. This book is in a sense a collaborative work with him.

Next, I am indebted to Jun-ya Watanabe. We have been collaborating with each other in the field of TAME (tense-aspect-modality-evidentiality) for more than ten years, during which we have exchanged comments on each other's studies. I have benefited much from him especially in comparing the English tense system with the French one.

Special thanks go to two Belgian linguists, Renaat Declerck and Bert Cappelle. A series of work on tense by Renaat inspired me to reconsider my model seriously in many respects and I adopted many ideas from his theory of tense in developing my own, to which his sound criticism and stimulating comments also contribute. Bert has been a friend of mine as well as a research collaborator since I was at KULAK (Katholieke Universiteit Leuven associatie Kortrijk) as a visiting scholar from September 2003 to July 2004. His comments and suggestions are insightful and he is always generous enough to spare time to talk with me about whatever topic I am interested in.

Furthermore, I need to thank all those who have discussed things with me about TAME and/or offered me encouragement. Not being able to name all of them, I would like to mention the following people in particular: Ronny Boogaart, Frank Brisard, Astrid de Wit, Naoyo Furukawa, Naoko Hayase, Yuko Horita, Michio Hosaka, Keita Ikarashi, Hidetake Imoto, Seizi Iwata, Theo Janssen, Nobuhiro Kaga, Masaru Kanetani, Fumitaka Kira, Satoru Kobayakawa, Hiroaki Konno, Kevin Moore, Yu-ichi Mori, Akiko Nagano, Minoru Nakau, Sadayuki Okada, Masao Okazaki, Mai Osawa, Toshi-aki Oya, Raphael Salkie, Kenji Sato, Masaharu Shimada, Kazuhiko Tanaka, Kazumi Taniguchi, Atsuro Tsubomoto, Taiko Tsuchihira, Johan van der Auwera, Norio Yamada, and Haruhiko Yamaguchi.

Finally, I would like to thank Masaru Kawata of Kaitakusha Publishing Co. for his patient editorial work and Haruka Shimura for helping to prepare the index.

This publication is supported in part by JSPS KAKENHI Grant Number JP19HP5057.

Naoaki Wada

Tsukuba
July 2019

Contents

Preface .... **v**

Chapter 1   Introduction **1**
  1.1.   The Background to My Theory of Tense 1
  1.2.   Comparison with Other Theories and the Spirit of My Framework ··· 11
  1.3.   Organization 16

PART I
THEORETICAL FRAMEWORK

Chapter 2   A Compositional Theory of Tense ································· **21**
  2.1.   Introduction 21
  2.2.   Tense Structure Level and Tense Interpretation Level ············· 21
  2.3.   Tense Structure 24
  2.4.   Tense Interpretation Process ··· 28
    2.4.1.   Fusion of the Speaker's T(emporal)-Viewpoint and
         Consciousness ··· 28
    2.4.2.   Viewpoint of Situation Description and Time of Orientation ··· 32
    2.4.3.   Various Factors Related to Tense Interpretation ····················· 36
      2.4.3.1.   Time Adverbials ·· 36
      2.4.3.2.   Auxiliaries ··· 38
      2.4.3.3.   Aspect and Situation Type ································ 41
      2.4.3.4.   Modality ··· 46

vii

viii　　　*The Grammar of Future Expressions in English*

      2.4.3.5.　Linguistic Environments ⋯⋯⋯⋯⋯⋯⋯⋯⋯⋯⋯ 48
    2.4.4.　Two Types of Event Time ⋯⋯⋯⋯⋯⋯⋯⋯⋯⋯⋯ 50
    2.4.5.　Temporal Focus ⋯⋯⋯⋯⋯⋯⋯⋯⋯⋯⋯⋯⋯⋯ 51
  2.5.　Conclusion and Theoretical Orientation ⋯⋯⋯⋯⋯⋯⋯ 53

Chapter 3　Modality, Mental Attitudes, and Related Phenomena ⋯⋯ 57
  3.1.　Introduction ⋯⋯⋯⋯⋯⋯⋯⋯⋯⋯⋯⋯⋯⋯⋯⋯⋯ 57
  3.2.　A Diversity of Studies on Modality ⋯⋯⋯⋯⋯⋯⋯⋯⋯ 59
    3.2.1.　Definition ⋯⋯⋯⋯⋯⋯⋯⋯⋯⋯⋯⋯⋯⋯⋯ 59
    3.2.2.　Classification ⋯⋯⋯⋯⋯⋯⋯⋯⋯⋯⋯⋯⋯⋯ 60
    3.2.3.　Type of Analysis ⋯⋯⋯⋯⋯⋯⋯⋯⋯⋯⋯⋯⋯ 62
  3.3.　Subjectivity and Objectivity of Modality and Modals ⋯⋯⋯ 63
  3.4.　Modality as Speaker's Mental Attitude and Semantic
     (De)Composition of Sentential Utterances ⋯⋯⋯⋯⋯⋯⋯ 65
  3.5.　Semantic (De)Composition of Sentential Utterances and
     the Three-Tier Model of Language Use ⋯⋯⋯⋯⋯⋯⋯⋯ 73
  3.6.　How to Treat Modal Phenomena ⋯⋯⋯⋯⋯⋯⋯⋯⋯⋯ 78
  3.7.　Subjective and Objective Use of Modality as Speaker's
     Mental Attitude ⋯⋯⋯⋯⋯⋯⋯⋯⋯⋯⋯⋯⋯⋯⋯⋯ 84
  3.8.　Modally Unmarked Forms and Assertive Modality ⋯⋯⋯⋯ 87
  3.9.　Concluding Remarks ⋯⋯⋯⋯⋯⋯⋯⋯⋯⋯⋯⋯⋯⋯ 92

Chapter 4　Tense Interpretation and Temporal Structures ⋯⋯⋯⋯ 95
  4.1.　Introduction ⋯⋯⋯⋯⋯⋯⋯⋯⋯⋯⋯⋯⋯⋯⋯⋯⋯ 95
  4.2.　The Simple Present Form ⋯⋯⋯⋯⋯⋯⋯⋯⋯⋯⋯⋯⋯ 96
    4.2.1.　Introductory Remarks ⋯⋯⋯⋯⋯⋯⋯⋯⋯⋯⋯ 96
    4.2.2.　The Polysemy of the Simple Present Form: A Variety of
       Uses/Functions ⋯⋯⋯⋯⋯⋯⋯⋯⋯⋯⋯⋯⋯⋯ 97
  4.3.　The Present Perfect Form ⋯⋯⋯⋯⋯⋯⋯⋯⋯⋯⋯⋯⋯ 108
    4.3.1.　Introductory Remarks ⋯⋯⋯⋯⋯⋯⋯⋯⋯⋯⋯ 108
    4.3.2.　Four Basic Uses ⋯⋯⋯⋯⋯⋯⋯⋯⋯⋯⋯⋯⋯ 108
  4.4.　Motivating the Polysemous Relationship among the Semantic
     Uses of a Tense Form with the Setting up of Temporal Structures ⋯ 118
  4.5.　Concluding Remarks ⋯⋯⋯⋯⋯⋯⋯⋯⋯⋯⋯⋯⋯⋯ 120

Contents   ix

PART II
APPLICATIONS

Chapter 5 *Will* ·· **125**
  5.1. Introduction ··· 125
  5.2. Uses and Functions of *Will*-Sentences ························· 128
  5.3. Toward Constructing the Temporal Structures of *Will*-Sentences ······ 130
    5.3.1. Tense Structure ··· 130
    5.3.2. Basic Temporal Structures ···································· 132
    5.3.3. The Core Meaning of *Will* ·································· 134
  5.4. Analysis ··· 137
    5.4.1. The Volitional Use ·· 138
    5.4.2. The Predictive-Future Use ···································· 148
    5.4.3. The Simple-Future Use ·· 151
    5.4.4. The Predictive-Present Use ··································· 154
    5.4.5. The Characteristic-Behavior Use ···························· 157
    5.4.6. Speech Act Uses ·· 160
    5.4.7. Conditional Clauses ·· 163
  5.5. The Relationship among the Temporal Structures Associated
        with the Semantic Uses of *Will*-Sentences ·················· 171
  5.6. Comparisons between *Will* and the French Simple Future ··········· 176
    5.6.1. Similarities and Differences ································· 176
    5.6.2. Tense Structure and Basic Temporal Structures of Simple
            Future Sentences in French ··································· 177
    5.6.3. Explanation ·· 180
      5.6.3.1. Temporal Clauses ··· 180
      5.6.3.2. Compatibility with Present Time Adverbials ·················· 181
      5.6.3.3. Present Time Reference ································· 182
      5.6.3.4. Indirect Speech Complements ························· 183
      5.6.3.5. Similarities ·· 187
  5.7. Concluding Remarks ·· 188

Chapter 6 *Be Going To* ·· **191**
  6.1. Introduction ··· 191
  6.2. Uses and Functions of BGT-Sentences ·························· 192
  6.3. Toward Constructing the Basic Temporal Structure of
        BGT-Sentences ··· 194

6.3.1.	Tense Structure and Characteristics of the Unit *Be Going To* ···	194
6.3.2.	Basic Temporal Structure ·················	196
6.4.	Analysis ···················	202
6.4.1.	The Typical Uses ···············	202
6.4.2.	The Immediate-Future Use ·············	210
6.4.3.	Semantic Bleaching and Derivative Uses ···········	212
6.4.4.	The Simple-Future Use ············	216
6.4.5.	Present Reference Uses ···············	219
6.4.6.	Speech Act Uses ···············	224
6.5.	The Relationship among the Temporal Structures Associated with the Semantic Uses of BGT-Sentences ··············	225
6.6.	Comparison between BGT-Sentences and *Will*-Sentences ··········	227
6.6.1.	Near Future, State Verbs ·············	227
6.6.2.	Volition ···············	229
6.6.3.	Ellipticality ···············	231
6.6.4.	Conditional Sentences ··············	233
6.6.5.	The Past Tense ···············	241
6.7.	Concluding Remarks ·················	249

Chapter 7　The Present Progressive ···············　**253**

7.1.	Introduction ···············	253
7.2.	Linguistic Characteristics Concerning PPF-Sentences ··············	254
7.3.	Toward Constructing the Basic Temporal Structure of PPF-Sentences ·················	256
7.3.1.	Tense Structure ···············	256
7.3.2.	Basic Temporal Structures ··············	257
7.3.3.	The Dual Structure of PPF-Sentences: In Comparison with BGT-Sentences ··············	269
7.4.	Explanation ··············	273
7.4.1.	PPF-Sentences ···············	273
7.4.2.	Present Progressive Sentences with Future Time Reference Other Than PPF-Sentences ·············	286
7.4.3.	The Past Tense ···············	288
7.5.	Concluding Remarks ·················	291

Contents   xi

Chapter 8   The Simple Present ···································· **293**
  8.1. Introduction ·· 293
  8.2. Uses and Functions of Simple Present Sentences with
        Future Time Reference ·· 294
  8.3. Temporal Structures of Simple Present Sentences with
        Future Time Reference and Their Analysis ···················· 295
    8.3.1. The Fixed-Future Use ···································· 296
    8.3.2. The Simple-Future Use ·································· 301
    8.3.3. The Future-Reference-in-Subordinate-Clause Use ·········· 303
    8.3.4. The "Note" Use ··· 307
    8.3.5. The Immediate-Future Use ······························ 308
    8.3.6. The "Instruction-Giving" Use and the "Either-Or" Use ····· 310
    8.3.7. The Stage-Direction Use ································· 314
  8.4. Concluding Remarks ·· 317

Chapter 9   *Be About To* ·· **319**
  9.1. Introduction ·· 319
  9.2. Linguistic Phenomena of BAT-Sentences ······················ 320
  9.3. Toward Constructing the Temporal Structures of BAT-Sentences ··· 325
    9.3.1. Combination Patterns of Constituents of BAT-Sentences and
            BGT-Sentences ·· 325
    9.3.2. Temporal Structures of BAT-Sentences ···················· 328
  9.4. Analysis ·· 334
    9.4.1. The Present Tense ·· 334
    9.4.2. The Past Tense ·· 338
      9.4.2.1. Environmental Characteristics of Descriptive Narrative
                Parts ·· 338
      9.4.2.2. BGT-Sentences ······································ 341
      9.4.2.3. BAT-Sentences ······································ 344
      9.4.2.4. Compatibility of BAT-Sentences with Time Adverbials
                Referring to the Future-in-the-Past ·················· 351
  9.5. Concluding Remarks ·· 353

Chapter 10   The Future Progressive ······························ **355**
  10.1. Introduction ··· 355
  10.2. Linguistic Facts to be Explained ······························ 356
    10.2.1. Three Uses of WBI-Sentences and Their Characteristics ····· 356

| 10.2.2. | Critique of Previous Studies | 361 |

10.3. Temporal Structures of the Three Uses of WBI-Sentences ········ 366

    10.3.1. Temporal Structure of the Future-Progressive Use ·············· 366

    10.3.2. Temporal Structure of the Future-as-a-Matter-of-Course Use ························· 369

    10.3.3. Temporal Structure of the Inferential Present-Progressive Use ························· 379

10.4. Comparison of (the Future-as-a-Matter-of-Course Use of) WBI-Sentences with Other Future Expressions ···················· 381

    10.4.1. Comparison with *Will*-Sentences ····························· 381

    10.4.2. Comparison with PPF-Sentences ···························· 385

10.5. Concluding Remarks ······································· 388

Chapter 11 Conclusion ······································· **391**

References ····························· **397**

Index ····························· **417**

THE GRAMMAR OF FUTURE EXPRESSIONS IN ENGLISH

Chapter 1

Introduction

1.1. The Background to My Theory of Tense

Languages have their own systems of describing temporal phenomena. In very many languages, tense, often defined as "grammaticalized expression of location in time" (Comrie (1985: 9)), plays a crucial role in such systems. However, how to treat it differs from linguist to linguist. For example, some linguists say that tense is represented by tense inflection (e.g. Smith (1978, 1997), Quirk et al. (1985)), but others say that it is represented not only by tense inflection but also by tense auxiliaries (e.g. Wekker (1976), Declerck (1991a, 1991b, 1997, 2006)).[1] For those who take the former position, only present and past tenses, as in (1a), are tenses, but for those who take the latter position, *will* (or *shall*) is also a tense morpheme (auxiliary) and represents future tense, as illustrated by (1b).[2]

(1) a. She {plays / played} the flute.
　　b. She will play the flute.

In either position, the term *tense* is usually used to refer to a tense form, but can be used as expressing a temporal meaning associated with it. In (1a), for example, the term *present tense* or *past tense* not only represents the present or past tense form, but is also used to refer to present time or past time. Given this, if we take the position that *will* is a future tense morpheme, the term *future tense* is used not only to designate the form with *will* but also to refer to

---

[1] This difference is closely related to whether *will* is a modal auxiliary or tense morpheme (auxiliary). In this book, *will* is treated as a modal auxiliary. With respect to how to treat it and arguments for that treatment, we will consider them in Chapter 3.

[2] In this and the following chapters, for the reason to be stated in note 1 of Chapter 5, I regard future *shall* as included in the reference range of future *will*.

1

future time, as in (1b).

The definition of tense often involves reference to the time of utterance, i.e. speech time, as deictic center (e.g. Lyons (1977: 678), Kortmann (1991: 15)). However, tense can be used to indicate the temporal relationship of a target situation to a base time (i.e. a "vantage point" from which to look at and/or pay attention to the situation at a time or during a time interval) other than speech time.[3] Tenses representing the temporal relationship between the target situation and speech time are called absolute tenses, while tenses representing the temporal relationship between the target situation and a base time other than speech time are called relative tenses (e.g. Comrie (1985), Declerck (2006)).

(2) a. Mary said that she was tired.   (Enç (1996: 350))
    b. Tomorrow, Frances will say that she was absent today.
                                        (Declerck (1991b: 161))
    c. John will say that Mary is upset.   (Enç (1996: 352))

For a better understanding, consider, first, (2a). The main clause verb *said* is an absolute past tense both formally and semantically. In contrast, on one reading of the subordinate clause verb *was*, the past form can represent a simultaneous relationship to the time of the main clause (cf. Enç (1996: 350)); the *was* in question is formally past tense because of the so-called sequence-of-tenses rule but is semantically present tense (in formal semantics, it is sometimes considered a "zero" tense), and is often referred to as a relative past tense (Declerck (1991a, 1991b, 2006)).

This *was* makes a contrast with the subordinate clause verb *was* in (2b). The latter represents an anterior relationship to the time of the main clause as the base time located in the future (i.e. the time of Frances's utterance) and is also regarded as a relative past tense.[4] Similarly, the base time for the present form *is* in (2c) is the time of the main clause located in the future (i.e. the time of John's utterance); the *is* in question represents a simultaneous relationship to the latter and is thus regarded as a relative present tense. Examples (2b) and (2c) show that even the choice of tense form can be based on a base time other than speech time.

From the observations about (2), we cannot say that the time information

---

[3] In this book, the term *situation* covers whatever is described by a verb (phrase) or clause including it (e.g. an action, event, state of affairs).

[4] Declerck calls such a past tense a "pseudo-absolute past tense" because it semantically represents an anterior relationship, as does an absolute past tense like *said* in (2a).

Chapter 1 Introduction

represented by tense morphemes always involves reference to speech time, even if we restrict them to verbal inflections. However, if we regard the deictic center as the base time with respect to which tense forms (i.e. verbs with a present or past tense inflection) are chosen, then the deictic center is not necessarily restricted to speech time.[5] In this case, we can still say that tense involves reference to the deictic center. A question, then, arises as to how the notion of deictic center is defined and what it theoretically means. We therefore need to explore a theoretical framework within which the deictic center is systematically defined, whereby we can deal with cases where the base time for the choice of tense form differs from the base time for evaluating or calculating temporal meanings as well as cases where the base time for the choice of tense form is a time point other than speech time, as we saw above.[6]

To this end, I have proposed elsewhere (Wada (2001a)) a framework which distinguishes two levels of time information, i.e. information concerning tense forms and information concerning temporal meanings, whereby one can treat the two types of time information separately, but in a related way.[7] The former level of time information relates to the schematic, or abstract, meaning of tense forms, based on which the speaker (i.e. the "chooser" of tense forms) chooses a tense form. The latter level relates to how to interpret tense forms, including how to determine the base time for the choice of tense form on the time line and the temporal value (including the temporal relation between the base time and the time of the situation involved, aspectual information, modification by time adverbials). As we will see in the next chapter, the former level corresponds to a tense level concerning grammatical time information and the deictic center at this level serves as the center of grammatical time; on the other hand, the latter level corresponds to a tense level concerning cognitive time information, including real, possible, or hypothetical time information, and the deictic center at this level is speech time, i.e. the center of cognitive time.

We now need to clarify how this framework treats future *will*. Within this framework, *will* is not a future tense morpheme, but a modal auxiliary verb (modal for short) with an implicit present tense morpheme. The reason for

---

[5] Such a base time is sometimes called "temporal zero-point" in the literature (e.g. Declerck (1991a, 1991b, 2006)).

[6] For the distinction in terminology between the two types of base times in my theory, see Section 2.2.

[7] As stated in the Introduction of Wada (2001a), the basic parts of the framework owe much to Nakau (1992, 1994). I also adopted many useful notions from other semantic analyses, especially a series of studies by Declerck, in constructing the framework.

this is that *will* is in a paradigmatic relationship to *would*, i.e. its past-tense counterpart in form, and behaves in a similar fashion to modals such as *may*, *can*, and *must* from a morpho-syntactic and semantic point of view (see Wada (2001a: Ch.1) for details).[8]

One might argue that *will* is future-time-oriented while other modals like *may* are present-time-oriented, and viewing *will* as a present tense modal may not explain why in most (at least very many) cases it refers to the future. However, to regard *will* as a present tense modal does not necessarily mean that sentences containing *will* cannot refer to a future situation. As implied above, my framework distinguishes the processes of tense-form choice and temporal value determination. Besides, it adopts a system in which the temporal reference of non-finite forms is independent of that of finite forms (cf. Nakau (1992, 1994), Janssen (1994, 1996)). Consider, for example, (3), where the sentences containing *will* and *may* as present tense modals both refer to a future situation.

(3) a.   Susan will bring her Finnish friend to the party.   (Enç (1996: 356))
    b.   Susan may bring her Finnish friend to the party.   (Enç (1996: 356))

In these sentences, it is the non-finite part (i.e. bare infinitive) that refers to future time; the finite part (i.e. modal) refers to the present. Sentences including a present tense modal can therefore systematically describe future situations. As for why *will* shows a strong inclination toward future time reference, I argue that it is mainly due to the core meaning of *will* as "high probability", which has an affinity for future time reference. We will see this point in some detail in Chapter 5.

In most studies on tense, the notion tense is only related to finite verbs, non-finite verbs being regarded as tenseless (e.g. Declerck (1991a, 1991b, 2006)). However, if we follow Comrie's (1985: 9) definition of tense—observed above—there is no a priori reason that non-finite verbs are excluded from tense forms.[9] Non-finite forms can also be grammaticalized expressions of location in time. Besides, as we saw above, tense does not necessarily involve reference to speech time as deictic center, and from this point of view,

---

[8] In Chapter 5, we will see how *will* as a modal works in my tense-interpretation system, which may also support my position that *will* is a modal.

[9] Comrie's definition of tense as given in the main text might enable us to regard the auxiliary *will* as a tense marker (e.g. Declerck (1991a, 1991b, 2006)). However, for the reasons given in the text and in Wada (2001a: Ch.1), I regard *will* as a modal. See also Huddleston (1995), Enç (1996), Klinge (2005), among others, which lend support to my position.

too, non-finite verbs are not excluded from tense forms.

It seems to me that one of the reasons why most linguists regard non-finite verbs as tenseless is that non-finite verbs do not express any fixed temporal value by themselves, but finite verbs do, even in the case of the relative tense interpretation. For example, the finite verbs *was* and *is* in (2b, c) above express, respectively, the temporal relations of anteriority and simultaneity with respect to the time of the main clause; by contrast, non-finite verbs can indicate any time relationship, namely, they do not express any fixed temporal value. Thus, the present participle expresses simultaneity (e.g. (4a)), anteriority (e.g. (4b)), and posteriority (e.g. (4c)) with respect to the time of the main clause.

(4) a. Trembling with fear, she recoiled into the bedroom.

(Declerck (1991a: 456))

   b. Opening the closet, he took out a bottle of whisky.

(Declerck (1991a: 456))

   c. The paint dripped onto the floor, completely ruining the fitted carpet.

(Declerck (1991a: 456))

From these observations, one might conclude that the temporal value of the present participle is not fixed by itself but determined depending on the temporal value of the finite verb and the context.

However, we have an intuition that the present participle is more or less related to the notion of simultaneity. In fact, De Smet and Heyvaert (2011: 495) state that like adjectives, present participles express states of affairs and thus simultaneity with respect to a reference point. In view of this, we may well be able to view the present participles in (4b) and (4c) as representing simultaneity in its broad sense, i.e. what Declerck calls "sloppy simultaneity". In fact, the distance between the two times is not so great. If we apply the distinction between the two levels of time information mentioned above to the temporal interpretation of non-finite forms like present participles, then we may assume that the present participle has simultaneity as its grammatical time value, which is represented by the present participle marker *-ing*, and what type of cognitive (real) time value it denotes depends on the situation type described by the verb (phrase) involved, the characteristics of the linguistic environment in which it occurs, and the contextual information involved.

Within my framework, a necessary condition for a verb or predicate to be regarded as a tense form is that it expresses a temporal relationship to a reference point. Given this condition, not only the present participle, but also the past participle, gerund, (*to-*)infinitive are tense forms.[10] Furthermore, even finite forms sometimes do not seem to have their own temporal meanings and are nevertheless still treated as tense forms. For example, as we saw above, *was* in (2a), when interpreted as formally past tense but semantically present tense, does not have any temporal value in some formal semantics approaches. For another example, the present forms used in synopses and stage directions are sometimes considered to show 'tenseless' uses (e.g. Huddleston and Pullum (2002: 129)).

From these observations, non-finite predicates (verbs) are also tense forms and non-finite markers represent temporal relations with respect to a reference point, i.e. relative time relations. Under this view, like the present and past tense morphemes, the present participle morpheme *-ing* is also a tense morpheme in that it contributes to constructing temporal relations. Although tense inflections and non-finite markers in English differ with respect to whether or not they are integrated with such deictic notions as person, number and mood, they both have their own grammatical time values and are therefore seen as tense morphemes. In this way, the present framework can treat temporal phenomena of finite and non-finite forms from a unified point of view.

One major merit of this framework is that it can, in a unified way, treat Japanese finite predicates whose tense morphemes are not integrated with the grammatical categories of deixis (i.e. person, number, mood) in the way English finite verbs are. Japanese finite predicates, as in (5), are classified into the same category as English non-finite verbs in terms of the type of tense morpheme, because, for example, Japanese finite predicates and English non-finite verbs do not agree with the person of the grammatical subject.

---

[10] In this connection, Williams (2002a: 132) observes that non-finite *-ing* forms (present participles) are used in sports commentary contexts, as in (i):

    (i) a. Rafter marching to the Royal Box end.   (Williams (2002a: 132))
        b. Ivanisevic serving ... off the top of the net.   (Williams (2002a: 132))

Because these sentences refer to ongoing situations in front of the reporter's eyes, the present participles in question represent temporal values. In these cases, the reference point is speech time and the present participles express simultaneity relative to speech time.

Williams (2002a: 133) further states that *to*-infinitives (non-finite forms) used in sports commentaries or newspapers' headlines explicitly represent a temporal relation, i.e. posteriority relative to speech time as reference point.

    (ii) a. Rafter to serve with new balls here.   (Williams (2002a: 133))
        b. IMF and World Bank to review meetings.   (Williams (2002a: 133))
        c. Cricket: Subba Row to retire next year.   (BNC A2S)

These examples lead support to the position that (at least some) non-finite forms have their own temporal values.

Chapter 1   Introduction   7

(5)   {Watasi / Kanozyo}-wa   furuuto-o   kanade-{ru / ta}.
       {I / she}-TOP   flute-ACC   play-{PRES / PAST}
       '{I / she} {play(s) / played} the flute.'

From this point of view, I have analyzed a number of temporal phenomena in English and Japanese in a unified way. For details, see, e.g. Wada (2009a, 2011b).

Let us now move to how to represent temporal semantics within my framework. Since Reichenbach (1947), one of the commonest ways to do so is to combine temporal parameters, usually three parameters, i.e. the point of the speech (speech time), the point of the event (event time), and the point of reference (reference time), with the help of the notions "dissociation" and "co-incidence".

As for the point of reference, it has been treated differently from linguist to linguist (partly because Reichenbach himself did not define it clearly). One such treatment is to regard it as an evaluation time, i.e. a time with respect to which one evaluates the truth value of the situation involved (e.g. Michaelis (1998), Partee (1973, 1984), Smith (1978, 1997), Sawada (2006)).

However, the point of reference in this sense is not reflected in the temporal semantics of tense forms within my framework. The information represented by the temporal semantics of tense forms includes the temporal relation between the event time (i.e. the time at or during which the situation involved obtains or occurs) and the time of orientation (i.e. the base time, or a vantage point from which to evaluate or calculate (the position of) the event time on the time line), the degree of specificity (i.e. the degree of connection between the situation involved and the time line), aspectual information (i.e. whether the situation involved is seen in its entirety (perfective aspect) or as incomplete or in progress (imperfective aspect)). The evaluation of the truth value of the situation is not directly relevant.[11]

A major reason for the exclusion of evaluation time from the temporal semantics is that we usually cannot evaluate the truth value of some sentences. For example, a performative sentence like *I name this ship Yamato*—regarded as one use of the simple present—is considered irrelevant to truth-value evaluation. We cannot use the point of reference as evaluation time to describe the temporal semantics of this type of sentence. Moreover, in my theo-

---

[11] This treatment does not necessarily imply that the evaluation time is irrelevant to the temporal interpretation of a given tense form. Within my framework, it can affect the tense-interpretation process if necessary (see Chapter 2).

ry of tense, modal sentences are treated on a par with non-modal sentences in that they both express temporal relations. However, the modal sentences describe situations in possible worlds. It is no use evaluating their truth values. Finally, although how to evaluate the truth value of sentences referring to future time is different from theory to theory (Stojanovic (2014: 26)), it is usually the case that we cannot evaluate the truth value of what has not been actualized yet. It is better to establish the temporal semantics of future expressions without recourse to the evaluation time in question.

There is another way to interpret the point of reference. Many linguists after Reichenbach (1947) have regarded it as a complex concept (e.g. Declerck (1986, 1991b, 2006), Kamp and Reyle (1993), Klein (1992, 1994), Huddleston and Pullum (2002)).[12] Within my framework, one concept constituting the point of reference, which functions as computing (or calculating or evaluating) the position of the event time on the time line, is referred to as the time of orientation.[13, 14] The time of orientation is, however, not a primitive temporal notion but a derivative one. That is, an event time or speech time can serve as the time of orientation for computing the target event time.

Let me illustrate the point by considering (6):

(6) a. Emily plays the violin.
   b. Emily played the violin.
   c. Emily has played the violin.
   d. Emily had played the violin when her husband came back.

In Reichenbachian approaches, the temporal relations of (the main clauses of) sentences (6a–d) are, respectively, schematized in (7a–d). In my approach, they are, respectively, schematized in (7a'–d').

(7) a. E, R, S   / a'.   E, S (=O)
   b. E, R—S   / b'.   E—S (=O)
   c. E—R, S   / c'. E_2—E_1 (=O_2), S (=O_1)
   d. E—R—S   / d'. E_2—E_1 (=O_2)—S (=O_1)

---

[12] In Huddleston and Pullum (2002: 126), for example, Reichenbach's reference time is divided into the "time referred to" and the "time of orientation", and the temporal relation between the two times is regarded as tense. The "time referred to" functionally corresponds to the event time in my sense (for its definition, see the main text).

[13] Henceforth, I use the phrase *calculate / compute / evaluate an / the event time* in the sense of 'calculate / compute / evaluate the position of an / the event time'.

[14] This concept corresponds to the time of orientation in the sense used in Declerck (1991a, 1991b, 2006) and Huddleston and Pullum (2002) or to the point of calculation in Helland (1995).

Chapter 1   Introduction   9

E stands for "event time", S for "speech time", R for "reference time", and O for "time of orientation". "X—Y" means that 'X is temporally anterior to Y'; "X, Y" means that 'X is temporally simultaneous with Y'; and "X (=Y)" means that 'X functions as Y' in temporal calculation.

Now I point out the differences between Reichenbach's and my notational systems (cf. Nakau (1994)). First, for the simple past in (6b), the evaluation time is located in the past, whereas the base time (i.e. a time from which to calculate the event time) is located in the speech situation at least in deictic contexts such as the conversational mode. In Reichenbach's notation (7b), the evaluation time is the reference time (R) in the past, i.e. the time with respect to which we evaluate the truth value of the situation involved; speech time (S) is the time from which to calculate the event time (E) or reference time (R) in the past. In my theory, however, the evaluation time—as stated above—is not reflected in the time structure of the simple past. In my notation (7b'), speech time (S) serves as the time of orientation (O), from which to calculate the (position of the) event time (E). My position here denies that the three temporal parameters, i.e. S, O, and E, are always necessary to construct time structures.[15] As we saw above, both finite and non-finite forms equally involve time information and in sentences consisting of a finite and a non-finite form, the two event times are therefore assumed, as in (7c', d'): both the present and past perfect sentences include the event time of the perfect *have* (E_1) and that of the past participle (E_2).[16, 17]

----

[15] This position is the same as Comrie's (1985) and Declerck's (1991a, 1991b, 1997, 2006) position. However, unlike Comrie and Declerck, I follow Nakau (1992, 1994) and Janssen (1994, 1996) to take the position that not only finite forms but also non-finite forms express their own event times. Boogaart (1999: Ch.4) also takes this position in the case of perfect tense sentences.

[16] In Comrie's notational system, the time information of the simple past and that of the present perfect are both represented as "E—S" and so he cannot distinguish between them. In Declerck's notational system, in the case of the simple past, E (=TSit) is calculated from a time of orientation (=TO) located in the past, which is in turn calculated from S (=TU) as another time of orientation. From these observations, it is clear that they do not take the position that every time structure consists of a set of the three temporal parameters. In Boogaart's notational system, the (simple) past tense has the time structure consisting only of E and S, i.e. "E—S", in the case of perfective situations, while it has a time structure consisting of E, R and S, i.e. "E , R—S", in the case of imperfective situations.

[17] Declerck (1991b: 92ff; 2006) allows a time of orientation to be implicit in some cases. In my theory of tense, as we will see in Chapter 2, I admit the existence of such an implicit time of orientation, but its distribution is more restricted than in Declerck's system. As shown in (i) below, for example, the time structure of the past perfect in his system is schematized as "E—O—S", where O is implicit in that it is determined based only on the context (he does not allow the perfect auxiliary *have* to have its own event time).

In my theory, an event time is defined as the time point or period of a relevant part of the situation expressed by a verb/predicate (phrase) or a clause/sentence including it. This notion corresponds to what Declerck (1997, 2006) calls the "time of the predicated situation".[18, 19] Take, for example, the sentence *Ken was sick yesterday*. The time structure of this simple past sentence is schematically represented in (7b') above. Although the time of Ken's being sick can possibly extend to speech time and beyond (e.g. Smith (1997: 70, 170–171)), the event time (E) of the sentence is restricted to a certain length of time in the past and hence anterior to S as the time of orientation.[20]

As for speech time, it is defined in my theory as the moment of speech (utterance) or thought as in the case of most theories. This notion corresponds to the momentary present and makes contrast with the durative present, a time span which includes speech time and extends into both the past and the future (cf. Nakau (1992, 1994)).[21]

The above observations may enable us to ask research questions like the following:

(i) Mary is sad because Jim had beaten John.   (Declerck (1991b: 92))
In my theory, on the other hand, the O in question is not implicit because the event time of *had* serves as the time of orientation for the event time of the past participle; the implicit time of orientation is needed, e.g. in a certain interpretational environment of descriptive narrative parts, i.e. an environment where the situations are described by the narrator out of the story world (see Wada (2015a)).

[18] With respect to stative predicates, Declerck's "time of the predicated situation" is momentary and coincides entirely with the time of orientation involved. With non-stative predicates, it corresponds to the time of the whole situation, whether momentary or durative. However, the event time in this study can be seen as the time corresponding to a part of the situation involved, irrespective of whether it is stative or non-stative.

[19] In Declerck (1986) and Huddleston and Pullum (2002), this notion corresponds to the "time referred to".

[20] The event time defined in this way may correspond to Klein's (1992, 1994) "topic time" as far as the time structure of lexical (main) verbs is concerned. In affirmative declarative sentences, the topic time is the time point or span of the topical part, i.e. the asserted part, of the situation involved. However, he takes the position that the three temporal parameters (i.e. the time of the situation (TSit), the topic time (TT), and the time of utterance (TU)) are necessary for every time structure. His analysis therefore differs from mine in analyzing sentences consisting of finite and non-finite verbs. Thus, in a present perfect sentence like the one in (6c), Klein's analysis would be as follows: TT is simultaneous with TU, to which TSit is anterior; the asserted part is in the posttime of the situation involved, i.e. TT, which includes TU. My analysis is like this: the event time of *have* (E_1) is simultaneous with S and the event time of the past participle (E_2) is anterior to E_1 (see Chapter 4 for more details).

[21] The length of time represented by the momentary present can be changeable based on our cognitive ability, though it is basically regarded as a very short time.

Chapter 1 Introduction 11

(8) a. How is the schematic temporal meaning (i.e. grammatical time information) of both finite and non-finite tense forms projected onto more
specific temporal meanings (i.e. cognitive time information)?

b. How can we finally obtain the temporal value (i.e. tense interpretation
value) of the tense forms through the tense-interpretation processes?

c. How are the time structures of tense forms represented at the levels
of grammatical and cognitive time?

I have thus far tried to answer these questions in previous studies. However,
future is a time area in which tense and modality/mental attitudes are closely
related to each other, and their uses or functions are often related to speech
acts. To give a more explanatory analysis of future expressions, we need to
develop a more comprehensive model of tense that can constructively consider
related areas such as modality, mental attitudes, and speech acts, which I will
do in Part I of this book. Before going further, however, I will briefly compare my theory of tense with other theories (models) of tense in the rest of
this chapter.

1.2. Comparison with Other Theories and the Spirit of My Framework

Let us first classify previous theories (or frameworks) of tense into major
eight groups according to theoretical stance:

(A) Descriptive or usage-/corpus-based approaches, such as Berglund (1997,
2000b), Declerck (1991a), Haegeman (1983), Kashino (1999), Kira
(2018), Leech (1987, 2004), Palmer (1974, 1988), Quirk et al. (1985),
Wekker (1976).

(B) Formal semantic approaches, such as Abusch (1988, 1997), Copley
(2009, 2014), Hatav (2012), Kamp and Reyle (1993), Ogihara (1996,
2007), Ogihara and Sharvit (2012), Partee (1973).

(C) Cognitive linguistic approaches, such as Brisard (1997, 2002, 2013),
De Wit and Brisard (2014), De Wit, Patard and Brisard (2013), Higuchi (1991), Langacker (1991, 2001, 2011a), Patard and Brisard (2011).

(D) Construction grammar approaches, such as Bergs (2010), Hilpert
(2008), Michaelis (1998).

(E) Non-compositional semantic approaches, such as Declerck (1986,
1991b, 1997, 2006, 2010), Depraetere (1996), Depraetere and Langford
(2012), Salkie (2010).

(F) Time schema-based, (compositional) semantic approaches, such as
Comrie (1985), Hirtle (1967), Hirtle and Curat (1986), Huddleston

(1969), Huddleston and Pullum (2002), Klein (1992, 1994), Smith (1978, 1997, 2007).

(G) Relevance-theoretic approaches, such as Haegeman (1989), Klinge (2005), Nicolle (1998).

(H) Generative syntactic approaches, such as Cowper (1998), Guéron and Lecarme (2004), Mihara (1992), Hornstein (1990), Stowell (2007, 2012), Thompson (2005).

In what follows, I will make a brief comment on each theoretical group. First of all, the studies in Group (H) do not directly compete with my framework, because they mainly focus on how temporal parameters and notions (e.g. operators) are related to syntactic structure or how temporal phenomena are explained in terms of tree diagrams. Moreover, these studies as they stand do not seem to be able to analyze, in detail, the uses and/or functions of a variety of future expressions in English. It seems that they are not interested in research questions like those in (8) above in the first place.

Although the studies in Group (A) are able to distinguish various interpretations and uses of tense forms, they do not provide a systematic explanation based on a general theory of tense. They do not seem to offer a "real" explanation.

The studies in Group (B) characterize the semantics of each tense form in terms of truth-conditionality. Thus, in analyzing a present tense sentence like *Adolphe plays the saxophone at seven*, a habitual reading and a futurate reading—which, respectively, illustrate different uses of this present tense sentence—have different truth conditions and are in a "homophonous" relationship. However, many studies (e.g. Goldsmith and Woistschlaeger (1982), Langacker (1991, 2001, 2011a), Brisard (2002), Wada (2015c), De wit (2017)) consider these two uses to be related to each other in terms of the cognitive mechanism of human beings. The studies in Group (B) do not seem to be able to treat this relation appropriately because their characterization of semantic uses (functions) of tense forms are not motivated by such a mechanism; they do not seem to be interested in such motivation in the first place and are thus not compatible with subjectivity and prototypicality, i.e. ideas to be dealt with in this book.[22] In addition, formal semantics approaches, like

---

[22] Copley (2009) gives a detailed formal semantics approach to English future expressions based on the Minimalist Program. She combines sentences with *will* and those with *be going to* into "futures", on the one hand, and the simple present and the present progressive with future time reference into "futurates", on the other. Her analysis assumes common and different parts constituting the truth conditions for both futures and futurates and hence may

Chapter 1   Introduction   13

generative syntactic approaches, do not extensively consider a variety of future expressions in English. For example, as Copley (2009: 60; fn.4) points out, formal approaches (including Groups (B) and (H)) do not even consider a variety of uses of *be going to* nor do they compare it with *will* in detail.

By contrast, Group (C), like Group (A), actively engages in this issue. However, the studies in Group (C) are more explanatory in that they consider and motivate tense-interpretation processes from a broader cognitive point of view.[23] On the other hand, analyses of this group tend to give an explanation from an "extremely cognitive" perspective and thus not to put weight on language-specific (grammatical) aspects of temporal semantics. Moreover, it seems that cognitive linguistic approaches in general pay less attention to unique characteristics of various uses (or semantic functions) of each tense form. Furthermore, these approaches often tend to focus on the common parts across different uses of a tense form, but usually have not considered seriously why and how such different uses have emerged from that tense form or in what sense one use of a tense form has come to differ from another use.[24, 25]

Let us move to the studies in Group (D). In this type of studies, linguistic units consisting of a pair of meaning and form, called "constructions", are assumed to consider temporal phenomena. Although construction grammar approaches can explain idiosyncratic characteristics of "temporal constructions" and grasp their relationships by means of general "linking rules", they sacrifice some important characteristics attributable to common elements that can appear across several temporal constructions. For example, the characteristics

---

escape from the criticism made in the main text. However, what still seems a problem for her analysis is that it cannot deal with meaning changes or diachronic aspects (e.g. grammaticalization) of tense forms, e.g. why a given tense form has come to obtain the semantic uses or functions that it has now. Moreover, formal semantics approaches in general put too much weight on detailed formalizations of the characteristics of tense forms and do not seem to pay much attention to the common parts across different tense forms.

[23] A series of studies by Jaszczolt (e.g. Jaszczolt (2009)) presents a framework called Default Semantics, which introduces a formal semantics approach (i.e. discourse representation theory) into a cognitive approach. This type of study is similar to my framework in that both assume the default interpretation of tense forms.

[24] Mental space analyses (e.g. Cutrer (1994), Dancygier and Sweetser (2005)), usually included in cognitive linguistic approaches in their broad sense, basically do not offer a detailed characterization of uses/functions of a given tense form nor do they reflect its time information in relation to the time line.

[25] Of course, not all cognitive linguistic approaches receive such criticism. For example, as we will see in Chapter 7, De Wit and Brisard (2014) consider these matters seriously, offering a detailed analysis.

associated with *will* seem to be reflected in the time structures of both the "*will* + infinitive" construction and the "*will* + *be* + present participle" construction, but in construction grammar approaches, the two constructions are taken as formally and semantically inseparable units and we cannot attribute certain common characteristics of the two constructions to the characteristics of *will*. Some construction grammarians might argue that the two constructions "inherit" such characteristics from *will* as another construction, but in that case they might need to assume as many "will" constructions as the number of its use (e.g. volitional, pure future, or epistemic use) and/or that of its formal variants (e.g. *will*, *'ll*, *would*, *'d*) and hence the undesirable increase of constructions. It seems that they sacrifice the merits of compositional approaches in some respects.

The studies in Group (E), like those in Group (D), provide a non-compositional analysis of temporal phenomena, considering the time information of a tense form in its entirety and not factorizing it into morpho-syntactic elements, though they do not assume "temporal constructions". Among them, a series of studies by Declerck and his proponents offers a more detailed, systematic, and comprehensive analysis than many construction grammarians. However, they may basically receive the same criticism as those in group (D), because they also sacrifice characteristics attributable to common elements that appear in different tense forms. As another example, we can point out *to* in sentences containing *be going to* and those containing *be about to*. Besides, Declerckian analyses do not regard *will* as a modal, which will be discussed extensively in Chapter 3.

Next, the studies in Group (F) give time schema-based, compositional semantic analyses. Many approaches of this type are too simple to describe a variety of temporal phenomena. What is worse, most of them are not so comprehensive in that they do not constructively consider information ascribed to grammatical fields other than tense (such as auxiliaries, modality, and mental attitudes) nor do they assume a tense system of treating finite and non-finite forms in a unified way (though the latter comment is applied to most of the previous studies in other groups).

Finally, the studies in Group (G) offer an analysis based on the principle of relevance depending on the context and consequently provide a versatile explanation. However, they are primarily devoted to how construal proceeds in a given context and do not seriously consider the temporal semantics of tense forms. They basically do not distinguish between tense forms referring to the same time category, e.g. the future, in terms of the temporal semantics which are made of the combination of the meanings of the elements consti-

Chapter 1 Introduction

tuting the tense forms. Moreover, some studies in this group do not distinguish semantic uses/functions from pragmatic uses/functions and therefore cannot enjoy the explanatory merits deriving from the distinction, as will be shown in e.g. Chapter 5. Furthermore, these studies alone cannot deal with differences in language-specific aspects of temporal semantics because they are basically a theory of utterance interpretation and communication, which should in principle be applied to any language.[26]

Taking into consideration the characteristics, merits and demerits of the studies considered above as well as the temporal mechanism and phenomena which I am interested in (including the research questions in (8) above), this book will further develop the tense model proposed in my previous book so that it will be explanatory enough to cover a diversity of phenomena concerning tense and related areas such as modality, mental attitudes, and speech acts. In so doing, I will construct "rich" time schemata based on a cognitive linguistic perspective (e.g. Jackendoff (1983), Langacker (1991, 2008)), namely a perspective where human cognition deeply affects tense interpretation, and in constructing the model, the following key concepts come into play: compositionality, comprehensiveness, systematicity, and cognitive schema.

First, by compositionality, I mean that the time information of semantic uses or functions denoted by a tense form consists—to a large extent—of the combination of the temporal meanings of its constituents, except for cases where the time information is extremely or completely grammaticalized. This compositionality is not necessarily carried out strictly in terms of truth conditions, but it can be carried out "loosely" in the speaker's mind—and thus sometimes not in a strict sense—in calculating the semantic value of a tense form. Next, comprehensiveness plays a key role in considering futurity because the time zone future is closely related to modality and mental attitudes (i.e. grammatical fields indispensable for analyses of future expressions) and only by introducing such grammatical fields into a general theory of tense can we give a more explanatory account of the temporal phenomena of future expressions. My framework is also comprehensive in that it is intended to cover the semantic uses and functions with a high degree of grammaticalization. As

---

[26] Unlike cognitive linguistic approaches, relevance-theoretic approaches allow "modules" such as the level of semantic representation, in which the coded meaning (which is underdetermined) is enriched by pragmatic processes such as saturation or disambiguation, and the level of pragmatic inference, in which implicature is dealt with. Since relevance-theoretic approaches are primarily a "hearer-based" theory, they cannot fully deal with the process of the choice of tense form by the speaker assumed in my theory of tense stated in the main text.

for systematicity, I intend to construct a tense model in which the field of tense is related in a systematic way to other grammatical fields, as well as to introduce "principle-based" and/or "default rule-based" explanations for tense and related phenomena. Finally, by using the concept of cognitive schema, I aim to reflect the schematized cognitive information in the time structures of tense forms.[27]

On the basis of this model, I will analyze various phenomena of sentences or clauses containing future expressions in English: sentences (clauses) containing *will* (i.e. *will*-sentences), those containing *be going to* (i.e. BGT-sentences), those containing the present progressive with future time reference, those containing the simple present with future time reference, those containing *be about to* (i.e. BAT-sentences), and those containing the *will* + *be* + *-ing* form (i.e. WBI-sentences). Using their time schemata, I will explain, from a unified and more comprehensive point of view, (i) how different tense forms (time expressions) having common constituents (e.g. *will, to-*) show similarities and differences in their temporal phenomena, (ii) how semantically or pragmatically different uses (functions) are derived from one and the same tense form, and (iii) why and how different tense forms without common constituents share similar but different uses (functions). In explaining these questions, I will also be answering the research questions in (8) above. Because of the theoretical stance of this study, I will occasionally refer to non-formal approaches such as groups (A), (C), (D), (E) and (G) above—when analyzing future expressions in Chapters 5 to 10—and clarify the differences between my analysis and theirs if necessary.

1.3. Organization

This book is divided into two parts, besides Introduction and Conclusion. The first part, consisting of Chapters 2, 3, and 4, is devoted to developing the compositional theory of tense proposed in my previous work (Wada (2001a)) in order to treat a variety of phenomena of tense and related areas such as modality, mental attitudes, and speech acts more systematically and comprehensively. Chapter 2 surveys the compositional theory of tense with some further clarifications and additions. Chapter 3 develops a theory of modality and the speaker's mental attitudes assumed in my previous work (Wada (2001a)) in terms of the semantic (de)composition of sentential utterances; a

---

[27] The concept of cognitive schema in this book basically corresponds to the concept of image schema in cognitive linguistics (cf. Yamanashi (2000: 140)).

Chapter 1   Introduction

sentential utterance consists of the speaker's attitude domain (subdivided into the addressee-oriented and the situation-oriented one) and the proposition domain. The former domain is related to the subjective aspect of the speaker and the latter to the objective scene, i.e. situations to be construed and/or described. This theory is further supported by the Three-Tier Model of Language Use, i.e. a general theory of language use dealing with the relation between grammar and pragmatics, which has recently been proposed by Yukio Hirose and developed by himself (Hirose (2013, 2015, 2016a, 2016b, 2017)) and his proponents (Ikarashi (2013, 2015), Konno (2015), Shizawa (2013, 2015), Wada (2013a, 2017b)). In this integrated model, the situation construal tier involves the propositional content and situation-oriented speaker's mental attitudes,[28] the latter being expressed by certain types of modality, including "predictive" and "assertive" modality in the sense of the present framework. The situation report tier involves the construed situation and addressee-oriented speaker's mental attitudes, at which the information from the situation construal tier interacts with that from the interpersonal relationship tier — dealing with the speaker's social or psychological relationship to the addressee(s) — to be conveyed to the addressee/hearer with some "extra" connotations such as (indirect) speech acts. This type of model is indispensable especially in treating, in a unified and systematic way, the tense-interpretation mechanism of future expressions in English and related phenomena such as those of modality, mental attitudes, and speech acts. In Chapter 4, I show how the tense model can deal with temporal phenomena and related issues, especially by showing the importance of the notion "temporal structure", a type of time schema. I take up the simple present and the present perfect as respective samples of simple and complex tense forms.

The second part, composed of Chapters 5–10, is devoted to considering sentences containing representative future forms in English in the developed model. Chapter 5 considers sentences containing *will*, i.e. *will*-sentences. It argues that the core meaning of *will* is "high probability", and *will*-sentences have a number of semantic uses/functions (including so-called predictive and volitional uses) to be analyzed based on their respective temporal structures in the situation construal tier and some pragmatic uses/functions (i.e. addressee-oriented uses or speech-act uses) to be derived in the communication process in the situation report tier. The merits of my temporal structure approach are also shown by an observation of the grammaticalization process of sentences

---

[28] A "tier" in this model is regarded as a kind of cognitive domain (Yukio Hirose (personal communication)).

with modal *will* and a comparison of *will*-sentences with their alleged counterparts in French, i.e. simple future sentences. Chapter 6 provides a temporal structure analysis of the temporal and modal phenomena of sentences containing *be going to*, i.e. BGT-sentences, arguing that a number of uses of BGT-sentences are basically derived from the combination of the temporal meanings of the constituents of this tense form and assertive modality; BGT-sentences are therefore sharply contrasted with *will*-sentences, which basically express predictive modality. However, BGT-sentences have not only uses where some parts of their semantic structures are semantically bleached but also uses where most parts of them are semantically bleached, their functions being very close to those of *will*-sentences. Comparison of BGT-sentences with *will*-sentences further clarifies their similarities and differences.

Chapters 7 and 8 deal with two present tense sentences with future time reference, i.e. sentences containing the present progressive and those containing the simple present, both of which are accompanied by assertive modality. Chapter 7 shows that the temporal structure of sentences containing the present progressive futurate (i.e. PPF-sentences) is derived from that of present progressive sentences in their aspectual use, providing an explanatory basis for their temporal phenomena. Comparison of the characteristics of PPF-sentences with those of BGT-sentences clarifies their similarities and differences in more detail. In Chapter 8, a number of future reference uses of sentences in the simple present form (including the simple present futurate) are analyzed based on their temporal structures.

Chapters 9 and 10 explore less typical future expressions in English, i.e. sentences containing *be about to* (i.e. BAT-sentences) and those containing the *will* + *be* + *-ing* form (i.e. WBI-sentences). Chapter 9 analyzes BAT-sentences, claiming that their temporal structure consists of the combination of the temporal meanings of the constituents of the form *be about to* + infinitive and assertive modality. Detailed comparison of BAT-sentences with BGT-sentences based on their temporal structures makes explicit the differences between the two sentences. In Chapter 10, the temporal structures of the three major uses of WBI-sentences, which are compositionally made of the temporal structures of *will*-sentences (in their predictive future or predictive present use) and present progressive sentences (in their aspectual or futurate use), systematically explain the temporal phenomena of the three uses. Comparison of WBI-sentences with *will*-sentences or PPF-sentences reveals the characteristics of the *will* + *be* + *-ing* form which inherit those of the latter two tense forms. Chapter 11 makes some concluding remarks.

PART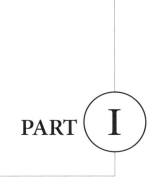

THEORETICAL FRAMEWORK

Chapter 2

A Compositional Theory of Tense

2.1. Introduction

This chapter surveys, with some further clarifications and additions, the essence of the theory of tense proposed and developed in previous works (e.g. Wada (2001a, 2009, 2013)), which aims to systematically analyze both finite and non-finite forms in English from a unified point of view. The theory distinguishes between two levels in the field of tense, i.e. the level concerning tense structure and that concerning tense interpretation, whereby one single tense form having an abstract core meaning can have a variety of semantic uses and/or functions. On the tense-interpretation level, the schematic time information of the tense form coming from the tense-structure level interacts with factors crucial for tense interpretation—such as time adverbials, auxiliaries, aspect and situation type, modality, linguistic environments (including syntactic positions and discourse modes)—to arrive at a given temporal value (including a temporal relation, aspectual information, specificity on the time line) through temporal calculation.

2.2. Tense Structure Level and Tense Interpretation Level

The two levels in the field of tense, i.e. the tense-structure (TS) level and the tense-interpretation (TI) level, are related to the two different types of time information associated with tense forms observed in Chapter 1. The TS level is concerned with the schematic time information of a tense form itself, i.e. grammatical time information. The structuralized grammatical time information is called *tense structure*. The TI level is concerned with cognitive time information, including time information in real, possible, or hypothetical worlds. This level is an interface in which tense-structure (i.e. grammatical time) information interacts with other information coming not only from the

21

factors mentioned in Section 2.1, but also from context and encyclopedic knowledge, to reach a temporal (or tense interpretation) value through temporal calculation. The structuralized cognitive time information of a tense form, which provides a basis for temporal calculation, is called *temporal structure*. The point here is that we distinguish between the two types of time structures (i.e. tense structure and temporal structure) based on the distinction between the TS and TI levels. How the tense-interpretation system works is schematically represented in Figure 1:

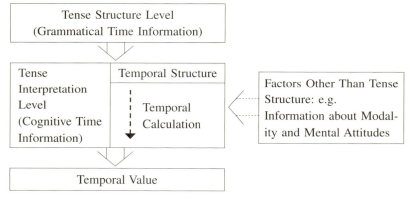

Figure 1: The Tense-Interpretation System

Most of the time schema-based, semantic approaches (such as those presented in Chapter 1) do not make this type of distinction.[1]

This distinction allows cases in which instances of one tense form share the same tense structure (i.e. abstract core meaning at the TS level) but can have different temporal structures for a variety of semantic uses and functions (we will consider how the system works by considering the simple present and present perfect as sample cases in Chapter 4). Moreover, the distinction under consideration enables us to give a related but separate treatment of the projection of tense-structure information of tense forms onto the TI level, on the one hand, and of their temporal calculation at the TI level, on the other, and consequently the base point in time for the choice of tense form (i.e. the time on

---

[1] Declerck (1997: 106–107) also distinguishes between two types of time structures with the same terms in his own theory. His and my theories share the same spirit with respect to the motivation for the distinction, but differ in that, for example, he does not make a distinction between the A- and the R-component nor does he allow an auxiliary verb (e.g. *will, have, be*) to have its own event time (more on this below).

Chapter 2   A Compositional Theory of Tense   23

which the core or cornerstone of tense-structure information is located) can be different from that for the process of tense interpretation (i.e. the time which serves as a time of orientation). Henceforth, I use the term *base point* to refer to the base point in time for choosing a tense form and the term *time of orientation* to refer to the base point in time for calculating the temporal value of that tense form.

Consider (1) for example.

(1)   Mary said that she was tired.   (Enç (1996: 350))

In my analysis, the past tense form *was* is chosen because the base point is speech time, but the time of orientation is normally (in the default case) identified to be the time of the main clause, i.e. the time of Mary's original utterance, because of the characteristics of the indirect speech complement. The event time involved is either (temporally) simultaneous with the time of orientation (i.e. the "simultaneous" reading) or (temporally) anterior to it (i.e. the "anterior" reading).[2]

The speaker (i.e. tense-form chooser) chooses a tense form whose tense structure is appropriate for the time information that s/he intends to express and convey to the hearer (addressee). In interpreting the chosen tense form, the hearer first identifies the base point, thereby the range of time reference of the form is determined. In the case of (1) above, the base point for the two simple past forms is the time of the report, i.e. speech time, so the range of time reference is a time domain in the past with respect to speech time. On the other hand, in the case of *was* in (2) below, the base point for the choice of tense form is the time of the main clause, i.e. the time of the (expected) original utterance located in the future, and the range of time reference is therefore a time domain in the past with respect to the time of the main clause.

(2)   Tomorrow, Frances will say that she was absent today.

                                                    (Declerck (1991b: 161))

The event time of *was* can be located in the future relative to speech time, especially when the time adverb *today* is taken away.

As a next step, the hearer identifies the time of orientation to calculate the temporal value of the tense form involved, especially the position of the event time. The process of tense interpretation is affected by the various factors

---

[2] In this book, I use the terms *anterior/anteriority*, *simultaneous/simultaneity*, and *posterior/posteriority* to express temporal relations between two times.

mentioned above (which we will see in detail in Section 2.4.3) and the finally-determined interpretation value (i.e. temporal value) of the tense form is obtained through temporal calculation. The process is based on a temporal structure (i.e. structuralized cognitive time information) of the tense form, which includes the grammatical time information as part of it.

As stated in Chapter 1, my position is based on a cognitive linguistic perspective and so the speaker as the subject of cognitive or mental activities is involved in this tense-interpretation process. We assume that both speaker and hearer share the process in mind. The speaker when using a tense form assumes the process in which the hearer infers and identifies the time information that the speaker intends to express and/or convey to the latter.

2.3. Tense Structure

This section considers the TS level, i.e. the level concerning tense structure, in more detail. Before going further, however, let us state that the terms *absolute tense* and *relative tense* are preserved exclusively for tense forms in this theory. This is to avoid confusion of terms which has often been seen in the literature (see Section 1.1). Tense forms whose tense structure involves the deictic center of grammatical time are absolute tense forms, whereas tense forms without such a tense structure are relative tense forms.

Two types of tense components play crucial roles in constructing tense structures: an A(bsolute tense)-component and R(elative tense)-component. The A-component is concerned with tense-structure information which is directly related to the deictic center of grammatical time; the R-component is concerned with other types of tense-structure information.[3] Absolute tense forms contain both the A-component and the R-component in their tense structure, while relative tense forms only contain the R-component.

West-European languages such as English and French have tense inflections (morphemes) that change according to person, number, and mood (i.e. grammatical categories encoding deixis). This type of tense morpheme is referred to as an A-morpheme in this study and assumed to involve reference to the deictic center of grammatical time, contributing to the A-component information; finite forms in West-European languages such as English and French are

---

[3] The A(bsolute tense)-component is named after the involvement of the deictic center of grammatical time, i.e. a time which will serve on the TI level as an absolute point of reference to which all time relations are finally attributed. The R(elative tense)-component is named after the lack of such a point.

Chapter 2   A Compositional Theory of Tense   25

therefore absolute tense forms. These observations enable us to argue that English only has two A-morphemes, i.e. the present tense morpheme (represented by -s) and past tense morpheme (represented by -ed), and hence two absolute tense forms, while French has four A-morphemes, i.e. the present tense morpheme, simple past tense morpheme, imperfect tense morpheme, and future tense morpheme, and hence four absolute tense forms.[4] Note that A-morphemes are the only element contributing to the A-component information.

Non-finite markers in West-European languages, which do not change according to person, number, and mood, are also tense morphemes for the reasons stated in Chapter 1, but of a different type. This type of tense morpheme is referred to as an R-morpheme. The present theory allows five R-morphemes in English: the present participle morpheme (represented by -ing), past participle morpheme (represented by -en), gerundive morpheme (represented by -ing), bare infinitive morpheme (represented by ø), and to-infinitive morpheme (represented by to). R-morphemes do not involve reference to the deictic center of grammatical time and contribute to the R-component information; the non-finite forms in English are relative tense forms because they do not have A-morphemes.

All tense forms, absolute or relative, involve in their tense structure the event time in the sense defined in Chapter 1, i.e. the time point or period of a relevant part of the situation involved, which contributes to the R-component information because it itself does not refer to the deictic center of grammatical time. An event time is the tense-structure information expressed by a verb (predicate) stem, so that the tense structure of absolute tense forms consists of the tense-structure information represented by an A-morpheme (i.e. A-component information) and that represented by the verb stem (i.e. R-component information), while the tense structure of relative tense forms consists of the tense-structure information represented by an R-morpheme and that represented by the verb stem, both of which contribute to the R-component information.

Based on these observations, the tense structures of the present and past tense forms in English (i.e. absolute tense forms) are schematically represented below.

---

[4] The simple past and imperfect tense morphemes might be integrated into one A-morpheme, i.e. the past tense morpheme, because their distinction is one of aspect, not of tense. I leave it for future research.

Figure 2: Tense Structures of (i) the Present Tense Form and (ii) the Past Tense Form

V_{SPK} stands for the *speaker's t(emporal)-viewpoint*, i.e. the deictic center of grammatical time; a rectangle with subscripted (shortened) words represents a time-sphere, i.e. grammatical time range; E denotes an event time. A vertical line indicates a temporal relation of simultaneity or inclusion, and a horizontal line a (temporal) before-after relationship. The tense-structure information represented by an A-morpheme is the positional relationship of a time-sphere to the speaker's t-viewpoint and the value of the time-sphere is determined in relation to the position of the latter. That is, a time-sphere including the speaker's t-viewpoint is a present time-sphere, or grammatical present (represented by the present tense morpheme) and a time-sphere excluding or anterior to the speaker's t-viewpoint is a past time-sphere, or grammatical past (represented by the past tense morpheme).[5] An event time (i.e. the tense-structure information represented by a verb stem) is necessarily included in a time-sphere. Since an event time is defined as the time point or period of a relevant part of the situation involved, we can assume that even in the case of stative or homogeneous situations, the event time is included completely and located somewhere in a time-sphere.

Let us now consider the tense structures of relative tense forms in English. As we saw above, R-morphemes do not represent tense-structure information involving the deictic center of grammatical time. Instead, they represent an intrinsic relation of grammatical time between an event time and potential time of orientation. The latter is a base time which will be identified as a time of orientation in the tense-interpretation process. Given that an event time is a temporal notion associated with the verb stem, the tense structure of relative tense forms—which consist of an R-morpheme and the verb stem—is merely a positional relationship in grammatical time between the event time and potential time of orientation. The tense structure of relative tense forms involves

---

[5] Declerck (2006: 147) states that "English tenses appear to reflect a mental division of time into past and nonpast," which correspond, respectively, to his notions of the past and present time-spheres. My notions of the present and past time-spheres are constructs of tense structures, but we could say that the distinction between the two grammatical time ranges reflects such a mental division.

Chapter 2   A Compositional Theory of Tense

only one base point in time, i.e. the potential time of orientation, and this time notion will therefore serve not only as the time of orientation for calculating the position of the event time but also as the base point for choosing a relative tense form in the tense-interpretation process.[6]

There are logically three types of relation between the two times in question: anteriority, simultaneity, and posteriority. Note that the relation of simultaneity includes that of inclusion or partial overlapping. The three types of time relations of relative tense forms are schematically represented below.

R: (i) E ——— (O)   (ii) E , (O)   (iii) (O) ——— E

Figure 3: Tense Structures of Relative Tense Forms:
(i) Anteriority; (ii) Simultaneity; and (iii) Posteriority

A parenthesized O stands for a potential time of orientation, and a comma for simultaneity. Relative tense forms can represent any of the three relations depending on the type of R-morpheme. The five non-finite markers in English (i.e. R-morphemes) represent the relations between the event time and potential time of orientation in the following manner.[7]

(3) a.   The present participle morpheme -*ing* represents simultaneity.[8]
    b.   The past participle morpheme -*en* represents anteriority.
    c.   The gerundive morpheme -*ing* represents unspecifiedness.
    d.   The bare infinitive morpheme ø represents unspecifiedness.
    e.   The *to*-infinitive morpheme *to*- represents posteriority.

---

[6] This characterization of the tense structure of relative tense forms is in keeping with Declerck's (1991b: 7) statement that non-finite forms represent single time relations, i.e. those of the time of the situation involved (i.e. event time) to some other time.

[7] In my previous book (Wada (2001a: Ch. 2)), the tense structure of bare infinitives was assumed to potentially cover the three time relations, i.e. anteriority, simultaneity, and posteriority, which is meant by the term *unspecifiedness* in this book. In that book, the tense structure of gerunds was assumed to represent non-posteriority — which was changed to represent unspecifiedness in Wada (2006a); gerunds expressing posteriority relative to the time of the main verb, as in *He considered giving her the keys* (Duffley (2000: 223); cf. Declerck (1999: 489)) were treated there in such a way that the event time of the gerund in question is interpreted as simultaneous with the (implicit) time of orientation established in the future relative to the event time of a main verb which can describe a future-oriented situation (e.g. *consider*).

[8] Some linguists (e.g. Huddleston and Pullum (2002: 80–81), Duffley (2006: 3–7)) do not distinguish between the present participle and gerund, but in my previous book (Wada (2001a)), I distinguished between them. This position is in keeping with De Smet and Heyvaert's (2011: 476) statement that "the constituent of which participles are the head stands in a distributional correspondence to an adjective phrase — a property not shared by

It should be stressed here that the grammatical-time relations in (3) can be co-erced on the TI level as far as such a coercion is motivated (more on this be-low).

2.4.   Tense Interpretation Process

2.4.1.   Fusion of the Speaker's T(emporal)-Viewpoint and Consciousness

Next, I will outline the tense-interpretation process of absolute tense forms with some specifications. The process begins when tense structures are proj-ected onto the cognitive time line — usually the real time line — to create tem-poral structures. The first task in this projection is to identify the starting point for calculating cognitive time relations.

As we have seen, the tense structure of absolute tense forms involves the speaker's t(emporal)-viewpoint, i.e. the deictic center of grammatical time (represented by an A-morpheme). Speech time is the absolute point of refer-ence on the (cognitive) time line, at which the (current) speaker's conscious-ness is always existent. This is because the speaker's consciousness is defined as the subjective aspect of the speaker, i.e. an activated part of the mind when engaged in any type of cognitive or mental activity such as communicating, uttering, thinking, perceiving or cognizing.[9, 10] Basing ourselves on a cogni-tive linguistic perspective and placing importance on the speaker as the center of cognition, the default case is when the speaker puts his/her viewpoint (i.e. a vantage point from which to "see" something) on the point in space and time at which his/her consciousness is existent, i.e. the spatiotemporal point at which he/she perceives and evaluates given situations or scenes. Therefore, unless otherwise specified or implied, the same speaker's consciousness and t-

---

gerunds, which are nominalizations." For a further discussion about the gerund/participle distinction, see De Swet (2014).

[9] My definition of consciousness is based on *Longman Dictionary of Contemporary Eng-lish*, which defines it as "the condition of being awake and able to understand what is hap-pening around you". It is similar to the definition of Chafe (1994: 38):

> "Consciousness, then, is regarded in this work as the crucial interface between the conscious organism and its environment, the place where information from the *envi-ronment* is dealt with as a basis for thought and action as well as the place where in-ternally generated experience becomes effective — the locus of remembering, imagin-ing, and feeling."

[10] My notion of speaker's consciousness may more or less correspond to the notion of "origo" (Bühler (1982)), the notion of "subject" (Lakoff and Johnson (1999)), the notion of "subject of consciousness" (Hirose (2002)), or the notion of "egocentric experience of now" (Evans (2013: 76)).

Chapter 2   A Compositional Theory of Tense   29

viewpoint (a viewpoint objectivized and internalized in the tense structure of absolute tense forms) are interpreted as occupying the same time.[11] Let us call this phenomenon *fusion*. A principle like (4) is thus operative in the default interpretation of absolute tense forms.

(4)   The speaker's t-viewpoint fuses with his/her consciousness at speech time.

Due to this principle, the base point for choosing absolute tense forms is identified as speech time by default.

An illustration might help here. Consider how the present and past tense forms in English (i.e. absolute tense forms) are interpreted with concrete examples.

(5) a.   James Bond is a secret agent. (Simple Present)
    b.   Akane played Piazzolla's "Oblivion". (Simple Past)

Because of the operation of principle (4), the speaker's t-viewpoint in the tense structures of the present tense form *is* in (5a) and the past tense form *played* in (5b) fuses with his/her consciousness in existence at speech time, and as a result, the present and past time-sphere correspond, respectively, to the non-past (present and future) time-area and the past time-area (i.e. cognitive time ranges on the time line).[12] By means of these correspondences, we obtain the basic temporal structures of the present and past tense forms, as shown in Figures 4 and 5.[13]

---

[11] The speaker's consciousness and t-viewpoint in this study seem to functionally correspond, respectively, to the "representing consciousness" and "represented consciousness" in the sense of Chafe (1994). This suggests that the speaker's consciousness is the "center of ego", but the speaker's t-viewpoint can be an object of consciousness and thus objectivized, so that it can be assumed to be internalized in tense structures.

[12] Strictly speaking, especially in philosophical terms, we have to consider and distinguish several types of time, as discussed in Jaszczolt (2009: Ch. 1). However, I only use a time line metaphor for convenience's sake to make a linguistic analysis of temporal phenomena based on a cognitive linguistic perspective. I utilize one of the simplest types of representation of the time line metaphor throughout the book. The notion of time line in this book corresponds to the time flow in human mind, i.e. the internal (psychological) time (Jaszczolt (2009: 30)).

[13] These basic temporal structures are elaborated under the influence of the properties of each use of both tense forms.

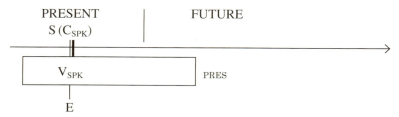

Figure 4: Basic Temporal Structure of the Present Tense Form

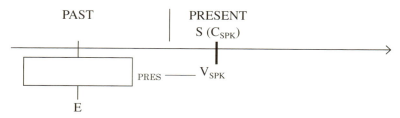

Figure 5: Basic Temporal Structure of the Past Tense Form

The horizontal arrow represents a time line and points to the future as the most likely direction of the time line;[14] C_{SPK} stands for the speaker's consciousness; S denotes speech time; the capitalized PAST, PRESENT, and FUTURE indicate the past, present, and future time-areas, respectively; the vertical line between two time-areas divides them; a heavy vertical line connecting V_{SPK} with C_{SPK} means a relation of fusion. The speaker of (5a) chooses the present tense form because he/she assumes that in the tense-interpretation process, the operation of principle (4) brings about the fusion of the speaker's t-viewpoint and consciousness and the event time located in the present time-sphere is located (somewhere) in the non-past (i.e. present and/or future) time-area. Using this basic temporal structure of the simple present form, he/she can convey the message that the situation of James Bond being a secret agent obtains now (for how the event time is "stuck" in the present time-area, we will see later). The same type of interpretation process applies to (5b).

---

[14] As stated in Jaszczolt (2009: 66-67), de Brabanter, Kissine and Sharifzadeh (2014: 2), among others, we have a number of future directions, so it might appear inappropriate to represent the future with a straight line. However, as stated in the main text, what the straight line represents in the future time-area is a most plausible future world, a world corresponding to the projected reality in the dynamic evolutionary model by Langacker (1991, 2008). Just because I adopt notations like the ones in Figures 4 and 5 does not necessarily mean that I am denying the so-called branching future hypothesis (see Dowty (1977), Watanabe (2014) and the relevant references cited in the latter).

Chapter 2   A Compositional Theory of Tense   31

The correspondence patterns shown above are justified by the following paradigms (cf. Hirtle (1967: 49), Quirk et al. (1985: 177)):

(6) a.   John is ill now. / a′. *John is ill yesterday.
    b.   Mary was ill yesterday. / b′. *Mary was ill now.[15]
    c.   After Yoko {*arrived / arrives} tomorrow, I will leave for my hometown.
(7) a.   I walk to work this year.   (Hirtle (1967: 49))
    b.   I walk to work this year and next year.   (Hirtle (1967: 49))
    c. *I walk to work last year, this year and next year. (Hirtle (1967: 49))

In the default case, the present tense form can refer to either the present time-area, as in (6a), or the future time-area, as in (6c), or both, as in (7b); the past tense form can only refer to the past time-area, as illustrated by (6b, b′, c). What is noticeable here is that even in the case of habitual readings, which can express situations in the durative present that extends into the past and the future, the present tense form is not compatible with a past time adverbial, as shown in (7c). This fact justifies my claim that in the default case the present time-sphere (grammatical present) corresponds to the present and future time-areas (cognitive present and future), but not to the past time-area (cognitive past). Because the event time involved is restricted into either the present or future time-area, it cannot be compatible with a past time adverbial even if the time range of the whole situation described by the present tense sentence extends into the past.

Let us now consider two non-default cases, i.e. the historical-present use, as illustrated in (8), and the past-in-the-future case, as shown in (2) above, repeated below.

(8) a.   At that moment in comes a message from the Head Office, telling me
         the boss wants to see me in a hurry.   (Leech (2004: 11))
    b.   I get home last night and find a note on my door.
                                                    (Langacker (2011a: 46))
(2)   Tomorrow, Frances will say that she was absent today.

In these cases, principle (4) does not work. In the case of the historical presents in (8), the speaker's t-viewpoint is located at a time point on the narrative time-line, which refers to—or is regarded as if referring to—the past relative to the time of narration. As a result, the present time-sphere (grammatical present) corresponds to part of the past time-area and the event time, which is

---

[15] Examples like (6b′) may be acceptable in past-tense, third-person narratives, but we are not assuming such contexts here.

restricted into the present time-sphere, is located in the past relative to the time of narration.

As for the past-in-the-future case (2), the speaker's t-viewpoint fuses with the consciousness of the (expected) original speaker Frances, which is assumed to be existent at the time of the (expected) original utterance in the future. The past time-sphere of the past tense form *was* therefore corresponds to a time range prior to the time of the (expected) original utterance. Without a time adverb referring to a specific time or further context, we cannot specify whether the event time of such a past tense form is located in the future, present, or past relative to speech time.

2.4.2. Viewpoint of Situation Description and Time of Orientation

Let us now move on to the calculation (computation) of the event time in the tense-interpretation process. For this purpose, the time of orientation for the event-time calculation (evaluation) needs to be identified. Just as the speaker's t-viewpoint is involved in the process of identifying the base point for the choice of tense form, so a certain viewpoint is involved in the process of identifying the time of orientation for calculating the event time. This is because such an involvement reflects a universal cognitive mechanism in which we use a point of view to calculate (evaluate) something. This ability is called a "reference point ability" in Langacker (1991, 1993). Since an event time is the time of a relevant part of the situation involved, the viewpoint operating in this process is the one from which to calculate the position of the relevant part of the situation on the time line. It is a type of viewpoint from which to see or evaluate situations or scenes and thus referred to as a viewpoint of situation description, or SD-viewpoint, in my theory. The time on which is put the speaker's SD-viewpoint serves as the time of orientation for calculating the event time.

As stated above, the default case is when the speaker puts his/her viewpoint on speech time, i.e. the spatiotemporal point at which his/her consciousness is existent. This default operation also works in identifying the time of orientation. When the relevant speaker is the speaker of the relevant utterance, the speaker's SD-viewpoint fuses with his/her consciousness at speech time, unless otherwise indicated (cf. Smith (2003), Smith and Erbaugh (2005)). Thus, in (5a), *James Bond is a secret agent*, the only relevant speaker is the speaker of this sentence and so the speaker's SD-viewpoint for evaluating the event time is put on speech time, which functions as the time of orientation. The same applies to (5b), *Akane played Piazzolla's "Oblivion"*. As we saw above, in the case of the present and past tense forms in main or independent clauses (e.g. (5a) and (5b)), the base point for the choice of tense form is also identified as speech time.

Considering these observations, we can schematically represent the temporal structures of the present and past tense forms in the default pattern of the event-time calculation in main or independent clauses, as shown in Figures 6 and 7.

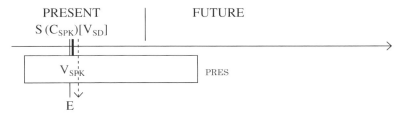

Figure 6: Temporal Structure of the Simple Present Form When the Speaker's T-Viewpoint and SD-Viewpoint Are Located at Speech Time

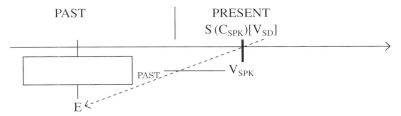

Figure 7: Temporal Structure of the Simple Past Form When the Speaker's T-Viewpoint and SD-Viewpoint Are Located at Speech Time

V_{SD} represents a speaker's SD-viewpoint and a broken arrow indicates an evaluation (calculation) path to the target event time.

It should be noted here that unlike in the case of the speaker's t-viewpoint, the speaker rather freely decides on the time point at which his/her SD-viewpoint is located, because one can describe a target situation from whichever point of view, unless otherwise restricted (cf. Iwasaki (1993: Ch.1)). However, this does not mean that the position of the SD-viewpoint on the time line is determined completely freely. If there are restrictions that regulate the position of the viewpoint from which to evaluate the situation involved, the determination of the position of the speaker's SD-viewpoint must conform to them. Thus, the properties of the linguistic environment involved play a crucial role in determining the position of the speaker's SD-viewpoint. They may allow or force the speaker's SD-viewpoint to be located at a time point other than speech time (see Section 2.4.3.5 for details).

Let us consider the indirect speech complement as a representative case. Indirect speech complements constitute the linguistic environment in which the reporter (i.e. the speaker of the whole sentence) conveys the original speech or thought with some reflection of his/her perspective (i.e. way of viewing or thinking about something) but without distorting the original (i.e. reported) speaker's intention or thought (Coulman (1986), Janssen and van der Wurff (1996), Quirk et al. (1985), Rigter (1982), Vandelanotte (2009), Yamaguchi (2009)). This suggests that the environment in question reflects both the reporter's perspective at the time of reporting the whole sentence (i.e. speech time) and the original speaker's perspective at the time of the original speech or thought (i.e. the time of the main clause). When the speaker's SD-viewpoint fuses with the consciousness of the original speaker at the time of the original speech or thought (and this is the default case because the primary function of indirect speech is to attribute "responsibility" to a person other than the reporter at the reporting time), the time of orientation for calculating the event time of the complement situation is the time of the original speech or thought. When the speaker's SD-viewpoint fuses with the consciousness of the reporter at the reporting time (in this case his/her perspective is given priority over the original speaker's), the time of orientation for evaluating the event time of the complement situation is the reporting time (i.e. speech time). The former case is referred to as a non-deictic interpretation, whereas the latter is referred to as a deictic interpretation.[16]

By way of illustration, consider (1) and (2) again, repeated below:

(1) Mary said that she was tired.
(2) Tomorrow, Frances will say that she was absent today.

In (1), the base point for the choice of tense form is the reporting time and the reporter can choose between the original speaker's perspective and his/her own perspective in interpreting the past tense form *was*. The temporal structure of the deictic interpretation of the past tense form is schematized in Figure 8; that of the non-deictic interpretation is schematized in Figure 9.

---

[16] Deictic and non-deictic interpretations are often referred to as absolute- and relative-tense interpretations, respectively. However, as stated in Section 2.3, the terms "absolute" and "relative" are reserved for tense forms. I use the terms "deictic" and "non-deictic" for tense interpretations/readings.

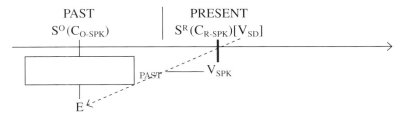

Figure 8: Temporal Structure of the Simple Past Form in the Indirect Speech Complement of (1) (Deictic Interpretation)

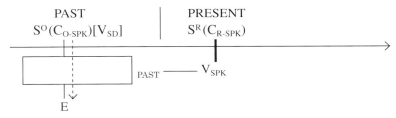

Figure 9: Temporal Structure of the Simple Past Form in the Indirect Speech Complement of (1) (Non-Deictic Interpretation)

S^O stands for the time of the original speech or thought; S^R represents the reporting time; $C_{O\text{-SPK}}$ denotes the consciousness of the original speaker; and $C_{R\text{-SPK}}$ symbolizes the consciousness of the reporting speaker (i.e. reporter).

The indirect speech complement of (2) is a different linguistic environment from that of (1) in that in the former case, the base point for the choice of tense form is the time of the (expected) original speaker's speech or thought in the future, but not the reporting time (i.e. speech time). This is due to the nature of this linguistic environment, i.e. a past-in-the-future context. Given that the complement clause situation refers to what the (expected) original speaker will say in the future and has not come into existence yet, it is difficult if not impossible for the reporter to convey it using his/her perspective of now without distorting the (expected) original speaker's intention or thought (Harder (1996: 438); cf. Wada (2001a: 296; note 23)); it is highly probable that by the time of the utterance in the future, the (expected) original speaker will change what he/she is now assumed to be intending to convey. This environmental characteristic may force the reporter to even give up the right to choose tense forms and devolve it to the (expected) original speaker. The base point for the choice of tense form is thus usually identified as the time of the (expected) original speaker's utterance or thought in the future. From these observations, in a linguistic environment like the complement clause in

(2), the reporter usually follows the perspective of the (expected) original speaker completely in choosing a tense form as well as in identifying the time of orientation and the speaker's t-viewpoint and SD-viewpoint are both situated at the time of the (expected) original speaker's utterance or thought. The temporal structure of the past tense form in this environment is schematized in Figure 10.

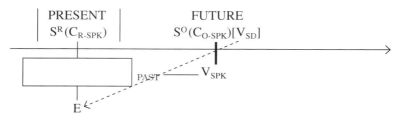

Figure 10: Temporal Structure of the Simple Past Form in the Indirect Speech Complement (the Past-in-the-Future Context Version)

2.4.3. Various Factors Related to Tense Interpretation

This sub-section considers various factors closely related to the tense-interpretation process outlined above. Although I have already mentioned them in my previous book (Wada (2001a)), I will here outline them with some further comments.

2.4.3.1. Time Adverbials

Let me start with how time adverbials work in the tense-interpretation process. They refer to the time at or during which the relevant part of a situation occurs or obtains. They may also express a time span in which is included the relevant part of the situation involved. In the former case, time adverbials specify an event time itself; in the latter case, they specify a time span including the event time. Note that even if they refer to the time associated with a non-specific (general) or schematic situation, they can specify it as an event time. However, if the situation involved is a semantically bleached type, then the event time referred to by time adverbials is not a pure type, but an orientational type (see Section 2.4.4).

Examples are shown in (9), where the underlines are mine:

(9) a. "They're falling faster now. Three days ago there were almost a hundred. It made me head ache to count them ... There are only five left now."   (O. Henry, *The Last Leaf*, p. 310)

b. Every afternoon of my college life I walked into that place, greeted

Chapter 2   A Compositional Theory of Tense   37

my buddies with friendly obscenities, shed the trappings of civiliza-
tion and turned into a jock.   (Erich Segal, *Love Story*, pp. 15‒16)

c.   "Uh—kind of negative on it, Phil," she said, now glancing at me for
support—which my eyes tried to give her.

(Erich Segal, *Love Story*, p. 93)

d.   "Yes, sir," I said. "Very unfortunate. But that's why I've come to
you, sir. 'I'm getting married next month. We'll both be working
over the summer. Then Jenny that's my wife—will be teaching in a
private school ...   (Erich Segal, *Love Story*, p. 98)

e.   When Michael came home, she [=Connie] gave him a big hug and a
kiss and looked at him admiringly and said, "Now you're my hand-
some brother again."[17]   (Mario Puzo, *The Godfather*, pp. 396‒397)

f.   {Now / At this moment / Today} John rehearses tomorrow.

(Smith (1981: 372))

In (9a, e), the past and present time adverbials, respectively, refer to the past
and present situations. In (9b), the time adverbial refers to the time of every
sub-situation constituting a habit. In (9c, d), time adverbials specify the time of
non-finite forms, i.e. *glancing* in (9c) and *(getting) married* in (9d). Recall that
both finite and non-finite verbs have their respective event times (see also the
next section). It should be noticed here that the time adverbial *next month* in
(9d) refers to the time span that includes the time at which the marriage cere-
mony occurs, i.e. the event time. In (9f), the future time adverbial *tomorrow*
specifies the event time associated with the situation of rehearsing. The present
time adverbials, by contrast, do not specify any event time because there is no
verb for it. However, considering that the functional purpose of time adverbials
is to specify a time at or during which some situation occurs or obtains, we
may assume that these present time adverbials refer to the time of the background to the speech situation, e.g. a present condition for the actualization of
the rehearsal (see Chapter 8 for a detailed mechanism of this modification).[18]

---

[17] This *now* is temporal, not a topic change marker. The background to this scene is that
Michael had got injured, but later he had an operation and then became a good-looking man
again. The *now* in question therefore refers to the present condition of Michael. In this
book, I will only consider temporal *now*.

[18] It is sometimes difficult to say which time adverbials are present or future. In this
connection, Haegeman (1983: 44) offers a criterion to distinguish them, stating that future
time adverbials are ones which can co-occur with imperative sentences, as in:

(i) a.   Come back!   (Haegeman (1983: 44))
    b.   Come back immediately / this very moment.   (Haegeman (1983: 44))
    c.   *Come back yesterday.   (Haegeman (1983: 44))

2.4.3.2. Auxiliaries

I assumed in my previous book (Wada (2001a: §1.2)) that auxiliaries as well as lexical verbs—both of which are incorporated into the category "predicate"—describe their own situations.[19] This assumption was based on prototype theory, which suggests that not all members of the same category need to have the same attributes. This position is not contradictory to Heine's (1993) position that auxiliaries are located at a middle position on the continuum with lexical verbs at one pole and affixes or clitics at the other.[20]

It is often said that auxiliary verbs differ from lexical verbs because they both behave differently with respect to the so-called NICE properties (Huddleston (1976); Palmer (1987)) or contraction. However, these properties are merely typicality conditions; the more typicality conditions of a category a given member satisfies, the more prototypical member it is. It is also sometimes said that lexical verbs are semantically contentful in comparison with auxiliaries, which seems to be used as one major criterion to distinguish them. However, one cannot say a priori that modal auxiliaries such as *may, must,* or *can* are not as semantically contentful as lexical verbs such as *seem* or *appear.* From these observations, we may be able to argue that auxiliary and lexical verbs are not classified into completely distinct categories, but constitute a "gradual" category of predicate, and thus describe their own situations. Situations described by verb or predicate phrases (and clauses or sentences containing them) can not only be specific or semantically contentful, but also sche-

---

The time adverbials which she calls "future time adverbials" refer to a time following speech time. Within my framework, however, as we will see in Chapter 5 and the following chapters, time adverbials establishing the present time-area are present time adverbials, not future ones, even if they refer to a time following speech time, as in (ii):

(ii) a.   Leave him alone now.   (BNC A4R)

   b.   Nephew ... from this moment on ... call yourself Vincent Corleone.

(quoted from Francis Ford Coppola's film *The Godfather Part III*)

[19] In my previous book, I used the term *main verb* for this category, but the term itself is not so important.

[20] Considering four types of grammaticalization processes, i.e. desemanticization, decategorialization, cliticization, and erosion, Heine (1993: 58–66) assumes seven overall stages of grammaticalization: Stage A is a stage "where the verb has its full lexical meaning" (Heine (1993: 59)), while Stage G is "the final stage where the verb is now purely a grammatical marker reduced typically to a monosyllable affix unable to carry distinctive tone or stress (Heine (1993: 65))". English modals "are Stage E items in most of their uses (Heine (1993: 63))"; Stage E is a "hybrid" stage that has both "the characteristics of lexical verbs and grammatical markers". This seems tantamount to saying that modal auxiliaries are less prototypical members of the category "predicate" than lexical verbs and share less characteristics of "main verb" than the latter.

Chapter 2   A Compositional Theory of Tense   39

matic or even semantically bleached.[21]

The above observations enable us to present a hypothesis like (10):

(10)   Members belonging to the category "predicate", whether lexical or aux-
       iliary, express their own event time.

The following examples all contain an auxiliary and a lexical verb and therefore have a temporal structure including two event times (boldface mine).[22]

(11) a.   I **must hand** those drawings in by to-morrow.
                                        (O. Henry, *The Last Leaf*, p. 311)
     b.   "That's Dandy Jim Valentine's autograph.   He**'s resumed** business...
                                  (O. Henry, *A Retrieved Reformation*, p. 120)
     c.   ... You grew up in Nevada, you know the state, you know the people.
          I**'m counting** on you being my right-hand man when we make our
          move out there."   (Mario Puzo, *The Godfather*, p. 400)
     d.   Listen, **can** you **meet** me at Twin Pines Mall tonight at one fifteen?
                                        (Screenplay, *Back to the Future*, p. 10)

It should be noted that a verbal unit also expresses one event time.[23]   By
"verbal unit", I mean a unit consisting of a verb (including an auxiliary) and
other items that as a whole expresses either a partially "opaque" meaning (e.g.
make headway 'make progress toward') or a totally "opaque" meaning (e.g.
kick the bucket 'die'), i.e. a meaning totally different from the original one
represented compositionally by its constituents (e.g. *kick the bucket* in its liter-
al sense). The degree of unification of a verbal unit is strengthened by
contraction.   Thus, *be going to, ought to,* and *have to* are verbal units having
contracted forms, e.g. *(be) gonna, oughta, hafta* (Collins (2009: 20)), developing new meanings concerning time and modality.

To illustrate the point, consider (12):

(12) a.   "... I'm going to go to this girl's family for dinner and I don't want
          them hanging around."   (Mario Puzo, *The Godfather*, p. 338)

---

[21] The view that a schematic or semantically bleached situation has its own semantic value is in keeping with the Langackerian view that even expletives or the preposition *of* have
their own semantic values.
[22] Strictly speaking, not only the auxiliary *do* in the use of *do*-support but also the *be*
used in passives expresses its own event time. However, in this book, to make the story
simpler, I do not consider auxiliaries other than aspectual and modal ones.
[23] For the reason stated in note 22, I will treat passive *be* + past participle as a unit. For
a unified, detailed analysis of sentences containing past participles, including passive sentences, see Wada (2006b).

b. "The best referees ought to be here, but some of them are not be-cause the SRA is cutting back on everything," said Davies.

(BNC A9H)

c. They have to earn £ 20,000 a year to qualify for the charge card.

(BNC A3J)

In the case of *be going to*, for example, the original meaning is spatial move-ment, but nowadays *be going to* as a verbal unit has lost it and expresses fu-ture meaning. This is supported by the fact that *be going to* co-occurs with spatial *go*, as in (12a).

What is particularly important in connection with the theme of this book is that auxiliaries contained in future reference sentences can describe their own situations and thus express their own event times. This is supported by at least two pieces of evidence (see also Wada (2001a: §1.2)): (i) auxiliaries con-tained in future reference sentences are specified by time adverbials, and (ii) they can be denied.[24]

(13) a. Now we are going to have no money at the end of the month.

(Haegemen (1989: 297))

b. Gentleman has nothing to say about the deficit, nothing to say about welfare, and nothing to say about growth. Now he is going to make a speech tomorrow, which he kindly invites me to, but if there are not any policies, what would be the point of coming?

(http://www.publications.parliament.uk/pa/cm201213/cmhansrd/cm130213/debtext/130213–0001.htm)

c. Now we will have no money at the end of the month.

(Huddleston (1969: 789))

d. Bye bye er that's that done, now we'll do another one tomorrow.

(BNC KM3)

(14) a. It won't not turn on. (/www.expansys.com/ft.aspx?k=75270/)

b. Obviously, the gunman is going to pick a gun-free zone of a "certain size" and isn't going to not carry out his plan.

(/www.independentsentinel.com/geraldo-says-the-2nd-amendment-is-bullsht/)

---

[24] These two criteria do not necessarily apply to all auxiliaries. For example, the pro-gressive *be* and the perfect *have* cannot be denied, as in (i):

(i) a. *He isn't not going.   (Brinton (1988: 70); cf. Heine (1993: 56))
    b. *He hasn't not gone.   (Brinton (1988: 70))

Heine (1993: 56) states that in sentences like these, the unification of the two verbs (i.e. auxiliary and lexical verbs) proceeds to a simple phase (cf. Brinton (1988: 70–71)).

Chapter 2 A Compositional Theory of Tense

2.4.3.3. *Aspect and Situation Type*

Let us next consider aspect and situation type. As is well known, there are (at least) two types of aspect, i.e. lexical or situation aspect (Aktionsart) and grammatical or viewpoint aspect (e.g. Smith (1983); Binnick (2006)).[25] The lexical or situation aspect, sometimes referred to as verb or predicate type, has been differently divided into sub-classes. Vendler (1967) assumes four sub-categories named states, activities, accomplishments, and achievements. Mourelatos (1978) makes a major distinction between states and occurrences; occurrences are further divided into processes and events with the latter further subdivided into developments and punctual occurrences.[26, 27] Nakau (1994) assumes three sub-categories of basic predicate types, i.e. states, actions, and processes. Huddleston and Pullum (2002) are similar to Mourelatos (1978) in that they primarily distinguish states from occurrences, but they finally support Vendler's classification because the category "occurrences" is subdivided into the punctual type (i.e. achievements) and the durative type (i.e. processes) with the latter further subdivided into activities and accomplishments. Smith (1997) and Brinton (1998) add one more category, i.e. "semelfactives", to the four categories of the Vendlerian classification.[28, 29]

As for grammatical (viewpoint) aspect, the distinction between perfective and imperfective aspect is important. I follow Kortmann (1991: 13), Smith (1997: 170), among others, to assume that perfective aspect is operative when the speaker views the situation involved—whether static or dynamic, telic or atelic—in its entirety or as a complete whole (De Wit (2017: 71)), while im-

---

[25] Kortmann (1991:13) states that the notion of aspect is concerned with the grammaticalized perfective-imperfective contrast, while the notion of Aktionsart is concerned with the semantic properties of verbs/predicates having to do with time. Unlike tense—a deictic notion for Kortmann—aspect and Aktionsart are concerned with situation-internal time (Kortmann (1991: 19)).

[26] Mourelatos (1978: 422) introduces the notion of "event"—which does not necessarily require human agency—to cover the verb *see* in a sentence like *I saw him run*, because such an example cannot but fall under states in Vendler's classification, which he claims provides a counterintuitive analysis in that the verb in question means 'sighting', an action or occurrence.

[27] Mourelatos's "processes" correspond to Vendler's "activities".

[28] For a simple but good summary of differences in classification of situation aspect, see Binnick (2006).

[29] In most studies on lexical aspect, semelfactives are incorporated into achievements. This is perhaps because the two categories share the same features, i.e. [+dynamic] [+punctual] and [+telic]. As a criterion to distinguish them, we can point out that when progressivized, achievements receive an "extended time" reading, e.g. *He was dying for weeks*, but semelfactives receive an "iterative" reading, e.g. *He was coughing* (Brinton (1998: 38)).

perfective aspect is operative when he/she focuses on a middle part of the situation involved without paying attention to its beginning and final parts or ignores both of the left and right bounds of the situation involved.[30,31] I assume with De Wit and Brisard (2014) and De Wit (2017) that in English, perfective aspect is expressed by the simple form, while imperfective aspect can be expressed by the progressive form.

It goes without saying that the characteristics of these lexical aspect categories as well as information represented by perfective and imperfective aspect crucially affect tense interpretation. What is particularly important to the present theory is that their interaction with each other or the context makes a distinction between stative and non-stative situation type.[32] This distinction corresponds to the distinction between boundedness and unboundedness on the time line, which has strong influence on temporal relations between the event time of the situation involved and the time of orientation. Note that, when I use the term "situation (type)", I am not restricting myself to (the type of) verb or predicate phrases, but referring to (the type of) situations which can be described by verbs or predicates alone, verb or predicate phrases, and clauses or sentences containing verbs/predicates, arguments, and even adjuncts.

Stative situations at a clausal (sentential) level consist of unbounded situations. They are referred to by the "open" reading of stative predicates, as Smith (1997) puts it, and the imperfective reading of non-stative predicates, i.e. predicates other than states (Comrie (1976), Smith (1997: Ch. 8, 2003: 68), Williams (2002a: §1.2)). In English, stative verbs such as *be tall* or *know*, pseudo-auxiliaries (auxiliary units) such as *be able to* or *have to*, and progressive aspect contribute to stative situations (Radden and Dirven (2007: Ch. 8)). In addition, a habitual (e.g. *John walks to school*) or generic (e.g. *Beavers build dams*) reading of non-stative predicates makes the situation involved stative.

Stative situations involve no change or are at least meant to ignore change

---

[30] Givón (2005: 157) defines perfective and imperfective aspect as follows:
"From a perfective perspective, an event is viewed *as if* from far away, as a compact, well-bounded small object. From an imperfective perspective, it is viewed *as if* from near by, as a protracted, unbounded span."

[31] For a good survey of the history of how the terms aspect and Aktionsart have been used, see Kortmann (1991).

[32] The notions of "stative situation" and "non-stative situation" intended in this study correspond, respectively, to the notions of "stative situation" and "dynamic situation" in the sense of De Wit and Brisard (2014). They use the terms *stative situation* and *dynamic situation* in the same way that I use the terms *stative situation* and *non-stative situation*.

Chapter 2   A Compositional Theory of Tense

of state on the time line—such a change of state is usually implied by the beginning and/or end points—and hence in theory extend endlessly, unless otherwise restricted. This characteristic enables stative situations to include in their time range a reference point from which to evaluate them. Within my framework, this reference point is identified as time of orientation (on which is located the speaker's SD-viewpoint). The temporal relation of the event time of stative situations and the time of orientation can therefore usually be that of simultaneity (or inclusion). However, the speaker can focus only on a part of the situation obtaining at a different time from the reference point (i.e. the time of orientation) if there are grammatical, linguistic, or contextual indications of that. From these observations, it is possible with stative situations that the event time is simultaneous with the time of orientation or occupies a different time position from the latter. I refer to the former case as a simultaneous reading and the latter as a time-gap reading. The simultaneous reading allows a case where the event time covers not only the time of orientation but can also extend into the time range before or after the latter.[33, 34] The time-gap reading logically allows two possibilities: an anterior and posterior reading. What is to be noted here is that stative situations can receive either a simultaneous or time-gap reading.

On the other hand, non-stative situations at a clausal (sentential) level consist of bounded situations. They are indicated by the "closed" reading of stative predicates, as Smith (1997) puts it, and the perfective reading of non-stative predicates (Comrie (1976), Smith (1997: Ch. 8, 2003: 68), Williams (2002a: §1.2)). Recall that perfective aspect requires the situation involved to be "viewed in its entirety, as something complete but not necessarily completed" (Comrie (1976: 18).[35] From a cognitive point of view, to evaluate some-

---

[33] The simultaneous reading includes cases where the time of the situation involved (i.e. event time) coincides with, totally includes, or partially overlaps, the time of orientation.

[34] For cases where the event time extends into another time-area, we can take up, for example, the continuative use of the present perfect, where the event time of the past participle covers the time range extending from the past to the present. Consider the following:

(i)   You've been under arrest for ten minutes, 'Silky' Bob.

(O. Henry, *After Twenty Years*, p. 190)

(ii) This year, 1959, marks the hundredth year that Welton Academy has been in existence.   (N. H. Kleinbaum, *Dead Poets Society*, p. 2)

In (i), for example, the event time of the past participle *been under arrest*, a stative situation, is interpreted as ranging from the past to the present time-area. We will see the detailed temporal structure of the continuative use of the present perfect in Chapter 4.

[35] The notion of "completed" means that the target situation is actually bounded on the time line. Thus, a situation that is complete but not completed would be a future situation that has a (natural) endpoint but is not actualized yet.

thing as a whole on the time line requires it to be bounded on both sides, though these sides do not have to correspond to the intrinsic (or natural) beginning and end points. This is because we cannot see the whole picture of the situation when it is unbounded or endless. Non-stative situations are expressed not only by telic predicates such as accomplishments (e.g. *destroy the city*) or achievements (e.g. *die*) but also by atelic predicates like activities (e.g. *run*) in their simple form, which reflect perfective aspect. In addition, the inchoative reading of stative predicates (e.g. *come to know*) or the bounded reading of stative predicates (e.g. *live somewhere from 1997 to 2003*) are also examples of non-stative situations. The properties of non-stative situations allow them to basically receive a time-gap reading. This is because to evaluate non-stative situations as something complete or closed from a time of orientation (i.e. a point in time), their event time must be located at a different position from the latter, unless they are totally included in the latter (this is a very special case, which we will see in Chapter 4); if the time of orientation is included in the situation involved, we cannot see its contour and in this case progressive aspect is to be in operation.

To summarize the relations between situation types and temporal readings, we can present the following generalization:

(15)   In the default case, non-stative situations receive a time-gap reading, while stative situations allow either a simultaneous or time-gap reading.

For a better understanding of this generalization, let us consider the following indirect-speech sentences.

(16)   Some people said that Mark was an actor, a hype-artist, an image-projector.   (BNC ASV)

(17)   I thought I married a gentleman.

(O. Henry, *The Defeat of the City*, p. 245)

The linguistic fact is that an indirect speech complement like that in (16) receives either a simultaneous or anterior reading, depending on context, while an indirect speech complement like that in (17) only receives an anterior reading (the time of orientation in question is the time of the main clause). This fact conforms to generalization (15) because the complement clause in (17) indicates a non-stative situation and thus receives an anterior reading, i.e. a type of time-gap reading, but the complement clause in (16) depicts a stative situation and can therefore receive either one of the two readings, depending on context. A question, then, arises as to why both complement clauses cannot receive a posterior reading, for the past tense form in this environment is

Chapter 2 A Compositional Theory of Tense

chosen with the reporting time (i.e. speech time) as the base point and it is logically possible for the event time of the complement clause to be located in the time range following the time of the main clause as far as that time range is restricted to the past time-area. To solve this problem, we need to consider a certain type of modality (i.e. what I call assertive modality) and thus postpone this matter until Section 2.4.3.5.

Before closing this sub-section, I will show how perfect aspect is treated within the present framework. Perfect aspect expresses a state at the time of orientation stemming from the occurrence of a prior situation (for evidence that perfect sentences entail state, see Wada (2001a: §4.1.2)).[36] In English, this aspect is represented by the perfect *have* followed by a past participle and the tense structure of the perfect form consists of the combination of the tense-structure information represented by the two verbs. To be more specific, the event time of the perfect auxiliary occupies the same time as the time of orientation and the event time of the past participle is located at a time before it.

We have several pieces of evidence to claim that perfect sentences consist of the two situations, i.e. the state at the time of orientation (associated with *have*) and the prior situation (associated with the past participle). First, as I have already mentioned in my previous book, both of the event times can be specified by time adverbials. For example, in a sentence like *John had left at 3 p.m.*, the time adverb can specify either the event time of *have* or that of the past participle (see Wada (2001a: §4.1.1) for details).

Let us present other pieces of evidence. Consider first the following:

(18) a.   He avoided getting caught.   (Kiparsky and Kiparsky (1970: 146))
     b. *He avoided having got caught.   (Kiparsky and Kiparsky (1970: 146))
(19) *I don't realize that he has gone away.

(Kiparsky and Kiparsky (1970: 148))

(20) a.??Hans intentionally has kissed Lin.   (Katz (2003: 207))
     b.   Hans has intentionally kissed Lin.   (Katz (2003: 207))

Let us start with (18). The reason why (18b) is unacceptable is this. The perfect in the gerundive form is not an example of the continuative use and the perfect *have* thus describes a resultant state (i.e. the subject referent's suffering from a cold) stemming from the occurrence of the past participle situa-

---

[36] The reason why I use the term *state*, but not *resultant state*, to refer to the situation obtaining at the time of orientation denoted by the perfect *have* is that in the case of the continuative use of perfect sentences, as illustrated in note 34, the state obtaining at the time of orientation is not a result of the occurrence of the prior event.

tion (i.e. his catching a cold). Since this perfect clause entails the resultant state obtaining at the time of avoiding as the time of orientation, it is a contradiction to say that someone avoids what is already existent.

Next, the unacceptability of (19) can also be explained along these lines. The complement clause entails that the resultant state stemming from the occurrence of his going away obtains at the time of the main clause. This indicates that the speaker of the whole sentence knows the male's situation now and cannot say he/she does not realize it now. Sentence (19) is therefore unacceptable.

Finally, let us consider (20). The adverb *intentionally* is generally said to only modify an agentive verb. In (20b), it occupies the syntactic position that can modify the non-finite verb *kissed* (i.e. complement verb), an agentive verb; hence (20b) is acceptable. In (20a), by contrast, *intentionally* occupies the syntactic position that can only modify the finite verb *have*, which is not an agentive verb and describes a resultant state; hence the low acceptability of (20a).

The above observations suggest that perfect sentences entail a (resultant) state in addition to the prior situation, stative or non-stative, and their tense structure thus contains two event times, i.e. the event time associated with *have* and that associated with the past participle. They therefore strengthen my position that auxiliary verbs can express their own situations and thus their own event times.

2.4.3.4. Modality

The next factor to be considered is modality. In my previous book, I defined modality as "a speaker's subjective mental state or attitude at the time of his or her utterance or thought (Wada (2001a: 22))",[37] assuming that a sentential meaning consists of the modality (or subjective) domain and the proposition (or objective) domain.[38] Predictive and assertive modality were considered to be particularly important to tense interpretation. In this book, that assumption is reconsidered and developed in terms of sentential utterances (see Chapter 3 for details) where the two types of modality are still important to tense interpretation. In what follows, I will summarize the statements about

---

[37] This definition is similar to Nakau's (1994) definition of modality. For some differences, see Wada (2001a: 29; note 25). Some other studies (e.g. Lyons (1977), Palmer (1979, 1986), Coates (1983)) also define modality in terms of the speaker's opinion or attitude.

[38] This distinction is similar to that between modality and proposition by Lyons (1977) and that between locutionary and illocutionary acts by Austin (1962) (cf. also Palmer (1986: §1.3)).

the two types of modality in English made in the previous book with some additions.

First, predictive modality is a mental attitude typically expressed by the modal *will*. For instance, the sentence containing *will* in (21), cited from a web page about a concert schedule, is semantically divided into the propositional content "Ian and Ani play a certain music" and the speaker's prediction about it, i.e. predictive modality.

(21) Ian & Ani will play Piazzolla's *Oblivion*, Rodion Shchedrin's *In the Style of Albeniz*, Ravel's *Habanera*, as well as the Sonata for Cello and Piano by Sergei Prokofiev.
> (http://blogs.wfmt.com/offmic/2014/11/07/ian-ani-live-on-wfmt/)

Next, assertive modality is the unmarked type of modality and usually represented by unmodalized forms, i.e. non-modal forms without modification by modal adverbs. For example, sentence (22) is generally said to describe a non-modalized situation, but in my analysis, it is semantically factored into the propositional content of Bach's Chaconne being an inexhaustible theme and the speaker's assertion about it, i.e. assertive modality.

(22) Bach's Chaconne is an inexhaustible theme.
> (http://www.lewiskaplan.net/news.htm)

Assertive modality can also accompany a modal sentence if the modal represents, say, Palmer's (1974, 1987, 2001) dynamic modality, which is an element belonging to the proposition domain within my framework. Consider (23) for example:

(23) He WILL do everything himself, although he has a secretary.
> (Declerck (1991a: 361))

Will in (23) expresses volition, i.e. a dynamic modality in Palmer's terminology, or "non-subjective" root modality; consequently, not only the situation of his doing everything himself but also his (strong) will to do so constitutes the propositional content, which combines with the speaker's assertive modality to describe what sentence (23) means.

In analyzing future expressions in English, it is of great importance to consider how modality is related to tense interpretation, because futurity and modality are inseparable from each other (Lyons (1977), Dahl (1985)). Thus far, very many studies have treated the notions of "prediction" and "assertion" differently based on their theoretical positions. In general, previous studies, including the previous version of my theory of tense, have not presented a

48   *The Grammar of Future Expressions in English*

comprehensive system for dealing with phenomena concerning tense, modality, mental attitudes, and speech acts, from a unified point of view, a system whereby the notions of prediction and assertion (including my notions of predictive and assertive modality) should be defined and treated in detail. Without such a broader theoretical point of view, it is not constructive, if not a nonsense, to say which analysis is better. In Chapter 3, I will therefore develop a theory that can, from a unified point of view, treat not only modality and mental attitudes but also speech acts in detail, which is further supported by a general theory of language use. My theory of tense will combine with this theory to provide a more comprehensive and systematic model, which in turn provides an explanatory basis for a variety of phenomena to be observed in Chapters 5 to 10.

2.4.3.5. Linguistic Environments

Let us next consider how the properties (characteristics) of linguistic environments have an influence on tense interpretation. In interpreting absolute tense forms (finite forms in English), principle (4) above works in the choice of tense form by default and usually gets preference over the influence by the properties of linguistic environments, as we saw in Section 2.4.1. Only in some special cases such as the historical present or the past-in-the-future context does principle (4) give way to the influence by the properties of the linguistic environment involved. In computing the event time, by contrast, the identification of the time of orientation—at which the speaker's SD-viewpoint is situated—is subject to the properties of the linguistic environment involved.

The properties of linguistic environments can sometimes affect the choice of the type of tense forms. For example, in the complement position of a verb, the complement verb is syntactically closely related to the head verb (they are in a "sister" relation), which requires the former verb to have a close relationship to the latter in terms of the tense structure. As we have seen, the tense structure of relative tense forms consists only of the (grammatical) time relation between the event time and the (potential) time of orientation, which is to be identified as the event time of the head verb in this case, and can thus show a closer relationship between the event time and time of orientation than that of absolute tense forms, in which the event time is not directly related to the time of orientation because of the intervention of a time-sphere. Relative tense forms are therefore chosen here.

Take, for example, the *will*-sentences in (21) and (23) above. A bare infinitive (a relative tense form) represents a tense structure expressing a grammatical time relation between the event time and potential time of orientation,

Chapter 2   A Compositional Theory of Tense

which will be identified as the event time of *will* as head verb in temporal calculation. In both examples, the contextual information finally allows the event time of the bare infinitive to be located at a time posterior to the event time of *will* (simultaneous with speech time), one usually located in the future time-area.

By contrast, in indirect speech complements, i.e. tensed clauses, such as those in (16) and (17) above, the position of the complement clause verb is syntactically in a distance from that of the verb in the main (i.e. reporting) clause, whose event time will serve as the time of orientation for the event time of the complement clause in temporal calculation. For this reason, the target verb in the complement clause is required to be an absolute tense form, whose tense structure involves a positional relationship between the speaker's t-viewpoint and a time-sphere (see Figures 2(i) and 2(ii) above) and therefore prevents one event time from directly relating to another event time as time of orientation.

As we saw in Section 2.4.2, the properties of indirect speech complements in past contexts (i.e. reporting clauses referring to the past) allow principle (4) to work (i.e. the default case), and both the deictic and non-deictic inter-pretations of the complement clause verb are available. On the other hand, the properties of indirect speech complements in future contexts (i.e. reporting clauses referring to the future) prevent principle (4) from working and there-fore force the time of orientation for computing the event time of the comple-ment clause verb to be identified as the time of the (expected) original utter-ance or thought in the future; only the non-deictic interpretation is allowed.

Now, we can answer the question raised in Section 2.4.3.3, i.e. why the complement clause verb does not receive a posterior reading, as in (1), (16), and (17). Take, for example, (1), i.e. *Mary said that she was tired.* This question is solved by the combination of the nature of assertive modality and properties of indirect speech complements, namely that modality in this envi-ronment is attributed to the original speaker or thinker (see Wada (2001a: Ch.8) for the justification and details). In (1), the assertive modality accom-panying the unmodalized form *was* in the complement clause is attributed to the original speaker Mary, whose perspective is put at the time of the original utterance (i.e. the time of the main clause). What we can usually make an as-sertion about is what is present or past relative to the time of the assertion. (Henceforth, this phenomenon will be referred to as the "restriction on assertion".) In this environment, the time of the assertion is the time of the original utterance. The event time of *was* therefore cannot be interpreted as located at a time later than the time of the original utterance. For this reason, the complement clause of an indirect speech sentence like that in (1) usually does not receive a posterior reading.

In independent or main clauses, it is usually the case that speech time doubles as the base point for the choice of tense form and as the time of orientation for the event-time computation. However, registers and discourse modes in the sense of Smith (2003) may affect the tense-interpretation process in independent or main clauses, especially the process of the event-time computation, although considering it is out of the scope of this book.

2.4.4. Two Types of Event Time

As we have already seen, within my framework, not only lexical verbs but also auxiliary verbs can express their own event times and an event time can serve as the time of orientation for calculating another event time. Thus, in (21) and (23) above, the event time of the modal *will*, i.e. the time at which prediction or volition occurs, functions as the time of orientation for computing the event time of the infinitive. In this sub-section, we will observe two types of event time which are distinguished based on whether a given situation is "contentful" or not.

As also seen above, both the situation whose semantic content is specific or lexically filled and the situation whose semantic content is schematic or semantically bleached can express an event time. We need to say something about the latter types of situations. The content of schematic situations can be specified with the help of the context in the tense-interpretation process and hence they can express so-called pure event times, as with specific situations or semantically contentful situations. However, the event time expressed by semantically bleached situations serves merely as the time of orientation for computing another event time because their semantic content is considerably or extremely "empty". This type of event time is referred to as an "orientational" event time within my framework.

There are two major cases where an event time is interpreted as an orientational type. One is that the event time of a semantically bleached situation occupies the same time as, or is included in, the event time of a specific situation, or a semantically contentful situation. A case in point is the progressive *be*.

(24)   I'm representing the New York Amalgamated Short Snap Biscuit Cracker and Frazzled Wheat Company.

(O. Henry, *A Retrieved Reformation*, p. 120)

In (24), the progressive *be* is not associated with a specific situation like the

Chapter 2   A Compositional Theory of Tense   51

one associated with the present participle *representing*. The event time of *be* is simultaneous with the event time of *representing*. The former therefore functions merely as the time of orientation for computing the latter, being an orientational event time.

The other case is the event time of the verb which itself has semantic content but is "coerced" to be semantically bleached by the context in the tense-interpretation process. Examples of this case are given in (25):

(25) a.   Tomorrow will be Sunday.   (Hornby (1975: 95))
      b.   Next century will begin on the first of January, 2001.
                                                             (Hornby (1975: 96))
      c.   I will be 83 next week and just can't be bothered any more ...
                                                             (BNC B11)

In these sentences, the modal *will* expresses a certain original value (which we will see in Chapter 3) but through the temporal calculation it is interpreted as functioning merely as a "space-filler", i.e. the mere place at which the speaker's SD-viewpoint is situated. This is because our encyclopedic knowledge tells us that the future occurrence of the infinitival situations in (25) is seen as self-evident and *will* seems to give a virtually null contribution to the sentential meaning. I argue that in this case, the semantic content of the situation associated with *will* is coerced to be semantically bleached in the process of temporal calculation. For example, in (25a), which is assumed to be uttered on Saturday, the situation of tomorrow's being Sunday is self-evident and therefore interpreted as occurring as a natural consequence of the common sense or encyclopedic knowledge available now. From these observations, the event time of the *will* in question serves merely as the time of orientation for calculating the event time of the infinitival situation.

2.4.5.   Temporal Focus

Finally, let us consider one more notion necessary for temporal calculation, i.e. temporal focus, which constitutes part of a temporal structure. When the speaker construes a scene consisting of a set of situations, he/she can possibly pay special attention to (or focus on) one specific situation. When this information is reflected in temporal structures, the notion of temporal focus comes into play and is directed at the event time of such a specific situation. Since it is a type of focus, it is by definition not directed at the orientational event time (cf. Section 2.4.4).

It is often said that the time specified by time adverbials is focused on or featured, but the temporal focus is not necessarily the same as such a focus.

Consider (9a) again, repeated here as (25):

(25) "They're falling faster now. Three days ago there were almost a hundred. It made me head ache to count them ... There are only five left now." (=(9a))

In the sentences except for the third one, the present and past tense forms are modified by time adverbials and the situations involved are therefore definite on the time line. This may suggest that such situations are focused on in that the speaker invites the hearer to pay attention to them by making the time of the relevant part of the situation involved (i.e. event time) definite. In these cases, the temporal focus is also directed at the event time involved. However, what should be stressed is that the temporal focus is also in operation in the third sentence, i.e. a sentence without any time adverbial. Even in this sentence, the speaker pays attention to the situation involved, i.e. a specific situation that the speaker invites the hearer to construe in such a way. The temporal focus is related to the specificity of the situation involved.

However, it should also be noted that the temporal focus can be directed at a situation whose position on the time line is not clearly specified. What is necessary for the operation of temporal focus is thus the speaker's concern about or reference to the situation directly related to the time line. This is confirmed by the following examples:

(26) a. I knew something dire was headed in his direction, but I didn't know when or where it would hit him.

(https://books.google.co.jp/books?isbn=0743213521)

   b. "I did actually divest, but I didn't know when I divested, nor would I have any reason to know that, given the fact that literally thousands of different investments are involved, given the fact that nobody brought it to my attention until I'm in the midst of a competitive campaign."

(https://www.counterpunch.org/2016/03/18/the-curious-case-of-alan-grayson/)

The time of the first sentence of each example is indefinite and non-specific with respect to its time position, for the speaker says he/she did not know the time at which the relevant situation occurred or obtained (which is indicated by the negative sentences following the first sentences). However, the speaker is paying attention to that situation in that he/she has in mind, or is concerned with, what actually occurred or obtained on the time line. For this reason, the temporal focus is directed at the event time of the situation in question.

Chapter 2   A Compositional Theory of Tense   53

Furthermore, the time at which the temporal focus is directed can some-times be different from the time specified by time adverbials, as in (27):

(27) a.   Now we are going to have no money at the end of the month. (=(13a))

   b.   Now we will have no money at the end of the month. (=(13c))

It is often pointed out in the literature (e.g. McIntosh (1966: 105), Wekker (1976: 126), Palmer (1979: 121), Haegeman (1983: 65); cf. Fleischman (1982: 95–98)) that future expressions with *will* are future-oriented while future ex-pressions with *be going to* are present-oriented. However, this distinction of the two future expressions in terms of time orientation is blurred by examples like those in (27), because they are both compatible with the present time ad-verb *now* and the future time adverb *at the end of the month*. The introduc-tion of temporal focus into the present theory clearly characterizes the present orientation of future expressions with *be going to* and the future orientation of future expressions with *will*. In the temporal structure of future expressions with *be going to*, the temporal focus is directed at the event time of *be going to* (a verbal unit) located in the present (including speech time); in the tem-poral structure of future expressions with *will*, it is directed at the event time of the bare infinitive located in the future. In either case, one event time specified by a time adverb does not receive temporal focus.

   Finally, it must be noted that the notion under discussion comes into play on the TI level, i.e. in the tense-interpretation process. This implies that, even if the relevant situation is originally schematic (e.g. the situation associated with *be going to*), its event time can receive a temporal focus if its content is "filled up" in the tense-interpretation process. (For how this notion concretely contributes to constructing temporal structures, see Chapters 5 to 10.)

2.5.   Conclusion and Theoretical Orientation

   In this chapter, we have outlined the theory of tense proposed in my previ-ous works with some clarifications and additions. We have especially ob-served the notions and factors necessary for tense interpretation and how they work.

   The present theory will be developed in Chapter 3 to explain a variety of synchronic aspects of temporal phenomena and related issues such as those concerning modality, metal attitudes, and speech acts from a more comprehen-sive and broader point of view, i.e. a point of view advanced by the semantic (de)composition of sentential utterances and supported by a general theory of language use.

The tense model to be developed will also take in the notion of semantic retention, which is related to diachronic aspects of temporal phenomena. Semantic retention is operative when meaning M continues to be one of the meanings expressed by form F even after a new meaning has been added to that form. This implies that it is not the case that the new meaning unites with the existing meaning to create a fused meaning, but that it continues to be an independent meaning expressed by that form.

This position is in keeping with a general tendency of meaning change, i.e. the idea that after the period when older and newer meanings coexist in a form, the older one disappears as grammaticalization proceeds. If a new meaning exists independently of an old one in a form, then the old meaning can easily disappear without affecting the meaning structure of that form. On the other hand, if it were the case that a new meaning unites with an old one to create a fused one, we could not explain why only a part of the fused meaning (corresponding to the old one) fades away—how can we pick out that part from the whole meaning which is already fused? (In this connection, see also Section 4.4.)

Moreover, the position under consideration enables us to explain cases where an old meaning of a given form survives in some linguistic environments, while a new meaning is dominant in other environments in the same period of the history of a given language. Take the form *will* for example. This form was once a lexical verb representing volition/will, but in present-day English it has gained another grammatical status, i.e. modal auxiliary, and expresses a number of uses/functions (i.e. meanings). Although its grammatical status has changed, the form still retains an older meaning (i.e. volition/will) in some contexts (e.g. a certain type of conditional clauses). This can be explained by our view that the older meaning of *will* still survives as an independent meaning in present-day English and comes to the fore in certain linguistic environments (we will see this matter in detail in Chapter 5).

In the present model, (at a synchronic level) those kinds of independent meanings (i.e. semantic uses and functions) are related to their own temporal structures: an independent semantic use/function has its own temporal structure. But how can we acquire the temporal structures of semantic uses/functions? I assume that when the speaker encounters a new semantic use of a given tense form, he/she considers it based on his/her cognitive knowledge as well as the temporal-structure and tense-structure information of that

Chapter 2   A Compositional Theory of Tense   55

form;[39] if the speaker recognizes it as related to but different from the existing semantic uses, then he/she acquires a new temporal structure typically by developing the temporal structure of an existing use (or more) into a revised or extended one.[40] In this way, temporal structures are gradually being stored in the speaker's mind.

---

[39] The tense-structure information serves as the "schema" in the sense of Langacker (1993), which prevents an unrelated and/or endless extension of the semantic range of the (tense) form involved.

[40] I assume that when the speaker encounters a first use of a given (tense) form, he/she does not follow the process but accepts it as the semantic meaning of that form.

Chapter 3

Modality, Mental Attitudes, and Related Phenomena

3.1. Introduction

Having seen my position on tense in the previous chapters, I will now consider modality, mental attitudes, and speech acts as tense-related phenomena. To be more specific, as I stated in Section 2.4.3.4, I develop a theory of modality and mental attitudes, focusing on predictive and assertive modality, which are closely related to the tense-interpretation process, and then introduce a general theory of language use called the Three-Tier Model of Language use to deal with the relation between mental attitudes and speech acts.

Before opening a discussion of this topic, let me make two basic assumptions explicit. One is that the category of modality is defined not merely in morpho-syntactic terms but also in semantic terms. This means that modality is not necessarily expressed by linguistic forms but can reflect semantic notions such as mental attitudes (cf. Nakau (1994), Jaszczolt (2009)). On this basis, I assumed in my previous book (Wada (2001a: §1.5)) and continue to assume in this book that assertive modality is a speaker's mental attitude toward the situation involved, which is not expressed by any linguistic marker in English.

The other assumption is that *will* is a modal and not a future tense marker. I argued for this assumption in a previous work (Wada (2001a: Ch. 1)), though there are still many proponents of the view that *will* is a future tense marker (auxiliary). I presented several arguments for my position there. However, as implied in Section 2.4.3.4, it is not constructive to defend one's position without recourse to a broader perspective which can account for the relevant phenomena more comprehensively. The category "future" is such a case. Considering (i) the characteristics of finiteness (e.g., finite verbs appear in the left-most position of finite verb phrases in English), (ii) the assumption that auxiliaries belong to the same category "predicate" as lexical verbs, and (iii) the theoretical consequence that English has two A-morphemes (the latter

57

two were already observed in Chapter 2), *will* is assumed to be a present (finite) tense form (i.e. a tense form with a present tense morpheme as A-morpheme) and thus establishes a present time-sphere (grammatical present) that will by default cover the present and future time-area (cognitive time range) in the tense-interpretation process. *Will* does not establish a future time-sphere (grammatical future) and is therefore not seen as a future tense marker (auxiliary) at least in the same way that present and past tense inflections (A-morphemes) are regarded as tense markers. I argue that this treatment of *will*, together with the fact that *will* behaves similarly to "real" modals such as *may*, *must*, and *can* (see also Wada (2001a: §1.2)), theoretically enables us to claim that *will* is a finite modal (cf. Blevins (2006: 519)).[1] However, to reinforce this claim as well as the first basic assumption above, I will need to introduce the semantic (de)composition of sentential utterances and a general theory of language use.

As already stated in my previous book as well as in Section 2.4.3.4, I assume that predictive and assertive modality are speaker's mental attitudes (occurring at speech time) toward the situation involved. However, these two modalities are closely related to—and often used in the same sense as—prediction and assertion, which are employed in different ways within different frameworks. For example, the term *assertion* is usually used as one type of speech act, or the term *assertive* is usually related to one type of illocutionary point in speech act theory (Searle (1969, 1975, 1979)).[2] For another example, the term *assertion* is often used to express a notion opposed to the term *presupposition*. As we will see later in this chapter, my notion of assertive modality is not equal (though related) to these notions. Furthermore, the term *prediction* is often used as another way of referring to the future (e.g. Torres-Cacoullos and Walker (2009), Declerck (1991a, 1991b, 2006), Gotti (2003)), whereas assertion is often used as another way of referring to a fact, a notion restricted to present or past time reference. My notions of predictive and assertive modality are not equal (though related) to these notions, either.

I therefore need to specify in what sense predictive and assertive modality are speaker's mental attitudes, i.e. elements belonging to the subjective aspect of sentential meaning, and how the idea is justified. In particular, I need to clarify at least the following two points.

---

[1] For arguments of the finiteness of *will*, see Section 5.3.1.

[2] In my previous book (Wada (2001a)), I used the terms (*modality of*) *prediction* and (*modality of*) *assertion* or *direct assertion* to refer, respectively, to predictive and assertive modality in this book.

Chapter 3   Modality, Mental Attitudes, and Related Phenomena   59

(1) a.   Under what system are predictive and assertive modality character-
         ized as speaker's mental attitudes?
    b.   In what framework and in what sense are the notions of "subjectivity"
         and "objectivity" concerning modality used?

To this end, I will construct a more comprehensive framework that can systematically deal with not only modality and mental attitudes but also speech
acts and which is supported by a general theory of language use. This is because, as Haegeman (1983: 99) also points out, describing the uses of linguistic items requires an account of them based on utterances in the relevant
speech situations and this is especially the case with modal elements in that
they are closely related to the speaker's judgment in the speech situation (including speech time). As a general theory of language use, I adopt the Three-
Tier Model of Language Use, a theory about the relation between grammar
and pragmatics proposed in a series of studies by Yukio Hirose (Hirose (2013,
2015, 2016a, 2016b, 2017)) and developed in studies by his proponents
(Ikarashi (2015), Konno (2015), Shizawa (2013, 2015), Shizawa and Hirose
(2015), Wada (2013a, 2017b)). By reconsidering predictive and assertive modality and related phenomena within this broader framework, I can give a
more convincing account of modal phenomena and therefore justify my position about predictive and assertive modality. In addition, this model will clarify in what sense subjectivity and objectivity related to modality are used. In
consequence, the combination of this model of modality, mental attitudes and
speech acts with the theory of tense outlined in Chapter 2 offers a more comprehensive and well-motivated model that provides a theoretical basis for temporal and modal phenomena of future expressions in English to be considered
in Chapters 5 to 10.

3.2.   A Diversity of Studies on Modality

3.2.1.   Definition

I will open up the discussion by considering the definition of modality in
more detail. There have been numerous studies on modality and modal expressions such as modal auxiliaries or adverbs even if we restrict them to

English.[3,4] We cannot survey and compare all of them in detail but will briefly outline major studies of them collectively.

First, modality in its narrow definition is related only to the notions of possibility and necessity. However, this position is not so prevalent. Many linguists, such as Nuyts (2005: 17) and Jaszczolt (2009), have a negative view on it.

Next, one of the most popular views on its definition seems to be the one in terms of non-factuality (Lyons (1977), Palmer (1979, 1990, 2001, 2003), Hoya (1997), Sawada (2006), Depraetere and Reed (2006), Depraetere and Langford (2012)). Under this definition, however, some members belonging to the category of modality have very different characteristics from other members. For example, using Heine's (1995) properties to characterize (German) modals, such as the notions "force" and "agent", Coates (1995) examines modals of possibility in English, arguing that *can* in its "existential" sense, as in (2a), shares no property with *must* in its "root obligation" sense, as in (2b), except that they are both non-subjective.[5]

(2) a. Lions can be dangerous.   (Coates (1993: 58))
    b. All students must obtain the consent of the Dean. (Coates (1995: 56))

This suggests that, as Nuyts (2005, 2006) points out, the definition of modality in terms of non-factuality is not of necessity (cf. also Palmer (1986: 18)). That is, we can extend the notion of modality to cover something other than non-factuality.

3.2.2. Classification

There are many ways to classify modality. Some studies tend to assume as many types of modality as possible; for example, von Wright (1951) assumes five categories (epistemic, deontic, dynamic, alethic and existential) and Rescher (1968) refers to eight (alethic, epistemic, temporal, boulomaic, deon-

---

[3] Traditionally, the central topic of the discussion about modality was on modal (auxiliary) verbs, but of course there have been extensive studies. For example, Perkins (1983) considers not only modal (auxiliary) verbs but also modal adverbs, adjectives, and nouns; Hoye (1997) gives an extensive analysis of the relation between modal verbs and adverbs.

[4] In this book, as Nuyts (2006: 8) puts it, mood is taken as a grammaticalized notion concerned with "formal categories of expressions of modal notions" (van der Auwera and Plungian (1998)), such as indicative vs. subjunctive (vs. imperative) or realis vs. irrealis. With respect to the relationship between mood and modality, Nuyts and van der Auwera (2016) deal with a variety of topics concerning it.

[5] The property "subjectivity" is introduced by Coates into Heine's system to characterize epistemic modality.

Chapter 3   Modality, Mental Attitudes, and Related Phenomena   61

tic, evaluative, causal, likelihood). Others allow only two categories, e.g. epistemic and root modality (R. Lakoff (1972), Hoffman (1976), Coates (1983, 1995), Sweetser (1990), Langacker (1991, 2008), Papafragou (1998, 2000)).[6, 7, 8] It seems that one generally accepted classification is a tripartite distinction of modality, i.e. epistemic, deontic, and dynamic modality (Palmer (1974, 1979, 1986, 1990),[9] Perkins (1983), Verstraete (2001), Huddleston and Pullum (2002), Nuyts (2005, 2006), Collins (2009)).[10] There are also many studies with a diachronic point of view that classify modality into the agent-oriented type,[11] the speaker-oriented type,[12] and the epistemic type (Bybee and

---

[6] Those who advocate Chomskyan syntax tend to take this dichotomy of modality perhaps because epistemic and root modals can be paraphrased differently in terms of syntactic structures. For example, the sentence containing *must* in (i) can be paraphrased into (iia) when it expresses an epistemic meaning and into (iib) when it expresses a root meaning.

    (i)   She must play the flute.

    (ii) a. It is necessary that she plays the flute. (epistemic)

       b. It is necessary for her to play the flute. (root)

[7] Sweetser (1990) assumes a third type of modality, i.e. what she calls speech-act modality, as an independent category. However, it is debatable whether this category is on a par with root and epistemic modality. Papafragou (2000), for example, denies the category of speech-act modality, arguing that it can be reanalyzed in terms of metarepresentation in relevance theory.

[8] Some linguists use the term *deontic* to cover all members of non-epistemic modality.

[9] In Palmer (2001), epistemic modality combines with evidential modality to form propositional modality, while deontic and dynamic modality constitute eventive modality.

[10] Dynamic modality—a term introduced by von Wright (1951: 8)—is sometimes not treated as modality in the literature. For example, Boyd and Thorne (1969: 71f.) and Palmer (1974: 115ff.) state that the following three types of dynamic sense do not constitute modality.

    (i) a. He can swim over a mile. ['ability']

       b. I can hear music. ['progressive' in Boyd and Thorne's use; 'sensation' in Palmer's use]

       c. Cocktail parties can be boring. ['sporadic' in Boyd and Thorne's use; 'characteristic' in Palmer's use]

[11] It is generally said that the agent-oriented type of modality has arisen first in the grammaticalization path of modals. Because it "reports the existence of internal and external conditions on an agent with respect to the completion of the action (Bybee, Perkins and Pagliuca (1994: 177))", it is often regarded as constituting part of the propositional content. Included in this type of modality are modals of obligation based on external or social conditions (e.g. *must, should*), modals of necessity based on physical conditions (e.g. *need*), modals of ability based on internal enabling conditions (e.g. *can*), modals of desire, intention or willingness based on internal volitional conditions (e.g. *will, would*), and modals of root possibility based on general enabling conditions (Bybee, Perkins and Pagliuca (1994: 177–178); cf. also Krug (2000: 42)). It seems that dynamic modality and (non-speaker-oriented) objective deontic modality correspond to the agent-oriented modality.

[12] The speaker-oriented type of modality includes "all such directives (commands, de-

Pagliuca (1987), Traugott (1989), Heine (1993), Bybee, Perkins and Pagliuca (1994), Krug (2000), Traugott and Dasher (2002)).

3.2.3. Type of Analysis[13]

Let us now turn to the type of analysis. Various types of analyses on modality and related issues have been offered thus far. A first group consists of descriptive polysemous approaches, some of which are corpus-based (Palmer (1974, 1979, 1986, 1987, 1990, 2001), Coates (1983), Quirk et al. (1985), Sawada (2006), Collins (2009), Depraetere and Langford (2012)). Second, we have force-dynamics analyses, such as Talmy (1988) and Sweetser (1990).[14] As a third group, we can point out relevance-theoretic analyses, such as Klinge (1993), Groefsema (1995), and Papafragou (1998, 2000, 2006).[15] A fourth group includes cognitive grammar approaches (e.g. Langacker (1991, 2008)),[16] while a fifth group is composed of analyses within original semantic frameworks, such as a hierarchical semantics analysis (Nakau (1992, 1994)). As a sixth type, we have a core semantics analysis based on speech act theory, such as Perkins (1983) and Nakano (1993). A seventh group is a hybrid type consisting of a monosemous and polysemous analysis, such as Depraetere (2010, 2014) and Cappelle and Depraetere (2016), while an eighth group consists of prototype approaches (e.g. Coates (1983), Quirk et al. (1985), Salkie (2009); cf. also Wada (2001a)). Finally, we have a group of diachronic analyses that consider the semantic change and development of modality and

---

mands, requests, warnings, exhortations, recommendations) as well as utterances in which the speaker grants the addressee permission (Bybee, Perkins and Pagliuca (1994: 179))". Speaker-oriented, subjective non-epistemic modality therefore corresponds to this type of modality (cf. Krug (2000: 42)).

[13] For surveys and criticisms of previous studies on modality and modal expressions, see, for example, Verstraete (2001), Nuyts (2005, 2006), and Depraetere and Reed (2006). Above all, Sawada (2006) offers a comprehensive summary of the previous studies and his own analysis of various phenomena concerning modality and related issues. In this book, we do not compare our framework concerning modality with others because the main purpose of this book is to justify the position we take with respect to predictive and assertive modality as speaker's mental attitudes.

[14] For criticisms of force-dynamics analyses, see Nuyts (2005: 18).

[15] For relevance-theoretic analyses, Sawada (2006: 178–189) points out some problems and/or insufficiencies deriving from lack of cognitive motivation.

[16] In Langacker's model, modals always link the situation described by the predicate involved to the speech situation (i.e. ground) and are thus not profiled on the "stage". However, as Sawada (2006: 154–155) points out, it seems that Langacker's model cannot deal with objective modals, because they do not seem to constitute grounding elements. Moreover, in other European languages such as German, modals can appear in non-finite position, a non-grounding position, so that Langacker's analysis as it stands cannot deal with this case.

Chapter 3   Modality, Mental Attitudes, and Related Phenomena   63

modals in terms of grammaticalization (e.g. Aijmer (1985), Baybee and Pagliuca (1987), Traugott (1989), Heine (1993), Bybee, Perkins and Pagliuca (1994), Krug (2001), Traugott and Dasher (2002)).

3.3.   Subjectivity and Objectivity of Modality and Modals

While, as we saw in the previous sub-section, the treatment of modality and modals is diverse, the matter of subjectivity vs. objectivity concerning modality and modals has been a central topic, or at least a topic worth considering, for most, if not all, studies of modality and modals. Traditionally, modality has been linked to subjectivity (Halliday (1970), Lyons (1977, 1995), Palmer (1979, 1990), Coates (1983, 1995), Perkins (1983), Nakau (1992, 1994), Nuyts (2001, 2005, 2006), Verstraete (2001), Collins (2009)). The subjectivity in question usually means 'speaker-relatedness' or 'speaker's involvement', defined as a matter of "whether or not the modal in question involves the speaker in the utterance" (Verstraete (2001: 1509)). Because this topic is crucially relevant in the attempt to develop my framework, we will survey, in this sub-section, how it has been treated in some representative studies.

First, Halliday (1970) reserves the term *modality* for the subjective modality which obtains only at speech time and has no tense distinction, i.e. epistemic modality (and part of subjective deontic modality); it is a linguistic element associated with the interpersonal component (related to the social role function).[17] Instances of the non-subjective (objective) modality are members of the category referred to as *modulation* and belong to the ideational component, constituting part of the content of the clause.[18, 19]

Second, Lyons (1977) claims that epistemic and deontic modality both have subjective and objective uses.[20] Developing Hare's (1970) tripartite distinction

---

[17] Within Halliday's framework, modality is characterized as "[t]he speaker's involvement at the speech event in the utterance" (Halliday (1970: 336)). He also defines it by saying that "[t]hrough modality, the speaker associates with the thesis an indication of its status and validity in his own judgment (p. 335)". Thus, not only epistemic modality but also subjective deontic modality, as in *Jones must resign*, involves the speaker's judgment and they therefore belong to members of modality in his sense (Halliday (1970: 349)).

[18] Halliday (1970: 349) defines modulation as "part of the ideational content of the clause".

[19] Verstraete's (2001) position is the same as Halliday's (1970) in that epistemic modality is always subjective but dynamic modality is objective, while deontic modality can be either subjective or objective.

[20] Lyons's (1977) objective epistemic modality is very close to alethic modality, because he himself states that "[i]t is also difficult to draw a sharp distinction between what we are calling objective epistemic modality and alethic modality" (p. 791). In this connection,

64   *The Grammar of Future Expressions in English*

between neustic, tropic, and phrastic components of the logical structure of utterances,[21] he argues that subjective epistemic modality contains a qualified neustic (or I-say-so) component while objective epistemic modality contains an unqualified neustic component but has a qualified tropic (or it-is-so) component (Lyons (1977: 800)). He also suggests that subjective deontic modality contains a qualified tropic (or so-be-it) component, but objective deontic modality is part of the phrastic (or propositional) component (Lyons (1977: 833)).[22]

Third, Perkins (1983) and Palmer (1979, 1990) both discuss subjectivity in relation to speech acts, but Palmer regards pseudo-modal auxiliaries as objective, while Perkins assumes that pseudo-modals can be viewed as subjective depending on context.[23] Note that Perkins considers modal expressions with an adjective, participle, and noun all to be instances of objective modality (e.g. *be possible, be to, be going to, be about to*).

Finally, Verstraete (2001) denies the definition of modality in terms of speaker's involvement (i.e. a definition shared by very many studies before him) and proposes a semiotic approach which relates the semantic distinction between subjectivity and objectivity to grammatical distinctions, in which the notion of "modal performativity" is used to characterize subjective modality. On this basis, he argues that epistemic modality is always subjective, dynamic modality is always objective, but deontic modality is either subjective or ob-

---

some linguists (e.g. Coates (1995), Verstraete (2001)) do not distinguish between objective and subjective epistemic modality, claiming that epistemic modality is always subjective. However, Celle (2009: 278–280) observes that only objective epistemic modality is compatible with hearsay adverbs, justifying Lyons's (1977) distinction between subjective and objective epistemic modality. For example, when its use is attributed to the reported speaker, not to the current speaker, *may* or *will* can co-occur with hearsay adverbs such as *reportedly* (but note that *must* cannot). For this reason, the distinction between subjective and objective epistemic modality is linguistically justifiable.

[21] The neustic is used for "the sign of subscription to an assertion or other speech act", the tropic is used for "the sign of mood", and the phrastic is used for "the part of sentences which is governed by the tropic and is common to sentences with different tropics", i.e. the propositional content (Hare (1970: 20–21)).

[22] Verstraete (2001: 1509) states that it was Lyons (1977) who first introduced "the terminological distinction between subjective and objective modality" (cf. Lyons (1977: 797ff)).

[23] Perkins (1983: 12) and Palmer (1990: 113–132) regard objective deontic modality as dynamic, which suggests that epistemic and deontic modality are all subjective in these studies.

Chapter 3   Modality, Mental Attitudes, and Related Phenomena   65

jective (p. 1525).[24, 25]

To sum up, in the previous studies, modality and modals are more or less related to subjectivity in the sense of speaker-relatedness or speaker's involvement and assumed to have objective as well as subjective uses.

3.4. Modality as Speaker's Mental Attitude and Semantic (De)composition of Sentential Utterances

The observations about the subjectivity of modality and modals in previous studies make us recognize the following points: (i) we need to reconsider and accommodate the ideas concerning subjectivity related to modality and modals, and (ii) the treatment of modality and modals is inseparable from the component of the interpersonal relationship between speaker and addressee (hearer), in which speech acts and evidentiality are deeply involved. Considering these points, in what follows I will reconsider and refine the semantic (de)composition of sentential meaning adopted in my previous book (see also Section 2.4.3.4), which consists of the modality (subjective) domain and the proposition (objective) domain.

First, we need to shift our attention from the level of sentential meaning to the level of sentential utterances. This is because sentential meaning (i.e. meaning at the sentence level) does not directly reflect the component concerning information about communication (or addressee-orientedness), including speech acts or evidentiality. We also need to change the term for the modality domain because in my previous work (Wada (2001a)) it was a little confusing to speak of dynamic modality while it actually does not belong to the modality domain.

We can thus assume the (de)composition of sentential utterances, as in (3):

(3)   Sentential Utterances: Speaker's Attitude Domain + Proposition Domain[26]

---

[24] Verstraete (2001: 1526) argues that both subjective deontic and epistemic modality in the sense of Lyons (1977) are characterized similarly in terms of tropic and neustic; they both involve modal performativity as well as "interactive performativity", or performativity in its general sense.

[25] Verstraete (2001: 1512–1513) compares the notion subjectivity in the sense of Halliday (1970) and Lyons (1977) with that in the sense of Langacker (1990, 1991, 2003, 2008) to argue that the latter is only related to the subjective pole of the subjective-objective scale while the former concerns the whole scale.

[26] A first version of this type of semantic (de)composition has already appeared in Wada (2011a: 38, 2013a: 37).

66   *The Grammar of Future Expressions in English*

The "speaker" here involves the subject of perception, cognition, thoughts, utterances, or communication. The speaker's attitude domain includes speaker's mental attitudes (sometimes refered to simply as speaker's attitudes in this study). A speaker's mental attitude is a mental behavior such as opinion, evaluation or judgment by the speaker as the subject of cognitive or mental activities (e.g. viewing, cognizing, thinking, uttering, and communicating); it always operates with the speaker's consciousness, i.e. an activated part of the mind when engaged in any type of cognitive or mental activity, which is always existent at speech time (see the definition in Section 2.4.1).[27] The speaker's attitude domain is subjective due to the definition of speaker's mental attitudes.

Elements other than speaker's mental attitudes, i.e. both external and internal situations (including the subject's experiences and internal thoughts) as scenes to be described or construed/evaluated, constitute the propositional content and hence the objective domain of sentential utterances. They belong to the proposition domain.

Let us next elaborate on the assumption in (3). Because speaker's mental attitudes are operative in both situation construal and communication, I subdivide the speaker's attitude domain into two types. One is associated with speaker's mental attitudes operative in situation construal; the other is associated with those operative in conveying the construed situation to the addressee (i.e. communication). The former type of speaker's mental attitude is called the situation-oriented mental attitude of the speaker (henceforth, referred to as "speaker's S-attitude" for short) and the latter type the addressee-oriented mental attitude of the speaker (henceforth, referred to as "speaker's A-attitude" for short).[28] The revised version of the semantic (de)composition of sentential utterances is shown in (4):[29]

---

[27] This statement concerning the speaker's mental attitude seems to be a detailed description of "speaker's involvement" or "speaker's relatedness". Lyon's (1977: 452) characterization of "opinion or attitude of the speaker" constitutes part of the speaker's mental attitude. Besides, Halliday's (1970: 335) definition of modality in note 17 suggests that the modality in his sense also constitutes part of the speaker's mental attitude.

[28] A similar distinction is made between the two types of speaker's attitudes in, e.g. Nakau (1994) and Sawada (1995), and I have benefited much from them.

[29] This semantic (de)composition is in keeping with Givón's notion of "modal shells", which "code the *speaker's attitude* toward the proposition" (Givón (2005: 149)). Note here that by the speaker's attitude, he means not only the speaker's attitude toward the proposition involved but also the hearer's attitude toward it as well as the speaker.

Chapter 3   Modality, Mental Attitudes, and Related Phenomena   67

(4)   Sentential Utterances: Speaker's Attitude Domain (Addressee-Oriented
      Speaker's Attitude Domain + Situation-Oriented Speaker's Attitude Do-
      main) + Proposition Domain[30]

Speaker's A-attitudes concern performativity in its general sense and therefore
include speech acts and illocutionary forces as well as evidentiality; Searle's
(1969, 1979) five general categories of speech acts, or illocutionary points (assertives, directives, commissives, expressives, declarations) are also speaker's
A-attitudes.[31]   They all belong to the addressee-oriented speaker's attitude domain (henceforth, abbreviated as ASA domain).   On the other hand, speaker's
S-attitudes include modality related to the speaker's judgment about, evaluation of, or opinion on, the situation involved, such as subjective epistemic and
deontic modality, i.e. elements belonging to the situation-oriented speaker's attitude domain (henceforth, abbreviated as SSA domain); it may also be characterized by the notion "modal performativity" in the sense of Nuyts (2001,
2005, 2006) and Verstraete (2001), which "brings into existence a particular
position of commitment with respect to the propositional content of the utterance" (Verstraete (2001: 1517)).   There are, however, some types of modality
that do not reflect the speaker's opinion, judgment or evaluation with respect
to the situation involved.   They belong to the propositional domain (henceforth, abbreviated as P domain).   It is generally the case that not only modality expressing the subject's ability or volition/intention/willingness (i.e. non-
subjective root modality, including dynamic modality) but also modality expressing possibility or necessity attributed to the external environment (i.e. objective epistemic modality) constitutes part of the propositional content (as to
the treatment of volition/intention in the tense-interpretation process within the
present framework, we will consider it in some detail in Section 5.4.1).[32]   In

---

[30] One might say that this trichotomy is comparable to Hare's (1970) tripartite distinction
between the neustic, tropic, and phrastic components (cf. Lyons (1977: 749–750)).   However, as we will see in Section 5.4.7 (see note 52 there), the two trichotomies are not the same.
[31] Searle (1979) defines the five categories as follows: assertives are used to "commit the
speaker (in varying degrees) to something's being the case, to the truth of the expressed
proposition" (p. 12); directives are "attempts (of varying degrees, and hence, more precisely,
they are determinates of the determinable which includes attempting) by the speaker to get
the hearer to do something" (p. 13); commissives are used to "commit the speaker (again
varying degrees) to some future course of action" (p. 14); expressives are used to "express
the psychological state specified in the sincerity condition about a state of affairs specified
in the propositional content" (p. 15); declarations are to show that "the successful performance of one of its members brings about the correspondence between the propositional
content and reality" (pp.16–17).
[32] Nuyts (2001, 2005, 2006) incorporates both epistemic and deontic modality into "atti-

this way, the distinction between modalities based on the semantic (de)composition of sentential utterances in (4) can potentially provide a more multi-layered and theoretically-motivated analysis than traditional modal distinctions, such as the "epistemic vs. root" one or the "epistemic vs. deontic vs. dynamic" one, at the sentence level. In addition, modal adjectives and nouns, as in *It is possible that Tom is a spy* or *It is a possibility that Tom is a spy*, are elements belonging to the P domain (cf. Perkins (1983)).[33] By assuming the semantic (de)composition in (4), we can answer the second point raised at the top of this section (i.e. point (ii)).

The semantic (de)composition in (4) is justifiable because it explains why subjective modalities, regarded by nature as speaker's S-attitudes, easily interact with addressee-orientation or performativity in its general sense. They are all concepts belonging to the speaker's attitude domain (i.e. the speaker's subjective aspect) composed of speaker's S-attitudes and A-attitudes, where both attitudes are closely related to each other. Thus, as Palmer (1990: 10) indicates, epistemic modals (expressing speaker's S-attitudes) easily signal assertives (i.e. speaker's A-attitudes) and deontic modals (expressing speaker's S-attitudes) easily denote directives (i.e. speaker's A-attitudes) by default.

Moreover, modalities as speaker's S-attitudes (occurring at speech time) are closely related to performativity in its general sense (cf. Papafragou (2006: §5)) and can even enable the morpho-syntactically past forms to refer to speech time, as in *John might {come/be there}* (Palmer (1990: 10)).

Furthermore, modalities as speaker's S-attitudes are sometimes linked with evidentiality when conveyed to the addressee (hearer). For example, consider (5):

(5) The door is unlocked and the lights are on, so somebody must be in here somewhere.   (Nuyts (2005: 16))

---

tudinal categories" and separate them from dynamic modality. This position is similar to the one in this book, but he appears to identify objectivity with intersubjectivity and thus cannot distinguish the two notions (Traugott (2010: 34)). I follow Traugott's (2010) definition below to argue that intersubjectivity is restricted to the relation between speaker and hearer.

"[I]ntersubjectivity in my views refers to the way in which natural languages, in their structure and their normal manner of operation, provide for the locutionary agent's expression of his or her awareness of the addressee's attitudes and beliefs, most especially their "face" and "self-image".   (Traugott (2010: 33–34))

[33] In the present model, evaluative or judgment adjectives (e.g. *a pretty girl, a lovely day*) are members of the proposition domain, not those of the speaker's attitude domain, because they are not used to evaluate or make a judgment about the situation described by a verb/predicate or a clause/sentence including it.

Chapter 3   Modality, Mental Attitudes, and Related Phenomena   69

Nuyts (2005: 16) states that this example exemplifies the case of inference/deduction based on information as evidence: by using epistemic *must*, the speaker derives an inference that somebody is now in the room from the situation in which the door is unlocked and the lights are on.[34] Evidentiality, by nature, is an addressee-related notion, for we do not have to clarify — or use a special means for — informational source unless we intend to convey it to the addressee.[35]

The observations made above imply that the ASA domain is separate from, but closely related to, the SSA domain; the two sub-domains are therefore subsumed under the same category "speaker's attitude domain", as indicated in (4).

Now, I will consider predictive and assertive modality — two modalities closely related to tense interpretation — in terms of the semantic (de)composition in (4). They are by nature members belonging to the SSA domain and hence two different types of speaker's S-attitudes, as defined below (cf. also Wada (2011a: 39–40)):

(6)   Predictive modality is a speaker's mental attitude operative when the speaker forecasts the situation involved on a reasoned basis (e.g. observations, experiences, scientific reasons).

(7)   Assertive modality is a speaker's mental attitude operative when the speaker construes and states the situation involved as a fact (or as if it is a fact).[36]

---

[34] It is usually the case that *must* in (5) is regarded as epistemic. However, when uttered, sentence (5) expresses inference/deduction based on information as evidence and so it seems difficult to treat it as representing a speaker's S-attitude alone. The semantic (de)composition in (4), however, combines speaker's S-attitudes and A-attitudes to form the speaker's attitude domain and *must* can therefore easily work together with addressee-oriented notions like evidentiality. Bybee, Perkins and Pagliuca (1994: 180) refer to a use of *must* like the one in (5) as "inferred certainty", which is relevant to evidentiality. Jaszczolt (2009: 39) makes a similar observation about epistemic *must* in a sentence like *Tom must have arrived in London by now*.

[35] Note that evidentiality, a semantic/functional notion, is often distinguished from the grammatical means called "evidentials" in the literature (Aikhenvald (2004), Murray (2017: Ch. 1)); English does not have evidentials, but can employ lexical expressions such as the modal *must* or hearsay adverbs to express evidentiality. For a comprehensive study of English expressions related to evidentiality, see Ikarashi (2015).

[36] Within Culioli's enunciative framework (e.g. Culioli (1995)), where "each utterance is located relative to a situation that is made up of two parameters, i.e. a spatio-temporal one, and a subjective [i.e. related to the original speaker] one, to which modality and commitment are attributed" (Celle (2008:16)), Celle (2008) states that assertion, the most basic level of modality, requires (at least) two features: (i) if a representation *r* for the target situation is

The term *forecast* means "calculate or estimate something conjecturally" (cf. also Close (1977: 131)) and the situation to be forecast is not necessarily restricted to a future one in this study. The term *fact* here means 'fact in the speaker's evaluation'. Predictive and assertive modalities are epistemic modalities in that they are speaker's S-attitudes related to the factuality or probability of the situation involved.[37, 38]

By characterizing predictive and assertive modality as speaker's S-attitudes in terms of the semantic (de)composition in (4), we can explain several phenomena concerning the notions of prediction and assertion. Since they are speaker's mental attitudes, it is not necessarily the case that predictive modality corresponds to futurity and assertive modality to presentness or pastness. It is true that in the default case, predictive modality—a typical type of modality expressed by *will* in English—tends to accompany a sentence with *will* describing a future situation, as exemplified by (8), and assertive modality—a typical type of modality expressed by modally unmarked (i.e. unmodalized) forms in English and the reason why this is the case will be stated in Section 3.8—usually accompanies an unmodalized sentence describing a present or past situation, but not a future one, as illustrated by (9).

(8) a. The parcel will arrive tomorrow.   (Leech (2004: 55))
    b. Tomorrow's weather will be cold and cloudy.   (Leech (2004: 57))
(9) a. *I know French next week.   (Prince (1982: 455))
    b. *Next month John knows Mary.   (Prince (1982: 455))
    c. *Men reach Mars in 1976.   (R. Lakoff (1970: 845))

---

the case, other than *r* is not the case; (ii) the speaker—usually the original one—commits him/herself to the truth of the utterance. This definition of assertion is basically comparable to my definition of assertive modality.

[37] This statement is in keeping with Palmer's (1986: 51) statement that "the term 'epistemic' should apply not simply to modal systems that basically involve the notions of possibility and necessity, but to any modal system that indicates the degree of commitment by the speaker to what he says".

[38] In this connection, Bybee, Perkins and Pagliuca (1994: 179) state:
    "The unmarked case in this domain [=epistemic modality] is total commitment to the truth of the proposition, and markers of epistemic modality indicate something less than a total commitment by the speaker to the truth of the proposition."
This statement implies that a type of epistemic modality can be expressed by something other than markers of epistemic modality and is therefore in keeping with my view that assertive modality as speaker's S-attitude accompanying unmodalized forms typically indicates a total commitment by the speaker to the factuality or probability of the situation involved and is thus a type of epistemic modality.

Chapter 3   Modality, Mental Attitudes, and Related Phenomena   71

However, predictive modality can accompany a present- or past-reference sentence containing *will*,[39] as in (10), while assertive modality can be used in unmodalized sentences to refer to the future if certain conditions are met, as in (11). (We will see the details of this mechanism in Chapters 7 and 8.)

(10) a. [Knock on door] That will be the plumber.
                                                (Huddleston and Pullum (2002: 188))
    b. They'll have arrived home by now.   (Leech (2004: 86))
(11) a. The parcel arrives tomorrow.   (Leech (2004: 55))
    b. The President gives his inaugural address tomorrow afternoon.
                                                (Leech (2004: 65))

As for assertive modality, several remarks are in order. First, since it is a type of speaker's mental attitude, the speaker can not only construe what was or is the case as a fact at the time of assertion but can also construe what will be the case as if it is a fact if he/she has enough evidence at the time of assertion,[40] as exemplified by (11).[41]

Second, unmodalized forms are accompanied by assertive modality typically in independent or main declarative clauses, as mentioned above. This is motivated by the semantic (de)composition of sentential utterances in (4), which implies that a speaker's S-attitude (belonging to the SSA domain) must be involved in situation construal. The SSA domain is usually semantically involved in independent or main clauses and assertive modality is the unmarked

---

[39] The notion of prediction (or predictive modality) in this book corresponds (or is very similar) to that used in Coates (1983), Ota (1998: Ch. 7), Leech (2004), and Collins (2009).

[40] This evidence can be subjective in that the speaker him/herself may judge it that way based on his/her belief and experience.

[41] Recently, an anthology of papers about assertion from a philosophical perspective was published (Brown and Cappelen (2011)). The papers discuss what assertion is or should be from various points of views. Although what they refer to by "assertion" is, in definition, similar to my notion of assertive modality in that they both refer to the factuality of the situation involved, the former type of assertion basically corresponds to a speech-act type, as with most linguistic studies. Therefore, even if some of them argue against the notion assertion itself, they do not directly affect my claim that assertive modality is a speaker's mental attitude toward the situation involved (i.e. speaker's S-attitude). For example, Cappelen (2011: 22) points out the possibility of the existence of an utterance without assertion ("saying" in his terminology), a speech-act-neutral notion. Although it is not clear whether proponents of this notion reject my notion of assertive modality as speaker's S-attitude, I argue that the notion at stake is linguistically defended in the main text and no serious problem will therefore arise in assuming it for linguistic purposes; on the contrary, it is very useful and tenable, as shown in the main text. For how assertive modality is related to assertion as a speech act, see Section 3.6.

type of speaker's S-attitude (for the reason why, see Section 3.8). However, just because a verb form is unmodalized does not necessarily mean that the clause or sentence including it is always accompanied by assertive modality. An unmodalized clause or sentence does not convey assertive modality if it contains a modal adverb and the like, as in (12):

(12) a. Time is possibly a more important limiting factor than storage space ...   (BNC ARR)

   b. It asserted that Steffi Graf made excuses for her losses. This is probably the most untrue statement I have heard in some time.

(BNC A0V)

Sentence (12a), for instance, is accompanied by the modality of possibility denoted by the modal adverb *possibly*; it is not accompanied by assertive modality. This is because it is only in the unmarked (i.e. default) case that an unmodalized form is accompanied by assertive modality and it is usually the case that the notion expressed by a marked expression is given preference over such an unmarked notion.

   Third, assertive modality in my use — often referred to as (direct) assertion in my previous studies — functionally corresponds to the notion of categorical assertion in Lyons (1977) and Perkins (1983), among others. However, while Lyons (1977: 809) claims that the speaker is making the cognitively strongest statement when making a categorical assertion, this is not always the case with assertive modality.[42] It may usually be the case that the speaker makes his/her maximum commitment to the truth of the proposition with assertive modality. In this case, the degree of assertiveness is strengthened by the addition of *do* to the declarative sentence, especially when conveyed to the hearer, as in (13a) below. However, he/she can sometimes merely make a tentative commitment to it by tentatively accepting it as a fact. This case is illustrated in (13b). In this example, the speaker tentatively accepts the semantic content of the first conjunct as a "fact" to someone for a communicative strategy, but what he/she really intends to convey is the semantic content of the second conjunct, which implies that the speaker does not actually believe what he/she says in the first conjunct and thus does not make a positive commitment to it.

---

[42] For this reason, I do not take Hoye's (1997: 60) position:
   "[W]hen making a modally unqualified assertion [=assertive modality] the speaker is signaling his maximum commitment to the truth of the proposition precisely by not qualifying it."

Chapter 3   Modality, Mental Attitudes, and Related Phenomena   73

(13) a.   The Great One does play some funny tricks sometimes.   (BNC G39)
     b.   Steve leaves tomorrow but I won't be surprised if he changes his
          mind.   (Smith (1997: 190))

It can safely be assumed that the assertive modality implied by modally unmarked (i.e. unmodalized) forms covers all cases other than those which the
speaker's S-attitudes expressed by modally marked forms cover.   In short, assertive modality is defined as covering a broader reference range than categorical assertion.

However, it can be said that the hearer usually assumes that the speaker,
when using unmodalized forms, considers the situation involved to be a
fact—whatever the evidence is—and conveys it to the hearer with a positive
and maximum commitment to it, unless otherwise indicated or implied.   Thus,
for example, only when the hearer assumes that the speaker has said (14A)
with a positive, maximum commitment and knows (or believes) that it is false
can he/she deny it, as in (14B).

(14)   A: Peter Parker is the Green Goblin.
       B: You're a liar!   I know he is Spider-Man.

This is a usual, unmarked pattern of the hearer's construal of sentences containing unmodalized forms.[43]   As for the relationship between unmodalized
forms and assertive modality, I will have more to say about it in Section 3.8.

3.5.   Semantic (De)Composition of Sentential Utterances and the Three-Tier Model of Language Use

In the previous section, we have shown that the semantic (de)composition
of sentential utterances is useful not only for characterizing predictive and assertive modality as speaker's S-attitudes (i.e. elements belonging to the SSA
domain), but also for accounting for why speaker's S-attitudes easily tend to
be linked to the phenomena of evidentiality or performativity (i.e. elements related to the ASA domain).   To further validate this model, our next task is to

---

[43] Cappelen (2011: 40) denies the position that assertion (as a speech act) presupposes
the asserter's knowledge of the situation involved because we can say *Your ticket did not
win* even before he/she knows the result of the lottery.   However, in this case, the speaker
violates Gricean maxims, especially the Maxim of Quality, for communication strategies;
even in this case, the hearer has to regard what the speaker is saying as what the latter
believes to be true, unless otherwise explicitly indicated or pragmatically implied.   Thus, a
usual, unmarked pattern of the hearer's construal is available here.

motivate it with a general theory of language use, i.e. one that can deal with the relation among grammar, semantics, and pragmatics, because the semantic (de)composition in (4) implicitly assumes the level of situation construal (mainly related to grammar and semantics) and the level of communication (mainly related to pragmatics).

There are many major pragmatic theories, such as speech act theory (e.g. Austin (1962), Searle (1969, 1975, 1979)), conversational implicature theory (e.g. Grice (1975), Horn (1984), Levinson (2000)), relevance theory (e.g. Sperber and Wilson (1986), Blakemore (1992)), but their main focus is on the level of communication and do not put much weight on the level of situation construal (cf. Shizawa and Hirose (2015: 114)).[44] They may indeed deal with phenomena showing close relationships between speaker's S-attitudes and A-attitudes (or speech acts), but cannot enjoy some merits which we can obtain by assuming the level of situation construal as an independent level; for example, they do not motivate the existence of assertive modality as speaker's S-attitude at the level of situation construal.[45]

Furthermore, they cannot explain some crucial differences between English and Japanese. This is particularly important, because theories concerning pragmatics should be universal, or at least cross-linguistic, and are thus supposed to explain them from a unified point of view, as far as the target languages share the same type of strategies, functions, and the like. Take (15), for example.

---

[44] As shown in the main text, just because we make a distinction between the two types of speaker's mental attitudes does not necessarily mean that they are not related to each other; on the contrary, as implied in (4), they constitute a super-category, i.e. the speaker's attitude domain, which can deal with some linguistic phenomena showing their close relationships, as we saw in Section 3.4.

[45] By contrast, a series of studies by Ronald Langacker (e.g. Langacker (1991, 2008)) elaborates on the cognitive mechanism of situation construal, but it seems that he does not clarify his position with respect to whether or not assertive modality accompanies unmodalized sentences in situation construal. Moreover, as is the case with the pragmatic theories mentioned in the main text, his theory of situation construal cannot deal with some crucial differences between English and Japanese linguistic phenomena; for example, while Langacker's notion of "subjectification" is useful for English, it is pointed out in Mori (1998) and Hirose (2002, 2013) that the notion of "objectification" plays a crucial role in describing lexico-grammatical phenomena in Japanese. This different linguistic behavior can also be explained by the Three-Tier Use of Language Use (see, especially, Hirose (2013, 2015, 2016a, 2016b, 2017) for details).

Chapter 3 Modality, Mental Attitudes, and Related Phenomena

(15) a. Today is Saturday.
    b. Kyoo-wa   Doyoobi da.
        Today-TOP   Saturday COP
        'Today is Saturday.'

It goes without saying that both English and Japanese (maybe all languages) have the "communicative" as well as "expressive" function. The English sentence (15a) when uttered is usually felt to convey the construed situation to the addressee. On the other hand, the Japanese sentence (15b), even when uttered, is usually felt to merely express what the speaker construes; for it to be in the communication mode, it usually requires the addition of a sentence-final particle such as *yo* 'I tell you', as in *Kyoo-wa Doyoobi-da yo* 'Today is Saturday, I tell you', or the change of the copula into a polite form like *desu*, as in *Kyoo-wa Doyoobi-desu* 'Today is Saturday (polite)'. Those pragmatic theories cannot explain this type of differences.

For these reasons, I will not adopt any of the pragmatic theories mentioned above to motivate (4). Instead, to motivate and lend support to the tripartite distinction between the three semantic domains in (4), I will introduce the Three-Tier Model of Language Use, or simply the Three-Tier Model, proposed by Yukio Hirose (Hirose (2013, 2015, 2016a, 2016b, 2017)). This model is a natural development of the theory of public/private self and public/private expression (Hirose (1995, 1997, 2000, 2002), Hasegawa and Hirose (2005), Hirose and Hasegawa (2010)).

This model is intended to explain differences between Japanese and English (and potentially other West-European languages), especially those of the relation between grammar and pragmatics in the two languages. In this model, one language is distinguished from another based on how to combine the three tiers, i.e. the situation construal tier, the situation report tier, and the interpersonal relationship tier, which are at least necessary for successful communication. In the situation construal tier, the (potential) speaker "construes a situation, forming a thought about it" (Hirose (2015: 123)). In the situation report tier, the speaker "reports or communicates his construed situation to the addressee" (Hirose (2015: 123)). In the interpersonal relationship tier, the speaker "construes and considers his interpersonal relationship with the addressee" (Hirose (2015: 123)).

Based on a number of linguistic facts about the differences between Japanese and English, Hirose makes the generalization that in Japanese, the situation construal tier is separated from the situation report tier, which is unified with the interpersonal relationship tier, whereas in English, the situation construal tier is unified with the situation report tier, which is separated from the interpersonal relationship tier. This different combination pattern reflects the public-self-centeredness of English and the private-self-centeredness of Japanese. The public self is the aspect of the speaker as the subject of (linguistic) communication, i.e. the speaker who has an addressee in mind, and thus involved in the situation report and interpersonal relationship tiers. The private self is the aspect of the speaker as the subject of thinking or consciousness, i.e. the potential speaker who has no addressee in mind, and thus involved in the situation construal tier.

English is a public-self-centered language in that many of its grammatical phenomena are "oriented to" or "center around" the public self. Because of this linguistic nature, even at the level of situation construal, where the subject involved is the private self, the public self can be relevant to or affect situation construal in that "one gives priority to the outside perspective from which to report a situation and linguistically encodes as much as is necessary to do so" (Hirose (2015: 123)). This is due to the view that in English the situation construal tier is unified with, and inseparable from, the situation report tier by default. On the other hand, Japanese is a private-self-centered language in that many of its grammatical phenomena are "oriented to" or "center around" the private self. Because of this linguistic nature, "the speaker can freely place himself in the situation and view it from the inside" (Hirose (2015: 124)) in situation construal. This is due to the view that in Japanese the situation construal tier is separate from the situation report tier by default.

In the Three-Tier Model, linguistic expressions used for thought expression or mental representation, i.e. those used in situation construal, are called private expressions, whereas linguistic expressions used for communication or situation report, i.e. those used in conveying the construed situation to the addressee, are called public expressions. Public expressions consist of private expressions and addressee-orientedness. The distinction between the two types of expressions enables us to explain the functional difference between direct and indirect speech. In this model, a direct speech complement can quote public expression while an indirect speech complement is a quotation of private expression. Consider (16):

(16) a.   John said, "Mary is sick."
     b.   John said that Mary was sick.

In (16a), the reporter (defined as public self) quotes the public expression of the original speaker John (defined also as public self); the reporter conveys not only the propositional content of Mary's being sick but also the original

Chapter 3   Modality, Mental Attitudes, and Related Phenomena   77

speaker's (i.e. John's) S-attitude and A-attitude. This means that the public expression of the original speaker consisting of the situation construal (by the original speaker) and addressee-orientedness is conveyed by the reporter. On the other hand, in (16b), the reporter quotes the private expression of the original speaker (defined here as private self);[46] the reporter reduces the original utterance of the original speaker to the level of the latter's private expression consisting of the propositional content and the original speaker's S-attitude. Note that in both cases, the speaker's S-attitude is attributed to the original speaker as private self, and consequently, the assertive modality (i.e. a speaker's S-attitude) accompanying the complement clause is that of the original speaker at the time of the original utterance (see Section 2.4.3.5).

It should be stressed here that in Hirose's model indirect speech is a linguistic device to quote the private expression of the original speaker, i.e. the original speaker's subjective thought existent in his/her mind. This indicates that the indirect speech complement does not necessarily represent the same wording as the original utterance (Quirk et al. (1985)); unless the original speaker's message is distorted, the reporter can choose wordings from his/her own point of view. Thus, for example, the original utterance for (16b) might be "My girlfriend feels bad" if Mary is John's girlfriend. (This characterization of indirect speech complements is in keeping with the statements about them in Section 2.4.2.) This is one merit of the distinction between public and private expression. For further justification of this phenomenon, see Hirose (1995, 2000) and Wada (2001a: Ch.8).

Now, we can show how the Three-Tier Model motivates the existence of assertive modality as speaker's S-attitude in situation construal. This model theoretically allows the situation construal tier as an independent language unit. This independence is necessary even in English, where the situation construal tier is unified with the situation report tier by default, because it can explain exceptional or marked behaviors. For example, in English diaries the first-person subject is often suppressed not only in main clauses but also in subordinate clauses, which is a major characteristic of Japanese — where the situation construal tier is independent of the situation report tier by default. By arguing that even in English the separation of the situation construal tier from the situation report tier is possible in marked cases, we can also explain marked characteristics like the subject-suppression phenomenon in English di-

---

[46] The original speaker in indirect speech is often referred to as the "reported speaker" in the literature.

aries (cf. also Konno (2015)).[47] As we have seen, linguistic expressions used in situation construal, i.e. private expressions, are semantically composed of the situation to be construed (i.e. propositional content) and the speaker's mental attitude toward it (i.e. speaker's S-attitude). Thus, even if there is no linguistic item expressing a speaker's S-attitude (e.g. modals), the sentence or clause must involve one. This is also a natural consequence of the cognitive linguistic view that situation construal necessarily reflects the speaker's or conceptualizer's perspective. In this way, the existence of assertive modality associated with modally unmarked forms is justified.

Our model can also explain why, as we saw with respect to (15) above, the default interpretation of English sentential utterances is situation report even if there is no element explicitly indicating the communication mode, while the default interpretation of Japanese sentential utterances is situation construal unless elements like addressee-oriented expressions are added or addressee-orientedness is implied contextually or in the speech situation. The answer would be that in the default case, the unification of the situation report tier with the situation construal tier allows the hearer to interpret the utterance as situation report in English, whereas the separation of the two tiers from each other causes the hearer to interpret it as situation construal in Japanese, unless there is an element indicating that the speaker is in the communication mode (including paralanguage such as gesture and tone). For other differences between English and Japanese that this model can deal with, I would like to refer readers to Hirose (2013, 2015, 2016a, 2016b, 2017) and studies based on his model (Ikarashi (2013, 2015), Konno (2015), Shizawa (2013, 2015), Wada (2013a, 2017b)).

3.6. How to Treat Modal Phenomena

I can now show how to treat modal phenomena in English based on the semantic (de)composition of sentential utterances in (4) supported by the Three-Tier Model. Let us first present the interpretation schema of the phenomena based on the relationship between the three semantic domains (the ASA, SSA, and P domains) and the three tiers (the situation construal, situation report, and interpersonal relationship tiers).

---

[47] Konno (2015: 148) refers to cases where the default grammatical behaviors of a language give way to marked ones as *default preference overrides*.

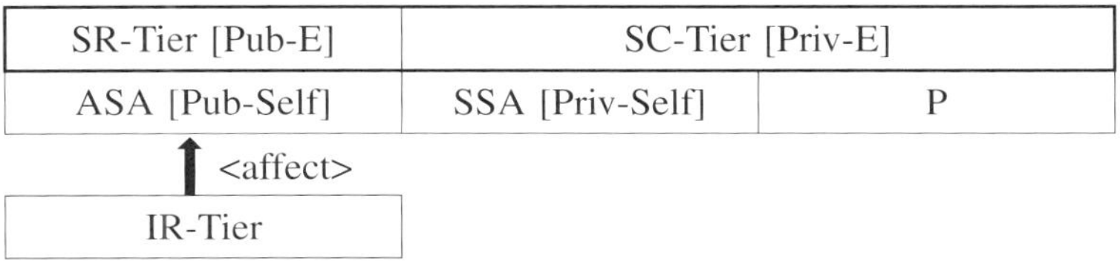

Chapter 3   Modality, Mental Attitudes, and Related Phenomena   79

SR-Tier [Pub-E]	SC-Tier [Priv-E]	
ASA [Pub-Self]	SSA [Priv-Self]	P

⬆ \<affect\>

IR-Tier

Figure 1: Interpretation Schema of Modal Phenomena in English

SC-Tier, SR-Tier, and IR-Tier stand, respectively, for the situation construal tier, the situation report tier, and the interpersonal relationship tier. Pub-E, Pub-Self, Priv-E, and Priv-Self, respectively, denote public expression, public self, private expression, and private self. ASA, SSA, and P, respectively, symbolize the addressee-oriented speaker's attitude domain, the situation-oriented speaker's attitude domain, and the proposition domain. The situation report tier and the situation construal tier are surrounded by one large box with bold lines, which suggests the unification of the two tiers, and the interpersonal relationship tier, which is independent of the other two tiers, can affect the situation report when the construed situation is conveyed to the addressee.[48, 49] Linguistic expressions used in the situation construal (SC) tier are private expressions (Priv-E), which semantically consist of the propositional content (P) and the speaker's mental attitude toward it, i.e. S-attitude. The speaker's mental attitude in the situation construal tier (SSA) is that of the private self (Priv-Self). Linguistic expressions used in the situation report (SR) tier are public expressions (Pub-E), which semantically consist of private expressions and addressee-orientedness, including the speaker's mental attitude directed at the addressee/hearer, i.e. A-attitude. The speaker's mental attitude in the situation report tier (ASA) is that of the public self (Pub-Self).

Let us now consider concrete examples with the interpretation schema in Figure 1. I will start with cases where the illocutionary force involved is neutral or not explicitly conveyed, but only a general category of speech act (illocutionary point) is implied.

---

[48] In the case of non-sentential utterances such as phatic communion (e.g. *Good morning!*), only the interpersonal relationship tier is relevant in that such expressions reflect, say, no more than the friendliness of the speaker to the addressee. In this case, the interpersonal relationship tier does not directly affect the situation report tier or situation construal tier because the expressions in question do not convey any content-specific information. Yukio Hirose (personal communication) brought this to my attention.

[49] This suggests that in English, "one can assume an unmarked (or neutral) level of communication which does not depend on any particular relationship between speaker and addressee" (Hirose (2015: 124)).

(17) a. Peter Parker may be Spider-Man.
   b. Peter Parker is Spider-Man.

In (17a), *may* is usually interpreted as expressing modality of possibility, a type of epistemic modality. This modality is a speaker's S-attitude (i.e. a mental attitude of the speaker as private self) which combines with the propositional content of Peter Parker being Spider-Man to form the private expression, i.e. the linguistic expression used in the situation construal tier. Since the situation report tier is normally unified with the situation construal tier in English, uttering sentence (17a) is normally accompanied by an ASA element, such as a speaker's A-attitude (i.e. a mental attitude of the speaker as public self); (17a) is thus interpreted as expressing the public expression, i.e. the linguistic expression used in the situation report tier. Unless otherwise specified or implied, the speaker's S-attitude is "automatically" conveyed to the addressee. That is, in a context where a specific illocutionary force is not clarified or irrelevant, the speaker's S-attitude doubles as the speaker's A-attitude. Thus, in this case, the modality of possibility functions as both the speaker's S-attitude and the speaker's A-attitude. Since this declarative sentence contains epistemic modality, the illocutionary point involved here is assertives, as we saw in Section 3.4. Finally, the interpersonal relationship tier does not affect the situation report here because this is an unmarked or neutral level of communication in which the speaker does not seem to have in mind any particular relationship between speaker and hearer. (This interpretation mechanism straightforwardly explains Palmer's (1990) indication that epistemic modals easily imply assertives, as observed in Section 3.4.)[50] The interpretation schema of this modalized sentence, which is henceforth slightly modified for convenience's sake, is presented below:

Figure 2: Interpretation schema of (17a)

---

[50] This explanation also applies to cases where deontic modals easily imply directives, for deontic modals are basically used to make someone perform something, i.e. the nature of the speech act category of directives.

Here, the unification of the SR tier and the SC tier is represented by the rectangle surrounding the two tiers. The bold and double underlines represent private expression and public expression, respectively.[51]

The same applies to the interpretation of unmodalized sentences like the one in (17b). As we saw above, an unmodalized form in main or independent clauses normally conveys assertive modality, a speaker's S-attitude. This modality and the propositional content form a private expression in the situation construal tier, to which a speaker's A-attitude is added to form a public expression in the situation report tier. In a context where a specific illocutionary force is not clarified or relevant, this speaker's S-attitude, i.e. assertive modality, doubles as the speaker's A-attitude. A sentence containing an unmodalized form, e.g. sentence (17b), conveys assertion (based on assertive modality) as a speech act. Finally, the general category of speech act is identified as assertives, because assertion, as well as prediction or possibility, constitute assertives as an illocutionary point (Searle (1979)). The interpretation schema of example (17b) is as follows:

Figure 3: Interpretation schema of (17b)

My claim that a speaker's S-attitude is taken over to the situation report tier to double as the speaker's A-attitude when a specific illocutionary force is not clarified or relevant is verified by the following examples:

(18) a.   Ann is pregnant, isn't she?
     b. #Ann is probably pregnant, isn't she? (Radden and Dirven (2007: 241))
     c. *Ann may be pregnant, isn't she?   (Radden and Dirven (2007: 241))

---

[51] In the situation report (i.e. communication) mode, the whole utterance expressed by the sentence usually corresponds to public expression, but in some linguistic environments, such as indirect speech complements, the sentence (clause) involved may correspond to private expression or only partially change into public expression. For this reason, we cannot say that situation report is equal to public expression and situation construal is equal to private expression. However, investigating such relations in detail is beyond the scope of this book.

Radden and Dirven (2007) state that tag questions are used to "ask the hearer to confirm an assertion made by the speaker" (p. 241). The assertion in this statement is regarded as a speaker's S-attitude in my analysis. This is because the speaker's asking the hearer to confirm the former's assertion directed at the latter (i.e. a speaker's A-attitude) is bizarre, while the speaker's asking the hearer to confirm that the situation construed by the former is a fact is reasonable. With this in mind, consider (18a) first. The speaker's S-attitude (i.e. assertive modality) operative in the situation construal tier is taken over to the situation report tier and doubles as the speaker's A-attitude, i.e. a speaker's mental attitude directed at the hearer. By using the tag question *isn't she*, the speaker asks the hearer to confirm his/her assertive modality, i.e. S-attitude, because the speaker is not so confident of his/her construing the situation involved as a fact. Sentences (18b) and (18c) are unacceptable or ungrammatical because the type of speaker's S-attitude expressed in the main clause is different from the type of speaker's S-attitude that the speaker asks the hearer to confirm by using the tag question.[52] The speaker's S-attitude expressed by the main clause is modality of probability in (18b), represented by *probably*, or modality of possibility in (18c), represented by *may*, while the modality targeted at by the tag question is assertive modality in both cases. A contradiction thus arises between the speaker's S-attitude expressed by the main clause and the S-attitude that the speaker asks the hearer to confirm by using the tag question.

Before concluding this section, let us consider a case where a modalized sentence is accompanied by an indirect speech act, as in (19):

(19)   You must visit us when you come to the United States.

In this utterance, the speaker intends to convey that the addressee will be welcome if the latter comes to the States. The inference mechanism behind this is as follows. First, in the situation construal tier, the speaker construes the addressee's visiting him/her as a must in his/her mind and the speaker's S-attitude is thus (strong) obligation. By letting the addressee know that it is an

---

[52] The examples in (18b, c), together with sentence (i), are originally intended by Radden and Dirven (2007) to explain the different degrees of subjectivity expressed by modal expressions.

(i)   I believe that Ann is pregnant, isn't she?   (Radden and Dirven (2007: 241))

Their explanation is that the higher the degree of subjectivity of a given expression becomes, the more difficult it becomes for the hearer to confirm it. According to Radden and Dirven, the reason why (i) is acceptable is that what is expressed by the mental expression *I believe* is on-stage information and thus more objective. In this connection, see note 56.

Chapter 3   Modality, Mental Attitudes, and Related Phenomena   83

obligation in the situation report tier (which is taken over from the situation construal tier and doubles as the speaker's A-attitude), the speaker intends to let the addressee get rid of the hesitation to visit him/her lest the latter should be afraid that his/her visit might annoy the former. Next, the information indicating that the situation involved is a benefit for the hearer (cf. Leech (1983)), which derives from the interpersonal relationship between speaker and addressee in this context, comes into play. The addressee can therefore infer that he or she is welcome to the speaker's home and the speaker intends to convey the notion of invitation as an indirect speech act to him/her. Because the invitation is a speaker's A-attitude different from the one originally expressed by the modal *must*, it is featured or focused on. The interpretation schema of sentence (19) is presented in Figure 4, where the obligation is taken over to the situation report tier as the speaker's A-attitude but interpreted as backgrounded (covered by the shaded area) and the notion of invitation as another speaker's A-attitude is superimposed as foregrounded information (represented in bold face).[53]

---

[53] Interestingly, a Japanese sentence containing the modal of obligation *nakerebanaranai* 'must', a counterpart of the English sentence (19), is difficult to regard as conveying invitation, as in (i):

(i)   Amerika-ni ku-ru   toki-wa   (anata-wa) wareware-o tazun-e
      America-to come-PRES   when-TOP   (you-TOP)   us-ACC   visit-CON
      nakerebanaranai.
      must
      'When you come to America, you must visit us.'

This is also explained by the analysis we are pursuing. Because in Japanese the situation construal tier is separated from the situation report tier by default, the speaker's S-attitude expressed by a modal verb is not "automatically" taken over to the situation report tier as the speaker's A-attitude. The speaker is thus required to decide on a certain A-attitude when changing the mode from situation construal to situation report. The hearer's reasoning therefore goes like this: the fact that the speaker of sentence (i) bothers to decide on obligation implies that he/she intends it to the hearer as his/her A-attitude and does not imply other speech acts. For more details, see Wada (2013, 2017b). In this connection, Kurotaki (2005: Ch. 1) has pointed out that a full-scale comparison of the modal systems in English and Japanese has not been conducted thus far. It is one of the first works of such a comparison, observing that unlike English, Japanese has developed an epistemic-centered modal system and deontic and epistemic modalities tend to be expressed by different expressions in Japanese. My analysis for a sentence like (i) can be relevant to the latter part of the observation, but I leave it for future research.

Figure 4: Interpretation schema of (19)

As Searle (1979: 13) states, the general speech-act category (illocutionary point) for the illocutionary force "invitation" is directives, which is also reflected in Figure 4.

3.7. Subjective and Objective Use of Modality as Speaker's Mental Attitude[54]

In Section 3.4, we observed that the modality expressed by modal auxiliaries and adverbs belongs to the subjective domain when it is a speaker's mental attitude (toward the situation involved) occurring at speech time. On the other hand, some types of modality (e.g. objective epistemic and deontic modality in the sense of Lyons (1977))—which can be felt as subjective in a sense because of the nature of modality—constitute part of the propositional content and therefore belong to the objective domain. How can we accommodate this apparent discrepancy? I argue that the semantic (de)composition in (4) supported by the Three-Tier Model can preserve the claim that modality as speaker's mental attitude is subjective and at the same time explain in what sense some uses of epistemic and deontic modality expressed by modal auxiliaries and adverbs are objective.

First, I argue that modality as speaker's mental attitude is always subjective at the level of situation construal alone, where the speaker in question is the private self, i.e. a (potential) speaker or thinker who has no hearer in mind.[55] This argument is in keeping with the view that modality as speaker's mental attitude is by nature a speaker's S-attitude (i.e. a mental attitude of the speaker as private self).

Next, I argue that whether a given use of modality is subjective or objective is a matter concerning the situation report tier, where the private expression

---

[54] In writing this section, I have benefited much from the discussion with Yukio Hirose.
[55] The notion "thinker" is included in the notion "speaker" in that speaking presupposes thinking.

Chapter 3   Modality, Mental Attitudes, and Related Phenomena   85

(the propositional content with the private self's mental attitude) is conveyed
to the addressee and the public self (i.e. the reporter) therefore comes into
play. Two types of relations between public self and private self are basically
available in the situation report tier. One relation is such that the private self
is identified with the public self. In this case, the two selves share the same
spatiotemporal point and the private self is not expressed linguistically. Unembedded clauses illustrate this case. Thus, in (17), repeated here as (20),

(20) a.   Peter Parker may be Spider-Man.
     b.   Peter Parker is Spider-Man.

the subject of construing these sentences (i.e. private self) shares the same
identity with the subject of conveying the construed situation to the addressee
(i.e. public self). Here, modality as speaker's S-attitude—which is ascribed
to the private self—is taken over as a mental attitude of the public self (i.e.
speaker's A-attitude) in the situation report tier and therefore attributed to the
very same person as the current speaker as public self. By "current speaker",
I mean the (potential) speaker who is engaged in, and finally responsible for,
the judgment about or evaluation of the situation described by the whole sentence involved. It is in this case that we speak of subjective modality and it is
in this sense that modality of possibility in (20a) and assertive modality in
(20b) are interpreted subjectively.

   The other relation between the two selves is such that the private self is not
identified with the public self. Indirect speech complements offer a case in
point.

(21) a.   John said that Mary was sick. (=(16b))
     b.   I said that Mary was sick.

Let us first consider (21a). The private self is not identified with the public
self because the former refers to John (i.e. a different person from the current
speaker as public self). Besides, the time at which the consciousness of the
private self is existent is different from the time at which the consciousness of
the public self (i.e. reporter) is existent, i.e. the time of the report. As we saw
in Section 3.5, the indirect speech complement is a quotation of the private
expression of the original speaker as private self and the assertive modality accompanying the past tense form *was* is thus attributed to John as private self;
this modality itself is a speaker's S-attitude. Unless the reporter as public self
makes a commitment to the semantic content of the indirect speech complement (i.e. in the case of the "neutral" reading of the indirect speech complement), even if the private expression in question is conveyed to the addressee

in the situation report tier, the assertive modality is not ascribed to the reporter and hence the expression described by the indirect speech complement basically remains private expression. Such a modality is therefore not "subjective" from the point of view of the current speaker, i.e. the reporter, because it is not his/her own S-attitude at the time of his/her report, i.e. speech time. For this reason, the assertive modality at issue is interpreted objectively.

Let us next consider (21b). In this case, the private self referred to by the first-person pronoun *I* appears to be identified with the reporter as public self, but this is not the case in my analysis. The time at which the consciousness of the private self is existent is different from the time at which the consciousness of the public self is existent, and in addition, the private self is linguistically expressed by *I*.[56] The assertive modality accompanying the past tense

---

[56] In my analysis, the private self is not identified with the public self when the former is linguistically expressed even if the referent is the same, i.e. in the case of the first-person pronoun. This is due to the following reasons. First, when the time at which the public self's point of view is located is different from the time at which the private self's point of view is located, as in (21), we can infer that the speaker wants to make a contrast between his/her point of view of now and his/her point of view of then; for if both points of view were entirely the same, the speaker would not have had to make his/her point of view of then linguistically explicit. For this reason, when the point of view of the public self is located at a different time from that of the private self, the two selves are not in an "identified" relationship.

Next, let us examine the case where the public self's point of view is located at the same time as the private self's point of view, as in (i):

(i) I say (that) Nancy is happy.

If the main clause verb is a verb of saying, then the sentence is usually interpreted as a performative one. In this case, a special nuance is conveyed because the addressee knows who is saying and it is redundant to make it explicit by using linguistic expressions. Thus, the reporting clause is taken here as a linguistic device to carry out a communication strategy— belonging to the ASA domain—and is therefore not a part of the propositional content anymore. In this connection, Ikarashi (2013, 2015), based on the Three-Tier Model, offers an analysis to this effect, using the performative clause (i.e. public expression) *I tell you*.

This type of analysis can also explain why sentence (i) in note 52, repeated here as (ii), is acceptable.

(ii) I believe that Ann is pregnant, isn't she?   (Radden and Dirven (2007: 241))

It is usually the case that the speaker believes what he/she asserts to be true (cf. Nakau (1994: 85–86)). The speaker does not have to express the phrase *I believe*. Nevertheless, it is expressed linguistically. This apparent discrepancy is explained by the present analysis. First, the situation described by the complement clause of sentence (ii) is construed with assertive modality by the current speaker as private self; the construed situation is the private expression of the current speaker. Second, by adding the apparently redundant phrase *I believe* to the private expression, the speaker is carrying out a communication strategy; i.e., the speaker is "hedging" his/her assertion (as a politeness strategy). At this point, the whole sentence is brought into the public expression mode because the speaker is now intending to

Chapter 3   Modality, Mental Attitudes, and Related Phenomena

form *was* is therefore interpreted objectively in the same way as in (21a).

The discussion in this section enables us to answer the first point raised at the beginning of Section 3.4, namely that we need to reconsider and accommodate the ideas concerning subjectivity related to modality and modals. Modalities as speaker's mental attitudes, which are always subjective in the situation construal tier, can be subjective or objective in the situation report tier, while other modalities are always objective in that they are elements of the proposition domain.[57] The semantic (de)composition in (4) developed by the Three-Tier Model offers a new way of distinction among modalities with general notions such as public and private self as well as spatiotemporal points.[58]

3.8.   Modally Unmarked Forms and Assertive Modality

Finally, I will consider the relationship between unmodalized forms (i.e. modally unmarked forms) and assertive modality in more detail. It seems safe to say that when construing (interpreting) a situation, we normally perceive the situation as it is and regard it as true (even if tentatively);[59] without evidence indicating otherwise, we usually commit ourselves to the truth of the situation involved. In this sense, we can say that assertive modality is the unmarked type of speaker's S-attitude. As we have stated, assertive modality typically accompanies unmodalized forms. I argue that this is due to a kind of iconicity: the semantically unmarked S-attitude, i.e. assertive modality, is associated with an unmodalized sentence as an unmarked form, i.e. the sen-

---

convey it to the addressee. Finally, by the tag question *isn't she*, the speaker asks the hearer to confirm his/her assertive modality.

[57] To be specific, modalities expressing the subject's internal state such as modality of ability are always objective and belong to the proposition domain. Modalities expressing root possibilities such as theoretical possibility can be speaker's S-attitudes because such notions indicate that the situation to be described can be believed to be true by people in general and therefore can be attributed to the private self of those people, which is not identified with the current speaker.

[58] Thus far, some linguists have considered volitional *will* as deontic but others as dynamic. In addition, it has not been clearly stated in what sense and under what condition *will* is regarded as expressing volitional meaning. As will be shown in Section 5.4.1, this new approach can systematically accommodate these problems.

[59] This statement is compatible with Nicolle's (1997: 370) claim that "[i]n the case of the existential status of an event the default assumption will usually be that the SR [=the semantic content of an utterance] represents a verified rather than an unverified event (speakers are more likely to talk about events which they know have occurred or are occurring than about potential or hypothetical events)."

tence without any modal element that expresses a speaker's S-attitude.[60] This is in keeping with Nicolle's (1997: 370) observation that operators which relate the propositional content to the realis (i.e. actual) world—such as assertive modality in my sense—are rarely encoded because they are linguistically an unmarked, or default, element. The speaker to whom a speaker's S-attitude is attributed is usually the current one because he or she is usually the one who is finally responsible for evaluating or making a judgment on the situation.

With these observations in mind, let us present the hypothesis about the default mental attitude of the current speaker:

(22)   In linguistic environments where a given (potential) speaker's mental attitude is involved, the unmarked mental attitude (i.e. speaker's S-attitude) is assertive modality attributed to the current speaker.

Recall that the attribution of modality as speaker's S-attitude to the current speaker means the subjective interpretation of it (see Section 3.7). This hypothesis is in keeping with Nuyts's (2005: 25) statement that the performative use of modals expressing mental attitudes of the current speaker at speech time (i.e. modals expressing modal performativity in his sense) is the default case.

Hypothesis (22) enables us to argue that assertive modality can also be considered to accompany sentences with modals that express modality belonging to the proposition domain. For example, in *She can play the violin*, the modality expressed by the modal *can* is a dynamic type (i.e. ability), and to meet the semantic (de)composition of this utterance, a certain type of speaker's S-attitude must be inserted in interpreting it. Due to hypothesis (22), such a sentential utterance is interpreted as accompanied by assertive modality in the situation construal tier (for the treatment of the volitional use of *will*, often re-

---

[60] In this connection, Jaszczolt (2009: 94) states:

"When a speaker utters an unqualified sentence [=unmodalized sentence], for example, stating that 2008 is a leap year, in accordance with Grice's maxim of truthfulness or any other post-Gricean principles of rational communicative behavior, the addressee assumes that the statement is true."

Similarly, Givón (2005: 150–151) seems to indicate that unmodalized sentences convey what he calls "R(ealis)-assertion", i.e. a type of epistemic modality used when "[t]he speaker *strongly asserted* the proposition to be true." However, as discussed toward the end of Section 3.8, my notion of assertive modality can be attributed to persons other than the (current) speaker. In addition, Givón's R-assertion seems to be a speech act or at least an intersubjective type of modality, while assertive modality in my sense is innately a situation-oriented mental attitude of the speaker (i.e. speaker's S-attitude).

Chapter 3   Modality, Mental Attitudes, and Related Phenomena   89

ferred to as a dynamic modal, see Section 5.4.1).

As hypothesis (22) suggests, assertive modality is usually attributed to the current speaker unless the existence of other speakers is indicated explicitly or implied in the context. A typical environment in which this attribution is available is independent or unembedded clauses. However, just because a given linguistic environment does not indicate the involvement of a speaker other than the current speaker does not necessarily mean that it automatically carries a mental attitude of the current speaker.

Recall here that (in English) assertive modality is not expressed by a linguistic item but interpreted as accompanying an unmodalized form. The unmodalized form itself is not a marker of assertive modality, but merely expresses part of the propositional content. Only in linguistic environments which reflect the mental attitude of a certain speaker (i.e. those semantically consisting of the situation-oriented speaker's attitude (SSA) domain and the proposition (P) domain) can we interpret the unmodalized form as accompanied by assertive modality.

Thus, temporal clauses or conditional clauses expressing "direct condition" (Quirk et al. (1985: 1088)) or "direct causation" (Copley (2014: 77)) are not linguistic environments consisting semantically of the SSA domain and the P domain; they semantically consist only of the P domain. In these environments, unmodalized forms are not interpreted as accompanied by assertive modality.[61] Consider (23):

(23) a.   When you wake up, you'll remember nothing.   (Leech (2004: 63))
     b.   If it rains tomorrow, the match will be cancelled.
                                          (Haegeman and Wekker (1984: 45))

A piece of evidence for the lack of the SSA domain in this type of clauses is that they turn out to be unacceptable if we insert *will* in its predictive sense into them, as in:

(24) a.   *We will begin dinner when my father will arrive.
                                                      (Sampson (1971: 587))
     b.   *If it will rain tomorrow, the match will be cancelled.
                                          (Haegeman and Wekker (1984: 45))

---

[61] For analyses of unmodalized forms in this type of linguistic environments, see Section 8.3.3. For justification of my claim that speaker's S-attitudes are not involved in this environment, especially with respect to conditional clauses, see Section 5.4.7.

Let us consider the two types of clauses one by one. First, temporal clauses provide a temporal setting for their main clauses, for which the occurrence of their situations is a presupposition (Hamann (1989: 39, 51)). This suggests that temporal clauses merely provide a time point or period with respect to which the truth value of main clause situations is evaluated, and their situations themselves are not the target of evaluation, or "assertion" in the sense of the opposite notion of "presupposition" (see Hooper (1975) for example).[62] It is in this sense that temporal clauses serve as a presupposition for the occurrence of main clause situations.[63]

Second, conditional clauses representing direct condition or causation (i.e. those of the direct cause-effect type) are similarly interpreted as a presupposition for the occurrence of main clause situations. This is because conditional clauses of the direct cause-effect type provide a condition for asserting the truth value of the content of their main clauses and the speaker does not make any commitment to, i.e. suspends the evaluation of, their content (Verstraete (2001: 1518); cf. Dancygier (1998)).

Let us recapitulate. Since the semantic content of independent or main clauses is the target of evaluation (or assertion) of the speaker involved, they reflect an S-attitude of the current speaker in the situation construal tier, unless otherwise indicated. These clauses constitute an "assertion" unit by themselves and therefore consist of the SSA domain and the P domain in situation construal. In the situation report tier, the ASA domain (to which speaker's A-attitudes belong) is added. By contrast, the semantic content of the presupposed parts of sentences is not the target of evaluation (or assertion) of the speaker involved. The temporal or conditional clauses observed above are therefore related to neither speaker's S-attitudes nor speaker's A-attitudes and consist only of the P domain. This indicates that the unmodalized forms in these linguistic environments (i.e. linguistic environments consisting only of the P domain) are not accompanied by assertive modality.

Moreover, the existence of linguistic environments without any speaker's mental attitude supports our position that the P domain is set up independently from the other two domains. The propositional content of the subordinate clauses in question combines with that of the main clauses to make the complex proposition, which may fall under the scope of the speaker's mental atti-

---

[62] In Murray (2017), this part of the propositional content is called the "not-at-issue content" or "not-at-issue restriction", which makes a contrast with the "at-issue content".

[63] Givón (2005:152–153) lists constructions that "display a high concentration of presupposed clauses", including adverbial clauses such as temporal ones.

Chapter 3   Modality, Mental Attitudes, and Related Phenomena   91

tude associated with the main clauses (cf. Lyons (1977: 750)).

From what we have observed thus far, we may conclude that the hypothesis about the semantic (de)composition of sentential utterances in (4) plays a crucial role in characterizing linguistic environments, i.e. one major factor indispensable to tense interpretation (cf. Section 2.4.3.5). Temporal clauses and conditional clauses of the direct cause-effect type are linguistic environments semantically consisting only of the P domain; indirect speech complements (in their "neutral" reading) semantically consist of the P domain and the SSA domain; and main or independent clauses, when their content is conveyed to the addressee in the situation report tier, semantically consist of the P domain, the SSA domain, and the ASA domain.

I will now give evidence for the validity of hypothesis (22), i.e. a linguistic phenomenon called Moore's Paradox, which is exemplified in (25):

(25) a. The cat is on the mat, and I don't believe it.   (Levinson (1983: 236))
     b. It's raining, but I don't believe it.

These examples are said to be unacceptable or inappropriate. First, suppose that an unmodalized form simply describes an objective situation, namely that it does not accompany any modality as speaker's S-attitude, but merely represents the propositional content. Then, it is difficult to explain the unacceptability of these sentences. Under this assumption, the first conjunct of (25a), for example, would express the propositional content of the cat's being on the mat alone and the speaker would not make any commitment to it, so that in the second conjunct he/she could make a denial of that propositional content. There is no contradiction between an objective description of the situation involved and the speaker's refusal to think of it as true. This line of analysis thus fails to explain the unacceptability of (25).

On the other hand, our analysis based on hypothesis (22) straightforwardly explains the unacceptability of the sentences in (25). Consider (25a) again. In our analysis, the first conjunct semantically consists of the assertive modality as speaker's S-attitude attributed to the current speaker and the propositional content. That is, the speaker considers the propositional content to be true on his/her responsibility. In the second conjunct, however, the same speaker states that he/she does not believe it is true and hence a contradiction. Sentences like those in (25) are therefore unacceptable.

Before closing this section, we will see that unmodalized forms do not always carry assertive modality attributed to the current speaker in independent or main clauses. Consider (26):

(26) a. According to Jack, Jill is pregnant.

b. We are the Austin area's largest consignment event and according to our community, JBF is the BEST!

(roundrock.jbfsale.com/homeView.jsp)

In these examples, the presence of the phrase *according to* clarifies that the information source for the semantic content is a person or persons other than the current speaker.[64, 65] Thus, in (26a), the assertive modality accompanying the unmodalized sentence *Jill is pregnant* is attributed to Jack, not to the current speaker. In this case, the assertive modality is interpreted objectively because it is not ascribed to the current speaker (see Section 3.7). From this, it follows that even in independent or main clauses, an objective reading of assertive modality is available if it is explicitly indicated.[66]

3.9. Concluding Remarks

In this chapter, we have developed the semantic (de)composition of sentential meaning into that of sentential utterances in (4) to be able to consider the two types of speaker's attitudes, i.e. the speaker's S- and A-attitudes, with the

---

[64] In making this statement, I follow Yamaguchi (2009) to define "quotation" and "speech/discourse" as follows:

(i)   A quotation is an act of introducing the wording of others into that of the current speaker in such a way that it is attributed to them.   (cf. Yamaguchi (2009: 1))

(ii) A speech/discourse is a linguistic means that is grammaticalized to make a quotation.   (cf. Yamaguchi (2009: 3))

Introducing the wording of others into the current speaker's is a communication strategy, so clauses containing linguistic means for quotation indicate that the speaker is conveying a situation to the addressee. Therefore, clauses including grammatical means for quotation—such as direct or indirect speech/discourse—or lexical means for quotation—such as *according to* (Yamaguchi (2009: 4))—semantically consist of the P domain, the SSA domain, and the ASA domain, i.e. the private expression + addressee-orientedness.

[65] Hearsay adverbs fulfill the same function as *according to* in that they both show the non-responsibility of the current speaker with respect to the information source (Celle (2008, 2009), Murray (2017)).

[66] Included in objective readings of assertive modality are cases where the notion is attributed to unspecified or general people, as in (i):

(i)   Steve leaves tomorrow but I won't be surprised if he changes his mind. (=(13b))

In this example, the assertive modality accompanying the first conjunct is not attributed to the current speaker because he/she does not make a maximum commitment to the situation involved; it is attributed to unspecified or general people as private self. The current speaker plays the role of public self in the first conjunct and tentatively accepts the assertive modality (attributed to others) for purposes of communication strategies or the like. For more details, see Wada (2017a).

Chapter 3   Modality, Mental Attitudes, and Related Phenomena   93

latter connected to speech acts, illocutionary forces, as well as evidentiality. Next, to motivate the semantic (de)composition in (4), we introduced the Three-Tier Model of Language Use, i.e. a general theory of language use that can treat the relation between grammar, semantics, and pragmatics cross-linguistically with different default patterns of combination of the three tiers, i.e. the situation construal tier, the situation report tier, and the interpersonal relationship tier. The tripartite division in the semantic (de)composition (i.e. the ASA, the SSA, and P domains), together with the three tiers of the Three-Tier Model, resolved the two points set up in the top of this chapter, repeated here as in (27):

(27) a.   Under what system are predictive and assertive modality characterized as speaker's mental attitudes? (=(1a))

  b.   In what framework and in what sense are the notions of "subjectivity" and "objectivity" concerning modality used? (=(1b))

As for (27a), since the situation construal tier—semantically consisting of the propositional content and a speaker's S-attitude—is recognized as an independent unit, sentences containing an unmodalized form and those containing *will* are taken as carrying a speaker's S-attitude in this tier, unless indicated otherwise. Under this system, assertive and predictive modality as speaker's S-attitudes accompany those sentences.

As for (27b), modal elements expressing speaker's mental attitudes are subjective in the sense that they are related to the judgment or evaluation of the speaker as private self in the situation construal tier. Linguistic elements unrelated to the judgment or evaluation of the speaker as private self are objective and belong to the proposition domain. As for the subjective vs. objective interpretation, modality as speaker's mental attitude is interpreted subjectively when it is attributed to the current speaker, e.g. when the private self who is responsible for the judgment about or evaluation of the situation involved is identified with the public self of the current speaker; it is interpreted objectively when it is attributed to a person or persons other than the current speaker, e.g. when the private self who is responsible for the judgment about or evaluation of the situation involved is not identified with the public self of the current speaker. The present framework showed the validity and usefulness of assuming assertive modality as a speaker's mental attitude, a unique point of the framework.

Chapter 4

Tense Interpretation and Temporal Structures

4.1. Introduction

Thus far, we have established a comprehensive model of tense and related issues such as modality, mental attitudes and speech acts by advancing my theory of tense (shown in Chapter 2) based on the semantic (de)composition of sentential utterances motivated by the Three-Tier Model of Language Use (shown in Chapter 3) to give a more systematic and far-reaching analysis of tense phenomena and related issues, especially those of future expressions. Before explicating the interpretation mechanisms of future expressions, however, we need to show in some detail how temporal structures contribute to the tense-interpretation process, including how they are constructed for various semantic uses/functions, in the established model—a crucial point for a temporal structure analysis of future expressions in Part II of this book.

As we saw in Chapter 2, temporal structures are "templates" for temporal calculation, providing a basis for interpreting tense forms (Section 2.2). In the situation construal tier, the speaker forms or constructs (and elaborates if necessary) a temporal structure in his/her mind by mentally referring to the list of stored temporal structures (Section 2.5). They are basically invariant through situation report because even if the information for communication is accumulated, it is addressee-oriented and usually does not affect the temporal calculation itself. The temporal value intended by the speaker is assumed to be the same throughout the communication process. It should be kept in mind that temporal structures, consisting of the combination of the temporal information and the cognitive schema (i.e. schematized cognitive information), reflect temporal relations, information from aspect, the semantics of its constituents (e.g. time adverbs, subjects and objects), contextual information, as well as information from the semantic (de)composition of sentential utterances (e.g. assertive modality) discussed in Chapter 3.

95

In this chapter, I will first consider the interpretation mechanism of the simple present as a sample case of the simple tense form, i.e. a tense form including only one event time (Section 4.2) and then the interpretation mechanism of the present perfect as a sample case of the complex tense form, i.e. a tense form including two event times (Section 4.3). It will be shown that in both cases, temporal structures play a crucial role in temporal calculation (i.e. tense-interpretation process).

4.2. The Simple Present Form

4.2.1. Introductory Remarks

There are numerous previous studies on the simple present form in English and all theoretical groups surveyed in Chapter 1 have considered this tense form. Even if we restrict ourselves to non-formal studies, there are still many. For example, descriptive approaches include Calver (1946), Declerck (1991a), Leech (1971, 1987, 2004), Palmer (1974, 1988), Quirk et al. (1985); Reichenbachian time-schema approaches include—besides Reichenbach (1947) himself—Comrie (1985), Huddleston and Pullum (2002), Klein (1994), Smith (1978, 1997, 2007);[1] Guillamean time-schema approaches include Hirtle (1967, 1995) and Hirtle and Curat (1986); non-compositional, temporal domain-based approaches include Declerck (1991b, 1997, 2003, 2006) and Williams (2002a, 2002b);[2] and cognitive approaches include Langacker (1991, 2001, 2011a), Brisard (2002) and De Wit (2017). By sketching how the present model deals with the simple present form in English, we can give a rough idea of what theoretical characteristics this study has as well as how it differs from the other previous studies, especially those of non-formal approaches. I will clarify the mechanism in which a variety of uses with non-future time reference are based on or derived from their temporal structures, which are in turn based on the tense structure of the simple present form (for uses with future time refer-

---

[1] Although Reichenbach himself was a formalist, his followers have not necessarily taken formal approaches.

[2] I have adopted many notions from a series of studies by Declerck in constructing temporal structures. However, there are several fundamental differences between his approach and mine: (i) my approach is partially compositional (in the sense that we saw in Chapter 1), while his approach is non-compositional; (ii) my approach allows auxiliaries to have their own event times, while his approach does not; and (iii) my approach considers *will* to be a modal, while his approach takes it as a future tense marker (auxiliary). For a criticism of his approach, see Wada (2001a: Ch. 9); for his criticism of my approach, see Declerck (1999); and for my reply to his criticism, see Wada (2001b).

Chapter 4   Tense Interpretation and Temporal Structures   97

ence, we will see them in Chapter 8).[3]

4.2.2. The Polysemy of the Simple Present Form: A Variety of Uses/Functions

Let us start by briefly considering the characteristics of uses (functions) of the simple present form that we are going to deal with in this section. How many uses the simple present form has depends on what type of position or theory one takes. Within my framework, differences in temporal meaning include those of time reference, aspectual information, types of mental attitudes, the position of temporal focus, and cognitive schemata closely related to temporal information; they are all reflected in different temporal structures, i.e. structuralized meanings of cognitive time information. Uses having their own temporal structures are semantic uses; uses deriving from the same temporal structure are pragmatic variants of one single semantic use.[4]

To illustrate the mechanism, I will consider seven uses of the simple present form (including both semantic and pragmatic uses) illustrated by (1a-g):

(1) a. "Edna, my wife is sick, very sick," he answered.   (BNC CDE)
    b. Adams intercepts, plays it up-field.   (Leech (2004: 7))
    c. My daughter is 9 and walks to school with her friends.
                    (Corpus of Global Web-Based English (=GloWbE) US)
    d. Beavers build dams.
                    (Corpus of Contemporary American English (COCA))
    e. This car runs on kerosene.
                    (Goldsmith and Woisetschlaeger (1982: 81))
    f. I name this ship Aurora.   (Leech (2004: 8))
    g. At that moment in comes a message from the Head Office, telling me the boss wants to see me in a hurry.   (Leech (2004: 11))

In the present model, the simple present form illustrates the stative-present use in (1a), the instantaneous-present use in (1b), the habitual-present use in the second conjunct of (1c), the generic-present use in (1d), the structural-description use in (1e), the performative-present use in (1f), and the historical-present use in (1g) (Wada (2015b, 2015c)).[5]

---

[3] For a detailed analysis of the simple present form in English within my framework and criticism of other semantic (non-formal) studies, see Wada (2015c).

[4] This suggests that my framework, though often adopting a cognitive linguistic perspective, makes a distinction between semantics and pragmatics. To support this view, see Depraetere and Salkie (2017).

[5] In the present model, the historical-present use is restricted to cases where a present

Let us next move to the tense-interpretation mechanism of these examples. First, in the model we are based on, simple present forms all share the same tense structure, namely that the event time is located in the present time-sphere (grammatical present), including the speaker's t(emporal)-viewpoint, i.e. the deictic center of grammatical time (Figure 2(i) in Chapter 2). This tense structure (i.e. grammatical time information) is projected onto the cognitive time line and provides a basis for tense interpretation in any of the following worlds, i.e. a real, possible, hypothetical, or fictional world. At the stage of tense interpretation, principle (2) below — which was already presented as (4) in Section 2.4.1 — works by default in all the cases above except for (1g).

(2) The speaker's t-viewpoint fuses with his/her consciousness at speech time.

Since the speaker's consciousness (i.e. an activated part of the speaker's mind when he/she is engaged in any type of cognitive or mental activity including thinking and uttering) exists at speech time, the operation of principle (2) causes the speaker's t-viewpoint to be located at speech time and therefore the basic temporal structure common to the simple present forms in (1a-f) is such

---

form refers to the past or to a time-area regarded as the past relative to the reference point (cf. Wolfson (1979), Schffrin (1981)). Note that the present progressive and the present perfect also have their own historical present uses, as illustrated in (i):

(i) ... and I said, "That's perfectly all right. I told you I drink it from the bottle at home."
And John HAS BACKED this up and Hellen IS LAUGHING. And so, um, then he PROCEEDS to pour it till it's filled to the top so it's about four ounces of brandy ...   (Wolfson (1979: 171))

Uses similar to the historical-present use include the narrative-present use (Fleischman (1990: 78)) and the fictional use (Leech (2004: 13)). Leech (2004: 13) considers a simple present form used in newspaper's headlines, as in (ii), to be an instance of the historical-present use.

(ii) Ex-champ dies.   (Leech (2004: 13))

Leech (2004: 12-13) also states that a simple present form with a verb of communication referring to the past, as in (iii), and one used for a historical summary, as in (iv), constitute a kind of historical-present use.

(iii) Francesca tells me you're a champion skier.   (Leech (2004: 12))
(iv) Germany invades Poland in 1939.

The three uses in (ii)–(iv) can all be regarded as reflections of the cognitive mechanism in which a situation that occurred in the past is interpreted as if it were ongoing or obtaining now in front of the speaker's eyes. They therefore belong to the historical-present use within my framework, too. Note, however, that although Leech (2004) views the stage-direction use as a member of the historical-present use (cf. Kashino (1999)), it does not belong to the historical-present use within my framework, because it does not refer to the past (or a time-area regarded as the past) but simply to a fictional world.

that the present time-sphere covers both the present and future time-areas and the event time is located in either of them or stretches over both time-areas (Figure 4 in Chapter 2).

With these in mind, let us first present the temporal structures of the stative-present and instantaneous-present uses, which are respectively shown in Figures 1 and 2.

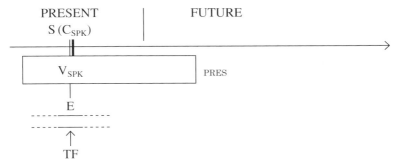

Figure 1: Temporal Structure of the Stative-Present Use

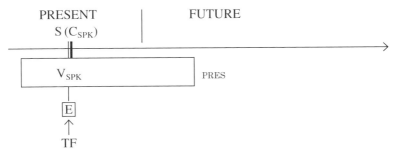

Figure 2: Temporal Structure of the Instantaneous-Present Use

In Figure 1, the solid-line and broken-line parts below E represent the foregrounded and backgrounded parts, respectively. Thus, in (1a), the state of the speaker's wife being sick itself may stretch from the past into the future, but the time of the relevant (i.e. foregrounded) part of the situation, i.e. the event time (E), is some span of time around speech time (S) within the present time-area. In Figure 2, on the other hand, the E surrounded by a square means that the whole of the situation involved is the relevant part and regarded as if it is a point.[6] Thus, in (1b), although the time of intercepting the ball

---

[6] It is usually the case that non-stative situations in the simple present form are not

and the time of playing the ball are, strictly speaking, not instantaneous, they are cognitively regarded as points in time in special linguistic environments like sports commentaries.

The stative-present use, as indicated by the name, is used only when the situation involved is stative, whereas the instantaneous-present use is an interpretation obtained when a non-stative situation receives a perfective reading.[7, 8] The difference between the two uses concerns that of the viewpoint aspect (perfective vs. imperfective) or situation type involved. Notice once again that temporal structures include not only tense-structure information, time notions (such as speech time, event time, time of orientation, temporal focus, time-area) and their relations, but also cognitive schemata reflecting time-related in-

---

viewed as occurring at the very same time as speech time (i.e. the moment of speech or thought) because "one cannot at the same time present a situation as bounded and as related to the punctual reference time [in this case speech time]" (Boogaart (1999: 198)). In this connection, Langacker (2001: 263) points out two reasons why a perfective event usually cannot coincide with the moment of speech: one is the "duration problem", which indicates "the length of an event is generally not equal to the length of a speech event describing it" (Langacker (2001: 263)); the other is the "epistemic problem", which states that it is usually the case that "[b]y the time the event is observed and identified, it is already too late to initiate a precisely coincident description" (Langacker (2001: 263)). Therefore, only when non-stative situations in the simple present form are able to be interpreted as coinciding with speech time for some reasons (e.g. because of the properties of linguistic environments such as sports commentaries) can we have the simultaneous reading.

[7] Leech (2004: 7) refers to the instantaneous-present use as an "event use", considering that it is only compatible with an event verb. This might appear to be contradictory to Williams's (2002a: 137) statement that some examples of this use contain a stative verb, as in (i):

(i)   ... and Safin remains alive in this quarter final.   (Williams (2002a: 137))
However, Williams (2002a: 137–138) also states that this type of stative verb has a limited time span. The situation described by this type of stative verb is therefore a bounded situation and can be viewed in its entirety.

[8] In this book, typical examples of the instantaneous-present use are represented by simple present forms used for sports commentaries or comments on what is occurring in front of the speaker's eyes. Unlike the structural-description use and the performative-present use, which we will see later, the instantaneous-present use has a characteristic showing that the speaker is reporting the situation involved as if it is an instantaneous one occurring at the same time as the time of seeing or hearing it. Therefore, when the reporter (i.e. speaker) regards the situation as requiring a time-span, i.e. a durative situation, the present progressive is used, as in (i):

(i)   The manager {is walking / *walks} slowly to the mound.   (Langacker (2011a: 60))
In this connection, Williams (2002a: §2.1) makes similar observations, but what is interesting in his findings is that the simple present form is used less frequently in TV broadcasting than in radio broadcasting. This may be due to the fact that since TV broadcasting is basically visible, the demand for comments on situation description decreases.

formation (represented by, for example, the solid and broken lines below E in Figure 1 and the square surrounding E in Figure 2).

Let us next consider the habitual-present and generic-present uses, whose temporal structures are schematized respectively in Figures 3 and 4.[9]

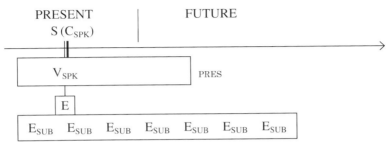

Figure 3: Temporal Structure of the Habitual-Present Use

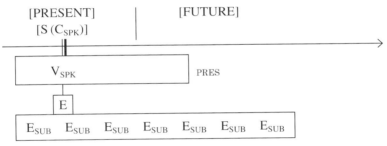

Figure 4: Temporal Structure of the Generic-Present Use

There are two major differences between Figures 1 and 2, on the one hand, and Figures 3 and 4, on the other. First, in Figures 1 and 2, the temporal focus is directed at the event time involved. This is due to the definition of this notion. The temporal focus is directed at the event time of the specific situation which the speaker is paying special attention to, i.e. the situation which is either highly informative or schematic by itself but specified by the interaction between the sentential meaning and the context. It can even be directed at the event time associated with a situation whose occurrence time is not clear if the speaker is interested in that situation and regards it as directly related to the time line (see Section 2.4.5).

---

[9] The uses of habitual present and generic present are different from the use of stative present in that in the former cases, the (sub)event involved does not necessarily obtain at speech time (Quirk et a. (1985: 180)).

On the other hand, in Figures 3 and 4, the temporal focus is not in operation, which is related to the second difference. The habitual-present and generic-present uses do not refer to specific situations but to a "superordinate" situation consisting of non-specific sub-situations of the same sort that ranges over a certain time span. The rectangle with seven E_{SUB}'s represents a cognitive schema indicating that type of superordinate situation. In (1c, d), the superordinate situation (i.e. the continuing state in which the speaker's daughter regularly walks to school with her friends and the continuing state in which beavers build dams whenever necessary) ranges over a certain time span of which speech time is the center. The event time — the time of the relevant part of the superordinate situation, symbolized by an E surrounded by a square — shares the same time point as speech time or is located in the time range including speech time, i.e. the present time-area (cognitive present). However, the superordinate situation itself does not reflect the notion of "specific on the time line" or "directly related to the time line". From these observations, I conclude that the temporal focus is not in operation in these two uses.

Both uses allow exceptional members, namely that the superordinate situation is still judged to be true even if there are some instances that do not conform to the characteristics of the uses in question.[10] However, they differ in that unlike the habitual-present use, the generic-present use is "super-temporal" or timeless, and time notions such as S (speech time), PRESENT (present time-area) and FUTURE (future time-area) — which are more or less related to the time line — are enclosed by square brackets in Figure 4. This is due to the following observation: the habitual-present use refers to a repetition of situations of the same type in the durative present (cf. Section 1.1), i.e. a situation ranging over a time span including speech time and extending into both the past and the future, whereas the generic-present use refers to general characteristics of a species or group, i.e. a situation in the everlasting present, as far as the species or group exists or unless it changes the characteristics.[11]

---

[10] For example, in the second conjunct of (1c), i.e. an instance of the habitual-present use, the superordinate situation of the speaker's daughter walking to school consists of tokens of that type of situation, but it is still true even if there are some days on which she goes to school by car or she walks to school alone. In the same way, in (1d), i.e. an instance of the generic-present use, the superordinate situation of beavers' building dams is still true even if some beavers do not build dams, as indicated by (i):

    (i)   Beavers build dams, but this one doesn't.

[11] The generic-present use, as indicated by the name, is not completely separated from the present time-area on the time line. For example, Bybee, Perkins and Pagliuca (1994)

Chapter 4 Tense Interpretation and Temporal Structures   103

This observation is verified by the following paradigm:

(3) a. My daughter walks to school {now/these days}.
    b. *Beavers build dams {now/these days}.
(4) a. My daughter {normally/usually/often} walks to school.
    b. *Beavers {normally/usually/often} build dams.

Let us now move to the structural-description use. Its temporal structure is schematically represented below:

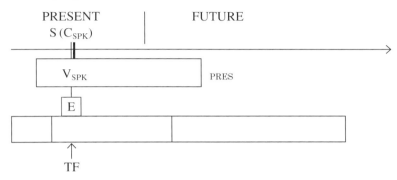

Figure 5: Temporal Structure of the Structural-Description Use

In Figure 5, the longer or outer rectangle below E surrounded by a square symbolizes the "structure of the world" and the shorter or inner rectangle below it represents the situation (around speech time) reflecting the characteristics of the (subject's) referent involved.[12] The structure of the world is defined

---

state that not only the habitual-present use but also the generic-present use refers to a situation available in the present time-area including speech time. This statement is exemplified by (i):

(i) Cows eat grass ... dinosaurs ate grass.
                              (http://www.freerepublic.com/focus/news/1350150/posts)

Since dinosaurs are extinct now, the past tense form has to be chosen here.

[12] The reason why the shorter rectangle stretches from the present to the future time-area is that the situation involved can include not only a present state but also a future situation. In this case, the time of the relevant part of the situation involved (i.e. event time) can correspond to the time span ranging from the present to the future time-area. Sentence (i) is just a case in point.

(i) This law raises the price of oil by 10 ¢ a gallon.
                                        (Goldsmith and Woisetschlaeger (1982: 82))

In this case, the relevant part of the situation is the combination of the present state (i.e. the likelihood of the passage of a specific bill) and the future situation brought about by the passage of that bill.

as a set of rules and constitutions of the society as well as the universe surrounding us (Goldsmith and Woisetschlaeger (1982), Langacker (1991), Brisard (2002)).[13] In this use, the speaker is paying his/her attention to a certain situation constituting part of the structure of the world. For example, in (1e), although it does not refer to a specific situation ongoing or obtaining at speech time, the situation (state) reflecting a certain vehicle's properties holds in the durative present and "characterizes" the society surrounding us in that it makes a contrast between that society and the society without such a vehicle. The speaker is in a sense paying attention to the situation in question and the temporal focus is therefore directed at the event time, i.e. the time of the relevant part of that situation corresponding to speech time. Since the time span under consideration is the durative present, i.e. some length of time centering on speech time, the time notions represented by S, PRESENT, and FUTURE are not enclosed by square brackets. A major difference between the structural-description use and the habitual-present use is whether the situation involved is interpreted as a situation characterizing a superordinate situation such as the structure of the world or as a superordinate situation consisting of non-specific sub-situations of the same type.

I now move on to the performative-present use. This use, exemplified in (1f) above, is usually seen as a special use of the simple present (Langacker (1991, 2001, 2011a)). In the present model, however, the performative-present use is the same as the instantaneous-present use in terms of the temporal structure. Indeed, unlike the instantaneous-present use, the performative-present use can co-occur with so-called "performative" adverbs such as *hereby*, as in *I hereby name this ship Aurora*. However, this compatibility is due to the properties of performative clauses and not related to the differences of temporal structures. In terms of the temporal structure, the event of the speaker's naming a certain ship Aurora described by (1f) is regarded as an instantaneous situation occurring at the very same time as speech time, i.e. the time of the

---

[13] The simple present forms in (i) are examples of what Prince (1982: 461) calls the "calculation" use, a use referring to a future situation. She distinguishes it from what she calls the "schedule" use, a use to be referred to as the fixed-future use in Chapter 8:

(i) a. [Climbing mountain] At this rate, we reach the top at 6:00. (Prince (1982: 461))
   b. The way things are going, I go below the poverty line in three years.

(Prince (1982: 461))

In the present analysis, this use is semantically categorized into the fixed-future use, though the superordinate situation constituting the structure of the world in this use is restricted to a more personal world. The calculation and schedule uses are pragmatic variants of the fixed-future use in my analysis.

Chapter 4   Tense Interpretation and Temporal Structures   105

locutionary act. The temporal structure of the performative-present use is therefore the same as that of the instantaneous-present use; the two uses in question are viewed as pragmatic variants stemming from the same temporal structure (Figure 2 above). In the present model, uses of a given tense form having different temporal structures are regarded as semantically different, but uses of a given tense form sharing the same temporal structure but behaving differently in some linguistic respects are pragmatic variants or uses.

One might realize that in the six uses that we have observed thus far, the event time associated with the situation involved is located in the present time-area (i.e. the time range centering on speech time), although it is possible in theory that it is located in the future time-area. The reason for the restriction of the time range is related to the nature of assertive modality (see Section 3.4). Within my framework, unmodalized forms in independent or main clauses normally receive the subjective interpretation of assertive modality, i.e. a reading in which the assertive modality is attributed to the current speaker (cf. hypothesis (22) in Section 3.8). This suggests that it is the speaker, i.e. the chooser of the simple present form, who judges the situation involved to be a fact. It is usually the case that the situation judged to be a fact (i.e. asserted situation) has already been actualized by, or is ongoing at, the time of assertion, i.e. speech time—this phenomenon was referred to as the restriction on assertion in Section 2.4.3.5. In the default case, the present time-sphere of a tense form with a present tense morpheme cannot cover the past time-area. It is therefore in the present time-area, i.e. a time-area including speech time as its center, that the event time can usually be located.

Finally, let us consider the historical-present use, exemplified by (1g). Its temporal structure is schematized in Figure 6.

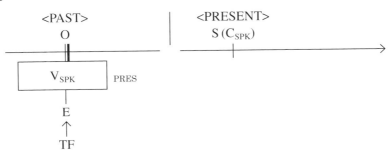

Figure 6: Temporal Structure of the Historical-Present Use

As observed in Section 2.4.1, this use is a non-default case, where principle (2) above does not work, namely that the speaker's t(emporal)-viewpoint (V_{SPK}) is not situated at speech time (S). In non-default cases, the position of the speaker's t-viewpoint on the time line is based on the characteristics of the linguistic environment in which the tense form involved occurs. In the environment we are considering here, the speaker is identified as the narrator and speech time is thus the time of narration. One phenomenon characteristic of the simple present form in its historical-present use is a so-called vividness effect, namely that the speaker (narrator) not only "focuses a camera on" a target situation (especially a non-stative situation) in the story or narration, but also represents it as if it were ongoing in front of his/her "eyes" (Quirk et al. (1985: 181), Fleischman (1990: 170)).[14]

To realize this effect, the speaker shifts his/her t-viewpoint (V_{SPK})—a viewpoint as a grammaticalized notion internalized in a tense form—onto the narrative now, or the story now (i.e. the central point on the time line of the story or narration) symbolized by O in Figure 6, which enables the hearer (reader) to see the situation involved as if it were occurring or obtaining in front of his/her eyes.[15, 16] As a result, the present time-sphere (grammatical present) corresponds to (part of) the past time-area, or a time area regarded as the past relative to the time of narration (S). The terms PAST and PRESENT are enclosed by angle brackets because the time area represented by PAST does not necessarily refer to the real-world past or the time area represented by PRESENT can possibly denote the present in a fictional world (cf. Fleischman (1990)). The reason why there is a break on the time line between PAST and PRESENT is that the time line of the story existent in the time area represented by PAST does not necessarily lead to the present relative to the time of narration, i.e. the central point in the narrator's world (this is the case espe-

---

[14] As Fleischman (1990: 23–24) points out, the historical-present use takes the place of the simple past when the target situation is focused on and foregrounded.

[15] In this connection, Langacker (1991: 269) argues that in the use of the historical present, the deictic center is detached from the speaker's here and now and shifted to a spatio-temporal site in the story. This statement is not contradictory to my claim in the main text, though in my account the speaker's t-viewpoint (corresponding to Langacker's deictic center) has not been linked to speech time (i.e. the speaker's here and now) in the first place before it is shifted to a time in the story.

[16] In Langacker (1991: 268, 2001: 269, 2011a: 61), this use is regarded as a type of use which represents a past event as if it were a mental reply at speech time. He extends this notion of mental replay to cover a simple present form used for describing pictures taken in the past, as in (i):

    (i)   Nixon says farewell from the steps of his helicopter.   (Langacker (2001: 270))

The same effect is obtained in my temporal structure analysis, because by situating the speaker's t-viewpoint at the same time as the time of taking this picture, the situation can be understood as if it were viewed from the speaker's present point of view.

Chapter 4   Tense Interpretation and Temporal Structures   107

cially with third-person novels). In general, in the case of fictions and narratives (spoken or written) the time of the world in which the narrator exists is
regarded as the present and the story itself is taken as if it happened in the
past. I will only consider such general cases in this book.[17, 18]

Our description of the historical-present use can straightforwardly answer
the question why the simple present form is chosen, while it does not refer to
the present: the tense-structure information of the simple present form is projected onto the temporal structure of this use. Moreover, since the historical-
present use refers to a foregrounded situation at a specific time in the time
area represented by PAST, the temporal focus is directed at the event time associated with that situation. The historical-present's reference to the past is
verified by the fact that this simple present form can be paraphrased into its
simple past counterpart, as in (5):

(5)   At that moment in came a message from the Head Office, telling me the
      boss wanted to see me in a hurry.

Before closing this section, we need to examine whether assertive modality is
in operation or not in the historical-present use. In the linguistic environment
we are considering, the narrator is assumed to describe situations in the story
line as if they occurred or obtained in the past. This suggests that assertive
modality, assumed to be attributed to the narrator existent at the time of narration, is in operation in this environment. The simple present forms in this use
are thus accompanied by assertive modality, which might explain why the factuality of the situations they describe is literally asserted, not suspended.

To recapitulate, this section has surveyed how the choice of the simple present form is made and how its uses (functions) are distinguished from one another, using the seven uses exemplified in (1). The same tense form can be
used for different uses because their temporal structures involve the tense-
structure information common to all instances of this form. Different semantic uses (functions) have their own temporal structures; different uses sharing
a temporal structure are pragmatic variants of the semantic use having that
structure: e.g. the instantaneous-present and the performative-present uses.
What should be stressed is that semantic uses are distinguished from pragmat-

---

[17] As Declerck (2003) points out, some novels or fictions are written in the present-tense-
based style, so the statement here is a tendency.

[18] Elsewhere (Wada (2015a)), I have given a rather detailed account of various past forms
(i.e. simple past, past progressive, past perfect, and expressions of future-in-the-past) in
third-person past fictions in English.

108   *The Grammar of Future Expressions in English*

ic ones in terms of the temporal structures.[19] In the next section, I will take up the present perfect as a sample tense form including two event times and show how the tense form is chosen and how its four basic uses are obtained.

4.3. The Present Perfect Form

4.3.1. Introductory Remarks

A great deal of attention has been paid to the present perfect.[20] I have analyzed it myself in my previous book (Wada (2001a: Ch. 4)), but after that various analyses of this tense form—often called "perfect aspect"—have been presented within various theoretical frameworks (e.g. Kiparsky (2002), Alexiadou, Rathert and von Stechow (2003), Portner (2003), Pancheva and von Stechow (2004), Rothstein (2008), Elsness (2009), Werner, Seoane and Suárez-Gómez (2016)).[21] Nevertheless, how many semantic uses or functions (meanings) should be identified in the present perfect is not agreed upon and can vary from framework to framework. In this section, I will offer the temporal structures of the four basic semantic uses of the present perfect form (i.e. the completive, continuative, experiential, and habitual uses) distinguished in my previous book and reanalyze them within the developed framework.

4.3.2. Four Basic Uses

The present perfect form consists of the perfect *have* as a finite verb and the past participle as a non-finite verb and its tense structure thus contains two event times. Let us first observe examples of the four basic uses of the present perfect.[22]

---

[19] It might be possible to regard the level of temporal structure in the present model as constituting a unit called "construction" in the sense of construction grammar. However, as far as I know, a construction is a pair of form and meaning and regarded as an independent unit, so the degree of independence of one construction from another in construction grammar is generally higher than that of one use from another in my approach. In my approach, one semantic use corresponds to one temporal structure that can cover more than one pragmatic variant, but they might form independent constructions in construction grammar.

[20] For bibliographic information about previous studies on the perfect before my previous book (Wada (2001a)), see the references cited there.

[21] Werner, Seoane and Suárez-Gómez (2016), using many corpora such as the Corpus of Global Web-based English or the International Corpus of English, deal with a variety of phenomena concerning the present perfect which have not received much attention thus far, such as the *to*-infinitival perfect in written American English or the narrative present perfect in Australian English.

[22] In (6), the underlines are mine.

Chapter 4   Tense Interpretation and Temporal Structures   109

(6) a.   "I thought I married a gentleman," the voice [=Alicia's voice] went
         on, ... "But I find that I have married"—was this Alicia talking?—
         "something better — a man — Bob, dear, kiss me, won't you?"
         [Completive]²³   (O. Henry, *The Defeat of the City*, p. 245)

    b.   In all competitions Arsenal have played seven times, won four, drawn
         three games and are still to lose. [Experiential]   (GloWeb GB)

    c.   "It sometimes changes a good man into a bad one," said the tall man.
         "You've been under arrest for ten minutes, 'Silky' Bob ..." [Continu-
         ative]   (O. Henry, *After Twenty Years*, p. 190)

    d.   Mr Phipps has sung in this choir for fifty years. [Habitual]
                                                              (Leech (2004: 39))

(6a), (6b), (6c), and (6d) are, respectively, examples of the completive, experiential, continuative, and habitual uses of the present perfect. In my previous
book, the four uses are not sharply distinguished, but characterized by the
combination of two scales as criteria.²⁴ One scale is the perfective-continuous
scale with one pole occupied by perfects whose two event times do not merge
with (and are thus separate from) each other—this is the "perfective" pole—
and the other pole occupied by perfects whose two event times merge with
each other—this is the "continuous" pole.²⁵ The other scale is the specific-
general scale with one pole occupied by perfects whose past participle refers
to a specific situation—this is the "specific" pole—and the other pole occu-

---

²³ (6a) is an example of the completive perfect with resultative overtones, but (i) is an example of the completive perfect with less resultative overtones.
   (i)   "You've found your way back at last, have you?"
                                              (O. Henry, *The Defeat of the City*, p. 242)

²⁴ For details about the criteria for the quadripartite distinction of the present perfect, see
Wada (2001a: Ch. 4), where the four uses were called pragmatic categories in that they
share the core semantics corresponding to the tense structure in this book and are brought
about by the interaction between the core semantics and other factors including pragmatic
and contextual ones. In that work, I did not clearly distinguish tense structures from temporal structures and thus failed to distinguish semantic uses (associated with temporal structures) from pragmatic variants. However, the essence of the previous analysis is still available, so I haven't abandoned but revise and develop it in this book.
   For the resultative perfect, it is (as well as was) a sub-category of the perfect whose temporal structure shows that the event time of the past participle does not reach the event time
of the perfect *have* obtaining at speech time—this type of perfect is either the completive or
experiential use. It is a prototypical member of the super-category "non-continuative" and
thus a pragmatic variant of it in my system.

²⁵ Note that the definition of "perfective" used with respect to the present perfect (i.e. the
sense of "bounded" or "separate") differs from that of the same term used in Section 2.4.3.3
and other chapters unless otherwise indicated.

pied by perfects whose past participle refers to a non-specific, general situation — this is the "general" pole. The combination of the perfective and specific poles brings about the basic (prototypical) use of completive perfects; the combination of the perfective and general poles brings about the basic (prototypical) use of experiential perfects; the combination of the continuous and specific poles brings about the basic (prototypical) use of continuative perfects; and the combination of the continuous and general poles brings about the basic (prototypical) use of habitual perfects. This approach allows fuzzy zones that have some characteristics of one use and those of another and so it can handle non-prototypical instances of the present perfect. The two scales are not ad hoc criteria because they are motivated: the perfective-continuous scale stems from the positional relation between one event time and the other preceding it; the specific-general scale is applicable to other tense forms, for example, the present and past tense forms in English, which can receive both specific and general readings.

Having seen some basic points, I will now present the temporal structures of the four basic uses and analyze their interpretation mechanisms. Let us first schematize the basic temporal structure common to the four semantic uses of the present perfect form.

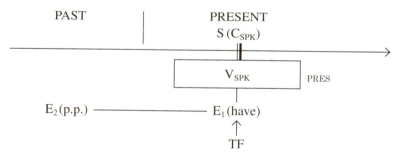

Figure 7: Basic Temporal Structure of the Present Perfect Form

Because the perfect *have* is a finite form with a present tense morpheme, it has the tense structure of the simple present form, namely that the event time is located in the present time-sphere (Figure 2(i) in Chapter 2). The past participle is a non-finite form and has the tense structure of anteriority relative to the potential time of orientation (Figure 3(i) in Chapter 2). The combination of the tense structures of the perfect *have* and the past participle constitutes the (combined) tense structure of the present perfect form: the event time of the past participle (E_2) is anterior to the event time of *have* (E_1) located in the

Chapter 4   Tense Interpretation and Temporal Structures   111

present time-sphere.[26] In the default case (which I will only consider in this section), principle (2) above necessarily works: the speaker's t-viewpoint (V_{SPK}) fuses with his/her consciousness (C_{SPK}) at speech time (S) and the choice of tense form is therefore based on speech time, the present time-sphere corresponding to the present and future time-areas.

The reason why E_1 is located at the same time as speech time in the present time-area (PRESENT) is the same as with the default case of the simple present form in independent or main clauses, i.e. due to the restriction on assertion observed in Section 2.4.3.5: the perfect *have*, a simple present form, carries assertive modality in this environment and a situation in the future relative to the time of assertion (speech time in this case) is difficult to make an assertion about. This is illustrated by the ungrammaticality of (7):[27]

(7) a. *John has left by the time you get there tomorrow.
                                                        (Huddleston (1977: 734))
    b. *John has come tomorrow.   (Hornstein (1990: 20))

In (7), the event time of the past participle is intended to be located at a future time because of the modification by a future time adverbial, which is contradictory to the restriction on assertion. Next, due to the properties of independent or main clauses (in the default case), speech time serves as the time of orientation for E_1, which in turn serves as the time of orientation for E_2 because the past participle occupies the complement position of the head verb *have* (for a more detailed observation of the temporal relation between the head verb and the verb in its complement position, see Section 5.3.1). In this way, E_1 — simultaneous with S — is located in the present time-area and E_2 — anterior to E_1 — is located in the past time-area (PAST). This basic temporal structure of the present perfect form brings about the so-called current-relevance effect; because the (resultant) state associated with E_1 occupies the same time as S, the past situation associated with E_2 is linked to S via E_1.[28]

---

[26] Boogaart (1999: Ch.4) also assumes that the English perfect form consists of two situations and hence two event times.

[27] As we will see in some detail in Chapter 8, assertive modality can accompany the simple present form in its fixed-future use only when the situation involved is a controllable type, i.e. a situation with what Copley (2009) calls "director" (i.e. a being which can potentially bring about the situation involved). In this case, there is a possibility that the speaker can construe the situation as certain to occur. However, the schematic situation represented by the perfect *have* is a resultant state, a non-controllable situation. Hence the present perfect with future time reference cannot be used in independent or main clauses, as in (7).

[28] Williams (2002a: 34) claims that a notion like the pre-present sector (stretching from the past to the present) — which is adopted in Declerck's theory of tense — is needed to ex-

112   *The Grammar of Future Expressions in English*

The situation associated with the perfect *have* itself is schematic. What type of state it expresses is determined in temporal calculation, depending on the interaction between the lexical content, the boundedness of the past participle situation and the context. Consider (8) for example:

(8) a.   Peter has injured his ankle.   (Leech (2004: 41))
    b.   We've known each other for years.   (Leech (2004: 36))

In (8a), the bounded nature of the past participle situation and its lexical content bring about the resultant state of Peter's ankle being bad now, unless otherwise indicated by the context.[29] In (8b), by contrast, the unbounded nature of the past participle situation and its lexical content usually bring about the continuing state of our knowing each other now. I will henceforth refer to the situation associated with the perfect *have* of the present perfect as "present state".

With respect to the temporal focus (TF), it is basically directed at E_1, i.e. the event time of the present state. This is because whatever the past participle situation refers to, the present state is finally identified as a specific state obtaining at speech time, which meets the condition for the operation of temporal focus (see Section 2.4.5). There is another reason for this position of temporal focus in the present perfect; if it is directed at E_2 in the past time-area, the difference between this case and the case where the simple past form refers to a specific past situation is minimized in that both cases focus on specific past events, which prevents the present perfect from being functionally differentiated from the simple past.[30]

---

plain a phenomenon like current relevance. He further argues that a framework which only allows the past and present sectors (and does not allow the pre-present sector) cannot explain the current relevance effect. However, as shown in the main text, my framework, which does not assume the pre-present sector, can handle the current relevance phenomenon. As shown in Figure 7, in the case of the present perfect the event time of the past participle and that of the perfect *have* are located respectively in the past and the present time-areas, and this duality in time reference brings about the current relevance effect.

[29] In my theory of tense, the resultant state is divided mainly into two types: the direct-result type and the indirect-result type (Wada (2001a: 101)). They both correspond to the "result in a narrow sense" and the "result in a broad sense" in Dahl (1985: 135). The former is a type of result stemming directly from the lexical meaning of the past participle involved, while the latter is a type of result based on the speaker's subjective judgment in the context (cf. Carey (1995: 83)).

[30] This type of functional difference between the present perfect form and the simple past form does not apply to such languages as French and German. In present-day French and German, the reference range of the simple past remarkably narrows and basically does not compete with that of the passé composé or the Perfekt. For this reason, the functional dif-

The basic temporal structure of the present perfect form in Figure 7 provides a basis for the temporal structures of its four basic uses, i.e. the completive, experiential, continuative, and habitual uses. In what follows, for simplicity's sake, I only treat prototypical cases of the four basic uses.

Let us start with the completive perfect. As we saw above, this use is characterized in the following manner: it is perfective in the sense that the past-participle situation is bounded and E_2 therefore does not reach E_1, and it is specific in the sense that the past participle describes a specific situation. The temporal structure of the completive perfect is therefore schematically represented below:

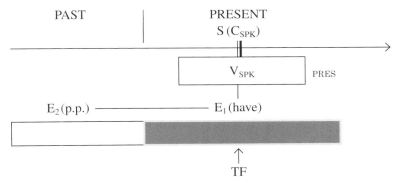

Figure 8: Temporal Structure of the Completive Use of the Present Perfect Form

In this figure, the cognitive schema below the two event times is added to Figure 7. The white rectangle below E_2 represents the past participle situation that is bounded and hence over before speech time; the dark-gray rectangle below E_1 represents the resultant state which obtains for a period of time including speech time. The two rectangles located side by side means that one occurs and the other follows it.

The past participle situation is bounded and the beginning of the present state coincides with (or is located just after) the end of the past participle situation. The end of the past participle situation is regarded as the end of the past time-area, while the beginning of the present state is seen as the beginning of the present time-area. However, E_2 (i.e. the time of the relevant part of the past participle situation) corresponds to a time point or span included in the past time-area, and similarly, E_1 (i.e. the time of the relevant part of the

---

ference does not come into play in these languages in the first place.

perfect *have*) corresponds to a time point or span included in the present time-area. E_2 thus does not reach E_1 and the completive perfect is situated at the perfective pole of the perfective-continuous scale.

The past participle situation, at the same time, refers to a specific event occurring at a point of time or in a span of time in the past time-area and the white rectangle therefore does not include any E_{SUB}'s (which symbolizes sub-situations of the same sort); the completive perfect is situated at the specific pole of the specific-general scale. The resultant state (i.e. the present state) is also specific in that it occurs as a direct result of the specific past event and the temporal focus can be directed at E_1.

For a better understanding of this temporal structure, consider the present perfect clause *I have married something better—a man* in (6a) above. From the context, it is interpreted in such a way that the speaker's getting married occurs in the past time-area and its resultant state (i.e. the state of their being married)—a specific present state—obtains thereafter. However, what is crucial here is that E_2 is located somewhere in the past time-area and E_1 is simultaneous with speech time in the present time-area, E_2 entirely preceding E_1; for this reason, the completive perfect is perfective. The past participle situation (i.e. the speaker's getting married) refers to a specific event occurring in the past time-area, the white rectangle representing a single specific situation. Hence this perfect is specific.

Second, let us consider the experiential perfect. This use is characterized in the following manner: it is perfective for the same reason as the completive perfect and general in the sense that the past participle describes a non-specific, or general, situation. The temporal structure of the experiential perfect is schematized below:

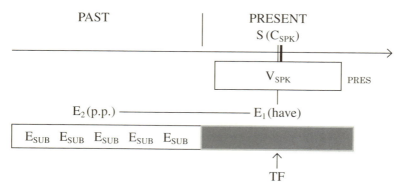

Figure 9: Temporal Structure of the Experiential Use of the Present Perfect Form

Chapter 4   Tense Interpretation and Temporal Structures   115

The major difference between the experiential use in Figure 9 and the completive use in Figure 8 is that in the former case, the past participle situation constitutes a superordinate situation consisting of non-specific sub-situations of
the same sort that obtains for a certain period of time, i.e. the time range
which starts at some time in the past time-area and reaches the end of the past
time-area, but excludes the present time-area. The superordinate situation is
thus seen as bounded or perfective. The (potential) repetition of sub-situations
of the same sort is symbolized by the repetition of E_{SUB}.[31] With respect to the
event time of the past participle (E_2), as with the completive perfect, it corresponds to a time point or span entirely included in the past time-area and
therefore does not reach E_1 (i.e. the event time of the perfect *have* included in
the present time-area). The present state of this perfect is the resultant state
in a broad sense, i.e. a state which the speaker, on his/her subjective grounds,
regards as deriving from the occurrence of the superordinate situation associated with the past participle. The resultant state refers to a specific state at
speech time and therefore the temporal focus is directed at E_1.

To illustrate the point, let us consider (6b), i.e. *In all competitions Arsenal
have played seven times, won four, drawn three games and are still to lose.*
The superordinate situation associated with the past participle of this perfect
sentence consists of the repetition of Arsenal's playing a football match
against a certain team, and its event time (E_2) corresponds to the time point or
span completely included in the past time-area at or during which the superordinate situation is true. The present state can, for example, be the state of
the football team being in mental superiority now (recall that the content of
the present state is specified by the interaction between the lexical content, the
boundedness of the past participle situation involved and the context). What
is important here is that even if the sub-situations constituting the superordinate situation associated with the past participle are repeatable at speech
time and beyond, the cognitive schema relevant here is such that the time
range of the superordinate situation does not continue up to speech time but is
restricted to the past time-area; the temporal structure says nothing about

---

[31] In this section, the number of E_{SUB} is five, but the number does not matter. What
does matter is that the superordinate situation involved presupposes the potential repetition
of non-specific sub-situations of the same type. Thus, the actual number could be one, as in
(i), or zero, as in (ii):

    (i)   England have played them once, in a warm-up before the 1986 World Cup when
        they won 4–0 in Cairo.   (BNC A9R)
    (ii) The churches have never objected to the existence of the vocational schools since
        their establishment in the early 1930s.   (BNC A07)

whether the superordinate situation actually obtains at speech time and beyond. In the experiential perfect, whether the past participle situation has (not) occurred and/or how many times it has occurred in the past time-area are questioned, and this information is reflected in the temporal structure in Figure 9.

Let us next move to the continuative perfect. This perfect is characterized in the following manner: it is continuous in the sense that E_2 continues up to E_1, which in turn coincides with speech time (S), and specific in the sense that the past participle refers to a specific situation. The temporal structure of this perfect is schematized below:

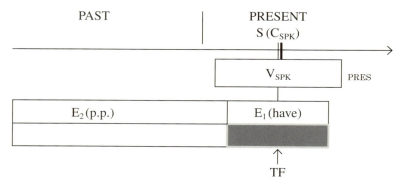

Figure 10: Temporal Structure of the Continuative Use of the Present Perfect Form

The completive and continuative perfects share the same characteristic, namely that the past participle situation is specific. However, they differ in that the continuative perfect requires the relevant time range of the situation involved (i.e. E_2) to stretch from the past to the present time-area and even to speech time. The past participle situation (symbolized by the white rectangle) is stative and unbounded and hence merges with the present state (symbolized by the gray rectangle) into a single, continuous state extending from the past to speech time; as a result, E_2—corresponding to the whole range of the past participle situation—continues up to E_1 (the event time of the perfect *have*) which is simultaneous with speech time.[32] The present state is a part of the

---

[32] One might argue that we should not allow the present state independently of the past participle situation because the latter situation is stative and unbounded. However, within my framework, one situation is associated with one verb, finite or non-finite. Moreover, the situation associated with the perfect *have* is schematic and the interpretation mechanism would be such that its content is specified only after we find the past participle situation stative and unbounded. From these observations, we can assume that the present state exists

specific unbounded situation described by the past participle and the temporal focus is thus directed at E_1.

Take, for example, the present perfect sentence in (6c), i.e. *You've been under arrest for ten minutes, 'Silky' Bob.* The past participle situation is the state of 'Silky' Bob's being under arrest and the relevant time range of that situation is ten minutes long, which reaches speech time. The past participle situation therefore merges with the present state. The schematic content of the latter situation — holding at speech time — is specified by the occurrence of the former situation, being recognized as the state of the man's being under arrest. These characteristics of the continuative perfect are reflected in the temporal structure in Figure 10.

Finally, let us consider the habitual perfect. This perfect is characterized in such a way that it is continuous for the same reason as the continuative perfect and non-specific (general) in the sense that the past participle describes a non-specific, or general, situation. The temporal structure of the habitual use is schematically represented below:

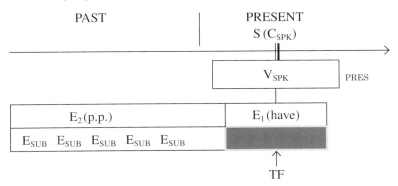

Figure 11: Temporal Structure of the Habitual Use of the Present Perfect Form

What the habitual perfect and the experiential perfect share in their temporal structures is a cognitive schema in which the past participle situation consisting of non-specific sub-situations of the same sort obtains for a certain period of time. However, unlike in the case of the experiential perfect, the superordinate situation of the habitual perfect is seen as unbounded or continuous

---

independently of the past participle situation from a theoretical and a cognitive point of view. In the process of tense interpretation, the past participle situation can merge with the present state into a single, continuous state, as assumed in the main text.

and the relevant time range of that situation stretches from the past time-area into the present time-area. The past participle situation (symbolized by the white rectangle containing five $E_{SUB's}$) merges with the present state (symbolized by the gray rectangle) into a single, continuous state extending from the past time-area to speech time. E_2—corresponding to the whole range of the past participle situation—therefore continues up to E_1 (i.e. the event time of *have*) which is simultaneous with speech time (S). The cognitive schema in this temporal structure indicates that the whole range of the superordinate situation stretches from the past to speech time and a sub-situation (i.e. a part of the superordinate situation associated with the past participle) is repeatable at speech time or beyond. The present state is still rather specific in that it refers to that part of the superordinate situation represented by the past participle which is derived from the repetition of the sub-situations involved and which obtains at speech time. The temporal focus is therefore directed at E_1.

For a better understanding of the interpretation mechanism of the habitual perfect, consider (6d), *Mr Phipps has sung in this choir for fifty years*. The past participle situation is the state of Mr Phipps's singing in a certain choir and the relevant range of time is fifty years, which leads up to speech time. The past participle situation merges with the present state, and the schematic content of the latter—obtaining at speech time—is specified by the occurrence of the former. The present state is thus such that the man's singing habit is still valid at speech time. From these observations, the temporal structure in Figure 11 reflects the characteristics of the habitual perfect.

4.4. Motivating the Polysemous Relationship among the Semantic Uses of a Tense Form with the Setting up of Temporal Structures

Thus far, we have seen how temporal structures contribute to tense interpretation by taking up the simple present and present perfect forms as sample cases. One single tense form has its own tense structure, which is shared by all of its semantic uses or functions having their own temporal structures. This instantiates a polysemous relationship because two or more related meanings (semantic uses) are associated with one single form. The setting up of more than one temporal structure for a single tense form motivates the polysemous relationship among its semantic uses (cf. Wada (2001a)).

We can also motivate the necessity of setting up temporal structures from other perspectives. First, as I have already stated, different temporal structures of a given tense form—which are distinguished based on differences not only

Chapter 4   Tense Interpretation and Temporal Structures

of temporal or aspectual factors but also of modal/mental attitude-related factors—are associated with its different semantic uses; on the other hand, pragmatic uses are distinguished based on factors other than the ones mentioned just above. In the present model, we can explicitly distinguish between semantic and pragmatic uses in terms of whether they have their own temporal structures or not—a distinction which has not been clearly stated in previous studies.

Second, if a tense form only allows one core meaning and pragmatics must take care of all derivative meanings (i.e. uses or functions deriving from the core meaning), then we have difficulty in explaining some temporal phenomena. For example, the simple present form is often said to be tenseless or almighty in that it refers not only to present situations but also to less specific or non-specific cases (e.g. the habitual and generic uses) and even to past situations (e.g. the historical-present use) and future situations (e.g. the future reference uses to be considered in Chapter 8). If we assume that the core meaning of the simple present form is tenselessness and its uses are all pragmatic variants deriving from that core meaning depending on "online" information—as do relevance-theoretic approaches in general—we cannot explain why the simple present form is restricted in usage, especially when referring to the past and future; for example, it can refer to the past only in the case of the historical-present use in its broader sense, i.e. only when it is related to the story now or a past time point, from which the vividness effect is derived from. If the simple present form were tenseless or almighty, it would be used to refer freely to past situations.

One might argue that the core meaning of the simple present would be such that the situation involved is in some sense or other related to the present. However, one single tense form cannot denote presentness while referring to the past at the same level of meaning. To avoid this contradiction, we have to assume at least two semantic levels and then claim that at one level it expresses the basic meaning of presentness and at another level it is extended to refer to past situations while preserving its basic meaning at the former level. This suggests that "pure" monosemous approaches to the simple present form are untenable and that we need at least two semantic levels. In our model, one level is associated with a rather schematic meaning (associated with the tense-structure information) and the other with a derivative or more specific meaning (associated with the temporal-structure information).

Third, by assuming temporal structures, we can easily and explicitly compare similar uses expressed by different tense forms. For example, both the simple present and present perfect forms have a habitual use ((1c) vs. (6d)), as

120   *The Grammar of Future Expressions in English*

we saw above. By comparing the temporal structures of the habitual use of the simple present form (Figure 3) and the present perfect form (Figure 11), we can clarify in what respects the semantic range of the former use is similar to, or different from, that of the latter use. In addition, using temporal structures also enables us to clarify the similarities and differences between similar but different uses of one single tense form. For example, the habitual-present and generic-present uses of the simple present form (Figure 3 vs. Figure 4) and the experiential and habitual use of the present perfect form (Figure 9 vs. Figure 11).[33]

Finally, as we saw in Section 2.5, our temporal structure approach can go along with a general pattern of grammaticalization (we will see briefly in later chapters how semantic uses or functions of future expressions are derived or newly obtained). It was stated there that when a given form acquires new meanings or uses, older meanings or uses fade away after some time during which they coexist (e.g. Hopper and Traugott (1993, 2003)). Within my framework, different semantic uses (functions) are associated with different temporal structures and in a polysemous relationship and so a given tense form acquires a new meaning (use) by constructing a new temporal structure based on older ones. Under this view, we can easily explain the mechanism in which a given tense form changes its semantic range: a tense form has lost an older meaning because the temporal structure associated with the older meaning has been lost, while it can maintain other newly-obtained meanings because it preserves their temporal structures.

4.5. Concluding Remarks

In this chapter, we have outlined how tense forms are interpreted, using the temporal structure approach within the framework developed in Chapters 2 and 3. To be more specific, we considered two tense forms, i.e. the simple present form (a tense form including only one event time in its basic temporal structure) and the present perfect form (a tense form including two event times in its basic temporal structure), showing what their temporal structures are like and how their semantic uses (functions) are characterized by those temporal structures as well as how pragmatic uses (functions) are treated. Moreover, toward the end of this chapter, we tried to defend and motivate the temporal

---

[33] A cognitive linguistic approach based on the configurations of binary features cannot deal with this point extensively. For details, see note 23 of Chapter 5 and note 13 of Chapter 6.

Chapter 4 Tense Interpretation and Temporal Structures

structure approach. In the chapters that follow, to further validate our comprehensive model, we will, along these lines, consider the six major future expressions in English, i.e. sentences containing *will*, sentences containing *be going to*, sentences in the present progressive, sentences in the simple present, sentences containing *be about to*, and sentences containing the *will* + progressive form.

PART II

APPLICATIONS

Chapter 5

Will

5.1. Introduction

This chapter gives a temporal structure analysis of sentences or clauses containing *will* (henceforth *will*-sentences) in the comprehensive model established in the previous chapters.[1] *Will* is often regarded as the primary future form in English and there have been numerous studies on *will*, including those on the comparison between *will* and *be going* to (e.g. Berglund (2000b), Binnick (1971, 1972), Boyd and Thorne (1969), Brisard (2001), Coates (1983), Collins (2009), Comrie (1989), Copley (2009), Declerck (1991b, 2006), Del Prete (2014), Fleischman (1982), Haegeman (1983, 1989), Kashino (1999, 2005), Leech (1971, 1987, 2004), McIntosh (1966), Nicolle (1998), Palmer (1988, 1990), Salkie (2010), Szmrecsanyi (2003), Torres-Cacoullos and Walker (2009), Tyler and Jan (2017), Wada (1996, 2001a, 2011a), Wekker (1976)).[2, 3, 4]

---

[1] Strictly speaking, *shall* should be treated differently from *will* because the former is etymologically different from the latter and in some cases they show different meanings. However, in contemporary English, especially in American English, *will* is basically used to refer to the future irrespective of person and number (Leech (2004: 56) notes that "*will* is at least 10 times more frequent than *shall*") and the aim of this chapter is to clarify the mechanism of tense interpretation of sentences with a so-called future modal. I will take *will* as a representative "future" modal and in principle do not refer to *shall*, unless absolutely necessary.

[2] It is reported in Berglund (1997) that in the three corpora of American, British, and Indian English, the frequency of *will* (including *'ll*) is much higher than that of *be going to* (including *gonna*). Such a report may support the statement that *will* is the primary future form.

[3] Here, I will very briefly outline some representative studies that have been published after my previous book (Wada (2001a)). Unlike previous studies that tend to focus on semantic or pragmatic differences between *will* and *be going to*, Szmrecsanyi (2003), using spoken corpora, points out that *will* and *be going to* show different tendencies with respect to four syntactic environments (i.e. negative contexts, subordinate contexts, *if*-clauses, and sentence lengths). Collins (2009) regards *will* as a modal, giving a detailed, corpus-based

They are primarily divided into two groups depending on their stance to *will*. One group takes the position that *will* is a future tense marker (auxiliary), e.g. Comrie (1985), Davidsen-Nielsen (1990), Declerck (1991b, 2006), Del Prete (2014), Hornstein (1990), Kissine (2008), Klein (1994), Reichenbach (1947), Salkie (2010), Wekker (1976);[5] the other group takes the position that *will* is a modal (auxiliary) verb, e.g. Brisard (1997), Collins (2009), Harder (1996), Huddleston (1995), Huddleston and Pullum (2002), Jaszczolt (2009), Klinge (2005), R. Lakoff (1972), Lyons (1977), Nakau (1994), Palmer (1979, 1990), Perkins (1983), Quirk et al. (1985).[6, 7] I take the latter position because within our framework, as we observed in Chapter 3, we have plenty of evidence to regard *will* as a modal which typically expresses predictive modality as speaker's

---

analysis of modals and quasi-modals including it. Torres-Cacoullos and Walker (2009), based on spoken corpora of Canadian English, present a multivariate analysis of *will*, *be going to*, and two types of futurate constructions, i.e. an analysis considering variables such as sentence type, clause type, temporal adverbials, and vicinity. Salkie (2010) compares the position that *will* is a future tense marker and the position that *will* is a modal auxiliary, arguing for the former position, which is the opposite to my position. One reason why he takes the former position is that in many cases *will* behaves in the same way as French future tense inflections. However, as we will see in Section 5.6, the fact is that at least in some cases English *will* and French future tense inflections behave differently. I will argue that such a different behavior reflects the differences between *will* as a modal and French tense inflections as real tense markers (i.e. A-morphemes in my terminology).

[4] For diachronic studies on *will*, see Aijmer (1985), Bybee and Pagliuca (1987), Bybee, Perkins and Pagliuca (1994), among others.

[5] Proponents of this position often argue that *will* is basically a future tense marker (auxiliary) because it preferentially refers to the future. However, as R. Lakoff (1972: 243) points out, epistemic *should* also preferentially refers to the future and such an argument does not support the position in question.

[6] This dichotomy is sometimes not clear-cut. For example, although Declerck (2006) argues that the form *will* + bare infinitive represents future tense, he admits that *will* more or less involves epistemic modality in its semantics (p. 103); he claims that the primary aspect of the meaning of *will* is the future tense, i.e. a tense indicating that the situation involved (i.e. the one represented by the bare infinitive) is located in the future. His stance is thus not necessarily contradictory to my treatment of *will*-sentences in this chapter.

[7] There seems to be a third type of stance to *will*. For example, Okamura (1996) claims that pure future *will* is a primary auxiliary verb, such as perfect *have* and progressive *be*, rejecting the two types of stance to *will* in the main text. However, his argument to reject the position that pure future *will* is an epistemic modal seems weak in many respects. First, he argues that pure future *will* expresses "the kind of futurity which is conceived of as disconnected from the present (p. 40)," but as we will see in Section 5.6, it is not so disconnected from the present in comparison with the French simple future. Second, he argues that volitional *will* can appear in conditional clauses of the direct cause-effect type while pure future *will* cannot, but epistemic modals generally cannot appear in that type of conditional clauses.

S-attitude.[8]

The meanings (uses) of modal (auxiliary) verbs have often been studied in terms of monosemy vs. polysemy. Monosemous approaches include Groefsema (1995), Haegeman (1989), Klinge (1993, 2005), Kissine (2008), Nicolle (1998), whereas polysemous approaches include Halliday (1970), Leech (1971, 1987, 2004), Palmer (1990, 2001), Sawada (2006), Sweetser (1990). Under the monosemous approach, *will* has a core meaning and its functions and uses are all pragmatic interpretations stemming from the core meaning. In contrast, under the polysemous approach, *will* itself has more than one semantically-related function or use (which can correspond to either semantic uses or pragmatic variants in my study) and the so-called future-tense use (a case where *will* serves as a future tense marker) is one such semantic use.

In this chapter, I combine the two types of approaches under the established model. To be more specific, in the same spirit as Depraetere's (2010, 2014) analysis of modals,[9] I assume three levels of "meanings", i.e. core meaning, semantic functions and uses, and pragmatic functions and uses—which are motivated by our dual time-structure approach—to analyze the meanings of the modal *will*. As implied in the analysis of the simple present form in Chapter 4, I argue that the core meaning of *will* corresponds to its tense structure, the semantic uses correspond to the temporal structures, and their pragmatic uses correspond to pragmatically different meanings sharing the same temporal structure.

This chapter is organized as follows. Section 5.2 observes (semantic and pragmatic) uses and functions of *will*-sentences. In Section 5.3, I offer the basic temporal structures of *will*-sentences in the default case and discuss the core meaning of *will*. Section 5.4 is devoted to a temporal structure analysis of the uses and functions of *will*-sentences. In Section 5.5, I briefly consider the relation among the temporal structures of the semantic uses and functions offered in Section 5.4 in terms of grammaticalization. In Section 5.6, to enhance the validity of this temporal structure analysis, I explain differences between *will*-sentences and their allegedly French counterparts, i.e. sentences

---

[8] Sarker (1998) states that the semantics of *will* is the combination of the predictive modality and the present tense, arguing that it cannot be taken as a modal alone or a (future) tense alone. However, this is basically the same position that the present study takes, as will be clear from the main text.

[9] Depraetere (2010, 2014) assumes the levels of "context-independent semantics", "context-dependent semantics", and "pragmatic meaning" to explain the behaviors of typical modals like *can*, *may*, and *must*, but not those of *will*.

128   *The Grammar of Future Expressions in English*

with French future tense inflections. Section 5.7 makes conclusions.

5.2. Uses and Functions of *Will*-Sentences

The uses and functions of *will*-sentences to be dealt with in this chapter are
illustrated by (1):

(1) a.   I will be back before six.   (Huddleston and Pullum (2002: 192))
    b.   It will rain tomorrow.   (Wekker (1976: 118))
    c.   He will be two tomorrow.   (Huddleston and Pullum (2002: 190))
    d.   That will be the milkman.   (Klinge (2005: 174))
    e.   Oil will float on water.
                (Huddleston and Pullum (2002: 194); Leech (2004: 87))
    f.   Private Jones will report at 08:00 hrs.   (Palmer (1990: 142))
    g.   If it rains tomorrow, the match will be cancelled.
                          (Haegeman and Wekker (1984: 45))
    h.   If the film will amuse them, I'll buy some tickets. (Close (1977: 143))

(1a) is an example of the volitional use.[10] This use expresses the subject's volition to pursue something controllable.

(1b) exemplifies the so-called simple-future or pure-future use, but the term
for this use in the present model is *predictive future* (e.g. Jaszczolt (2009: 50,
54)). The reason for this naming is this: not only is the term *simple future* in
my model restricted to a smaller reference range in terms of the definition just
below, e.g. a case like (1c), but instances of the use in question are restricted
to the ones accompanied by predictive modality (see Section 3.4).

(1c) is an example of the simple-future use in my terminology. The speaker
using this use construes the target situation as a future fact because it is regarded as absolutely certain to occur or obtain as a result of the present situation or fact; for example, age-related situations, calendar-related events.

(1d) is an instance of the epistemic use, often termed *predictability* (e.g.
Coates (1983: 177–178)) or *epistemic prediction* (e.g. Dancygier (1998)). In
the present model, it is called *predictive present*. This is because this use of
will conveys predictive modality, as with the predictive-future use in (1b), but
the infinitival situation occurs or obtains at the same time as, or in the time-

---

[10] This use is sometimes further divided into subtypes. For example, Leech (2004: 87–
88) assumes three subtypes, i.e. the uses of intention ('intermediate volition'), willingness
('weak volition'), and insistence ('strong volition'). For the treatment of the subtypes of
this use, see Section 5.4.1.

Chapter 5   *Will*

span including, speech time located in the present time-area.[11]

(1e) exemplifies a use expressing the grammatical subject's properties or tendencies, often referred to as *propensity* or *characteristic behavior* and sometimes as *predictability*. In the present model, it is referred to as the use of characteristic behavior.[12]

(1f) is an example used to illustrate a case where the speaker gives an order or instruction to the second or third person. This use is termed *order* in this book, though it is sometimes referred to as deontic *will* in the literature (Huddleston and Pullum (2002: 194), Collins (2009: 134)).

(1g) shows that epistemic or non-volitional *will* usually does not occur in typical conditional clauses (i.e. *if*-clauses of the direct cause-effect type) with future time reference (see Section 3.8); by contrast, (1h) shows that such a *will* can occur in certain *if*-clauses.[13, 14] Close (1977: 143) states that the *will* in the *if*-clause of (1h) does not convey volition. Note that volitional *will* can occur even in *if*-clauses of the direct cause-effect type, as in *If he'll pay, I'll go with him* (Quirk et al. (1985: 1009)).[15]

In what follows, I will show how the temporal structure analysis figures out the mechanism of interpreting each use. Before going into the analysis, how-

---

[11] For those who consider future *will* to be a future tense marker (e.g. Depraetere and Reed (2006)), the epistemic use of *will* is often restricted to the use of "inference" with present or past time reference. In the present model, prediction in situation construal is one type of modality as speaker's S-attitude (see Chapter 3). Thus, if the target situation is evaluated or judged with such a mental attitude, then it conveys predictive modality as a type of epistemic modality, irrespective of whether it refers to the non-future or the future, because it is related to the degree of probability or factuality of the situation involved. Proponents of the position that prediction is a type of epistemic modality include Coates (1983), Kytö (1990), Hoye (1997: 113), Dancygier (1998: 45), and Collins (2009: 126ff). Notice that some linguists regard future *will* as an instance of deontic use (e.g. Gotti (2003: 288)).

[12] Although the way of using the term *predictability* sometimes differs from linguist to linguist, it is often used for a case where the speaker is confident about the truth of a present or past situation based on evidence or knowledge (Coates (1983: 178), Collins (2009: 127)).

[13] Note in passing that the *will*'s in the main clauses of conditional sentences are usually instances of the predictive use (e.g. (1g)). This is illustrated by the following example:

(i) *If it rains, the match will be canceled, and I predict it will. (Dancygier (1998: 47))
As Dancygier (1998: 47) indicates, because the *will* in the main clause of the first conjunct conveys predictive modality, it is redundant and therefore unacceptable to add an expression that lexicalizes the notion of prediction, i.e. *I predict*.

[14] Szmrecsanyi (2003: 296) proves, based on spoken corpora, that *will* tends to appear in main clauses, but not in *if*-clauses, whereas *be going to* can appear in *if*-clauses much easier.

[15] In the present model, the volitional use of *will* in *if*-clauses of the direct cause-effect type is treated differently from that in independent or main clauses, e.g. *will* in (1a) (see Sections 5.4.1 and 5.4.7).

ever, I will first construct the basic temporal structures of *will*-sentences—which are assumed to be stored in our mind and referred to in the tense-interpretation process—and clarify the core meaning of *will*.

5.3. Toward Constructing the Temporal Structures of *Will*-Sentences

5.3.1. Tense Structure

To construct the basic temporal structures of *will*-sentences, we first need to consider the tense structure of *will*-sentences, which is the combination of the tense structures of the modal *will* and the bare infinitive. I will begin with *will*. *Will* is a finite verb, because it has the past-tense counterpart *would*, as lexical verbs do—illustrated by, e.g. *plays* vs. *played*—and occupies the left-most position of a verb phrase in a tensed clause, i.e. the finite position in present-day English, as exemplified by *Akane {will/would} play the flute* vs. *Akimi {intends/intended} to play the piano*. This indicates that *will* has the same tense structure as, say, the present tense form *plays*, as shown in Figure 2(i) in Chapter 2. In the default case, as a result of the operation of principle (4) in Section 2.4.1, the present time-sphere (grammatical present) associated with the present form *will* covers both the present and future time-areas (cognitive present and future) and excludes the past time-area (cognitive past). This is supported by the ungrammaticality of (2):

(2) *Yesterday I will be happy.   (Ludlow (2013: 179))

The *will* in (2) is assumed to receive the default interpretation, namely that the speaker's t-viewpoint internalized in the tense structure of *will* fuses with the speaker's consciousness at speech time; as a result, the present time-sphere in question does not cover the past time-area and the event time included in the present time-sphere cannot be situated in the past time-area. A time adverb when fronted is usually seen as referring to the time position of the finite verb, i.e. *will* in this case. The adverb *yesterday* is a past time adverb referring to the past time-area. Hence a contradiction arises and (2) is ungrammatical.

Let us next consider the bare infinitive, a non-finite verb. Its tense structure is such that the temporal relation between the event time and potential time of orientation is unspecified (see (3d) in Section 2.3). In *will*-sentences, the bare infinitive occupies the complement position of the head verb *will* and the potential time of orientation internalized in the tense structure of the bare infinitive is therefore identified as the event time of *will*. In this way, the event time of the bare infinitive is calculated relative to the event time of *will* as the relevant time of orientation.

In the process of tense interpretation, the properties of this linguistic environment (i.e. the complement position of a modal as head verb) play a crucial role. The situation described by the bare infinitive is situated in the potential world created by the modal; this potential world "comes into existence" only after the time of the modal is identified and specified on the time line, so the event time of the bare infinitive cannot be located in the past relative to the event time of the modal (cf. Duffley (1992, 2006)).[16] This relationship is schematized in Figure 1:

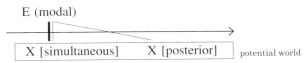

Figure 1: The Relationship between the Event Times of the Modal and the Bare Infinitive in the Potential World Created by That Modal

X symbolizes the position of the event time of the bare infinitive. The bold solid line shows that the potential world symbolized by the rectangle comes into existence at the time when the speaker's S-attitude expressed by the modal occurs. The solid lines represent the possible time relations between the two event times.

Thus, modals in the present form, such as *may*, *must*, or *will*, bring the potential worlds into existence at the event time of the modal — i.e. the same time as speech time in this case — and the event time of the bare infinitive is located somewhere in the time range during which the potential world obtains, i.e. a time range corresponding to both the present and the future time-area. This is illustrated by the following examples:

---

[16] One might argue, presenting the following examples, that the event time of the bare infinitive can be located in the past relative to that of the modal and thus speech time.
  (i) a. Doc may have overdone the dynamite a bit.
                                          (C Gardner, *Back to the Future III*, p.19)
     b. "The last meeting must have been fifteen years ago," Keating recalled.
                                        (N. H. Kleinbaum, *Dead Poets Society*, p.47)
However, what is in the bare infinitive form is the perfect *have*, which — within my framework — has its own event time (see section 2.4.3.2); the tense interpretation of these examples is such that the event time of the resultant state associated with *have* is simultaneous with the event time of the modal *must* or *may*. What is located in the past time-area is the event time of the past participle. These examples are therefore not counterexamples to the present tense model; on the contrary, they lend support to it.

(3) a.　Nancy {must / may / will} come.

　　b.　John {must / may / will} be in his office.　　　(cf. Palmer (1987: 137))

As we saw in Section 2.4.3.3, stative situations usually prefer the simultaneous reading to the posterior reading. Thus, in (3b), unless otherwise stated or implied, the event time of the bare infinitive is interpreted as simultaneous with the event time of the present tense modal as the time of orientation, which is, in turn, simultaneous with speech time. In the case of non-stative situations, as in (3a), the only available reading in this environment is the posterior reading, namely that the event time of the bare infinitive is posterior to the event time of the modal as the time of orientation. Incidentally, the fact that *will* behaves in the same way as typical modals such as *must* or *may* in this respect also lends support to the view that *will* is a modal.

Furthermore, as shown in (4) below, the VP-internal modification of a fronted time adverbial is not excluded: the fronted time adverbial can specify the time position of the infinitival situation on the time line.

(4)　One day I'm going to be famous, too.　　　　　　　(BNC ADR)[17]

This observation, together with the ungrammaticality of example (2) above, supports my claim that the bare infinitive in the complement position of the modal (and quasi-modal) as head verb cannot have an anterior relationship to the event time of that modal. In (2), even if *yesterday* is seen as referring to the time of the bare infinitive *be happy*, it is ungrammatical, which suggests the impossibility of the anterior relationship between the modal as head verb and the bare infinitive in its complement position.

5.3.2.　Basic Temporal Structures

In the default case, i.e. when principle (4) in Chapter 2 is in operation, the speaker's t(emporal)-viewpoint (V_{SPK}) in the tense structure of *will* as a present tense form fuses with his/her consciousness (C_{SPK}) at speech time (S). This fusion allows the tense structure of *will*-sentences (consisting of the tense

---

[17] In (4), *be going to* involves the stative verb *be* with a present tense inflection (though in the case of irregularly conjugated verbs, the verb stem and tense inflection are fused). As stated in note 27 in Chapter 4, the schematic stative situation of a present tense sentence is difficult to interpret as located in the future time-area. The *be* in question is also schematic and stative and its event time is thus difficult to view as located in the future time-area. For this reason, the event time of *be going to* as a unit is located at the same time as speech time in the present time-area (for the claim that *be going to* is a unit as a tense form, see Section 6.3.1) and the indefinite future-time adverb *one day* has to specify the event time of the infinitival situation.

structures of *will* and the bare infinitive) to bring about two basic temporal structures: the basic temporal structure of *will*-sentences with future time reference and that of *will*-sentences with present time reference. The two temporal structures are schematically represented in Figures 2 and 3, respectively.

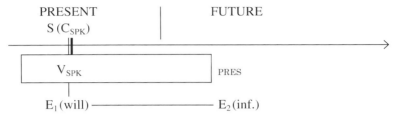

Figure 2: Basic Temporal Structure of *Will*-Sentences with Future Time Reference (Default Case)

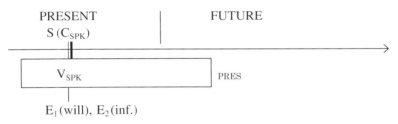

Figure 3: Basic Temporal Structure of *Will*-Sentences with Present Time Reference (Default Case)

Each use of the *will*-sentences exemplified by (1) has its respective temporal structure based on either of the two basic temporal structures, unless it is a pragmatic variant. Uses and functions associated with their own temporal structures are in a temporally (i.e. in terms of temporal semantics) polysemous relationship to each other, but they share a core meaning, i.e. an abstract meaning common to all instances of *will* outside the field of tense in the English grammar.[18, 19]

---

[18] This idea is similar to that of Depraetere (2010) except that the determination of the semantic meanings of *will* is based on their temporal structures within my framework. However, I am not sure that this approach is equally applicable to all modals in English. For example, Depraetere (2010) is skeptical about the position that all instances of *shall* have a core meaning. I leave it for future research.

[19] My approach is basically the same as Haegeman's (1983: 9), where *will* has derivative meanings stemming from its basic (i.e. core) meaning and future *will* (i.e. the simple-future use in my terminology) is one of them.

5.3.3. The Core Meaning of *Will*

Let us next move to the core meaning of *will*. I assume that the core meaning of *will* is "high probability".[20, 21, 22, 23] This is in keeping with Palmer's

---

[20] This core meaning of *will* is similar to Rigter's (1982) "confident assumption" or Haegeman's (1983) "actuality", "subjective certainty", or "maximal likelihood".

[21] Boyd and Thorne (1969) provide the first study which constructively uses Austin's (1962) speech act theory to analyze modal phenomena, claiming that *will* expresses prediction even in the case of the characteristic-behavior use. However, unlike the Three-Tier Model, i.e. a general theory of language use for explaining the relation between grammar and pragmatics, speech act theory does not clearly distinguish between the levels corresponding to the situation construal tier and the situation report tier and therefore cannot distinguish modality as speaker's S-attitude—operative in the situation construal tier—from modality as speaker's A-attitude—operative in the situation report tier. In this connection, Sawada (2006: 68) criticizes Boyd and Thorne's (1969) analysis, arguing that *will*-sentences do not always perform a direct speech act, i.e. prediction; for example, *will*-sentences can convey promises, i.e. indirect speech acts. In fact, Leech (2004: 87) notes that *will*-sentences with a first-person subject when conveying volition can be interpreted as expressing promises, threats, offers, shared decisions, and the like. Thus, the *will*-sentence in (i) is usually seen as representing a volitional use, but can be interpreted in such a way that the speaker promises the addressee that the former will write a letter to the latter.

(i) I'll write tomorrow. (Leech (2004: 87))

In the present model, predictive modality as speaker's S-attitude can interact with the contextual information to create a different type of indirect speech act, e.g. promise, as speaker's A-attitude (see Section 3.6). My analysis is thus better than Boyd and Thorne's in this respect. Moreover, in my analysis, unlike Boyd and Thorne's (1969), prediction is a key notion common to a number of uses of *will*-sentences and not the core meaning of *will*; the core meaning of *will* is high probability. See Section 5.4.6 for more details about how to interpret so-called speech act uses of *will*-sentences.

[22] Torres-Cacoullos and Walker (2009) have found, using Canadian spoken corpora, that *will* tends to co-occur with indefinite time adverbials in comparison with *be going to*. They regard this finding as a reflection of the semantic retention of *will* and therefore as evidence for claiming that it expresses "uncertainty about the prediction or, rather, about the timing of its realization" in comparison with *be going to* (Torres-Cacoullos and Walker (2009: 346)). My analysis is in keeping with Torres-Cacoullos and Walker's finding because *will*, whose core meaning is high probability, has an affinity for uncertainty in comparison with *be going to*, which is taken as accompanied by assertive modality. Moreover, they observe that *will* is preferable to other future expressions in the main clause of conditional sentences, where the subordinate clause (i.e. *if*-clause) is semantically dependent on the main clause. This characteristic is related to their finding mentioned above.

[23] Brisard (1997) presents a similar approach within a cognitive grammar framework. He defines the core meaning of *will* (a modal) as consisting of the features NON-GIVEN and NON-PRESENT, stating that "based on the knowledge that a certain state of affairs holds in the world in which the conceptualizer finds her/himself, she/he can confidently predict another state of affairs that is epistemically dependent upon the presumed truth value (or givenness) of this initial set of conditions" (p. 281). He suggests that the futurity associated with *will* emerges through the interaction between the epistemic values of the modal in question and the temporal frame indicated by Langacker's (1991) "time-line" and "dynamic

Chapter 5   *Will*

(1990: 57–58) statement that *will* indicates what is a reasonable conclusion.[24]

It might appear that *will* can co-occur not only with adverbs of degree of higher probability, as in (5) and (6), but also with those of not-so-high degree of probability, as in (7):

(5) a.   "You'll probably want a steak," said another familiar voice.

(E. Segal, *Love Story*, p. 28)

   b.   "No!" Todd shouted. "Oh, I don't know. I'll probably never know ..."

(N. H. Kleinbaum, *Dead Poets Society*, p. 65)

(6) a.   But they will certainly be disappointed by the style of Rockies skiing above valley level.   (BNC A5X)

   b.   It will certainly take a great deal of time.   (BNC ADP)

(7) a.   "... Maybe you'll think of something to win her love."

(N. H. Kleinbaum, *Dead Poets Society*, p. 37)

   b.   "Why don't you ask him first? Maybe he'll say yes," Todd suggested.

(N. H. Kleinbaum, *Dead Poets Society*, p. 64)

However, Diagram 1 reveals that *will* tends to co-occur with adverbs expressing a higher degree of probability, which can be taken as an argument for the core meaning of high probability associated with *will*.

Adverbs	Sequence of 'modal verb-modal adverb'	number	Sequence of 'modal adverb-modal verb'	number
certainly	will certainly	515	certainly will	92
probably	will probably	1826	probably will	139
perhaps	will perhaps	80	perhaps will	23
maybe	will maybe	6	maybe will	2
possibly	will possibly	25	possibly will	3
seldom	will seldom	24	seldom will	3
surely	will surely	160	surely will	17
definitely	will definitely	89	definitely will	4

Diagram 1: Co-occurrence Frequency of *Will* and Adverbs Expressing
Degree of Probability or Possibility Based on the BNC

---

evolutionary" models. Under the influence of syntactic, semantic, pragmatic, and discourse criteria, this core meaning leads to specific uses depending on context.

[24] Brisard (1997: 282) notes that "the use of WILL suggests a stage of deduction, similar to that involved in the (epistemic) usage of the deontic modal MUST". This implies that *will* is also concerned with a mental calculation of the speaker involved and thus supports our view that *will* is a modal expressing a mental attitude toward the proposition or situation involved, i.e. speaker's S-attitude.

This diagram is a list of the numbers of the co-occurrence frequency of *will* and adverbs expressing degree of probability or possibility in the British National Corpus (BNC). These numbers come only from those cases where *will* and such adverbs are located side by side with each other, but they are sufficient for our purposes. All we need here is to know the tendency of the co-occurrence frequency of the two items. As is clear from Diagram 1, the frequency of co-occurrence of *will* and the adverbs in question (e.g. *probably, certainly*) is extremely higher. In this connection, Lyons (1977: 807) says, based on Halliday (1970: 331), that "the adverb and the modal verb may, and normally do, 'reinforce each other' in a modally harmonic combination".[25, 26] These observations enable us to assume that *will* itself has the core meaning of high probability.[27]

This assumption is empirically supported by the following data:

(8) a. *It will rain tomorrow, and if it does we won't go for a walk.

(Haegeman (1983: 60))

    b. *It will rain tomorrow, but if it doesn't we'll go for a walk.

(Haegeman (1983: 60))

(9) a. ?We will send the manuscript on 31 March, and we will not send it by then.   (De Brabanter, Kissine and Sharifzadeh (2014: 10))

    b. #The Red Sox will play the Yankees tomorrow, but (all else being equal) they won't.   (Copley (2014: 83))

The sentences in (8) indicate that *will*-sentences suggest "a higher degree of certainty of future occurrence" (Haegeman (1983: 58)) and it is rather contradictory for one single speaker to assert that a certain situation will certainly occur, but then again to "conditionalize" it; an *if*-clause of a conditional sen-

---

[25] Halliday (1970: 331) observes two types of combination between modal verbs and adverbs: (i) when the degree of probability of modal verbs is the same as, or similar to, that of modal adverbs, they "reinforce each other"; (ii) when the degree of probability of modal verbs is different from that of modal adverbs, they bring about cumulation in meaning.

[26] In this connection, Coates (1983: §7.1.2.5) claims that *will* is compatible with adverbs expressing any degree of probability ranging from certainty to uncertainty, but only the combination of epistemic *will* (expressing the speaker's confidence) and adverbs expressing certainty (or high probability) is an instance of modally harmonic combination. Hoye (1997: 118), on the other hand, argues that the combinations between *will* and *possibly, probably* or *definitely* are all modally harmonic combinations. Brisard (1997: 281–282) seems to stand for the latter position, stating that "the high degree of epistemic certainty" (i.e. high probability in my terminology), typically related with the use of *will*, can be lowered in cases where the context allows such modification.

[27] Lakoff (1972: 243) claims that epistemic *will* expresses future certainty and occupies the top position on the epistemic scale.

Chapter 5   *Will*

tence expressing a direct cause-effect relationship represents a neutral condition and is therefore not compatible with the notion of high probability. Similarly, the sentences in (9) show that because of the high probability accompanying the *will*-sentences, it is contradictory for one single speaker to affirm the
occurrence of a future situation with a higher degree of certainty and negate it
with a higher degree of certainty at a time in one utterance.

This makes a sharp contrast with the case of sentences with *may*, whose degree of probability or possibility is at most fifty percent. This assumption
about the degree of probability or possibility of *may* is verified by the acceptability of (10a), which makes a contrast with the unacceptability of the *will*-
version in (10b):

(10) a.   John may come back tomorrow but I'm not certain.

(Haegeman (1983: 58))

   b. *John will come back tomorrow but I'm not certain.

(Haegeman (1983: 58))

From this we predict that by using *may*-sentences, one can assume the possibility of a certain situation and at the same time its opposite possibility in the
same utterance. This prediction is borne out by (11):

(11) a.   The canon may or may not be oppressive.   (BNC A1B)
   b.   These may or may not progress to cervical cancer.   (BNC A1Y)

By arguing that *may* and *will* express modalities of different degrees of
probability or possibility, we can account for the phenomena observed in this
sub-section from a unified point of view. This is one merit of our position
that *will* is a modal whose core meaning expresses high probability. In the
next section, I will verify this position by confirming that the core meaning of
high probability is reflected in the temporal structures of all semantic uses
(functions) of *will*-sentences, based on which I will explain the temporal phenomena of the uses of *will*-sentences observed in Section 5.2.

5.4.   Analysis

The temporal structures of *will*-sentences to be proposed reflect the combined tense structure of *will* and the bare infinitive and include the cognitive
schema which schematizes both the tense/aspect-related information and the
modality/mental-attitude-related information, on one hand, and the characteristics of the semantic uses necessary for temporal calculation, on the other.
When two temporal structures share similarities, they motivate each other as

the semantic uses associated with one single tense form (i.e. *will*-sentences in this case). Let us start with the volitional use.

5.4.1. The Volitional Use

This sub-section will show how my framework can effectively deal with various phenomena concerning the volitional use of *will*, as exemplified by *John will help you to find a job* (Palmer (1987: 138)). Volitional *will* has been treated differently in the literature,[28] but as far as I know, few studies have focused on and extensively considered this use. Within the present framework, volitional *will* is originally regarded as expressing a mental state or activity of the grammatical subject as potential speaker at the first stage (or earlier stages) of the tense-interpretation process, but in the course of that process, i.e. at the stage when the public self of the current speaker (the speaker of the whole sentence involved in the relevant scene) is relevant to the process, it is identified either as an element belonging to the current speaker's attitude domain or as an element belonging to the proposition domain (observed in Section 3.4). However, the temporal-structure information of volitional *will* reflecting the grammatical subject's mental state is invariant in temporal calculation (Section 4.1) even when the volition associated with *will* is identified as the current speaker's S-attitude. The reason for this is as follows: differences as to the temporal-structure information—a necessary condition for an appropriate construal of the relevant situation—are already discerned in the situation construal tier and the temporal structure of the volitional use, once fixed, basically cannot be changed thereafter; the information about whether the volition in question is attributed to the current speaker or not is only relevant to the "mental-attitude area" in the situation report tier—when the notion of public self comes into play—and does not affect the temporal structure already fixed in the situation construal tier. In what follows, we will consider these observations in more detail.

Let me start by constructing the temporal structure of the volitional use of *will*-sentences in the present tense. To this end, I will first clarify what the notion of volition means. Volition is defined as a mental activity of making a practical decision (cf. Zhu (2004: 178)) or "the faculty or capacity of conscious choice, decision, and intention" (Collins Free Online Dictionary);[29] in

---

[28] For example, Coates (1983) and Hoffman (1976) consider volitional *will* a root modal; Palmer (1987), Huddleston and Pullum (2002) and Collins (2009) classify it into a dynamic type; and Ziegeler (1996) and Gotti (2003) regard it as expressing deontic modality.

[29] http://www.collinsdictionary.com/dictionary/english/volition.

the volitional use, the notion can therefore be seen as a mental state or activity of the grammatical subject that serves as a precondition for the actualization of the situation involved. The volitional interpretation of *will*-sentences is obtained typically when the grammatical subject is animate, especially human, and the situation involved is a controllable type. A situation is "controllable" if the grammatical subject can determine whether or not to carry out the relevant situation on his/her own will.[30] When a grammatical subject's volition is available at a time of orientation (in the case of present-tense *will*-sentences, the time of orientation is speech time), the infinitival situation (i.e. the situation that the grammatical subject decides to carry out), if actualized, will come into existence in the future relative to that time of orientation.

Taking these observations into consideration, I present the temporal structure of the volitional use below, which is based on the basic temporal structure of *will*-sentences with future time reference in Figure 2 above.

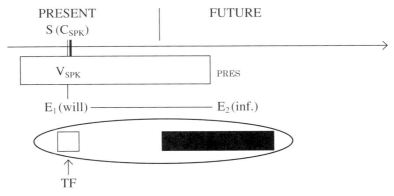

Figure 4: Temporal Structure of the Volitional Use of *Will*-Sentences

E_1 and E_2 denote the event time of *will* and the event time of the bare infinitive, respectively. The white square below E_1 indicates a grammatical subject's volition; the black rectangle below E_2 stands for the infinitival situation; and the oval including the two quadrangles represents a mental world created by the grammatical subject which comes into existence only after his/her decision to do something is made.

In the case of *will*-sentences in the present tense, the volition of the grammatical subject constitutes part of his/her present state of mind (Leech (2004: 62)). The volition at issue is assumed to occur at the very time of the utter-

---

[30] This is comparable to Haegeman's (1983: 85–89) "volitional proposition".

ance or just before it, and the event time associated with the volition (i.e. E_1) is construed as coinciding with (or occurring just before) speech time (S).[31] This is because the volition of the grammatical subject is taken as an embodiment of his/her reaction to the speech situation or the preceding context, which occurs at the time of utterance or just before it (Celle (1997)). The white square below E_1 connected to $S(C_{SPK})$ by a solid vertical line is intended to express this (virtual) coincidence. This makes a contrast with the case of the volition (of the grammatical subject) conveyed by *be going to*, whose length of time corresponds to a longer time span (we will return to this matter in the next chapter). As we saw above, the infinitival situation can come into existence only after the decision to carry it out is made and the event time of the bare infinitive (E_2) is thus located at a time in the future relative to E_1 as the time of orientation, which is, in turn, seen as simultaneous with S. The positional difference between E_1 and E_2 causes the volitional use to always convey futurity.

Let us next consider the position of temporal focus (TF) in this use. The temporal focus is directed at E_1 because the speaker pays his/her special attention to the volition of the grammatical subject; volition has predominance over the infinitival situation in that the actualization of the latter presupposes the fulfillment of the former.

It should be noted here that in constructing the temporal structure of the volitional use in the situation construal tier, the speaker's S-attitude involved is assertive modality. In this tier, volitional *will* is an element belonging to the proposition domain and does not express any speaker's S-attitude (i.e. an element belonging to the speaker's attitude domain). Within my framework, situation construal must involve a speaker's S-attitude and hypothesis (22) in Chapter 3 works, assertive modality as the unmarked speaker's S-attitude coming into play. Thus, in Figure 4, unlike in the case of the predictive-future use that we will see in the next section (Figure 5), E_1(will) is not surrounded by a box with the subscript SA, i.e. a marker denoting an element belonging to the speaker's attitude (SA) domain.

Let us next examine whether the volitional use is compatible with the notion of high probability, the core meaning common to all uses of *will*-sentences. When one decides to carry out something, one will usually accomplish it unless such an accomplishment is prevented by external factors or something more urgent happens. That is, if the volition of the grammatical

---

[31] This means that the volition involved is interpreted as simultaneous with speech time in a broad sense (cf. Declerck's (1991a, 1991b, 1997, 2006) "sloppy simultaneity").

Chapter 5   *Will*   141

subject occurs at (or just before) speech time, it implies that the infinitival situation involved (i.e. the target situation to be carried out) is very much likely to come into existence. In this way, this use satisfies the "high probability" condition. This is in keeping with Jaszczolt's (2009: 59) statement that "strong intentionality results in strong probability".[32]

Before moving to the matter of whether the volition of the grammatical subject is identified either as an element belonging to the speaker's attitude domain or as an element belonging to the proposition domain, let me briefly consider the relationship between volition and notions similar or related to it. In the literature, volition is often classified into subgroups or named differently, e.g. "intention". In this book, following Coates (1983: 173) and Kytö (1990), I use the term *volition* to cover not only instances of *will* referred to as *intention* and those referred to as *willingness* but also those in-between.[33] In Kytö (1990: 278), willingness is defined as "a state of mind of the subject" and intention as "a single dynamic event in future". In the present model, these two uses are derived from the volitional use (a semantic use) depending on which of the two situations involved the speaker is inclined to put more emphasis on, i.e. a volition occurring at speech time or the infinitival situation to be actualized in the future;[34] they are therefore pragmatic variants that share the same temporal structure in Figure 4 above. Leech (2004: 87–88) also assumes subcategories of the volitional use, but he allows three types, i.e. intention (=intermediate volition), willingness (=weak volition), and insistence (=strong volition), exemplified respectively by (12a–c).

---

[32] Our assumption that high probability is the core meaning of *will* is empirically supported by a sentence like (i).

    (i) ?I'll cut the grass but unfortunately I won't be able to.   (Salkie (2010: 211))

In the first conjunct, the current speaker as private self takes the volition of the grammatical subject as his/her S-attitude and asserts that his/her decision to cut the grass occurs at speech time. This suggests that the infinitival situation is highly likely to occur. In the second conjunct, however, the modal *won't* represents a negative prediction and thus the same speaker predicts that the possibility of occurrence of the target situation is denied. Since the first *will*-sentence shows a high degree of probability of the future occurrence of the target situation, denying its occurrence with a high degree of probability in the second conjunct leads to a kind of self-contradiction.

[33] *Will* in its volitional use can be paraphrased into *want, wish, desire, intend, be willing* and so on, depending on context (Haegeman (1983: 80)), although they do not have exactly the same meaning (Huddleston and Pullum (2002: 192)). This suggests that *will* itself is associated with the modality of volition as an independent use.

[34] The focus operative here is a "phase focus", a pragmatic focus used to show which phase (sub-situation) the speaker puts more emphasis on, based on the presupposition that the temporal focus is directed at E_1, the event time of the volition represented by *will*.

142   *The Grammar of Future Expressions in English*

(12) a.   I'll write tomorrow.   (Leech (2004: 87))
     b.   Jim'll help you — he's always ready to oblige a friend.
                                                                  (Leech (2004: 87))
     c.   He WILL go swimming in dangerous waters
          ('He insists on going swimming ...')   (Leech (2004: 88))

They are all pragmatic variants, i.e. subtypes of the volitional use, too.[35] This is because the three uses — as indicated by the parenthesized parts in the above statements — are distinguished from one another depending on the strength of volition, which does not affect the temporal information expressed by the *will*-sentence in its volitional use.

I will now consider in detail the process in which the volition of the grammatical subject is identified either as a speaker's S-attitude or as an element belonging to the proposition domain in the situation report tier. My framework allows us to assume (at least) two different types of speakers in the volitional use: one is the current speaker, i.e. the speaker responsible for construing and conveying the target situation; the other is the grammatical subject, i.e. a potential speaker serving as the "cognizer" (i.e. thinker or conceptualizer) of his/her mental world forming (part of) the propositional content, who is responsible for the mental activity involved, i.e. volition. As we saw in Chapter 3, a speaker can be dissolved into two aspects, i.e. the public self and the private self, and so the two selves of the current speaker are relevant to the process under consideration. However, the grammatical subject as a potential speaker does not actually communicate or report something to the addressee in the relevant utterance and therefore only the aspect of private self is relevant. The identification process in question is carried out in the situation report tier, when the public self comes into play for the first time. Note again that any operation in this process basically does not affect the construction of the temporal structure of the volitional use.

Let us start with cases where the volition of the grammatical subject is identified as a speaker's S-attitude, an element belonging to the situation-

---

[35] As formal diagnostics to distinguish between the three categories, Leech (2004) points out that the uses of intention and willingness, but not the use of insistence, allow the contracted form *'ll*, and that the use of willingness usually does not allow a stress to be put on *will*, but the use of insistence does. Coates (1983: 173) states that a focus is put on the state of mind of the grammatical subject at present in the case of willingness, but on the future situation in the case of intention — a similar explanation adopted in the main text. Note, however, that this "focus" is different from the temporal focus. The focus in Coates's sense does not affect the temporal structure of the volitional use and therefore serves as a diagnostic to distinguish pragmatic variants.

Chapter 5   *Will*   143

oriented speaker's attitude domain. This case happens when the grammatical subject is the same as the current speaker, as indicated by means of the first-person subject. Examples of this case are given in (13):

(13) a. I will be back before six. (=(1a))
   b. I WILL solve this problem.   (Huddleston and Pullum (2002: 193))
   c. I will look after you till you die.   (BNC AHG)
   d. Before passing on, I will introduce a piece of terminology of my own and call central-system thinking.   (BNC A0T)
   e. "We'll continue next time, boys," Keating said. "Good effort."
                                    (N. H. Kleinbaum, *Dead Poets Society*, p. 71)
   f. "I will write to her [=mother-in-law] myself," answered Alicia, with a faint foreshadowing of enthusiasm.
                                    (O Henry, *The Defeat of the City*, p. 241)

Take (13a) for example. In the situation construal tier, the current speaker as private self construes the subject's volition to come back before six with assertive modality. This (grammatical) subject is the private self, i.e. cognizer of the mental world. When the current speaker conveys the construed situation to the addressee (i.e. in the situation report tier), the public self of the current speaker comes into play. At this stage, the function of the grammatical subject as private self completely overlaps with that of the current speaker as private self, because the current speaker and the grammatical subject share the same identity, which is indicated by the first-person subject *I*. The private self of the current speaker is therefore regarded as functionally redundant and less than necessary in that its function can be covered by the grammatical subject and other functions of the current speaker can be covered by the public self, the private self of the grammatical subject being the only aspect of him/her in operation. For this reason, the private self of the grammatical subject is foregrounded and the private self of the current speaker is backgrounded. The backgrounding of the private self of the current speaker reduces the effect of assertive modality (attributed to this self) and thus causes the assertive modality to be backgrounded, which enables the volition attributed to the private self of the grammatical subject to move to the site for a speaker's S-attitude. As a result of this process, the volition as a speaker's S-attitude can double as a speaker's A-attitude, an element belonging to the addressee-oriented speaker's attitude domain (cf. Section 3.6). In this way, the notion of volition is brought to the fore in conveying the content of the target sentence (in this case sentence (13a)) to the addressee.

   Unless otherwise indicated, the unmarked message conveyed by this type of sentence is such that the speaker S-attitude is volition (as a modality) and the speaker's A-attitude is also volition. However, in appropriate contexts, illocutionary forces such as promise can be added as a speaker's A-attitude by way of the interpretation mechanism discussed in Section 3.6. We will consider this matter in some detail in Section 5.4.6.

I argue that only in cases where the grammatical subject and the current speaker share the same identity can *will*-sentences receive a truly volitional interpretation, and only this *will* should be interpreted as the volitional use.[36] This is compatible with the view that the speaker usually knows completely what the mental world is like only when it is his/her own mental world (Ziegeler (1996: 418)). (Note, however, that this conclusion is only true of independent or complement clauses consisting of the speaker's attitude domain and the proposition domain. We have a different explanation for the "volitional" use of *will* in *if*-clauses of the direct cause-effect type, i.e. a subordinate clause consisting only of the proposition domain, as we will see in Section 5.4.7.)

Now, let us consider cases where the grammatical subject is not first-person, i.e. where the current speaker and the grammatical subject do not share the same identity, as shown in (14).

(14) a. He'll go on holiday next week. (Haegeman (1983: 100))
 b. John will help you to find a job. (Palmer (1987: 138))
 c. Jill won't sign the form. (Huddleston and Pullum (2002: 192))

---

[36] Note that in indirect speech, free indirect speech, and linguistic environments which can be interpreted as such, the grammatical subject is not necessarily represented by a first-person pronoun for the relevant situation to satisfy the condition that the current speaker and the grammatical subject share the same identity.

    (i) a. Mary says that she'll be back by ten o'clock.
       b. (Mary says) She'll be back by ten o'clock.

The referential relationship between the original speaker of the complement clause situation (corresponding to the speaker in the main or independent clause) and the grammatical subject in the complement clause in (i) is the same as that between the current speaker and the grammatical subject in the case of the first-person subject discussed in the main text. These *will*-sentences can therefore be regarded as instances of the volitional use in my system. In short, I am arguing that the volitional use of *will*-sentences is available only when the speaker of the sentence in question and its grammatical subject share the same identity. This implies that a sentence like *This door won't open*, often presented as an instance of the strong-volition (i.e. insistence) use of *will*-sentences in grammar books, does not express a truly volitional meaning in my analysis; the volitional overtones emerge through personification and are thus pragmatic. My argument here has benefited much from the discussion with Yukio Hirose (personal communication).

In cases of this kind, the current speaker, who is responsible for the judgment about or evaluation of the situation involved, does not decide to do something him/herself; for the situation to be interpreted as expressing volitional overtones, the current speaker must know the volition of the grammatical subject in advance or needs a contextual clue to know that. This is a premise for the volitional interpretation of *will*-sentences without a first-person subject.

With this premise in mind, consider (14a) as an example. In the situation construal tier, the current speaker as private self interprets the subject's volition to go on holiday next week, and in the situation report tier, his/her public self comes into play. In the case under consideration, the function of the (grammatical) subject as private self does not overlap with that of the current speaker as private self because the current speaker and the grammatical subject do not share the same identity. The private self of the current speaker thus has its raison d'etre and remains foregrounded, playing the role of the observer of the mental world of the grammatical subject. Hence, neither the backgrounding of the private self of the current speaker nor the foregrounding of the private self of the grammatical subject—discussed above—is in action. A question, then, arises as to what kind of S-attitude of the current speaker as private self is relevant here. I assume that the S-attitude working here is not assertive modality but predictive modality. Because "the speaker is less likely to have explicit knowledge of the subject's volition" (Ziegeler (1996: 418)), the current speaker usually cannot make an assertion about the situation with the other person's volition but is more or less required to make a prediction about it; even if the current speaker knows the volition of the grammatical subject in advance, he/she does not exactly know the present mental state of the latter at speech time unless it is uttered explicitly in front of him/her—a very unlikely situation. This suggests that *will*-sentences of the type under discussion are no longer instances of the (true) volitional use, but they are, in functional terms, instances of the predictive-future use and the *will* in this type of *will*-sentences is to be associated with predictive modality (we will consider the tense-interpretation process of the predictive-future use in detail in the next sub-section); the volition accompanying this type of *will*-sentence is an implicature deriving from the interaction between the content of the sentence and the context.

The explanation above is verified by the following examples, all of which are cited from Haegeman (1983: 101):

(15) a. ?I'll go on holiday next week, although I don't intend to now.
  b. He'll go on holiday next week, although he doesn't intend to now.

(16) a. ?I'll break the cups to annoy my sister-in-law although I don't intend to now.

    b. He'll break the cups to annoy his wife although he doesn't intend to now.

Take (15) for example. In the main clause of (15a), in the situation construal tier the current speaker as private self asserts that he/she (as the grammatical subject) has a volition to carry out the infinitival situation (describing his/her mental world); in the situation report tier the volition at issue is interpreted as a speaker's S-attitude and the current speaker as public self conveys the situation with that volition to the addressee. However, in the subordinate clause, the same speaker denies his/her intention to do so. A kind of contradiction arises and hence the low acceptability of (15a). In (15b), by contrast, the current speaker and the grammatical subject do not share the same identity and therefore the *will* in the main clause is interpreted as representing predictive modality; the current speaker (as private self) restricts him/herself to the role of the observer, merely making a prediction about a man's going on holiday. Since the *will*-sentence in question is an instance of the predictive-future use, it is not a contradiction if the subject's volition to carry out the infinitival situation in the main clause is denied by the content of the subordinate clause. In this way, my theory of modality and mental attitudes, supported by the Three-Tier Model, can systematically distinguish instances of the true volitional use from those of the predictive-future use with volitional overtones. Note, however, that when we do not bother to distinguish between the (true) volitional use and the predictive-future use with volitional overtones but refer simply to a reading in which the target sentence conveys volition, we use the term *volitional reading* in what follows to cover all types of "volitional" meanings including the above two.

Before closing this sub-section, let us consider a possible counterargument by those who take the position that all uses of *will*-sentences (including the volitional and predictive uses) are contextual meanings, or pragmatic variants.[37] One argument for this position could be that the volitional use also

---

[37] Haegeman (1983) takes the position that *will* has the core meaning consisting of non-factuality, actuality (=subjective certainty), and event time orientation (=future orientation), considering that interpretations such as volition or prediction are contextual or pragmatic ones (a monosemous approach). However, in an approach like mine, which allows two semantic levels to be set according to two different levels of time structure, i.e. tense structure and temporal structure, meanings other than the core meaning are not necessarily regarded as pragmatic ones but can be classified as semantic ones. One argument against the monosemous approach is that it cannot explain why the volitional use, but not the predictive-future (pure-future) use, can appear in *if*-clauses expressing a direct cause of the main clause

Chapter 5   *Will*   147

conveys futurity or the speaker's prediction and is therefore not independent of
the pure-future use (corresponding to the predictive-future and simple-future
uses in my terminology).

My position would be like this. First, as shown in Figure 4 above, the
temporal structure of the volitional use of *will*-sentences involves the event
time of the infinitival situation (E_2) located at a time later than speech time
(typically in the future time-area). My analysis can thus give a solution to
Huddleston and Pullum's (2002: 193) observation that "one has no feeling of
ambiguity between volitional and non-volitional future in examples like [(13a)]".
Sentences like those in (13) all convey both volitionality and futurity.

Second, as for the possibility that *will*-sentences can convey both volitionality and predictivity, it can be exemplified by sentences like those in (14)

---

situation, because such *if*-clauses are future-oriented and both volitional and predictive interpretations should equally be available. The present framework can deal with this matter.
Let us first confirm that *will* in such *if*-clauses expresses a different type of volitional reading from the ones dealt with in this sub-section. Because *if*-clauses of the type under consideration semantically consist only of the proposition domain, i.e. P-domain, the *will* in this
environment is an element belonging to the P-domain throughout temporal calculation. This
will can thus appear in the *if*-clauses of the direct cause-effect type. On the other hand, *will*
in its predictive use belongs to the speaker's attitude domain, i.e. SA-domain. Since predictive *will* expresses predictive modality as speaker's S-attitude (an SA element), it cannot appear in such *if*-causes, i.e. a linguistic environment consisting only of the P-domain.

Analyses based on relevance theory (e.g. Haegeman (1989), Nicolle (1998)) cannot explain the difference in question, either, because they are basically monosemous approaches.
For example, Nicolle (1998: §5) assumes that the core meaning of *will* as grammatical
marker is "potentiality", but not "futurity" (p. 235); an optimally relevant value is determined depending on context. He seems to suggest that the procedural content of *will* (i.e.
potentiality) and a similar function of *if* bring about a functional redundancy, so the hearer
makes an adjustment and regards it as expressing volition. However, why is *will* able to appear in a functionally redundant linguistic environment like such *if*-clauses before the adjustment is made? He might argue that the volitional *will* occurring in the *if*-clause is a lexical
or semi-modal expression and thus homophonous with the grammatical marker *will*, but then
it must be addressed what type of relationship exists between the two *will*'s. In addition,
characterizing *will* merely as potentiality cannot distinguish it from other modals such as
may and thus cannot explain the different behaviors of *will* and *may* observed in Section
5.3.3.

The present framework assumes the level of core meaning (i.e. tense structure) of *will*-
sentences and can therefore enjoy the merits of the monosemous approach; at the same time,
it allows a number of semantic and pragmatic uses of *will*-sentences and can thus avoid criticism on polysemous approaches, which usually assume two or three semantic uses (i.e.
epistemic vs. root, or epistemic vs. deontic vs. dynamic) and are criticized in that they cannot deal with subtle distinctions of uses (see, e.g. Papafragou (1998: 5–8)). Moreover, as
we have seen above, my approach can explain some linguistic phenomena that the monosemous approach cannot explain.

148   *The Grammar of Future Expressions in English*

above. My framework can solve the second case by treating the sentences as instances of the predictive-future use with volitional overtones, as we saw above.

5.4.2. The Predictive-Future Use

Let us now move to the predictive-future use. As shown in Section 3.4, predictive modality as a speaker's S-attitude is associated with *will* when the speaker forecasts the situation on a reasoned basis (e.g. observations, experiences, scientific reasons). In the situation construal tier, *will* is interpreted as expressing predictive modality and the event time of *will* in its predictive use (E_1) is located at the same time as speech time (S) due to the definition of modality as speaker's S-attitude. The temporal position of the infinitival situation construed by the (current) speaker as private self with predictive modality is affected by the environmental properties of the complement position of a modal, as schematically represented in Figure 1 above (see Section 5.3.1); the event time of the bare infinitive (E_2) is located at the same time as E_1 or at a time later than E_1. This sub-section is concerned with the predictive-future use and the relevant temporal structure is therefore based on the basic temporal structure of *will*-sentences with future time reference in Figure 2 above.

Any use accompanied by predictive modality requires that the temporal focus (TF) be directed at the event time of the infinitival situation (E_2) in constructing the temporal structure. As stated in Section 2.4.5, the temporal focus is in operation in the temporal structure of the tense form involved when the speaker pays special attention to a (specific) situation in the scene to be described. It must therefore be directed at the event time of a situation belonging to the proposition domain, but not one belonging to the speaker's attitude domain (in the situation construal tier). This is supported by Nakau's (1994: 156) or Sawada's (1995: 173) observation that subject-related elements (i.e. speaker's attitudes) in principle cannot be the target of focus. Since predictive modality is a speaker's mental attitude, the event time associated with *will* in its predictive use (E_1) cannot receive the temporal focus. This observation characterizes the so-called future-orientation of the predictive-future use of *will*-sentences (Coates (1983: 201), Fleischman (1982)).[38]

The predictive-future use is also compatible with the core meaning of *will*-sentences (i.e. high probability) because the speaker construes the relevant situation with predictive modality when he/she regards it as very likely to occur

---

[38] This characteristic makes a sharp contrast with that of the basic use of sentences containing *be going to*, i.e. a present-oriented future expression, which we will see in Chapter 6.

or obtain.

The above observations enable us to present the temporal structure of the predictive-future use below.

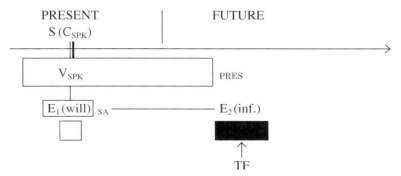

Figure 5: Temporal Structure of the Predictive-Future Use of *Will*-Sentences

The white square below E_1 indicates predictive modality and the black rectangle below E_2 represents the infinitival situation. Unlike in the case of Figure 4 (i.e. the temporal structure of the volitional use), in Figure 5 the event time of *will* (E_1) is surrounded by a box with subscript SA, which means that it is associated with a speaker's mental attitude (in the situation construal tier) and the oval — which, in Figure 4, symbolizes a mental world created by the grammatical subject that comes into play after his/her decision to do something is made — is missing because the infinitival situation can come into existence without the grammatical subject's control. The infinitival situation needs to express the semantic content that can be the target of prediction, which implies that the situation in question should be differentiated from the one that is sure to come into existence when the time comes. The use with the latter type of situation is named *simple future*, which will be considered in the next sub-section.

To illustrate the predictive-future use, let us consider the examples in (17):

(17) a. It will rain tomorrow. (=(1b))
 b. Tomorrow's weather will be cold and cloudy.   (Leech (2004: 57))
 c. "Come on," Charlie encouraged. "It will help you get Chris."
        (N. H. Kleinbaum, *Dead Poets Society*, p. 49)
 d. Base rates hit eight-year high: Rise to 15% will lead to increase in mortgage payments, lenders say.   (BNC A34)
 e. Mr Reilly will have to make his own bureaucracy reform itself.

150   *The Grammar of Future Expressions in English*

(BNC ABK)[39]

f.   "We'd better get going," Charlie said. "Before you know it, we'll have to be in class."   (N. H. Kleinbaum, *Dead Poets Society*, p. 59)

g.   "... But if I give Watson demerits, I will also have to give Perry demerits ... and I like Perry."

(N. H. Kleinbaum, *Dead Poets Society*, p. 70)

This use imposes no restrictions on the choice of grammatical person or situation type. However, when the situation involved is a non-controllable type with a third-person subject, the *will*-sentence basically does not convey volitional overtones. Take (17a) for example. Since the grammatical subject is impersonal and rainfall is a non-controllable situation, the sentence definitely receives a predictive-future reading. It may be the case here that the speaker makes a prediction based on personal experience or meteorological data. If *will*-sentences co-occur with future time adverbials or nouns, as in (17a, b), the event time of the infinitival situation (E_2) is automatically located in the future time-area; if they do not, as in the other examples, whether or not E_2 is located in the future time-area depends on context. In these examples, the temporal focus is directed at the event time (E_2) of the infinitival situation, not the event time (E_1) of predictive modality (as speaker's S-attitude) occurring at speech time, for the reason we have already seen.

Before going further, let us once again confirm cases where the grammatical subject is human and non-first-person, especially third-person, and the infinitival situation is a controllable type. Consider (18):

(18)   She will beat him easily.   (Huddleston and Pullum (2002: 188))

As discussed in the last sub-section, in a case like this, the volition of the grammatical subject (an element belonging to the proposition domain) and the predictive modality attributed to the current speaker as observer are both involved and in play. This type of instance therefore receives a predictive-future reading, even if it is regarded as conveying a volitional nuance. The volition relevant here is merely pragmatic.[40] In my analysis, for a sentence with a

---

[39] When *will* is followed by semi-modals like *have to* or *be able to*, it is difficult to regard the relevant *will*-sentence as conveying volition.

[40] The reason why volitional overtones are obtained pragmatically in a sentence with a human subject and a controllable situation, as in (18), may be due to the transitivity of the situation involved. Hopper and Thompson (1980) state that one factor contributing to transitivity is volitionality, namely that volitional acts receive more saliency than non-volitional ones.

Chapter 5   *Will*   151

controllable situation to indicate an instance of the volitional use as an independent semantic use, the condition discussed in the last sub-section must be
met: the current speaker and the grammatical subject share the same identity.

5.4.3.   The Simple-Future Use

I now turn to the simple-future use. Let me stress again that the simple-future use to be discussed in this study is not a collective term for non-volitional, future reference uses. It is restricted to instances of *will* in which the
speaker construes the target situation as a future fact, i.e. a situation regarded
as absolutely certain to come into existence as a necessary result of the present situation. This notion of simple future corresponds to Close's (1977: 132)
"statement of future fact", Palmer's (1979, 1990) "future fact", or Collins's
(2009: 128) "minimal degree of prediction".[41] The typical situations involved
in this use are those referring to calendar-related events or describing human
age. These situations are absolutely certain to come into existence when the
time comes. It is thus inappropriate, or even meaningless, for the speaker to
evaluate or judge them with predictive modality.

Then, what type of modality as speaker's S-attitude is expressed by *will*-
sentences of the simple-future use? This question arises because the simple-
future use does not express predictive modality due to the characteristics of
the situation involved in this use — a factor which coerces the semantic content of this *will* to be "bleached" in the tense-interpretation process or, more
precisely, in the situation construal tier.[42] The answer to this question is that
the simple-future use of *will*-sentences expresses assertive modality as a
speaker's S-attitude because this environment semantically involves the situation-oriented speaker's attitude domain (see (4) in Section 3.4) and the situa-

---

[41] With respect to the modal notion of "not-yet-factual-at-t_0" conveyed by *will* (as a future
tense marker), Declerck (2006: 103) distinguishes three subcategories, i.e. "pure future",
"prediction", and "predictability". My notion of simple future might appear to correspond
to his notion of pure future, because he defines it as "the least subjectified" prediction "clos-
est to a statement of plain fact." By way of illustration, he offers an example like (i):

    (i)   The seventh annual European Biotech Crossroads — "Biotech Nantes 2003" — *will
be held* at the Cité des Congrès conference centre, Nantes, France, on September
25–26.   (requoted from Declerck (2006: 103))

However in fact, my notion of simple future is more restricted in the range of its use, because even in (i), there is a low possibility that the future situation in question will not happen and the *will*-sentence in (i) is thus not a prototypical example of the simple-future use
in my sense.

[42] It is presupposed that the situation for the simple-future use is a non-controllable type
and thus cannot be construed as volitional in the situation construal tier. On this presupposition, the semantic bleaching of *will* is carried out.

tion involved is absolutely certain to come into existence and thus assertable.

What is important with this use is that the situation associated with *will* is coerced to be semantically bleached and its event time is an orientational type, i.e. E^O (cf. Section 2.4.4). This *will* itself does not express assertive modality, but the whole sentence is interpreted as indicating it in temporal calculation. The E^O in question is originally the event time of *will* (expressing high probability), thus inheriting the characteristics of speaker's S-attitudes when its position on the time line is determined. As a consequence, the orientational event time (E^O_1) associated with *will* is situated at speech time.

With respect to the temporal focus (TF), we have no choice but to direct it at the event time of the infinitival situation (E_2) because the situation associated with *will* is semantically bleached. For an event time to receive a temporal focus, the situation associated with that event time must have semantic content (cf. Section 2.4.5).

A possible semantic criterion to distinguish the simple-future use from the predictive-future use is like this: if there is some doubt as to whether the propositional content of a *will*-sentence will occur or obtain, then such a *will*-sentence receives a predictive-future reading; if not, it receives a simple-future reading. For the compatibility with the core meaning of *will*-sentences, this use refers to a situation absolutely certain to occur or obtain as a necessary result of the present situation surrounding the speaker and thus reflects the notion of very high probability, or more precisely, certainty — a notion compatible with the core meaning of *will*.

From the observations made thus far, we can present the temporal structure of the simple-future use below:

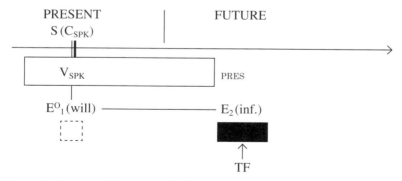

Figure 6: Temporal Structure of the Simple-Future Use of *Will*-Sentences

E^O_1 is an orientational event time and the square with broken lines represents a semantically bleached situation. E^O_1 is not surrounded by a box with subscript SA, for assertive modality is not directly related to *will*, but is inserted in the course of the tense-interpretation process when the infinitival situation turns to be a type of situation appropriate for the simple-future use and the situation associated with *will* is coerced to be semantically bleached. The *will* in this use does not represent any semantic content and merely serves as a "space-filler";[43] E^O_1, located at the same time as speech time (S), merely serves as a viewpoint from which to compute the event time of the infinitival situation in the future (E_2).

For a better understanding of this use, consider (19):[44]

(19) a. He will be two tomorrow. (=(1c))
   b. Tomorrow will be Monday.   (GloWeb BD)
   c. There will be a public holiday on Friday.   (Close (1977: 132))
   d. Next century will begin on the first of January, 2001.

                                                                  (Hornby (1975: 96))
   e. The stop after Minami-Nagareyama will be Kita-Senju.
                       ("a train announcement" of the Tsukuba Express line)

In (19a), for example, the speaker knows that the birthday of the person referred to by *he* is the next day. For a person to become a certain age is inevitable and there is no room for the speaker to question whether it will happen. The person is sure to become two years old when tomorrow comes. The situation associated with *will* is therefore coerced to be semantically bleached and serves merely as a "space-filler", its event time merely functioning as an orientational event time from which to calculate the event time of the infinitival situation. Since the orientational event time coincides with speech time, the event time of the infinitival situation is located at a time later than speech time, usually in the future time-area.

As supporting evidence that this use of *will*-sentences refers to a future fact accompanied by assertive modality, I will point out that the sentences in (19)

---

[43] What is to be emphasized is that the notion of simple future is not a particular type of modality expressed by *will* alone, but it is derived in temporal calculation from the interaction between the basic temporal structure of the *will*-sentence involved and its semantic content.

[44] Reference to a calendar-related event or a situation describing age does not automatically make possible the simple-future reading of *will*-sentences, as in (i):

(i) *Christmas will be in December this year.   (Williams (2002a: 200))
I leave the reason for this unevenness for future research.

can have their simple present counterparts, as in (20), with virtually no change of meaning (cf. Huddleston and Pullum (2002: 190), Collins (2009: 128)).

(20) a. He is two tomorrow.   (Huddleston and Pullum (2002: 190))
   b. Tomorrow is Saturday.   (BNC GUE)
   c. There is a public holiday on Friday.   (Close (1977: 134))
   d. This is the year of the Horse. Each month of a Chinese year begins at new moon and has 29 or 30 days.   (COCA NEWS)
   e. The stop after Shinjuku-Sanchome is Shibuya.
                    ("a train announcement" of the Tokyo Metro subway)

Within my framework, an utterance with the simple present form in independent clauses is accompanied by assertive modality unless otherwise expressed or implied. Therefore, the fact that *will*-sentences in their simple-future use can be paraphrased into their simple present counterparts implies that the *will*-sentences in question are accompanied by assertive modality. (However, this does not mean that *will*-sentences and simple present sentences in their simple-future use have exactly the same meaning. We will point out subtle differences in nuance between the two tense forms in Chapter 8.)

This paraphrasability test is also useful to distinguish the simple-future use from the predictive-future use of *will*-sentences, because in the latter case the paraphrase of the *will*-sentence into the simple present counterpart involves change of meaning. For example, when (17a), i.e. *It will rain tomorrow*, is paraphrased into its simple present counterpart, the result is that the simple present sentence is unacceptable, as in **It rains tomorrow* (Wekker (1976: 85)), because it is interpreted as making an assertion about a future fact while nobody usually can make an assertion about tomorrow's weather.

5.4.4. The Predictive-Present Use

The next to be considered is the predictive-present use of *will*-sentences. In this use, as with the predictive-future use, *will* is interpreted as expressing predictive modality and the event time of *will* is located at the same time as speech time due to the definition of predictive modality as speaker's S-attitude in the situation construal tier. The only difference between the two uses is that the predictive-present use, as its name indicates, requires the infinitival situation to obtain at (or around) speech time and thus the event time of the infinitival situation is located at the same time as the event time of *will* in the present time-area.[45]

---

[45] In the present model, the predictive-present use includes *will*-sentences used to infer a

To verify that *will* in its predictive-present use and the so-called future *will* are both epistemic modals, we can present the following phenomena (cf. Collins (2009: 128–129)): both types of *will* (i) co-occur with the epistemic modal adverb *probably*, (ii) allow the perfect infinitive, (iii) allow the progressive infinitive, (iv) appear in existential *there*-constructions, and so on. These phenomena are shared by other epistemic modals and therefore can be taken as evidence that the two types of *will* are both epistemic modals. Given this, in the predictive-present use — as with the predictive-future use — the temporal focus (TF) is directed at the event time of the infinitival situation (E_2), because *will* here expresses predictive modality (a speaker's S-attitude) and cannot be focused on. For the compatibility of the type of modality expressed by this use of *will* with the core meaning of *will* (i.e. high probability), we have already confirmed it (in Section 5.4.2), because the *will* under consideration expresses predictive modality.

From the above observations, the temporal structure of the predictive-present use of *will*-sentences — which is based on the basic temporal structure of *will*-sentences with present time reference in Figure 3 above — is presented in Figure 7:

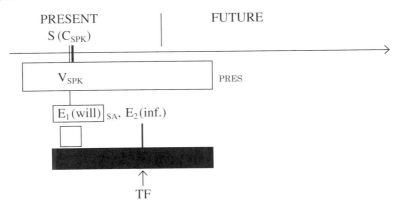

Figure 7: Temporal Structure of the Predictive-Present Use of *Will*-Sentences

---

past situation, as in (i), because in this type of *will*-sentences, what refers to the past is the past participle and the perfect *have* describes a present situation:
    (i) a. They'll have arrived home by now.   (Leech (2004: 86))
        b. You'll have heard all the results last night, so I won't read them out again.
                                                             (Close (1977: 126))
Our approach can, in a unified way, treat these cases as well as other modals followed by the perfect form, as seen in note 16 of this chapter.

The white square below E_1 indicates predictive modality occurring at speech time (S) and E_1 shares the same time as S. The black rectangle below both E_1 and E_2 represents the infinitival situation ranging from the time simultaneous with speech time to the future time-area, but E_2 — which is linked to the black rectangle by the bold line — is restricted to the time of the relevant part of the situation included in the present time-area. The temporal focus (TF) is directed at E_2 for the same reason stated in Section 5.4.2. This use does not have a volitional reading, which presupposes the posterior relationship between the volition of the grammatical subject and its target situation.

By way of illustration, consider (21):[46]

(21) a. That will be the milkman. (=(1d))
   b. [Knock on door] That will be the plumber.
                                    (Huddleston and Pullum (2002: 188))
   c. John will be in his office.   (Palmer (1987: 137))
   d. That'll be the electrician — I'm expecting him to call about some rewiring [on hearing the doorbell ring].   (Leech (2004: 86))
   e. The plane will be ready for its test flight by now.   (Leech (2004: 87))

Take (21b) for example. The speaker, based on solid ground, judges to be highly probable the situation in which the person on the other side of the door is the plumber. It would be appropriate to utter (21b) when the speaker has been waiting for a plumber because he/she asked the plumber to visit him/her at a certain time and hears someone knocking on the door around that time. The time at which predictive modality occurs (E_1) is restricted to the same length of time as speech time (S) and the time of the relevant part of the infinitival situation (E_2) — at which the temporal focus (TF) is directed — is restricted to a certain time span included in the present time-area. Since the relevant situation is stative, E_2 can be simultaneous with E_1 and hence S (recall the discussion with respect to the temporal relationship between the event time

---

[46] *Will* in its predictive-present use can basically be paraphrased into epistemic *must* (Leech (2004: 86)). However, they do not have exactly the same meaning. Palmer (1990: 57–58) states that *will* is used for "what is a reasonable conclusion" while *must* is used for "the only possible conclusion on the basis of the evidence available" (cf. Palmer (2001: 28)). This statement is illustrated by the following example:

   (i)   John will be in his office now. Yes, the lights are on, so he must be there.
                                                              (Palmer (1990: 58))
Coates (1983: 177) makes a similar statement, saying that a sentence with epistemic *must* refers to a situation "based on a process of logical inference", whereas epistemic *will* refers to a situation "based on common sense, or on repeated experience".

Chapter 5   *Will*   157

of stative situations and the time of orientation in Section 2.4.3.3).

5.4.5. The Characteristic-Behavior Use

Now, we will consider the characteristic-behavior use of *will*-sentences. A characteristic behavior is a superordinate situation consisting of non-specific sub-situations of the same sort, which obtains for a certain time span and characterizes a tendency or the nature of an animate or inanimate entity. This use is similar to the predictive-present use in that they both require (part of) the infinitival situation to obtain at speech time in the present time-area. In fact, Leech (1987, 2004) integrates them into one use. However, while the predictive-present use refers to a single specific situation, the characteristic-behavior use refers to the repetition of non-specific sub-situations that stretches for a considerable period. As we saw with respect to the simple present form in Section 4.2.2, this difference is attributed to the difference between the temporal structures of the two uses under consideration. The characteristic-behavior use is therefore a different semantic use from the predictive-present use (as we will see in Section 5.5, this is also supported diachronically).

In Section 4.2.2, I distinguished the habitual-present use from the generic-present use of simple present sentences, because in comparison with the habitual-present use, the generic-present use was "super-temporal" or timeless, which was reflected in the differences between the temporal structures of the two uses. Along these lines, I divide the characteristic-behavior use of *will*-sentences into two subtypes: one subcategory of the characteristic-behavior use is referred to as the "W-habitual" use and refers to a repetition of situations of the same type in the durative present; the other subcategory of the characteristic-behavior use is referred to as the "W-generic" use and describes general characteristics of a species or group continuing as long as that species or group continues. As far as I know, no previous studies have made this distinction explicitly in terms of the temporal structures.

Next, let us consider what type of modality is operative in these two subcategories. Leech (2004: 86) states that they both express "predictability", i.e. an objectified type of prediction. Within my framework, this modality is classified into an objective use belonging to the P-domain because it is attributed to the private self of general people, which is not identified with the current speaker as public self. This is convincing in terms of "habitat isolation". Compare the *will*-sentence (22a) with the simple present sentence (22b):

(22) a. Oil will float on water. (=(1e))
      b. Oil floats on water.   (Leech (2004: 87))

Although these two sentences depict similar generic situations (Leech (2004: 87)), they are different in terms of whether predictability is relevant or not. (22a) would express a predictability about the superordinate situation consisting of the repetition of oil's floating on water, which obtains in the everlasting present (including speech time), although the predictability is an element of the P-domain and thus assertive modality, i.e. the unmarked speaker's S-attitude, comes into operation. (22b), by contrast, would simply express the speaker's assertion about the nature of oil, a fact gained by the repetition of experiments and/or observations. However, the difference in meaning between the two sentences is subtle,[47, 48] and they virtually describe almost the same situation. Because *will*-sentences in their W-habitual and W-generic uses involve predictability, i.e. a type of prediction, they are compatible with the notion of high probability.[49]

In the W-habitual and W-generic uses, the temporal focus (TF) is not operative in their temporal structures for the same reasons that we saw with respect to the present-habitual and present-generic uses in Chapter 4: since the superordinate situation consists of the repetition of non-specific sub-situations of the same type, its event time is not linked to the notion of "specificity" or "relatedness to the time line".[50] With these in mind, let us first consider the temporal structure of the W-habitual use, schematized in Figure 8:

---

[47] In this connection, Boyd and Thorne (1969: 64) have given a similar explanation. They state that habitual *will*-sentences convey an illocutionary potential named *prediction* (corresponding to predictability in my terminology) and habitual simple-present sentences convey an illocutionary potential named *statement* (corresponding to assertive modality in my terminology), but they are more or less the same in terms of illocutionary force.

[48] Palmer (1987: 136) claims that what he calls habitual/characteristic *will* — corresponding to the characteristic-behavior *will* in this study — is a type of dynamic modality. However, in my opinion, habitual/characteristic overtones are not attributed to *will* itself but derived from the infinitival situation consisting of sub-situations of the same type. This claim is supported by the fact that sentences without *will* can also receive habitual/characteristic overtones when the repeated occurrence of the same type of situation constitutes a superordinate situation characterizing the grammatical subject, as in (22b) in the main text.

[49] This does not necessarily mean that the characteristic-behavior use guarantees the actualization of the infinitival situation. Leech (2004: 87) states that *will*-sentences indicating the notion of prediction or predictability allow a possibility of the non-actualization of the infinitival situation.

[50] Besides, it is unlikely that the state of something general being predictable is focused on.

Chapter 5 *Will* 159

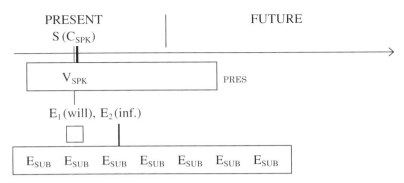

Figure 8: Temporal Structure of the W-Habitual Use of *Will*-Sentences

The square below E_1 represents predictability and the event time of *will* (E_1) is located at the same time as speech time (S). The rectangle containing E_{SUB}'s stands for the superordinate situation consisting of non-specific sub-situations of the same sort (symbolized by E_{SUB}) which characterizes an entity in the sentence involved, especially the grammatical subject.

For a better understanding of this use, observe the following examples:

(23) a. She'll go all day without eating. (Leech (2004: 86))
   b. At weekends, he'll be in the club by 7 o'clock, and there he'll stay till they close. (Leech (2004: 86))
   c. That parrot will chatter away for hours if you give him a chance. (Leech (2004: 86))

In (23a), for example, it is predictable that the superordinate situation consisting of the repetition of a woman's going all day without eating obtains in the durative present, i.e. a certain length of time including speech time. (23a) does not refer to any single sub-situation at a specific time; it indicates that a set of sub-situations of the same type constitutes a habit. This example thus exemplifies the temporal structure of the W-habitual use.

Let us next consider the temporal structure of the W-generic use, which is schematically represented in Figure 9:

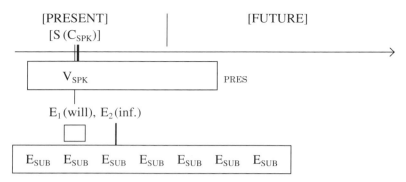

Figure 9: Temporal Structure of the W-Generic Use of *Will*-Sentences

The only difference in temporal structure between this use and the W-habitual use is that in this use the superordinate situation is "super-temporal" or timeless; the notions related to the time line, i.e. the present time-area (PRESENT), the future time-area (FUTURE), and speech time (S), are all enclosed by brackets.

The W-generic use of *will*-sentences is illustrated by the following examples:

(24) a. Oil will float on water. (=(1e))
  b. Boys will be boys. (R. Lakoff (1970: 848))
  c. A lion will attack a human being only when hungry.
  (Leech (2004: 86))

As we have seen, (24a) expresses a predictability about the superordinate situation consisting of the repetition of oil's floating on water in the everlasting present. In this connection, Leech (2004: 86) states that the W-generic use can be paraphrased by the following formula: whenever x happens, it is predictable that y happens. This paraphrasability implies that it is the case for people in general that if we try the same type of event (e.g. an experiment on oil) repeatedly, we will see the same result repeatedly. A similar observation applies to (24b, c). The examples in (24) thus illustrate the temporal structure of the W-generic use.

5.4.6. Speech Act Uses

Next, I will deal with how speech act uses are obtained within the framework we have advanced in Chapter 3. Within this framework, speech act uses are pragmatic variants of certain semantic uses of *will*-sentences. Several types of speech acts are to be considered.

Chapter 5   *Will*   161

First, Leech (2004: 87) points out that especially in the case of first-person subjects, *will*-sentences can be interpreted as conveying speech act meanings such as a promise, a threat, an offer, or a shared decision. As a sample case, let us consider the interpretation mechanism of *will*-sentences conveying promises. Observe (25):

(25) a.   Trust me. I will be back in less than ten.
(A. Gilyard, *Bartholomew Nelson and the World of Zathya*, Ch. 3)

   b.   "There will be a consumer watchdog to deal with the whole range of consumer rights and needs," he promised.   (BNC A88)

In (25a), the *will*-sentence is interpreted as conveying the sense of 'promise' because of the presence of the sentence *Trust me* before it. Within my framework, in the situation construal tier the current speaker (as private self) construes and describes, with assertive modality as a speaker's S-attitude, the situation in which he/she (as the private self of the grammatical subject) has the volition to come back soon. In the situation report tier, when the construed/described situation is conveyed to the addressee, the private self of the current speaker and his/her assertive modality become backgrounded because the current speaker and the grammatical subject share the same identity and therefore the volition in question is now seen as the current speaker's S-attitude, which doubles as his/her A-attitude (cf. Section 5.4.1). In the process of communication (i.e. situation report), given an appropriate context the speaker's having the volition to do something (i.e. the construed situation with the speaker's A-attitude) can metonymically imply that he/she will surely realize it, which may lead to a promise (cf. the discussion in Section 3.6).[51] The meaning of promise is therefore added as a speech act depending on context. In this case, the presence of the preceding sentence *Trust me* promotes such a speech act interpretation. Note that when a certain speech act is added, not only the speaker but also the addressee utilizes information from the interpersonal relationship tier. This use, called the *promise* use, shares the same temporal structure (i.e. the one in Figure 4 above) with the volitional use, as we can infer from the interpretation process observed above. The use of promise is thus a pragmatic variant of the volitional use.

The speech act of promise can also be derived from *will*-sentences with predictive modality, as shown in (25b). The *will*-sentence in (25b) can be inter-

---

[51] Leech (2014: 185) states that the speech act of promise (or 'undertaking') arises when the situation involved implies cost to the speaker but benefit to the hearer and there is no optionality on the part of the hearer.

preted as an instance of the predictive-future use, for the presence of the expletive subject *there* excludes the possibility of the volitional use. In the situation construal tier, the current speaker as private self observes the situation in question with predictive modality as speaker's S-attitude, which doubles as his/her A-attitude in situation report. The fact that the speaker's prediction about a future situation is addressed to the hearer can imply that he/she strongly hopes that the situation will be realized, which may also lead to a promise in an appropriate context. In this case, the reporting clause *he promised* fixes the speech act value. In this way, the meaning of promise can be superimposed onto the construed situation with predictive modality. Note that this type of *promise* use shares the same temporal structure (i.e. the one in Figure 5 above) with the predictive-future use and is therefore a pragmatic variant of the latter.

The observation that the speech act of promise can be derived from both the volitional use and the predictive-future use suggests that the use of promise is different from both the volitional and predictive-future uses. However, they do not constitute uses or functions at the same level: the volitional and predictive-future uses are semantic and their differences are reflected in their temporal structures, whereas the use of promise is pragmatic, not affecting the temporal structures of the *will*-sentences with future time reference.

Let us next consider cases of other speech act meanings, such as an order, an instruction, or a commission. Due to the nature of these speech act meanings, the *will*-sentence involved tends to have a second-person subject, as in (26), but a third-person subject is also possible depending on context, as in (27).

(26) a. You will report back for duty on Friday morning.

(Huddelston and Pullum (2002: 194))

b. You will do as I will tell you. (Klinge (2005: 174))

c. "Welton can forgive, Mr. Dalton, provided you have the courage to admit your mistakes. You will make your apology to the entire school." (N. H. Kleinbaum, *Dead Poets Society*, p. 107)

(27) a. Private Jones will report at 08:00 hrs. (=(1f))

b. "These meetings will be conducted by me and by the rest of the new initiates now present. Todd Anderson, because he prefers not to read, will keep minutes of the meetings."

(N. H. Kleinbaum, *Dead Poets Society*, p. 53)

Take (26a) for example. The speech act of this sentence is an order. In the situation construal tier, the speaker makes a prediction about the situation of

Chapter 5   *Will*   163

the addressee's reporting back for duty at a future time. This sentence is typically uttered in a military context and the speaker is a military superior, e.g. a commander. From this, we can say that the speech act of order as a speaker's A-attitude is added when the predicted situation is communicated to the addressee (i.e. in the situation report tier), depending on this context as well as information from the interpersonal relationship tier. Similarly, (27a), for example, can be interpreted as conveying the speech act of indirect order or instruction because the person to whom the order (instruction) is directed is a third person, not the addressee. These uses share the same temporal structure (i.e. the one in Figure 5 above) as the predictive-future use in the situation construal tier. They are thus pragmatic variants stemming from the temporal structure of the predictive-future use.

As far as I know, few previous studies have considered speech act phenomena of *will*-sentences systematically from both the points of view of tense interpretation and modality/mental attitudes. This is an advantage of the present framework.

5.4.7. Conditional Clauses

Before closing this section, let us show how my analysis explains the fact that the so-called future *will* cannot occur in some *if*-clauses, but can appear in others.[52] I argue that *if*-clauses in which future *will* can occur differ in

---

[52] It is generally said that *will* cannot occur in conditional clauses. However, it is only true of predictive or future *will* (i.e. a use generally referred to as "pure future" or "simple future"); conditional clauses containing *will* allow volitional readings (cf. Dowty (1977: 70; fn.11)), whether they precede the main clause, as in (30) in the main text, or follow the main clause, as in (i):

    (i)   I intend to leave next month, if my father will let me.   (Close (1977: 142))

With respect to (i), Close (1977: 142) states that the sequence *my father will* is paraphrased into *my father is willing*. As we have already stated, the volitional reading of *will*-sentences is available typically when the subject is a human being and the predicate is a controllable type (and *will*-sentences represent the (truly) volitional use in main or independent clauses only when the current speaker and grammatical subject share the same identity), but the decisive factor is contextual. For example, Close (1977: 143) states that *will* in the conditional clause of (ii) can also receive a volitional reading; the context tells us that the delivery of the car requires a deliverer.

    (ii)   If the car will be delivered tomorrow, I'll stay an extra day.   (Close (1977: 143))

The following examples, all cited from Haegeman (1983: 87), are unacceptable, because it is usually difficult, or perhaps impossible, to assume a volitional reading when the situation described by the predicate involved is not regarded as controllable:

    (iii) a. *If John will resemble his father ...

         b. *If John will faint ...

         c. *If the storm will destroy the building ...

164   *The Grammar of Future Expressions in English*

terms of linguistic environments from those in which future *will* cannot occur. More specifically, the two linguistic environments relevant here stem from the different combination patterns of the three domains of the semantic (de)composition of sentential utterances in (4) observed in Section 3.4.

If-clauses in which future *will* cannot occur are conditional clauses of the direct cause-effect type (henceforth, type A conditional clauses); they were discussed briefly in Section 3.8, and correspond to Haegeman's (1983) "standard type conditionals", Haegeman and Wekker's (1984) "central *if*-clauses", and Dancygier's (1998) "predictive conditional clauses".[53] On the other hand, *if*-clauses in which future *will* can occur are often called closed conditionals (henceforth, type B conditional clauses), corresponding to Haegeman's (1983) "conclusion type conditionals", Haegeman and Wekker's (1984) "peripheral *if*-clauses", and Dancygier's (1998) "non-predictive conditional clauses".[54, 55, 56] Note that in this study conditional sentences consisting of type A conditional clauses and main clauses are referred to as type A conditional sentences, and conditional sentences consisting of type B conditional clauses and main clauses are called type B conditional sentences.

As we saw in Section 3.8, type A conditional clauses consist only of the

---

    d. *If John will break the bottle by accident ...

[53] Palmer (1987: 150) names this type of *if*-clause the *predictive* or *causal* type, allowing the following three types—cited from Palmer (1987: 151)—to be subsumed under this name.

    (i) a. If it rains, the match will be cancelled. (real)
        b. If it rained, the match would be cancelled. (unreal)
        c. If it had rained, the match would have been cancelled. (unreal)

[54] Type B conditional clauses, i.e. *if*-clauses with future *will*, sometimes require another conditional clause—which is usually unspecified. Declerck and Reed (2001: 82) divide this case into two subtypes: a case where the interpretation of the conditional clause is complemented by a clause like *as I believe* in the front position of that clause, as in (i); and one where the interpretation of the conditional clause is complemented by a clause like *as you say* in the front position, as in (ii):

    (i) If (as I believe) there will be trouble <if we go to the pub>, then we'd better not
        go to the pub.   (Declerck and Reed (2001: 82))
    (ii) If (as you say) it will help you <if I lend you ten pounds>, I am willing to lend
        you £10.   (Declerck and Reed (2001: 82))

[55] I am not arguing that there are only two types of conditional clauses in English. For example, we have Sweetser's (1990) "speech act" types or Copley's (2009) "relevance conditionals". A major characteristic of this third type of conditional sentence is that it does not allow the conditional clause, or protasis, to be put in front of the main clause, i.e. apodosis (Iatridou (1994), Copley (2009)).

[56] Some studies on the compatibility of future *will* with conditional sentences (e.g. Jacobsson (1984)) consider the past form (i.e. *would*) as well, offering a more comprehensive analysis.

Chapter 5 *Will*

proposition (P) domain and exclude both situation-oriented and addressee-oriented mental attitudes of the speaker (belonging, respectively, to the SSA and ASA domains).[57] On the other hand, type B conditional clauses consist of the P domain and a speaker's attitude (SA) domain (we will see later whether this SA domain is the addressee-oriented or situation-oriented type). A decisive piece of evidence for this constitutional pattern of type B conditional clauses is their co-occurrence with epistemic modals including future *will*.[58] Within the framework developed in this study, (subjective) epistemic modals express speaker's S-attitudes (i.e. elements belonging to the SA domain) in the situation construal tier. It is thus predictable that future *will* as epistemic modal can occur in type B conditional clauses, but not in type A conditional clauses.[59] This prediction is borne out by the following examples:

---

[57] My tripartite distinction of semantic (de)composition of sentential utterances presented in Section 3.4 is different from Hare's (1970) and Lyons's (1970). For example, type A conditional clauses have a sign of indicative mood (i.e. tropic) as well as the propositional content (i.e. phrastic) in their distinction, while they consist only of the proposition domain in my distinction. It seems that their distinction as it stands cannot distinguish type B from type A conditional clauses, because the neustic "is not applicable to the component simple proposition [*if*-clauses in this case], but only to the complex proposition taken as a whole [i.e. the whole of conditional sentences in this case]" (Lyons (1977: 750)) and therefore both types of conditional clauses should include the tropic and phrastic components, but not the neustic component. In my distinction, type B conditional clauses consist of the situation-oriented speaker's attitude domain and the proposition domain, whereas type A conditional clauses consist only of the proposition domain.

[58] Studies such as Gotti (2003) cannot straightforwardly explain this fact. Because they consider future *will* to be a dynamic or root modal, they cannot account for why both type A and type B conditional clauses allow a volitional reading of *will*, but only type B conditional clauses allow future *will* (i.e. the predictive use) to occur in them.

[59] As shown in note 37 of this chapter, this difference supports my temporal structure analysis, in which semantic uses or functions are associated with their respective temporal structures. If *will*-sentences had only one abstract meaning common to all interpretations, as the monosemous approach puts it, we would not be able to explain why only volitional *will* can occur in type A conditional clauses. My analysis, by contrast, explains it straightforwardly. As we will soon see in the main text, *will*-sentences have retained a temporal structure like the one for the volitional use in Figure 4—as shown in Figure 10—as an independent semantic use in the history of the English language; the use in question can occur in type A conditional clauses because they constitute a linguistic environment where reference to SA-domain elements is irrelevant and its evolution to subjective meanings (e.g. predictive uses) has not happened (see section 5.5). This conclusion is also justified by Ziegeler's (1996: 434) observation that "older, volitional senses still constrain its [=*will*'s] use as a future auxiliary in certain grammatical environments" such as the complement clause of the hypothetical predicate, as shown in *I wish there would be no fighting at the party* (Ziegeler (1996: 442)). Although sentences like this are rejected by many of her informants, they are accepted by many as well, which she claims may be a reflection of the

(28) a. *John will do it if he will have time.   (Declerck and Reed (2001:132))

b. *If she will ask me for an explanation, I will tell her everything.

(Declerck (1991a: 428))

c. *If it won't rain tomorrow, we will have a picnic.

(Declerck and Reed (2001: 137))

d. *If John will come, Mary will leave.   (Palmer (1987: 151))

(29) a.   If the film will amuse them, I'll buy some tickets.   (=(1h))

b.   If the lava will come down as far as this, all these houses will have to be evacuated.   (Close (1977: 144))

c.   If Claude will be here tomorrow, there's no need to call him now.

(Close (1977: 145))

d.   If he'll be left destitute, I'll change my will.   (Palmer (1987: 157))

The conditional clauses in (28) are type A conditional clauses and those in (29) are type B conditional clauses.

We can now argue that the volitional reading of *will*-sentences is possible with type A conditional clauses because volitional *will* exclusively expresses a modality belonging to the P domain in a linguistic environment without the SA domains, one consisting only of the P domain.[60, 61] This is illustrated by the acceptability of (30):

---

volitional meaning of the past form of *will*.

[60] In addition to the case of the volitional reading, *will* can occur in *if*-clauses when they express atemporal situations or prediction about habits, as in (i), or predictability at speech time about the occurrence or non-occurrence of future situations, as in (ii):

(i)   If drugs will cure him, this drug should do the job.   (Quirk et al. (1985: 1009))

(ii) a.   If you won't arrive before six, I can't meet you.   (Quirk et al. (1985: 1009))

b.   If the water will rise above this level, then we must warn everybody in the neighbourhood.   (Quirk et al. (1985: 1009))

These *if*-clauses are classified into either type A or type B conditional clauses depending on whether the modality expressed by *will* belongs to the P domain or the SSA domain.

[61] As a traditional test to distinguish volitional *will* from pure/simple-future *will*, passivization has often been presented. Observe (i):

(i) a.   John won't meet Mary.   (Haegeman (1983: 140))

b.   Mary won't be met by John.   (Haegeman (1983: 140))

According to the test, if the *will* is interpreted as expressing pure/simple future, the (cognitive) meanings of the two sentences are the same; if the *will* is interpreted as expressing volition, it is John's will that is relevant in (ia), but Mary's in (ib), and the two sentences have different meanings. However, this test is not actually a test for the distinction between the two uses in question. For example, the active-voice version of the W-generic use of *will*-sentences is different from its passive-voice counterpart with respect to genericity, as shown in (ii).

(ii)   A beaver will build dams. ≠ Dams will be built by a beaver. (Haegeman (1983: 141))

In order for the test in question to be more reliable, it must also deal with this type of use.

Chapter 5   *Will*   167

(30) a. If you'll wait here for a second, the doctor will see you immediately.
    (Haegeman (1983: 22))
   b. If you'll excuse me now, I must go.   (Haegeman (1983: 22))
   c. If he'll pay, I'll go with him.   (Quirk et al. (1985: 1009))
   d. If John'll come, Mary will leave. [= If John is willing to come, ...]
    (Palmer (1987: 157))
   e. If you will get her to ask one question about the new winter styles in
       cloak sleeves I will promise you a one-in-five chance for her, instead
       of one in ten."   (O. Henry, *The Last Leaf*, p. 309)

It must be stressed here that type A conditional clauses do not convey any type of speaker's S-attitude. In Section 5.4.1, we observed that assertive modality is inserted when *will* represents the volitional use or predictive modality is identified when the *will*-sentence illustrates the predictive-future use with volitional overtones. However, it is only in linguistic environments reflecting speaker's mental attitudes (e.g. main or independent clauses) that such an operation occurs. Since type A conditional clauses do not reflect any speaker's mental attitude, they do not convey assertive modality or predictive modality.

This suggests that the volitional reading of *will* in type A conditional clauses is different from that of *will* in independent or main clauses, as mentioned beforehand in Section 5.4.1. I argued there that only when the current speaker and the grammatical subject share the same identity and the predicate is a controllable type can *will*-sentences in independent or main clauses receive a truly volitional reading (i.e. the volitional use). The reason for this argument is attributed to the linguistic-environmental characteristics of independent or main clauses, namely that these clauses involve both the speaker's attitude (SA) and proposition (P) domains. With respect to type A conditional clauses, the subjective aspect of the speaker (e.g. speaker's mental attitudes) cannot be involved in them because they semantically consist only of the P-domain. Hence neither the backgrounding of the speaker as private self nor the foregrounding of the grammatical subject as private self is in action and thus the volition involved is not re-interpreted as a speaker's S-attitude in the interpretation process of type A conditional clauses. In what follows, to avoid possible confusion between the volitional use (used in main or independent clauses) and the volitional reading of *will* in type A conditional clauses, I refer to the latter as "P(roposition domain)-volitional use". This use is named after their linguistic-environmental characteristics and so can cover all volitional readings of *will* in linguistic environments consisting only of the proposition (P) domain, including type A conditional clauses and temporal clauses.

How, then, can we treat this type of volitional *will* (i.e. the P-volitional use) in type A conditional clauses? As anticipated in Section 2.5, the P-volitional use of *will* is a remnant of the former meaning of *will*, namely that the P-volitional use is an older meaning of *will* and has not yet been encroached by a newer meaning, i.e. prediction (for more on this, see the discussion in the next section).[62] This semantic retention is convincing, because grammaticalization often goes hand in hand with subjectification and type A conditional clauses—consisting only of the P domain—do not involve the speaker's attitude domain, a domain reflecting the speaker's point of view, whereas main or independent clauses—in which *will*-sentences can represent the volitional use and the predictive-future use with volitional overtones—reflect the speaker's point of view.

The temporal structure of the P-volitional use is schematized in Figure 10:

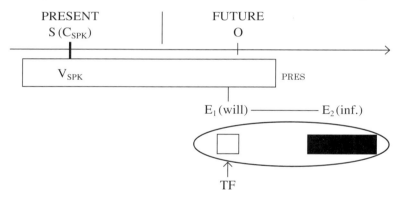

Figure 10: Temporal Structure of the P-Volitional Use of *Will*-Sentences in Type A Conditional Clauses

The temporal structure in Figure 10 is different from that in Figure 4 in that in the P-volitional use (i.e. the volitional reading of *will*-sentences in type A conditional clauses) the position of the event time of *will* (E_1) is determined with respect to the event time of the main clause (lexical) verb as the time of

---

[62] Dancygier and Sweetser (2005: §4.3) stress that volitional *will* and "positive-interest" *will* (representing willingness and desire) should be distinguished from predictive *will* because only the former can occur in type A conditional clauses (i.e. their "predictive" conditional clauses). This suggests, within my framework, that the former two meanings of *will* belonging to the P domain survive in this linguistic environment, which is a different linguistic environment from main or independent clauses, and an appropriate temporal structure must therefore be given to sentences containing volitional *will* (and positive-interest *will*) in type A conditional clauses.

Chapter 5 *Will* 169

orientation (O), which is certainly located in the future relative to speech time (S). (It is possible that E_1 and O are located at a time later than S in the present time-area, but for simplicity's sake we do not consider such a possibility here.) The oval including the white square and the black rectangle is also a mental world attributed to the grammatical subject of the *if*-clause, a linguistic element belonging to the P domain. When the *will* in the *if*-clause refers to a specific volition, as in (30) above, the temporal focus (TF) is directed at its event time. Take, for example, (30c), i.e. *If he'll pay, I'll go with him.* In this case, the context tells us the position of the event time of *will* in the *if*-clause with respect to the event time of the lexical verb *go* in the main clause, which is located in the future relative to speech time (note, in passing, that the *will* in the main clause is an instance of the volitional use). In this way, the P-volitional use has its own temporal structure and is an independent semantic use within my framework.

Now, let us consider in more detail the semantic (de)composition of type B conditional clauses (e.g. (29)). In the beginning of this sub-section, I simply stated that they consist of both the P and SA domains. However, I must here state that the SA domain of type B conditional clauses only contains the situation-oriented speaker's attitude domain (SSA domain) and lacks the addressee-oriented speaker's attitude domain (ASA domain). That is, type B conditional clauses consist of the SSA domain and the P domain. This is because we assume, following Dancygier (1998: 18–19), that *if* is a non-assertion marker, namely that *if* requires the non-assertion of the assumption referred to by the *if*-clause.[63] Note that the term *assert(ion)* used there refers to a speech act in the sense of Searle (Searle (1969, 1975, 1979)); this notion of assertion requires "that the speaker have evidence to support her belief and actually believe the assumption to be true, and that the hearer not be known to share the same belief (needs to be told or reminded about it)" (Dancygier (1998: 18)). Type B conditional clauses thus lack the ASA domain because they lack assertion as an addressee-oriented speaker's mental attitude (speaker's A-attitude).[64]

---

[63] Declerck and Reed (2001: 67) reject the view that *if* is a non-assertion marker, because this view is not applicable to the case of what they call "factual P-conditionals", a type of *if*-clause whose situation "is represented and interpreted as factual, i.e. as forming part of the actual world" (Declerck and Reed (2001: 67)). However, as they also admit, this type of *if*-clause is exceptional and the way of assumption adopted in this conditional is very special. Besides, I am not considering factual P-conditionals in this book. For these reasons, I assume that *if* is a non-assertion marker, at least as far as the two types of conditional clauses considered in this book are concerned.

[64] Another possible piece of evidence for my claim here is that type B conditional clauses

170   *The Grammar of Future Expressions in English*

On the other hand, the fact that epistemic modals, including predictive *will*, appear in type B conditional clauses indicates that this linguistic environment involves an SSA-domain element, i.e. situation-oriented speaker's mental attitude (speaker's S-attitude). Hence it is the SSA domain, but not the ASA domain, that is contained in the semantic (de)composition of type B conditional clauses.

Many, if not most, of type B conditional clauses, at least what Declerck and Reed (2001) call "closed P-conditionals"—i.e. conditional clauses in which the supposition is given in the context and the speaker takes it as true—are echoic. When the content of a conditional clause is echoic, it does not "have to be echoes of actual utterances", but can "be echoes of an internal or mental proposition (thought) such as the interpretation of an experience, perception, etc." (Declerck and Reed (2001: 83); cf. Verstraete (2001: 1519)). In our model, type B conditional clauses consist of the SSA and P domains and therefore refer to private expression. However, the private expression in this echoic type of conditional clause is attributed to the speaker of the preceding utterance (i.e. the present hearer) or the potential speaker (i.e. the assumed thinker) who is the (cognitive) subject of an internal or mental proposition; the current speaker "reduces" the two types of speakers to the private self as the subject of construing the conditional clause situation. The current speaker as public self quotes as the supposition the conditional clause situation, i.e. the private expression of the present hearer or the potential speaker, and regards it as a condition for his/her own assertion (as a speech act); when he/she regards the supposition or assumption as correct, the current speaker can assert the content of the main clause in the situation report tier, i.e. when communicating it to the addressee/hearer.[65] This way of reasoning is in keeping with

---

cannot go without their main clause counterpart. This may suggest that this type of conditional clause alone does not have a communicative function and thus lacks an ASA-domain element.

[65] In this connection, let us consider another type of example of type B conditional sentences:

    (i)   If you will be alone on Christmas Day, get in touch with us now. (Close (1977: 144)) According to Close, (i) is displayed outside a social institution and the only paraphrase of it is: "[i]f, at the present time, you have no plans for spending Christmas in company with other people, get in touch with us now" (Close (1977: 144)). In my analysis, the person to see this notice is regarded as a potential speaker or thinker of the internal or mental proposition described by the *if*-clause, and the current speaker or writer of this notice assumes that the person referred to by *you* when seeing it thinks that he/she will be alone on Christmas Day. The internal or mental proposition in question is a private expression of the person under consideration as private self. The speaker (or writer) of (i), regarded as the public self because he/she is reporting the whole sentence to the assumed addressee, is assumed to

Haegeman's (1983: 148) statement that type B conditional clauses (her "conclusion type") are paraphrased into 'If (I assume A) then (I conclude B)', which suggests that the quoted conditional-clause situation (i.e. the A part in the paraphrase) is the target of the current speaker's assumption.

For a better understanding of this point, consider, for example, (29a), i.e. *If the film will amuse them, I'll buy some tickets*. This sentence can be interpreted in such a way that the prediction about the situation of the film's amusing them is ascribed to the private self of the original speaker of the preceding sentence, i.e. the present hearer. This interpretation is justified because (29a) can be paraphrased by (31):

(31) If you think the film will amuse them, I'll buy some tickets so that they can see it.   (Close (1977: 143–144))

In the Three-Tier Model (which motivates our unified model of tense and modality/mental attitudes), a private expression is a thought or mental representation of a (potential) speaker and can occupy the position of verbs of thinking. Thus in (31), the complement clause of the verb of thinking (i.e. *think*) is the predicted situation as the private expression attributed to the present hearer. In the situation report tier, when communicating with the addressee (hearer), the current speaker of (31) as public self echoes it and assumes that the private expression in question is a condition for the assertion of the main clause situation as a speaker's A-attitude.

From these observations, it should be clear now that an approach within the framework developed in this study can systematically explain temporal and modal phenomena concerning *will* in conditional clauses. This would enhance the validity of the present framework and hence the temporal structure analysis of *will*-sentences proposed in this chapter.

5.5. The Relationship among the Temporal Structures Associated with the Semantic Uses of *Will*-Sentences

Having presented the temporal structures associated with a number of semantic uses (functions) of *will*-sentences in the previous section, this section

---

be a member of the social institution; he/she judges that the private expression in question may possibly bring about the situation in which the person in question wishes to get in touch with him/her. Because the main clause is in the imperative form, its semantic content, by definition, constitutes public expression and the semantic content of the whole sentence is definitely interpreted as a situation report conveying the speech act of invitation.

172   *The Grammar of Future Expressions in English*

briefly considers their relationship in terms of grammaticalization.[66] As is well known, the origin of *will* was a lexical (main) verb expressing desire, which has changed into an auxiliary expressing futurity by way of grammaticalization (e.g. Aijmer (1985), Bybee and Pagliuca (1987), Bybee, Perkins and Pagliuca (1994)). Bybee, Perkins and Pagliuca (1994: 256) observe that a grammaticalization pathway to futurity beginning with the notion of desire is like the one in (32a):

(32) a.   DESIRE → WILLINGNESS → INTENTION → PREDICTION
      b.   VOLITION → PROCLIVITY → PROBABILITY → PREDICTION

However, Ziegeler (2006: 110), adducing ample data of *will*-sentences, revises the pathway, as in (32b), where the VOLITION stage subsumes the stages of DESIRE, WILLINGNESS and INTENTION and the stages of PROCLIVITY and PROBABILITY—including *will*-sentences having generic/habitual (characteristic-behavior) meanings, i.e. examples of what Ziegeler (2006) calls omnitemporal *will*—are added between the VOLITION and PREDICTION stages (cf. Hilpert (2008: 86)). She offers a K(nowlege)-operator-based analysis of modals and justifies her pathway in terms of the parallelism between the transition from deontic meanings to epistemic meanings with respect to modals such as *may* and *must*, on one hand, and that from omnitemporal (i.e. characteristic-behavior) meanings to epistemic meanings with respect to the modal *will*, on the other, by claiming that both the deontic and characteristic-behavior uses are characterized in such a way that the speaker knows that the proposition involved is not realized at the reference time (Ziegeler (2006: 85, 90)). Her point is that it was the characteristic-behavior uses of *will* that triggered the rise of the future reference use of *will* in the process of grammaticalization; she denies the general view that the characteristic-behavior uses of *will* have been derived from the future reference uses.

   Given this revision, it follows that the temporal structure of the "volitional" uses belonging to the stages of DESIRE, WILLINGNESS and INTENTION (cf. Figure 4) was first established, followed by the temporal structures of the characteristic-behavior uses including the W-habitual use (Figure 8) and the W-generic use (Figure 9), i.e. uses belonging to the stages of PROCLIVITY and PROBABILITY, and finally the temporal structures of the future reference uses including the predictive-future use (Figure 5) and the simple-future use

---

[66] Nesselhauf (2010) offers a corpus-based analysis of the development of the future expressions *will*, *shall*, *'ll*, *be going to*, the present progressive with future time reference, and *be to* in late modern English.

(Figure 6), i.e. uses belonging to the stage of PREDICTION, were established. Note that in the present model, the volitional readings at the VOLITION stage in the grammaticalization pathway are assumed to cover all uses of *will* indicating volitions with or without assertive modality, including the P-volitional use (Figure 10).

It is also assumed that the inferential use with non-future time reference (i.e. the predictive-present use) has been derived from the pure-future/simple-future use in the sense used generally. The PREDICTION stage is therefore divided into at least two sub-stages: one is associated with future reference uses and has been established before the other sub-stage, a stage associated with non-future reference uses. Included in the former sub-stage are the predictive-future use (Figure 5) and the simple-future use (Figure 6); included in the latter sub-stage is the predictive-present use (Figure 7).

These semantic shifts are motivated and newer meanings (uses) are established by way of pragmatic strengthening. For example, it is highly possible that *will*-sentences describing a grammatical subject's desire or willingness to carry out a future situation can be extended to imply that such a situation is likely to occur at other times or happens to many other similar subjects,[67] and if such an implication occurs repeatedly, the situation involved finally comes to be interpreted as a superordinate situation consisting of sub-situations of the same type through pragmatic strengthening. In this way, characteristic-behavior uses may have been established as a new use of *will*-sentences. Similarly, as stated in Ziegeler (2006: 109) as well as above, since generic/habitual situations are based on the speaker's generalization about something that can potentially be pursued volitionally, they can easily induce us to predict the future actualization of a sub-situation (i.e. token) of the superordinate situation. The actualization of the situation may have been merely a pragmatic implicature of the *will*-sentence involved in older English, but the frequent repetition of such an actualization can have established a new use referring to the future.

The fact that both the P-volitional use (e.g. (30)) and the characteristic-behavior uses (e.g. (i) in note 60 of this chapter) of *will*-sentences can appear in type A conditional clauses lends indirect support to our position that they have come into existence at earlier stages than the PREDICTION stage in the revised (grammaticalization) pathway. In type A conditional clauses, i.e. a linguistic environment semantically consisting only of the P domain, *will*-sentences cannot develop uses belonging to the PREDICTION stage, which are accompanied by predictive modality, i.e. an SSA-domain element. As we saw

---

[67] Ziegeler (2006: §5) adduces diachronic data supporting this extension.

above, this is partly because grammaticalization is often accompanied by subjectification. Thus, since *will*-sentences cannot undergo subjectification in this environment, they remained at the stage of volitional readings and characteristic-behavior uses.

I have already argued elsewhere (Wada (2001a: Ch. 7)) that the operation of temporal focus shift is one factor triggering grammaticalization. The explanation was as follows. In the temporal structure of the volitional readings in older English, the temporal focus (TF) is directed at the event time of *will* (E_1) located at the same time as the time of orientation (O), especially speech time (S) in main or independent clauses. By shifting the TF to the event time of the infinitive (E_2) located in the future, the future part of the temporal structure is foregrounded and the present part—associated with the volition—is backgrounded, so that the future-orientation comes into play. As a result, the predictive-future use has emerged.

Now I consider how to treat the characteristic-behavior uses in terms of the temporal focus. As shown in Section 5.4.5, the temporal structures of these uses do not receive any temporal focus because of their non-specific nature: the uses under consideration refer to a superordinate situation consisting of sub-situations of the same type, not to a specific sub-situation. We can thus say that dropping the temporal focus from the temporal structure of the volitional readings facilitates non-specificity or generality of the situations described by *will*-sentences of this type. In this way, the "TF drop" triggers the advent of the stages of PROCLIVITY and PROBABILITY.

Next, I will state how the PREDICTION stage arises. There is always a possibility that the speaker can focus on a sub-situation of the superordinate situation described by *will*-sentences at the stages of PROCLIVITY and PROBABILITY. When he/she actually does, the event time involved can be interpreted as associated with that sub-situation and the temporal focus can thus be directed at such an event time. The repetition of this operation may have led to the advent of the PEDICTION stage. Note that in this grammaticalization process, another factor is crucially involved: the stativity of the relevant sentence. Since the superordinate situation is stative, it can extend into the future; as a result, some sub-situations can be located in the future and the temporal focus can thus be directed at the event time associated with a sub-situation in the future. I conclude that restoring the temporal focus into the temporal structure of the relevant uses, or "TF restoring", together with the nature of stativity, triggered the advent of the future reference uses.

Although whether the predictive-future use emerged before the simple-future

Chapter 5   *Will*   175

use or vice versa is pending in this book,[68] they are the same with respect to the position of the TF (in both cases the TF is directed at E_2); such a question does not matter as far as the temporal focus shift is concerned. The simple-future use is a special case of the predictive-future use in that the type of situation appropriate for the simple-future use is restricted (see Section 5.4.3). The TF's being directed at E_2 can cause the semantic content of *will* (associated with E_1) in the simple-future use to be bleached.

Let us next consider the extension from the future reference uses to the present reference uses. In this extension, too, the stativity of the relevant sentence plays a role. Given that the finite form (i.e. *will*) is present and the non-finite form (i.e. infinitive) describes a stative situation, we can carry out the following calculation in our mind: if stative situations obtain at a future time, it is highly possible that they have already obtained at speech time because of their homogeneous nature, or unboundedness. In fact, this correlation is implied in the temporal structure of the predictive-present use in Figure 7; the infinitival situation itself ranges from the present to the future time-area. If such correlation happened repeatedly, then it may have been the case that by way of pragmatic strengthening the predictive-present use came to be established as a new use. These observations enable us to conclude that the stative nature of the infinitival situation—which is a necessary condition—motivates such an extension of use; by shifting our attention to that part of the state encompassing speech time, we can restrict the event time (i.e. the time of the relevant part of the state) to the time span encompassing speech time in the present time-sphere.

As we have seen, my temporal structure approach assumes that more than one semantic use is associated with a tense form (i.e. the *will*-sentence) and is therefore compatible with an "overlap model" of grammaticalization, which states that a shift from an older meaning (use) to a newer one is a continuum and there is a stage at which more than one meaning (use) coexists (Heine (1993: 48–48); cf. Hopper and Traugott (1993: 35–36)); for example, when a present reference use (e.g. the predictive-present use) emerged from a future reference use (e.g. the predictive-future use), the newer use and the older use coexisted and still do. Our model predicts, along the lines of the "overlap model" of grammaticalization, that if an older use vanishes away in the future, the temporal structure associated with that use will vanish away, but the core meaning and other semantic uses are intact. The monosemous approach, es-

---

[68] I argued elsewhere (Wada (2001a: Ch. 7)) that the predictive-future use has derived from the simple-future use, but here I leave open which of the two uses has emerged earlier.

pecially relevance-theoretic analyses, may be weak in this respect. This type of approach would predict that once a new use is added to a given form, the core meaning of that form has changed to be common to all uses, including the newly added use, and so it might not explain how the older uses vanish away.

5.6. Comparisons between *Will* and the French Simple Future

Before concluding this chapter, let us confirm the validity of the comprehensive model developed in this book from a cross-linguistic point of view. To be specific, I will show that the model can straightforwardly explain the similarities and differences between *will*-sentences in English and their alleged counterparts in French, i.e. simple future sentences.

5.6.1. Similarities and Differences

The *will*-sentence in English is often considered to behave similarly to the simple future sentence in French, which leads some linguists to the conclusion that *will* is a future tense marker (e.g. Salkie (2010)).

(33) a. Anne Hathaway will play the role of Catwoman, ...
      (http://www.ibtimes.com/dark-knight-rises-viral-campaign-features-go-thams-hunt-batman-new-posters-hint-upcoming-film-photos)

   b. Emma Fesneau figurera Jeanne d'Arc durant les fêtes johanniques à Orléans du 29 avril au 8 mai 2016.
      'Emma Fesneau will represent Joan of Arc during the festival for Joan in Orléans from April 29th to May 8th, 2016.'
      (http://www.clodelle45autrement.fr/2016/01/emma-fesneau-figurera-jeanne-d-arc-durant-les-fetes-johanniques-a-orleans-du-29-avril-au-8-mai-2016.html)

In (33), for example, to describe the situation of someone playing the role of a character in the future, *will* is chosen in English and the simple future form in French. This might suggest that *will*-sentences are equivalent to simple future sentences in French in describing a future situation.

However, there are cases where *will*-sentences do not correspond to simple future sentences and vice versa, as illustrated below:

(34) a. When Jules returns, he will be rich.

   b. Quand Jules {reviendra / *revient}, il sera riche.   (Jones (1996: 171))
      'When Jules {will return / *returns}, he will be rich.'

Chapter 5 *Will*   177

(35) a. John will leave now.
     b. *Jean partira maintenant.   (Hornstein (1990: 19))
        'Jean will leave now.'
(36) a. That'll be the postman.
     b.(?)Ce sera le facteur.   (cf. Celle (2005: 192))
        'That will be the postman.'
(37) a. Yesterday he predicted that it'll be nice out tomorrow.
     b. ?Hier il a prévu qu'il fera beau demain.   (Fleischman (1982: 10))
        'Yesterday he predicted that it'll be nice out tomorrow.'
(38) a. Mary will say that she will be tired.   (Enç (1996: 350))
     b. Léon dira vendredi qu'il partira dans trois jours. (Smith (1997: 211))
        'Leon will say on Friday that he will leave in three days.'

Two remarks are in order here. It is rather obsolete in present-day standard
French to take example (36b) as illustrating an inferential use with present
time reference (cf. Celle (2005), Watanabe (2014: 142)), although it can be
used that way. As for (38), the English sentence indicates that the time of the
complement situation, i.e. the situation of Mary's being tired, is located at a
time later than the time of her utterance in the future, whereas the French sentence can suggest that the time of the complement situation, i.e. the situation
of Leon's leaving, is situated at a time later than speech time as well as the
time of his utterance in the future (Smith (1997: 211)).

In the present model, the (basic) temporal structures of *will*-sentences consist of the combination of the tense-structure information of the modal *will* as
finite form and that of the infinitive as non-finite form, whereas those of simple future sentences in French consist only of the tense-structure information
of the future-tense form as finite form. This implies that we can attribute the
different behaviors of the *will*-sentences and the simple future sentences observed in (34)-(38) to the different tense and temporal structures of the two
forms. In what follows, we will demonstrate it.

5.6.2. Tense Structure and Basic Temporal Structures of Simple Future Sentences in French

I will first present the tense structure and the basic temporal structures of
simple future sentences in French for the purpose of comparison with the
tense structure and the basic temporal structures of *will*-sentences. Let us
start with the tense structure. In (33b) above, *figurera* is the third-person singular future form of *figurer* 'represent'. In my system, a tense inflection such
as -*ra* is by definition an A(bsolute tense)-morpheme and represents the future

time-sphere (grammatical future) in constructing the tense structure of simple future sentences. Because the simple future form consists only of one (finite) verb, it has only one event time in its tense structure. The tense structure of simple future sentences in French is therefore such that the event time is located in the future time-sphere.

In the default case, the principle in (4) presented in Section 2.4.1 works and the speaker's t(emporal)-viewpoint thus fuses with the same speaker's consciousness at speech time, the future time-sphere corresponding to the present and future time-areas (cognitive time ranges). This predicts that when the time of orientation is identified as speech time (i.e. in the case of the deictic interpretation), the French simple future form can refer not only to future situations but also to present situations, and this is actually the case, though the reference to present situations is rather obsolete in present-day French, as we saw in the comments on (36b) above. Consequently, the French simple future form represents two basic temporal structures, i.e. those of the future-time-reference version and the present-time-reference version, as shown in Figures 11 and 12, respectively.

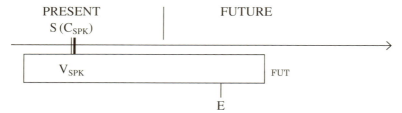

Figure 11: Basic Temporal Structure of Simple Future Sentences in French with Future time Reference (Default Case)

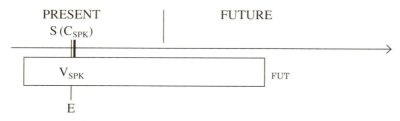

Figure 12: Basic Temporal Structure of Simple Future Sentences in French with Present Time Reference (Default Case)

To make the story simpler, we avoid representing the temporal focus (TF) in these schemata. The rectangle with subscript FUT represents a future time-

Chapter 5 *Will*   179

sphere, which covers both the future and present time-areas—as the present time-sphere in English does—but primarily refers to the future time-area (this is partly because this time-sphere is termed *future*). These schemata capture the intuition that we conceptually distinguish between the future and present time-spheres and explain why the French simple future form mostly does not refer to a present situation (for when and how this time reference is allowed, see Section 5.6.3.3). In fact, Celle (2005: 192; fn. 36) reports that she could not find any examples of the simple future form with present time reference in the data she had collected.

One possible argument for this claim is Copley's (2009: 141) observation that when simple future sentences in French are interpreted as conveying speech act meanings such as offers and promises, there is some time lag before such speech acts happen, which is not the case with *will*-sentences. Observe the following:

(39) a. Je t'attendrai (#dans cinq minutes).
         'I will wait for you (in five minutes).'   (Copley (2009: 140))
     b. I'll wait for you (in five minutes).   (Copley (2009: 141))

In (39a), if the adverbial *dans cinq minutes* 'in five minutes' (i.e. an adverbial referring to the immediate future) is added to the French simple future form, an expected reading would be that the offer is supposed to occur in five minutes.[69] However, such an addition makes the simple future sentence unacceptable or at least marginal. This suggests that the French simple future form does not tend to refer to the near future (even in the future time-area), let alone the present time-area. We can take this phenomenon as indicating that the future time-sphere in French primarily refers to the rather distant future (in the future time-area) in the default case (i.e. deictic interpretation) and does not refer to the present time-area unless certain conditions are met (Section 5.6.3.3).

Before going further, let us briefly consider the relationship between the simple future form and modality as speaker's S-attitude. As we saw above, in the default case, the future time-sphere of the French simple future form tends to refer to the future time-area, so that they are usually interpreted as accompanied by predictive modality in linguistic environments reflecting speaker's

---

[69] Copley (2009: 141) notes that the simple present version, as in (i), can be used for this purpose. In this case, the relevant speech act is a promise.

(i) Je t'attends (dans cinq minutes).   (Copley (2009: 140))
     '(Lit.) I wait for you (in five minutes)'

mental attitudes, e.g. independent or main clauses. The French simple future form as a modally unmarked form is not a marker of predictive modality and does not express it by themselves, but can be accompanied by it in the process of tense interpretation. This may provide another reason why although both the present and the future time-spheres can cover the present and the future time-areas in the default case, the future time-sphere exists in the grammatical system of French independently from the present time-sphere, which is assumed to be accompanied by assertive modality in the unmarked interpretation of the French simple present form as a modally unmarked form (as with the English simple present form).

5.6.3. Explanation

5.6.3.1. Temporal Clauses

Having constructed the two basic temporal structures of simple future sentences in French, we are now in a position to give a temporal structure account of the similarities and differences of English and French observed in Section 5.6.1. Let us start by explaining why in the two languages different tense forms are chosen in temporal clauses referring to the future, as in (34), repeated below.

(34) a.   When Jules returns, he will be rich.
   b.   Quand Jules {reviendra / *revient}, il sera riche.   (Jones (1996: 171))
        'When Jules {will return / *returns}, he will be rich.'

In this linguistic environment, the simple present form is chosen in English while the simple future form is chosen in French. This difference is explained in the following manner. First, as discussed in Section 3.8, temporal clauses are a type of linguistic environment semantically consisting only of the proposition (P) domain. Since *will* is a modal auxiliary, it is supposed to express a speaker's S-attitude, usually predictive modality. However, the linguistic environment in question does not allow the occurrence of speaker's S-attitudes and therefore *will* cannot occur there. Hence the simple present form is chosen because it can be interpreted as not accompanied by any speaker's S-attitude.

On the other hand, the French simple future form is, by definition, a modally unmarked form and does not express any speaker's S-attitude itself. As we have seen, English simple present forms as modally unmarked forms can convey a speaker's S-attitude (i.e. assertive modality) in linguistic environments reflecting the mental attitude of a certain speaker (e.g. main or independent clauses), but they themselves are not markers of assertive modality, and this is

Chapter 5   *Will*   181

true of the French simple future form. They are thus not accompanied by any speaker's S-attitude in this linguistic environment (the assumed speaker's S-attitude is predictive modality). Just as English simple present forms can occur in temporal clauses, as shown in (34a), so the French simple future form can appear in temporal clauses, as shown in (34b).

A question, then, arises as to why the French simple present form does not appear in this linguistic environment. An answer lies in the French tense system, a tense system having the future time-sphere (grammatical future). As we have seen, although the future time-sphere covers both the present and future time-areas in its basic temporal structures in Figures 11 and 12 above, it primarily refers to the future time-area. This is because the Gricean maxims of conversation come into play. For example, the maxim of Quantity, i.e. "make your contribution as informative as is required for the current purposes of the exchange" (Levinson (1983: 101)), enables the speaker to conventionally choose the simple future form (i.e. a tense form with the future time-sphere that primarily refers to the future time-area) to refer to a future situation described by the temporal clause. In a similar fashion, when referring to a present situation, the speaker chooses the simple present form, a tense form with the present time-sphere that primarily refers to the present time-area.

5.6.3.2.   *Compatibility with Present Time Adverbials*

Next, we will consider the compatibility of *will*-sentences or simple future forms with present time adverbials. Let us observe (35) again, repeated here.

(35) a.   John will leave now.[70]
  b. *Jean partira maintenant.   (Hornstein (1990: 19))
   'Jean will leave now'

The time adverbials *now* and *maintenant* 'now' in (35) refer to the immediate future. What is interesting here is that *now* is compatible with the *will*-form, whereas *maintenant* 'now' is not compatible with the French simple future form. If *will* and the simple future inflection were equally future tense markers, we would not explain this compatibility difference.

My framework can explain it in the following manner. First, both adverbials (i.e. *now* and *maintenant*) establish the present time-area. In the case of

---

[70] I will present an authentic data of the *will*-sentence with a present time adverbial, as in (i):

 (i) "I will now read the traditional opening message from society member Henry David Thoreau."   (N. H. Kleinbaum, *Dead Poets Society*, p. 53)

will-sentences, the infinitive is a non-finite form which itself establishes no time-sphere and its event time can be located at any time in the non-past time-area which is covered by the present time-sphere associated with the present form (i.e. *will*) as head verb. In cases like (35a), the event time in question is located at a time later than speech time because the situation type is non-stative (Section 5.3.1). Putting all these together, we may say that the *will*-sentence in (35a) can refer to a time in the future relative to speech time but in the present time-area—a necessary condition for the non-stative infinitival situation to be modified by this use of *now*.

On the other hand, the French simple future form, i.e. a tense form with the future time-sphere, has only one event time in its tense structure. When this tense structure is projected onto the cognitive time line, the event time is usually located at a time in the future time-area because the future time-sphere of the French simple future form primarily refers to the future time-area, as we saw above. In contrast, the present time adverbial *maintenant* 'now' refers to the immediate future, which is included in the present time-area. A kind of contradiction then arises. For this reason, the French simple future form cannot go with a present time adverbial, as shown in (35b).

5.6.3.3. *Present Time Reference*

Let us next consider cases where *will*-sentences and simple future sentences in French refer to the present, i.e. a time simultaneous with speech time. Consider (36) again, repeated below.

(36) a.   That'll be the postman.
     b.(?)Ce sera le facteur.   (cf. Celle (2005: 192))
      'That will be the postman.'

Although both sentences can refer to present situations, present time reference is highly restricted in the case of simple future sentences in French, as we saw above.

Let us show how my temporal structure approach deals with this difference. I will start with the English example (36a). As indicated by the basic temporal structure of *will*-sentences with present time reference (Figure 3) in Section 5.3.2, in the default case the event time of the modal *will* (E_1) is located at the same time as speech time (due to the definition of modality as speaker's S-attitude) and serves as the time of orientation for the event time of the infinitive (E_2), which is also located in the present time-area. In this case, E_2 is interpreted as simultaneous with E_1 under the condition that the infinitival situation is a stative type.

Chapter 5   *Will*   183

By contrast, in the case of simple future sentences in French, the event time located in the future time-sphere is primarily situated in the future time-area. The event time can be located in the present time-area only when simple future sentences in French satisfy the two conditions observed by Celle (2005: 192): (i) the establishment of clear reference to the speech situation, and (ii) future verification.[71] In (36b), for example, we can easily verify whether the situation involved is true at a future time because the verification occurs immediately after speech time (condition (ii)); in addition, the situation involved is clearly related to the speech situation in which the speaker and hearer are engaged (condition (i)). The speaker and hearer can easily inter at the verification time that the relevent situation may have already obtained at speech time. Hence the situation can be referred to as an inferential present situation.

It is important to note that this type of verification requires the situation involved to be a stative type; if the situation has already changed before the verification time in the future, we usually cannot confirm that it has been the case at speech time. This "stative" requirement accounts for why an example like (35b) above cannot satisfy the future-verification condition and thus cannot be interpreted as a case of the present reference use. We thus conclude that the future-time preference of the tense structure of simple future sentences in French, together with the two conditions for the present time reference, restricts their present reference use.

5.6.3.4.   *Indirect Speech Complements*

Let us now move to differences between *will*-sentences in English and simple future sentences in French in indirect speech complements. First, we will observe cases where the main clause is past, as in (37), repeated below.

(37) a.   Yesterday he predicted that it'll be nice out tomorrow.
   b.   ?Hier il a prévu qu'il fera beau demain.   (Fleischman (1982: 10))
        'Yesterday he predicted that it'll be nice out tomorrow.'

As shown in Section 3.5, an indirect speech complement is a quotation of the private expression of the original (potential) speaker, which consists of modality as the original speaker's S-attitude and the propositional content. The

---

[71] It is sometimes claimed that *will* is a future tense marker in English because *will*-sentences are more or less related to future verification; for example, a present reference use of *will* induces the speaker to verify the truth of the proposition in the future. However, as Lakoff (1972: 234–235) points out, the epistemic modal *should* is also used for future verification (cf. also Papafragou (1998: 35)). The claim made above is therefore not convincing.

choice of tense form here is the default case and speech time is the base point for it (Section 2.2).[72]

With these in mind, let us first consider the English case (37a). The use of the present tense form *will* allows the complement clause to receive the so-called double-access reading, a reading in which the complement clause situation represented by the finite verb (in this case the prediction expressed by *will*) obtains not only at the time of the original speaker's prediction (in the past) but also at speech time (i.e. the time of reporting the whole sentence). Since the choice of tense form is the default case here, the present time-sphere associated with the present tense form *will* covers the present time-area (i.e. a cognitive time range including the time of the report) and its event time (i.e. the time of the predictive modality expressed by *will*) is located at the same time as the time of the report because of the definition of modality as speaker's S-attitude. The prediction involved is originally attributed to the original speaker, whose consciousness is existent at the time of the original speaker's prediction in the past. By using the present tense form, the reporter expresses that he/she regards the prediction as the original speaker's S-attitude as continuing to be valid until the time of his/her report, when the reporter him/herself believes that the infinitival situation involved is predictable. To put it differently, the reporter superimposes his/her prediction onto the original speaker's when reporting the complement clause situation: the mental attitude of the original speaker toward the complement clause situation (i.e. the original speaker's S-attitude) is interpreted as continuing up to the time of the report and hence the prediction (made in the past by the original speaker) about the complement clause situation is still valid at the time of the report. There is thus no temporal gap between the time of the prediction itself (described by the main clause verb) in the past and the time at which the predicted situation (described by the infinitive of the complement clause) will obtain in the future; for the reporter's taking over the original speaker's prediction—at the time of the report—serves as a "bridge" between the prediction in the past and the predicted situation to occur in the future relative to the time of the report. This is how a sentence like (37a) is interpreted.

Let us next consider the French case (37b), whose complement clause contains the simple future form. For the same reason we saw above, as shown in Figure 11 above, in a default case like this, its event time is normally located in the future time-area and the base point for choosing the simple future form

---

[72] For a detailed and more extensive analysis of tense and modal phenomena in indirect speech complements, see Wada (2001a: Ch.8).

is speech time (in this case, the time of the report). This means that the complement clause situation occurs in the future relative to speech time. On the other hand, the original speaker's S-attitude occurs at the time of the original speaker's prediction in the past relative to speech time because the event time represented by the past participle *prévu* is located in the past. In the present model, it is also assumed in French that the past participle represents anteriority relative to the time of orientation, i.e. the event time of the perfect *avoir*, which is in turn simultaneous with speech time. There is no "bridging element", such as the original speaker's prediction taken over by the reporter at the time of the report (i.e. speech time) and hence there is a temporal gap between the time of the prediction made in the past and the time of the predicted situation to occur in the future. Thus, the acceptability of (37b) is low.

Let us now move to cases where the original utterance is assumed to be made in the future, as in (38), repeated below

(38) a. Mary will say that she will be tired.   (Enç (1996: 350))
     b. Léon dira vendredi qu'il partira dans trois jours. (Smith (1997: 211))
         'Leon will say on Friday that he will leave in three days.'

Let us start with the English (38a). As Enç (1996: 350) observes, the predictive modality expressed by the *will* in the complement clause is attributed to the (expected) original speaker (i.e. Mary) and thus assumed to occur at the time of the original speaker's utterance.

The temporal calculation goes as follows. The present tense form *will* in question expresses predictive modality attributed to the (expected) original speaker Mary and is chosen with the time of Mary's saying as the base point in this linguistic environment, a non-default environment where absolute tense forms are not chosen with speech time being the base point.[73] The event time of the infinitive *be tired* is located in the future relative to the event time of the *will* in the complement clause, which is simultaneous with the time of the

---

[73] In the complement clause of a future reporting clause in English, the choice of tense form is basically based on the time of the (expected) original speaker's utterance located in the future (cf. Wada (2001a: Ch.8)). The tense forms used here are called "pseudo-absolute tense forms" in Declerck (1991b, 2006). One of the reasons why this is the case may be that, as Harder (1996: 438) puts it, when the complement clause situation is evaluated from the time of the (expected) original speaker's utterance, shifting the perspective (including the speaker's t-viewpoint) from the original speaker's to the report's (existent at speech time) would distort the intended message by the original speaker because the whole content of the complement clause is in the mental world to be created in the future by the original speaker. Only in the case where such a distortion might not happen can we choose absolute tense forms with speech time being the base point in this linguistic environment.

(expected) original speaker's utterance represented by *say*. The time of the original speaker's utterance is situated in the future relative to the event time of the *will* in the main clause, which is simultaneous with the time of the report (i.e. speech time). This calculation is a natural consequence of our approach, where the bare infinitive can represent its event time as posterior to the time of orientation (in this case the event time of *will* as head verb) and *will* is a modal that expresses a speaker's S-attitude (in this case predictive modality) attributed to the cognitive subject (i.e. private self) of the respective linguistic environment (i.e. the indirect speech complement or the main clause).

On the other hand, as Smith (1997: 211) observes, the complement clause situation in the French (38b) can receive two temporal readings: (i) the time of the complement clause (i.e. the event time of *partira*) is located in the future relative to the time of the main clause (i.e. the event time of *dira*), and (ii) the time of the complement clause is located in the future relative to speech time, i.e. the time of reporting the whole sentence.

These observations are explained in the following manner. In reading (i) as with the *will*-sentence in the complement clause of (38a), the simple future form as an absolute tense form is chosen with the time of the (expected) original speaker being the base point. The event time of the complement clause verb *partira* is located later than the event time of the main clause verb *dira* (i.e. the time of the expected original speaker) as the time of orientation, which is itself located in the future time-area (cf. Figure 11).

Unlike *will*-sentences, however, simple future sentences in French like the one in (38b) do not contain a linguistic element explicitly expressing a speaker's mental attitude, i.e. a modal. This suggests that in this linguistic environment, speaker's S-attitudes implied by modally unmarked forms do not necessarily constitute part of the private expression attributed to the (expected) original speaker (as private self) from the beginning of temporal calculation.[74] As implied in Section 3.5, the indirect speech complement is a linguistic environment in which both the original and reporting speaker's perspectives are available. It is thus possible that the predictive modality implied by the simple future form is interpreted as attributed to the reporting speaker in the course of temporal calculation unless the intended message by the original

---

[74] This does not mean that modally unmarked sentences in French are not accompanied by any speaker's S-attitude (see Section 5.6.2). What I am arguing here is that the fact that the sentence in question is modally unmarked opens up a path to the choice of tense form based on the reporter's point of view in this linguistic environment.

Chapter 5   *Will*   187

speaker is distorted. In this case, the reporter's perspective at speech time is foregrounded and the simple future form (i.e. a modally unmarked form) in the complement clause of (38b) is chosen with speech time (i.e. the time of the report at which is located the reporter's perspective) being the base point. The temporal relationship of the event time of *partira* to the time of orientation is the same as in the case of reading (i), i.e. that of posteriority. Hence (38b) allows reading (ii).

The idea that modally unmarked sentences do not necessarily require the base point (for choosing tense forms) to be the time of the original speaker's utterance is borne out by the following English example, where the complement clause contains a modally unmarked sentence.

(40)   Tomorrow I will tell your father that Bill refuses to pay us.

(Declerck (1991b: 190))

Declerck (1991b: 190) states that the simple present form *refuses* (i.e. a modally unmarked form) can refer either to the time of the speaker's utterance in the future, i.e. the reporting-clause time, or to the time of reporting the whole sentence, i.e. speech time. In my analysis, the simple present form as a modally unmarked tense form can be chosen with speech time being the base point, as long as the relevant situation refers to the time zone that the reporting speaker can make an assertion about on his/her responsibility, i.e. a time zone past relative to the time of the reporting clause and present relative to speech time.

From these observations, we may conclude that the difference of the temporal structures between the *will*-sentence in English and the simple future sentence in French plays a crucial role in explaining the different behaviors of the two languages in indirect speech complement clauses.

5.6.3.5.   *Similarities*

In the last four sub-sections, we have examined the different behaviors of *will*-sentences in English and simple future sentences in French. We found that the differences between the relevant temporal structures of the two tense forms provide a basis for explaining them. Now, I will briefly mention when the two tense forms are used to refer to a similar situation, as exemplified by (41):

(41) a.   It will rain tomorrow.
    b.   Il pleuvra demain.
         'It will rain tomorrow.'

Since the (basic) temporal structures of the two tense forms (with future time reference) contain the event time located in the future time-area (Figure 2 vs. Figure 11), they can potentially be interchangeable. If the speaker concentrates on the occurrence of a future situation, *will*-sentences, especially in comparison with sentences including *be going to*, are chosen in English,[75] and simple future sentences, especially in comparison with sentences including *aller* + infinitive, are chosen in French.[76] The sentences in (41) are used for making a prediction about a future event (without volition) and the main concern here can be what the future situation is like. Thus, in cases like this, a future situation is the speaker's main concern and tense forms with future orientation are chosen in both English and French, i.e. *will*-sentences and simple future sentences.

5.7. Concluding Remarks

In this chapter, I have explained a variety of temporal phenomena concerning *will* in terms of its temporal structures. Future time is often said to be a "gray" zone in which tense is intermingled with mood and modality and sometimes they are indivisibly united (Dahl (1985: 103), De Brabanter and Sharifzadeh (2014: 15)). For this reason, the phenomena concerning future time cannot be explained properly without a framework like the one we have developed in this book. In this chapter, we assumed three levels of meaning associated with *will*, i.e. the core meaning, semantic uses/functions, and pragmatic variants. The core meaning of *will* is high probability, which is reflected in all instances of *will*-sentences. Different semantic uses have their own temporal structures, i.e. temporal "templates" for calculating the temporal value of a given tense form. Pragmatic variants are independent uses but share a temporal structure with other variants and so they are not distinguishable in terms of temporal calculation. All instances of *will*-sentences share the combination of the tense structure of the present tense form *will* and that of the infinitive, which motivates why the same tense form (i.e. *will* + infinitive) is

---

[75] In the case of English, we are only assuming typical uses of sentences with *be going to* here. As we will see in Chapter 6, some uses of sentences containing *be going to* are more future-oriented these days.

[76] It seems that *aller*-futures in French are more present-oriented than *be going to*-futures in English; the former often correspond to *will*-futures in English (cf. Celle (1997), Larreya (2001), Lansari (2009)). I myself made a brief comparison between *aller*-futures and *be going to*-futures or *will*-futures elsewhere (Wada and Watanabe (2016)), but a more detailed exploration is needed.

used to express different uses or functions.

Thus far, linguists and grammarians have had different opinions about what is regarded as tense. Some consider only tense inflections to be tense markers; others take the position that linguistic items other than tense inflections, such as auxiliaries, can be tense markers. De Brabanter, Kissine and Sharifzadeh (2014: §1.3) compare linguistic items such as inflections or auxiliaries in many languages, coming to the conclusion that tense markers should not be restricted to inflections. However, as they themselves point out (p. 16), tense and modality are deeply related to each other and necessarily go together. This suggests that no matter what claim one makes about future-related phenomena, it is a basic premise that one's explanation should be based on a comprehensive framework treating both tense and modality/mood in a unified way. My framework at least satisfies this basic premise and has explained a variety of tense and modal phenomena of *will*-sentences in this chapter. It might appear that in my analysis only tense inflections (A-morphemes) are regarded as tense markers, but this is not true. What my framework assumes is that A-morphemes are special in that they establish time-spheres (i.e. grammatical time ranges) in tense structures; they are distinguished from other tense markers, R-morphemes, which merely express a temporal relation between the event time and the (potential) time of orientation. Auxiliaries, including *will*, are themselves tense forms. In West European languages, when a verb or predicate appears in finite position, it is accompanied by an A-morpheme (English modals are always finite forms); when it appears in non-finite position, it is accompanied by an R-morpheme. English has only two A-morphemes, i.e. the present and past tense morphemes, so that *will* is regarded as a present tense form, which morpho-syntactically consists of the present tense morpheme (A-morpheme) and verb stem; *will* itself is not a future tense marker. French, by contrast, has the future tense morpheme as an A-morpheme. The simple future form is a modally unmarked (i.e. unmodalized) form and does not itself express any modality as speaker's mental attitude. However, because tense and modality are indivisibly united especially in future expressions, the simple future form must convey a certain mental attitude of the speaker. Since unmodalized forms in English are either present or past, the modality accompanying them in a linguistic environment in which a speaker's mental attitude is available is assertive modality, i.e. a speaker's mental attitude toward the situation in the present or past relative to the time of assertion.

However, things are a little complicated in the case of the French simple future form. The unmarked mental attitude of the speaker toward the situation which will occur or obtain in the future is predictive modality and the simple future form (an unmodalized form) is therefore in principle interpreted as accompanied by predictive modality. However, since such predictive modality is not the one expressed by a linguistic item like *will*, the simple future form can behave differently from the *will*-form, as in the complement clause of a future reporting clause (e.g. (38)). Although the simple future form is accompanied by predictive modality by default, what type of modality as speaker's S-attitude is actually conveyed by it depends on context. In independent or main clauses, the simple future form usually implies predictive modality. However, as in the case of (33b) above, which says that the festival period has already been determined when this sentence is uttered (written) and a girl named Emma Fesneau has been selected to play the role of Joan of Arc during that festival, the modality as speaker's S-attitude accompanying this utterance may possibly be assertive modality.

As observed thus far, only by taking a comprehensive framework that can treat both tense and modality/mood (including mental attitudes and speech acts) from a unified point of view can we give a systematic and promising explanation to the temporal phenomena of future expressions. We will also take this stance to explain temporal phenomena of other future expressions in the following chapters. By so doing, we can confirm and enhance the validity of the present framework.[77]

---

[77] Needless to say, to prove that the present framework is cross-linguistically valid, we have to show not only that it can explain more temporal and modal phenomena of English and French, but also that it can be extended to those of other languages such as German and Dutch. For some comparisons of the differences of temporal phenomena in English and Japanese, the present model (including my previous theory) has already been adopted to explain them (e.g. Wada (2001a, 2001c, 2009b)).

Chapter 6

Be Going To

6.1. Introduction

As with *will*-sentences, there have been numerous studies on sentences or clauses containing *be going to* (henceforth BGT-sentences); e.g. Berglund (2000a), Brisard (2001), Bybee, Perkins and Pagliuca (1994), Danchev, Pavlova, Nalchadjan and Zlatareva (1965), Danchev and Kytö (1994), Eckardt (2006), Gesuato and Facchinetti (2011), Hilpert (2008), Hopper and Traugott (1993, 2003), Kashino (1993), Langacker (1990), Nicolle (1997), Sato (2016), Tagliamonte, Durham and Smith (2014), Traugott (1995), Traugott and Dasher (2002).[1, 2, 3] In this chapter, based on the comprehensive model established in this book, I give a temporal structure analysis of temporal and modal phenom-

---

[1] Here, I only mention the studies on BGT-sentences which were not taken up in Chapter 5 in comparison with *will*-sentences.

[2] While there are so many studies comparing BGT-sentences with *will*-sentences (as we saw in Chapter 5), there are much fewer studies comparing BGT-sentences with sentences in the present progressive with future time reference, as we will see in Chapter 7.

[3] There are many studies, especially in terms of relevance theory, arguing that *will* and *be going to* are truth-conditionally (i.e. semantically) equal, but pragmatically different (e.g. Haegeman (1989), Nicolle (1998)). This is a different position from mine, where *will*-sentences and BGT-sentences are semantically different in that they represent different (basic) temporal structures. Theoretical positions like Haegeman's (1989) are also criticized by Declerck (1991b: 382–383), because as she herself admits, her analysis cannot, for example, explain why the past-tense versions of the two sentences are semantically different (cf. Wada (2001a: §7.7)), as in (i):

    (i) a.   The Queen would arrive three hours later.   (Haegeman (1989: 313))

       b.   The Queen was going to arrive three hours later.   (Haegeman (1989: 313)

Sentence (ia) indicates the actualization of the infinitival situation while sentence (ib) tends to indicate its non-actualization. However, we are not arguing that all uses of *will*-sentences and BGT-sentences are completely different in semantic terms. In some uses (e.g. the simple-future use in the sense used in this book), the temporal structures (i.e. semantics) of *will*-sentences and BGT-sentences are almost equal with only a very slight difference.

ena of BGT-sentences.[4]

This chapter is composed of seven sections. In Section 6.2, we first observe several uses of BGT-sentences. Section 6.3 is devoted to constructing the tense structure and basic temporal structure of BGT-sentences, followed by their justification. Section 6.4 explains the uses observed in Section 6.2, using their respective temporal structures. Section 6.5 touches, in terms of grammaticalization, on the relations among temporal structures associated with different semantic uses. Section 6.6 considers differences between BGT-sentences and *will*-sentences, including those in *if*-clauses, and enhances the validity of my analysis. Section 6.7 makes concluding remarks.

6.2. Uses and Functions of BGT-Sentences

The uses and functions of BGT-sentences to be considered in this chapter are exemplified by the following:

(1) a. I'm going to stay at home and write letters.   (Leech (2004: 58))
  b. She's going to have twins.   (Leech (2004: 59))
  c. I turned to face Kathleen ... We had a good long hug. "It's going to be all right now," I told her.   (BNC A0F)[5]
  d. I'm going to be forty in a few years.
          (S. Sheldon, *Master of the Game*, p.204)
  e. Even though we've got this wretched document we're talking about there's always going to be an Asterix book by the bedside or something like that.   (requoted from Collins (2009: 144))
  f. Petaluma is going to be sixty miles north of here.
          (Traugott (2006: 115))

---

[4] Berglund (2000a), investigating the spoken component of the British National Corpus, has found that there are differences between uses of *be going to* and *gonna* with respect to factors such as text type, generation, and social class. We will not be focusing on such factors; we simply follow Collins (2009), among others, to regard (*be*) *gonna* and *gunna* (contracted versions of *be going to*) as variants of *be going to*, and basically regard all of them as semantically (i.e. in terms of their temporal structures) equal.

[5] This use of BGT-sentences has a temporal structure similar to the one for the basic use of sentences containing *be about to*, which will be considered in detail in Chapter 9. Sentences containing *be about to* are, in principle, incompatible with time adverbials establishing the future time-area and require the event time of the infinitive to be located in the present time-area. In this connection, Leech (2004: 59) points out that BGT-sentences, when referring to the immediate future, have an almost equivalent value that sentences containing *be about to* have.

g. I'll ring you up if I'm going to be late for dinner.
                    (requoted from Declerck and Reed (2001: 157))

(1a) exemplifies the use termed *intention* in Coates (1983), the FUTURE OF PRESENT INTENTION in Leech (2004), or *dynamic* in Collins (2009). This use conveys the volition of the grammatical subject and is usually obtained in the case of human subjects, especially first-person subjects, and agentive verbs expressing controllable situations. In this book, I refer to this use of BGT-sentences as the volitional use. (1b) exemplifies the use termed *prediction* in Coates (1983), the FUTURE OF PRESENT CAUSE in Leech (2004), or *epistemic* in Collins (2009). This use can be obtained irrespective of the animacy of the subject involved or the agentivity of the verb phrase involved, indicating that something is already ongoing or in progress—objectively or subjectively—at the time of orientation toward the actualization of the infinitival situation in the future. In this book, I refer to this use as the predictive-future use. (1c) shows that BGT-sentences can co-occur with time adverbials referring to the present time-area. This use is referred to as the immediate-future use in this study. (1d) is used when the situation involved refers to the aging of human beings or calendar-related events, i.e. situations which are absolutely certain to occur or obtain in the future. This use is named the simple-future use in this book (cf. Section 5.4.3). (1e) contains an instance of the so-called predictability use of BGT-sentences, which refers to a general state obtaining in the present. (1f) exemplifies what Traugott (2006: 115) calls "inferential" *be going to*. According to her, this use is equivalent to a use of *would*, as in *That would be sixty miles north of here,* and expresses "speaker's certainty and expectation of hearer's future information state." I refer to this use of *be going to* as the "predictive-present" use. A difference between the predictability use and the predictive-present use is that although both uses depict a situation obtaining in the present, the former refers to a less specific or nonspecific situation while the latter is used to draw an inference to a specific situation. The BGT-sentence in (1g) occurs in type A conditional clauses, i.e. conditional clauses denoting a direct cause for the occurrence of the main clause situation, in which *will*-sentences in their predictive use cannot occur (cf. Section 5.4.7).

6.3. Toward Constructing the Basic Temporal Structure of BGT-Sentences

6.3.1. Tense Structure and Characteristics of the Unit *Be Going To*

We next turn to constructing the basic temporal structure of BGT-sentences in the default case. For this purpose, we will have to observe not only the tense structure of BGT-sentences — consisting of the two verbal units, i.e. *be going to* and the (bare) infinitive — but also the characteristics of *be going to*, whose temporal information crucially affects the temporal structures of BGT-sentences.

It is usually said that the origin of BGT-sentences was composed of the progressive form of *go* and a purposive clause headed by *to*, but as grammaticalization proceeds, *be going to* has been reanalyzed as a unit and now established as a grammatical marker of futurity (cf. Hopper and Traugott (1993, 2003: 68–69)). Whether *be going to* is a grammatical marker of futurity or semi auxiliary, or whether it is an operator or an element belonging to the propositional content, what is important is the idea that the spatial movement indicated by the movement verb *go* has given way to the temporal movement toward the future by way of metaphorical or metonymic extension (Sweetser (1988), Hopper and Traugott (1993, 2003: 92–93), Traugott (1995)); *be going to* is nowadays a verbal unit indicating that something is ongoing (or in progress) at a time of orientation (i.e. speech time in the case of the present tense form) toward the actualization of the infinitival situation in the future relative to the time of orientation.

With respect to the *to* component, I adopt Duffley's (1992, 2000, 2006) view that the so-called infinitive marker *to* was once a preposition representing a spatial path, i.e. a notion consisting of a course and goal, and more or less preserves the original meaning (Wada (2001a, 2009a)). More specifically, in the grammaticalization process the infinitival *to*, preserving part of the meaning of the preposition *to*, has developed to exclusively represent a temporal path (consisting of a process and end point) by way of metaphor and/or metonymy.[6] The *to* in question includes the notion "end point" (i.e. the goal of the temporal path) because it has been derived through metaphor from the preposition *to* (i.e. the origin of the infinitival *to*) which includes the goal of the spatial path, as illustrated by a sentence like *Neri, take a train to Rome* (cited from Francis Ford Coppola's film *The Godfather Part III*). The entailment of the end point of the infinitival *to* is also indirectly supported by the

---

[6] Sweetser (1988) gives a metaphor-based analysis, while Traugott (1995) offers a metonymy-based analysis.

Chapter 6 *Be Going To*

fact that the progressive form of dynamic verbs, which depicts imperfectivity and hence excludes the end point from its reference range, is more likely to occur with *toward(s)* than with *to* (*Taishukan's Unabridged English-Japanese Dictionary*), as illustrated by *[T]he value of your house is heading towards the basement* (BNC ABS).

Let us next support the view that the verbal unit *be going to* is a semantic unit expressing futurity. A semantic unit is a unit whose constituents are semantically closely related to and basically cannot be separated from each other. As for the unit *going to*, we can first point out that no element intervenes between *going* and *to*, as in **Mary is going not to dance with Tom* (in the intended reading). Second, there are contracted forms of *going to*, such as *gonna* and *gunna*. Third, as shown in (2), the *to* in BGT-sentences cannot be deleted by way of VP-deletion.

(2) a.   John's willing to come, but he's not going to.   (Palmer (1987: 140))
    b. *John is willing to come, but he's not going.[7]

Next, *be* and *going* form a semantic unit, too, which is justified for (at least) two reasons.[8] First, the combination of the two items originally meant progressive aspect, a semantic concept. Second, the original meaning of a given form or unit is generally becoming (more) opaque in the course of grammaticalization, which is usually referred to as idiomatization (e.g. *make headway*), and this is indeed the case with *be going* (*to*) (for linguistic evidence, see Chapter 9, where we compare BGT-sentences and sentences containing *be about to*). From these observations, we conclude that in BGT-sentences, the sequence *be going to* constitutes a semantic unit, which consequently allows the (bare) infinitive (and its complements and/or adjuncts) to form an independent unit.

Because BGT-sentences contain a finite verb (i.e. *be*), the unit *be going to* has an A-morpheme and is an absolute tense form. The tense structure of *be going to* in the present tense is therefore the same as that of other present tense forms: the event time is located in the present time-sphere (see Figure

---

[7] The ungrammaticality of (2b) is due to Joyce Cunningham, Mary Lee Field, and Nina Padden (all north American).

[8] It is true that certain elements like the negative marker can intervene between *be* and *going*, as in *Mary is not going to dance with Tom*. However, this position is reserved for syntactic adjuncts and accordingly such an intervention stems from the syntactic requirement, not showing that the two items do not constitute a semantic unit. For example, the semantic unit *have to*, which has the contracted form *hafta*, can be intervened by certain elements such as *only*, as in *have only to*.

2(i) in Chapter 2). In the default case, the present time-sphere (grammatical present) covers both the present time-area (cognitive present) and the future time-area (cognitive future), excluding the past time-area (cognitive past). As observed in Chapter 5, when the (bare) infinitive, a relative tense form, occupies the complement position of a modal as head verb, it represents the temporal relationship between its event time and the event time of the head verb as the time of orientation. Whether a head verb is a modal or not, we can generally assume that the verb in the (direct) complement position of the head verb represents a (direct) temporal relationship to the latter because of the nature of that position. Thus, in BGT-sentences, too, the (bare) infinitive represents the temporal relationship between its event time and the event time of *be going to* as the head verb. However, the characteristics of *be going to* observed above enable the temporal relationship represented by BGT-sentences to differ from that represented by *will*-sentences (we will see linguistic evidence for this statement in Section 6.6.4). To be more specific, *to* indicates a temporal path and so the temporal relationship between the *be going* part and the infinitive part must be restricted to a before-after one (note, however, that this is not the case when the content of *be going to* is semantically bleached in the course of grammaticalization).

From these observations, the tense structure of BGT-sentences consists of those of *be going to* and the infinitive, in which the event time of the infinitive (which occupies the complement position of *be going to*) is located at a point on the time line later than the event time of *be going to* as the head verb.

6.3.2. Basic Temporal Structure

Let us now consider the basic temporal structure of BGT-sentences. In the tense-interpretation process of BGT-sentences, the principle for the default interpretation of absolute tense forms—given in (4) in Section 2.4.1—causes the speaker's t(emporal)-viewpoint (V_{SPK}) included in the tense structure of the verbal unit *be going to* to fuse with his/her consciousness (C_{SPK}) existent at speech time (S). The basic temporal structure of BGT-sentences in the default case is schematized in Figure 1:

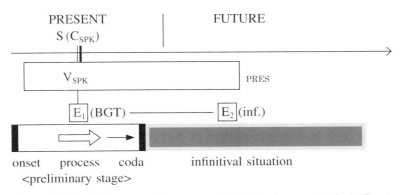

Figure 1: Basic Temporal Structure of BGT-Sentences (Default Case)

Here, I omit the comments on the parts shared with the basic temporal structure of *will*-sentences presented in Chapter 5. The situation described by *be going to* is regarded as a preliminary stage leading to the actualization of the infinitival situation and its semantic content is determined by way of the interaction between the semantic content of the BGT-sentence involved and the context. For example, in the case of (1b), i.e. *She's going to have twins*, a possible preliminary stage for the actualization of the birth of twins is the situation in which the grammatical subject has a pregnant belly.

As stated above, my framework takes a compositional analysis in which the semantic content of the whole entity is basically composed of the semantic content of its parts, unless the entity is highly or completely grammaticalized. Given this perspective, the basic temporal structure of BGT-sentences—which is assumed to preserve the original meanings of their constituents, such as *go* and *to*, due to semantic retention—reflects the temporal information indicated by the progressive form of *go* (i.e. the situation in which something is ongoing at a time of orientation) and that represented by *to* (i.e. a temporal path consisting of a process and end point on the time line).[9] These meanings are reflected especially in the cognitive schema involved. In the case of the present

---

[9] As stated by Bybee, Perkins and Pagliuca (1994: 269) and Langacker (2002: 330–333), it is possible to assume that the future orientation of BGT-sentences has arisen not by way of metaphorical extension, but through a process in which only the spatial meaning of the verbal unit *be going to*—which originally had both the spatial and temporal meanings—has bleached. Even in this assumption, my position—presented in the main text—is still valid because we can say that the temporal meaning of *be going to*, which originally coexisted with its spatial meaning, comes to the fore because of its foregrounding and the semantic bleaching of the spatial meaning.

tense, the first time of orientation (i.e. the starting point for temporal calculation) is identified as speech time (S), as indicated in Figure 1. That something
is already ongoing or in progress at speech time entails that its beginning part
(i.e. the onset represented by the left bold line of the rectangle symbolizing
the preliminary stage in Figure 1) has been actualized in the past. The preliminary stage (i.e. the *be going to*-situation already ongoing or in progress at
speech time) will come to an end at some future time unless intervened (the
end point of the preliminary stage is the coda represented by the right bold
line of the rectangle in Figure 1). The infinitival situation, which is considered to happen after the preliminary stage without interruption in terms of the
cognitive schema, will come about (represented by the grey rectangle in Figure 1). Objectively speaking, there are cases where the infinitival situation
cannot come about immediately after the end of the preliminary stage; there
can be a considerable time gap between the two situations. However, what is
intended by the cognitive schema is that we (subjectively) construe the relation between the preliminary stage and the infinitival situation as such. In
Figure 1, the notion of "ongoing" or "in progress" is represented by the wide
arrow in the rectangle with bold lines on both sides, and the notion of "temporal path" by the arrow in the same rectangle.

In its basic temporal structure, *be going to* represents the preliminary stage,
i.e. a part of the propositional content, which suggests that *be going to* in its
basic use does not express a speaker's mental attitude. As we saw in Section
3.4, however, main or independent clauses are typically accompanied by a
speaker's mental attitude due to the semantic (de)composition of sentential
utterances. The hypothesis about the default mental attitude of the current
speaker — introduced in (22) in Section 3.8 — enables main or independent
clauses to be accompanied by assertive modality as speaker's S-attitude (i.e.
speaker's mental attitude toward the situation involved). Thus, when using
BGT-sentences in their basic use, the speaker, with assertive modality, construes the preliminary stage represented by *be going to*, whose semantic content is specified in temporal calculation. It is the preliminary stage that is asserted because it is simultaneous with speech time as the time of orientation
and is therefore assertable. Because the preliminary stage ongoing at speech
time toward the actualization of the infinitival situation is construed with assertive modality, the infinitival situation is usually interpreted as certain to occur, unless interrupted externally or implied otherwise. Hence BGT-sentences
are typically chosen in the case of the higher probability of occurrence of the
future situation in comparison with *will*-sentences (cf. Binnick (1971), Brisard
(2001), Declerck (1991a), Leech (2004)). This characteristic is a natural con-

Chapter 6 *Be Going To*

sequence of the basic temporal structure of BGT-sentences in Figure 1.

This view is borne out by the following examples, which show that BGT-sentences are more difficult to "conditionalize" than *will*-sentences.

(3) He'll cry, and if he does ...   (Haegeman (1983: 35))
(4) ?He's going to cry, and if he does ...[10]   (Haegeman (1983: 35))

Conditional clauses cast doubt on, or at least neutralize, the possibility of occurrence of the situation involved (McIntosh (1966: 306–307); cf. Haegeman (1983: 35)), and therefore, the higher possibility of occurrence of the situation the relevant tense form indicates, the less acceptable its conditionalized version becomes. Hence the less acceptability of the example with the BGT-sentence in (4).

It should be noted that within my framework, basic uses of BGT-sentences, which apparently seem to express a prediction, are actually accompanied by assertive modality as speaker's S-attitude. As we will see later in some detail, the prediction is a nuance stemming from an "indirect" reference to the infinitival situation via the preliminary stage at speech time, which is the target of the speaker's judgment or evaluation, i.e. assertive modality in this case.

As shown in Figure 1 above, the two situations constituting BGT-sentences (i.e. the preliminary stage and the infinitival situation) have their own event times. The event time of the preliminary stage, i.e. E_1 (BGT), is located at the same time as speech time as the time of orientation. The event time of the infinitival situation, i.e. E_2 (inf.), is located at a time later than E_1 as the time of orientation because of the temporal path represented by *to*. As a result, E_2 is typically located in the future time-area, though it can be located in the present time-area (see the next paragraph). All the temporal relation between E_1 and E_2 has to preserve is a relation of posteriority.

The posterior relationship of E_2 to E_1 is borne out by the fact that even if BGT-sentences co-occur with time adverbials establishing the present time-area (e.g. *now*), such adverbials never fail to situate E_2 at a time later than E_1—simultaneous with speech time—when they modify E_2, as in (5b) below. This makes a sharp contrast with the case of *will*-sentences, where E_2 can be located at the same time as E_1 and thus speech time, as shown in (5a).

---

[10] The question mark here indicates the less acceptability of the *be going to*-sentence in terms of relative probability in comparison with the *will*-sentence, not the low acceptability of the *be going to*-sentence itself.

200   *The Grammar of Future Expressions in English*

(5) a. Chelsea players will be happy now they can do whatever they want (go for a pint in 'The Plough' after training). (GloWbE GB)

    b. The Water Works Board wants to make sure that the water supply is going to be safe now and for future years, ... (GloWbE US)

In (5b), the situation of the water supply's being safe occurs just after the time of this utterance; *now* establishes the present time-area, in which the event time of that situation (E_2) must be located at a time later than speech time.

There are at least two reasons why the basic temporal structure of BGT-sentences in their basic use entails that an event time simultaneous with speech time is associated with one situation and an event time later than it with another. First, BGT-sentences are compatible with time adverbials referring to two different times, as illustrated by (6):

(6) a. Now we are going to have no money at the end of the month.

                                          (Haegemen (1989: 297))

    b. Now I'm going to wake up tomorrow.
       (query.nytimes.com/gst/fullpage.html?res=9D02E0DF1F3AF932A357 57C0A961958260)

    c. ... She thought she was doing it for just a year, but she kept going with it. Now she is going to display all her best expressions tomorrow, so if you don't have any plans come and check it out ...

                                      (http://halboor.com/photoshow)

    d. ... I'm going to marry the finest girl on earth two weeks from now.
                     (O. Henry, *A Retrieved Reformation*, p. 123)

    e. "It's all set up. I'm going to meet Barzini a week from now. To make a new piece now that the Don is dead." Michael laughed.
                       (M. Puzo, *The Godfather*, p. 413)

A second reason is that the *be going to*-situation itself can be negated, as shown in (7):

(7) Obviously, the gunman is going to pick a gun-free zone of a "certain size" and isn't going to not carry out his plan.
(/www.independentsentinel.com/geraldo-says-the-2nd-amendment-is-bullsht/)

Before closing this section, it is worth pointing out that the ongoingness of the preliminary stage is part of the cognitive schema of BGT-sentences. To claim that the preliminary stage is ongoing at the time of orientation toward the actualization of the infinitival situation involved does not necessarily mean

Chapter 6   *Be Going To*

that a concrete situation is in existence at that time. It can be an abstract situation like the one in our mind.

Consider (8) for example.[11] The background scene for (8) is as follows: a hit-man called Leon, who came across a murder case and happened to protect a girl called Mathilda, is bothered by a drastic change in his life and begins to tell her that he wants to stop living with her; Mathilda, an orphan, has no way to live if she is abandoned by him, so she asks him to play Russian roulette with her and loads a gun with one bullet.[12] (8) is an exchange of conversation immediately after Mathilda has aimed a gun at her head.

(8)   Mathilda: If I win, you keep me with you ... for life.
      Leon: And if you lose?
      Mathilda: You'll go shopping alone, like before.
      Leon: You're gonna lose, Mathilda. There's a round in the chamber,
                  I heard it.   (quoted from Luc Besson's film *Leon*)

With respect to this BGT-sentence, no concrete event or state of affairs is ongoing at the time of Leon's utterance toward the actualization of Mathilda's losing the game, i.e. her death. However, as implied by the semantic content of the following sentence, he is sure that she is already on the way to losing the game. We can thus assume that Leon takes such an abstract situation (i.e. his assurance) as the preliminary stage already ongoing toward her death. In this way, the semantic content of the preliminary stage stems from the interaction between the semantic content of the BGT-sentence and the context. The preliminary stage can refer to such a "subjective", or abstract, ongoing situa-

---

[11] While it is possible to assume that BGT-sentences with the contracted forms *gonna* and *gunna* are more grammaticalized instances (cf. Hopper and Traugott (1993, 2003)), such instances do not always describe semantically bleached situations. As Berglund (2000a) observes, contracted versions of BGT-sentences may be more popular among younger generations, but they seem to preserve the basic temporal structure of BGT-sentences in many cases, as far as we can tell.

[12] Russian roulette is defined as "a very dangerous game of chance where each player aims at their own head with a gun that has one bullet in it and five empty chambers" (Cambridge Dictionaries Online).

202 *The Grammar of Future Expressions in English*

tion in one's mind.[13, 14, 15]

6.4. Analysis

6.4.1. The Typical Uses

We are now in a position to analyze the uses of BGT-sentences observed in Section 6.2 using their temporal structures. Let us first consider two typical uses of BGT-sentences, i.e. the volitional use and the predictive-future use, which are two of their basic uses. As we saw in Chapter 5, the two uses of *will*-sentences constitute different sematic uses based on different temporal structures (see Figures 4 and 5 in Chapter 5). However, I claim that the two uses of BGT-sentences are pragmatic variants sharing one temporal structure.[16]

---

[13] Within the framework of cognitive grammar, Brisard (2001) characterizes BGT-sentences in terms of referentiality and epistemicity. To be more specific, he claims that BGT-sentences have characteristics of non-givenness (−G) and presentness (+P). He criticizes previous analyses based on a temporal path or temporal metaphor by claiming that a sentence like (i) does not indicate that something actual is ongoing at the time of orientation toward the actualization of the infinitival situation, i.e. the occurrence of the earthquake.

(i)   The earthquake is going to destroy that town.   (Brisard (2001: 279))

Because my analysis is based on the temporal structures reflecting a temporal path by way of temporal metaphor or metonymy, I have to refute the criticism. As I claimed in the main text, the notion of ongoingness is part of a cognitive schema; it is not necessarily the case that the preliminary stage is actually ongoing, i.e. some concrete event or state of affairs that is ongoing. Moreover, Brisard's two notions characterizing BGT-sentences, i.e. non-givenness and presentness, can be derived from the (basic) temporal structure of BGT-sentences in my analysis (in this connection, Tyler and Jan (2017: 418−412) criticize Brisard's binary semantic feature analysis by arguing that he cannot explain where the features non-givenness and presentness associated with *be going to* come from). The notion presentness is derived from the preliminary stage (i.e. the *be going to*-situation) already ongoing at speech time (i.e. at present) and the notion non-givenness is derived from the infinitival situation that is not given yet at present, i.e. has not occurred yet at speech time. Thus, my analysis can not only avoid his criticism but also accommodate his two notions characterizing BGT-sentences.

[14] Tyler and Jan (2017) give a cognitive analysis of the five meanings of *be going to* (i.e. neutral future, prior intention, imminence, assumption, and inevitability) based on embodied experience, especially by appealing to the notion of the human walk cycle.

[15] The preliminary stage is sometimes interpreted subjectively when BGT-sentences co-occur with expressions referring to the source of the speaker's judgment or evaluation at speech time, as in (i) and (ii):

(i)   "I hear we're going to be roommates," he said. "I'm Neil Perry."

(N. H. Kleinbaum, *Dead Poets Society*, p. 12)

(ii) "Those seventh graders look like they're going to make in their pants, they're so nervous."

(N. H. Kleinbaum, *Dead Poets Society*, p. 20)

[16] In this respect, Haegeman (1989) also correctly indicates that BGT-sentences are not ambiguous between the volitional and predictive uses.

Chapter 6   *Be Going To*

There are at least three pieces of evidence for this claim. First, unlike the volitional use of *will*-sentences, the volitional use of BGT-sentences indicates that the subject's referent has already decided on something and therefore what obtains or is ongoing at speech time as the time of orientation is a mental state of the grammatical subject that comes about after his/her decision made before the time of orientation (Declerck (1991a), Celle (1997), Leech (2004), Wekker (1976)).[17]   Consider (9) for example:

(9) a.   I'll give you a hand.   (Leech (2004: 87))
    b.   I'm going to give you a hand.   (Leech (2004: 87))

(9a) expresses the speaker's volition that takes places when he/she utters this sentence; (9b) indicates that the speaker as the grammatical subject is already in the mental state of helping the addressee at the time of the utterance. This suggests that the BGT-sentence of the type under consideration has a temporal structure including the preliminary stage ongoing at speech time that has started before it (see Section 6.6.2 for details). In this respect, the temporal structure of the volitional use of BGT-sentences is the same as that of the predictive-future use (e.g. (1b)).

Second, BGT-sentences (in their basic use) do not contain any modals and are therefore accompanied by assertive modality in linguistic environments reflecting speaker's mental attitudes, especially in main or independent clauses. This is true whether BGT-sentences represent the volitional or predictive-future use. As in the case of other modally unmarked forms, in this type of BGT-sentence assertive modality is not expressed by a linguistic element but inserted in interpreting the BGT-sentence to meet the requirement that a sentential utterance semantically contain the speaker's attitude domain (cf. (3) in Section 3.4). Besides, with respect to the prediction associated with this type of BGT-sentences, it is a nuance deriving from its temporal structure, as shown below. By contrast, we saw that *will*-sentences contain a modal and the two uses in question have different temporal structures. In the predictive-future use, e.g. *It will rain tomorrow*, the event time of *will* is represented as an element related to the speaker's attitude domain in the temporal structure; in a volitional use like the one in (9a) above, the event time of *will* is repre-

---

[17] It is said, e.g. in Danchev et al. (1965), that with respect to the volitional use, BGT-sentences are more popular in American English than in British English. They suggest that the reason would be attributed to the fact that *will* is used with all persons in American English, which weakens the modal connotation (i.e. the nuance of volition) of *will*, and accordingly, *be going to* has substituted for *will* for that purpose in American English.

sented as an element associated with the proposition domain (in the situation construal tier). The two uses of *will*-sentences have differences in their temporal structures.

Third, unlike in the case of *will*-sentences, in the case of BGT-sentences not only the volitional use but also the predictive-future use can occur in type A conditional clauses, i.e. conditional clauses of the direct cause-effect type. (10) is an instance of the volitional use; (11) exemplifies the predictive-future use.

(10) If you are going to double student numbers, then the extra students are going to come from lower-income families and they will need a full grant.   (BNC A4V)

(11) a. If there's going to be a hard frost I'll put some protection over the camellia.   (Declerck and Reed (2001: 157))
     b. I'll ring you up if I'm going to be late for dinner. (=(1g))
                                             (requoted from Jacobsson (1984: 132))
     c. If John is going to come, Mary will leave.   (Palmer (1990: 179))

As stated above, *be going to* (i.e. an element of BGT-sentences) itself does not express any speaker's mental attitude. Thus, in type A conditional clauses, assertive modality (i.e. the unmarked type of speaker's S-attitude) is not inserted in interpreting them because they semantically consist only of the proposition domain (cf. Section 3.8) and hypothesis (22) in Section 3.8 is not relevant here.[18]

The third evidence, at the same time, lends support to our view that unlike the predictive-future use of *will*-sentences, the predictive-future use of BGT-sentences does not express predictive modality (as a speaker's S-attitude). The nuance of prediction associated with this type of BGT-sentence stems from the cognitive schema in which the infinitival situation occurs after the end of the preliminary stage ongoing at speech time. When the speaker judges or evaluates the infinitival situation, he/she makes an assertion about the semantic content of the preliminary stage, but not about that of the infinitival situation itself; he/she judges or evaluates the latter "indirectly". This indirectness brings about prediction-like nuances, because the occurrence of the

---

[18] This line of argument also accounts for the fact that BGT-sentences (in their typical uses) can appear in temporal clauses, as in (i), because they also consist only of the proposition domain and are not accompanied by any speaker's mental attitudes (cf. Section 3.8).

(i) When something is going to happen to me, I prefer to know about it.
                                   (A. Camus, *The Outsider*, p.102, translated by Sandra Smith)

infinitival situation is inferred based on the preliminary stage already obtaining at speech time and we usually expect such a situation to occur with high probability (see the definition of predictive modality in (6) in Section 3.4).

As we have seen, the two uses of BGT-sentences (i.e. the volitional and predictive-future uses) share not only the preliminary stage—which is ongoing at speech time in the case of the present tense form in main or independent clauses—followed by the infinitival situation, but also assertive modality in linguistic environments to which speaker's S-attitudes are relevant. This reflects the way that BGT-sentences are typically used and so I speak of the two uses as typical uses of BGT-sentences. The temporal structure for the two uses is schematically represented in Figure 2.

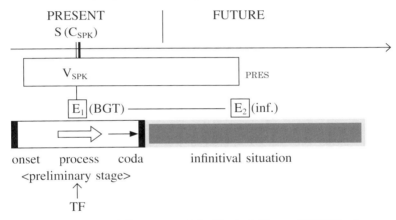

Figure 2: Temporal Structure of the Typical Uses of BGT-Sentences

Figure 2 basically inherits Figure 1. The only difference is that the information about temporal focus (TF) is added in Figure 2. The reason why the temporal focus is directed at E_1 (the event time of the verbal unit *be going to*) is as follows: the speaker bothers to choose a tense form with future time reference that can refer to the preliminary stage triggering the occurrence of a future situation and it is therefore natural to focus on such a marked part, i.e. the preliminary stage. The position of temporal focus accounts for a generally accepted characteristic of BGT-sentences, i.e. present-orientation (Coates (1983: 201), Fleischman (1982: 18-19), McInrosh (1966), Palmer (1988: 146, 1990: 144), Quirk et al. (1985: 48), Wekker (1976: 126)).

There is one more important thing to note here. The cognitive schema symbolizing the relationship between the preliminary stage and the infinitival situation in Figure 2 implies that the infinitival situation is required to be non-stative. More specifically, it evokes an image in which the end of the preliminary stage (represented by the coda) brings about the beginning of the infinitival situation—even if there is actually some time gap between the two situations—and therefore the infinitival situation must be bounded at least on its beginning side.

For a better understanding of the schema in Figure 2, let us consider some examples of the typical uses of BGT-sentences in (12):

(12) a. I'm going to stay at home and write letters. (=(1a))
   b. She's going to have twins. (=(1b))
   c. "This match is going to help me. To beat the World No. 1, even in an exhibition, gives me confidence for the future." (BNC A2E)
   d. Roger Poole, chief union negotiator, said there was a real risk of a major breakdown in the 999 service. "Someone is going to get hurt. That's bound to happen in a dispute like this," he said. (BNC A2P)
   e. "Excuse me, Mr President. Mr President, there is going to be a nuclear test on Tuesday," he yelled. Springer's group organises an annual Easter protest against the nuclear testing programme in the Nevada desert, 65 miles from Las Vegas. (BNC AKR)
   f. I am going to leave this job. I have worked loyally, shown you respect, but I too expect to be treated with respect. (BNC A6V)
   g. Sollozzo said placatingly to the captain, "I am going to talk Italian to Mike, not because I don't trust you but because I can't explain myself properly in English ... (M. Puzo, *The Godfather*, pp. 149–150)
   h. Michael said to Tommasino, "I want you to tell those two sheep herders to leave me alone Sunday. I'm going to go to this girl's family for dinner and I don't want them hanging around."

   (M. Puzo, *The Godfather*, p. 338)
   i. "They are going to cut someone's leg off and then pour some hot oil on a bird." (BNC AAH)

As for (12c-i), the contexts imply that they refer to some kind of preliminary stage ongoing at speech time. Assertive modality (i.e. a speaker's mental attitude when he/she views or construes the relevant situation as a fact or absolutely certain to occur) is inserted in the process of the speaker's judging or evaluating the situation (i.e. situation construal). The speaker describes, with assertive modality, the preliminary stage leading to the actualization of the infinitival situation and the possibility of the actualization of the latter is thus considerably high. Moreover, the preliminary stage's being already ongoing at speech time normally implies that its end will come about soon and accordingly the infinitival situation will occur in the near future (Coates (1983: 198), Leech (2004: 59)).

Whether or not a given BGT-sentence has a volitional overtone finally depends on the context. However, semantic factors often serve as guideline values for non-volitional readings. BGT-sentences with an inanimate subject, as in (12c), or an expletive subject, as in (12e), usually do not invite volitional interpretations; even if BGT-sentences have an animate subject, they usually do not imply volitional overtones when occurring with an uncontrollable type of situation, as shown in (12d).[19] As discussed with respect to the volitional use of *will*-sentences in Section 5.4.1, it is assumed within my framework that in independent clauses only a first-person animate subject can, in principle, bring about the (truly) volitional use. This also applies to BGT-sentences.[20] Thus, the BGT-sentences in (12f) and (12g) illustrate the volitional use because they refer to a first-person animate subject and a controllable type of situation.

As we have seen, however, it is the context that finally determines whether a BGT-sentence of the typical type is interpreted as indicating the volitional or predictive-future use. In (12h), for example, Michael, the speaker of the BGT-sentence, has already been invited to a dinner the next Sunday and therefore the preliminary stage is already ongoing at speech time toward the actualization of his participation in the dinner. On the other hand, in a preceding context—which is not shown in the text—there is an indication that it is he who wants to visit the girl's home and so the BGT-sentence in question is supposed to receive a volitional reading. However, without such an indica-

---

[19] Even if the grammatical subject is first person, BGT-sentences with an uncontrollable type of situation do not carry volitional overtones, as illustrated by (i):

    (i)   ... I'm so in love, I feel like I'm going to die!"

                                     (N. H. Kleinbaum, *Dead Poets Society*, p. 67)

[20] Note, however, that the volitional use of BGT-sentences is a pragmatic variant of their typical uses and makes a sharp contrast with the volitional use of *will*-sentences. With *will*-sentences (in their volitional use), *will* as a modal presupposes the existence of the grammatical subject as a potential speaker, i.e. private self, and when the current speaker and the grammatical subject share the same identity, the volition involved can be shifted into a speaker's S-attitude of the current speaker. However, BGT-sentences (in their volitional use) do not contain any modal and the grammatical subject is merely a part of the situation to be construed; their propositional content does not involve any private self. The volition involved stems from the interaction between the semantic content of the BGT-sentence (including the first-person subject and a controllable type of situation) and the context. Due to this difference, I basically do not use the term *current speaker* in the use of BGT-sentences, for unlike *will*-sentences, BGT-sentences (in their volitional use) do not involve any other (potential) speaker (i.e. grammatical subject as private self) in their interpretation process.

tion, it is possible that he was forced to join the dinner irrespective of his own will. In this case, the BGT-sentence would receive a predictive-future reading.

Unlike *will*-sentences, BGT-sentences in their volitional use express a grammatical subject's mental state (at speech time) that has come about as a result of his/her decision made before speech time.[21] (12f) is a case in point. The context tells us that the subject's referent has decided to resign the job and his/her mental state continuing after that decision (i.e. the preliminary stage toward the actualization of his/her resignation) is ongoing at speech time.

It should be noticed here that just because the preliminary stage of BGT-sentences is ongoing or obtains at speech time does not necessarily mean that the infinitival situation never fails to be actualized in the near future (Leech (2004), Wekker (1976: 133); cf. also Wada (2001a: Ch. 7)). As indicated in (13), BGT-sentences can refer to the actualization of an infinitival situation in a very far future.

(13) a. If Winterbottom's calculations are correct, this planet is going to burn itself out 200,000,000 years from now.   (Leech (2004: 60))
    b. The whole idea of the digital computer is going to be obsolete in fifty years.   (Leech (2004: 60))
    c. "One day, hard as it is to believe, each and every one of us is going to stop breathing, turn cold, and die!"

(N. H. Kleinbaum, *Dead Poets Society*, p. 26)

What is common to BGT-sentences in their typical uses is that the speaker has in mind the preliminary stage ongoing now—which can be taken as something subjectively ongoing in the speaker's mind—leading finally to the actualization of the infinitival situation.

Before closing this sub-section, let us present two arguments showing that the temporal structure of the typical uses of BGT-sentences schematized in Figure 2 above has the temporal path denoted by *to* in the cognitive schema represented by *be going to*.[22] As a first argument, consider (14):

---

[21] I will make a detailed comparison between *will*-sentences and BGT-sentences in their volitional uses in Section 6.6.2.

[22] The notion "temporal path" is expressed in different ways in the literature. For example, Danchev et al. (1965: 381) states:

"*Going to* very frequently encompasses a period of longer duration, a whole series of events leading up to the final result, and is better suited for denoting changes in the state not taking place abruptly."

They attribute these characteristics to the imperfectivity represented by the form and the semantic field of *go*.

(14) a. I am going to leave tomorrow.   (Leech (2004: 59))
     b. I intend to leave tomorrow.   (Leech (2004: 59))
     c. I want to cut the grass but unfortunately I won't be able to.

                                                          (Salkie (2010: 211))

As we have seen, the *to* in BGT-sentences is semantically part of the verbal unit *be going to* and thus the temporal information represented by *to* (i.e. the temporal path) constitutes part of the temporal information represented by *be going to* (i.e. the preliminary stage). With this in mind, let us consider Leech's (2004: 59) observation that the sentence with *intend* in (14b) says nothing about whether or not the departure will be actualized, but the BGT-sentence in (14a) strongly implies that the subject's referent carries out the in-finitival situation. As for the BGT-sentence, the temporal focus (TF) is direct-ed at the event time of *be going to* (E_1) associated with the preliminary stage — i.e. the mental state obtaining after the grammatical subject's decision has been made before speech time — part of which is contributed by the tem-poral path denoted by *to*. This suggests that the end of the temporal path (i.e. the coda) is also foregrounded. The infinitival situation is thus naturally as-sumed to come into existence as a result of the completion of the preliminary stage.

As for the sentence with *intend*, by contrast, *to* constitutes part of the infini-tival clause. The temporal focus is directed at the event time of *intend* be-cause the volition of the grammatical subject represented by *intend* has pre-dominance over the infinitival situation in that the actualization of the latter presupposes the existence of the former (this is the same reason we saw with respect to *will*-sentences in Section 5.4.1). However, the temporal path indi-cated by *to* in the sentence with *intend* is not part of the semantics of the verb *intend* and thus not foregrounded; the path simply indicates that the infinitival situation in theory follows the volition of the grammatical subject. Therefore, in the temporal structure of the sentence with *intend*, there is no implication that the infinitival situation involved will actually occur.

A similar explanation applies to the sentence with *want* in (14c). For the same reason we saw with respect to (14b), the temporal path denoted by *to* is not foregrounded and merely implies that the infinitival situation of cutting the grass itself in theory follows the grammatical subject's wish. The actualiza-tion of the infinitival situation is thus not necessarily indicated by this sentence. Hence the speaker him/herself can make a negative evaluation on the possibility of the occurrence of the infinitival situation by using a sentence like the second conjunct, i.e. *but unfortunately I won't be able to*.

210   *The Grammar of Future Expressions in English*

As a second argument for our claim that the temporal path represented by *to* is part of the preliminary stage depicted by *be going to*, consider (15):

(15) ?She's going to have twins, but she isn't pregnant yet.

(Nicolle (1998: 230))

Although the BGT-sentence in (15) is an instance of the predictive-future use, its temporal structure is the same as that of the volitional use in my model. As we saw in Section 5.4.2, *will*-sentences in their predictive-future use require the temporal focus to be directed at the event time of the infinitive. With BGT-sentences, however, the temporal focus is directed at the event time of *be going to* even in the case of the predictive-future use and the preliminary stage, assumed to include the temporal path represented by *to*, is foregrounded. This strongly suggests that the infinitival situation (i.e. the birth of twins) will be actualized as a result of the completion of the preliminary stage. Thus, negating the pregnancy of the woman referred to by *she* (i.e. the preliminary stage) in the second conjunct is somehow contradictory to using the BGT-sentence in the first conjunct.

6.4.2. The Immediate-Future Use

Next, we will consider the immediate-future use of BGT-sentences. This use has basically the same temporal structure as the two typical uses (i.e. the volitional and predictive-future uses) except for one point: the event time of the infinitive (E_2) is located in the present time-area, not in the future time-area. This indicates that given an appropriate context, BGT-sentences in their immediate-future use can convey volitional overtones. To situate E_2 in the present time-area, we usually need adverbials referring to the present. The temporal structure of the immediate-future use is schematically represented by Figure 3.

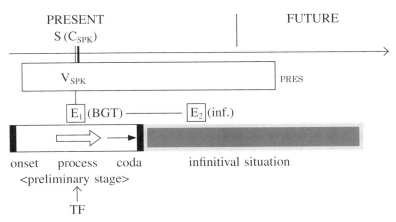

Figure 3: Temporal Structure of the Immediate-Future Use of BGT-Sentences

This use also includes in its temporal structure the preliminary stage ongoing at speech time which leads to the actualization of the infinitival situation. The situation, however, will come about in the present time-area. The temporal structure of the immediate-future use differs from that of the typical uses with respect to the position of E_2, which indicates that the immediate-future use is semantically different from the typical uses within my framework.

To illustrate the point, consider (16):[23]

(16) a. I turned to face Kathleen... We had a good long hug. "It's going to be all right now," I told her. (=(1c))
    b. I am going to make the scones now. Perhaps you should have a rest. (BNC AD1)
    c. Oh yes, dear magazine, I was a victim. But not any more. Things are going to be different now. (BNC BMS)

These examples contain present time adverbials such as *now* or *right now*.

---

[23] Our claim that some present time adverbials refer to a time later than speech time but still in the present time-area is supported by the existence of the following examples:
    (i) Now I'm going to show you now how you going to put it away again, fold it, afterwards, opening it up alright, everyone open their bandage up? (BNC F8D)
    (ii) Now I'm going to come now, I think, it will be the mind of the assembly to take the vote on, for deliverance number four and Mr's counter motion. (BNC F86)
Within my framework, these sentences indicate that *now* at the beginning position of a sentence (clause) specifies the position of the event time of *be going to* (simultaneous with speech time) while *now* at the end or inside position of the sentence (clause) specifies the position of the event time of the infinitive.

212   *The Grammar of Future Expressions in English*

While they do not actually clarify the distance of the event time of the infinitival situation from speech time, the speaker (subjectively) construes the event time as located in the present time-area (cognitive present). In (16c), for example, the context implies that the situation of the speaker's being a victim is over now and the preliminary stage leading to the actualization of the infinitival situation (i.e. the speaker's being in better condition) is now ongoing in his/her mind. The infinitival situation is construed to be actualized at a time (later than speech time) in the present time-area, i.e. a time-area established by the present time adverb.

6.4.3. Semantic Bleaching and Derivative Uses

I now turn to a consideration of the BGT-sentences that came to have some "bleached" parts in their temporal structures through semantic bleaching.[24]

Let us first consider BGT-sentences whose infinitival situation is stative. As shown in Figure 1 above, the basic temporal structure of BGT-sentences, which retains the temporal path represented by *to*, requires the boundedness of the preliminary stage (because of the existence of the coda) and thus the boundedness of the infinitival situation in that the infinitival situation comes into existence after the completion of the preliminary stage.[25] However, quite a number of BGT-sentences are used to show that a certain situation is ongoing toward the actualization of the infinitival situation which seems to be purely or highly stative; e.g. BGT-sentences with state verbs with a very high degree of stativity such as *know* or *need*, semi modals such as *have to* or *be able to*, and the progressive auxiliary *be*, in their infinitival position (cf. also Kashino (1993: 175–176); Hilpert (2008: 118–121)). This type of state verb basically describes an unbounded situation and in this case at least the coda part of the preliminary stage must be backgrounded and semantically bleached. The temporal structure of this type of BGT-sentences is schematically represented in Figure 4.

---

[24] As I repeated in the main text, the preliminary stage of BGT-sentences itself is schematic and its content is specified by the interaction between the semantic content of the rest of the sentence and the context. Readers might be confused when I use the term *bleach* to refer to cases where some part of a schematic notion is backgrounded. However, within my framework, temporal structures, including schematic parts, constitute a semantic level. For this reason, I use the term *semantic bleaching* to cover the backgrounding of a schematic notion in a temporal structure.

[25] There are some sentences like (i), in which a copula in the infinitive form apparently seems stative but in fact expresses a change of state and is usually paraphrased by the verb *become*.

(i)   You know I am going to be a doctor, Mufundishi.   (BNC BLY)

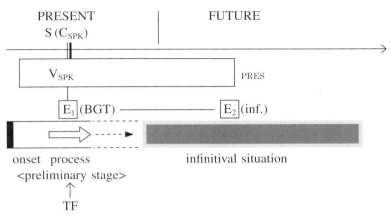

Figure 4: Temporal Structure of the Bleached-Coda Use of BGT-Sentences

I refer to this use as the "bleached-coda" use. This is because the coda part, i.e. a part of the temporal path represented by *to*, is semantically bleached and thus shows the "trace" of future orientation (represented by the broken arrow in Figure 4).

By way of illustration, consider (17):

(17) a. ..., in New Jersey, the people of New Jersey are going to know for the next three years every year their taxes are going to go down.
(COCA)

b. There will probably be a lull over the winter, followed by a resurgence of activity next spring. Nevertheless, the market is going to remain very depressed throughout next year ... (BNC A5T)

c. Eurotunnel's only hope seems to lie in satisfying the banks' technical adviser that his forecast can be reduced — which means at least to the contractors' £7.5bn, if not to Eurotunnel's own £7bn estimate. Even then there is going to have to be £300m-350m rights issue.
(BNC A1S)

d. ..., and maybe we're going to be able to teach the world something about authenticity and truth and love. (COCA)

e. "The Government should be forced to change its mind. I don't accept there is no public money. I'm going to be arguing and voting for a no-toll bridge."[26] (BNC A1Y)

---

[26] Gesuato and Facchinetti (2011), a corpus-based analysis, observe that BGT-sentences allow the infinitive part to be in the progressive form these days, as in (i):

Take (17e) for example. The semantic content of the sentence preceding the BGT-sentence indicates that the speaker does not agree that there is no public money. This enables us to assume that the preliminary stage (i.e. the speaker's positive attitude toward the construction of a no-toll bridge) already obtains in the speaker's mind. As for the infinitive part, it is in the progressive form, i.e. a grammatical means to "defocus" the beginning and end points of the situation involved and make it similar to state verbs in that they are both unbounded. In order to accommodate this situation, the semantic bleaching of the temporal path occurs in the temporal structure of the BGT-sentence involved, making the preliminary stage unbounded with its end side. As a result, there is no obstacle to the choice of state verbs or state-like verbs in the infinitive position.[27]

Let us next consider another use of BGT-sentences that has undergone semantic bleaching. In contrast to the bleached-coda use, the use to be considered has a temporal structure in which the beginning portion of the preliminary stage (i.e. onset) is bleached (in pragmatic terms, of course, something ongoing at a time of orientation implies that it has started). This use has emerged through the following process: when a BGT-sentence whose temporal structure includes the preliminary stage ongoing at speech time co-occurs with a time adverbial referring to both speech time and the time range after that (e.g. *from now on, from now onwards*), only the adverbially specified portion of the preliminary stage is "featured" and foregrounded; by contrast, the portion of the preliminary stage before speech time — including the onset part — is backgrounded because it is not featured and the onset is therefore semantically bleached. I speak of this use as the "bleached-onset" use, whose temporal structure is schematized in Figure 5:[28]

(i)   "Does he know I'm going to be babysitting him when he gets to New York?"

(requoted from Gesuato and Facchinetti (2011: 62))

However, they admit that the form of *be going to + be -ing* "is not fully established yet" (p. 84) and is "typical mainly of oral dialogic, spontaneous communication" (p. 87). Within my framework, examples like the BGT-sentences in (i) and (17e) exemplify the bleached-coda use and their observation suggests that such a use is gradually spreading these days because of the progress of grammaticalization.

[27] Hopper and Traugott (1993: 61) show that the grammaticalization process of BGT-sentences develops by analogy from the stage in which non-stative verbs occupy the infinitival position to the stage in which stative verbs occupy that position. In the analysis presented in the main text, this analogy brings about the semantic bleaching of the temporal path so that stative situations can occur in the infinitival position.

[28] The bleached-onset use corresponds to a middle-stage use which is located between the stage of the typical uses and that of the simple-future use (to be considered in Section 6.4.4) on the grammaticalization scale of BGT-sentences. This type of use was considered in my

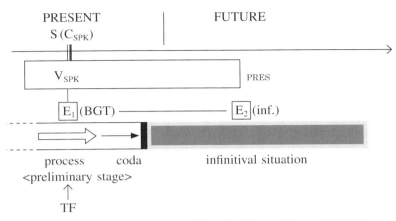

Figure 5: Temporal Structure of the Bleached-Onset Use of BGT-Sentences

Unlike the bleached-coda use, the bleached-onset use entails the end (i.e. coda) of the preliminary stage in its temporal structure. This suggests that the infinitival situation will come into existence after the preliminary stage is over.

To illustrate the point, consider (18):

(18) a. "I am going to do great cinema from now on. I will not do any movie as a favour to anyone or out of compulsion ... .
(http://indianexpress.com/article/entertainment/bollywood/will-not-do-films-as-favour-to-anyone-from-now-sanjay-dutt/)

b. Actor Sidharth recently revealed that the film took him back to his family loving roots. While confirming, he said "Every year, from now onwards, I am going to make at least a two-week plan with my family."
(http://www.desimartini.com/news/bollywood/kapoor-and-sons-has-brought-sidharth-closer-his-family/article31003.htm)

Take (18b) as an example. Judging from the semantic content of the first sentence, we can assume that the background for the speaker of the BGT-sentence to carry out a certain plan has already been given and the preliminary stage for the actualization of the infinitival situation is ongoing at speech time. The

---

previous work (e.g. Wada (2001a: 247-248, 2009a)), where the use corresponding to it was derived from a subjective re-location of the onset to the same time as the time of orientation (i.e. speech time), triggered by the co-occurrence with a time adverbial referring to both the time of orientation and the time range after that, such as *from now on*, or the context implying such a reference range.

216   *The Grammar of Future Expressions in English*

time adverbial *from now onwards* features the portion of the preliminary stage ranging from speech time to the time thereafter. This allows the foregrounding of the adverbially specified portion of the preliminary stage and the backgrounding of its onset.

The bleached-coda and bleached-onset uses include in their temporal structures a preliminary stage which has a semantically bleached portion. However, the content of the preliminary stage is specified by the interaction between the semantic content of the rest of the BGT-sentence involved and the context. The event time of the preliminary stage of the two types of BGT-sentences in question is therefore a pure type and can receive a temporal focus. These examples are different from those of the simple-future use, which we will consider in the next section.

6.4.4. The Simple-Future Use

The simple-future use of BGT-sentences has a temporal structure which includes more "bleached" parts than the bleached-coda and bleached-onset uses. To be more specific, the preliminary stage becomes a "mere shell" with all parts constituting it (i.e. the onset, process, and coda parts) bleached; only the trace of future orientation is left in the temporal structure. The event time associated with this type of preliminary stage therefore serves merely as the time of orientation, qualifying as an orientational event time (E^O). Like the simple-future use of *will*-sentences (see Section 5.4.3), the simple-future use of BGT-sentences is employed when the sentence involved refers to a calendar-related event or describes human age. Since these types of situations are absolutely certain to occur when the time comes, the speaker can normally evaluate or judge them with assertive modality. The preliminary stage of BGT-sentences of this type is almost bleached and so we cannot specify its content through the interaction between the semantic content of the rest of the BGT-sentence involved and the context; after all, unlike a schematic situation, a bleached one cannot be specified. As we saw in Chapter 5, the temporal focus (TF) is not directed at the orientational event time (E^O1) and thus automatically directed at the event time of the infinitival situation (E_2).

The temporal structure of BGT-sentences in their simple-future use is schematized in Figure 6:

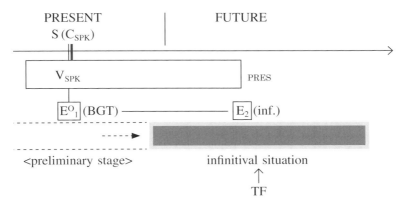

Figure 6: Temporal Structure of the Simple-Future Use of BGT-Sentences

In the cognitive schema part, the rectangle under E^O_1 with broken lines on the top and bottom sides symbolizes the bleached preliminary stage; the broken arrow in the rectangle indicates the trace of future orientation.

By way of illustration, let us consider (19):[29]

(19) a. I'm going to be forty in a few years. (=(1d))
 b. My name is Pat Marshall. I am going to be 73 in another week, and I live in Cedar Rapids, Iowa. (COCA)
 c. Next Monday is going to be the twentieth anniversary of my parents' wedding. (Kashino (1993: 177))[30]
 d. It's two fifty-five now. It's going to be three o'clock soon.[31] (Kashino (1993: 169))

---

[29] Williams (2002a: 199) explains the difference in acceptability between the sentences in (i) and sentence (ii) in terms of whether the situation involved is "fixed" or not. The infinitival parts in (i) are intended to describe what day of the month the target day is or in which month Christmas Day falls. The fact that these situations are fixed on the calendar may lie behind the unacceptability of the sentences. In (ii), on the other hand, the day on which Easter Day falls differs from year to year, which may cause the sentence to be acceptable.
  (i) a. *Tomorrow's going to be June 10th. (Williams (2002a: 199))
     b. *Christmas is going to be in December this year. (Williams (2002a: 200))
  (ii) Easter is going to be in April this year. (Williams (2002a: 199))
In this connection, Kashino (1993: 177–178) points out that some native speakers judge sentence (iii) to be acceptable, but others do not.
  (iii) Tomorrow is going to be Sunday. (Kashino (1993: 177))
Kevin Moore (personal communication), North American, judges this to be acceptable.

[30] Kashino (1993: 178) reports that four out of the five informants he asked regard (19c) as acceptable.

[31] Kashino (1993: 169) reports that his American informant judges (19d) to be acceptable.

e. "I'm going to be four years old, Mommy. I'm a big boy, right?"

(A. Corman, *Kramer vs. Kramer*, p. 41)

In (19a), for example, it is difficult to assume that some arrangements for the speaker to turn forty are already ongoing toward the actualization of the infinitival situation. For this reason, the preliminary stage of this use is bleached.

However, it should be noted here that as suggested in Figure 6, the preliminary stage under discussion implies the trace of future orientation (represented by the broken arrow). This indicates that the simple-future use of BGT-sentences and that of *will*-sentences are not completely the same in terms of the temporal structures — as we saw in Figure 6 in Section 5.4.3, there is no trace of future orientation in the temporal structure of the simple-future use of *will*-sentences.

This difference is indirectly supported by the fact that *will*-sentences allow the event time of the infinitival situation (E_2) to be simultaneous with the event time of the finite verb (E_1), whereas BGT-sentences do not. Compare (20) and (21), both of which are taken from Ota (1998: 274):

(20) a. He'll have come yesterday.
　　b. He'll have come by now.
　　c. He'll be traveling now.
(21) a. *He's going to have come yesterday.
　　b. *He's going to have come by now.
　　c. *He's going to be traveling right now.

As observed in Section 5.3.1, when the bare infinitive in the complement position of *will* as the head verb describes a stative situation, its event time (E_2) can be simultaneous with the event time of the head verb (E_1). The perfect form describes a stative situation due to the stative nature of the perfect *have* (Section 4.3.2; Wada (2001a: §4.1.2)). Progressive aspect turns the situation involved into an unbounded one due to its imperfective nature (Section 2.4.3.3). As shown in Section 5.5, the present reference uses of *will*-sentences derive from their future reference uses by way of grammaticalization, which is triggered by the inference based on the homogeneous nature of stative situations: when stative situations obtain at a future time, it is highly possible that they have also obtained at speech time because of their homogeneous nature, and therefore, the focus can be shifted to the part of the infinitival situation surrounding speech time as well as E_1 and finally the time of that relevant part comes to be identified as the event time, i.e. E_2 (see Figure 7 in Chapter 5).

Chapter 6   *Be Going To*

This is how E_2 comes to be interpreted as simultaneous with E_1.[32]

However, the future reference uses of BGT-sentences include future orientation in their temporal structures and it is therefore difficult for them to go through the same grammaticalization process as those of *will*-sentences. Even in the case of the simple-future use, the trace of future orientation is left in the cognitive schema of its temporal structure, which prevents the focus from shifting to the part of the infinitival situation surrounding speech time. This explains why BGT-sentences basically do not allow E_2 to be simultaneous with E_1, which in turn coincides with speech time (but see the next subsection). In this way, the contrast in acceptability between (20) and (21) lends indirect support to our claim that the simple-future use as well as the bleached-coda use of BGT-sentences retain future orientation, a remnant of the temporal path heading for the future, in their temporal structures.

6.4.5.   Present Reference Uses

In the previous sub-sections, I have shown that the (trace of) future orientation in the cognitive schema of the temporal structure of the future reference uses makes it difficult for BGT-sentences to allow the infinitival situation to refer to the present. However, there are some exceptional cases. More specifically, BGT-sentences nowadays seem to have at least two present reference uses, i.e. what I call the predictability and inferential-present use. How can we resolve this apparent discrepancy? It is our task here to show that the existence of the two present reference uses of BGT-sentences is not necessarily contradictory to the existence of the trace of future orientation.

Let us start with the predictability use. This use of BGT-sentences is similar to the characteristic-behavior use of *will*-sentences in that it describes a su-

---

[32] Within my framework, in the case of modal sentences with the progressive or perfect (including the forms *will* + *have* + past participle and *will* + *be* + present participle), the event time of the non-finite verb (i.e. the progressive *be* or the perfect *have*) can be simultaneous with the event time of the head verb (i.e. a modal), which in turn is simultaneous with speech time due to the nature of the modal involved. The use in question is a present reference use. In the perfect case, the event time of the past participle is located at a time earlier than the event time of the perfect *have* due to the anterior relationship represented by the past participle morpheme *-en* and the situation expressed by the past participle finally refers to the past relative to the time of orientation (which coincides with speech time when the finite verb is present). In the progressive case, the event time of the present participle is located at the same time as the event time of the progressive *be* due to the simultaneous relationship represented by the present participle morpheme *-ing* and the situation expressed by the present participle finally refers to the present relative to the time of orientation (which coincides with speech time when the finite verb is present).

perordinate situation consisting of the repetition of sub-situations of the same type, though the former use does not necessarily characterize a tendency or the nature of a given entity (see Section 5.4.5). When BGT-sentences of this type are compatible with an adverb indicating that the situation involved occurs all the time (e.g. *always*), they come closer in meaning to the W-generic use of *will*-sentences in that the two uses describe "super-temporal" situations.[33] Given that the W-generic use can be paraphrased by a *whenever*-clause—as shown in Section 5.4.5—the predictability use of BGT-sentences is expected to have the same meaning as the clause paraphrased with *whenever*. This implies that each time we assume the occurrence of the infinitival situation of this use, we subjectively recognize a "time gap" between a causing situation and the caused situation (i.e. the situation evoked by it in the speaker's mind). The repetition of this type of "cause-effect" relationship in the speaker's mind constitutes a superordinate situation obtaining in a longer time span including speech time. Put differently, the individual relationship in question serves as a token and the repetition of such a relationship constitutes a type. We can thus assume that the trace of future orientation holds for individual occurrences of the infinitival situation (as a sub-situation) in the speaker's mind, but does not affect the simultaneous relationship between the event time of the infinitive associated with the superordinate situation and the event time of *be going to*. The latter serves as an orientational event time, i.e. the event time of a semantically bleached preliminary stage, because there is no (subjective) process leading to the actualization of the infinitival situation.

These observations lead us to the temporal structure of the predictability use of BGT-sentences, schematically represented in Figure 7:

---

[33] Copley (2009: 76) states that when combined with *always*, BGT-sentences can receive an interpretation in which the speaker makes a prediction about a future generic situation. I assume that as in the case of the grammaticalization mechanism of *will*-sentences discussed in Section 5.5, the predictability use of BGT-sentences (a present reference use) stems from this interpretation by way of the following reasoning: a situation predicted to potentially occur repeatedly in the future constitutes a generic state of affairs as a superordinate situation that will obtain in the future and it is highly possible to infer that such a state of affairs has already obtained at speech time due to its homogeneous nature. This motivates the semantic extension of BGT-sentences from the future-generic interpretation to the present-generic interpretation.

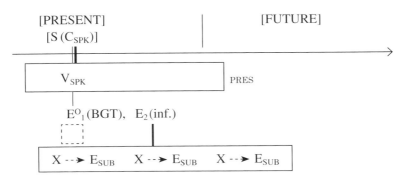

Figure 7: Temporal Structure of the Predictability Use of BGT-Sentences

Specific time notions such as S, PRESENT, and FUTURE are enclosed by square brackets because this use refers to a rather "super-temporal" situation. The long rectangle beneath E_2 symbolizes the superordinate situation involved (connected by a bold line) and E_2 is a time at which the situation holds. The square consisting of broken lines beneath E^O_1 indicates a semantically bleached preliminary stage, which merely serves as a place to view the superordinate situation associated with the infinitive. The trace of future orientation is reflected as a time gap (represented by a broken arrow) in an individual relation between a causing situation X and the caused situation E_{SUB}. The reason why this use of BGT-sentences is somehow considered to convey predictive nuances is that it can be paraphrased by the formula observed in the case of the W-generic use of *will*-sentences, i.e. 'whenever x happens, it is predictable that y happens' (Section 5.4.5). Since a specific situation is not under consideration here, the temporal focus is not in operation.

By way of illustration, consider (22):

(22) a. Even though we've got this wretched document we're talking about there's always going to be an Asterix book by the bedside or something like that. (=(1e))
  b. You could have the worst day of practice, competition—never give up. There is always going to be something better. (COCA)
  c. But you know, that's capitalism, you know. There is always going to be that gulf and there aren't very many rich people in America. (COCA)

(22b), for instance, refers to a superordinate situation (e.g. the speaker's belief that every time something bad happens, something better follows) consisting of the repetition of the same type of individual relationship between a causing situation (e.g. experiencing something bad)—triggered by the preceding sentence *You could have the worst day of practice, competition*—and the caused situation (e.g. experiencing something better). The trace of future orientation is reflected in this relationship, but not in the relationship between the fully bleached situation (associated with E^O_1) and the superordinate situation (associated with E_2). The superordinate situation modified by a time adverb meaning 'all the time' holds for a longer time span including speech time and there is therefore no before-after (and cause-effect) relationship between the event times of the infinitive and *be going to*, which coincides with speech time. The presence of *always* enables the superordinate situation to be rather supertemporal and thus a generic state of affairs.

I now turn to the other present reference use, i.e. the inferential-present use. This use of BGT-sentences is characterized by the observation that it expresses "speaker's certainty and expectation of the hearer's future information state" (Traugott (1995: 35, 2006: 115)). This characterization is closely related to the notion of future verification associated with the French simple future with present time reference discussed in Section 5.6.3.3. Let me clarify how this use of BGT-sentences obtains such a characterization. As with their simple-future use (Section 6.4.4), the preliminary stage becomes a "mere shell" with all parts constituting it (i.e. the onset, process, and coda) bleached, retaining the trace of future orientation alone, and the event time of *be going to* therefore serves as an orientational event time (E^O_1). The infinitival situation is specific and stative (i.e. a single continuing state). Again, we can guess that stative situations that will obtain in the future may have already obtained at speech time and E^O_1. Hence the present time reference of this type of BGT-sentences arises. The trace of future orientation here allows the speaker to be assured that the situation already obtaining at speech time will be verified when he/she confirms it in the (immediate) future, on the one hand, and to expect that the hearer will notice it when thinking of it, on the other. It is, so to speak, retained in our mental calculation.

The temporal structure of this use of BGT-sentences is schematized in Figure 8.

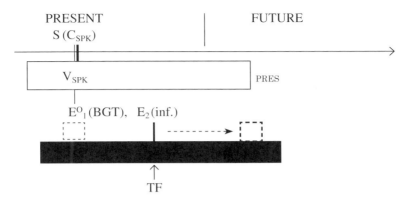

Figure 8: Temporal Structure of the Inferential-Present Use of BGT-Sentences

The semantic content of the situation associated with *be going to* is fully bleached (represented by the square with thin broken lines), which is associated with $E^O{}_1$. The infinitival situation obtaining at speech time, associated with E_2, is symbolized by the black rectangle. The trace of future orientation, represented by the broken arrow, links the present portion of the situation (corresponding to E_2) to the future portion corresponding to the time when the speaker will confirm it and the hearer will notice it, i.e. the portion represented by the square with bold broken lines. Unlike the predictability use, the inferential-present use refers to a specific infinitival situation and the temporal focus (TF) is thus directed at the event time of the infinitival situation (E_2).

To illustrate the point, consider (23):

(23) a. Petaluma is going to be sixty miles north of here. (=(1f))
 b. An accident has been reported on Crockett Boulevard. — That is going to be South of Crockett. (requoted from Traugott (1995: 35))

In (23a), for example, the speaker is confident that if not only he/she but also the hearer actually calculates the distance to Petaluma after this utterance, they will verify the truth of the information at that time.[34] The infinitival situation itself refers to the present, but the speaker has in mind the future time when

---

[34] The BGT-sentences in (i), which Williams (2002a: 201) considers to be able to be paraphrased into sentences with epistemic *will*, can be explained along the lines sketched here.
 (i) a. He's going to be having lunch at this time, isn't he? (Williams (2002a: 201))
 b. Manchester United beat Chelsea earlier this afternoon. Keith's going to be furious about that. He drove up specially from London to see the match.
 (Williams (2002a: 201))

he/she will confirm it and the hearer will notice it. The trace of future orientation contributes to the process of future verification.

I speak of the use in question as the inferential-present use, not the predictive-present use, because BGT-sentences in main or independent clauses do not convey predictive modality but are accompanied by assertive modality. Predictive nuances, i.e. "non-assertive" nuances, conveyed by this type of BGT-sentences are derived from the nature of inference: inference is always accompanied by some uncertainty.

Before closing this sub-section, let us briefly compare the inferential-present use of BGT-sentences with the predictive-present use of *will*-sentences. Although basically similar to each other, they are different in at least two respects. First, the future orientation and the future portion of the situation expected to be verified — represented respectively by the broken arrow and the square with bold broken lines in the cognitive schema of Figure 8 — are not reflected in the temporal structure of the predictive-present use of *will*-sentences (see Figure 7 in Section 5.4.4). Second, BGT-sentences in their inferential-present use do not carry predictive modality, whereas *will*-sentences in their predictive-present use do.

6.4.6. Speech Act Uses

Before moving to the relationship among the temporal structures of semantic uses of BGT-sentences, let us briefly consider some speech act uses (Coates (1983: 202–203), Collins (2009: 148–149)). Above all, I will deal with what Collins (2009) calls "deontic uses". Consider (24):

(24) a.   You're going to try and be bit earlier.

(requoted from Collins (2009: 148))

  b.   Now with your hand still on the front brake we're going to put the bike on its side stand.   (requoted from Collins (2009: 148))

These BGT-sentences are interpreted as giving an order or instruction to someone, usually the addressee. This notion is based on an obligation under which the speaker places someone to actualize the infinitival situation (Collins (2009: 148)). Within my framework, these deontic uses are pragmatic variants stemming from the typical uses of BGT-sentences when they are addressed to the addressee/hearer (i.e. in the situation report tier).

Take, for example, (24a), whose speech act meaning is an instruction or order. In the situation construal tier, i.e. when the private self of the current speaker judges or evaluates the situation involved, he/she makes an assertion about the preliminary stage (e.g. an imagined situation in which the addressee is "under way" to change his/her action pattern) ongoing at speech time to-ward the actualization of the infinitival situation (i.e. the addressee's being a little earlier). This is an instance of the typical use of BGT-sentences because it has the same temporal structure as the one in Figure 2 above. In the situa-tion report tier, however, the speech act meaning of instruction or order, i.e. an addressee-oriented speaker's mental attitude, is conveyed due to the interaction between the second-person subject, the semantic content of the BGT-sentence involved, and the context: by referring to the result situation which the speaker wants to actualize, he/she can metonymically imply the instruction or order which brings about that situation (cf. Panther and Thornburg (1998)).

6.5. The Relationship among the Temporal Structures Associated with the Semantic Uses of BGT-Sentences

Now, we will briefly consider, in terms of grammaticalization, the relation-ship among the temporal structures associated with the semantic uses of BGT-sentences observed in the previous sub-sections. First, it is well known that the basic meaning of BGT-sentences is derived through grammaticalization from the spatial meaning of 'agent on a path toward goal' (Traugott (1995: 36), Torres-Cacoullos and Walker (2009: 331)) and the first use of BGT-sen-tences would be the volitional one. This is in keeping with the observation by Danchev, et al. (1965: 376) that at the beginning, BGT-sentences had only the volitional (i.e. modal) use. Next, when BGT-sentences came to express men-tal experiences and/or be used with an inanimate subject, they developed the predictive-future use by means of pragmatic strengthening (Traugott (1995: 35–36); cf. also Langacker (1990: 23)). BGT-sentences at an earlier stage of grammaticalization were thus used to indicate that the preliminary stage is on-going at speech time toward the actualization of the infinitival situation and its schematic situation is specified by the interaction between their temporal structure, other semantic factors and the context. These characteristics are common to the volitional use, the predictive-future use, and the immediate-fu-ture use, as we saw above.

Now, as grammaticalization proceeded further, BGT-sentences came to be compatible with stative situations described by the infinitive (Hopper and Traugott (1993: 61, 2003: 69)). This stage may correspond to the bleached-coda and simple-future uses in this study. Since at least the coda is bleached in the temporal structures of these uses, stative situations can appear in the in-finitival position. With respect to the bleached-onset use, as far as I know, no previous studies have pointed it out. I do not have enough empirical data now, but theoretically speaking, it is desirable that the bleached-onset use should have arisen before the advent of the simple-future use. This is because the degree of semantic bleaching of the bleached-onset use is less than that of the simple-future use (cf. also Wada (2001a: §7.6.2)).

Furthermore, this study has observed two present reference uses, i.e. the predictability use and the inferential-present use, the latter corresponding to the one referred to as inferential *be going to* in Traugott (2006: 115). As observed in Section 5.5, the present reference uses of *will*-sentences have stemmed from their future reference uses. By analogy, we can assume that the present reference uses of BGT-sentences have also stemmed from their future reference uses. This assumption is at least conceptually motivated, because BGT-sentences first developed future reference uses and the present reference uses considered in this chapter then occurred through semantic bleaching, retaining only the trace of future orientation in their temporal structures.

If grammaticalization has proceeded the way we observed above, we can explain (i) why the present reference uses of BGT-sentences have not been described thus far in most grammar books and monographs, but have only recently been dealt with in some studies concerning grammaticalization, and (ii) why we can only find a few examples of the present reference uses in corpora such as the BNC and COCA. Because BGT-sentences started going through the grammaticalization process later than *will*-sentences and are therefore rather new members of the category "future" (Bybee and Pagliuca (1987)), we can explain the fact that the number of examples of the predictability and inferential-present uses of BGT-sentences is smaller than that of the characteristic-behavior and predictive-present uses of *will*-sentences; after all, the uses in question are located at a later stage on the grammaticalization path.

It must be repeated here that this study attempts to provide a temporal structure analysis of future expressions in English from a synchronic point of view. For this reason, we have mainly dealt with which uses of BGT-sentences are semantic (i.e. have different temporal structures) and which uses are pragmatic (i.e. share the same temporal structure) in present-day English. However, notions such as semantic retention and semantic bleaching (i.e. notions used to describe the grammaticalization path) contribute to the construction of the temporal structures of semantic uses and so we cannot avoid touching on the relationship among the semantic uses of BGT-sentences on the grammaticalization path. Unlike this study, many (at least some) studies argue that in present-day English BGT-sentences have fully grammaticalized, constituting a future tense form in that they place no restriction on future time reference, or a modalized form in that they can be used to make inference with re-

Chapter 6   *Be Going To*

spect to a present situation. These studies, however, cannot answer (i) why certain uses of BGT-sentences are not so developed in comparison with the corresponding uses of *will*-sentences, as we have seen, and (ii) why many native speakers still need at least the notion of future orientation in order to choose BGT-sentences or prefer BGT-sentences to *will*-sentences in some cases. These matters will be discussed in the next section.

6.6.   Comparison between BGT-Sentences and *Will*-Sentences

6.6.1.   Near Future, State Verbs

As announced at the end of the last section, this section explores a number of differences between BGT-sentences and *will*-sentences to more clarify the characteristics of BGT-sentences.[35] By showing that the differences can be explained systematically in our model, we will enhance its validity.

Let us start with two phenomena which were hot topics at least a few decades ago but are rather obsolete now. It was once argued that in comparison with *will*-sentences, BGT-sentences (i) tend to refer to the near future (Binnick (1972), Coates (1983: 199–200), Declerck (1991a: 114–115), Eckardt (2006: Ch. 4), Fleischman (1982), Wekker (1976: 132–133)),[36] and (ii) hardly co-occur with state verbs (Leech (1971: 55), Declerck (1991a)). Recent studies tend not to mention such differences, but many of them instead regard the two future expressions as semantically almost the same, i.e. interchangeable with each other with little change of meaning, at least as far as the two phenomena are concerned (Leech (2004), Copley (2009), Torres-Cacoullos and Walker (2009); cf. Coates (1983: 199–201)).[37]

---

[35] It is often reported that BGT-sentences are preferred to *will*-sentences in spoken language (e.g. Wekker (1976: 124)). On the other hand, it is pointed out (e.g. Berglund (2000a)) that *be gonna* tends to be used in spoken language while *be going to* tends to be used in written language. These differences seem to be related to the grammaticalization of BGT-sentences.

[36] As observed with respect to (13) in this chapter, the fact that BGT-sentences can co-occur with time adverbials referring to the remote future suggests that an analysis of BGT-sentences based on a notion like near future or imminence, e.g. Eckardt (2006: 120)— which is a truth-conditional semantic approach—is not tenable.

[37] As a piece of evidence for this position, both *will*-sentences and BGT-sentences can refer to the remote future and in that case the two future expressions are interchangeable with each other with little change of meaning, as illustrated by the following pair of examples (Leech (2004: 60)):

(i) a.   The whole idea of the digital computer will be obsolete in fifty years.

(Leech (2004: 60))

   b.   The whole idea of the digital computer is going to be obsolete in fifty years.

228   *The Grammar of Future Expressions in English*

However, we should pay attention to the fact that such differences were certainly observed in the literature (e.g. Wekker (1976)) a few decades ago or more. To simply say that the semantics of BGT-sentences have come closer to those of *will*-sentences these days does not explain why there were once differences between the two future expressions with respect to the two phenomena mentioned above, or even why there are still differences between them with respect to the linguistic phenomena to be observed in the following sub-sections. In my temporal structure analysis, they will be explained systematically and in a motivated way.

Let us first explain the two phenomena concerning BGT-sentences. As for the reference to the near future, it is natural to infer that the preliminary stage already ongoing at speech time toward the actualization of the infinitival situation will come into existence in the near future. For this reason, BGT-sentences refer to the near future by default. However, this is a pragmatic implicature and cancellable. Given an appropriate context, the preliminary stage can extend further into the future, as exemplified by (13) above. From a cognitive point of view, we can safely reason that if the preliminary stage is extremely prolonged, we tend not to regard it as ongoing any more (because we usually relate ongoingness to tentative or timely limited situations); the notion of ongoingness is virtually nullified in the case of the prolonged preliminary stage. Those who stick to the ongoingness of the preliminary stage find it difficult for BGT-sentences to refer to the remote future; those who give priority to the cognitive reasoning mentioned above find it easier for BGT-sentences to refer to the remote future. We can therefore explain the first question by claiming that more people adhered to the aspect of ongoingness of the preliminary stage a few decades ago, but less people do so now.

As for the compatibility with state verbs, we may assume that the grammaticalization of BGT-sentences has proceeded further in these several decades. There seemed to be a tendency that more people give priority to the typical uses over the bleached coda and simple-future uses when using BGT-

---

(Leech (2004: 60))

However, Wekker (1976: 133), a rather classical work, observes some differences between them. For example, in the case of *will*-sentences the speaker has in mind a possibility that the infinitival situation will not come true, but it is not the case with BGT-sentences. In the analysis we are developing, this is due to the temporal structure of the typical uses of BGT-sentences, which suggests that the preliminary stage for the actualization of the infinitival situation is ongoing at speech time and the infinitival situation will therefore come about unless prevented by external factors. Note, in passing, that I have already explained elsewhere (Wada (2001a: 234)) how BGT-sentences refer to the remote future.

Chapter 6 *Be Going To*

sentences. However, as time went by, the bleached-coda and simple-future uses came to be used more and more (Sections 6.4.3 and 6.4.4). The absence of the coda does not require change of state and hence allows state verbs— representing an unbounded situation—to appear in infinitive position.

Now, I turn to the two phenomena concerning *will*-sentences. In the temporal structures of the three future reference uses of *will*-sentences, i.e. the volitional use, the predictive-future use, and the simple-future use (Figures 4, 5 and 6 in Chapter 5), what obtains at speech time is not the preliminary stage ongoing toward the actualization of the infinitival situation, but a volition, prediction, or assertion with respect to the infinitival situation. These temporal structures do not entail the notion of something already ongoing toward the future actualization of the situation involved, nor do they require the infinitive in the complement position of *will* to express change of state.[38] These differences in the temporal structures of the two future expressions suggest that the *will*-sentences are, in the first place, not subject to the restrictions that the BGT-sentences are potentially subject to.

6.6.2. Volition

A third difference between BGT-sentences and *will*-sentences is concerned with volition. The present framework can systematically deal with the difference. As shown in Section 6.4.1, the volitional use of BGT-sentences indicates that the grammatical subject has already made a decision and what obtains or is ongoing at speech time is a mental state of the grammatical subject that comes into existence after that decision. That is, all of the content of the BGT-sentence in question belongs to the proposition (P) domain and the private self of the speaker construes it with assertive modality; BGT-sentences themselves do not contain any modal and the grammatical subject is not a potential speaker, not playing the role of private self. On the other hand, as observed in Section 5.4.1, the volitional reading of *will*-sentences indicates that the grammatical subject is a potential speaker (serving as private self) and makes a decision at the very time of the utterance (i.e. speech time), or just

---

[38] For Wekker (1976: 132–133), BGT-sentences cannot be paraphrased into *will*-sentences because the former refer to the near future but the latter do not. In my analysis, the reason why *will*-sentences do not refer to the near future by default is due to the characteristics of their temporal structures shown in the main text. Such a reference is an implication deriving from the characteristics. Thus, when adverbials referring to the very immediate future such as *in a minute* or *in a moment* are added, such an implication is overridden and therefore *will*-sentences with future time reference can refer to the near future, as in (i):

    (i)   "In a minute I'll lose my nerve. What's the number?" (E. Segal, *Love Story*, p. 123)

before it, in reaction to the speech situation or the preceding context (Coates (1983: 200), Declerck (1991a: 112–113), Leech (2004: 87), Wekker (1976: 127)). When the current speaker and the grammatical subject share the same identity, the volition in question is regarded as an S-attitude of the current speaker in the situation report tier and the volitional reading involved is the volitional use of *will*-sentences. What is crucial is that the volition associated with BGT-sentences in their volitional use is part of the situation to be described (i.e. a P-domain element) while the volition associated with *will*-sentences in their volitional use is a speaker's S-attitude (i.e. an element of the situation-oriented speaker's attitude domain). This difference is nicely reflected in the different temporal structures of BGT-sentences in their typical uses and *will*-sentences in their volitional use: the preliminary stage associated with *be going to* has started before and is ongoing at speech time, whereas the volition associated with *will* occurs only at or just before speech time in reaction to the speech situation or preceding context.

To illustrate the point, observe (25)–(27):

(25) a. I've bought a typewriter. I'm going to do the paperwork myself in future. (Declerck (1991a: 112))

    b. It's dark in here. —Don't worry. I'll fetch a torch.

(Declerck (1991a: 113))

(26) a. I'm going to give you a hand. (=(9b))

    b. I'll give you a hand. (=(9a))

(27) a. I've sold my car; I'm going to take up cycling. (Wekker (1976: 127))

    b. "I can't open this box." "I'll do it for you." (Wekker (1976: 127))

For example, the BGT-sentence in (26a) can be interpreted as suggesting that the grammatical subject has already made up his/her mind about what he/she proposes to do and the mental state following that decision is ongoing or obtains at speech time. The point here is that the speaker construes the situation in question in such a way that the volition is seen as ongoing at speech time. This is compatible with the temporal structure of BGT-sentences of the volitional use (Figure 2 in Section 6.4.1) which includes the preliminary stage ongoing at speech time (e.g. the speaker is in preparation for helping the addressee in his/her mind).

As for the volition accompanying *will*-sentences, consider (25b) and (27b), for instance. It is implied that in reaction to the preceding utterances, the grammatical subject (as private self) of the *will*-sentences makes a decision at speech time or just before it and the volition is finally regarded as an S-attitude of the current speaker (because the current speaker and the grammatical

Chapter 6   *Be Going To*

subject share the same identity). The temporal structure in Figure 4 in Section 5.4.1 indicates that the volition in question occurs at or just before speech time and the infinitival situation involved will be actualized in the future relative to the time of the decision in the grammatical subject's mental world created by his/her decision. In this way, the third difference can be straightforwardly explained by the temporal structures of BGT-sentences in their typical uses and *will*-sentences in their volitional use.

6.6.3.   Ellipticality

A fourth difference between BGT-sentences and *will*-sentences is that *will*-sentences sound "somewhat odd" as they stand (Wekker (1976: 124)) or "elliptical" (Binnick (1972: 3)), whereas BGT-sentences sound "perfectly normal" as they stand (Binnick (1972), Wekker (1976)).[39]   Compare (28) and (29):

(28) a.   The rock'll fall.   (Binnick (1972: 3))
    b.   In fact, she will die.   (Binnick (1972: 3))
(29) a.   The rock is going to fall.   (Binnick (1972: 3))
    b.   As it happens, she's going to die.   (Binnick (1972: 3))

The "ellipticality" problem is resolved if a conditional clause is added or a condition is retrievable from the preceding context (Binnick (1972: 3), Wekker (1976: 127)). For example, (28a) would be perfect if embedded in a context like (30a) or (30b).

(30) a.   The rock'll fall if you pull the wedge out from under it.

(Binnick (1972: 3))

    b.   Don't pull the wedge out from under boulder, you nitwit! The
       rock'll fall.   (Binncik (1972: 3))

Although this type of difference is often regarded as a pragmatic implicature, I argue that it stems from the differences of their temporal structures. Let us assume that some *will*-sentences contain the "elliptical" part in their semantics. We can then claim that the elliptical part provides a condition for the actualization of the infinitival situation of the *will*-sentences and the speaker judges with predictive modality that there is a causal relation between the

---

[39] Wekker (1976: 127) explains this difference by appealing to the future orientation of *will*-sentences and the present orientation of BGT-sentences. Since BGT-sentences are present-oriented, all necessary conditions for the occurrence of the situation involved are met at speech time. By contrast, since *will*-sentences are future-oriented, such conditions are not met at speech time and therefore sound elliptical unless they are explicitly given.

"elliptical" (or implied) condition and the content of the infinitival situation. In Section 5.4.2, I presented the temporal structure of the predictive-future use of *will*-sentences (Figure 5 in Chapter 5), which reflects predictive modality as a speaker's S-attitude. As implied in the definition of predictive modality (see (6) in Section 3.4), for the speaker to make a prediction about the infinitival situation, external or internal factors are necessary as conditions which enable the speaker to believe that the infinitival situation will be actualized. The addressee (hearer) is supposed to identify the conditions in interpreting the *will*-sentence at issue. Since the infinitival situation of the *will*-sentence is assumed to occur in the future, the condition for it is assumed to occur before it, usually at a time later than speech time, due to the nature of direct causation. The condition is clarified when specified by an *if*-clause or preceding sentence, as in the case of (30) above.

The temporal structure of *will*-sentences with elliptical conditions is thus schematized in Figure 9, where the capitalized E-CONDITION means an elliptical condition and the bold vertical arrow indicates that the condition is assumed to occur just before, or occur (conceptually) simultaneously with, the infinitival situation represented by the black rectangle. If such a condition cannot be identified, the causal relation in question is not met and hence the sense of ellipticality arises.

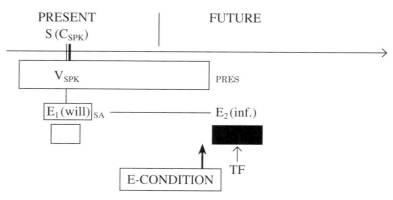

Figure 9: Temporal Structure of the Future Reference Uses of *Will*-Sentences with "Elliptical" Conditions

On the other hand, BGT-sentences in their typical uses have a temporal structure (Figure 2 in this chapter) which includes the preliminary stage ongoing at speech time toward the actualization of the infinitival situation. Since the preliminary stage can serve as a cause—whether subjective or objective—

Chapter 6   *Be Going To*

for the actualization of the infinitival situation, this type of BGT-sentence as it stands satisfies the condition for the actualization of the infinitival situation and therefore other conditions are not necessary. Thus, in (31a) below, the first sentence is not interpreted as providing a condition for the actualization of the infinitival situation; the rock is already about to fall and the sitting on that rock is not a cause for the rock's fall (Binnick (1972), Wekker (1976)).

(31) a.   Don't sit on that rock.   It's going to fall.
                                    (Wekker (1976: 128); cf. Palmer (1974))
     b.   We're going to get rid of our teacher and then we're going to be happy.
                                    (Wekker (1976: 128))

Similarly, in (31b), there is no causal relation between the two BGT-sentences: the situation of the speaker and his/her fellows getting rid of their teacher does not cause the situation of their being happy. The preliminary stages of the two BGT-sentences are separately on their way to the actualization of the infinitival situations.

6.6.4.   Conditional Sentences

As a fifth difference between BGT-sentences and *will*-sentences, let us consider their behaviors with respect to conditional sentences. As stated in many grammar books and monographs (e.g. Leech (1987, 2004), Palmer (1988: §7.4), Wekker (1976: §7.2)), it is generally the case that BGT-sentences (as main clauses) cannot be used with *if*-clauses intended to refer to the future fulfillment of a condition, as in (32) (Declerck (1991a: 115), Leech (2004: 60)), while *will*-sentences can, as in (33).

(32) a. *You are going to learn to drive a car proficiently if you take this
            course.   (Declerck (1991a: 115))
     b.?*If you pay by cash you are normally going to obtain a receipt as
            proof of payment.   (Leech (2004: 60))
(33) a.   You will learn to drive a car proficiently if you take this course.
                                                       (Declerck (1991a: 115))
     b.   If you pay by cash you will normally obtain a receipt as proof of
            payment.   (Leech (2004: 60))

However, if *if*-clauses are intended to refer to the present fulfillment of a condition, then BGT-sentences can be used with them, as in (34).

(34) a. ["I've lost my passport."] — "If you have lost your passport, you're going to have a lot of trouble with the police."

(Declerck (2006: 354); cf. Declerck (1991a: 115))

b. We're going to find ourselves in difficulty if we go on like this.

(Leech (2004: 60))

c. "Oliver, you're gonna flunk out if you just sit there watching me study." "I'm not watching you study. I'm studying." "Bullshit. You're looking at my legs." "Only once in a while. Every chapter."

(E Segal, *Love Story*, p. 47)

I have already explained the compatibility of the two future expressions with conditional clauses elsewhere (Wada (2001a: §7.5.2.1)), but for convenience's sake, I will repeat the point of my explanation there. First, when *will*-sentences appear in the main clauses (i.e. apodoses) of type A conditional sentences (i.e. conditional sentences of the direct cause-effect type), the situation described by the conditional clause (i.e. protasis) as a cause is interpreted as coming (just) before that described by the main clause. Such a causal relation is predicted to hold in the future by the speaker at speech time. We can thus modify the temporal structure in Figure 9 in Section 6.6.3 by replacing the E-CONDITION part with the conditional clause situation representing a condition for the occurrence of the main clause situation and regard the modified temporal structure as the one for *will*-sentences in the main clause of type A conditional sentences. Hence (33) is acceptable.

On the other hand, the temporal structure of the typical uses of BGT-sentences (Figure 2 in this chapter) includes the preliminary stage ongoing at speech time toward the actualization of the infinitival situation. This suggests that when conditional clauses refer to the future fulfillment of conditions, they cannot serve as the conditions for the actualization of the infinitival situations of BGT-sentences because the preliminary stage for the actualization of the infinitival situation is already ongoing at speech time; in other words, the preliminary stage serves as a cause for the infinitival situation involved. Therefore, another condition serving as a cause for the infinitival situation cannot be added without contradiction. Hence the unacceptability of (32).

By contrast, as shown in (34), if conditional clauses refer to conditions which have already been given before speech time or are already ongoing (or obtain) at speech time, we can regard them as causes for the preliminary stages which have occurred before speech time (e.g. (34a)) or as "specifiers" of the preliminary stages obtaining at speech time (e.g. (34b) and (34c)). This observation is compatible with the temporal structure of the typical uses of

Chapter 6 *Be Going To*

BGT-sentences. What we have thus far seen with respect to the compatibility between the two future expressions and type A conditional clauses has already been stated in my previous work.

However, in fact, there are cases where BGT-sentences co-occur with conditional clauses referring to the future fulfillment of a condition. For example, Copley (2009: 105) observes that the conditional clauses in (35) can be interpreted as open conditionals expressing direct causation.[40, 41, 42]

---

[40] This suggests that the examples in (35) can basically express the same meaning as their *will* counterparts; the situation referred to by the conditional clause can serve as a cause for the occurrence of the situation referred to by the main clause. Whether a given conditional clause refers to the future or the present depends ultimately on the interaction between the semantic content of the conditional clause, its relationship to the semantic content of the main clause, and the context. However, even in the case of the future fulfillment of the condition involved, the occurrence of the infinitival situation of the BGT-sentence is sometimes not based on the *if*-clause situation. For example, Copley (2009) states that the more natural reading of (35a) is such that at the time when the baby comes to cry, we will find that the sign of the baby's vomiting (i.e. the preliminary stage for the actualization of her vomiting) was already indicated at speech time. She calls this reading an "indication" reading. In the indication reading, the conditional sentence involved is interpreted in such a way that "IF P, IT INDICATES Q", and there is no direct causal relation between P and Q. This implies that the conditional clauses in question are type B conditional clauses within my framework, i.e. conditional clauses consisting not only of the proposition (P) domain but also of the speaker's attitude (SA) domain. On the other hand, a conditional clause like the one in (35b) can refer to a type of situation that the addressee is supposed to carry out in the future and hence (35b) usually does not receive an indication reading. In a case like (35b), the reading in which the occurrence of the infinitival situation is based on the *if*-clause situation is preferable. This reading of conditional sentences with *be going to* is basically the same as that of type A conditional sentences with *will*.

[41] Copley (2009) offers a formal semantic analysis with such notions as "scope" in the spirit of minimalist program.

[42] The following example, taken from Sato (2016), is an authentic example of the indication reading, cited from a film scenario.

(i) "Look, George. I'm telling you, George, if you do not ask Lorraine to that dance, I'm *gonna* regret it for the rest of my life." (Screenplay, *Back to the Future*, p. 102)

In this science fiction film, before this scene, the speaker of this BGT-sentence, Marty, came from the future with a time machine and happened to interfere with the first meeting of his parents, i.e. George and Lorraine. At the time of this scene, Lorraine begins to be attracted to Marty, her future son. If she does not marry George, she will not give birth to Marty. Marty is now worrying about that. To avoid such a situation, he must arrange the meeting of his parents. However, George is shy and seems not to ask Lorraine to a certain dance. Under this context, something like his unwillingness to ask her for a date can regarded as the preliminary stage ongoing at speech time and Marty is already on the way to regretting the unfulfillment of the date.

(35) a. If the baby cries, she's going to spit up. (Copley (2009: 105))
b. If you hold the baby horizontally, she's going to spit up.
(Copley (2009: 105))

In the present analysis, these BGT-sentences (in the intended reading) basically have the temporal structure of the simple-future use (Figure 6 in this chapter), a rather recent use derived through further grammaticalization.[43] In this temporal structure, the verbal unit *be going to* does not describe a full-fledged preliminary stage ongoing at speech time toward the actualization of the infinitival situation but a semantically bleached one, and as a result, the event time associated with *be going to* is seen as an orientational type. This suggests that as long as a before-after relationship—the presupposition for a causal relation—is preserved, the situation described by the conditional clause can refer to the future and serve as the condition for the actualization of the infinitival situation. Therefore, BGT-sentences of this type can co-occur with type A conditional clauses, as exemplified by (35) above.

Henceforth, I refer to BGT-sentences used in the main clause of type A conditional sentences as the "future-condition" use. The temporal structure of this use of BGT-sentences is schematized in Figure 10.

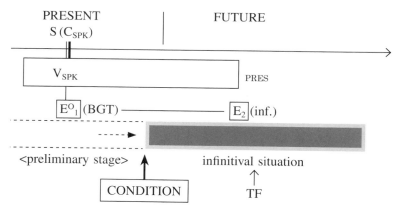

Figure 10: Temporal Structure of the Future-Condition Use of BGT-Sentences

---

[43] In Wada (2009a: 127), I argued that the BGT-sentence in (i)—for at least some native speakers a type-A-conditional reading is possible—has a temporal structure which corresponds to that of the simple-future use in this study with one difference, namely that the speaker's S-attitude accompanying the BGT-sentence was predictive modality.
(i) You're going to break that chair if you're not careful. (Close (1981: 83))
In the present analysis, the speaker's S-attitude in question is regarded as assertive modality.

Chapter 6   *Be Going To*

This temporal structure is basically the same as that of the simple-future use in Figure 6 above, except that the temporal information concerning the conditional clause situation (represented by CONDITION) is added. The preliminary stage is semantically bleached and does not depict a semantically contentful situation. In this respect, this use is equivalent to the simple-future use. Moreover, both uses are accompanied by assertive modality because they appear in main clauses, i.e. clauses involving a speaker's S-attitude in their semantic (de)composition, and this modality is the unmarked one in this environment. However, the addition of information about the condition for the actualization of the infinitival situation to the temporal structure has an influence on the degree of certainty of the future-condition use. That is, although the future-condition use of BGT-sentences is accompanied by assertive modality, it conveys the lesser degree of certainty about the infinitival situation, i.e. predictive overtones. This is because the actualization of the infinitival situation depends crucially on the type of condition and the infinitival situation is not a direct target of the assertion (cf. Section 6.3.2).

To illustrate the point, take, for example, (35b) above. When evaluating the situation described by this sentence, the speaker construes it with assertive modality: he/she asserts that when the condition (i.e. the addressee's holding the baby horizontally) is imposed at a time later than speech time, carrying it out leads to the actualization of the infinitival situation (i.e. the baby's vomiting). Because the preliminary stage of this use of BGT-sentences is semantically bleached and only the trace of future orientation is implied in the temporal structure, the use in question is freed from the restriction imposed on the typical uses of BGT-sentences, namely that a condition for the actualization of the infinitival situation has already been given before speech time or is already given at speech time, as illustrated by (34) above. In this type of BGT-sentences, the asserted situation is based on whether or not the condition is fulfilled and therefore they convey predictive overtones. This is the mechanism in which BGT-sentences co-occur with conditional clauses describing the condition which will be fulfilled in the future.[44]

---

[44] Dancygier and Sweetser (2005: 82) make an interesting observation that BGT-sentences (as main clauses) describing first-person actions can indicate predictions about negative outcomes (such as threats) closely connected to the causes represented by the conditional clauses, as exemplified in (i):

(i)   "If I break another nail I'm going to scream."

(requoted from Dancygier and Sweetser (2005: 82))

Dancygier and Sweetser (2005: 82) state that in cases like the one in (i), a threat accompanying the BGT-sentence is "construed as inevitably causally tied to the antecedent". This

I have more to say about the type of speaker's mental attitude associated with the future-condition use of BGT-sentences. As indicated in Figure 10, the actualization of the infinitival situation is based on the condition indicated by the *if*-clause, which triggers a lesser degree of certainty, or prediction-like nuances, of the future-condition use in comparison with the simple-future use. This statement is supported by Copley's (2009: 105) observation that the future-condition use of BGT-sentences can be paraphrased into *will*-sentences co-occurring with type A conditional clauses, i.e. *will*-sentences in their predictive-future use. The situation to be actualized based on a certain condition is usually not viewed as absolutely certain to occur, because its actualization depends on the fulfillment of that condition. From these observations, I conclude that the BGT-sentence at issue takes on prediction-like nuances (i.e. a lesser degree of certainty), while it is accompanied by assertive modality.[45] The theoretical model adopted in this study accommodates this apparent paradox in the following manner: in temporal calculation, the BGT-sentence itself is accompanied by assertive modality, but when it is used with a type A conditional clause, it can convey prediction-like nuances due to the characteristics of the dependency relation between the conditional clause situation (as cause) and the infinitival situation of the BGT-sentence (as effect).

To further support the view that the future-condition use of BGT-sentences is accompanied by assertive modality, we can provide Wekker's (1976: 130–131) observation about the following examples (cf. also Palmer (1974)):

(36) a. If he comes in, I shall leave.   (Wekker (1976: 130))
     b. If he comes in, I'm going to leave.   (Wekker (1976: 130))

According to Wekker's informant, (36b) is more emphatic and expresses greater certainty than (36a). In my analysis, this is due to the difference of modality as speaker's S-attitude between the BGT-sentence and the *will*-sentence (the *shall*-sentence in this case). Since the BGT-sentence is accompanied by assertive modality, the speaker regards its infinitival situation as more certain to occur than the infinitival situation of the *shall*-sentence accompanied

---

might imply that BGT-sentences like the one in (i) have a temporal structure similar to the one for the typical uses of BGT-sentences, which involves an explicit preliminary stage triggering and thus causally tied to the occurrence of the future situation described by the infinitive. I leave this for future research.

[45] As we saw in Section 6.4.1, one of the typical uses of BGT-sentences, which are accompanied by assertive modality, can convey predictive overtones and thus be regarded as a predictive use, but it is a pragmatic variant within my framework.

Chapter 6 *Be Going To* 239

by predictive modality.[46]

In this connection, Sato (2016: 146–148) observes that when BGT-sentences like those in (35) above receive the intended reading (i.e. when they exemplify the future-condition use), they convey an intention or sign (or evidence) already in existence or ongoing at speech time, based on which the speaker argues that the causal relation between the conditional clause situation and the infinitival situation of the main clause will come into existence. Within my framework, the preliminary stage, though semantically bleached, induces the speaker (i.e. the chooser of this tense form) to have in mind a sign or piece of evidence at speech time, based on which he/she asserts that the causal relation will be actualized. In (35b), for instance, we may say that a certain sign or piece of evidence already existent at speech time is some background knowledge about the baby, which enables the speaker to assert that the addressee's holding the baby horizontally causes the baby's vomiting. As evidence that BGT-sentences in their future-condition use convey the sign or piece of evidence, Sato points out that BGT-sentences of this type when used with a future-oriented conditional clause often follow an expression like *X know(s)*. This expression suggests that the grammatical subject X knows something in existence or ongoing at speech time (which indicates the intention or sign available at speech time) and so does the speaker, whereby the speaker is able to assert that the causal relation in question will come into existence in the future. The following examples are requoted from Sato (2016: 154–155):

(37) Frankie: You are in a position to negotiate?
      Maggie: Yes sir, because I know if you train me right, I'm gonna be a
                champ.
(38) You know darned well that if it rains we're going to get wet. So we'd
      just better go prepared.

These examples may provide a linguistic motivation for the rise of the future-condition use of BGT-sentences.

---

[46] Wekker (1976: 131) further states that the BGT-sentence in (36b) is more likely to indicate warning or threat. This is also explainable within my framework. In the situation construal tier, the causal relation to hold in the future is asserted as if it were a fact and the degree of speaker's S-attitude is therefore higher in the BGT-sentence in (36b) than in the *shall*-counterpart in (36a). When the situation involved is conveyed to the addressee (i.e. in the situation report tier), it can be accompanied by speech acts based on the modality as speaker's S-attitude (in the case of the BGT-sentence, assertive modality). For this reason, the BGT-sentence is interpreted as conveying a strong speech act, such as stronger warning or threat, in comparison with the *will*-version (i.e. the *shall*-sentence).

240   *The Grammar of Future Expressions in English*

However, it must be noted that the predictive-future use of *will*-sentences in type A conditional sentences (i.e. a use corresponding to the future-condition use of BGT-sentences) can also follow an expression like *X know(s)*, as exemplified by (39) and (40).

(39)   I know that if my feet leave the floor of the cave then I'll float upwards and my head'll hit the ceiling and my skull'll get bashed in and I'll die.

                                                                   (BNC BMS)

(40)   Try to discipline yourself to work contracted hours only. If you want to indulge, get in half on hour early. Try to set the example for the rest of your organization. You know that if you kill yourself with fatigue, you'll have no hours left at all.   (BNC EW5)

This fact must also be explained from a unified point of view. In my approach, the combination of the BGT-sentence in its future-condition use with the expression *X know(s)* produces a different nuance from that of its *will*-sentence counterpart with the same expression with respect to the degree of certainty of the situation involved, whereas both of them have a higher degree of certainty or probability than the versions of BGT-sentences and *will*-sentences without the expression *X know(s)*.

First, as seen above, the BGT-sentence in question is accompanied by assertive modality, but the addition of a type A conditional clause to it reduces the certainty of the infinitival situation and the BGT-sentence thus conveys prediction-like nuances. In the same vein, the *will*-sentence in question is accompanied by predictive modality, but the addition of the same type of conditional to it produces a lower probability. On the other hand, the presence of an expression like *X know(s)* suggests a sign or piece of evidence available at speech time; by bothering to express who knows that the situation involved will be the case, the speaker tries to emphasize the existence of the sign or evidence. We can thus argue that the conditional sentences (including the BGT-sentence and the *will*-sentence) with the expression *X know(s)* are regarded as conveying a higher degree of certainty or probability than those without such an expression.

Before closing this sub-section, we will briefly consider BGT-sentences that appear in type B conditional clauses, i.e. conditional clauses consisting of the situation-oriented speaker's attitude (SSA) domain and the proposition (P) domain, as seen in Section 5.4.7. As observed in Section 6.4.1, when BGT-sentences appear in type A conditional clauses, they are not accompanied by any speaker's mental attitude. However, when they appear in type B conditional clauses, they are accompanied by a speaker's S-attitude, i.e. assertive modality.

Chapter 6   *Be Going To*   241

Consider (41):

(41) a. [Mrs. Thatcher at her first press conference after being elected leader
          of the Conservative Party]: "One will obviously consult with those in
          the Shadow Cabinet who will be responsible for economic policy.
          And, if you're going to ask me who those will be, I don't know. <Vo-
          lition>   (Wekker (1976: 131))
     b.   If you are going to turf a site, ask for a sample and make sure of be-
          ing at home when the turf is delivered. <Volition>
                                                                     (Wekker (1976: 132))
     c.   If uranium prices are going to swing in favour of fast reactors, they
          have a long way to go. <Prediction>   (BNC AB6)
     d.   ... if a prisoner is going to get after-care, he should know it as soon
          as he starts his sentence. <Prediction>
                                                        (requoted from Coates (1983: 202))

The protases are not in a direct causal relationship to the apodoses and hence
type B conditional clauses. Although the BGT-sentences in (41a, b) convey
volitional nuances and those in (41c, d) predictive (epistemic) nuances, both
types of BGT-sentences share the temporal structure of the typical uses, which
involves the preliminary stage (consisting of the onset, process, and coda
parts) ongoing at speech time. The conditional clauses in (41) can all be interpreted as indicating that something is already ongoing at speech time toward the actualization of the infinitival situation involved and the speaker's assertion is directed at the preliminary stage followed by the infinitival situation.
In (41c), for example, the speaker asserts that the sign of the change of uranium prices (indicated by the preliminary stage) is already in existence at
speech time, which leads to the actualization of the infinitival situation (i.e.
the swing of uranium prices) unless implied otherwise. The speaker regards
the infinitival situation as very likely to be actualized and therefore chooses
the BGT-sentence.

6.6.5. The Past Tense

Finally, let us compare BGT-sentences and *will*-sentences in the past tense.
I have already explained some basic differences between them elsewhere
(Wada (2001a: 259–260). In this section, I will consider more differences us-
ing the developed model.

It is generally said that in unembedded clauses, BGT-sentences in the past
tense often imply non-fulfillment of the infinitival situation at a time later than
the time of orientation in the past, whereas *will*-sentences in the past tense of-

ten imply fulfillment of the infinitival situation (Binnick (1971), Coates (1983), Quirk et al. (1985: 218–219), Declerck (1991a: 120–121, 2006: 453–455), Copley (2009: 87–88)), as exemplified by (42) and (43):[47]

(42) a. [Soon after that war ended,] another one would begin.

(Declerck (2006: 455))

    b. [He entered Parliament at the age of 31.] Five years later he would be the youngest Prime Minister the country had ever had.

(Declerck (2006: 455))

(43) a. The vase was going to fall, but at the last moment I caught it.

(Copley (2009: 88))

    b. I {was going to / *would} pay you a visit this afternoon, [but I have to attend an emergency meeting of the board.] (Declerck (2006: 453))

In both future expressions, the event time of *be going to* or *will* in the past tense is located in the past time-area, which serves as the time of orientation, i.e. a time from which to compute the event time of the infinitival situation in the future relative to that time of orientation. In this connection, Declerck (2006: 453) makes an interesting observation that in referring to "a past intention that was never fulfilled", the *will*-sentence is not allowed, and the BGT-sentence must be employed instead, as shown in (43b).

The observations made above involve two issues. One is why BGT-sentences in the past tense tend to imply non-fulfillment of the infinitival situation, whereas *will*-sentences in the past tense tend to imply fulfillment of the infinitival situation (issue (i)). The other issue is why *will*-sentences in the past tense are not allowed, but BGT-sentences in the past tense must be chosen, to imply a past volition (intention) leading to the non-fulfillment of the infinitival situation (issue (ii)). Some studies consider these differences to be pragmatic. For example, relevance-theoretic analyses (e.g. Haegeman (1989), Nicolle (1998)) do not regard the differences as semantic. However, within my framework, such differences are attributed to temporal structure differences and hence they are semantic. But this does not mean that pragmatic factors are irrelevant to the differences. The different temporal structures of BGT-

---

[47] The *will*-sentence in the past tense in (i) conveys the volition of the grammatical subject referred to by *he*, but whether the infinitival situation was fulfilled or not is unclear.

(i) He said that he would return and inform Will Douglas. (BNC CD8)

This is not a counterexample to the tendency shown in the main text because the linguistic environment here is different from the one we are discussing. Since the indirect speech complement is a quotation of private expression (Hirose (1995, 1997); cf. Section 3.5), it is not a linguistic environment where the speaker looks back at a past situation as a fact.

Chapter 6   *Be Going To*   243

sentences and *will*-sentences in the past tense interact with the characteristics of the relevant linguistic environment (including pragmatic factors) to bring about the differences in issues (i) and (ii).

As a premise, I assume that in choosing between competing expressions in the same linguistic environment, we tend to make semantic distinctions between them based on their prototypical uses or functions, which identify the raison d'etre of the expressions in question (this assumption will also be in operation in the following chapters). In the present theory, the semantic distinctions between temporal expressions (i.e. tense forms) are reflected in differences of their temporal structures. The comparisons in Sections 6.6.1 to 6.6.4 enable us to assume that BGT-sentences and *will*-sentences are competing future expressions in present-day English. In fact, Copley (2009) classifies both expressions into the same category "futures". This may be supported by the fact that numerous studies have thus far compared them as two major future expressions. Given these observations, BGT-sentences and *will*-sentences are competing expressions in "past contexts", i.e. contexts where the speaker looks back at past situations as facts.

Let us begin by explaining issue (ii). In general, especially in independent or main (i.e. unembedded) clauses, when the speaker sees a past situation as a fact from his/her own point of view situated at speech time (or the time of narration), he/she has already known whether it was actualized or not. In this case, the speaker can pinpoint a grammatical subject's volition (in the past) to pursue the past situation in question. Now, the Gricean maxim of Quantity comes into play. When the speaker knowing whether or not the past situation came into existence bothers to pinpoint the volition to pursue it, the implication would be that the speaker intends to convey that the situation itself did not happen or obtain; if it did or if what the speaker wanted to convey were the actualization of the situation itself, he/she would have chosen the simple past form, i.e. a tense form which can straightforwardly indicate the actualization of that situation.

One major reason for the speaker's reference to the volition of the grammatical subject in past contexts would be a communicative strategy. Within the present framework, this strategy works in the situation report tier and the public self of the speaker or narrator comes into play. By referring only to the past volition—which implies the non-actualization of the infinitival situation for the reason we saw above—the speaker as public self makes a strategic move so that he/she can introduce what he/she really wants to convey. In this communicative strategy, the past volition in question serves as a "base", or "reference point" in the sense of Langacker (1993), from which to have access to what the speaker really wants to convey, i.e. the target situation. In fact, in (43b) above, what the speaker really intends to convey to the addressee is the second sentence, i.e. the reason why the infinitival situation of the first sentence does not come into existence. The point here is that a sentence in the volitional use of the *will*-sentence or BGT-sentence in the past tense is used as a reference point for the target situation, often indicated by the sentence following the *will*-sentence or BGT-sentence in the past tense.

With these in mind, let us first consider the case of *will*-sentences in the past tense. Recall that in the present tense form, the volition associated with *will*-sentences occurs at the time of utterance (i.e. speech time) or just before it. In the past tense form, therefore, the time in question is a past time of orientation and the volition of the grammatical subject as private self occurs at or just before the past time of orientation from which to evaluate the target situation. From a cognitive point of view, we have easier access to an entity which has already been existent than an entity which has just happened or is just happening. This is because in the latter case, the two different cognitive processes, i.e. identifying the entity as a target and regarding it as a reference point for evaluating another target entity, occur (almost) simultaneously—a burden for the speaker and hearer. It is thus easier to regard the entity which has already been existent as a reference point for the target entity than the entity which has just happened or is just happening. This view is in keeping with the cognitive linguistic view that the target entity and the reference point correspond, respectively, to the Figure and the Ground, and entities characterized by the notion "more recently on the scene/in awareness" are the Figure, while those characterized by the notions "more backgrounded" or "once Figure is perceived" are the Ground (Talmy (2000: 316)). It is therefore difficult for the volition accompanying the *will*-sentence in the past tense (in the past context) to serve as a reference point for the target situation, e.g. the sentence headed by *but* in (43b) above, because the volition in question occurs at or just before the past time of orientation and tends to be regarded as the Figure.

Let us turn to the case of BGT-sentences in the past tense. As we have seen, BGT-sentences imply the volition of the grammatical subject which is already in existence at a time of orientation, i.e. a mental state of the grammatical subject that comes about after his/her decision to do something; the volition at issue is not an S-attitude of the grammatical subject as private self because the *be going to* in question is not a modal, i.e. an element evoking a cognizer or potential speaker, but an element belonging to the proposition domain, i.e. what is to be perceived. This characteristic is not compatible with the characteristics of the Figure mentioned above. The mental state accompanying the volitional use of BGT-sentences therefore serves as the Ground and qualifies as a reference point for the target entity as the Figure. For this reason, BGT-sentences in the past tense serve as an appropriate tense form to indicate the past volition of the subject's referent leading to the non-fulfillment of the relevant infinitival situation in the past context.

I now turn to issue (i). Let me start with BGT-sentences. As observed in Section 6.4.1, both the "volition" and "prediction" meanings accompanying BGT-sentences are based on the temporal structure in which the preliminary stage (consisting of the onset, process, and coda) is already ongoing at speech time toward the actualization of the infinitival situation; they are not speaker's S-attitudes. Among the semantic uses of BGT-sentences in the present tense observed above, the uses whose temporal structures preserve the essential parts of the preliminary stage (i.e. the portions expressing ongoingness) are the typical, immediate-future, bleached-onset, and bleached-coda uses, which are candidates for the use of BGT-sentences in the past context (implying something ongoing at the past time of orientation). Recall that what is at issue with respect to issue (i) is whether the infinitival situation is actualized in the past or not. This implies that the most important perspective with respect to the distinction among the four uses is whether or not there is a "break" between the preliminary stage and the infinitival situation. If there is one, it is conceptually possible that focusing on the preliminary stage does not lead to the actualization of the infinitival situation in terms of the temporal structure. The break occurs when the coda of the preliminary stage is bleached. Thus, the distinction based on whether the coda (a part of the temporal path represented by *to*) is bleached or not may affect the temporal calculation of BGT-sentences in the past tense in the past context, especially when we consider the matter of the fulfillment of their infinitival situation.

The temporal structure of the bleached-coda use of BGT-sentences in the past tense, which is relevant in explaining when and why BGT-sentences imply non-fulfillment of the infinitival situation in the past context, is schematically represented in Figure 11:

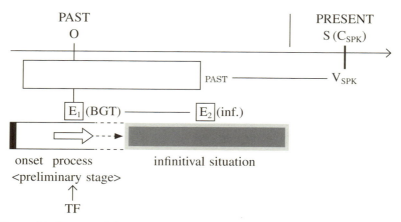

Figure 11: Temporal Structure of the Bleached-Coda Use of BGT-Sentences in the Past Tense

In this figure, the event time of the past tense verb (E_1) is located in the past time-sphere (grammatical past). In the default case, the speaker's t(emporal)-viewpoint (V_{SPK}) fuses with his/her consciousness (C_{SPK}) at speech time (S)— and this applies in the past context here—so that E_1 (i.e. the event time of the preliminary stage with which predictive or volitional nuances are associated) is located in the past time-area (cognitive past). The event time of the infinitive (E_2), which comes later than E_1, is not necessarily located in the past time-area. However, in this section, we are discussing the past context (i.e. whether the infinitival situation is actualized in the past or not) and so we are assuming that E_2 is located in the past time-area.

Figure 11 suggests that since the coda is semantically bleached, the actualization of the infinitival situation is not guaranteed in terms of the temporal structure. In addition, as implied above, the use of BGT-sentences in the past tense in the past context implies that the speaker focuses on the preliminary stage, not the infinitival situation itself. Putting these together, we may conclude that the speaker is assumed to have in mind the temporal structure in Figure 11 when he/she is certainly intending the non-fulfillment of the infinitival situation in the past context. For example, in (43a) above, the first conjunct is represented by the BGT-form in the past tense, not the simple past form, so that the speaker intends to focus on the preliminary stage (e.g. the situation of the vase's being in the process of falling) but not on the infinitival situation itself (i.e. the vase's fall); the second conjunct indicates that the infinitival situation is not actualized. The temporal structure of the bleached-coda use of BGT-sentences in the past tense does not guarantee the coming about of the infinitival situation. From these observations, we may conclude that the speaker employs the temporal structure in Figure 11—a temporal structure which does not guarantee the coming about of the infinitival situation—to explicitly indicate the non-fulfillment of the situation in question.

However, especially in some linguistic environments, e.g. third-person past-tense narratives, BGT-sentences in the past tense often imply fulfillment of the infinitival situation, as in (44).

(44)   ... Apollonia stumbled and fell against him [=Michael] so that he had to hold her and her body so warm and alive in his hands started a deep wave of blood rising in his body. They could not see the mother behind them smiling because ... And smiling because this was the only way this young man was going to get his hands on her daughter [=Apollonia] until the marriage.   (M. Puzo, *The Godfather*, p. 342)

Here, the demonstrative *this* in the fourth line refers to the act of Apollonia's stumbling and falling against Michael. This scene is what Apollonia's mother saw just before Michael's getting his hands on Apollonia, i.e. the situation indicated by the infinitive part of the BGT-sentence involved, and therefore serves as the preliminary stage for the infinitival situation, which can be judged to be actualized in this context.

In my analysis, the BGT-sentence in question is interpreted as a typical use of BGT-sentences in the past tense, whose temporal structure is schematized in Figure 12.

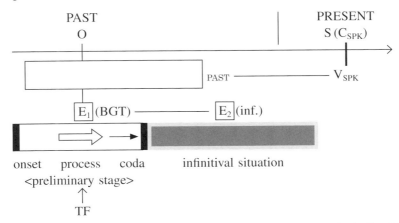

Figure 12: Temporal Structure of the Typical Uses of BGT-Sentences in the Past Tense

As this figure suggests, there is no break between the preliminary stage and the infinitival situation and so focusing on the former can lead to the actualization of the latter in terms of the temporal structure. In addition, the properties of third-person past-tense narratives are relevant here: the perspective of the narrator (as public self) at the time of narration is usually "out of focus" and the perspective of a character (as private self) at the narrative now in the "past" relative to the time of narration is crucially relevant to the temporal calculation of tense forms referring to the narrative world. The effect seen with respect to the past context exemplified by (43) above does not apply here. Given these observations, focusing on the preliminary stage at the narrative now—which is indicated by the position of the temporal focus— can lead to the actualization of the infinitival situation of the BGT-sentence involved. We will consider this matter in more detail in Section 9.4.2.2.

I now turn to *will*-sentences. Since we are considering future-in-the-past situations (i.e. past contexts), as illustrated by (42) above, the use to be considered must be a future reference one. I argue that among the three future reference uses of *will*-sentences (i.e. the volitional, predictive-future, and simple-future uses), the past-tense version of the simple-future use provides an appropriate temporal structure to refer to a future-in-the-past situation.[48] We have already seen that the volitional use is not chosen in this case (and perhaps the same observation applies to *will*-sentences with volitional overtones). The reason why the predictive-future use is not appropriate here is basically the same as in the case of the volitional use. The past-tense version of *will*-sentences in their predictive-future use conveys prediction assumed to occur at or just before a past time of orientation. When the speaker sees a past situation as a fact from his/her own point of view (i.e. the public self's point of view) at speech time (or the time of narration), he/she is usually supposed to know whether or not it actually happened or obtained. Thus, in a case like this, if the speaker bothers to choose the predictive-future use to pinpoint the prediction at the past time of orientation, it would be implied that the infinitival situation itself did not happen or obtain.

For these reasons, the past-tense version of *will*-sentences appropriate for

---

[48] As with BGT-sentences, *will*-sentences also allow the "immediate-future" use, a use that co-occurs with a present time adverbial like *now*, as we briefly saw in Section 5.6.3.2. However, in the temporal structure of its past-tense version, E_2 (the event time of the infinitival situation) is located at a time later than E_1 (the event time of *would*), which is, in turn, simultaneous with a past time of orientation. There is therefore no distinction of time-area between the predictive-future and immediate-future uses in the past tense, the two uses being classified into one and the same use within my framework.

this environment is that of the simple-future use, schematically represented in Figure 13:

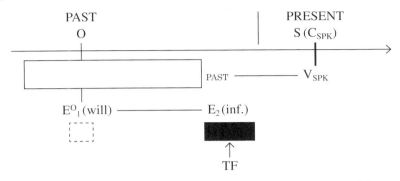

Figure 13: Temporal Structure of the Simple-Future Use of *Will*-Sentences in the Past Tense

The event time of the *will* in the past tense is not associated with a semantically contentful situation, such as volition or prediction, and thus serves as an orientational event time (E^O_1)—represented by the square with broken lines—i.e. an event time that merely functions as the time of orientation for E_2. For the same reason we saw with respect to the simple-future use of *will*-sentences in the present tense in Section 5.4.3, the temporal focus (TF) is directed at E_2. Since the infinitival situation (represented by the black rectangle) is in the past relative to the speaker's point of view at speech time (or the time of narration), it was a fact to the speaker even if it happened or obtained in the future relative to E^O_1. From these observations, we conclude that the temporal structure schematized in Figure 13 appropriately symbolizes the mechanism of fulfillment of the infinitival situation in the case of *will*-sentences in the past tense.

6.7. Concluding Remarks

This chapter has been devoted to explaining a variety of temporal phenomena of BGT-sentences in terms of their temporal structures. It has been generally assumed in the literature that BGT-sentences have two major uses, i.e. the predictive and volitional uses, but as far as I know, it has not been examined theoretically whether the two uses of BGT-sentences correspond, respectively, to the predictive-future and volitional readings of *will*-sentences. It goes without saying that an analysis of future expressions should be based on a model that is able to cover not only tense but also closely related areas such as modality, mood, and mental attitudes. It is much better if the model is more comprehensive and systematic.

Using the model developed for that purpose, I have argued that unlike the volitional and predictive-future uses of *will* sentences — which were regarded in Chapter 5 as semantic uses reflecting different temporal structures — the volitional and predictive-future uses of BGT-sentences are pragmatic variants sharing the same temporal structure (Figure 2), which includes the preliminary stage already ongoing at the time of orientation (in the case of the present tense, speech time). In both uses, in the situation construal tier the speaker (as private self) chooses assertive modality in making a judgment about the infinitival situation of BGT-sentences via the preliminary stage. It is in the situation report tier (i.e. when the speaker as public self conveys the construed situation to the addressee) that the volitional/non-volitional distinction comes to the fore, depending on the interaction between the semantic content of the BGT-sentence involved and the context or characteristics of the linguistic environment involved. It is also in the situation report tier that BGT-sentences can receive speech act readings, in which addressee-oriented speaker's mental attitudes are conveyed. The speech act meanings accompanying BGT-sentences are pragmatic information added in the situation report tier.

In this chapter, we have also focused on other uses of BGT-sentences, in particular, uses that have been derived through semantic bleaching in the course of grammaticalization, such as the bleached-coda, bleached-onset, and simple-future uses. Their differences are especially reflected in the parts concerning the cognitive schemas of the temporal structures and therefore these three uses are semantically different within my framework. The temporal structures of BGT-sentences discussed thus far are mainly divided into two types: (i) the temporal structures of one type reflect the semantics of the constituents (e.g. the progressive form of *go*, *to*) with their original meanings conceptually (metaphorically) preserved, and (ii) the temporal structures of the other type include semantically bleached parts that come about as a result of grammaticalization. Within my framework, BGT-sentences are further grammaticalized by the addition of new temporal structures to the existing ones whenever new uses are recognized. The grammaticalization of BGT-sentences do not proceed through the re-schematization or leveling of one single meaning after the addition of new uses or functions. It has been clear now that the proposed analysis reflects the spirit of compositionality, at least in some major cases.

Finally, to enhance the validity of this model, we have considered the differences between BGT-sentences and *will*-sentences in several linguistic phenomena. By explaining them based on the temporal structures of BGT-sentences and *will*-sentences, we were able to provide a more systematic analysis of the similarities and differences between the corresponding uses of the two sentences from a wider point of view.

Chapter 7

The Present Progressive*

7.1. Introduction

The present progressive form with future time reference, often referred to as the progressive futurate/futurate progressive (form), is described in almost all the studies concerning progressive aspect (Declerck (1991a, 2006), De Wit and Brisard (2014), De Wit and Patard (2013), Dowty (1977), Goldsmith and Woisetschlaeger (1982), Kranich (2010), Landman (1992), Langacker (1991), Leech (1987, 2004), Palmer (1974, 1988), Quirk et al. (1985), Swan (1995, 2005)). Numerous previous studies have compared the present progressive futurate form (the PPF form) with the simple present form with future time reference (Copley (2009), Goodman (1973), Hirtle and Curat (1986), Huddleston (1977), Prince (1982), Smith (1981), Wekker (1976), Williams (2002a)). There are also many studies discussing the diachronic development of the PPF form (Hundt (2004), Nesselhauf (2007)).

In this chapter, I first clarify, using the model explored in this book, how the PPF form has developed from the present progressive form in its aspectual use (i.e. the normal present progressive form) and what temporal structures sentences or clauses containing the PPF form (henceforth PPF-sentences) have in present-day English, and then explain a number of synchronic behaviors of PPF-sentences based on the temporal structures.

This chapter is composed of five sections. After looking at linguistic characteristics of PPF-sentences in Section 7.2, I present in Section 7.3 the temporal structures of sentences containing the normal present progressive form

---

* This chapter is a radically revised version of Naoaki Wada (2009a), "The Present Progressive with Future Time Reference vs. *Be Going To*: Is Doc Brown Going Back to the Future Because He Is Going to Reconstruct It?", volume 26.1, pp 96–131, *English Linguistics*, 2009 © The English Linguistic Society of Japan, reproduced with permission.

(simply present progressive sentences) and PPF-sentences, showing how the latter have stemmed from the former and how the temporal structure of PPF-sentences differs from that of BGT-sentences in their typical uses, both of which share something ongoing at speech time. Section 7.4 provides a temporal structure analysis of the linguistic characteristics observed in Section 7.2, especially by comparing PPF-sentences with BGT-sentences in their typical uses. Section 7.5 offers a brief summary.

7.2. Linguistic Characteristics Concerning PPF-Sentences

This section looks at some linguistic phenomena concerning PPF-sentences. Let us first briefly outline the characteristics of PPF-sentences observed in previous studies.[1] For example, Leech (2004: 61) states that PPF-sentences describe the "FUTURE EVENT ANTICIPATED BY VIRTUE OF A PRESENT PLAN, PROGRAMME OR ARRANGEMENT". Similarly, Swan (1995:

---

[1] Although providing a comprehensive analysis of various uses of present progressive sentences (i.e. non-future reference uses) is not a target of this book, they are closely related to PPF-sentences. I therefore need to say some words about the general treatment of the present progressive form within my framework. Let us start with a look at De Wit and Brisard's (2014: 51) criticism of the previous studies on the English progressive. They argue that those studies generally have two drawbacks: (i) they only focus on the purely temporal and aspectual concepts of the progressive form, including PPF-sentences; (ii) they do not stipulate the core meaning and therefore cannot provide a comprehensive and unified account of its uses. For example, as De Wit and Brisard point out, Dowty (1975) himself admits that the core meaning of the progressive form (i.e. temporality) is not applied to all uses of this form; Goldsmith and Woistschlaeger (1982: 80) do not regard the notion of "phenomenal description" as directly relevant to the aspectual uses of the progressive form (cf. also Kranich (2010: 58)). My framework can avoid such criticisms because it can solve the two drawbacks at issue. First, drawback (ii) is not problematic to my framework, which assumes the core meaning of the present progressive form, i.e. the tense structure shared by all uses of the present progressive form. Drawback (i) is not problematic, either, because what De Wit and Brisard refer to as the purely temporal and aspectual notions are in operation on the tense-interpretation level (including temporal structures) and unlike the temporal and aspectual uses, the modal (or subjective) uses of the progressive form can be linked to possible or mental worlds on the tense-interpretation level, as we saw in connection with several uses of the simple present form in Chapter 4. Moreover, my framework may explain the observation that the modal uses have been derived from the temporal and aspectual uses in a similar way that I have explained a variety of uses of *will*-sentences and BGT-sentences in Chapters 5 and 6. In this connection, Williams (2002a) proposes a similar approach in which a variety of uses of the progressive form come about as a result of the interaction between factors such as the context and its core meaning, i.e. "susceptibility to change" (p. 87). He also states that all uses of the progressive (including the present perfect progressive) more or less reflect the sense of "in progress" (§1.4.1 and §1.4.2).

Chapter 7   The Present Progressive   255

210, 2005: 189) observes that PPF-sentences usually refer to "personal arrangements" or "fixed plans".[2] For such situations to obtain at speech time,
the decision must have been made before that time.

(1) a.   We're having fish for dinner.   (Leech (2004: 61))
    b.   "Yes, sir," I said. "Very unfortunate. But that's why I've come to
         you, sir. I'm getting married next month. We'll both be working
         over the summer ..."   (E. Segal, *Love Story*, p. 98)
    c.   "We're meeting at the cave after dinner," Cameron said to Neil.
                                    (N. H. Kleinbaum, *Dead Poets Society*, p. 87)
    d.   My car's going in for a service next week.   (Swan (2005: 189))
    e.   THE National Theatre is breaking its long repertory tradition next
         March to stage a straight 16-week run of the Sondheim musical Sun-
         day In The Park With George.   (BNC A93)
    f.   He's dying next week.   (Quirk et al. (1985: 215))

It is generally the case that PPF-sentences require the subject's referent to be
the agent of the plan or personal arrangement involved, as in (1a–c). However,
especially in cases where the grammatical subject is inanimate or where it is
not an agent if it is human, the arrangement involved is attributed to someone
closely related to the subject's referent or made by the authority of someone
other than the subject's referent, as in (1d–f). Following Copley (2009: 29), I
refer to as "director" someone who has the ability or authority to cause the arrangement or plan to happen and is committed to the actualization of such
events. In (1f), for instance, although the subject's referent is human, he is
not a director; the director is someone else (e.g. the Minister of Justice or an
executioner authorized to carry out a death sentence) and the arrangement for
his execution next week has already been made.

When PPF-sentences refer to fixed arrangements, they tend to imply the
near future and hence be associated with the notion of "imminence", as in (2).
However, this is merely a tendency and not a requirement, as shown in (3).

(2) a.   I'm taking Mary out for dinner this evening.   (Leech (2004: 62))
    b.   I'm visiting them tonight.   (Declerck (2006: 184))
(3) a.   When I grow up, I'm joining the police force.   (Leech (2004: 62))
    b.   Those groups combined—84 percent of Americans—"appear to rep-
         resent the highest level of belief that the climate is changing in at

_____

[2] This suggests that unlike BGT-sentences and *will*-sentences, PPF-sentences do not receive predictive readings (Swan (1995: 211), Kashino (1999: 84)).

least five years, ...
(http://www.naylornetwork.com/app-ppd/newsletter-v2.asp?issueID=
26956)

It is also pointed out that PPF-sentences cannot be used with verbs describing situations that human beings cannot control (Close (1981: 83), Copley (2009: 29), Declerck (2006: 184), Kashino (1999: 76), Swan (2005: 215))).

(4) a. *It's snowing before long.   (Swan (2005: 190))
    b. *I'm sneezing in a moment.   (Close (1981: 83))

On the other hand, present progressive sentences can be used with such verbs, as in (5):

(5) a. It's been a long winter around here, it's snowing now.
                                 (http://bitterrootriverguides.com/?m=201603)
    b. ... but today I have a sore throat too and am sneezing (not a good sign) these symptoms often lead to me getting a chest infection.
                                                            (GloWbE GB)

This suggests that PPF-sentences have more restrictions on their use than present progressive sentences.

Furthermore, PPF-sentences are usually incompatible with conditional clauses with future time reference, whereas *will*-sentences and BGT-sentences can occur with them, as in (6):[3]

(6) a. *You're breaking that chair if you're not careful.
                                 (Close (1981: 83); cf. Kashino (1999: 84))
    b. You {will / are going to} break that chair if you're not careful.
                                 (Kashino (1999: 84); cf. Close (1981: 83)

7.3. Toward Constructing the Basic Temporal Structure of PPF-Sentences

7.3.1. Tense Structure

Having observed the linguistic phenomena to be discussed, I will construct the basic temporal structure of PPF-sentences, considering their characteristics. Let us first observe the tense structures of the two verbal units constituting

---

[3] As seen in Section 6.6.4, BGT-sentences in their typical uses do not co-occur with conditional clauses with future time reference. BGT-sentences like that in (6b) are instances of the future-condition use (which has a semantically-bleached preliminary stage) within my framework.

Chapter 7   The Present Progressive

PPF-sentences, i.e. *be* in the present tense and the present participle. The combination of the two tense structures constitutes the tense structure of PPF-sentences, which is the same as that of present progressive sentences. Within my framework, the fact that PPF-sentences and present progressive sentences share the same tense form (i.e. *be* + present participle) indicates that they share the same tense structure. On the other hand, they have different basic temporal structures because they are regarded as representing different semantic uses (functions).

Let me start by considering the tense structure of the progressive *be* as a finite verb. In the case of present tense forms, the *be* is in the present tense and the tense structure is therefore such that its event time is located in the present time-sphere (grammatical present). I now move to the tense structure of the present participle. As seen in Section 2.3, the tense-structure information represented by the present participle morpheme *-ing* is a simultaneous relationship to the time of orientation (cf. Wierzbicka (1988));[4] the present participle is in the complement position of the progressive *be* as the head verb and its event time is thus computed with respect to the event time of the progressive *be* as a time of orientation.[5]

7.3.2.   Basic Temporal Structures

Now I turn to constructing the basic temporal structures of present progressive sentences and PPF-sentences, clarifying how the latter type of sentences stem from the former. Let us first take a look at present progressive sentences. The progressive auxiliary *be* itself does not refer to any specific situation. In terms of the semantic function, it merely serves as a time position for the speaker's viewpoint of situation description (i.e. SD-viewpoint) from which to evaluate or describe the present participle situation. The event time of this *be* is therefore an orientational type.

By contrast, the present participle indicates a specific situation with full se-

---

[4] See also Hayase (2002) and Tomozawa (2003), who give an argument to the effect that the basic meaning of the present participle is simultaneity. In this connection, De Smet and Heyvaert (2011: 479) state that the time stability of the adjectival slot tends to cause the participle situation to be interpreted as involving simultaneity. Besides, Killie (2014: 379) notes that the inherent nature of the present participle is durativity. When its durativity is computed with respect to a given time as the time of orientation, the participle situation can be interpreted as including the latter and hence a simultaneous relationship arises.

[5] This treatment of the progressive form is compatible with the cognitive grammar view (e.g. Langacker (1991: 211–212)) that the progressive *be* simply connects the present participle situation to the time line.

mantic content and therefore represents the event time as a pure type. The present participle morpheme -*ing* is in general assumed to be an imperfective marker, backgrounding the beginning and end portions of the situation involved and foregrounding the middle portion (Declerck (1991a), Williams (2002a)). In my model, this imperfectivity comes from the idea that the present participle morpheme -*ing* (i.e. an R-morpheme) represents simultaneity relative to the time of orientation at which the present participle situation itself is ongoing (in progress).

The present progressive form we are considering in this chapter does not co-occur with any modal auxiliary and so both present progressive sentences and PPF-sentences are accompanied by assertive modality, i.e. a speaker's S-attitude at work when the speaker makes a judgment about the relevant situation (in the situation construal tier). In the default case (i.e. when the speaker's t(emporal)-viewpoint fuses with his/her consciousness at speech time), the present time-sphere (i.e. the tense-structure information represented by the progressive *be* in the present tense) corresponds to both the present and future time-areas (i.e. cognitive time ranges). The (orientational) event time of *be* (E^O_1) is located at the same time as speech time (in the present time-area). This is partly due to the restriction on assertion (cf. Section 2.4.3.5) and partly because the progressive *be* in the present tense does not satisfy the conditions for the future time reference by the simple present form, namely that it does not indicate a situation specific enough to be interpreted as part of the structure of the world in the sense of Goldsmith and Woisetschlaeger (1982)—i.e. a set of rules and constitutions of the society as well as the universe surrounding us (which we have already discussed in Section 4.2.2 and will consider in more detail in Chapter 8).[6] Therefore, the operation of assertive modality, together with the "schematicity" of the situation associated with the progressive

---

[6] This line of reasoning enables us to explain, from a unified point of view, the fact that the event time of the verbal unit *be going to* of BGT-sentences in the present tense and the event time of the perfect *have* of present perfect sentences usually cannot be located in the future time-area, especially in main or independent clauses. Observe:

(i)   She is going to play Beethoven's "Moonlight Sonata" on the piano.

(ii) She has played Beethoven's "Moonlight Sonata" on the piano.

It is not the case that the preliminary stage indicated by *be going to* or the resultant state denoted by *have* is ongoing or obtains at a future time and the situation described by the non-finite verb in their complement position is positioned with respect to that future time, as shown in e.g. **Tomorrow, the conference has already ended* (Rothstein (2008: 29)). This can be attributed to the view that the *be going to* and *have* in question do not indicate a situation specific enough to constitute part of the structure of the world, as discussed in the main text.

be, causes its event time to be located at the same time as speech time.[7] The present participle is in the complement position of the progressive *be* and the event time of the latter thus serves as the time of orientation for computing the event time of the former; the relationship of the two event times is that of simultaneity.[8]

The above observations enable us to schematize the basic temporal structure of present progressive sentences in their aspectual use in Figure 1:

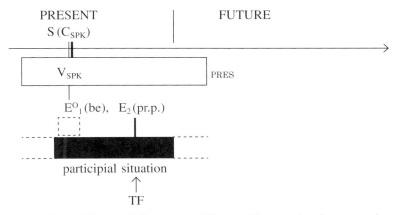

Figure 1: Basic Temporal Structure of Present Progressive Sentences in Their Aspectual Use

---

[7] The auxiliary verb or verbal unit can describe its own situation within my framework and so not only the *be* of PPF-sentences, the *be going to* of BGT-sentences and the *have* of perfect sentences, but also the *be* of present progressive sentences can indicate their own situations, even if they are schematic. However, the type of schematic situation of present progressive sentences, which is deemed to be semantically bleached in temporal calculation, differs from that of the other three for the following reason. The schematic situation of present progressive sentences does not serve as an "earlier stage" leading to the occurrence of another situation or a resultant state stemming from the occurrence of a prior situation, but it obtains at the same time as the present participle situation, i.e. a specific situation with full semantic content; it is, so to speak, semantically valueless information. The event time of the *be* of present progressive sentences is therefore regarded as an orientational event time. By contrast, in the other three types of sentences, the schematic situation associated with the auxiliary or verbal unit is ongoing or obtains at a different time from the time of the non-finite situation and has a raison d'etre in semantic terms. In this way, the event times of the *be* of PPF-sentences, the verbal unit *be going to*, and the perfect *have* are those of the pure type.

[8] Boogaart (1999: 173) also regards the English progressive as consisting of two situations and thus two event times.

The square with broken lines below E^O_1 represents a schematic situation, i.e. one without specific semantic content. The black rectangle symbolizes the present-participle (pr.p.) situation, connected to E_2 by the heavy vertical line. The broken line portions extending from both sides of the black rectangle indicate that the beginning and end portions of the present participle situation are backgrounded. The event time of the progressive *be* (E^O_1) is an orientational type and the temporal focus (TF) is thus directed at the event time of the present participle situation, i.e. a situation with full semantic content (E_2).[9, 10]

---

[9] De Wit and Brisard (2014), extensively discussing a variety of uses of the English progressive within the framework of Langacker's cognitive grammar, argue that the uses stem from the interaction between the schematic core meaning of the progressive and cognitive branching principles. This analysis is salient because, as stated in Chapter 1, most — at least very many — of cognitive linguistic approaches tend to focus on common parts of the forms to be compared. It seems to share the same spirit as my analysis. However, the core meaning assumed in their analysis is different from that in my analysis. In their analysis, the core meaning of the English progressive is epistemic contingency, which itself expresses a modal value. The aspectual and temporal value (which is the combination of the tense information of *be* and the aspect information of *-ing*) comes about when the core meaning is projected onto what Langacker (1991: 244) calls "Time-Line Model" (p. 58). Their classification of uses of the progressive is based on explicit criteria which are general concepts used for cognitively motivated classifications (e.g. singular vs. multiple, actual vs. virtual) (De Wit and Brisard (2014: 87)). In my analysis, the core meaning is the combined tense structure of the progressive *be* and present participle, namely that the event time of the progressive *be* is located in the present time-sphere and the event time of the present participle is computed with respect to the event time of *be* as the time of orientation. When projected onto the cognitive time line on the tense-interpretation level, this tense-structure information interacts with other factors to bring about a variety of semantic uses which have their own temporal structures in the situation construal tier and to further bring about speech act uses (i.e. pragmatic variants) in the situation report tier.

Lying behind their claim that the core meaning of the present progressive is a modal value is the idea that an emotional use like the one in (i) — a kind of speech act use — cannot be explained by a temporal value-based analysis.

(i) [On how to punish children] Well, I'm telling you, withholding goodies works.

(requoted from De Wit and Brisard (2014: 84))

However, my framework can also handle this example. This type of use is derived from the interaction between the tense-structure information and factors such as the semantics of the rest of the sentence involved, the context, or the information from the interpersonal relationship tier. In my analysis, the core meaning of the present progressive form is neither a modal value nor a value on the cognitive or real time line; it is the combined tense structure of the progressive form (i.e. grammatical time information). This suggests that my analysis can avoid their criticisms and at the same time provide a different explanation from theirs. We thus conclude that although the two approaches differ in terms of the nature of the core meaning of the progressive form, they are similar to each other in that they adopt a core meaning-based explanation and place emphasis on the motivation for the classification of uses of the progressive form.

[10] The present progressive in present-day English has a habitual use, as in (i), or subjec-

Chapter 7   The Present Progressive

Examples of present progressive sentences in their aspectual uses are given in (7):

(7) a.   However, the American method is now gaining popularity. (BNC A6A)
    b.   "I'm not watching you study. I'm studying."

(E. Segal, *Love Story*, p. 47)

To see how the temporal structure analysis deals with concrete examples of the present progressive sentence in its aspectual use, consider, for instance, (7b). The situation represented by the progressive *be* (i.e. *am*) is semantically bleached. The assertive modality accompanying the finite verb *be* (i.e. a speaker's S-attitude) as well as the schematic nature of its situation observed above causes its event time (i.e. orientational event time) to coincide with speech time. The present participle situation (e.g. the speaker's studying) is ongoing at the event time of *be* as the time of orientation and its event time is thus simultaneous with the latter.

Next, let us turn to the basic temporal structure of PPF-sentences, as exemplified by the PPF-sentence in (1c), i.e. *We're meeting at the cave after dinner*, which indicates the future actualization of the meeting. I claim that PPF-sentences are semantically derived from present progressive sentences. This claim is supported both diachronically and synchronically. As diachronic evidence, I present Nesselhauf's (2007) observation that the progressive in its aspectual use started to be prevalent in the early Modern English period (cf. also Killie (2014)), but PPF-sentences started to be prevalent only in the late Modern English period. This implies that PPF-sentences are diachronically based on present progressive sentences.[11] As synchronic evidence for the claim, I present De Wit and Patard's (2013:125) observations: (i) the frequency of present progressive sentences is higher than that of PPF-sentences;[12] (ii) present progressive sentences have more uses than PPF-sentence;[13] and (iii) there

---

tive use, as in (ii) (Wright (1994, 1995), Killie (2004)):

(i)   I'm taking dancing lessons this winter.   (Leech (2004: 32))
(ii) They're always cracking jokes.   (Leech (2004: 34))

Since this study mainly concerns the present progressive as a future expression, I leave for future research my explanation of such uses within my framework.

[11] There are many diachronic studies on the English progressive (e.g. Nesselhauf (2007), A. K. Smith (2007)). For a comprehensive study from a diachronic point of view, see Kranich (2010).

[12] De Wit and Patard (2013: 125) note that in their corpus study, the "pure current ongoingness" use (a typical use of normal progressive sentences) occupies 27.43% of all tokens of the progressive, while the "futurate" use (i.e. PPF-sentences) occupies 13.57%.

[13] According to De Wit and Patard's (2013) classification, the progressive with present

are less restrictions on present progressive sentences than PPF-sentences, as illustrated in (4) and (5) above.

Now, we will be able to see how PPF-sentences have derived from present progressive sentences in terms of their temporal structures. Let me first present the temporal structure of present progressive sentences which is located at the middle stage of the grammaticalization process developing from present progressive sentences in their aspectual use toward PPF-sentences. The temporal structure of the present progressive sentence in question is schematized in Figure 2:

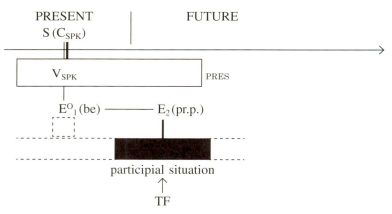

Figure 2: Temporal Structure of Present Progressive Sentences at the Middle Stage of the Grammaticalization Process toward PPF-Sentences

In Figure 1 above, the present participle situation itself is interpreted as ongoing or obtaining at the event time of *be* as the time of orientation, which is in turn simultaneous with speech time. In Figure 2, by contrast, a "cognitive shift" enables us to restrict the actualization part of the present participle situation to a time span — represented by the black rectangle — in the future relative to E^O_1 (i.e. the event time of the semantically bleached situation represented by the progressive *be*). As a result, the portion of the present participle situation corresponding to E^O_1 — represented by the broken line portion on the left side of the black rectangle — is backgrounded and "out of focus".

The restriction process goes as follows. The present participle marker *-ing* in the progressive form represents imperfective aspect and the present partici-

---

time reference has at least six uses, i.e. "pure current ongoingness", "temporary validity", "limited duration", "incompletion", "iteration", and "habitual".

Chapter 7   The Present Progressive

ple situation involved is thus interpreted as unbounded and homogeneous not only at the time of orientation but also before and after it unless bounded by other factors. It is highly possible that the situation ongoing or obtaining at the time of orientation (in the case of the present tense form, speech time) is still ongoing or obtains at a later time and therefore the portion of the present participle situation corresponding to the time of orientation can potentially "represent" the portion after it or vice versa. This serves as a trigger for the cognitive shift observed above, which potentially enables us to pay attention only to the portion of the participial situation corresponding to a future time without reference to other portions.[14, 15] If it actually happens, then the portion corresponding to the time of orientation (i.e. speech time) can be backgrounded and "out of focus". In this way, the event time of the present participle situation (E_2), which receives the temporal focus (TF), is restricted to the portion corresponding to a time in the future time-area (represented by the black rectangle).

This temporal structure is further developed into the basic temporal structure of PPF-sentences, which is schematically represented in Figure 3.[16]

---

[14] This cognitive shift is a kind of profile shift in Langacker's cognitive grammar. Yamanashi (1999: Ch. 3) considers the profile shift as a cognitive process that triggers grammaticalization.

[15] One might argue that for a similar reason we can pay attention to the portion corresponding to a past time. However, the range of the present time-sphere plays a role here. In the default case—and this applies here—the present time-sphere of the present progressive covers both the present and future time-areas, but not the past time-area. This restriction as to time ranges prevents such a shift of attention to the past from arising.

[16] The claim that PPF-sentences have a different temporal structure from present progressive sentences in their aspectual use suggests that the progressive form is semantically ambiguous (or polysemous), which is supported by the fact that a sentence like (i) has two temporally different readings (cf. Dowty (1977: 69)).

   (i)   Lee was going to Radcliff until she was accepted by Parsons.   (Dowty (1977: 69))
Based on Ellen Prince's observation, Dowty argues that the imperfective (i.e. aspectual) reading of sentence (i) is such that "Lee's going to Radcliff was in progress until she was accepted by Parsons", while the futurate reading is such that "Lee's going to Radcliff (at some future date) was the plan until she was accepted by Parsons", implying that Lee did not go to Radcliff.

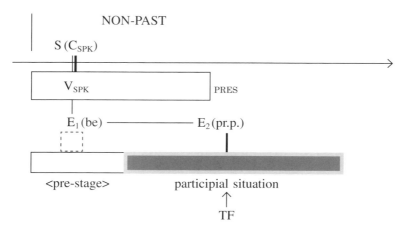

Figure 3: Basic Temporal Structure of PPF-Sentences

Within my framework, several semantic uses (functions) of PPF-sentences stem from this basic temporal structure in interaction with such factors as the semantic content of the rest of the sentence involved and the context.

Let us comment on how to read this schema. First, NON-PAST symbolizes the non-past time-area—corresponding to the present and future time-areas—which is intended to cover not only the case where the event time of the present participle (E_2) is located in the future time-area but also the case where E_2 is located at a time later than speech time in the present time-sphere.

Second, the backgrounded, or "out of focus", part in Figure 2 is replaced by an earlier stage of the present participle situation termed *pre-stage* in Figure 3. This replacement is motivated by Smith's (1981: 374–375) statement that the simple ongoing process of normal progressive sentences—consisting only of imperfective aspect—is re-interpreted as an extended process consisting of both perfective and imperfective aspect (cf. Williams (2002a: 51–52)).[17] Within my framework, Smith's notion of extended process is regarded as a complex notion consisting of the pre-stage of a present participle situation obtaining at speech time and the main part of that situation to occur at a later time. In the cognitive schema part, the pre-stage is seen as ongoing (related to imperfective aspect) at a certain time and the end of the pre-stage triggers

---

[17] Williams (2002a: §1.4.3) refers to this type of earlier stage as "precondition". In his study, progressive sentences consisting of two situations, i.e. PPF-sentences, are called type two progressives; progressive sentences consisting of only one situation, i.e. progressive sentences in their aspectual use, are called type one progressives. The extended process in Smith's terms corresponds to a "wider situation" in Williams's terms.

Chapter 7   The Present Progressive   265

the occurrence of the present participle situation itself viewed in its entirety (related to perfective aspect).

Let us observe in more detail the process of the replacement mentioned above. The event time represented by the progressive *be*—associated with a semantically bleached situation represented by the square with broken lines— functions merely as the time of orientation and the function of the verb is reduced to a minimum. On the other hand, the pre-stage, i.e. an earlier stage of the present participle situation—sharing the same time with the semantically-bleached situation described by *be*—requires its own event time, not only because the semantic content of the pre-stage will be specific enough by way of the interaction between the semantic content of the rest of the PPF-sentence involved and the context, but also because it is different from the semantic content of the main part of the present participle situation. From a cognitive point of view, it is natural to assume that one event time (of the pure type) is allocated to one distinct situation with specific semantic content. It is true that the pre-stage is closely related to the main part of the present participle situation and in that sense is not entirely independent of the latter, but its semantic content is determined in temporal calculation to be a pre-condition (or pre-situation in a broad sense) leading to the present participle situation itself (i.e. the main part) and the pre-stage thus constitutes a different situation in terms of the cognitive schema.

From these observations, we argue that the event time of the progressive *be* (E_1) is re-interpreted as linked to the pre-stage, i.e. a schematic situation in progress or obtaining at speech time, whose semantic content will be specified in temporal calculation. In parallel to the re-interpretation process observed above, only the foregrounded part of the present participle situation in Figure 3, which is restricted to the range corresponding to a time span in the future relative to E_1, is interpreted as associated with the event time of the present participle situation (E_2).

It should be noted that like the preliminary stage of BGT-sentences, the pre-stage of PPF-sentences is not necessarily related to a concrete situation actually ongoing or obtaining in the real world, but it can be an abstract situation regarded subjectively as ongoing or obtaining in the speaker's mind. The earlier stage in PPF-sentences (i.e. pre-stage) is distinguished from the earlier stage in BGT-sentences (i.e. preliminary stage) for reasons to be clarified later (see Section 7.3.3).[18]

---

[18] In Wada (2009a), I referred to both of the earlier stages in BGT-sentences and PPF-sentences by the term preliminary stage. However, as will be clarified in the main text, the

Next, since PPF-sentences do not contain any modal form, they are accompanied by assertive modality as the unmarked speaker's S-attitude (cf. the semantic (de)composition of sentential utterances in (4) in Section 3.4 and the hypothesis about the default mental attitude of the current speaker in (22) in Section 3.8). This modality is by definition operative at the time of assertion, i.e. the time simultaneous with speech time, or at least in the time-area including it (i.e. the present time-area) and thus occurs at or around E_1, i.e. the event time of the pre-stage.

Let us finally consider the position of the temporal focus (TF). As we will see later, the pre-stage of PPF-sentences is more closely related to and therefore less independent of the main (part of the) situation involved than the preliminary stage of BGT-sentences. (I will henceforth use the term *main situation* to refer not only to the infinitival situation of BGT-sentences but also to the main part of the present participle situation of PPF-sentences, unless confusion occurs.) In addition, the pre-stage is a so-called presupposed part constituting part of the present participle situation, which is inferable from the above observation that the pre-stage and the main situation of PPF-sentences are related to one verbal unit, i.e. the present participle. E_1 is associated with the pre-stage as a presupposed part of the present participle. The temporal focus is thus not directed to E_1 but to E_2, i.e. the event time associated with the main situation.

Now, a question arises as to what is the driving force for the development of PPF-sentences? I argue that a certain type of metonymy is at work here, applying to the predicational part of a proposition (e.g. Panther and Thornburg (1998), Fabiszak (2012)). In this connection, Panther and Thornburg (1998: 757) present the POTENTIALITY FOR ACTUALITY metonymy as a type of metonymy in point, stating that in (8), by referring to the ability to nail down the championship (8a), the speaker implies the actualization of winning the championship (8b).[19]

(8) a. The Chicago Bulls were able to nail down their fifth NBA championship ...
    b. The Chicago Bulls nailed down their fifth NBA championship ...

(Panther and Thornburg (1998: 757))

---

two types of earlier stages are different in some respects and hence different terms are given to them in this study.

[19] As another relevant "predicational" metonymy, the OBLIGATORY ACTION FOR ACTUAL ACTION metonymy can be presented (Panther and Thornburg (2007)), as in (i):

(i) a. The saxophone player had to leave early.   (Panther and Thornburg (2007: 246))
    b. The saxophone player left early.   (Panther and Thornburg (2007: 246))

Chapter 7   The Present Progressive

Along these lines, I argue that the EARLIER STAGE FOR MAIN SITUA-TION metonymy is operative in the grammaticalization process from the temporal structure in Figure 2 to that in Figure 3. This metonymy means that the earlier stage of a situation leading to or bringing about the main situation stands for the latter. The metonymy observed in reference to (8) is subsumed under this metonymy.

Let us reconsider the differences in the temporal structures in Figures 2 and 3 from this perspective. The backgrounded part of the present participle situation (represented by the broken line portion on the left side of the black rectangle) and the foregrounded part of the present participle situation (represented by the black rectangle) in Figure 2 correspond, respectively, to the pre-stage and the main situation (i.e. the main part of the participial situation) in Figure 3. This suggests that the temporal structure in Figure 2 is, in terms of the cognitive schema, ready for the occurrence of the metonymical reasoning. Thus, the EARLIER STAGE FOR MAIN SITUATION metonymy comes into play and triggers the re-interpretation of the situation associated with E_1 as the pre-stage — discussed above — so that the earlier stage can serve as a pre-situation (pre-condition) leading to the main situation. In this way, the basic temporal structure of PPF-sentences in Figure 3 is derived from the temporal structure of present progressive sentences at the middle stage in Figure 2.

Thus far, we have seen the conceptual motivations for the derivative process from the temporal structure in Figure 1 to that in Figure 3 via that in Figure 2. Let us next observe linguistic phenomena contributing to the bridging between present progressive sentences in their aspectual use (Figure 1) and PPF-sentences (Figure 3) via present progressive sentences at the middle stage (Figure 2). I assume that so-called transitional event verbs play a crucial role in bringing about the cognitive shift and metonymical reasoning observed above.[20] As Leech (2004: 63) notes, in the case of present progressive sentences in their aspectual use, transitional event verbs such as *arrive, die, land, stop* refer to an event ongoing now — a situation which requires some range of time. For example, to say that one is in the process of arriving at some place at a given time of orientation (e.g. speech time) amounts to say that one is already in the "cumulative process" (at least for some time) leading to the arriving time; in this type of process, a portion of the situation corresponding to a

---

[20] An argument for this assumption is Torres-Cacoullos and Walker's (2009: 337) observation that in spoken Canadian English, transitional event verbs such as *go* and *come* are often used in "futurate sentences", including PPF-sentences. Kashino (1999: 75) makes a similar observation.

given time span is, in terms of its quality, more or less the same as a portion corresponding to a later time span, unless the latter is the end point of the process.[21] This linguistic phenomenon therefore motivates the cognitive shift in the derivation process from the aspectual use (Figure 1) to the middle stage (Figure 2).

Now we turn to the motivation of the metonymical reasoning. Because the transitional event verbs refer to gradual change of states, the distinction between the earlier stage and the main situation described by verbs of this type is sometimes not clear-cut when they are used in the progressive form. That is, the gradual change of state of this type of present progressive sentences does not make clear the distinction between the earlier stage and main situation and we can regard them as if they were a series of situations. However, we can assume as many steps of the earlier stage as possible and the further back one goes, the easier the distinction between the earlier stage and the main situation becomes.

For a better understanding of the statements above, consider, for example, a transitional verb *leave*, as in *She is leaving for Europe*. In this progressive sentence, an earlier stage may be the situation of the woman's checking in at an international airport, which is followed by the taking off itself (i.e. the main situation), and in this case the two stages are not clearly distinguished. However, the earlier stage may include the situation of her heading for the airport and can be extended even to the situation of her calling a taxi to go to the airport. If we assume the calling of a taxi to be an earlier stage (i.e. pre-stage), then the departure itself (i.e. main situation) is located explicitly in the future relative to the time of the telephone call in terms of our encyclopedic knowledge. This provides a basis for a conceptual distinction between the earlier stage and the main situation, which serves as a motivation for the operation of the EARLIER STAGE FOR MAIN SITUATION metonymy observed above. I therefore conclude that this type of metonymical reasoning underlies the derivation process from the temporal structure in Figure 2 to that in Figure 3 above.

Before closing this sub-section, I present examples from the BNC that illustrate the temporal structure of present progressive sentences at the middle stage in Figure 2.

(9) a.   TOWARDS the end of a week of stocktaking at the Stuttgart Classic, in which some of the world's leading male players have expressed

---

[21] The result is the same even if the time of orientation is shifted to a past or future time.

Chapter 7   The Present Progressive   269

mixed feelings about the way professional tennis is moving into the
next decade, Boris Becker was asked to name his player of the 1980s.
(BNC A3L)

b.   There will not be a final dividend. Pre-tax profits in 1988 were £5.3m.
The shares stand at 65p against a high for 1989 of 127p. Shares of
Armour Trust, the sugar confectionery and car accessories business
headed by Andrew Balcombe, slipped 0.5p to 47p yesterday. Following recent confectionery takeovers, UBS Phillips & Drew believe the
trust has a break-up value of 100p. Analyst Mark Simpson is looking for profits of £2.4m this year and £2.85m next year.   (BNC A5G)

The progressive sentence in (9a)—containing the progressive form *is moving
into*—is interpreted in such a way that the direction in which professional
tennis is heading is already set at the time of orientation (simultaneous with
speech time) and the direction still obtains or is ongoing at a later time in the
future. (9b) is an excerpt from a text published in 1989 and the phrase *this
year* refers to 1989. The situation represented by the present progressive *is
looking for* is seen as covering both 1989 (the present) and 1990 (the future);
in other words, the situation of looking for profits is not only ongoing at
speech time but still ongoing in the next year.

7.3.3.   The Dual Structure of PPF-Sentences: In Comparison with BGT-Sentences

I now turn to a consideration of the characteristics of PPF-sentences, including the dual structure of their temporal structure, in comparison with those of
BGT-sentences of the non-bleached type.[22] Although both sentences consist
of an earlier stage and the main situation, PPF-sentences are composed of the
pre-stage and the main part of the present participle situation, while BGT-sentences are composed of the preliminary stage and the infinitival situation.

First, as Leech (2004: 62) points out, PPF-sentences do not necessarily co-
occur with future time adverbials (e.g. *tomorrow*) or present time adverbials
referring to the immediate future (e.g. *now*), if future time reference is indicated in the context.[23] This characteristic is due to the cognitive schema in the

---

[22] Henceforth, when I refer to BGT-sentences in this chapter, I mean BGT-sentences of
the non-bleached type, especially BGT-sentences in their typical uses, unless otherwise indicated.

[23] In this connection, Williams (2002a: 198) makes a similar statement, from a different
angle, that unlike BGT-sentences, sentences containing the present progressive form must
co-occur with future time adverbials in order to be interpreted as PPF-sentences, unless the

temporal structure of PPF-sentences (Figure 3 above), which suggests that the main situation is regarded as occurring as a natural consequence of the completion of the pre-stage. The temporal structure of PPF-sentences clearly indicates that the event time of (the main part of) the present participle situation (E_2) is located at a later time than the event time linked to the pre-stage (E_1)— coinciding with speech time—and hence PPF-sentences are future-oriented by themselves. In this respect, PPF-sentences are similar to BGT-sentence, which also have a future-oriented temporal structure (Figure 1 in Section 6.3.2).

Next, PPF-sentences, like BGT-sentences, have an earlier stage leading to the occurrence of the main situation in their temporal structure and the cognitive schema therefore implies that the main situation following it is likely to occur in the near future. For this reason, PPF-sentences tend to refer to a near-future situation, as seen with respect to (2), repeated below.

(2) a. I'm taking Mary out for dinner this evening.   (Leech (2004: 62))
    b. I'm visiting them tonight.   (Declerck (2006: 184))

However, the cognitive schema is subjectively based, as repeatedly stated, and so the pre-stage can continue for a rather long time, as we saw in (3), repeated here.

(3) a. When I grow up, I'm joining the police force.   (Leech (2004: 62))
    b. Those groups combined—84 percent of Americans—"appear to represent the highest level of belief that the climate is changing in at least five years, ...
        (http://www.naylornetwork.com/app-ppd/newsletter-v2.asp?issueID=26956)

I turn then to two arguments for the dual structure of PPF-sentences consisting of the pre-stage and the main situation. First, PPF-sentences can co-occur with both a present time adverb and a future time adverb at the same time, as in (10):

(10) a. "Now I'm flying down there tomorrow night."
        (C. Webb, *The Graduate*, p. 155)
    b. "Now we're going down in the morning and get the blood tests."

---

context clarifies future time reference. This means, within my framework, that sentences containing the present progressive form are interpreted as present progressive sentences in their aspectual use if future time reference is not clarified by way of the context or future time adverbials.

Chapter 7   The Present Progressive   271

(C. Webb, *The Graduate*, p. 155)

c.   Right now, John is coming home tomorrow, but I doubt that he will.

(Binnick (1991: 344))

d.   Right now she's leaving tomorrow and that's that.

(boards.babycenter.com/bcus1525975/messages/4754/16)

In (10a), for example, *now* specifies the event time of the progressive *be* (E_1), which is linked to the pre-stage (e.g. the state of the speaker's being ready for the departure) and simultaneous with speech time; *tomorrow* specifies E_2, the time of the main situation (i.e. the flying itself). The fact that the two situations (i.e. the pre-stage and the main situation) are specified by two different time adverbials indicates that they occupy different times on the time line and hence are distinct (though closely related).

As a second argument, I point out Declerck's (2006: 187–188) observation that when PPF-sentences co-occur with certain adverbs expressing probability (e.g. *perhaps, possibly, maybe, probably*), the probability expressed by those adverbs refers either to the probability of the main situation or to the less certainty about the arrangement or intention associated with the situation involved.

(11)   Jim's probably leaving tomorrow.   (Declerck (2006: 187))

Declerck (2006: 187) notes that sentence (11), for example, receives at least the reading of 'Jim {intends / has arranged} to leave tomorrow, and he says he probably will' and that of 'I am not sure Jim {intends / has arranged} to leave tomorrow, but he probably {does / has}'. This suggests that in addition to the main situation, the PPF-sentence contains another situation as the target of probability judgment, i.e. a schematic situation to be specified as the intention or arrangement in temporal calculation. Because a schematic situation can have its own event time within my framework, PPF-sentences have a dual structure consisting of two situations associated with two event times.

Recall, however, that the pre-stage of PPF-sentences (Figure 3 above) is more closely related to the main situation than the preliminary stage of BGT-sentences (Figure 1 in Section 6.3.2). This is a natural consequence of our position that the pre-stage and the main situation are connected with one verb (i.e. the present participle)—as we saw above—while the preliminary stage and the infinitival situation are connected with two different verbal units, i.e. *be going to* and the infinitive. This line of reasoning may come from a pattern of cognition in which two related entities in different positions tend to co-operate less closely than the same two related entities in a single position.

There are several linguistic phenomena supporting this statement.

First, I point out as evidence that BGT-sentences, but not PPF-sentences, can co-occur with two negatives.

(12) a. She also added: "But I am not going to not go out because people care ... You are human, you have to go out and eat."   (GloWbE GB)

b. ?He isn't not going.   (Brinton (1988: 70); cf. Heine (1993: 56))

The co-occurrence of BGT-sentences with two negatives, as in (12a), implies that the preliminary stage and the main (i.e. infinitival) situation are independently negated, while the fact that it is difficult for PPF-sentences to co-occur with two negatives, as in (12b), indicates that the pre-stage of the present participle situation cannot be negated independently of the main situation. This difference suggests that the degree of independence of the preliminary stage from the main situation is higher than the degree of independence of the pre-stage from the main situation.

A second argument for the higher degree of closeness of the pre-stage to the main situation is that unlike BGT-sentences, PPF-sentences cannot go with state verbs expressing permanent states (Prince (1982: 455); cf. Swan (1995: 212, 2005: 190)).

(13) a. *I'm knowing the answer tomorrow.   (Prince (1982: 455))

b. So we think of them as being descriptive, but in reality, if you're going to say to somebody, you're very responsible, they're probably not going to know what you mean, unless you come up with a few examples of what you're talking about, of how they've demonstrated that type of behaviour.   (BNC K74)

(14) a. *Their new house is looking over the river.   (Swan (2005: 190))

b. Their new house is going to look over the river.   (Swan (2005: 190))

As we saw in Sections 6.4.3 and 6.4.4, BGT-sentences in their coda-bleached or simple-future use are compatible with (permanent) state verbs, or stative situations, because they semantically bleach the coda of the preliminary stage in their temporal structures and accordingly do not require a clear-cut boundary between the preliminary stage and the main (i.e. infinitival) situation. To be able to blur the boundary between two entities presupposes that they are fully independent of each other in the first place. Thus, for the boundary between the preliminary stage and the main situation to be able to be blurred indicates that they are originally two independent situations. Seen from this perspective, the reason why it is difficult for such bleaching or backgrounding to happen in the pre-stage of PPF-sentences is that the pre-stage and the main situa-

Chapter 7 The Present Progressive

tion are closely related to and not fully independent of each other.[24] The insufficient differentiation between the two situations does not meet the preconditions for the operation of the blurring of the boundary between the two situations and hence PPF-sentences basically do not have such bleached uses.[25]

In addition, in cases where future time reference is not clear from the context or pragmatic information, PPF-sentences must co-occur with future time adverbials (Chilton (2013: 246)), while BGT-sentences need not. This difference also reflects the difference in degree of closeness of the earlier stage to the main situation between the two types of sentences.

(15) a. *Henry is visiting Calais. [future time reference, no pragmatic or lexical indicator]   (Chilton (2013: 246))
     b. Mr. Piggy's body said: "Legalize Drugs, No more guns, Bush is going to visit his farm Colombia, no walls for people, etc ..." (GloWbE GB)

The temporal structure of BGT-sentences involves a cognitive schema in which the preliminary stage existent independently of the main situation is ongoing or obtains at speech time. We can easily understand without the help of future time adverbials that the main situation is located at a time clearly later than speech time. By contrast, the temporal structure of PPF-sentences involves a cognitive schema in which the pre-stage is not fully independent of but closely related to the main situation. Without the help of future time adverbials, the main situation can possibly be located at a time stuck to speech time, which may result in an ambiguity between future and present time reference.

To sum up, although both PPF-sentences and BGT-sentences involve an earlier stage in their temporal structures, the degree of closeness to the main situation is different between the pre-stage and the preliminary stage.

7.4. Explanation

7.4.1. PPF-Sentences

Now, we can present the temporal structures of the typical and immediate-future uses of PPF-sentences based on their basic temporal structure in Figure 3 above, whereby I will explain the temporal phenomena of the two uses.

---

[24] But see exceptional cases where the pre-stage of PPF-sentences is semantically bleached when they co-occur with *if*-clauses in the next section.
[25] This perspective is in keeping with my claim that by way of the cognitive shift or the metonymical reasoning observed in the main text, PPF-sentences—which consist of two closely-related situations, i.e. the pre-stage and the main situation—are derived from present progressive sentences (in their aspectual use) which consist only of the present participle

Let us start with the temporal structure of the typical use, which is schematized in Figure 4:

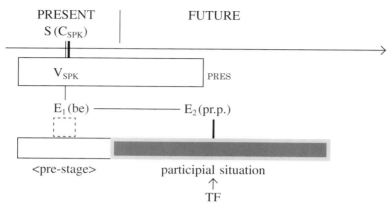

Figure 4: Temporal Structure of the Typical Use of PPF-Sentences

The only difference between this temporal structure and the temporal structure in Figure 3 is that in this temporal structure, the present time-area is distinguished from the future time-area, in which the event time of the present participle situation (E_2) is located.

Next, let us present the temporal structure of the immediate-future use, which is schematically represented in Figure 5:

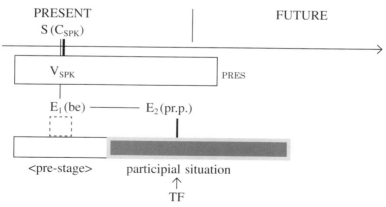

Figure 5: Temporal Structure of the Immediate-Future Use of PPF-Sentences

situation. The point here is that unlike BGT-sentences, the "ancestor" of PPF-sentences has only one situation.

Chapter 7　The Present Progressive

The only difference between this temporal structure and the temporal structure of the typical use in Figure 4 is that in this temporal structure, the event time of the present participle situation (E_2) is located in the present time-area. This is supported by the fact that PPF-sentences in their immediate-future use are modified by a present time adverb like *(right) now*, which establishes the present time-area, as illustrated by (16):[26]

(16) a.　She left the stove, grabbed her holdall and began packing everything back into it. "I'm leaving right now! If I stay in this house with you for another minute I'm going to go quite mad." 　(BNC HGT)

　　 b.　"Neil, how are you gonna do this?" Todd asked. "Ssshh! That's what I'm taking care of now," Neil explained.

(N. H. Kleinbaum, *Dead Poets Society*, p. 72)

In (16a), for instance, it is clear from the context that the speaker of the present progressive sentence has not left the house yet nor is she already in the actual process of moving out of the house; she will leave it very soon. The time of her leaving is located in the present time-area established by *right now*, but at a time later than speech time.

Now, let us consider how the differences between the two temporal structures of PPF-sentences in Figures 4 and 5 and the temporal structure of BGT-sentences (in their typical uses) affect the temporal behaviors of the two types of sentences. I will start with the differences of semantic notions with respect to the earlier stages, i.e. the pre-stage of PPF-sentences and the preliminary stage of BGT-sentences.[27] As observed in Section 7.2, PPF-sentences tend to represent semantic notions such as plans, programs, and arrangements. I will

---

[26] Just because present progressive sentences co-occur with a present time adverb like *(right) now* does not always mean that they are present progressive sentences in their immediate-future use. Such adverbs can modify the present participle situation ongoing at speech time, as in (i):

(i)　It was I who spoke those words, although for a split second I wasn't sure I really had. "Who said anything about marriage?" "Me. I'm saying it now."

(E. Segal, *Love Story*, p. 57)

In this case, they are present progressive sentences in their aspectual use.

[27] Goodman (1973) presents three semantic conditions for "futurate" sentences and one of them is called the "current-state-of-affairs" condition, which seems to be able to explain linguistic phenomena that my notion of "pre-stage" can. The other two conditions are the "definite-upper-time-bound" condition and the "no-speaker-control" condition. Although these conditions can explain a variety of differences between *will*-sentences and futurate sentences, he does not distinguish PPF-sentences from sentences containing the simple present form with future time reference and thus basically cannot give an explanation of their differences.

276   *The Grammar of Future Expressions in English*

here repeat the examples in (1), all of which exemplify one of those notions.

(1) a. We're having fish for dinner.   (Leech (2004: 61))

    b. "Yes, sir," I said. "Very unfortunate. But that's why I've come to you, sir. I'm getting married next month. We'll both be working over the summer ..."   (E. Segal, *Love Story*, p. 98)

    c. We're meeting at the cave after dinner," Cameron said to Neil.

                    (N. H. Kleinbaum, *Dead Poets Society*, p. 87)

    d. My car's going in for a service next week.   (Swan (2005: 189))

    e. THE National Theatre is breaking its long repertory tradition next March to stage a straight 16-week run of the Sondheim musical Sunday In The Park With George.   (BNC A93)

    f. He's dying next week.   (Quirk et al. (1985: 215))

These examples suggest that irrespective of whether the volition of the subject's referent is involved or not, the present participle situation is highly likely to occur in the future because of the ability or authority of the director involved (who is not necessarily the current speaker).[28]

On the other hand, BGT-sentences tend to represent semantic notions such as the grammatical subject's intention (i.e. the state after the grammatical subject has made a decision) or his/her decision made previously, which serve as a cause for the occurrence of the main (i.e. infinitival) situation. The use of BGT-sentences does not presuppose the presence of the director.

I argue that the reason why PPF-sentences and BGT-sentences have an affinity for the respective semantic notions observed above is attributed to the interaction between the nature of the semantic notions involved and the differences of the cognitive schemata in the temporal structures of the two sentences, especially those between the pre-stage and the preliminary stage. Let us first observe the following examples, which illustrate the differences of the semantic notions expressed by the two sentences.

(17) a. I'm taking Mary out for dinner this evening.   (Leech (2004: 62))

     b. I'm going to take Mary out for dinner this evening.

                                (Leech (2004: 62))

(18) a. ?I'm watching TV this evening.   (Leech (2004: 62))

     b. I'm going to watch TV this evening.   (Leech (2004: 62))

---

[28] In a similar vein, Williams (2002a: 198) states that PPF-sentences describe controllable situations such as plans and arrangements, while BGT-sentences denote intention and prediction. Hence (i) is unacceptable.

  (i) *The situation's getting worse tomorrow afternoon.   (Williams (2002a: 198))

Chapter 7   The Present Progressive

(19) a.   I'm getting a new job. (It's already arranged.)   (Swan (1995: 211))
     b.   I'm going to get a new job. (I've decided to.)   (Swan (1995: 211))

Leech (2004: 62) notes that "[a]n intention is part of one's present state of mind, while an arrangement is something socially predetermined in the past". Given this, sentence (17a), i.e. a PPF-sentence, could be used to indicate "some reluctance by someone who now regrets the arrangement" (p. 62). He also comments that because someone's watching TV alone does not have an affinity for the social nature of arrangements, he finds (18a) somewhat strange. Similarly, Swan (1995: 211, 2005: 186) observes that sentence (19a), i.e. a PPF-sentence, tends to indicate a personal arrangement, whereas sentence (19b), i.e. a BGT-sentence, tends to refer to a personal intention or decision.

There are many studies (e.g. Leech (1987, 2004), Swan (1995, 2005), Williams (2002a)) pointing out the differences between PPF-sentences and BGT-sentences observed above. However, as far as I know, no previous study has provided a detailed explanation for why PPF-sentences and BGT-sentences have an affinity for the respective semantic notions in terms of the different types of earlier stages in their temporal structures, which I will proceed to now.

As discussed above, the pre-stage and the main situation of PPF-sentences are connected with one verb (the present participle) and thus the degree of closeness between the two situations (or stages) is high in comparison with the degree of closeness between the preliminary stage and the infinitival situation of BGT-sentences. In addition, the pre-stage is regarded as the presupposed part for the main situation of PPF-sentences and thus backgrounded, which prevents the temporal focus (TF) from being directed to the event time associated with the pre-stage (E_1) because of the presence of the event time of the main situation (E_2), i.e. a more appropriate candidate to receive it. One reason why unlike the preliminary stage of BGT-sentences, the pre-stage of PPF-sentences is presupposed (and so cannot be negated, as in (12b) above) is that basically there is only one type of pre-stage — as indicated in Figures 3, 4, and 5 above — whereas there are several types of preliminary stages, including partially or fully bleached ones, as shown in Figures 2, 4, 5, and 6 in Section 6.4.[29] It is usually the case that if there are several possibilities for the pre-

---

[29] The pre-stage of PPF-sentences is a schematic situation, but not semantically bleached. This is justifiable by the fact that unlike BGT-sentences, PPF-sentences do not have the simple-future use. For example, a sentence like (i) is unacceptable.

   (i) *He is being two tomorrow.

The pre-stage leading to or bringing about the main situation is at work here and its semantic content is specified through temporal calculation. The use of PPF-sentences therefore

supposed part, it is difficult for the hearer to decide on one without further contextual information. Hence the preliminary stage of BGT-sentences would not be presupposed. To argue that the pre-stage is presupposed and not the object of assertion implies that one usually cannot control it, i.e., it is "un-touchable"; therefore, once the pre-stage goes underway, the main situation, which is closely linked with the pre-stage and whose event time (E_2) receives the temporal focus, is regarded as highly likely to occur.

On the other hand, as observed in Section 6.3.2, the preliminary stage and the main situation of BGT-sentences are connected, respectively, with *be going to* and the infinitive (i.e. two different verbal units) and so the degree of close-ness between the two situations is lower than in the case of PPF-sentences. The preliminary stage of BGT-sentences is not a presupposed part, as we saw above, and can be negated, as shown in (12a) above; the temporal focus is directed to E_1, i.e. the event time of the preliminary stage, which is foregrounded. These observations enable us to claim that even if the prelimi-nary stage is under way, the main situation following that stage is not very likely to occur in comparison with the main part of the present participle situ-ation in PPF-sentences, especially when the coda is bleached.

We can now consider why the semantic notions of arrangements and (fixed) plans tend to be associated with the pre-stage, while the semantic notions of intentions and previously-made decisions tend to be associated with the pre-liminary stage. Considering the definitions of those notions common to sever-al dictionaries (e.g. Crowther et al. (1995), Sinclair et al. (2006)), we can de-fine them as follows: an arrangement is defined not only as a plan or prepara-tion but also as an agreement with someone to do something; a plan is an idea thought about in detail in advance or something that one has decided to achieve; an intention is an aim or something that one proposes or plans to do; and a decision is a conclusion reached or a judgment. Indeed it is difficult to distinguish completely between these notions, but the definitions above at least enable us to argue that the former two notions (arrangements and plans) tend to make the occurrence of the situation more certain than the latter two, i.e. previously-made intentions and decisions (the phrase "previously made" is added because of the characteristics of the preliminary stage observed in Chapter 6). An agreement with someone (i.e. arrangement) and something

---

requires us to assume something ongoing toward the actualization of the main situation, i.e. some semantic content of the pre-stage. However, with the simple-future use the main situ-ation is regarded as absolutely certain to occur without the speaker's assumption of such se-mantic content. A discrepancy arises and hence the unacceptability of (i).

Chapter 7 The Present Progressive 279

thought about in detail beforehand (i.e. plan) are generally more difficult to halt or cancel than a mere aim (i.e. intention) or a conclusion reached or a mere judgment (i.e. decision) in that the former two notions — arrangements normally cannot be canceled unilaterally and plans have been considered carefully before one has decided to achieve — require more effort (physically or psychologically) for interruption or cancellation than the latter two notions, which can be cancelled relatively easily because the speaker usually has not done much effort or consulted others to arrive at them. The observations thus far suggest that the situations based on the notions of arrangements and plans are more certain to occur than those based on the notions of previously-made intentions and decisions.

From the above discussion, I conclude that the notions of arrangements and plans are more compatible with the pre-stage in the temporal structure of PPF-sentences, whereas the notions of intentions and previously-made decisions go better with the preliminary stage in the temporal structure of BGT-sentences. As far as I know, only by assuming the temporal structures of PPF-sentences and BGT-sentences constructed above can we explain, from a unified and broader perspective, why notions such as arrangements and plans tend to be associated with PPF-sentences and notions such as previously-made intentions and decisions tend to be associated with BGT-sentences.

Let us next explain another difference between PPF-sentences and BGT-sentences which reflects the differences between their temporal structures, i.e. why PPF-sentences require the presence of the director (i.e. someone who has the ability or authority to carry out the arrangement or plan and is committed to their actualization) while it is not necessarily the case with BGT-sentences. This can also be explained by the degree of closeness between the earlier stage and the main situation. As we have seen, PPF-sentences have a higher degree of closeness between the pre-stage and the main situation, which brings about a higher degree of actualization of the main situation. If there is someone or some organization having the ability or authority to carry out the target situation, it is more likely to be actualized. PPF-sentences thus go well with the nature of the notion director. It must be noted, however, that the director is a derivative notion that can be attributed to the temporal-structure information of PPF-sentences, namely the high degree of closeness between the pre-stage and the main situation. By contrast, the degree of closeness between the preliminary stage and the main situation is not so high in the case of BGT-sentences and hence their use does not necessarily require the existence of a director.

This line of explanation enables us to account for some further differences

280 *The Grammar of Future Expressions in English*

between PPF-sentences and BGT-sentences. First, we do not usually regard uncontrollable situations (including natural phenomena) as occurring with very high probability and PPF-sentences are therefore basically incompatible with such situations, as exemplified by (20):[30]

(20) a. *Things are getting better soon.   (Swan (1995: 211))
     b. *He's having an accident one of these days.   (Swan (1995: 211))
     c. *It's snowing before long. (=(4a))

Since BGT-sentences are not affected by such a higher-degree-of-occurrence constraint, they are compatible with uncontrollable situations, as in (21):

(21) a. Things are going to get better soon.   (Swan (1995: 211))
     b. He's going to have an accident one of these days. (Swan (1995: 211))
     c. It's going to snow before long.   (Swan (2005: 190))

Second, since the chooser of PPF-sentences construes the pre-stage (leading to the occurrence of the main situation) with assertive modality, PPF-sentences denoting uncertainty of the main situation are less acceptable. Directing the assertive modality to the pre-stage, so to speak, brings the main situation into its target range because the two stages (situations) are considered as inseparably connected. It is usually the case that one cannot construe as a fact the situation whose position on the time line is not clear and/or whose semantic content is not clear enough. That is, we cannot make a confident assertion about the situation without knowing when it occurs.[31] Thus, sentences like (22a) are less acceptable.

---

[30] Goodman (1973) points out the fact that some sentences describing natural phenomena are compatible with PPF-sentences, but others are not, as illustrated in (i), claiming that the notion "plan" cannot explain some linguistic phenomena concerning PPF-sentences.
    (i) a. The sun is setting at 8:39 tomorrow.   (Goodman (1973: 81))
        b. An eclipse is occurring tomorrow morning.   (Goodman (1973: 81))
        c. *It is raining tomorrow.   (Goodman (1973: 81))
He convincingly states that the reason for the difference in question is that "the position of the sun and the moon are believed to be predictable by current technology, while the state of the weather is not believed to be predictable". In my analysis, sentences (ia) and (ib) are acceptable because our present-day science and technology enable us to predict the actualization of their main situations and thus have the pre-stages in mind, even if they are subjectively ongoing in our mind; however, our present-day science and technology are not so reliable with respect to weather forecast and so it is difficult to assume an appropriate pre-stage for tomorrow's weather conditions.

[31] In this connection, Goodman (1973: 85–86) observes the following examples:
    (i) a. *Joe is cooking dinner tomorrow when he's unexpectedly shot.
                                                              (Goodman (1973: 85))

Chapter 7   The Present Progressive   281

(22) a. ?Henry is visiting Calais in the future.   (Chilton (2013: 246))

   b.   ... and these costs are going to rise in the future.
                     (https://www.ncbi.nlm.nih.gov/pmc/articles/PMC1409849/)

On the other hand, in the case of BGT-sentences, the degree of closeness between the preliminary stage and the main situation is not so high and they can
thus escape from such a constraint, as shown in (22b).

It must be stressed again that the presence of the director in the case of
PPF-sentences is derived from the characteristics of their temporal structure,
especially the nature of the pre-stage. If the director came directly from the
nature of PPF-sentences itself, we would not explain why the acceptability
judgment differs from native speaker to native speaker with respect to sentences referring to uncontrollable situations, as in (23):[32]

(23) a. *The sun is rising at 5 o'clock tomorrow.
                              (Leech (2004: 63); cf. Wekker (1976: 103))

   b.   The sun is setting at 6:31 tomorrow.
                              (Prince (1982: 458); cf. Goodman (1973: 81))

Within my framework, the notion director is a strong pragmatic implicature,
an implicature available in most contexts where PPF-sentences are used; however, it is the higher degree of actualization of the main situation of PPF-sentences that characterizes the linguistic behaviors of PPF-sentences. We thus
argue that native speakers who accept (23b) only place emphasis on the high-
er-degree-of-actualization aspect in choosing PPF-sentences, which is due to
the close relationship between the pre-stage and the main situation, and do not
pay attention to the aspect of the director, i.e. someone or an organization
having the ability or authority to carry out the main situation.

─────────────

   b. *Sue is mowing the lawn tomorrow when she discovers the body.
                                                        (Goodman (1973: 86))
In my opinion, these sentences are unacceptable for the following reason. The scene introduced by the *when*-clause is a temporal setting and thus presupposition for the occurrence of
the main clause situation (cf. Section 3.8). However, the *when*-clauses in (i) refer to an ac-
cidental situation and it is thus difficult to anticipate when it will be actualized. In short,
the semantic content of the *when*-clause is indefinite future-oriented. On the other hand, as
repeated in the main text, the degree of actualization of the main situation of PPF-sentences
is very high and the speaker makes a confident assertion about it. The semantic content of
the PPF-sentence is more present-oriented. Thus, a kind of contradiction arises between the
two clauses.
   [32] Copley (2009) views the presence of the director as one of the core meanings of PPF-
sentences, but this view cannot explain why some native speakers accept a sentence like
(23b), which refers to an uncontrollable situation.

Furthermore, the difference between the temporal structures of PPF-sentences and BGT-sentences observed above, i.e. the distinction between the pre-stage and the preliminary stage, can explain Swan's (2005: 190) observation that unlike BGT-sentences, PPF-sentences cannot emphasize the intention of the subject's referent holding at speech time.

(24) a. *I'm really telling him what I think of him.   (Swan (2005: 190))
     b. I'm really going to tell him what I think of him. (Swan (2005: 190))

In (24), the adverb *really* is assumed to modify an earlier stage ongoing at speech time in both sentences. The earlier stage in BGT-sentences is the preliminary stage, which is conceptually seen as separate from the main situation in the future; the stage can thus be emphasized as an independent entity. By contrast, the earlier stage in PPF-sentences is the pre-stage, which is conceptually seen as inseparably connected to the main situation and in addition as a presupposed part of it. Thus it cannot be emphasized as an independent entity.

Let us now turn to a description of how our model accounts for the correlation between PPF-sentences and conditional clauses with future time reference — a common but intriguing topic concerning future expressions. To this end, we must first recall that *will*-sentences are much more likely to occur in the apodosis of conditional sentences with future time reference (i.e. type A conditional sentences) than BGT-sentences, as in (25):

(25) a.   You will learn to drive a car proficiently if you take this course.
                                            (Declerck (1991a: 115))
     b. *You are going to learn to drive a car proficiently if you take this
        course.   (Declerck (1991a: 115))

The reason why BGT-sentences usually cannot co-occur with *if*-clauses with future time reference was this: the preliminary stage already ongoing at speech time in the temporal structure of BGT-sentences in their typical uses — which serves as a kind of condition for the actualization of the main (i.e. infinitival) situation — contradicts a condition to be given in the future and therefore the BGT-sentences usually can co-occur only with *if*-clauses with present time reference, as shown in (26).

(26)   We're going to find ourselves in difficulty if we go like this.
                                            (Leech (2004: 60))

However, as observed in Section 6.6.4, the BGT-sentences whose temporal structure includes the bleached preliminary stage (Figure 10 in Section 6.6.4) and is thus similar to that of *will*-sentences in their future reference uses can

Chapter 7   The Present Progressive

appear in this linguistic environment, as shown in (27b).

(27) a. *You're breaking that chair if you're not careful. (=6a))
      b.   You {will/are going to} break that chair if you're not careful. (=(6b))

Now a question arises as to why sentence (27a), which includes a PPF-sentence in the main clause, is unacceptable. The model developed in this study can explain this fact. Since PPF-sentences include the pre-stage (i.e. an earlier stage ongoing at speech time to be semantically contentful in temporal calculation) in their temporal structure, a sentence like (27a) is unacceptable for the same reason that conditional clauses co-occurring with the typical uses of BGT-sentences in the main clause, such as (25b), are unacceptable.

However, things are not so simple as they seem. As with *will*-sentences and BGT-sentences, PPF-sentences sometimes can co-occur with conditional clauses with future time reference, as illustrated below:[33]

(28)   If you break that chair, {a. you're paying/b. you're gonna pay/c. you'll pay} for it.
(29)   If he brings a gun in here, {a. I'm calling/b. I'm gonna call/c. I'll call} the police.

I will explain this fact in the same way that we did with respect to BGT-sentences. To be specific, I argue that some native speakers, by analogy, interpret the pre-stages of the PPF-sentences in (28) and (29) as semantically bleached. However, this argument appears to be contradictory to the claim made above that PPF-sentences basically cannot allow a bleached type of pre-stage. How can we accommodate this apparent discrepancy? A key to solve this question lies in a general view that we prefer marked to unmarked cases. In this case, type A conditional sentences serve as a kind of "construction" and constitute a marked linguistic environment in that they specifically require the cause-effect relationship between the conditional and main clauses. I assume that for some native speakers, such a linguistic environment "coerces" the PPF-sentences to behave in a marked way by means of the operation of the analogy.

With this observation in mind, let us take a look at the temporal structure of PPF-sentences in the main clause of type A conditional sentences, which is schematized in Figure 6.

---

[33] I owe the examples in (28) and (29) to an anonymous *EL* reviewer.

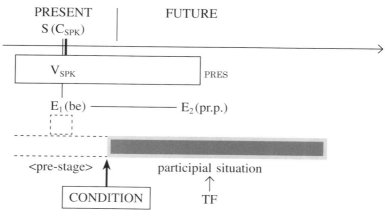

Figure 6: Temporal Structure of the Future-Condition Use of PPF-Sentences

In this linguistic environment, the future-oriented condition of type A conditional sentences (i.e. a marked construction) affects part of the temporal structure of PPF-sentences. More specifically, the pre-stage ongoing at speech time is coerced to be semantically bleached and only the main part of the present participle situation, i.e. main situation — which is located at a time later than speech time — is "activated" in the cognitive schema of the temporal structure of the PPF-sentence under consideration. As a result of such a coercion, the PPF-sentence can co-occur with an *if*-clause referring to a future condition for the actualization of the main situation. This temporal structure is basically the same as that of BGT-sentences co-occurring with type A conditional clauses, i.e. conditionals with future time reference, as seen in Figure 10 in Section 6.6.4.

A question still remains as to why the pre-stage is able to be semantically bleached in this linguistic environment. My answer is as follows. Without the influence of the properties of type A conditional sentences, as we saw above, the temporal structure of PPF-sentences implies that the pre-stage depicts a situation as a kind of condition leading to the actualization of the main situation. However, in type A conditional sentences, as in (28) and (29), the semantic content supplied by the *if*-clause preferentially functions as a condition for the actualization of the main situation, namely that the condition supplied by the pre-stage is overridden by the one supplied by the *if*-clause. This override is motivated by a general idea that we usually place priority on what is explicitly stated rather than what is implied when interpreting what the speaker is conveying. The content of the *if*-clause situations in (28) and (29)

Chapter 7   The Present Progressive

is explicitly stated, while that of the pre-stages is merely implied by the PPF-sentences. I thus conclude that for those who accept sentences like (28) and (29), under such a general idea the co-occurrence of a PPF-sentence with a conditional clause with future time reference is a driving force bringing about the semantic bleaching of its pre-stage.[34]

For a better understanding of what we have observed, consider (28a) as a concrete example. If the conditional clause were removed, the PPF-sentence would be interpreted "normally", namely that the pre-stage (e.g. the situation in which the addressee has been arranged to pay for something) is the precondition for the actualization of the main situation (i.e. the addressee's payment itself). Actually, however, the conditional clause provides a condition (i.e. the addressee's breaking a chair) for the actualization of the main situation and the condition implied by the pre-stage is "forced away" from the interpretation process. In other words, the implied condition supplied by the pre-stage is overridden by the explicit condition supplied by the *if*-clause and hence the stage is semantically bleached. In this way, PPF-sentences like those in (28) and (29) are regarded as those having a semantically bleached pre-stage.

Before closing this sub-section, let us briefly consider the mechanism in which PPF-sentences convey speech act meanings. As with *will*-sentences and BGT-sentences, PPF-sentences often convey speech act meanings, such as orders, commands or refusals (Swan (1995: 212, 2005: 190), Kashino (1999: 79–80)). Consider (30):

(30) a.   You're finishing that soup if you sit there all afternoon!

(Swan (2005: 190))

b.   "Actually, I think I should go home," Terese said. "You're staying right here," Colleen ordered.   (requoted from Kashino (1999: 79–80))

c.   "You're staying for dinner. That's an order."

(E. Segal, *Love Story*, p. 69)

d.   She's taking that medicine whether she likes it or not!

(Swan (2005: 190))

e.   I'm not washing your socks — forget it!   (Swan (2005: 190))

---

[34] Viewed from a different angle, the closer relationship between the pre-stage and the main situation indicated in the temporal structure of PPF-sentences prevents the semantic bleaching of the pre-stage, unless a substitute for the pre-stage, such as a type A conditional clause, is explicitly shown.

Sentences (30a-c) imply the speaker's order or command; sentence (30d) implies the speaker's indirect order; and sentence (30e) implies the speaker's refusal. The mechanism in which these PPF-sentences convey indirect speech acts is basically the same as the mechanism in which *will*-sentences and BGT-sentences do. Within my framework, these speech act uses are pragmatic variants derived from the temporal structure of PPF-sentences in their typical or future-condition use in the situation report tier, where the speech acts in question are conveyed to the addressee. Take (30d) for example. In the situation construal tier, the main situation of the typical use of the PPF-sentence (i.e. the ingestion of a certain medicine) is highly likely to occur because the situation is affected by the assertive modality directed to the pre-stage, i.e. a presupposed part inseparably connected to that situation. In the situation report tier, the information about the interpersonal relationship between speaker and addressee and the contextual information (e.g. the presence of the exclamation mark, the implication stemming from the semantic content of the *whether* clause) are added for the interpretation of the PPF-sentence and thus the speech act meaning, namely that the subject's referent is required to take that medicine, is obtained.

The interpretation mechanism for (30a) may be a little different from that for (30d), for the PPF-sentence is of the future-condition type. In this case, as we saw above (cf. Figure 6), the condition specified by the *if*-clause serves as the precondition for the actualization of the main situation of the PPF-sentence—while the pre-stage is interpreted as semantically bleached—and the interpretation mechanism is therefore very similar to that of *will*-sentences with type A conditional clauses (Section 5.4.7). Considering the information about the interpersonal relationship between speaker and addressee and the contextual information (e.g. the presence of the exclamation mark, the second-person subject), we can interpret the sentence as conveying a speech act meaning such as order in the situation report tier.

7.4.2. Present Progressive Sentences with Future Time Reference Other Than PPF-Sentences

Thus far, we have considered temporal phenomena concerning PPF-sentences. In this section, we will take a brief look at another type of present progressive sentences with future time reference. Observe (31):

(31)   You are now entering a nuclear-free zone.   (Williams (2002a: 32))

This sentence is used for a road sign. Williams (2002a: 32) notes that a present progressive sentence like this merely describes an ongoing situation at a

Chapter 7   The Present Progressive

future time; such a sentence is a future version of the present progressive sentence in its aspectual use. The present form *are* does not refer to speech time, i.e. the time of writing the road sign, but to the time when a "construer" is assumed to see it, e.g., when he/she is driving in a certain district.[35]

The point here is that the speaker chooses the present tense form with the base point situated at a time in the future relative to speech time.[36] This certainly reflects the characteristics of an aspectual use of present progressive sentences. Unlike in the default case, however, the speaker's t(emporal)-viewpoint (V_{SPK}) included in the tense structure of this present tense form does not fuse with his/her own consciousness at speech time, but with the consciousness of the assumed construer; as a result, the event time of the progressive *be* (i.e. E^O_1) is located at a future time of orientation (O) when the construer is assumed to see the road sign, with which the event time of the present participle (i.e. E_2) is simultaneous.

The temporal structure of present progressive sentences in their aspectual use with future time reference is schematized in Figure 7:

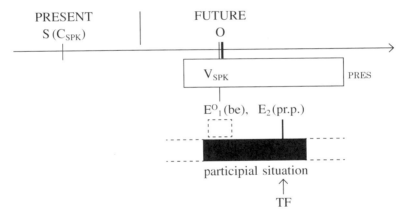

Figure 7: Temporal Structure of Present Progressive Sentences in Their Aspectual Use with Future Time Reference

The only difference in temporal structure between the aspectual use with future time reference and the aspectual use with present time reference of pres-

---

[35] This use corresponds to the use of "note" in the case of sentences containing the simple present form, which we will consider in Chapter 8.
[36] Generally, the form *will* + *be* + *-ing* is chosen for a time reference like this, as in (i):
   (i)   This time next week they will be sailing across the North Sea.   (Leech (2004: 66))
We will discuss this form in detail in Chapter 10.

ent progressive sentences is that in the former use the speaker's t-viewpoint is located at a time of orientation in the future while in the latter it is located at speech time; with respect to the other parts, the two temporal structures are the same.

7.4.3. The Past Tense

Finally, I will explain the often-made observation that like BGT-sentences in the past tense, past progressive sentences with future time reference, i.e. past progressive futurate sentences—which refer to a situation in the future relative to a past time of orientation—tend to imply non-fulfillment of the main situation (Leech (1987, 2004: 52), Kashino (1999: 83)). Compare (32a) with (32b):

(32) a. The beauty contest was taking place on the next day.

(Leech (2004: 52))

 b. The beauty contest was going to take place on the next day.

(Leech (2004: 52))

The mechanism in which the BGT-sentence in the past tense in (32b) indicates non-fulfillment of the main (i.e. infinitival) situation was already discussed in Section 6.6.5: when it is interpreted as an instance of the bleached-coda use, it implies non-fulfillment of the infinitival situation because of the break in the cognitive schema between the preliminary stage (with its coda bleached) and the infinitival situation.

How about the past progressive futurate sentence in (32a), then? As observed above, PPF-sentences (i.e. the present tense counterpart of past progressive futurate sentences) tend to refer to a present participle situation that is highly likely to occur. Isn't this tendency contradictory to the tendency of past progressive futurate sentences observed above? My answer would be that the interaction between the temporal structure of past progressive futurate sentences and a reference to a specific past situation in the real world implies non-fulfillment of past progressive futurate sentences.[37]

Before starting our discussion, let me first present the two types of temporal structures of past progressive futurate sentences. Figure 8(i) schematizes the temporal structure of past progressive futurate sentences for the non-fulfillment case and Figure 8(ii) represents that for the fulfillment case:

---

[37] The idea that PPF-sentences in their typical use tend to imply fulfillment of the main situation comes from the interaction between their temporal structure and a reference to a specific future situation in the projected world located on the extended time line of the real world.

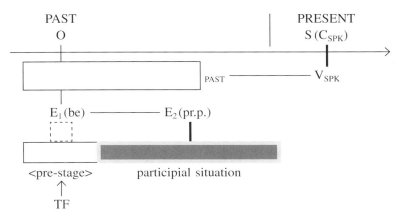

Figure 8(i): Temporal Structure of Past Progressive Futurate Sentences (Non-fulfillment Version)

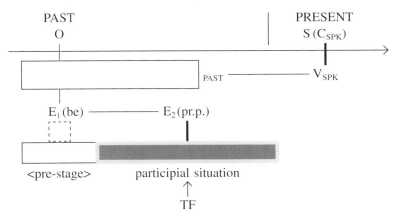

Figure 8(ii): Temporal Structure of Past Progressive Futurate Sentences (Fulfillment Version)

Note that the temporal structure of past progressive futurate sentences in Figure 8(i), unlike that of PPF-sentences in Figure 3 above, requires the temporal focus (TF) to be directed at the event time of *be* (E_1), whereas the temporal structure of past progressive futurate sentences in Figure 8(ii), like that of PPF-sentences, requires it to be directed at the event time of the main situation (E_2). What motivates such a temporal focus shift in the use of past progressive futurate sentences in Figure 8(i)?

The mechanism is as follows. We have already seen that PPF-sentences basically refer to cases where the pre-stage is inseparably connected to the main situation and regarded as a presupposed part, which is hard to make foregrounded. The temporal focus is therefore directed at the event time associated with the main situation (E_2) in PPF-sentences. However, we are here considering cases where a past specific situation is referred to in the real world and the speaker is usually assumed to know whether the past situation involved was actualized or not. These cases were referred to as past contexts (i.e. contexts where the speaker looks back at past situations as facts) in Section 6.6.5. We may thus reason: if the speaker intends to convey that the situation was really actualized, he/she can use the simple past form, i.e. a tense form straightforwardly indicating its actualization. Using a past progressive futurate sentence, therefore, would imply something that a simple past sentence cannot indicate, i.e. a reference to an earlier stage (i.e. pre-stage) which serves as a precondition for the main situation. Due to the special characteristics of this environment, the pre-stage is now the target of the assertion and thus coerced to be more separated from the main situation and foregrounded with the temporal focus shifted to the event time of *be* (E_1), which occupies the same time as the past time of orientation, as shown in Figure 8(i) above.[38] The idea that the pre-stage is foregrounded by means of the temporal focus shift suggests that it is no longer merely the presupposition for the main situation but is more focused than the main situation itself. We would thus obtain the following reasoning. The speaker bothers to use past progressive futurate sentences whose temporal structure includes the event time of the pre-stage receiving the temporal focus because he/she intends to refer only to the semantic content of the pre-stage; the main situation is thus coerced to be "forced away" from the main focus in temporal calculation and hence its non-fulfillment is implied.

However, as with BGT-sentences in the past tense, non-fulfillment of the main situation of past progressive futurate sentences is merely an implicature deriving from the above reasoning. If there are factors interrupting the reasoning process, past progressive futurate sentences can indicate fulfillment of the main clause (Figure 8(ii)). In past contexts, this interpretation of past progressive futurate sentences is a marked case, though.

To illustrate the point, let us consider (32a) above. Here, the pre-stage (e.g. the state after the decision has been made by the director to hold a beauty

---

[38] As indicated in the main text, this temporal focus shift does not occur with PPF-sentences. This is partly because the main situation cannot be referred to as a (past) fact; since it is located in the projected world, i.e. a world located on the extended time line of the real world, we cannot know, at speech time, whether the main situation is actualized or not.

Chapter 7   The Present Progressive   291

contest) is taken as foregrounded, because we may assume that if the speaker had wanted to show that the contest has really happened, he/she would have chosen the simple past form, which would straightforwardly indicate its actualization.   The reason why the speaker chooses a tense form whose temporal structure includes the pre-stage would be that he/she intends to focus on the precondition for the main situation and refer only to it, which implies that the speaker wants to convey that the main situation (i.e. the beauty contest) itself did not happen.   Hence the use of the type of past progressive futurate sentences schematized in Figure 8(i).   We conclude that this use is motivated by the temporal focus shift based on the pragmatic reasoning triggered by the special characteristics of past contexts observed above and has come to be an independent semantic use of past progressive futurate sentences through pragmatic strengthening.   A sentence like (32a) is interpreted as indicating the actualization of the main situation only when the context explicitly indicates that (where the temporal structure in Figure 8(ii) is in operation).

7.5.   Concluding Remarks

In this chapter, we have discussed a variety of temporal phenomena concerning PPF-sentences, especially in comparison with BGT-sentences.   The characteristics of PPF-sentences observed above are the following: (i) they tend to be associated with semantic notions like arrangements or plans, i.e. notions more likely to occur and less likely to be cancelled or halted than intentions or decisions; (ii) they typically require the presence of the director and the co-occurrence with controllable situations; and (iii) it is basically hard for them to co-occur with type A conditional clauses, i.e. conditionals of the direct cause-effect type with future time reference.   We showed that these characteristics are all derived from the characteristics of the temporal structure of PPF-sentences.   The temporal structure of PPF-sentences (Figure 3) is conceptually derived from that of present progressive sentences in their aspectual use (Figure 1) via that of the middle-stage use of present progressive sentences (Figure 2).   Although PPF-sentences have been grammaticalized through this derivation process, the three semantic uses associated with their respective temporal structures are synchronically acquired by native speakers of English and stored in their grammar.

We compared PPF-sentences with BGT-sentences—both sentences include tense forms which have two situations in the cognitive schema of the temporal structure and are assumed to refer to situations in the rather near future—and found that the three characteristics of PPF-sentences pointed out above are attributed to the nature of the pre-stage (i.e. an earlier stage of the present participle situation) or, more precisely, the higher degree of closeness between the pre-stage and the main part of the present participle situation. Although the pre-stage is a similar notion to the preliminary stage of BGT-sentences, the former is conceptualized as more closely connected to the main situation and expressing notions like a cause or precondition for the main situation. The pre-stage is a presupposed part for the main situation, which indicates that it basically cannot be foregrounded. In marked environments, however, the characteristics associated with the pre-stage surveyed just above can be coerced. For example, for some native speakers, PPF-sentences co-occurring with type A conditional clauses can have a semantically-bleached pre-stage. In reference to a past specific situation in the real world (i.e. past contexts), the pre-stage of past progressive futurate sentences can usually be foregrounded. I stress again that my framework can, in a motivated way, bring about new temporal structures that might appear to be contradictory to those of the basic or typical uses and can explore language dynamism (i.e. change or variation of meanings and uses)—a strong point of my framework.

Chapter 8

The Simple Present

8.1. Introduction

As Williams (2002a: 127) puts it, "[s]ince we live in the present moment, it is not surprising to find that the present tense is the one we use most in verbal communication." This statement may account for why the simple present form has so many uses and functions. What concerns us in this chapter is a variety of uses/functions indicated by sentences containing the simple present form with future time reference. Included in them are uses/functions referring to fixed or scheduled future events. The simple present form describing a fixed or scheduled event is often termed the simple futurate and dealt with in almost all grammar books as well as articles and monographs concerning tense (e.g. Brisard (2002), Copley (2009), Declerck (1991a, 2006), De Wit (2017), Goodman (1973), Hirtle (1967, 1995), Hirtle and Curat (1986), Huddleston and Pullum (2002), Langacker (1991, 2001, 2011), Leech (1987, 2004), Palmer (1974, 1988), Prince (1982), Quirk et al. (1985), Swan (1995, 2005), Vetter (1973), Wekker (1976), Williams (2002a)). Henceforth, I refer to sentences containing the simple futurate in the present tense as SFP-sentences. Since we have already discussed a number of non-future reference uses of the simple present (see Section 4.2), we focus on its future reference uses, including SFP-sentences, in this chapter. To be more specific, I investigate how and under what circumstances the temporal structures of SFP-sentences as well as other simple present sentences with future time reference are constructed in our mind.

In this chapter, we mainly consider synchronic characteristics of simple present sentences with future time reference, including SFP-sentences. In Section 8.2, we observe linguistic facts concerning several uses of the simple present sentences with future time reference. In Section 8.3, we consider the types of uses observed in Section 8.2 in more detail, presenting their respec-

294   *The Grammar of Future Expressions in English*

tive temporal structures, from which their respective characteristics stem. Moreover, we compare some uses of SFP-sentences with similar uses of other future expressions and explain how they are similar to or different from one another in terms of the similarities and differences in the temporal structures involved. Section 8.4 makes concluding remarks.

8.2. Uses and Functions of Simple Present Sentences with Future Time Reference

This chapter considers the eight uses/functions of simple present sentences with future time reference, as illustrated in (1):

(1) a. The train leaves at eight o'clock tomorrow.   (Leech (2004: 11))
    b. Tomorrow's Saturday.   (Leech (2004: 65))
    c. When you wake up, you'll remember nothing.   (Leech (2004: 63))
    d. I am in room 2114.   (Declerck (2003: 86))
    e. We go to Headington now and George, hello George.   (BNC KRL)
    f. You take the first turning on the left past the roundabout, then you cross a bridge and bear right until you reach the public library.
                   (Leech (2004: 17))
    g. Either that alligator goes or I go.   (R. Lakoff (1970: 845))
    h. Biff and his friends hop into a car parked outside. Marty stares at George as George is eating. George becomes very uncomfortable and turns to Marty.   (Screenplay, *Back to the Future*, p. 62)

Sentence (1a) indicates that the situation involved is judged to occur at a specific future time, based on a certain situation obtaining at speech time which forms part of the structure of the world, i.e. a set of rules and constitutions of the society as well as the universe surrounding us (cf. Section 4.2.2). This use is called the *fixed-future* use (a typical use of SFP-sentences) in this study.[1, 2] The simple present form in (1b) is a special instance of the fixed-future use. It refers to a situation at a specific future time that comes into existence as a natural result of a present situation constituting the structure of the world and its actualization is not subject to the speaker's judgment. This use is called the *simple-future* use in this study. The fixed-future and simple-fu-

---

[1] The structural-description use observed in Chapter 4 describes a characterizing situation constituting part of the structure of the world that obtains in the present, so it differs from the fixed-future use.

[2] This use was referred to as the futurate-construction use in Wada (2015b, 2015c).

Chapter 8   The Simple Present

ture uses differ in that it is possible with the former use that the situation will not occur, but this is not the case with the latter. The simple present form in the subordinate clause of (1c) refers to a situation in the future. This use is here referred to as the *future-reference-in-subordinate-clause* use. The simple present form in (1d) is an instance of a special use called *note*. The "encoder" or writer chooses this use of the simple present form when imagining a scene in which the "decoder" or reader sees the note at a time later than the time of writing it (i.e. speech time). The simple present form in (1e) refers to a situation at a time immediately after speech time, located in the present time-area (cognitive present) established by a present time adverbial such as *now*. I refer to this use as the *immediate-future* use. The simple present forms in (1f) are used in a context where the situations involved are conveyed to the hearer as instructions and so this use is termed the *instruction-giving* use. All this use requires is that the situation involved occur or obtain in a time range later than speech time, i.e. the time of giving the instruction, irrespective of whether the time range is the present or the future time-area. The simple present forms in (1g) appear in a construction consisting of *either A or B*, in which the speaker regards either one of the two as absolutely certain to occur in his/ her mind. This use is named the *either-or* use in this study and requires, as with the instruction-giving use, that the situation involved be located in the time range later than speech time, irrespective of whether the time range is the present or the future time-area. Finally, the simple present forms in (1h) express stage directions and are thus instances of the *stage-direction* use. This use is a type of the simple present form with future time reference in that the situations involved are assumed to occur or obtain in the fictional worlds created by playwrights or dramatists, which will be opened to the public in the future relative to the time of writing plays or dramas, i.e. speech time. As is clear from the observations so far, SFP-sentences are part of simple present sentences with future time reference. The simple present form in English has a variety of uses even if we restrict them to uses with future time reference.

8.3.   Temporal Structures of Simple Present Sentences with Future Time Reference and Their Analysis

Having shown the uses of simple present sentences with future time reference to be dealt with, I will in this section consider their characteristics in more detail and offer their temporal structures, whereby I will analyze the uses one by one. Before going further, however, it should be stressed again that within the present framework, instances sharing the same tense form have the same tense structure in common. Therefore, as with the simple present sentences with non-future time reference observed in Chapter 4, the simple present sentences with future time reference to be observed in this chapter all share the tense structure schematized in Figure 2(i) in Chapter 2. This tense structure is projected onto the cognitive time line and develops into the temporal structure of each use under the influence of the characteristics of the relevant factors. The cognitive time line is basically identified as the real time line but can be seen as the time line in a possible, imaginative, or fictional world. The principle repeated below, which worked as the default principle in the case of simple present sentences with non-future time reference in Chapter 4, is also in operation as the default principle in the case of simple present sentences with future time reference.

(2)   The speaker's t-viewpoint fuses with his/her consciousness at speech time.

Strictly speaking, simple present sentences with future time reference should be restricted to sentences expressing a situation located in the future time-area on the real time line (i.e. the projected world), but in this book they are intended to cover all simple present sentences expressing a situation that will occur or obtain at a time later than speech time, irrespective of the time is on the real, imaginative, or fictional time line.

8.3.1. The Fixed-Future Use

Let us start with the fixed-future use of simple present sentences with future time reference, illustrated by (1a), i.e. *The train leaves at eight o'clock tomorrow*. This use is seen as a typical use of SFP-sentences, referring to a single situation at a specific time in the future time-area that will occur or obtain as a natural result of a situation or scene valid in the structure of the world (Calver (1946: 323)). Because the situation involved is specific and the target of the speaker's focus, the temporal focus is directed at the event time associated with that situation.

Recall that within the present framework, unmodalized forms in independent or main clauses are normally accompanied by assertive modality. I thus argue that this SFP-sentence is accompanied by assertive modality. At a first glance, this argument might appear to violate the "restriction on assertion", namely that we can normally only make an assertion about what is present or past relative to the time of assertion (cf. Section 2.4.3.5), but this is not the case. This use involves the situation obtaining at speech time which constitutes part of the structure of the world. The situation in question is one characterizing the world structure and henceforth referred to as a WS (world structure)-characterizing situation. What is asserted in this use is the WS-characterizing situation, a situation in the present relative to the time of assertion (i.e. speech time). Thus, the simple present form in its fixed-future use can be accompanied by assertive modality, a speaker's mental attitude toward the situation involved.[3]

The temporal structure of the fixed-future use of simple present sentences is schematically represented below:

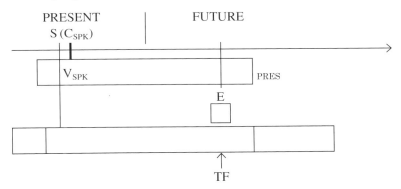

Figure 1: Temporal Structure of the Fixed-Future Use of Simple Present Sentences

The default principle in (2) works in this use and the speaker's t-viewpoint (V_{SPK}) fuses with his/her consciousness (C_{SPK}) at speech time (S), i.e. the deictic center for the cognitive (real) time line. The present time-sphere (grammatical present) corresponds to the present and future time-areas (cognitive time ranges) and in this case the relevant event time (E) is located in the future time-area. In the cognitive schema, the square below E denotes the target (specific) situation to occur or obtain in the future and the relevant event time is associated with that situation. The longer rectangle below the square symbolizes the structure of the world, while the shorter rectangle refers to a WS-characterizing situation. The vertical line connecting S and the rectangles indicates that the structure of the world and the WS-characterizing situation both obtain in the time range including speech time.

By way of illustration, consider some concrete examples, shown in (3):

---

[3] The assertive modality in this use can be regarded as a mental attitude of the speaker when he/she views the situation to occur or obtain as if it were a fact now (cf. Fleischman (1982)).

(3) a. The train leaves at eight o'clock tomorrow. (=(1a))
   b. I retire from work next month. (Leech (2004: 11))
   c. The new album is out early next year, and should provide another couple of minor classics. (BNC A83)
   d. The South Americans have come from a five-nation tournament in Hamburg, where they beat Spain 2–1 and lost to Australia 3–2. Tomorrow, England play the Dutch and on Sunday, Australia. (BNC A33)
   e. Thank God for dome tents with two bays: you collect snow from one end for tea, pass it through the middle-man, and then deposit it at the other end. Next morning the worst is over. Outside there are scudding clouds, but they are high up and the sun occasionally breaks through. (BNC A6T)
   f. "By the way, there's a meeting this afternoon," Neil said.
   (N. H. Kleinbaum, *Dead Poets Society*, p. 64)
   g. The first twenty problems at the end of Chapter One are due tomorrow.
   (N. H. Kleinbaum, *Dead Poets Society*, p. 21)

Take (3a) as an example. In this example, the relevant time table available now can be a WS-characterizing situation, entailing the situation of a certain train's departure at a certain future time as its constituent; the time table in question as a WS-characterizing situation is valid in the time range including speech time (i.e. the present time-area) and constitutes part of the structure of world. This WS-characterizing situation provides a basis for us to argue, with assertive modality, that the train's departure is certain to occur at a specific future time. The temporal structure of the fixed-future use in Figure 1 reflects the observations made above.

I turn now to a number of linguistic phenomena that validate this temporal structure. First, as observed above, simple present sentences in their fixed-future use (i.e. SFP-sentences) contain a situation in the present time-area (i.e. a WS-characterizing situation) and one in the future time-area. This is verified by the fact that the two situations can be, respectively, modified by a present time adverb and a future time adverb, as in (4):

(4) a. {Now / At this moment / Today} John rehearses tomorrow.
   (Smith (1981: 372))
   b. The match now starts next Monday, not Tuesday, as I said in my last letter. (Huddleston and Pullum (2002: 133))
   c. Now I miss the tie with Portugal at Ibrox next month, and there's a hint that I might even be out against Italy in November. (BNC HAE)
   d. Davis, who hasn't won a world ranking event for 13 months, now

Chapter 8   The Simple Present

faces Devon's Andy Hicks for a place in tomorrow's final.[4]

(BNC K5A)

Next, simple present sentences in their fixed-future use normally must be used with an adverbial referring to a specific future time.[5] This is illustrated by (5):

(5) a.   Henry visits Calais this Thursday.   (Chilton (2013: 246))
    b. *Henry visits Calais. [future time reference, no pragmatic or lexical indicator]   (Chilton (2013: 246))
    c.??Henry visits Calais in the future.   (Chilton (2013: 246))

As indicted by the temporal structure in Figure 1, the speaker of (5a) judges the situation denoted by the simple present form (i.e. Henry's visiting Calais) to be certain to occur as a natural consequence of a WS-characterizing situation obtaining now (e.g. Henry's schedule available now). From a cognitive point of view, in order for the speaker to judge that a given situation is certain to occur, it would be necessary that the target situation is to be specific and located at a specific time. This is because it is hard to judge whether non-specific situations and/or situations separated from a specific time and place will certainly be actualized or not (cf. the discussion in Section 7.4.1). (5b) is thus unacceptable in the intended reading. The reason for the low acceptability of (5c) is that to merely say that the situation involved will occur in the future does not guarantee that it is situated at a specific future time and therefore does not satisfy the conditions for the use of SFP-sentences.

I argue against an analysis in which PPF-sentences (i.e. sentences containing the present progressive futurate) and SFP-sentences are put together into one category called *futurate* (e.g. Goodman (1973), Torres-Cacoullos and Walker (2009), Copley (2009)), because I give different temporal structures to PPF-sentences and SFP-sentences (see Figure 4 in Chapter 7 and Figure 1 in this chapter). In this respect, let us examine Copley (2009), who seems to assume that both types of sentences can be explained by the notion "director" (i.e. someone who has the ability or authority to make the arrangement or plan

---

[4] In (4d), although the situation described by the simple present form is not modified by a time adverb, the future-time noun *tomorrow* clearly specifies the event time of the situation in question.

[5] Wekker (1976: 80) reports that about 75% of SFP-sentences (71 instances out of 95) co-occur with a future time adverbial. Bergs (2010: 224) makes a similar statement: when SFP-sentences do not co-occur with future time adverbials, future time reference must be implied in the preceding context or inferable from the present context (see also Dowty (1977: 72)).

happen and is committed to the actualization of such events). I use the term only to explain PPF-sentences (see Chapter 7), whereas she uses it to explain SFP-sentences like those in (3) and (5a) as well as PPF-sentences like *Henry is visiting Calais this Thursday* (Chilton (2013: 246)), though in the case of SFP-sentences she defines the director as "law-like properties of the world-time pair" (Copley (2009: 40–41)).[6] However, she also argues that the director in this sense is at work only when simple present sentences refer to a future event as a token of regular events that are predictable from the fixed properties of the universe (i.e. the structure of the world in our terminology), as illustrated in (6). If such a prediction is not possible, the director is not at work and thus the simple present sentence involved cannot refer to a future situation, as in (7):

(6) a. The sun rises tomorrow at 5:13 a.m.   (Copley (2009: 39))
    b. The meteorite impacts tomorrow at 5:13 a.m.   (Copley (2009: 40))
(7) #It rains tomorrow at 5:13 a.m.   (Copley (2009: 40))

As we can infer from Copley's statements above, when she refers to 'law-like properties' by speaking of the director, the notion is comparable to something which stems from (a WS-characterizing situation in) the world structure in this study. The director as a human authority in the case of PPF-sentences is thus different in meaning from the director as law-like properties in the case of SFP-sentences. Extending a key notion like the director to cover two different notions not only amounts to blurring the nature of that notion, but it also does not straightforwardly explain the difference in acceptability between (6a) and (8).

(8) ?The sun is rising tomorrow at 5:13 a.m.   (Copley (2009: 39))

In this regard, Copley states that "[s]peakers I consulted differ as to unacceptability". In fact, some linguists, for example Leech (2004: 63), regard a sentence like (8) as unacceptable, while others, for example Goodman (1973: 81), regard it as acceptable. This suggests that for some native speakers of English, the type of notion referred to by the term director in PPF-sentences may differ from that referred to by the same term in SFP-sentences. At least, for those who recognize the difference in acceptability between (6a) and (8), the distinction between the term for a human authority and that for law-like properties is useful.

---

[6] Copley (2009: 41) refers to the director for SFP-sentences as "the world".

Chapter 8   The Simple Present   301

I therefore restrict the notion director only to the case of PPF-sentences and adopt the notion of the structure of the world in the case of SFP-sentences. In the analysis we are pursuing, the temporal structure of PPF-sentences (Figure 4 in Chapter 7) differs from that of SFP-sentences in Figure 1 above and it is therefore natural that they reflect different notions characterizing the respective sentences. On the other hand, both temporal structures contain, in the cognitive schema, not only a situation to occur or obtain at a specific future time, but also a situation obtaining at speech time (i.e. the pre-stage in the case of PPF-sentences and the WS-characterizing situation in the case of SFP-sentences) and it is therefore possible for them to share similar notions, e.g. an external "stimulator", which induce the coming about of the relevant situation in the future.

8.3.2.   The Simple-Future Use

I turn next to the simple-future use,[7] illustrated by (1b), i.e. *Tomorrow's Saturday*. One difference between the simple-future use and the fixed-future use is that in the former, the speaker's consideration of the possibility of non-occurrence of the situation involved does not make any sense. The target situation is seen as derived automatically from a WS-characterizing situation obtaining now (i.e. a situation constituting part of the world structure). This characteristic enables the simple-future use of simple present sentences to be accompanied by assertive modality, which is the strongest type because the situation involved is the type that never fails to happen. From these observations, we conclude that while the simple-future and fixed-future uses differ with respect to whether or not the speaker's consideration of the possibility of non-occurrence of the situation involved makes sense — which does not affect the temporal-structure differences — they are the same in other aspects and share the same temporal structure in Figure 1 above. The difference in question is a pragmatic one and not a temporal-structure one. The two uses thus belong to the same semantic use, constituting pragmatic variants.

For a better understanding of the point, observe the following examples:

---

[7] The simple-future use of simple present sentences may refer to what Quirk et al. (1985: 215–216) call "statements about the calendar" or "immutable events or 'fixtures'."

302   *The Grammar of Future Expressions in English*

(9) a. Tomorrow's Saturday. (=(1b))
    b. Next Christmas falls on a Thursday.   (Leech (2004: 65))
    c. This Friday is Abigail's birthday.   (Leech (2004: 65))
    d. It's Sunday tomorrow.   (BNC A0R)
    e. In the next chapter it is Sarah's turn to hear the happy news (Abraham
        does not seem to have passed it on!)   (BNC ACG)

In (9a), for example, the situation of tomorrow being Saturday described by
the simple present sentence is based on a calendar (i.e. a WS-characterizing
situation obtaining now) and thus never fails to occur (unless the earth
disappears). The speaker (i.e. the chooser of the tense form) can therefore
make an assertion about that situation.[8]

In this connection, recall that *will*-sentences and BGT-sentences had this
use, too. Compare (9) with (10):

(10) a. And I will be forty years old next month.   (COCA SPOK)
     b. I'm going to be forty seven in a month.   (COCA SPOK)

The difference between the simple-future uses of *will*-sentences and BGT-sentences was this: the temporal structure of the BGT-version includes the trace
of future orientation in the speaker's mind (i.e. a remnant of the temporal path
represented by *to*) as part of the cognitive-schema information—which prevents a simultaneous or anterior relationship between the infinitival situation
and speech time from occurring—whereas that of the *will*-version does not
(See Section 6.4.4).

The question then arises as to whether *will*-sentences and simple present
sentences in their simple-future use—both do not have *to*, a linguistic element
implying (the trace of) future orientation—show any semantic difference. As
anticipated in Section 5.4.3, they are semantically different in that their temporal structures are different.

To show this type of difference, note first Close's (1977: 134) statement that
will-sentences in their simple-future use refer to future events that will certainly occur, whereas simple present sentences in their simple-future use represent
present certainty. Within my framework, this difference reflects the difference
between the two temporal structures. As Figure 1 above shows, simple present sentences in their simple-future use involve a WS-characterizing situation

---

[8] Our claim that the simple-future and fixed-future uses belong to the same semantic use
is in keeping with Leech's (2004: 65) classification, which classifies the two uses into the
same group. His classification implies that the two uses are the same at some level.

Chapter 8   The Simple Present

obtaining at speech time and providing a necessary basis for the occurrence of a specific situation in the future. They thus represent present certainty.

On the other hand, as shown in Figure 6 in Section 5.4.3, *will*-sentences in their simple-future use contain a bleached situation associated with *will* obtaining at speech time — which serves merely as a space-filler — in their temporal structure. Its event time (i.e. an orientational event time) only provides a viewpoint from which to compute the event time of the infinitival situation in the future. This type of *will*-sentence is accompanied by assertive modality, as seen in Section 5.4.3, but it involves a bleached situation associated with *will* and there is thus a temporal gap between the speech situation, i.e. the time of assertion, and the infinitival situation, i.e. the target of the modality. These observations lead us to conclude that this type of *will*-sentence does not represent present certainty, but future events that will certainly occur.

In this way, the differences in temporal structure between the simple-future uses of simple present sentences and *will*-sentences account for the subtle differences in nuance observed above. However, in both sentences the speaker regards the situation involved as absolutely certain to come into existence based on the type of situation and encyclopedic information available in the speech situation. There is virtually no difference in meaning between the two sentences and they are thus often interchangeable, as we saw in Section 5.4.3.

8.3.3.   The Future-Reference-in-Subordinate-Clause Use

We now turn to the future-reference-in-subordinate-clause use. As shown in (1c), i.e. *When you wake up, you'll remember nothing*, this use describes a future situation in certain types of subordinate clauses, which depends on the future reference in the main clause. By certain types of subordinate clauses, I mean subordinate clauses constituting the presupposition for the asserted part in the main clause (cf. Leech (2004: 63–64)). In my model, they semantically consist only of the proposition domain, not accompanied by any mental-attitude elements (cf. the semantic (de)composition of sentential utterances in (4) in Section 3.4). Examples of this type of subordinate clause are temporal clauses providing a temporal setting for specific situations on the time line and conditional clauses providing a direct cause for the occurrence of specific situations.

As an explanatory basis, let us first present the temporal structure of the future-reference-in-subordinate-clause use, schematically represented in Figure 2:

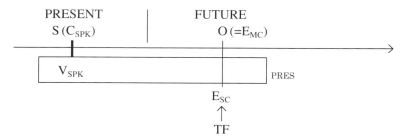

Figure 2: Temporal Structure of the Future-Reference-in-Subordinate-Clause Use of Simple Present Sentences

Here, E_{SC} stands for the event time of the subordinate clause situation and E_{MC} for that of the infinitival situation in the main clause, which serves as the time of orientation (O) for the former.

In this linguistic environment, too, the default principle for the fusion of the speaker's t-viewpoint and consciousness comes into play. The situation described by this type of subordinate clause depends on the infinitival situation of the main clause in terms of the tense interpretation. This temporal phenomenon corresponds to what Declerck (1991b, 2006) calls the "temporal subordination."

The reason for the temporal subordination is two-fold. First, as we saw, the situations described by these subordinate clauses are "necessary conditions" (preconditions) for the actualization of main clause situations. Put differently, the subordinate clause situations are regarded as presupposed parts for the main clause situations, i.e. asserted parts. In this sense, the former situations are semantically subordinate to the latter.

Second, since the situations described by the subordinate clauses semantically consist only of the proposition domain, they need to be incorporated into the type of clauses involving the speaker's attitude domain so that they can be construed by the speaker (as the private self) and conveyed to the hearer (by the speaker as the public self). The second point explains why the event time of the subordinate clause situation (E_{SC}) can be located in the future time-area without restrictions. Because this type of subordinate clause consists only of the proposition domain, the relevant situation is not accompanied by assertive modality.

In this way, the event time in question is computed with the event time of the main clause verb referring to the future (E_{MC}) as the time of orientation (O). Subordinate clauses of the type under consideration refer to specific situations and the temporal focus (TF) is therefore directed at their event times.

Chapter 8   The Simple Present

To illustrate, consider (11):

(11) a.   When you wake up, you'll remember nothing. (=(1c))
   b.   Cherry will throw a party after she passes her exams.

(Declerck (2006: 749))

   c.   The design of the (relevant) building, particularly its bulk and size. Any loss of daylight and sunlight to adjoining properties. These matters will be looked at before a firm decision is taken. (BNC A3K)
   d.   If he runs he'll get there in time. (Thomson and Martinet (1986: 197))
   e.   If that approach prevails in the higher courts, it will amount to a major reverse, making it more difficult for the ordinary citizen to complain of unlawful action by a public authority.   (BNC A31)

In all examples of (11), the (relevant) main clause is a *will*-sentence with its infinitival situation referring to the future. As a representative of temporal clauses, let us consider the *when*-clause in (11a). The temporal clause situation is the presupposition for the occurrence of the infinitival situation of the main clause, i.e. the asserted part of the sentence. The situation of the addressee's waking up serves as a temporal setting to provide a time point or period with respect to which the truth value of the situation of the addressee's remembering nothing is evaluated.

On the other hand, due to the temporal subordination, the temporal calculation of the subordinate clause situation (i.e. the evaluation of its event time) is based on the event time of the relevant situation in the main clause (E_{MC}), which serves as the time of orientation (O). The event time of the simple present form *wake* in the *when*-clause (Esc) is interpreted as (virtually) simultaneous with that time of orientation because of the lexical properties of the temporal connective *when* representing "sloppy simultaneity" in the sense of Declerck (1997, 2006).[9] The event time of the infinitival situation (E_{MC}) as the time of orientation is located in the future relative to the event time of *will*, which in turn coincides with speech time (S), and so the event time of the *when*-clause situation (E_{SC}) is located in the future. The temporal focus (TF) is directed at the event time of the subordinate clause situation (E_{SC}) because the subordinate clause refers to a specific situation as a temporal setting for the occurrence of the infinitival situation of the main clause, which is assumed to be actualized in the future (Hamann (1989: 51)).

---

[9] In the case of stative situations, the temporal relation between the two situations is that of strict simultaneity. In the case of non-stative situations, especially, bounded situations, the temporal relation is that of virtual (or sloppy) simultaneity.

Let us next consider the tense interpretation of conditional clauses of the direct cause-effect type, i.e. type A conditional clauses. Take (11d) as a sample case. The type A conditional clause (i.e. the situation of a man's running) serves as a kind of presupposition for the infinitival situation (i.e. the situation of his reaching somewhere in time) to occur.[10] The tense-interpretation process of type A conditional clauses like this is similar to that of the *when*-clause observed above, with the proviso that the situation of the conditional clause provides a specific condition (not a temporal setting) for the occurrence of the infinitival situation of the main clause in the future. A cognitive schema representing a cause-effect relationship is such that the cause comes before the effect, and accordingly, the event time of the subordinate clause situation (E_{SC}) as a cause is seen as coming before that of the infinitival situation of the main clause (E_{MC}) as the effect or result, which serves as the time of orientation (O) for E_{SC}. However, a prototypical case should be that the cause occurs immediately before the effect and this small time difference is adjusted in the process of the event-time evaluation in the name of sloppy simultaneity. The event time of his running (E_{SC}) is thus interpreted as (sloppy) simultaneous with the event time of his reaching somewhere in time (E_{MC}), both of which are located in the future relative to speech time (S). The temporal focus is directed at the event time of the *if*-clause situation, which describes a (assumed) specific situation as a condition for the occurrence of the infinitival situation of the main clause.

As observed in Section 5.4.7, this type of subordinate clause is semantically composed only of the proposition domain, so that the simple present form in this linguistic environment is not accompanied by assertive modality. Thus, in linguistic environments where principle (2) above (i.e. the speaker's t-viewpoint fuses with his/her consciousness at speech time) is at work, the tense interpretation of the simple present form (i.e. an unmodalized form) of the subordinate clause is not affected by the restriction on assertion. This means that the situation involved can in theory be not only simultaneous with, but also posterior to, speech time as the time of assertion, because the present timesphere of the simple present form covers the future time-area as well as the present time-area when principle (2) is in operation. In this way, in the subordinate clauses under consideration, the simple present form can refer to a future situation, i.e. a situation posterior to speech time as the time of assertion.

---

[10] Declerck (1991b: 193) refers to this type of conditional clause as an open conditional. He defines it as "a condition which may or may not be fulfilled in the future, but whose fulfilment is seen as a real possibility."

8.3.4. The "Note" Use

Let us now briefly touch on the "note" use, exemplified by (1d), i.e. *I am in room 2114*. In this use, the speaker or writer (i.e. "encoder") chooses the simple present form with the decoding time of the sentence functioning as the base point for the choice of tense form. The decoding time, or the time of reading the note, is assumed to be located in the future. It doubles as the time of orientation for calculating the event time.

These observations enable us to present the temporal structure of simple present sentences in their "note" use below:

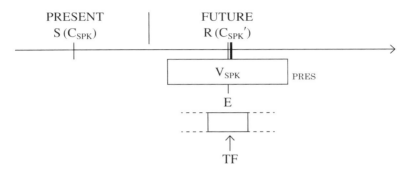

Figure 3: Temporal Structure of the "Note" Use of Simple Present Sentences

The default principle in (2) does not work here and the speaker's t-viewpoint (V_{SPK}) does not fuse with his/her consciousness (C_{SPK}) at speech time (S). Instead, as a marked case, the speaker's t-viewpoint fuses with the consciousness of the speaker as he/she speaks to the expected reader in his/her mind—represented by C_{SPK}'—which is located at the time of the reading (R) in the future. That is, by choosing the present tense form of this type, the speaker behaves as if he/she were conveying the message to the reader in front of the latter at the time of the reading. As a result, the present time-sphere in the tense structure of the present tense form corresponds to the time range including the time of the reading, i.e. the future time-area, in which is located the relevant event time (E). Because we are considering a specific situation at a future time, the temporal focus (TF) is directed at the event time. The situation indicated by the note is a stative one which will obtain around the time of the reading and thus the temporal structure of this use is basically the same as that of the stative-present use observed in Section 4.2.2 (see Figure 1 in Chapter 4) expect for one difference, namely that the base point for the simple present form of this use is the time of the reading in the future, not speech time. The solid-line part below E represents the foregrounded part of the situation involved and the broken-line part denotes the backgrounded part. The assertive modality accompanying the simple present (i.e. unmodalized) form is attributed to the speaker (as the private self) whose consciousness is located at the time of the reading when he/she is assumed to speak to the expected reader in his/her mind. The situation involved is thus interpreted as obtaining at the time of the reading as the time of assertion and there is no violation of the restriction on assertion.

For a better understanding of the above observations, consider in some more detail (1d), repeated here as (12):

(12)   I am in room 2114. (=(1d))

The speaker or writer of this sentence chooses the simple present form *am*, assuming that the base point for the choice of tense form is the time of the reading, i.e. the time of the expected reader's seeing the memo in the future. The time of the reading doubles as the time of orientation. The event time involved is the relevant time span of the writer's being in a certain room when the reader reads the simple present sentence. This simple present form can be accompanied by assertive modality because the modality is attributed to the speaker as he/she speaks to the expected reader in his/her mind at the time of the reading. The use of this present tense form thus preserves the restriction on assertion.

8.3.5.   The Immediate-Future Use

Let us next consider the immediate-future use of simple present sentences, illustrated by (1e), i.e. *We go to Headington now and George, hello George.* As with the immediate-future uses of *will*-sentences and BGT-sentences, the immediate-future use of simple present sentences also refers to a situation at a time later than speech time located in the present time-area, i.e. a time range cognitively regarded as the present, which is usually established by a present time adverbial like *now*.[11, 12]

The temporal structure of the immediate-future use of simple present sentences is schematized in Figure 4:

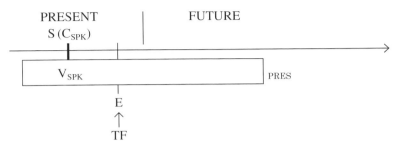

Figure 4: Temporal Structure of the Immediate-Future Use of Simple Present Sentences

The base point for the choice of tense form is speech time (S); principle (2) above is in operation and the speaker's t-viewpoint (V_{SPK}) fuses with his/her consciousness (C_{SPK}) at speech time. Because this use is concerned with a specific situation, the temporal focus (TF) is directed at the event time of the situation (E). The point here is that the event time involved is located in the present time-area (though at a time later than speech time). The temporal structure of this use does not include a cognitive schema showing the structure

---

[11] If we admit two types of *now*, i.e. one with present time reference and one with future time reference, then we must motivate why the same form can refer to two different time ranges. Within the present framework, *now* is always a present time adverb establishing the present time-area (except for the use as topic-change marker) and specifies the event time in the present time-area, irrespective of whether it is simultaneous with or posterior to speech time. One of the merits of this treatment of *now* is that we can treat *will*-sentences and BGT-sentences with *now* in a unified way, as in (i) and (ii):
    (i) They will now renew their application for asylum.   (BNC A2P)
    (ii) I am going to make the scenes now.   (BNC AD1)
In (i) and (ii), the event time of the infinitive is located at a time later than speech time, but still in the present time-area established by *now*.

[12] Bergs (2010: 224) points out a future reference use of the simple present form in the beginning part of TV or radio programs which does not co-occur with a time adverbial. The simple present form *look* in (i) is a case in point.
    (i) A new study shows that only one in 20 women undergoes an annual mammogram as recommended by doctors. We look at that and other health stories with our medical contributor ...   (requoted from Bergs (2010: 224))
This instance can be regarded as a kind of immediate-future use in that it appears in a similar linguistic environment in which the simple present form in (1e) appears and refers to the immediate future, a time which can be seen as part of the present time-area.

310   *The Grammar of Future Expressions in English*

of the world, so that we do not have any basis (e.g. a WS-characterizing situation) on which to make an assertion about the situation to occur or obtain at a time later than speech time. At first glance, this might seem to lead to the violation of the restriction on assertion. However, the present time-area is a cognitive time range including speech time, i.e. the center of cognitive time at which the speaker's mental attitude exists. We can thus assume that the whole of the present time-area is under the influence of the speaker's mental attitude at speech time and this time-area is regarded as the so-called "assertable" time range. Under this assumption, we can make an assertion about the situation to occur or obtain at a time later than speech time as if it were asserted at the time of assertion, as long as it is located in the present time-area.

For a better understanding of this use, observe (13):

(13) a.   We go to Headington now and George, hello George. (=(1e))
      b.   "Since our design center has started using GObookings I leave earlier now and have more time for my daughter ...."

(https://www.gobookings.com.au/client-feedback/)

Consider, for example, (13a), which was uttered in a radio program when a broadcaster wanted to broadcast live from Headington. The situation expressed by this simple present sentence is non-stative and bounded and so its event time cannot be interpreted as simultaneous with the time of orientation because of its aspectual properties (see Section 2.4.3.3). Since the tense form is present, the event time of the relevant situation can in theory be located at speech time and in the time range thereafter, but because of the aspectual properties in question, the event time is interpreted as located at a time later than speech time as the time of orientation. The time in question is, however, situated in the present time-area established by *now*, and for the reason we saw above, the relevant situation can be asserted as if it were a fact or to occur definitely.

8.3.6. The "Instruction-Giving" Use and the "Either-Or" Use

Now we consider two uses of simple present sentences which refer to a time later than speech time. One use is the "instruction-giving" use, exemplified by (1f), i.e. *You take the first turning on the left past the roundabout, then you cross a bridge and bear right until you reach the public library*. The other is the "either-or" use, exemplified by (1g), i.e. *Either that alligator goes or I go*. In the former case, we imagine a scene containing a series of consecutive situations, whereas in the latter case, we assume a scene in which either one of the two situations will occur. Both scenes constitute superordinate situations (consisting of two or more specific sub-situations) created when the speaker expresses his/her mental world. What deserves attention here is that the individual sub-situations described by the simple present forms under consideration are not directly related to the cognitive (i.e. real) time line; it is the superordinate situation created at speech time (in the present time-area) and extending into the following time interval—henceforth referred to as the "present scene"—that is directly linked to the time line in the real world. The distinction between the present and future time-areas is thus blurred within the present scene. The sub-situations constituting the present scene will be actualized in the time range after speech time, but not at specific points on the real time line.

As we will see later, it is certain that there are some differences between the two uses under consideration, but such differences are not directly reflected in their temporal structures. This suggests that the two uses are pragmatic variants of the same semantic use within my framework and thus share the same temporal structure, schematically represented in Figure 5.

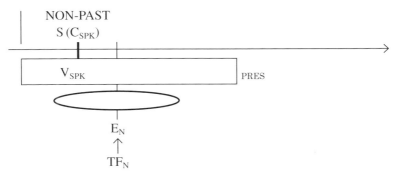

Figure 5: Temporal Structure of the Instruction-Giving Use and the Either-Or Use of Simple Present Sentences

The present time-sphere (grammatical present) corresponds to the non-past time-sphere symbolized by NON-PAST, in which there is no clear distinction between the present and future time-areas. The oval represents a present scene—created at speech time and extending into the following time interval—which contains sub-situations: a series of consecutive situations in the instruction-giving use and two complementary situations in the either-or use. E denotes the event time of a sub-situation to be actualized at a time later than speech time in the present scene. Both uses depict specific sub-situations and the temporal focus (TF) is thus at work here. The subscript N means that there is more than one set of E and TF.

With these observations in mind, let us consider the two uses in some detail. I will begin by characterizing the instruction-giving use. The speaker (i.e. the giver of the instructions) employs this use when he/she imagines the scene in which the addressee (i.e. the receiver of the instructions) carries out his/her instructions at times later than the time of giving instructions (i.e. speech time). This characterization is justified by the fact that if the individual instructions are specified by time adverbials referring to different times on the real time line, the simple present forms have different meanings and no longer represent the instruction-giving use. When giving instructions at speech time, the speaker imagines a present scene containing a series of consecutive instructions which will be actualized if the addressee carries them out, but he/she is not necessarily interested in their actualizations. Meanwhile, the speaker has specific individual situations in mind, for one usually does not give instructions about what one cannot specify. Hence the event time associated with each instruction in the non-past time-area receives the temporal focus.

Let us now discuss whether or not the instruction-giving use is accompanied by assertive modality. While the present scene itself (i.e. the superordinate situation) is created at speech time and linked to the real time line, the individual instructions themselves are "mental products", i.e. specific situations that the speaker assumes the addressee to carry out in his/her mind when uttering them as instructions. In one's own mind, one can freely imagine each sub-situation (i.e. instruction) as if it were a fact and it is thus assertable.[13] For these reasons, the simple present form under discussion is accompanied by assertive modality without violating the restriction on assertion.

By way of illustration, consider the following:[14]

---

[13] Similar statements apply to the simple present form used in itineraries, as below:
  (i) Today the train takes us to London. (Declerck (2003: 87))
  (ii) Across a stile begins the descent to the river. At first the way is between confining trees. Then, suddenly, they are behind us and we find ourselves held enraptured by a vista of exquisite beauty. The hillside falls away to a tree-lined meadow which spreads flatly to the River Eden. (Leech (2004: 17))

[14] Simple present sentences like those in (14a) might be seen as imperative sentences with the second-person subject, but they are actually not. A difference between imperative sentences with the second-person subject and simple present sentences in their instruction-giving use with the second-person subject lies in the fact that a stress is put on *you* in the former case, but not in the latter case (cf. Leech (2004: 17)). In addition, when *you* in (14a) is paraphrased into impersonal *one*, the result is that the sentence in question receives a habitual reading and can be paraphrased as "Every time you want to get to the library, ..." (Leech (1987, 2004: 17), Hirtle (1995: 266-267)). In this case, the situations in the paraphrased version of (14a) are non-specific (recall that sub-situations constituting a habit are

Chapter 8   The Simple Present   313

(14) a. You take the first turning on the left past the roundabout, then you
         cross a bridge and bear right until you reach the public library.
         (=(1f))
     b. You test an air-leak by disconnecting the delivery pipe at the carbu-
         rettor and pumping petrol into a container.   (Leech (2004: 17))

In (14a), for example, when the speaker gives instructions, he/she imagines
the present scene in which the situation of the addressee's turning left at the
first corner past the roundabout, that of the addressee's crossing a bridge, and
that of the addressee's bearing right will occur if the addressee carries them
out. The sub-situations in the speaker's mental world look as if they are providing his/her simulated experiences. This suggests that the speaker—interested in them—regards them as if they were ongoing or had occurred in his/
her mental world and thus facts. Hence the temporal focus is directed at the
event time of the simple present form (describing an instruction) accompanied
by assertive modality.

   I will next consider the either-or use. This use appears in the "either-A-or-
B" construction, which suggests that in the speaker's mental world either one
of the two situations indicated by A and B never fails to occur at a time later
than speech time, but whether it occurs in the present time-area or the future
time-area does not matter. The speaker assumes a present scene—created at
speech time—in which two alternative situations can potentially occur at a
time later than speech time. This present scene, which can be regarded as a
superordinate situation consisting of two sub-situations, is linked to the real
time line via speech time. The speaker is interested in the two sub-situations,
for we can safely say that selecting two as alternative options implies that the
selector (i.e. the speaker of the either-A-or-B construction) pays attention to
them. The temporal focus (TF) therefore comes into operation in this use and
directed at the event time of a sub-situation (E) (we can assume two sets of
the event time and temporal focus for this use).

   As to the restriction on assertion, the either-or use of the simple present
form does not violate it, either. The explanation goes as follows. First, the
necessary and sufficient condition for the present scene of the either-A-or-B
construction is that one of the two sub-situations involved (i.e. the sub-situations referred to by A and B) will certainly come about and the other will not.
This suggests that the speaker can regard the present scene (created at speech

---

non-specific); the temporal focus is not in operation and the simple present forms associated
with such situations represent the habitnal-present use within my framework.

time) as always true because it is the mental world of the speaker where either one of the two sub-situations will come true with a probability of 50%; in this sense it is assertable. Hence the simple present form in its either-or use can be accompanied by assertive modality.

For a better understanding of what we have observed, consider concrete examples of this use, as in (15):

(15) a.   Either that alligator goes or I go. (=(1g))

b.   "Isn't the truth that the Chancellor said to you "either the adviser goes by the end of the year or I go now"? Why can't you admit to that truth?"   (BNC A7W)

Note that in the "either-A-or-B" construction of (15b), the situation represented by A is specified by *by the end of the year*, i.e. a future time adverb, and the situation represented by B is specified by *now*, i.e. a present time adverb. This implies that the speaker of this use is concerned not with the distinction between the present and future time-areas, but with the present scene in which either one of the two sub-situations constituting the superordinate situation never fails to occur at a time later than speech time in the non-past time area.[15]

To illustrate the point, take (15a) as a sample. The superordinate situation (i.e. present scene) is that either the alligator or the speaker is regarded as certain to go in the speaker's mental world and the speaker thus takes it as true at speech time. Hence the two simple present forms used in this construction are accompanied by assertive modality. The speaker is interested in the two sub-situations because he/she selects them as alternative options and the relevant event time thus receives a temporal focus.

8.3.7. The Stage-Direction Use

Finally, let us consider the stage-direction use of simple present sentences, illustrated by (1h): *Biff and his friends hop into a car parked outside. Marty stares at George as George is eating. George becomes very uncomfortable and turns to Marty.* This use is employed to describe the scenes of dramas, plays, films, and the like; they are composed of situations constituting parts of fictional worlds.[16] Unlike the instruction-giving use, this use emphasizes the

---

[15] This type of treatment is in keeping with Wekker's (1976: 85) statement that what is important in the use of the simple present futurate is "the speaker's presuppositions about the future event or activity." In addition, Hirtle and Curat (1986: 64–65) propose as a necessary condition for the simple present futurate the notion of inevitability, which is also in keeping with my statement in the text.

[16] The simple present forms used for the summary of stories, as shown in (i), basically

Chapter 8   The Simple Present   315

perspective of the audience (i.e. receiver) because of its nature. The writer—
subsumed under the category "speaker" for convenience's sake—employs
simple present forms in their stage-direction use to describe situations in the
fictional worlds that will be open to the public (i.e. audience) in the future relative to the time of writing (i.e. speech time). The simple present forms refer
to the fictional worlds "accessible" in the future in that the release date of the
dramas, plays, or films is in the future relative to the time of writing. That is,
the scenes represented by the simple present sentences are located in the fictional worlds to "come into existence" at the time of viewing (V) in the future, i.e. the time when the audience watches the dramas, plays, or films.[17]
The situations or scenes in the fictional worlds themselves are disconnected
from the real world including speech time, but they are linked to the time line
in the real world through the time of the audience's viewing and the simple
present forms are chosen to describe them with the center of the fictional
world (identified with the time of the audience's viewing on the real time line)
being the base point (cf. Leech (2004: 16)). This is verified by the fact that if
the simple present forms go with expressions referring to a specific time, the
time refers to the center of the fictional world, but not speech time, as illustrated in (16).

(16)   The clock changes from 12:27 to 12:28. The radio plays music. Marty
       sleeps soundly with his bedside lamp still on ...

                              (Screenplay, *Back to the Future*, p. 34)

From the above observations, we may schematize the temporal structure of
the stage-direction use of simple present sentences in Figure 6:

---

have the same characteristics as those for stage direction.
     (i)   Les Misérables: Jean Valjean, a simple peasant, steals a loaf of bread to feed his
           sister's starving children. Condemned to five years of hard labour, he tries to es-
           cape, is caught, and has to serve nineteen years in the galleys.   (Leech (2004: 16))
   [17] These characteristics of the stage-direction use suggest that it should not be regarded as
the same use as the historical-present use or the narrative-present use observed in Section
4.1.2. A piece of linguistic evidence for this distinction is that the latter two uses, but not
the former, can usually be paraphrased into past tenses.

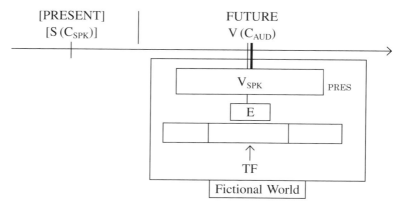

Figure 6: Temporal Structure of the Stage-Direction Use of Simple Present Sentences

In this temporal structure, the speaker's (i.e. writer's) t-viewpoint (V_{SPK}) does not fuse with his/her consciousness (C_{SPK}) at speech time (S) in the real world, but with the consciousness of the audience (C_{AUD}) at the time of viewing (V), the time simultaneous with the center of the fictional world. The simple present form in question is typically used to refer to the center of the fictional world and therefore suitable for a description of the scenes (consisting of specific situations) in the fictional world existent at the time of viewing. As a result of the fusion of the speaker's t-viewpoint with the consciousness of the audience at the time of viewing, the present time-sphere (i.e. grammatical present) associated with the simple present form corresponds to a time range including the time of viewing simultaneous with the center of the fictional world. This fictional world is assumed to occur at a future time in the real world, and the event time involved (symbolized by the surrounded E) is located at the same time as the time of viewing, which advances as the story line progresses. Since this use is utilized in scene settings (symbolized by the shorter rectangle below E), it presupposes the structure of the world (symbolized by the longer rectangle below E), i.e. a set of rules and constitutions of the society in the fictional world. Because this use refers to a specific situation constituting an individual scene, the temporal focus is at work. Speech time is not directly relevant to the choice and interpretation of this use of simple present forms and so the present time-area as well as speech time is enclosed by brackets (for the same reason as with the historical-present case).

To illustrate the point, consider (17):

Chapter 8   The Simple Present   317

(17) a.   Biff and his friends hop into a car parked outside. Marty stares at
          George as George is eating. George becomes very uncomfortable
          and turns to Marty.   (Screenplay, *Back to the Future*, p.62)
     b.   Oliver is walking amidst the crowd. He comes up to the window of
          a travel agency. He stops and looks in at a poster advertising trips to
          Paris. He stands there thinking for some time.
                                          (requoted from Kashino (1999: 17))

In (17a), for example, the simple present forms are used to describe specific
situations constituting a scene in the fictional world of the film *Back to the
Future*. As background information for the fictional world in question, we
can point out that time machines exist, time travels to the past can affect the
future, and so on. In this scene, the main character named Marty encounters
George, his future father, and each simple present form describes each situation constituting this scene. The simple present forms are used here because
the situations are ongoing or obtaining in front of the "eyes" of the audience,
i.e. at the time of viewing the film, which functions both as the base point for
choosing the tense form and as the time of orientation for evaluating the event
times of the situations.

Since the world under consideration is fictional, the writer of stage directions (i.e. specific scenes) is omniscient, freely setting scenes and describing
situations in them. The writer can therefore refer to the scenes and situations
as facts in such fictional worlds, so that he/she can use unmodalized forms accompanied by assertive modality without violating the restriction on assertion.

8.4.   Concluding Remarks

In this chapter, we have shown how my temporal structure approach analyzes a number of future reference uses of simple present sentences. Sentences
containing the simple futurate in the present tense, or SFP-sentences, correspond to the fixed-future and simple-future uses in my terminology, i.e. major
uses of the simple present form with future time reference. The tense structure of these future reference uses is the same as that of the non-future reference uses observed in Chapter 4, because they share the same tense form. The
simple present form can have different temporal structures under the influence of the properties of co-occurring elements and the linguistic environment in which it occurs. The temporal structure involves schematically-repre-
sented time information characterizing the properties of the use involved. Different uses having different temporal structures are semantically different, but

those sharing the same temporal structure are pragmatic variants (e.g. the instruction-giving and either-or uses).

The fixed-future use of simple present sentences is sometimes not distinguished from PPF-sentences, i.e. sentences including present progressive futurate forms. However, the approach we are advancing in this study distinguishes between them as a natural consequence, because the temporal structure of the former (Figure 1 in this chapter) is different from that of the latter (Figure 3 in Chapter 7). On the other hand, the two future expressions have similarities in their temporal structures, which could lead to their functional similarities.

The present framework also distinguishes the simple-future use of simple present sentences from the simple-future use of *will*-sentences or BGT-sentences, because they have their own temporal structures (Figure 6 in Chapter 5, Figure 6 in Chapter 6, and Figure 1 in this chapter). Thus my approach can explain, from a unified point of view, Close's (1977) intuition that *will*-sentences are more likely to express a nuance of futurity than simple present sentences. However, the two expressions refer to situations regarded as absolutely certain to occur or obtain in the future and may thus express a virtually equal value from a functional perspective.

Chapter 4 and this chapter have shown that the present framework enables us to extensively treat various types of uses of simple present sentences from a unified point of view. The framework, which comprehensively takes in information not only from tense but also from other related areas, was able to distinguish semantic uses/functions from pragmatic variants as well as provide a fine-grained analysis of uses of simple present sentences by constructing temporal structures reflecting various types of information concerning temporal calculation. Moreover, the framework was also able to systematically compare simple present sentences with future time reference and other future expressions such as PPF-sentences, *will*-sentences, and BGT-sentences. I hope this study has provided a more general and comprehensive analysis of simple present sentences with future time reference than before.

Chapter 9

*Be About To**

9.1. Introduction

Sentences containing *be about to* (henceforth BAT-sentences), as illustrated in (1) below, are referred to in many grammar books and monographs concerning tense (e.g. Collins (2009: 155–156), Declerck (1991a: 116, 2006: 356), Leech (1987, 2004: 70), Perkins (1983: 72–73), Quirk et al. (1985: 217), Swan (1995, 2005: 3), Thomson and Martinet (1986: 118)).[1]

(1) a. "Excuse me, we're about to have a wedding. Do you think you could come back later?" (BNC A0F)

　 b. AS THE dust settles on the surprising, but widely approved decision to appoint Claudio Abbado chief conductor of the Berlin Philharmonic Orchestra to replace Karajan, a new round of speculation is about to begin. (BNC A4W)

　 c. "It's not been a failure of the organic principle, it's been a failure of people," says Melville unhappily. Johnson is about to explain with lots of big words but it's agreed he should shut up. (BNC AAF)

In comparison with the four future expressions we have observed thus far, there have been far fewer detailed studies on BAT-sentences;[2] as far as I know, no comprehensive and systematic studies of this type of sentences have been

---

* This chapter is a largely revised version of Naoaki Wada (2000), "*Be Going To* and *Be About To*: Just Because Doc Brown Was Going to Take Us Back to the Future Does Not Mean That He Was About to Do So", volume 17.2, pp 386–416, *English Linguistics*, 2000 © The English Linguistic Society of Japan, reproduced with permission.

[1] Some detailed studies on future forms in English, such as Wekker (1976) and Huddleston and Pullum (2002), basically do not deal with BAT-sentences.

[2] But Watanabe (2011) is an exception, providing a detailed, diachronic analysis of BAT-sentences in terms of grammaticalization.

conducted in the model which have also dealt with other future expressions.

BAT-sentences are often compared to BGT-sentences (i.e. sentences containing *be going to*) in the literature.[3] It is often stated that both sentences refer to the near future and thus have similar meanings, with the proviso that BAT-sentences refer to the nearer future than BGT-sentences (e.g. Coates (1983: 200), Collins (2009: 155), Leech (2004: 70), Perkins (1983: 72), Thomson and Martinet (1986: 118)).[4] This suggests that comparing the two sentences provides a good reference point for investigating BAT-sentences. In this chapter, I will clarify the temporal properties of BAT-sentences and construct their temporal structures by comparing them with those of BGT-sentences, and then explore in depth a number of linguistic phenomena concerning BAT-sentences.

The remainder of this chapter is organized as follows. In Section 9.2, I first point out a number of differences in linguistic behavior between BAT-sentences and BGT-sentences. Next, in Section 9.3, I show that the combination patterns of constituents of the two sentences — both of which contain the form of *be* + X + *to*-infinitive — are different and present the temporal structures of BAT-sentences in the present and past tense. Section 9.4 is devoted to a temporal structure analysis of the differences between BAT-sentences and BGT-sentences observed in Section 9.2. Section 9.5 makes concluding remarks.

9.2. Linguistic Phenomena of BAT-Sentences

Let us first observe the linguistic phenomena of BAT-sentences which behave differently from those of BGT-sentences. As a first difference, it is often stated that BAT-sentences generally tend to refer to the nearer future than BGT-sentences, though both tend to refer to the near future (Collins (2009: 155), Leech (1987, 2004: 70), Thomson and Martinet (1986: 118)).[5] In fact, Quirk et al. (1985: 217) claim that BAT-sentences can be paraphrased into BGT-sentences co-occurring with *just* (meaning 'very soon' (Quirk et al. (1985: 582)). However, BGT-sentences can occur with adverbs referring to the re-

---

[3] Some studies note that the BAT-sentence is used as a synonym for the *be on the point of* construction, while others point out some differences between them. For example, Declerck (1991a, 2006: 356) notes that the *be on the point of* construction basically allows an animate subject alone. We do not consider this construction in this book.

[4] In some periods of the history of the English language, BAT-sentences were regarded as synonymous with BGT-sentences. For example, Kytö (1994: 67) observes that in the 17th century work, the two sentences both had the meanings of 'near future' and 'intention'.

[5] BAT-sentences, like BGT-sentences in their typical uses, never fail to locate the infinitival situation in the future.

Chapter 9 *Be About To*   321

mote future, as shown in (13) in Section 6.4.1. Their reference to the near future is merely an implicature deriving from the temporal structure of BGT-
sentences in their typical uses, although it is the default case unless otherwise
implied. Meanwhile, BGT-sentences can co-occur with adverbs referring to
the immediate future, such as *now* and *in a minute*, as illustrated in (2).

(2) a. I'm going to get dressed now.   (BNC FRS)
    b. I'm going to scream in a minute!   (BNC KBF)
    c. I'm going to go to England very soon.   (BNC HJ4)

Unless we clarify in what sense BAT-sentences refer to the nearer future than
BGT-sentences, we cannot judge whether the above statement is valid or not.

On the other hand, the idea that BAT-sentences refer to the (very) near future is justified by linguistic facts. This is because BAT-sentences are compatible with *just* in the sense of 'very soon' (Collins (2009: 255)), as shown in
(3), or *now* in the sense of 'immediately', as exemplified in (4), whereas they
cannot or can hardly co-occur with future time adverbs such as *tomorrow* or
next week, as illustrated in (5):[6]

(3) a. Willard is just about to propose to Angelica!   (BNC CH4)
    b. The girl is just about to turn.   (BNC G0F)
    c. The agreement is just about to be reached.   (BNC HHW)
(4) a. The mystery kept secret from all eternity is now about to be made
        clear.   (BNC CCG)
    b. I am now about to mix the two together.   (BNC J52)
    c. The towering 25-year-old Dungannon man is now about to break
        through the elusive century barrier on the Sony ladder.   (BNC K2D)
(5) a. *Doc Brown is about to leave tomorrow.
    b. *Mana is about to play the *koto* next week.

In fact, in the British National Corpus (BNC), I input the sequence "about to *
tomorrow / next" or "tomorrow / next * about to" in the search box, and found
only two instances of them, as shown in (6).[7]

---

[6] The ungrammatical examples in this chapter are all judged by Joyce Cunningham, Mary
Lee Field, Kevin Moore and/or Nina Padden—all of them are North American—unless
otherwise indicated.

[7] In this study, when using the asterisk in the search box of the BNC, I always made the
maximum number of words for the asterisk part "nine".

(6) a. We've been running the management skills courses since nineteen eighty-six, and since then, more than seven hundred and fifty people, from groups such as yours, have taken a part, and we're about to launch a phase two in the next er, year or so. (BNC JNK)

b. First they happen in June that's that's a good starter for one, and they're really not that big a problem and I guess people in London would just laugh at the prospect of the noise which which May Balls cause and not worry about it in one way and would not have telephone calls to the local council and lots of stories in my newspaper every year. We're about to start them again probably in the next week or two. (BNC KRP)

In contrast, I found more than thirty instances of the sequence "about to * now" or "now * about to".

Interestingly, the native speakers who judged the examples in (5) to be unacceptable judged the examples in (7) to be better.

(7) a. ?I am about to leave for America tomorrow, so I am afraid I cannot see you this afternoon.

b. ?We are about to move next week, so we are very busy preparing.

The above observations lead us to consider how the notion of near future associated with BAT-sentences is treated and distinguished from that associated with BGT-sentences.

Let us next consider Perkins's (1983: 73) observation that unlike BGT-sentences, BAT-sentences do not "comfortably co-occur with the progressive aspect", as in (8):

(8) a. The plane is about to take off. (Perkins (1983: 73))

b. ?The plane is about to be taking off. (Perkins (1983: 73))

This phenomenon cannot be explained in terms of whether BAT-sentences refer to the nearer future than BGT-sentences or not. This must also be explained.

Finally, there are differences between the ways in which BAT-sentences and BGT-sentences in the past tense are used in descriptive narrative parts. Descriptive narrative parts consist of sentences in non-conversational parts describing situations in both the outer world and the inner world of the characters, including events and states, and can correspond to both the foreground and background parts in the sense of Hopper (1979) or Reinhart (1984). It is generally said that in unembedded (i.e. independent) clauses, BAT-sentences as

Chapter 9   *Be About To*   323

well as BGT-sentences in the past tense pragmatically imply unfulfillment of the infinitival situation (Declerck (1991a: 113), Quirk et al. (1985: 218)), as exemplified below:

(9) a.   You were going to give me your address.   ['... but you didn't ...']
(Quirk et al. (1985: 218))

   b.   The police were going to charge her, but at last she persuaded them she was innocent.   (Quirk et al. (1985: 218))

(10) a.   I was about to protest when Mr. Smith interrupted me.
(Jespersen (1931: 362))

   b.   I was about to go to bed when the telephone rang.   (Swan (2005: 3))

However, this statement is only partially true, for example, when the two types of sentences are used in conversational texts. At least, this is not true for descriptive narrative parts of third-person fiction. In descriptive narrative parts (of third-person fiction), where the situations are narrated as if they were past experiences from the narrator's perspective, BAT-sentences in the past tense make a sharp contrast with BGT-sentences in the past tense.[8] To be more specific, the infinitival situation tends to be actualized in the case of the BGT-sentence, whereas it tends to be halted or not to be actualized in the case of the BAT-sentence. For example, in M. Puzo's novel *The Godfather*, all of the seven relevant BGT-sentences in the past tense are used to indicate fulfillment of the infinitival situation, while five out of six relevant BAT-sentences in the past tense are used to indicate non-fulfillment or halt of the infinitival situation.[9]

To illustrate the point, let us observe the following sentences:

(11) a.   And now, finally, Albert Neri, alone in his Bronx apartment, was going to put on his police uniform again.   He brushed it carefully.   Polishing the holster would be next ...   (M. Puzo, *The Godfather*, p. 426)

   b.   Nothing was going to stop him from owning this girl, possessing her, locking her in a house and keeping her prisoner only for himself.
(M. Puzo, *The Godfather*, p. 340)

   c.   She was head of a great conglomerate, she was married to the man she loved and she was going to have his baby.
(S. Sheldon, *Master of the Game*, p. 201)

---

[8] Henceforth, the term *narrative* is used in the sense of 'third-person narrative', unless otherwise indicated.

[9] Watanabe (2011: 77) confirms this point by investigating more data.

(12) a. Michael was touched. He was about to tell the young man to go away again, but then he thought, why not let him stay?

(M. Puzo, *The Godfather*, p. 127)

   b. The man didn't move. Benjamin bent his knees slightly and was about to move toward the door when he felt an arm closing around his neck. He thrashed away.   (C. Webb, *The Graduate*, p. 191)

   c. Marty was about to ask another question — something about paradoxes and Doc always talking about their responsibility to the past — when he heard the woman scream.

(C. S. Gardner, *Back to the Future Part III*, p. 112)

(11) includes examples of BGT-sentences in the past tense in descriptive narrative parts; (12) includes examples of BAT-sentences in the past tense in descriptive narrative parts. The BGT-sentence in (11a), for example, indicates that Albert Neri, a former policeman and now a guard for a mafia boss, actually kills another mafia boss with his police uniform on at a time later than this scene. That is, the infinitival situation of the BGT-sentence is actualized. On the other hand, the BAT-sentence in (12a), for example, indicates that Michael does not actually tell the young man to leave the place where they are. This is inferable from the content of the clause following the BAT-sentence and the infinitival situation involved is thus not actualized.

Note, however, that the above observations are merely tendencies and it is therefore possible that BGT-sentences in the past tense imply non-fulfillment of the infinitival situation, as shown in (13), whereas BAT-sentences in the past tense suggest fulfillment of the infinitival situation, as in (14).

(13) ... The sharks surrounded the raft now, ... Each nudge tilted the raft at a precious angle. It was going to capsize at any moment.

(S. Sheldon, *Master of the Game*, p. 67)

(14) A storm, which had been brewing all evening, was about to break ... The clock tower read 10:04 ... And lightning struck the clock tower.

(C. S. Gardner, *Back to the Future Part II*, p. 1)

In (13), the raft's capsizing does not come about later than the time of this scene, whereas in (14), the break of the storm does come about later than the time of this scene. As far as I know, this type of difference has not been pointed out in previous studies and thus should be explained.

The above three differences between BAT-sentences and BGT-sentences have never been given a systematic and unified explanation. Within my framework, they are derived from the interaction between the different tem-

Chapter 9   *Be About To*   325

poral structures of the two sentences and the properties of the linguistic environments in which they appear. In what follows, I will restrict myself to the typical uses of BGT-sentences when comparing them with BAT-sentences, unless otherwise mentioned.

9.3.   Toward Constructing the Temporal Structures of BAT-Sentences

This section is devoted to constructing the temporal structures of BAT-sentences in the present and past tenses. As with BGT-sentences (in their typical uses), the temporal-structure information of BAT-sentences is always determined "compositionally", i.e. composed of the temporal meanings of their constituents. BAT-sentences basically do not allow "bleached" parts in their temporal structure. This seems to be due to the fact that BAT-sentences have a lower degree of grammaticalization than BGT-sentences (Collins (2009: 156)). Generally speaking, a higher degree of grammaticalization is accompanied by (a higher degree of) semantic bleaching (cf. Traugott (1988: 407), Heine, Claudi and Hünnemeyer (1991: 40)), which makes the degree of compositionality weaker. The above statements about the difference in compositionality and grammaticalization provide a basis for the following discussion.

9.3.1.   Combination Patterns of Constituents of BAT-Sentences and BGT-Sentences

Before constructing the temporal structures of BAT-sentences, we first need to look at how the constituents of this type of sentences make semantic units. Both BGT-sentences and BAT-sentences belong to the "*be* + X + *to*-infinitive" construction (Perkins (1983: Ch.5)) and contain two verbs (including verbal units), but they differ with respect to how their constituents make semantic units. To be specific, BGT-sentences are divided into the *be going to* part and the (bare) infinitive part—as we saw in Chapter 6—whereas BAT-sentences are divided into the *be* part and the *about* + *to*-infinitive (i.e. A-infinitive) part. Thus, in the case of BGT-sentences, the verbal unit *be going to* is associated with an event time (i.e. E_1) and the infinitive with another event time (i.e. E_2); in the case of BAT-sentences, on the other hand, *be* is associated with an event time (i.e. E_1) and the A-infinitive with another event time (i.e. E_2). The combination patterns of constituents of BGT-sentences and BAT-sentences are summarized in (15):

(15) a.   *Be Going To*-Sentences: E_1 (*be going to*) + E_2 (infinitive)

    b.   *Be About To*-Sentences: E_1 (*be*) + E_2 (*about* + *to*-infinitive)

There are a number of syntactic phenomena which support the difference in combination pattern between the two sentences. First, *about to* can co-occur with copulas other than *be*, as in (16), but *going to* cannot, as shown in (17):[10, 11]

(16) a. ... , and at times the sheer cliffs seemed about to close in.

(The Brown Corpus (Brown))

   b. When the Plymouth neared, it veered toward him and seemed about to run him down. (Brown)

   c. ... ; while in an early Attic scene, he appears about to cut off the monster's tongue. (BNC EB7)

(17) a. *... , and at times the sheer cliffs seemed going to close in.

   b. *When the Plymouth neared, it veered toward him and seemed going to run him down.

   c. *... ; while in an early Attic scene, he appears going to cut off the monster's tongue.

Next, the combination of *as if* and the A-infinitive is impeccable, as shown in (18), but the combination of *as if* and *going to* is basically impossible, as exemplified in (19):[12]

(18) a. Maude swooped up the cup and hiked up her top hoop as if about to take off with a racing start. (Brown)

   b. Marc took a step forward as if about to restrain his younger brother by sheer force, but ... (BNC JXU)

   c. ... Many photos appear to capture something that is about to be lost. Families camp as if about to move on. (GloWbE GB)

---

[10] In the BNC, I could not find any instance of the sequences *seem(s)/seemed going to* and *appear(s)/appeared going to*. By contrast, I found four instances of the sequence *appear(s)/appeared about to* and 51 instances of the sequence *seem(s)/seemed about to*.

[11] Kevin Moore (personal communication) comments that although the sentences in (16) are not part of his dialect, he recognizes them as English. He continues to say that he prefers, say, *seemed to be about to* to *seemed about to* in (16a), but even if (17a) is changed into the *seemed to be going to* version, it is still bad. This may imply that BGT-sentences are more grammaticalized than BAT-sentences.

[12] In GloWbE US and GloWbE GB, I found in total 19 instances of the sequence *as if about to*, but only one instance of the sequence *as if going to*, as in (i):

   (i) According to Mr. Bulmer the Australians, when surprised, utter the exclamation korki,

   "and to do this the month is drawn out as if going to whistle." (GloWbE GB)

For the time being, I regard this example as an exception.

Chapter 9   *Be About To*   327

(19) a. *Maude swooped up the cup and hiked up her top hoop as if going to take off with a racing start.

   b. *Marc took a step forward as if going to restrain his younger brother by sheer force, but ...

   c. *... Many photos appear to capture something that is about to be lost. Families camp as if going to move on.

Thirdly, head nouns can be modified by the A-infinitive, as illustrated in (20), but not by *going to*, as shown in (21):

(20) a. Someone threw a beer bottle at me, and hit a guy who was behind me about to pour a pint over my head.   (BNC ACN)

   b. This is the story of Firdaus—as told to the author in the condemned cell of a prison in Cairo. Firdaus is a prostitute about to die for the murder of her pimp.   (BNC HH3)

   c. They're only statues—I know that—but they look really real, just like a real family sitting round a table just about to eat their Christmas lunch.   (BNC A74)

(21) a. *Someone threw a beer bottle at me, and hit a guy who was behind me going to pour a pint over my head.

   b. *This is the story of Firdaus—as told to the author in the condemned cell of a prison in Cairo. Firdaus is a prostitute going to die for the murder of her pimp.

   c. *They're only statues—I know that—but they look really real, just like a real family sitting round a table just going to eat their Christmas lunch.

As assumed in Section 6.3.1, a semantic unit is a unit whose constituents are semantically closely related to each other, expressing a kind of idiomatic meaning in a broad sense. This type of expression ranges from true idiomatic expressions (e.g. *kick the bucket*), to what Nunberg, Sag and Wasow (1994) call idiomatically combining expressions (e.g. *take advantage of*). Under this assumption, the observations made above, together with the observations in Section 6.3.1, enable us to claim that in the case of BGT-sentences, *be going to* and the infinitive part form their respective semantic units, whereas in the case of BAT-sentences, *be* and the A-infinitive (i.e. *about* + *to*-infinitive) form their respective semantic units.

9.3.2. Temporal Structures of BAT-Sentences

Having seen how the constituents of BAT-sentences make semantic units, we can now move on to the construction of the temporal structures of BAT-sentences. Let us start with the temporal information represented by the *be* part of BAT-sentences. The nature of this *be* is the same as that of the copula *be*. This is supported by the fact that the *be* in BAT-sentences allows the co-ordination of an adjective and A-infinitive in its complement position, as shown in (22):

(22) a. They have had the benefit of such an education and now it is over or about to end, together with almost all paramedical help. (BNC A7Y)

    b. This can be an especially useful consideration if you are unhappy in a job or about to change direction. (BNC CEF)

    c. This showed that we have now implemented the majority of the rec-ommendations while the remainder are either well in hand or about to be tackled. (BNC GX2)

Moreover, just as the present participle of present progressive sentences is coordinated with a preposition phrase, as illustrated in (23), so an A-infinitive can be coordinated with a present participle, as in (24).

(23) Its former head, Mr Erick Mielke, for years the man who knew all the secrets and pulled all the strings, is under arrest and facing corruption charges. (BNC A9M)

(24) a. Consider a helicopter which is flying forwards and about to make a turn. (BNC CAY)

    b. ... the dog is worrying or is about to worry the livestock and there are not other reasonable means of ending or preventing the worrying; ...

        (BNC FSS)

This fact suggests that *be* in BAT-sentences has the same status as the copula *be*.[13]

As already seen in Section 7.3, the *be* of present progressive sentences in their aspectual use, which is in nature the same as the copula *be*, denotes a schematic situation without specific semantic content, i.e. semantically bleached situation (Figure 1 in Chapter 7). In the same vein, the *be* of BAT-sentences, which is also the same as the copula *be*, depicts a semantically

---

[13] Huddleston and Pullum (2002: 526–527) define the copula *be* as follows: "As a lex-eme, *be* makes little if any contribution to the meaning, but serves the syntactic function of carrying the tense inflection (and showing agreement with the subject)."

Chapter 9 *Be About To*

bleached situation and its event time is thus an orientational event time (E^O).

I turn now to the consideration of the temporal information associated with the A-infinitive (i.e. *about* + *to*-infinitive) part. I follow two dictionaries, i.e. *Collins Online English Dictionary* and *Longman Dictionary of Contemporary English, 5th edition*, to assume that *about* in BAT-sentences is a predicative adjective. This can be justified by the fact that some types of "copula + X + *to*-infinitive" constructions — which include the *be about to* construction — are future expressions with the X position occupied by a predicative adjective (e.g. *sure, certain*), as indicated by (25) and (26) (Hornby (1975: 98)).

(25) a. Time is sure to bring a lot of changes.   (BNC G2T)
     b. He was disappointed to learn that there was no such event on last season's European Tour calendar, but seems sure to get his wish next year.   (BNC AAN)
(26) a. Hankin is certain to announce a clear-out when he presents his retained list next week.   (BNC K4T)
     b. Implementation of the Cadbury Committee's proposed code of best practice for improving boardroom procedures in UK listed companies looks certain to be put back until next year.   (BNC CBV)

Predicative adjectives occur in the complement position of the copula (Huddleston and Pullum (2002: 526)) and the predicative adjective *about* in BAT-sentences is thus regarded as occurring in the complement position of *be*.

On the other hand, *about* in BAT-sentences combines with the *to*-infinitive to form a semantic unit, i.e. A-infinitive, which as a whole occupies the complement position of *be*. In their temporal structure, the A-infinitive serves as a semantically "opaque" unit (i.e. a kind of idiomatic expression) providing certain temporal information. In this semantic unit, *about* functions as an adverb modifying the *to*-infinitive because adverbs modify a verb or predicate.[14] Thus, the predicative adjective *about*, so to speak, doubles as an adverbial modifier (including a preposition as well as an adverb) in the A-infinitive.[15] As defined in online dictionaries such as *Macmillan Dictionary* and *Collins English Dictionary*, the adverbial *about* has a meaning like 'near or close to' or 'nearby'. This implies that when mapped into the domain of time, the *about* in question expresses 'nearness in time' or 'near or close to a time'. We can therefore assume that in BAT-sentences, *about* indicates that the event time of the infinitival situation (E_2) is temporally near or close to a certain

---

[14] *The Oxford English Dictionary* defines the *about* in BAT-sentences as an adverb.
[15] In this sense, the semantic unit *be about to* is a kind of amalgam construction.

time. As stated in Section 2.3, the *to*-infinitive represents its event time as posterior to the potential time of orientation at the tense-structure level. Since the A-infinitive occupies the complement position of the copula *be* as the head verb, the potential time of orientation is identified as the orientational event time associated with the head verb *be* ($E^O{}_1$). From these observations, I conclude that BAT-sentences in the present tense include the event time of the infinitive located in the near future relative to the orientational event time of *be*, which is in turn simultaneous with speech time.

A question then arises as to which time-area the notion of near future refers to. This is because in my model the time range from now onward is divided into the present time-area, including speech time, and the future time-area (in the real world). I assume that the near future represented by BAT-sentences refers to a time later than speech time in the present time-area. However, if the infinitival situation involved is durative, the whole of time range covered by the situation is not necessarily restricted into the present time-area. As defined in Section 1.1, an event time in our model is the time point or period of a relevant part of the situation involved, so that the event time of the infinitive can correspond to the time of a certain part of the infinitival situation, not the whole of it. From these observations, I argue that in constructing the temporal structures of BAT-sentences, a kind of profile shift in the sense of cognitive grammar (e.g. Langacker (2008: 69)) comes into play. That is, the beginning part (i.e. onset) of the infinitival situation is foregrounded through such a shift and the time corresponding to it is coerced to be located in the present time-area to make a sharp contrast with the time of the rest of the situation located in the future time-area. We can say this because from a cognitive point of view, two entities (e.g. the onset of the infinitival situation and the reset of it) at two different places (e.g. the present and the future time-area) can make a sharper contrast with each other than do the two entities at the same place. It is therefore the time of the onset of the infinitival situation that is recognized as the time of the relevant part of the infinitival situation in this construction, i.e. the event time of the A-infinitive (E_2). This claim is empirically verified by the fact that as shown in (5) above, BAT-sentences in the present tense basically cannot go with adverbials referring to the future time-area.

These observations enable us to schematically represent the basic temporal structure of BAT-sentences in the present tense in Figure 1:

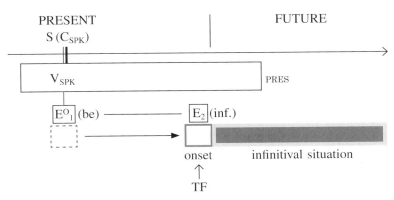

Figure 1: Basic Temporal Structure of BAT-Sentences in the Present Tense

Several comments are in order here. The square with broken lines below E^O_1 represents the situation expressed by *be*, a semantically bleached situation. The square with solid lines below E_2 denotes the beginning part (i.e. onset) of the infinitival situation. This is the default case and the speaker's t-viewpoint (V_{SPK}) therefore fuses with his/her consciousness (C_{SPK}) at speech time (S), which is represented by the bold vertical line. Since the situation associated with *be* is semantically bleached, the temporal focus (TF) is directed at the other event time, i.e. the event time of the infinitive (E_2), whose time length corresponds to the time of the onset of the infinitival situation. In Section 6.3.1, I followed Duffley (1992, 2000, 2006) to argue that the *to* of the *to*-infinitive represents a temporal path (represented by the horizontal arrow). We take the same position here and E_2—located in the present time-area (PRESENT)—is thus posterior to E^O_1, which is in turn simultaneous with S (represented by the vertical line connecting E^O_1 with S). Because BAT-sentences are much less grammaticalized than BGT-sentences in general, the meanings of the constituents of BAT-sentences are basically retained and the infinitival situation therefore never fails to be situated at a time later than speech time (cf. Collins (2009: 155)). This case makes a contrast with the case where the highly grammaticalized versions of BGT-sentences (i.e. the present reference uses discussed in Section 6.4.5) can refer to situations obtaining at speech time.

The BAT-sentences that we are dealing with in this chapter are all unmodalized forms, which are accompanied by assertive modality in linguistic environments reflecting speaker's mental attitudes, i.e. independent or main clauses. As we saw with respect to the immediate-future use of simple present sentences in Section 8.3.5, the present time-area is a cognitive time range in which the influence of the speaker's mental attitude—holding at speech time—is prevalent and thus considered an assertable time range. Given this perspective, the speaker can construe, with assertive modality, the relevant situation to occur or obtain at a time later than speech time, as long as it is located in the present time-area. Because the onset of the infinitival situation of BAT-sentences—corresponding to the event time in question (E_2)—is confined to the present time-sphere, the situation can be the target of assertion.

Our assumption that the onset of the infinitival situation is located in the present time-area may lead us to a cognitive schema in which the event time in question (E_2) and the orientational event time (E^O_1)—simultaneous with speech time in the case of the present-tense version—are very close to each other on the time line. That is, the two event times can be treated as if they were located around the same area. This is supported by the linguistic phenomenon in which the A-infinitive can occur in the predicate part of the complement of perception verbs, as in (27):

(27) a. The day before, she told me, the hospital staff had been dismayed to see a young girl about to deliver, shackled in leg-irons and handcuffs, escorted to the maternity ward by armed guards.   (BNC CJP)
   b. He looked around and saw Pete about to go out the door. (BNC HJC)
   c. While waiting in the floodlit colonnade of the mansion for his car, Hagen saw two women about to enter a long limousine already parked in the driveway ...   (M. Puzo, *The Godfather*, p. 61)

It is generally said that the complement position of perception verbs is subject to the so-called coincidence restriction concerning perception, namely that the time of what is perceived must coincide with the time of perceiving it. This is not an objective, strict restriction, but a subjective, cognitive one and the coincidence between the two times can therefore be extended to what Declerck (1991b, 2006) calls the sloppy simultaneity case (Section 1.1), in which two events or event times are almost or nearly simultaneous with each other. Given this perspective, the fact that the A-infinitive appears in the complement position of perception verbs lends support to our claim that the time associated with a part of what is perceived (i.e. the onset of the infinitival situation) is located around the same time as the time of perceiving it (i.e. the time of orientation). In other words, the former time is recognized as "sloppily simultaneous" with the latter.

This way of reasoning is supported by the linguistic fact that aspectual verbs expressing inchoative aspect can appear in the complement position of perception verbs, as exemplified by (28):

(28) a. Knox felt his head begin to swim.
(N. H. Kleinbaum, *Dead Poets Society*, p. 94)
b. He saw Maisie start to open her mouth and, ... (BNC ASS)
c. At the second attempt she made the connection and heard the telephone begin to ring at the other end. (BNC BMW)

These examples suggest that the beginning part (i.e. onset) of the situation described by the complement clause of a perception verb can be regarded as obtaining at (almost) the same time as the perception itself. In this way, the coincidence restriction concerning perception can work in the case of the relationship of sloppy simultaneity.

Let us next move to the basic temporal structure of BAT-sentences in the past tense, which is schematically represented in Figure 2:

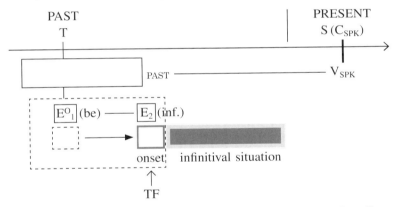

Figure 2: Basic Temporal Structure of BAT-Sentences in the Past Tense

Because the tense is past, the event time of the finite verb, i.e. the orientational event time of *be* (E^O_1), is located at a time (T) in the past time-area (represented by PAST). In this temporal structure, the event time of the A-infinitive (E_2) is located at a time later than E^O_1 but recognized as included in the same time range in which E^O_1 is included—the time range represented by the rectangle with broken lines including both E^O_1 and E_2. What is crucial here is that unlike in the case of the present-tense version in Figure 1 above, the time range including the past time T (corresponding to the present time-area in Figure 1) is not conceptually distinguished from the time range thereafter (corresponding to the future time-area in Figure 1). We will see later that this difference between the present-tense and past-tense versions plays a crucial role in analyzing their behaviors. Two derived temporal structures of BAT-

334   *The Grammar of Future Expressions in English*

sentences in the past tense, i.e. the one for conversational texts and the one for descriptive narrative parts, will be provided in Section 9.4.2.3.

9.4. Analysis

9.4.1. The Present Tense

We are now in a position to explore the linguistic phenomena of BAT-sentences observed in Section 9.2. Let us start with the observation that BAT-sentences tend to refer to situations in the nearer future than do BGT-sentences.

As discussed in Chapter 6, BGT-sentences allow the event time of the infinitival situation (E_2) to be located either in the future time-area in the case of the future reference uses, e.g. the typical uses (Figure 2 in Chapter 6), or in the present time-area in the case of the immediate-future use (Figure 3 in Chapter 6). In the latter case, BGT-sentences typically co-occur with a present time adverb like *now*, as in (2a) above. However, they can also be classified into the immediate-future use when co-occurring with time adverbs referring to a time after now, such as *very soon*, as in (2c), or *just*, as in (29) below, because these time adverbs indicate immediacy but do not explicitly refer to the future.

(29) a.   I'm just going to walk down the hill with this lady—her husband's there—she's had rather a shock ...   (BNC APR)
      b.   It's just going to be a long, slow process.   (BNC BPD)

As for *in a minute* in (2b), if interpreted as 'one minute later', it explicitly refers to the future time-area even if it is very close to speech time. BGT-sentences with *in a minute* in this sense are instances of the future reference use. By contrast, if *in a minute* is interpreted as 'very soon', it does not explicitly refer to the future. BGT-sentences with *in a minute* in this sense are instances of the immediate-future use.

In sum, the near future represented by BGT-sentences (in the present tense) is an implication deriving from their temporal structure, especially the cognitive schema in which the infinitival situation—without a break—follows the preliminary stage holding at speech time. Since the notion near future is an implication, it can be canceled and BGT-sentences thus can go with time adverbs referring to the remote future, as shown in (13a, b) in Chapter 6. In order to be classified as instances of the immediate-future use (i.e. a use denoting a situation in the very near future), BGT-sentences need to occur with present time adverbs or time adverbs expressing immediacy as well as avoid an explicit reference to the future time-area.

Chapter 9   *Be About To*

On the other hand, BAT-sentences (in the present tense) are basically considered to co-occur with present time adverbs like *now*, as in (4) above, or time adverbs which indicate immediacy but do not explicitly refer to the future, such as *very soon* or *just*, as in (3) above. They basically cannot go with future time adverbs like *tomorrow* or *next week*, as shown in (5) above. These observations are explained by the characteristics of the basic temporal structure of BAT-sentences in the present tense (Figure 1 above). The location of the event time of the A-infinitive (E_2) in the present time-area is conceptually contradictory to the specification of E_2 by a future time adverb referring to the future time-area. Hence the low acceptability of the sentences in (5). The very near future implied by BAT-sentences is derived from the above claim that in terms of the temporal structure, the onset of the infinitival situation is regarded as situated at a time very close to E^O_1 as the time of orientation, which is simultaneous with speech time.

However, we must recall here that there are cases where BAT-sentences occur with future time adverbs, as in (6) — repeated below — and (30).

(6) a.   We've been running the management skills courses since nineteen eighty-six, and since then, more than seven hundred and fifty people, from groups such as yours, have taken a part, and we're about to launch a phase two in the next er, year or so.   (BNC JNK)

 b.   First they happen in June that's that's a good starter for one, and they're really not that big a problem and I guess people in London would laugh at the prospect of the noise which which May Balls cause and not worry about it in one way and would not have telephone calls to the local council and lots of stories in my newspaper every year. We're about to start them again probably in the next week or two.   (BNC KRP)

(30) a.   Jim Grandison, Export Manager, has recently returned from the Middle East and Fraser Gordon, European Manager, is about to visit Paris and Austria in the near future.   (BNC HS0)

 b.   ... it's just about to come out in three weeks time oh really because it would have been nice if you could have put something in the corpus about the prisoners who help with the corpus actually or a bit in the B A I E Communicators Newsletter in Scotland you know here's a member that's launched a new publication for the Scottish prison service.   (BNC KGK)

A careful observation reveals that these instances of BAT-sentences with future time adverbs have a common denominator. They do not straightforwardly express a definite future time, as in (6) and (30a), or they are "subjectively" interpreted as referring to the time close to now, as in (30b). In the former three examples, the presence of *or so* in (6a) and *probably* in (6b) prevents us from putting a focus on a definite point in the future, and the expression *in the near future* in (30a) does not refer to a definite time point or period in the future. In (30b), although the expression *in three weeks time* itself refers to a definite time in the future, the presence of *just* (meaning 'very soon') gives the impression that the occurrence of the infinitival situation involved is subjectively close to now. From these observations, we assume that although the infinitival situation is objectively located in the future time-area, in the cognitive schema of BAT-sentences of this type the factors observed above coerce the present time-area to be expanded into the future to cover the onset of the infinitival situation.

Let us elaborate on this expansion mechanism by considering the four examples step by step. In the case of (6a), which is excerpted from the text published in 1991, the context tells us that the relevant project has been continuing more than five years; in comparison with that time span, one year from now on — implied by the time adverb *in the next year or so* — is a relatively shorter time span. Besides, due to the presence of *so*, the time of launching a phase two is blurred. We can thus subjectively construe the future situation as close to now and expand the present time-area to cover its onset.

Next, in the case of (6b), the presence of *probably* indicates that the speaker is not confident of the exactness of the time referred to by *in the next week or two*. In addition, the future time referred to by this time adverb is not so distant from now. We can therefore subjectively expand the present time-area to cover the onset of the future situation.

We now turn to (30a). The future time adverb *in the near future* does not refer to a definite time in the future; it lexically implies that the relevant time is not so far away from now. Hence the subjective expansion of the present time-area is easy.

Finally, let us consider (30b). The presence of the adverb *just*, which indicates the meaning 'very close', implies that the speaker regards the occurrence time of the relevant situation as close to now. This allows him/her to subjectively incorporate the relevant part (i.e. onset) of the future situation specified by *in three weeks time* into the present time-area by means of the present-time-area expansion.

From these observations, I conclude that the subjective expansion under the influence of the factors considered above makes it possible for the event time

Chapter 9   *Be About To*

of the infinitival situation (E_2)—which corresponds to the time covered by the onset of that situation—to be located in the (expanded) present time-area, which sanctions a special use of BAT-sentences in these contexts.

Before going further, we must still explain why apparently unacceptable BAT-sentences become improved when embedded in wider contexts, as in (7), repeated here.

(7) a. ?I am about to leave for America tomorrow, so I am afraid I cannot see you this afternoon.
    b. ?We are about to move next week, so we are very busy preparing.

As is evident from (7), these BAT-sentences are embedded in the contexts where the semantic content of the second sentence is clearly relevant to the speech situation and hence the infinitival situation of the BAT-sentence is also taken as relevant to the speech situation. This motivates us to incorporate the onset of the infinitival situation—corresponding to its event time (E_2)—into the subjectively expanded present time-area, while the rest of the infinitival situation remains in the future time-area. However, (7) is not completely acceptable. Because the time adverbs *tomorrow* and *next week* refer to specific time points in the future, the subjective expansion of the present time-area is not made complete without the help of expressions indicating immediacy, such as *just*.[16]

In our model, the present time-area and the future time-area are not absolutely distinguished from each other, but their boundary can be flexible in the cognitive schema of temporal structures. It is therefore possible to subjectively expand the present time-area to cover the onset of the future situation. This is one merit of my temporal structure approach, where the temporal-structure information can interact with information from other factors such as the context or environmental characteristics to produce a context-driven, subjective interpretation, such as the one based on the subjective expansion of the present time-area.

I now turn to an explanation of why BGT-sentences allow the infinitive part to be in the progressive form, while BAT-sentences do not, as illustrated by (8), repeated here.

---

[16] Unlike (30b), the BAT-sentences in (7) do not co-occur with *just*, an indicator of the notion "very close in time", and therefore the subjective expansion in question does not apply perfectly here.

(8) a. The plane is about to take off. (Perkins (1983: 73))

b. ? The plane is about to be taking off. (Perkins (1983: 73))

My temporal structure approach straightforwardly accounts for this phenomenon. As observed in Chapter 6, grammaticalization has proceeded considerably in the case of BGT-sentences in general. They have developed some uses in which (part of) the preliminary stage has been semantically bleached (e.g. the bleached-coda and simple-future uses) with the result that the coda (i.e. right boundary) is blurred or disappears in the cognitive schema of the temporal structures of these BGT-sentences. Stative situations can thus appear in the infinitival position of these sentences. This allows the progressive form—which describes a stative (unbounded) situation (Section 2.4.3.3)—to appear in this position. By contrast, as observed in Collins (2009: 156), BAT-sentences are less grammaticalized than BGT-sentences in general.[17] The *to* of BAT-sentences thus preserves the meaning of temporal path, which implies that the infinitival situation must be non-stative, or at least the left side of the situation must be bounded (recall that *to* contributes to part of the situation described by the A-infinitive in BAT-sentences). This is conceptually contradictory to the generally accepted idea that the progressive form refers only to the middle part of the situation. For this reason, the acceptability of BAT-sentences combined with the progressive form in the infinitival position is lower, as exemplified by (8b).

9.4.2. The Past Tense

We now move to the observation made in Section 9.2 that in descriptive narrative parts (of third-person fiction), BGT-sentences in the past tense tend to indicate fulfillment of the infinitival situation, while BAT-sentences in the past tense tend to result in non-fulfillment of the infinitival situation. To explain this difference, we first need to look at the characteristics of this linguistic environment.

9.4.2.1. *Environmental Characteristics of Descriptive Narrative Parts*

At least two types of "person" and two types of "world" play crucial roles in characterizing this linguistic environment (see Wada (2015a)). The two types of person relevant here are the narrator(s) and characters. The mechanism of

---

[17] Collins (2009: 155–156) points out that BAT-sentences have epistemic uses, but not volitional uses except for the negative volitional use expressing refusal—an omen of the gradual grammaticalization of BAT-sentences.

Chapter 9 *Be About To*

narration can be very complex because, for example, sometimes more than one narrator is involved or the relationship between the writer and narrator must be considered (e.g. Genette (1980), Chafe (1994), Ehrlich (1990), Fleischman (1990), Fludernik (2009)). Here, I only describe the essence of the mechanism because it is enough for our purposes.

Let us start with the observation of the narrator. The narrator does not belong to the fictional world but is an omniscient being outside of it—or in the narrator's world—and knows everything concerning the former world, including the mental states or attitudes of the characters. The two worlds are of a different nature. The narrator's consciousness is always present at the time of narration. He/She narrates the story from his/her perspective in his/her world as if the situations in the fictional world were past relative to the time of narration (Prince (1982), Fleischman (1990: 23–24)). The default principle concerning the choice of the English tense forms in (4) in Section 2.4.1 is also at work here and therefore the fusion of the speaker's (i.e. narrator's) t(emporal)-viewpoint and consciousness at the time of narration triggers the narrator to choose the past tense forms to refer to the fictional world.

Both types of persons (i.e. narrator(s) and characters) have the ability to do mental or cognitive activities such as thinking or uttering. This implies that in addition to the narrator—who is by definition the speaker—characters are also depicted as (potential) speakers. Because of their ability to do such activities, they also serve as viewers or recognizers of situations and can think and utter based on the viewed and/or construed situations. Both types of persons thus have their own viewpoints of situation description, i.e. SD-viewpoints, from which to see or evaluate the target situation. While the narrator's consciousness is always present at the time of narration, his/her SD-viewpoint can be situated either at the time of narration, i.e. the central point of the time line in the narrator's world, or at any time on the time line in the fictional world because of his/her omniscient nature. By contrast, the characters always belong to the fictional world and their SD-viewpoint must be situated at a point on the time line in the fictional world, usually at the narrative (story) now, though it can move forward or backward on the time line.[18]

---

[18] From the perspective of the Three-Tier Model adopted in Chapter 3, the narrator as the speaker at the time of narration is, by definition, always depicted as the public self, whereas the characters are regarded as the private selves in the represented speech and thought of descriptive narrative parts because they function as the subject of thought or mental activities in this environment. It is expected that the public self / private self distinction has a great influence on the explanation of temporal phenomena in narrative, but as far as the temporal phenomena concerning BGT-sentences and BAT-sentences in the past tense are concerned,

340   *The Grammar of Future Expressions in English*

The parameter of the narrator's vs. character's SD-viewpoint is crucially related to the classification of descriptive narrative parts.[19] First, represented speech and thought (free indirect speech) can be distinguished from the scene description parts (i.e. the rest of the descriptive narrative parts) in that the former basically allow only the character's SD-viewpoint to be foregrounded because they describe the mental (inner) world or consciousness of the characters.

Second, the scene description parts are divided into at least two, i.e. the part where only the narrator's SD-viewpoint is relevant, as exemplified by (31a), and the part where both the narrator's and character's SD-viewpoints are relevant and fuse with each other, as illustrated in the underlined part of (31b).

(31) a.   The bloody victory of the Corleone Family was not complete until a year of delicate political maneuvering established Michael Corleone as the most powerful Family chief in the United States. For twelve months, Michael divided his time equally between his headquarters at the Long Beach mall and his new home in Las Vegas ...

(M. Puzo, *The Godfather*, p. 441)

b.   ... She stood there up on her toes poised like a deer to run. She was very close now, close enough for the men to see every feature of her face. <u>She was all ovals—oval-shaped eyes, the bones of her face, the contour of her brow.</u> Her skin was an exquisite dark creaminess and her eyes, enormous, dark violet or brown but dark with long heavy lashes shadowed her lovely face ...

(M. Puzo, *The Godfather*, pp. 333–334)

(31a) only recounts, objectively from the narrator's perspective, situations that are regarded as if they happened in the past. There is no room for the character's perspective to be involved and only the narrator's SD-viewpoint is relevant here. On the other hand, the underlined part of (31b) describes the scenes as seen from the perspective of the characters referred to by *the men*. However, the underlined part is not a represented speech and thought environment. We thus feel that in addition to the characters' (i.e. the two men's) SD-viewpoint, the narrator's SD-viewpoint is somehow at work here

---

such a distinction does not seem to be so crucial and therefore I do not appeal to it here, though an explanation based on that distinction is necessary for a contrastive study of narratives in English and Japanese (Wada (2017b)).

[19] The classification here is based on Wada (2015a), which analyzes the mechanism of interpreting four verb forms with a past tense morpheme in English (i.e. simple past, past progressive, past perfect, and future-in-the-past) in four types of "interpretive environments".

because of the omniscient nature of the narrator. In either case, the narrator's SD-viewpoint is relevant to the scene description parts. What we are treating as examples of narrative texts in this chapter are basically those in the scene description parts.

Before going further, let us briefly mention the correlation between my notions of t-viewpoint and SD-viewpoint, on one hand, and Chafe's (1994) notions of the representing consciousness (i.e. the deictic center for tense and person) and the represented consciousness (i.e. the deictic center for adverbials of space and time), on the other. He defines consciousness as a small segment of human mind which is active when the experiencer refers to the surrounding world (Chafe (1994: 28)). Considering the definitions of the two types of consciousness, we may conclude that the representing and the represented consciousness correspond, respectively, to the speaker's t-viewpoint and SD-viewpoint, at least in tense interpretation.

9.4.2.2. BGT-Sentences

We can now explain the differences between the ways in which BAT-sentences and BGT-sentences in the past tense are used in descriptive narrative parts (of third-person fiction), which we observed in Section 9.2. First, I will explain why in conversational texts, BGT-sentences in the past tense tend to imply non-fulfillment of the infinitival situation, while in descriptive narrative parts they tend to imply fulfillment of the situation. (9a) and (11a)—representing, respectively, examples of BGT-sentences in the past tense in conversational texts and those in descriptive narrative parts—are repeated here as (32a) and (32b).

(32) a. You were going to give me your address. ['... but you didn't ...']
    (=(9a))

   b. And now, finally, Albert Neri, alone in his Bronx apartment, was going to put on his police uniform again. He brushed it carefully. Polishing the holster would be next ... (=(11a))

The difference in question is due to the environmental differences between conversational texts and descriptive narrative parts.[20]

Conversational texts contain the current speaker and the hearer as well as the time line in the real world whose central point is the speech situation (including speech time). This suggests that in the default case, situations in the

---

[20] This difference can be dealt with in the interpersonal relationship tier of the Three-Tier Model, which I leave for future research.

past are seen from the perspectives of the speaker and hearer located in the speech situation and thus what occurred or obtained in the past is on the same time line with which the speech situation is associated. It is therefore usually the case that as of now (i.e. at speech time) the speaker and hearer already know whether the relevant situation was actualized or not. These environmental characteristics play a crucial role.

Now, recall that the BGT-sentence in the past tense having the temporal structure of the bleached-coda use (Figure 11 in Section 6.6.5) can receive an interpretation in which the infinitival situation is not fulfilled. What then leads the hearer to assume that the speaker has the bleached-coda use in mind when using BGT-sentences in the past tense? We can answer this question in the following manner. To refer to situations in the past in this linguistic environment, the speaker has at least three options. One is to use the simple past, which directly refers to the relevant situation itself. Another option is to employ the *will*-form or *be to*-form in the past tense, which guarantees the actualization of the relevant situation from a point of view in the past. The third option is to utilize the BGT-sentence in the past tense, a tense form involving the preliminary stage in its temporal structure. The choice of BGT-sentences provides a presupposition for the non-fulfillment of the situation, because choosing the other two options automatically leads to the actualization of the relevant situation and does not leave any room for the non-fulfillment of the situation involved. The hearer may therefore infer that the speaker chooses the BGT-sentence in the past tense, but not the version whose temporal structure includes the coda of the preliminary stage, because such a version of the BGT-sentence tends to indicate fulfillment of the infinitival situation, as suggested by Figure 12 in Section 6.6.5. It is thus most likely that in conversational texts, the speaker chooses the bleached-coda use of BGT-sentences in the past tense to express non-fulfillment of the relevant situation in the past.

Why, then, in descriptive narrative parts, especially the scene description parts, do BGT-sentences in the past tense tend to imply fulfillment of the infinitival situation? In other words, why in this linguistic environment do we tend to use the BGT-sentence in the past tense whose temporal structure includes the coda of the preliminary stage, which allows the actualization of the infinitival situation? To answer these questions, we need to point out some essential differences between descriptive narrative parts and conversational parts.

In descriptive narrative parts (of third-person fiction), the time line of the story is entirely different from that of the narrator (see Fludernik (2009: 31)). Usually, at least in the course of recounting the story, the narrator tends to

Chapter 9   *Be About To*

concentrate on describing situations in the fictional world as seen from his/her SD-viewpoint shifted into that world and the reader or hearer accepts the story as it is.[21, 22] This suggests that in this linguistic environment, unlike in conversational texts, the reader's or hearer's inferences are irrelevant which would otherwise be in operation at the time of narration; the reader or hearer "blindly" accepts the narrator's SD-viewpoint shifted into the story world (i.e. the fictional world), whose central point is the narrative now. The case under consideration is thus similar to the case where BGT-sentences in the present tense are used in conversational texts, because the narrative now here is virtually treated as if it were speech time in conversational texts.

These observations allow us to assume that the same type of analysis provided in Chapter 6 to account for BGT-sentences in the present tense in conversational texts is available here. The results of the comparison of BGT-sentences and *will*-sentences in Section 6.6 enabled us to claim that the primary purpose of use of BGT-sentences in the present tense is to show that the speaker pays attention, or makes the hearer pay attention, to the preliminary stage leading to the actualization of the infinitival situation in the future — a case which *will*-sentences cannot indicate. In this way, we can explain why BGT-sentences in the past tense tend to imply fulfillment of the infinitival situation in descriptive narrative parts, especially in the scene description parts.

It should be stressed again, however, that the behaviors of the BGT-sentences observed above are merely tendencies. It is therefore possible that BGT-sentences in the past tense indicate fulfillment of the infinitival situation in conversational texts, but imply non-fulfillment of the infinitival situation in descriptive narrative parts, as indicated in (13) above. I argue that in the former case, the speaker chooses BGT-sentences whose temporal structure includes the full-fledged coda of the preliminary stage (which implies actualization of the infinitival situation in terms of the cognitive schema), whereas in the latter case, the speaker chooses BGT-sentences whose temporal structure includes the bleached coda (which implies non-actualization of the infinitival situation). This is a strong point of our model because it allows more than one temporal

---

[21] In narrative, my notions of "speaker's SD-viewpoint" and "speaker's t-viewpoint" partially correspond, respectively, to Genette's (1980: 186) "mood" — related to the question of "who is the character whose point of view orients the narrative perspective?" or "who sees?" — and "voice" — related to the question of "who is the narrator?" or "who speaks?"

[22] This linguistic environment is what I call "Interpreting Environment B", where scenes and events/states are described in terms of the narrator's SD-viewpoint shifted into the story world and the character's SD-viewpoint is not directly relevant to the tense interpretation (Wada (2015a: 304)).

344   *The Grammar of Future Expressions in English*

structure for one tense form. We can say which temporal structure is preferred, depending on both the characteristics of the linguistic environment in
which the tense form involved appears and the contextual information.

9.4.2.3. BAT-Sentences

Let us next explain why BAT-sentences in the past tense tend to imply non-
fulfillment of the infinitival situation not only in conversational texts but also
in descriptive narrative parts (of third-person fiction). (10a) and (12a)—representing, respectively, examples of BAT-sentences in conversational texts and
those in descriptive narrative parts—are repeated here as (33a) and (33b).

(33) a.   I was about to protest when Mr. Smith interrupted me.   (=(10a))
      b.   Michael was touched. He was about to tell the young man to go
            away again, but then he thought, why not let him stay?   (=(12a))

I start with the mechanism in which BAT-sentences in the past tense tend to
imply non-fulfillment of the infinitival situation in conversational texts. As in
the case of BGT-sentences in the past tense, both the perspectives of the
speaker and the hearer located in the speech situation are relevant to the interpretation of BAT-sentences in the past tense and the hearer assumes that the
speaker knows whether the relevant past situation is actualized or not. On
this basis, the hearer's reasoning goes as follows. If the speaker wants to
show that the target situation has been actualized, the speaker is able to
choose the simple past form, which can straightforwardly refer to that situation, or a *will*-form (or *be to*-form) in the past tense, which can indicate the
actualization of the situation from a point of view at a preceding time.

As we have seen, the onset of the infinitival situation of BAT-sentences is
foregrounded through a profile shift. Thus, in the default case, the onset part
is representative of the whole situation in temporal calculation and the time
corresponding to the former is viewed as the event time of the situation involved (E_2). In the present-tense version, the onset part (associated with E_2)
is coerced to be incorporated into the present time-area, but the core part remains located in the future time-area (Figure 1 above). The present time-area
is an assertable time range, while the future time-area is not, and the two
time-areas are thus different in quality. Hence the present time-area makes a
contrast with the future time-area.

In the past-tense version, the onset part (associated with E_2) is similarly coerced to be incorporated into the time range in which the orientational event
time associated with the *be* of BAT-sentences (E^0_1) is located (Figure 2
above). Unlike in the case of the present-tense version, however, in a context-

Chapter 9   *Be About To*

free setting, the time range including the onset of the infinitival situation and the one including the core part constitute (part of) the same time range (i.e. the past time-area) in the case of the past-tense version and the two time ranges are both assertable in that the situations in them are located in the past relative to the time of narration, i.e. the time of assertion. For these reasons, the two time ranges in question are not clearly distinguished from each other and thus the basic temporal structure of BAT-sentences in the past tense observed in Figure 2 must be elaborated on and revised to make a conceptually clear distinction between them.

Two steps are necessary for this purpose. One step is to place the two event times involved in this construction (i.e. the event time of *be* and that of the A-infinitive) in two different time ranges. From a cognitive point of view, contrasting two entities at different places with each other is easier than contrasting two entities at the same place (unless they are too far apart). The other step is to make a sharp distinction between the foreground and background areas. Generally speaking, distinguishing a spotlighted area from a shadowed area is an easier task than distinguishing between two spotlighted areas or two shadowed areas. Based on these observations, I argue that two cognitive shifts, or coercions, closely related to these two steps are in operation in constructing the derived versions of the temporal structure of BAT-sentences in the past tense.[23]

A first cognitive shift concerns the target shift with respect to the event time associated with the infinitival situation, i.e. the E_2 shift. In the basic temporal structure of BAT-sentences in the past tense (Figure 2 above), E_2 corresponds to the time of the onset of the infinitival situation. In the derived version, however, E_2 is coerced to correspond to the time of the core part of the situation located in the time range different from the one including the onset part. Thus, the orientational event time of *be* (E^O_1) remains in the time range including the onset part and E_2 is located in the time range following it (see Figures 3 and 4 below). By situating the two event times (i.e. E^O_1 and E_2) in two different time ranges, we can strengthen the contrast between the two time ranges in terms of the temporal positions of E^O_1 and E_2.

Let us next consider the second cognitive shift, which comes into play after

---

[23] These cognitive shifts are not in operation with BGT-sentences in the past tense because the two situations (i.e. the preliminary stage and the infinitival situation) of BGT-sentences are, in the first place, independent of each other in terms of the cognitive schema of the temporal structure. Hence the inference pattern observed with respect to BAT-sentences in the past tense is not in operation in the case of BGT-sentences in the past tense.

the E_2 shift. At this stage, the onset of the infinitival situation as the foreground part is not linked to any event time, which brings about a cognitive discrepancy because a foregrounded entity is salient and from a cognitive point of view should be linked to an event time, i.e. a salient mark on the time line, due to iconicity (cf. Taylor (2002: 46–48)). There is only one event time left in the time range in question, i.e. the event time of *be*, which is an orientational type and not associated with a semantically contentful situation, let alone a foregrounded one. How can we solve this problem? An answer seems to lie in Langacker's (2011b: 183) observation that "a spotlight illuminates not only its [=a scene's] target, but also the immediately surrounding area." If we equate the foregrounding with the spotlighting, we can argue that the foreground area expands and thus incorporates the semantically bleached situation associated with *be*—which is located in the vicinity of the onset (i.e. foreground) part because of the properties of *about*—into it. As a result of this expansion, the whole of the time range including both the situation associated with *be* and the onset part of the infinitival situation is foregrounded and thus makes a sharp contrast with the time range including the core part of the infinitival situation, which is not foregrounded. Now that the situation associated with *be* is incorporated into the foreground area, its event time is "conceptnally" linked to the onset of the infinitival situation and coerced to be a pure type (i.e. E_1) and can thus receive a temporal focus. In this way, the expansion of the foreground area to cover the situation associated with *be* resolves the cognitive discrepancy observed above. Since the temporal focus by its nature tends to be directed at an event time (a pure type) in a foreground area, it can be directed at E_1 in this case.

Having observed the two cognitive shifts common to the derived temporal structures of BAT-sentences in the past tense in conversational texts and descriptive narrative parts, we can now consider the temporal structures themselves in some detail. Let us start with the version for conversational texts, which is schematized in Figure 3:

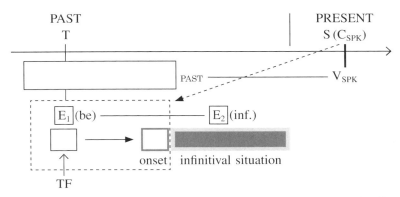

Figure 3: Temporal Structure of BAT-Sentences in the Past Tense in Conversational Texts

This temporal structure stems from the interaction between the basic temporal structure in Figure 2, the two cognitive shifts discussed above, and the environmental characteristics of conversational texts observed in Section 9.4.2.2. The broken arrow from S (C_{SPK}) to the past time-area (PAST) suggests that the speaker's and the hearer's inferences at speech time are relevant to the interpretation of the past situations. The T in the past time-area serves as a past time with which the event time of *be* in the BAT-sentence (E_1) is simultaneous. E_1 is a pure type of event time, i.e. the event time associated with the situation of *be* incorporated into the foreground area because of the second cognitive shift and thus represented by the square with solid lines below E_1. Due to the first cognitive shift, the event time of the infinitival situation (E_2) is coerced to be associated with the time of the core part in the time range different from the one including E_1 and the time of the onset part (represented by the rectangle with broken lines). The temporal focus (TF) is coerced to be directed at E_1.

Now we are in a position to explain, with this temporal structure, why BAT-sentences in the past tense tend to imply non-fulfillment of the infinitival situation in conversational texts. The explanation goes as follows. As we have seen, in this linguistic environment the speaker is assumed to know whether the relevant situation in the past is actualized or not. The temporal structure of the BAT-sentence under consideration allows us to be able to feature the onset of the relevant situation as the foreground part, which is conceptually separated from the core part of the situation described by the A-infinitive. If the speaker wants to indicate fulfillment of the situation itself (corresponding to the core part), he/she can choose the simple past or the *would*-form, as we saw with respect to the similar case of BGT-sentences. We can therefore reason that the speaker chooses the BAT-sentence in the past tense because he/she intends to show that only the onset of the situation occurred and the core part did not happen.

By way of illustration, consider (33a) above. The speaker is assumed to have in mind, say, a scene in which he/she uttered a few syllables, when his/her utterance was suddenly interrupted. The syllables are regarded as the onset of the infinitival situation of the BAT-sentence in question and the protesting words (i.e. the main body of the utterance) as the core part. Due to the temporal structure schematized in Figure 3 above, the use of BAT-sentences in the past tense usually leads to the non-fulfillment of the (core part of the) relevant situation in this linguistic environment. A possible difference between the non-fulfillment cases of the BAT-sentences and the BGT-sentences may be that in the former case, part of the infinitival situation comes into existence, but in the latter, only the preliminary stage (which is not a part of the infinitival situation) comes into existence. This difference will be considered later in relation to the difference as to the fulfillment of the infinitival situation between BAT-sentences and BGT-sentences in descriptive narrative parts.

Let us next consider the derived temporal structure of BAT-sentences in the past tense for descriptive narrative parts, which is schematically represented below.

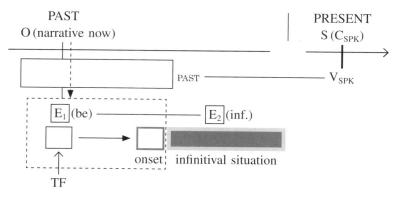

Figure 4: Temporal Structure of BAT-Sentences in the Past Tense in Descriptive Narrative Parts

This temporal structure derives from the interaction between the basic temporal structure in Figure 2, the two cognitive shifts discussed above, and the environmental characteristics of descriptive narrative parts observed in Sec-

Chapter 9   *Be About To*   349

tions 9.4.2.1 and 9.4.2.2. The time line of the story is entirely different from
that for the narrator and so there is a break on the time line represented by the
horizonal long arrow. As we saw above, especially in the course of recounting the story, the narrator tends to concentrate on describing situations in the
story world as seen from his/her SD-viewpoint shifted into it and the narrative
now, i.e. the central point of that world, serves as the time of orientation for
computing the target event time. Hence the broken arrow starts from the time
of orientation (O) in the past time-area (PAST), i.e. the story (i.e. fictional)
world. This suggests that the two situations involved in BAT-sentences (i.e.
the infinitival situation and the situation expressed by *be*) are both located in
the fictional world and evaluated from the narrator's SD-viewpoint situated at
the narrative now. As for the other parts of the temporal structure, this version is the same as the version for conversational texts represented in Figure 3
above.

I will now explain why BAT-sentences in the past tense tend to imply non-
fulfillment of the infinitival situation even in descriptive narrative parts, while
BGT-sentences in the past tense tend to imply its fulfillment. The explanation
goes as follows. First, as we saw with respect to BGT-sentences in the past
tense in descriptive narrative parts, the reader or hearer of the story does not
pay attention to the time of narration, except for some special parts (i.e. those
describing the scene or background at the time of narration). In most parts of
the story line, he/she concentrates on situations at the narrative now (in the
story world) and accepts them as they are. This implies that the reader's or
hearer's perspective at the time of narration is usually irrelevant in this linguistic environment and therefore his/her inferences at the time of narration do
not have any influence on the story line (i.e. the fictional world). From these
observations, we may conclude that the narrative now is, in functional terms,
comparable to speech time in the case of conversational texts. So far there
are no differences between the two sentences under comparison with respect
to the characteristics of the linguistic environment in which they appear.

However, there is a crucial difference between the temporal structures of
BAT-sentences and BGT-sentences in question. In the case of the BAT-sentences, the speaker bothers to divide the target situation into the onset and
core parts and feature the former part, while in the case of the BGT-sentences,
what is foregrounded is the preliminary stage, which is regarded as separate
from the infinitival situation in the first place. From a cognitive point of view,
we can safely say that the speaker's emphasis on the occurrence of the onset
(i.e. foreground) part of the target situation, i.e. the part that the speaker bothers
to divide from the core part of that situation, leads the reader/hearer to reason

that the speaker does not intend to indicate the actualization of the core part (i.e. rest) of the situation. As a result of this process, the core part of the situation is driven into the background. This is a kind of paradoxical phenomenon, because the actualization of the part of the target situation (i.e. the onset part)—which strongly implies the actualization of the following part in the case of the present-tense version—prevents the core part (i.e. the following part) from happening.[24] Consider the BAT-sentence in (33b) above, i.e. *He was about to tell the young man to go away again*, for example. The onset part of the infinitival situation is such that he almost said something to instruct the young man to go away and the halt of the actualization of the saying itself (i.e. the core part) is implied by the semantic content of the following sentence, i.e. *but then he thought, why not let him stay?*. The reader/hearer— whose attention is paid to the narrative now—expects only the foreground onset part to be actualized, and thus the background core part tends to be halted for the reason mentioned above.

On the other hand, in the case of BGT-sentences in the past tense in this linguistic environment, the preliminary stage (i.e. the foreground part) is an independent situation from the infinitival situation (i.e. the background part) and interpreted as followed by the latter in terms of the temporal structure. As explained in Section 6.6.5, if the relevant BGT-sentence is interpreted as indicating fulfillment of the infinitival situation, it is given the temporal structure of the typical uses in Figure 12 in Chapter 6, whereas if it is interpreted as indicating non-fulfillment of the infinitival situation, it is given the temporal structure of the bleached-coda use in Figure 11 in Chapter 6. The former structure corresponds to the present-tense version with a higher probability of the actualization of the infinitival situation, e.g. the typical-use version (Figure 2 in Chapter 6), which is a more prototypical case. The BGT-sentence in the past tense is thus interpreted as having the temporal structure in Figure 12 in Chapter 6 and tends to indicate fulfillment of the infinitival situation in descriptive narrative parts.

---

[24] As observed in Section 9.3.2, we do not bother to distinguish between two time ranges in one and the same time-area, i.e. the foreground and the background areas, in the case of the present-tense version of BAT-sentences and therefore the paradoxical phenomenon observed in the main text does not happen.

Chapter 9   *Be About To*

9.4.2.4.   Compatibility of BAT-Sentences with Time Adverbials Referring to the Future-in-the-Past

We have thus far shown that the distinction between the two time ranges in the temporal structure of BAT-sentences in the past tense (i.e. the time range including the onset of the infinitival situation and the one including the core part) is conceptually not very clear in a context-free setting (Figure 2 above). I contended that since the two time ranges as they stand are not clearly distinguishable compared to the present/future time-area distinction, the two cognitive shifts come into play in constructing the temporal structures of BAT-sentences in the past tense in conversational texts and descriptive narrative parts so that the two time ranges can clearly be distinguished.

Before closing this chapter, I will further justify the above contention. To this end, I will explore the fact that the restriction on the compatibility of BAT-sentences in the past tense with time adverbs referring to a time later than the time of orientation is weaker than the restriction on the compatibility of BAT-sentences in the present tense with such adverbs.

As discussed in Section 9.4.1, one major factor allowing BAT-sentences in the present tense to go with future time adverbs is the subjective expansion of the present time-area — as exemplified in (6) and (30) above — which states that the present time-area is expanded into the future. This subjective expansion occurs when the boundary between the present time-area and the future time-area is rather blurred because of the presence of time adverbs which do not refer to a specific future time or which make a vague reference to a future time.

However, it seems that such a restriction is relaxed when BAT-sentences in the past tense go with a time adverb referring to a time later than the past time of orientation, as illustrated by (34).

(34) a.   State intervention, collectivism and political consensus, which had characterized politics after 1945, were seen as significant causes of economic decline and social dependency. A new ideology based on individualism, a diminution in public activity and intervention, free enterprise and selective welfarism prevailed within a Conservative party that was about to gain electoral success in 1979 and throughout the 1980s.   (BNC B1U)

b.   Half a minute later the airframe gave one final creak and his stomach fell away as the Hercules lifted off, whining into the night sky. It finally came home then to Delaney what they were about to do in several hours' time.   (BNC BPA)

c. Just as he was about to travel to Paris in November, to open a book exhibition and make a speech at the Bibliothèque Nationale, he caught a heavy cold which turned to bronchitis with congestion of the lungs; a nurse was called in and he took a course of penicillin, but he still managed to make the journey.   (BNC EFX)

d. Despite widespread protests, the government was about to launch its third structural adjustment programme in May 1991.   (BNC HL7)

As is clear from these examples, BAT-sentences in the past tense can go with time adverbs referring to a specific or definite past time which is later than the past time of orientation.

I argue that the difference between the present-tense and past-tense versions depends on whether or not the two time ranges involved are by nature distinguishable from each other. The conceptual boundary between the present time-area and the future time-area is clear by nature in that they are identified as different time zones in the first place. By contrast, the conceptual boundary between the two time ranges involved in the basic temporal structure of BAT-sentences in the past tense is not so clear in that they belong to the same time-area, i.e. the past time-area, and so the contrast between the two time ranges is not so sharp. One can thus use BAT-sentences in the past tense with time adverbials referring to a time later than the time of orientation, i.e. those indicating a different time range, as long as he/she subjectively regards the time distance between the time of orientation (E_1) and the event time of the A-infinitive (E_2) as close. In this way, BAT-sentences in the past tense, as shown in (34), are more likely to go with a specific or definite time adverbial than those in the present tense.[25]

---

[25] In the case of BAT-sentences in their historical-present use, the speaker's t-viewpoint fuses with a past time of orientation and the present time-sphere (grammatical present) corresponds to part of the past time-area (cognitive past). Therefore, unlike in the default case of the present-tense version, the time range including the past time of orientation and the time range thereafter are not distinguished clearly. This predicts that BAT-sentences of this type can go more easily with time adverbs referring to a specific or definite time which comes later than the past time of orientation. This is borne out by (i):

(i)   G. S. Perrin, Collection
      Another picture taken from the York-Bournemouth as it is about to pass through Staveley Central in 1965.   (BNC AMR)

This text was published in 1991 and the year 1965 refers to the future relative to the past time of orientation. Although the BAT-sentence in (i) is present tense, the conceptual distinction between the time range including the past time of orientation and the time range thereafter is not so clear, as is the case with BAT-sentences in the past tense.

9.5. Concluding Remarks

This chapter has investigated the linguistic phenomena of BAT-sentences in detail, especially in comparison with those of BGT-sentences. With BAT-sentences in the present tense, the characteristics of their (basic) temporal structure allow the event time of the infinitival situation (E_2) to correspond to the time of the onset part, which is incorporated into the present time-area. Hence BAT-sentences in the present tense can hardly go with time adverbs referring to a definite future time. However, if the time adverbs refer to the future indefinitely or vaguely, or are subjectively interpreted as referring to a near future, the conceptual boundary between the present and the future time-areas becomes less clear, which induces the expansion of the present time-area into the future. In this case, the compatibility of BAT-sentences in the present tense with future time adverbs is allowed.

The temporal structures of BGT-sentences in the past tense interact with the characteristics of the relevant linguistic environments and tend to imply non-fulfillment of the infinitival situation in conversational texts, but its fulfillment in descriptive narrative parts. By contrast, the temporal structure of the past-tense version of BAT-sentences in a context-free setting (i.e. basic temporal structure) has the following characteristic: the onset and core parts of the infinitival situation (i.e. two parts inherently constituting a single situation) are divided into two different time ranges which are not clearly distinguishable by nature. This characteristic interacts with the environmental characteristics of conversational texts or descriptive narrative parts to bring about the derived temporal structures in which the foreground time range (i.e. the time range including the onset part) is coerced to be clearly distinguished from the background time range (i.e. the time range including the core part), which systematically explains why the (core part of the) infinitival situation of BAT-sentences in the past tense is basically halted to occur in both conversational texts and descriptive narrative parts.

This type of explanation is possible within the present framework, where the basic temporal structure can interact with other factors such as the context or the characteristics of the relevant linguistic environment to bring about the semantic uses having the respective temporal structures.

Chapter 10

The Future Progressive*

10.1. Introduction

Thus far, we have analyzed a variety of temporal phenomena concerning *will*-sentences, BGT-sentences, present progressive and simple present sentences with future time reference (i.e. futurate sentences), and BAT-sentences within the framework that has been developed in this book. This chapter deals with one more future expression, i.e. sentences in the future progressive form, or sentences containing the form *will* + *be* + *-ing* (henceforth WBI-sentences), as illustrated in (1).[1]

(1) a. "Established organisations are often stretched in satisfying these varied needs which Tennis Interlink can help resolve through its London based operation. We will be expanding opportunities by promoting existing tennis resources around the world and improving communications between members so an extensive and thriving network is created." (BNC A0V)

b. JESSLYN PARKES, the England goalkeeper, will be hoping to guide her new team, Middlesex, to a winning start when the new season of English county league matches opens tomorrow, writes Liz Round. (BNC A33)

c. The company has sent an invitation to Mr Graham Bright, the Tory

---

* This chapter is a revised and extended version of Naoaki Wada, (2013b), "On the so-called future-progressive construction", volume 17.3, pp 391–414, *English Language and Linguistics*, 2013 © Cambridge University Press 2013, reproduced with permission.

[1] As indicated in note 1 of Chapter 5, this study regards (future) *shall* as an allomorph of (future) *will*. The form *shall* + *be* + *-ing* is thus also a variant of the form *will* + *be* + *-ing*. This is because the two constructions basically behave in the same way (at least with respect to the data that this chapter is considering), except that the *shall*-version does not have an epistemic use referring to the present.

MP for Luton South, whose bill seeks to ban all-night parties. "We want him to see what the reality is, compared with the tabloid myth," said a party organizer. British Rail will be running Sunday services on New Year Day.

(BNC AAU)

Most grammar books, monographs or pedagogical works about English tenses (e.g. Coates (1983), Declerck (1991a, 1991b, 2006), Hornsby (1975), Huddleston and Pullum (2002), Leech (1987, 2004), Nehls (1988), Palmer (1988, 1990), Quirk et al. (1985), Swan (1995, 2005), Thomson and Martinet (1986), Wekker (1976), Whittaker (1983)) include descriptions of this tense form. Nevertheless, WBI-sentences are one of the least discussed tense forms. As far as I know, most previous studies have merely referred to uses and characteristics of WBI-sentences with some comments and have not analyzed them in detail. A few studies (e.g. Celle and Smith (2010), Sawada (2006), Williams (2002a)) have provided detailed descriptions of them, but they have drawbacks and/or do not explain their temporal phenomena in a general theory of tense combined with a theory of modality and mental attitudes.

This chapter therefore analyzes the temporal phenomena (i.e. characteristics and behaviors) of WBI-sentences systematically within the proposed framework. First, Section 10.2 observes linguistic facts concerning three major uses of WBI-sentences (i.e. the future-progressive use, the future-as-a-matter-of-course use, and the inferential present-progressive use) and points out problems with the previous studies. Section 10.3 constructs the temporal structures of the three uses by combining those of the *will* + infinitive form and of the progressive form, whereby we explain the linguistic facts and solve the problems observed in Section 10.2. Section 10.4 compares the future-as-a-matter-of-course use of WBI-sentences—whose temporal structure is constructed by combining the temporal structures of the *will*-form and the non-finite version of PPF-sentences (i.e. non-finite sentences containing the progressive futurate form)—with either *will*-sentences or PPF-sentences. Section 10.5 makes concluding remarks.

10.2. Linguistic Facts to be Explained

10.2.1. Three Uses of WBI-Sentences and Their Characteristics

Let us first observe some linguistic facts concerning WBI-sentences. This construction is generally said to have three major uses. The first use refers to ongoing situations in the future. This use is dubbed the future-progressive use in this book. Examples of this use are given in (2):

Chapter 10   The Future Progressive   357

(2) a.   This time next week they will be sailing across the North Sea.

(Leech (2004: 66))

b.   The whole factory will be working overtime next month.

(Leech (2004: 67))

c.   This time tomorrow I'll be lying on the beach.   (Swan (2005: 195))

d.   The Arsenal striker, who scored in both north London derby games last season, refused to be drawn into a slanging match after the game but responded forcefully yesterday. He said: "Monkou is a whinger and I will be waiting for him when Southampton come to Highbury.

(BNC CBG)

e.   This means there will be time to get everything down but that your brain will have to work at full speed and concentration to analyse all the words. While your brain is doing that it will be storing the words so that when you look at your sheet of nouns you will recall what was said for some while after it was actually said.   (BNC CBU)

The future-progressive use involves progressive aspect and usually shows the so-called "framing effect", namely that the situation referred to by WBI-sentences occupies a time span encompassing a time point in the future (i.e. future time of orientation), especially specified by a future time adverbial, as in (2a, c, d). However, in some cases this use of WBI-sentences simply describes a situation ongoing for a certain length of time in the future, as in (2b, e).[2]

The second use refers to a future situation that occurs as a matter of course. This use is referred to as the future-as-a-matter-of-course use in this study. Examples of this use are given below.

(3) a.   Professor Baxter will be giving another lecture on Roman glass-making at the same time next week.   (Swan (2005: 195))

b.   David Lawrence will be staying with the county after signing a new four-year contract.   (BNC A8N)

c.   Tonight until December 16 The Scottish Ballet will be dancing the popular Peter Pan.   (BNC A9T)

d.   "Established organisations are often stretched in satisfying these var-

---

[2] Killie (2014) gives weight to the distinction between two uses of the present progressive (i.e. the so-called "focalized" and "durative" uses) in her diachronic study, observing that only the focalized use has become obligatory in present-day English. The focalized use denotes an event ongoing at a time of orientation and thus brings about the framing effect, while the durative use indicates that an event is continuing for a certain length of time. The two uses seem to be inherited by WBI-sentences.

ied needs which Tennis Interlink can help resolve through its London based operation. We will be expanding opportunities by promoting existing tennis resources around the world and improving communications between members so an extensive and thriving network is created." (=1a)

e. Christien knows Tony and Tracey and mum Sheila will be rooting for him on Monday night when the series starts. (BNC CBC)

f. "Get the car," Michael called down to him. "I'll be leaving in five minutes. Where's Calo?" (M. Puzo, *The Godfather*, p. 351)

This use is generally considered not to reflect progressive (imperfective) aspect and regarded as a special and characteristic use of WBI-sentences. In (3e), for example, the presence of an expression like *X know(s)* implies the presence of something for us to say that we know a future situation.[3] That is, it makes easier for us to interpret WBI-sentences in such a way that the present participle situation will come about in the future as a natural course of a certain situation obtaining at speech time. In what follows, we will observe further characteristics of this use.

First, the future-as-a-matter-of-course use is said not to describe a future situation conveying volition at speech time. Instead, it is said to indicate that some prerequisites for the occurrence of a future situation have already been set up or fixed (Declerck (1991a, 2006), Huddleston and Pullum (2002), Leech (2004)), as exemplified by (4):

(4) a. Your son will be staying with the other first formers in block D.
(Declerck (1991a: 165))

b. Shall I take you to the station?—Oh, I don't want to trouble you.—That's all right. I'll be driving past it anyway. (Declerck (1991a: 165))

c. BIG Brother will be watching you from the end of this week when spy cameras start to operate in north-east Essex. Stretches of road such as Mersea Road, Colchester, have been selected for the installation of the cameras which can record the registration number of speeding motorists and could lead to fines. (BNC CFC)

Second, as explicitly shown by the time adverbials in (3a, c, e) above, this use tends to refer to the near but not too immediate future (Leech (2004: 68)). However, this is only a rough guideline. This use can refer not only to the immediate future, as in (5), but also to the somewhat distant future, as in (6):

---

[3] Recall the discussion in Section 6.6.4.

Chapter 10   The Future Progressive

(5) a.   The train will be leaving in a second.   (Leech (1987: 69))
    b.   Miranda will be coming in in a minute.   (BNC H0F)
    c.   It will be taking place immediately beside, behind and in front of the
         homes of a large number of my constituents.   (BNC HHX)
(6) a.   I'll be meeting him next year.   (Kashino (1999: 103))
    b.   "At last we are getting the reward for our hard work and we will be
         challenging for the world title ourselves in a couple of years," he
         said.   (BNC A2E)
    c.   Without pilots gaining experience at the lowest level, we will be
         shaping up for another chronic pilots shortage in a few years' time.
                                                              (BNC CAU)

Third, the future-as-a-matter-of-course use is usually incompatible with situations that are not normal or occur suddenly (Declerck (1991a: 165), Leech
(2004: 68)), as illustrated in (7):

(7) a.?*Margot will be poisoning her husband when he gets home.
                                                       (Leech (2004: 68))
    b. ?We'll be catching a huge pike tomorrow.   (Declerck (1991a: 165))

Fourth, the use under consideration is compatible with stative verbs which
are not normally progressivized.[4]   The following examples are cases in point.

(8) a.   He'll be owning his own house next.   (Quirk et al. (1985: 217))
    b.   "Will you be needing your car?"   "I don't think so."
                                                 (requoted from Kashino (1999: 95))
    c.   Soon they will be needing a personal loan, perhaps for the first time
         ever, to pay for the carpets, the curtains and the new kitchen.
                                                              (BNC G28)

---

[4] Leech (2004: 68) considers the future-as-a-matter-of-course use to be incompatible with
stative verbs, arguing that a sentence like (i) is interpreted as an instance of the future-progressive use.
    (i)   We'll be living in London next year.
However, this view is questionable, as illustrated in the text (see also Kashino (1999), Sawada (2006)). It should be noted that *live* in (i) is not a purely stative verb because it can appear in the progressive form, whereas purely stative verbs such as *own* or *need* cannot
(Declerck (1991a: 167–175), Leech (2004: 20)), as shown in the following:
    (ii)   I am living in Wimbledon.   (Leech (2004: 20))
    (iii) *He is owning a couple of horses.   (Declerck (1991a: 169))
    (iv) *She is needing a car.   (Kevin Moore (personal communication))

Fifth, this use, as exemplified by (9), can indicate that the participial situation will occur as a daily routine or regular activity.

(9) a. Bill will be driving to London tomorrow. Why don't you ask him to deliver the parcel? (Declerck (1991a: 116))

b. When will you be seeing her again? (Declerck (1991a: 116))

Sixth, the use under discussion is sometimes utilized to describe natural and physiological phenomena, as in (10).

(10) a. The cherry blossom will be falling in a few days.
(Sawada (2006: 471))

b. *When the speaker sees John enter a dusty room.*
He will be {coughing / sneezing} in a minute. (Sawada (2006: 479))

c. Erm the, there is an annex to the hotel, so some of us will be sleeping in the annex but taking all our meals in the, and it's just round the corner. (BNC FUJ)

Before going further, note that WBI-sentences can be ambiguous between the future-progressive use and the future-as-a-matter-of-course use when they co-occur with a future time adverbial, as in (11) below. With the future-progressive use, the time adverbial specifies a future time included in the time span of an ongoing situation, whereas with the future-as-a-matter-of-course use, it specifies the very time when (the beginning of) a participial situation occurs in the future.

(11) a. When the meeting ends we'll be flying to Bonn.
(Huddleston and Pullum (2002: 171))

b. I'll be visiting my aunt at lunchtime. (Leech (2004: 68))

I turn now to the third use, an epistemic use referring to a current, ongoing situation. This use is termed the inferential present-progressive use in this study. Consider, for instance, (12):

(12) a. By now they'll be eating dinner [looking at one's watch].
(Leech (2004: 86))

b. Don't phone them now—they'll be having dinner. (Swan (2005: 194))

c. MOST self-respecting museum directors will now be counting up the takings from the holiday season. (BNC ABD)

d. "You could easily slip over to his lodgings, in Tan House Lane. He will be having his breakfast now. It would be more efficient if you were to bring him straight here." (BNC ANL)

Chapter 10   The Future Progressive   361

e. "But this man here has a temper." "His factor will be feeling it now,
    for letting us through the gates." James Menzies laughed.

                                                              (BNC A0N)

These examples show that like the future-progressive use, the inferential present-progressive use also involves progressive aspect.

10.2.2. Critique of Previous Studies

As shown in Section 10.1, most previous studies of WBI-sentences simply
note the characteristics of the three uses with some comments and do not explain systematically why they have such characteristics and/or why one single
form appears to express two contrasting aspectual values, i.e. progressive and
non-progressive. In this sub-section, I will survey Williams (2002a), Sawada
(2006), and Celle and Smith (2010) as representative studies of WBI-sentences
and point out some problems and/or insufficiencies with them.

First, Williams (2002a) provides an exhaustive study of the simple present
and present progressive, arguing that the concept inducing the speaker to
choose the progressive form is "susceptibility to change" (p. 87).[5] On this basis, he considers the three uses of WBI-sentences discussed in Section 10.2.1.
According to him, both the future-progressive and inferential present-progressive uses reflect progressive aspect directly in their meanings. By contrast, in
the case of the future-as-a-matter-of-course use—as with the present progressive futurate—it is a precondition that is ongoing at speech time and the progressive aspect is thus reflected in an "earlier" situation, but not in the "main"
situation (in this case the participial situation). His analysis provides a unified
perspective in understanding WBI-sentences because the three uses all share
the notion "in progress" in their meanings (Williams (2002a: 217)).[6]

His analysis is similar to my analysis—to be presented in Section 10.3—in
a number of respects and as far as they are concerned, I agree with him.
However, his analysis is not based on a general theory of tense. Moreover, it
is sometimes not clear how the concept of susceptibility to change is relevant
to the explanation of WBI-sentences, especially the future-as-a-matter-of-
course use. Let us consider this with concrete examples.

In Williams's analysis, the present progressive futurate, a type of progres-

---

[5] Williams (2002a: 87) states that the speaker chooses the simple present when he/she is
not interested in "susceptibility to change".

[6] The future-progressive use and the future-as-a-matter-of-course use in this study correspond, respectively, to type one future progressive and type two future progressive in
Williams (2002a).

sive form, is related to the concept of susceptibility to change and thus tends to describe a changeable situation compared to the simple present futurate (which is unrelated to this concept). This implies that the situation described by progressive aspect (i.e. the earlier situation) is tentative and can possibly change in the future. We therefore tend to view the participial situation (i.e. the main situation) of the present-progressive version as less likely to occur or be actualized than the situation of the simple-present version, as exemplified in (13a, b):

(13) a. The parcel arrives tomorrow.   (Leech (2004: 55))
     b. The parcel is arriving tomorrow.   (Leech (2004: 55))
     c. The parcel will arrive tomorrow.   (Leech (2004: 55))
     d. The parcel will be arriving tomorrow.   (Leech (2004: 55))

However, when the future-as-a-matter-of-course use of WBI-sentences is compared with the predictive-future use of *will*-sentences, as illustrated in (13c, d), the WBI-sentence often refers to a future situation which is more likely to occur than the one described by the *will*-sentence, i.e. a sentence without the progressive form, because the former sentence includes a precondition obtaining at speech time, but the latter does not. In this pair of sentences, the implications derived from the concept of susceptibility to change seem to be reversed. In any case, it should be clarified how susceptibility to change influences the interpreting mechanism of WBI-sentences.[7]

Next, I will outline Sawada's (2006) analysis and point out some problems with it. He characterizes the three uses with some linguistic tests and, like many other studies, argues that only the *will* of the inferential present-progressive use is an epistemic modal referring to the present. For him, the *will* in the future-progressive and future-as-a-matter-of-course uses is a future tense marker.

One weak point is that his temporal schemata for the three uses are intuitive and not motivated theoretically. Moreover, his approach cannot explain why future *will* and other epistemic modals (including epistemic *will*) behave similarly with respect to a number of linguistic phenomena. First, as we have seen, future *will* and other modals such as *may* and *must* share the same morpho-syntactic properties (e.g. the so-called NICE properties).[8] Second, as stated in

---

[7] Since Williams (2002a: 89) states that the only exception to the "susceptibility to change" rule is the passive progressive, the notion should be applied to all of the three uses of WBI-sentences discussed in this chapter.

[8] Salkie (2010) argues that the same morpho-syntactic behaviors of future *will* and other

Chapter 10   The Future Progressive   363

Coates (1983) and Collins (2009), future *will* can easily be followed by the perfect form or the progressive form, which is a common characteristic of epistemic modals. Third, future *will*, as well as other epistemic modals such as *may*, usually cannot occur in conditional clauses of the direct cause-effect type, i.e. type A conditional clauses (see Section 5.4.7), as in **If it {will/may} rain tomorrow, I'll stay home.* Last but not least, future *will* can co-occur with a modal adverb such as *probably*, which typically corresponds in the degree of modality to *will* (Section 5.3.3; cf. also Halliday (1970: 334)).

Within my framework, future *will* is a modal—which has already been discussed in Chapter 3—and typically expresses predictive modality as a situation-oriented mental attitude of the speaker (i.e. speaker's S-attitude), whereby the linguistic phenomena concerning future *will* observed above are explained naturally. In addition, we have already discussed and justified how modality as a speaker's mental attitude is positioned in the semantic (de)composition of sentential utterances (see Chapter 3), based on which we have analyzed a variety of tense phenomena and related issues (especially modality and viewpoint aspect). The present framework thus provides a systematic analysis of tense-aspect-modality phenomena, including those of WBI-sentences, from a more comprehensive perspective.

What is worse, Sawada's approach cannot explain the existence of sentences such as (14).

(14) a.   This book will be in her library now and for years to come.

(/www.makereadingfirst.com/Parts.html/)

   b.   In this way, through Christ and his work in us, we will be living in God's presence now and eternally.

(/www.theseed.info/sermon.php?id=337/)

---

modals do not necessarily mean that they belong to the same category, reaching the conclusion that future *will* is not a modal. His argument is based on Salkie (2009), where he proposes four semantico-pragmatic criteria to verify his prototype analysis of modality. However, what is important is that ability *can*, which does not meet the criteria as with future *will*, is viewed as having a low degree of modality and thus as a peripheral member of the category "modal"; ability *can* still expresses modality in his prototype analysis. This implies that if he is consistent in his own analysis, future *will* should be viewed as a modal expressing a certain type of modality even if it is a peripheral member. In fact, Salkie (2009: 99) himself seems to regard future *will* as a non-prototypical modal and at the same time as a non-prototypical tense, which is not incompatible with our claim that *will* is a modal which can express pure futurity depending on the interaction between the basic temporal structure of *will*-sentences with future time reference and the context (i.e. the case of the simple-future use in Chapter 5).

In these examples, sentences containing a single instance of *will* refer to a time range covering both the present and the future. It is usually the case (e.g. Schachter (1972: 92), Okada (2002: 18–19)) that a single form cannot signify two different meanings at a time.[9] Therefore, if *will* were ambiguous between a future tense marker and an epistemic modal referring to the present, as Sawada assumes, the sentences in (14) would be unacceptable, because the two different semantic notions are represented by a single instance of *will*. Sawada's analysis cannot straightforwardly explain these data.

My analysis, by contrast, can straightforwardly explain them. *Will* is always a modal expressing the core meaning of high probability (Section 5.3.3) and can express predictive modality, irrespective of whether the infinitival situation refers to the future or the present, as shown in (14) above. Moreover, within my framework the infinitive in the complement position of modals allows both the simultaneous and posterior relationship to the time of modals — which is in turn simultaneous with speech time — and the infinitival situation can therefore cover both the present and the future time-area at a time (Sections 5.3.1 and 5.3.2).

Finally, let us examine Celle and Smith's (2010) analysis. They argue that the future-as-a-matter-of-course use is underspecified for aspect, which means that it can express any type of aspect depending on the context. Therefore, they are not motivated to allow the future-progressive use as an independent category because the future progressive can be expressed by the future-as-a-matter-of-course use in their system.

Moreover, they argue that the notion of "predetermination", which triggers an "already decided (started)" reading, is not a distinctive factor for the future-as-a-matter-of-course use, but can also be observed in the future-progressive use, as illustrated by (15):

(15)   He gave the address of the destination to him.
       "Axel will be waiting for you," he said to her in a whisper. "He'll take you to the boat. I'll be there shortly after six."

(Celle and Smith (2010: 253))

However, this is no more than a pragmatic implicature deriving from the context in which the WBI-sentence occurs (cf. Williams (2002a: 205)), because the same expression does not convey predetermination in a context like

---

[9] This does not exclude Salkie's (2010) position that *will* is a future tense marker even if it is utilized to refer to the present; he argues that this use is based on "future verification". However, Celle (2004/2005) notes that this is not always the case with English *will*.

Chapter 10   The Future Progressive

(16):

(16) He gave the address of the destination to him.
      "We haven't made the arrangements yet, but Axel will be waiting for
      you when you get there," he said to her in a whisper.

This WBI-sentence indicates that the arrangements (i.e. preparations) will be
made between the time of uttering this sentence and the time of the arrival.
The point here is that the "already decided" reading is not due to the future-
progressive use itself, but induced by other factors, e.g. the contextual information.

This reasoning is strengthened by the following example, where the use of
still triggers an "already decided" reading.

(17) Output has fallen more slowly this time, and unemployment has risen
      less fast ... The decline in output seems to be coming to an end, so the
      economy is at or near the trough. Unemployment will still be rising this
      October (and for months after that)—but output should be expanding.

                                                                    (BNC ABG)

In (17), the rise of unemployment is ongoing at the future time specified by
this October, so this WBI-sentence is an instance of the future-progressive
use. The presence of the temporal *still* implies a state's continuation to the
reference time in question (Michaelis (1993: 193))—a future time of orientation in this case—and what should be noticed here is that it is also implied
that the participial situation is also ongoing now and the situation is therefore
considered to have started before now. Hence, the WBI-sentence in question
receives the "already decided" reading.

By contrast, in the case of the future-as-a-matter-of-course use, cancelling
the predetermination causes a contradiction, as illustrated in (18):

(18) a. *Professor Baxter will be giving another lecture on Roman glass-mak-
         ing at the same time next week, but it has not been decided yet.
                                                      (adapted from Swan (2005: 195))
     b. *This train will be calling at Preston, Chorley, ... but it has not been
         decided at which stations it will make a stop.
                                                (adapted from Celle and Smith (2010: 240))

The above observations suggest that the alleged predetermination associated
with the future-progressive use is of a different type from that associated with
the future-as-a-matter-of-course use. They should be distinguished from each
other.

366   *The Grammar of Future Expressions in English*

10.3. Temporal Structures of the Three Uses of WBI-Sentences

Now I will show how our framework analyzes the linguistic facts as well as the problems with the previous studies observed in Section 10.2. Our approach is, here again, temporal structure-based. As we have seen, the temporal structure of a given tense form is determined compositionally by the meanings of its constituents, unless it does not contain parts that have become highly opaque or completely semantically bleached due to grammaticalization. As for the three uses of WBI-sentences observed above, their temporal structures are determined by the combination of the meanings of the modal *will* and the progressive form.[10] To be more specific, the temporal structure of the future-progressive use consists of that of the modal *will* expressing predictive modality and that of the non-finite version of the aspectual use of the progressive form with future time reference (cf. Figure 7 in Chapter 7); the temporal structure of the future-as-a-matter-of-course use consists of that of the modal *will* expressing predictive modality and that of the non-finite version of the PPF form, i.e. the present progressive futurate (cf. Figure 3 in Chapter 7); and the temporal structure of the inferential present-progressive use consists of that of the modal *will* expressing predictive modality and that of the non-finite version of the aspectual use of the progressive form with present time reference (cf. Figure 1 in Chapter 7).[11] Because WBI-sentences involve (at least) three verbs, their temporal structures include (at least) three event times: the event time of *will* (E_1), the event time of *be* (E_2), and the event time of the present participle (E_3).

10.3.1. Temporal Structure of the Future-Progressive Use

Let me start by constructing the temporal structure of the future-progressive use of WBI-sentences, whereby the participial situation is predicted to be ongoing at the future time specified by a future time adverb or implied by the context. The temporal structure of this use is schematically represented in Figure 1:

---

[10] This characterization of WBI-sentences implies that this type of construction cannot have the simple-future use, which refers to cases where the infinitival situation is considered to be absolutely certain to occur or obtain in the future, regardless of the speaker's judgment or evaluation (see Section 5.4.3). This implication is borne out by the ungrammaticality of a sentence like **He will be being two tomorrow*.

[11] WBI-sentences do not have the temporal structure made by the combination of that of *will*-sentences with future time reference and that of PPF-sentences, simply because PPF-sentences by nature have a temporal structure rooted in the present.

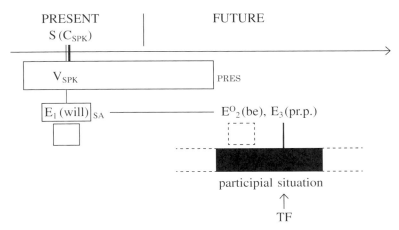

Figure 1: Temporal Structure of the Future-Progressive Use of WBI-Sentences

In this temporal structure, the *will* + infinitive part reflects the temporal structure of the predictive-future use of *will*-sentences (Figure 5 in Chapter 5). *Will* expresses predictive modality as a speaker's S-attitude (represented by the square below E_1), which by definition occurs at the same time as speech time (S), with the result that its event time (E_1) coincides with speech time.[12] The event time of the infinitival *be* (E^O_2), located in the future time-area, is regarded as an orientational type because the *be* + *-ing* part reflects the temporal structure of the non-finite version of the aspectual use of the progressive form, in which the infinitival situation expressed by *be* is semantically bleached (symbolized by the square with broken lines). The participial situation — represented by the black rectangle — is interpreted as unbounded (ongoing or in process) and as indicating no change in time; the initial and final boundaries are backgrounded (represented by the broken-line portions). The event time of the participial situation (E_3) corresponds to the time simultaneous with or including E^O_2 (i.e. the time of orientation) because of the tense-structure information of the present participle (i.e. simultaneity). As we have seen, the temporal focus (TF) cannot be directed at E_1, i.e. the time at which occurs a

---

[12] It is usually impossible to intentionally make what is already ongoing (in process) come about. For this reason, *will* in the future-progressive use dose not express volition or intention. Note, however, that as implied by the discussion in Section 5.4.1, if the situation denoted by the future-progressive use involves factors for the volitional reading (e.g. a human subject or a controllable type of situation), it can pragmatically take on volitional colors.

speaker's mental attitude — because the temporal focus must be associated with the event time of a situation in the proposition domain (Section 5.4.2) — nor can it be directed at E^O_2, i.e. an orientational event time — because the temporal focus must be directed at the event time of a situation that the speaker's attention is paid to, i.e. a specific situation or a situation that the speaker regards as related to the time line even if its temporal location is not clear (Section 2.4.5). The temporal focus is thus automatically directed at E_3, i.e. the event time of the present participle. In this way, we can justify the temporal structure in Figure 1 as that of the future-progressive use of WBI-sentences.

This temporal structure explains the linguistic facts about the future-progressive use observed in Section 10.2. The pure progressivity (imperfectivity) expressed by this use is a consequence of the temporal structure in Figure 1, in which the participial situation itself is unbounded (imperfective) and indicates no change in time and its event time (E_3) is simultaneous with the event time of *be* (E^O_2) as the time of orientation. For example, in (2a), i.e. *This time next week they will be sailing across the North Sea*, the temporal structure only indicates that the situation of their sailing across the North Sea will be ongoing or in progress at the event time of *be* (E^O_2) as the future time of orientation specified by the time adverb *this time next week* and the beginning and end parts of the participial situation involved are backgrounded.

However, although only the middle part of the present participle situation — which includes a time of orientation — is foregrounded in the aspectual use of the progressive form, the beginning and end (i.e. backgrounded) parts are relevant to the tense interpretation in that they constitute a "background" (i.e. "base" in the sense of Langacker's (1991) Cognitive Grammar) based on which the relevant (i.e. middle) part of this situation is interpreted. Generally, for the speaker to be able to predict that a non-stative situation is ongoing or in progress at a given time, such a situation has already started or come into existence by that time and an earlier stage for the ongoing situation must have been in existence. However, this is a pragmatic implicature because the earlier stage itself is not the information included in the temporal structure of the use under consideration. This observation is in keeping with the discussion about examples (15)-(17) in Section 10.2.2. (We can therefore argue that the temporal structure reflecting the notion of predetermination or an earlier stage is reserved exclusively for the future-as-a matter-of-course use, which will be shown in the next sub-section.)

To illustrate this point, let us consider again (15) above. This context enables us to infer that an "earlier stage" (i.e. predetermination in Celle and

Chapter 10   The Future Progressive

Smith's (2010) terminology) has already come into existence not only at the future time of orientation but also at the time of uttering the WBI-sentence; the earlier stage for the infinitival situation of Alex's waiting for the addressee has already started by now and the infinitival situation itself is ongoing at the future time of orientation. This is because the situation involved is related to a type of situation which usually requires an arrangement or plan for its actualization. Because this information is pragmatically inferable from our knowledge about the type of situation at issue, it is a pragmatic implicature. This is compatible with the temporal structure in Figure 1, which itself does not say anything about the beginning part of the situation involved, let alone an earlier stage causing the situation to come into existence, but does not exclude the possibility that the earlier stage (as an implicature) obtains.

In addition, the temporal structure in Figure 1 straightforwardly accounts for the framing effect indicated by the future-progressive use observed in Section 10.2.1. As we saw, sentence (2a), i.e. *This time next week they will be sailing across the North Sea*, shows the framing effect, but sentence (2b), i.e. *The whole factory will be working overtime next month*, does not. Both phenomena can be explained by the interaction between the temporal structure in Figure 1 and the length of time referred to by the time adverb involved. In (2a), the present participle situation (i.e. sailing across a sea) occupies a certain period of time, its event time (E_3) corresponding to a certain period of time. On the other hand, the time indicated by *this time next week*, i.e. the orientational event time associated with *be* (E^O_2), is a shorter time. E^O_2 is thus interpreted as included in E_3. A sentence like (2a) therefore shows the framing effect. In (2b), by contrast, the time span of the present participle situation (i.e. working overtime)—corresponding to E_3—does not include, but is included in, the time span indicated by *next month*. For this reason, a sentence like (2b) does not show the framing effect.

10.3.2.   Temporal Structure of the Future-as-a-Matter-of-Course Use

I turn now to the temporal structure of the future-as-a-matter-of-course use of WBI-sentences, whereby the speaker predicts that the present participle situation will come about as a natural consequence of the pre-stage (i.e. an earlier stage) ongoing or obtaining at speech time.[13] The temporal structure of this use is schematically represented in Figure 2:

---

[13] Recall that in Chapter 7, we named the earlier stage of the present participle situation of the progressive form the "pre-stage".

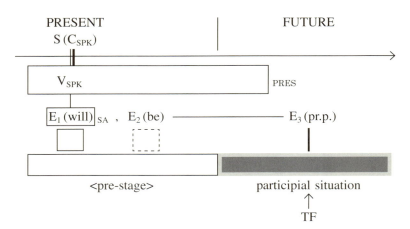

Figure 2: Temporal Structure of the Future-as-a-Matter-of-Course Use of WBI-Sentences

In this temporal structure, the *will* part reflects the temporal structure of the present form of *will*. Here again, *will* expresses predictive modality, which by definition occurs at the same time as speech time (S), and the event time of *will* (E_1) is therefore simultaneous with speech time.

The *be -ing* part reflects the non-finite version of the temporal structure of PPF-sentences, i.e. the present progressive futurate (Figure 3 in Chapter 7). The cognitive schema concerning this part includes not only the main part of the participial situation, i.e. the main situation (represented by the grey rectangle below E_3), but also the pre-stage (represented by the rectangle on the left side of the grey one), which denotes the presupposition or precondition regarded as preceding that situation. The time length of the pre-stage is regarded as including the event time of *be*. It is true that the pre-stage itself is a schematic situation, but its semantic content is specified in the course of interpretation. There was good reason to assume that the pre-stage — which refers to a specified situation whose semantic content is related to but different from that of the main situation — is re-interpreted as taking the place of the semantically bleached situation (symbolized by the square with broken lines) and so linked to the event time of *be* (Section 7.3.2). The event time of *be* thus comes to be a pure type (E_2). The main situation occurs or obtains at a time later than E_2 and the time of its relevant part corresponds to its event time (E_3). Since the pre-stage refers to the presupposition or precondition obtaining at present (which brings about the main situation in the future), E_2 (i.e. the event time coerced to be linked to the pre-stage) is viewed as simultaneous

Chapter 10   The Future Progressive

with speech time (S), which is also simultaneous with E_1 (i.e. the event time of *will*).

Let us finally look at the position of the temporal focus (TF). For the same reason we saw in Section 5.4.2, it is not directed at the event time of *will*. Thus, as we saw in the annotations with respect to Figure 3 in Chapter 7, it is directed at the event time of the main situation (E_3) in this construction. In this way, the temporal structure in Figure 2 is motivated and justified.

The temporal structure in Figure 2 explains why viewing the pre-stage for the main situation as ongoing at speech time presupposes that a decision to carry it out has already been made. The temporal structure of this use implies that the pre-stage covers the time period extending into the past in the cognitive schema and so guarantees the occurrence of the decision in the past. Therefore the pre-stage cannot be canceled, as illustrated by (18) above. An "already decided" reading is a semantic entailment, not a pragmatic implicature, in the future-as-a-matter-of-course use.

In addition, the temporal structure in question explains why this progressive form implies progressive (imperfective) aspect as well as perfective aspect. It implies progressiveness because the pre-stage is regarded as ongoing at the time of orientation simultaneous with speech time. On the other hand, it implies perfectiveness because the end of the pre-stage leads to the occurrence of the main situation, which is viewed in its entirety, and in addition, there is a change from the pre-stage to the main situation. These two implications are basically the same as those of PPF-sentences observed in Chapter 7 because, as stated above, the temporal structure of the future-as-a-matter-of-course use inherits that of (part of) PPF-sentences. The reasoning goes as follows. The event time of the main situation (E_3) is located later than the event time of *be* (E_2), which is associated with the time of the pre-stage. The two sub-situations, i.e. the pre-stage and the main (part of the participial) situation, are related to their respective event times, i.e. E_2 and E_3, which are typically located in the present and future time-areas, respectively, so that the conceptual boundary between them is made clear for the reason we discussed in Section 9.4.2.3 (recall the discussion about the two time ranges with respect to the past-tense version of BAT-sentences). This supports our claim that the main situation is construed as a separate unit from the pre-stage. Hence the main situation can be viewed in its entirety at a different time from the time of its pre-stage, which suggests the completion of the pre-stage and thus change of state.

However, the future-as-a-matter-of-course use of WBI-sentences differs from PPF-sentences in that the former conveys predictive modality while the latter conveys assertive modality. I contend that the difference concerning the speaker's mental attitude between the two sentences explains the observation that the main situation of WBI-sentences is less certain to occur than that of PPF-sentences (recall the definitions of the two types of modality as speaker's mental attitude in Section 3.4), having much to do with the controllability of the situation involved. As discussed in Section 7.4.1, the notion of assertion, together with the ongoingness of the pre-stage at speech time as a presupposed part, allows PPF-sentences to give an affinity for controllable situations such as an arrangement or fixed plan. On the other hand, what is predicted to happen as a matter of course or as a natural progression is not restricted to human (agentive) actions, which are preconditions for controllability. Regardless of whether a given situation is controllable or not, we can make a prediction. This contention is supported by the difference in acceptability between a sentence like *It's raining tomorrow* (Wekker (1976: 110)) and a sentence like *It will be raining tomorrow* (Wekker (1976: 118)).

The pre-stage in the future-as-a-matter-of-course use is prototypically viewed (by the speaker) as a direct condition for the occurrence of the main part of the participial situation (i.e. main situation). For example, in (3b), i.e. *David Lawrence will be staying with the county after signing a new four-year contract*, the speaker predicts that the pre-stage at speech time (e.g. a state after David Lawrence has decided to sign a new four-year contract) as a direct condition will bring about the future situation (i.e. David's staying with the county) and the hearer also interprets it that way. In a less typical case, the pre-stage can refer to what the speaker regards as a solid basis for predicting the occurrence of the main situation, for example, a situation constituting part of the structure of the world (i.e. a set of rules and constitutions of the society as well as the universe surrounding us). In any case, the pre-stage serves as a precondition for the occurrence of the main situation. What type of pre-stage is assumed depends on the type of context in which the WBI-sentence involved occurs. What is important here is that the future-as-a-matter-of-course use entails the pre-stage in its temporal structure (cf. Williams (2002a: 203)).

There are at least two phenomena supporting our claim that the temporal structure of the future-as-a-matter-of-course use in Figure 2 above contains the pre-stage ongoing at speech time as well as the main situation occurring at a later time. A first phenomenon concerns the compatibility with a time adverbial with *in* (e.g. *in two hours*). This type of time adverb is said to co-occur only with a delimited or bounded event (Vendler (1967: 101), Tenny (1994)). The *in X* type of time adverb indicates that the relevant situation occurs at a time distant from the base time specified by X. Thus in (10a), i.e. *The cherry*

Chapter 10   The Future Progressive

blossom will be falling in a few days, the base time is speech time and the main part of the participial situation (i.e. the situation of cherry blossoms falling itself) is predicted to occur a few days later than speech time—the temporal distance between the base time and the time at which the situation involved occurs is specified by *a few days*. The pre-stage ongoing at speech time is, for example, the situation of cherry blossoms being in full bloom, and in terms of the cognitive schema, the end of the pre-stage (i.e. the time when the pre-stage is "delimited") leads to the actualization of the main part of the participial situation. Because the *in X* type of time adverb involves reference to two different (though related) times at a time, its compatibility with this use of WBI-sentences suggests that the temporal structure of this use entails two situations corresponding to two different times. The *in X* type of time adverb "delimits" the pre-stage available at the base time and at the same time specifies the very time when the main situation viewed in its entirety occurs (Smith (1981: 378), Sawada (2006)). This explains why the future-progressive use and the inferential present-progressive use cannot co-occur with this type of time adverb. Their temporal structures do not include the pre-stage as well as the main situation viewed "holistically".

Let us next consider the phenomenon in which the time adverbial *next* implies two consecutive periods of time or events. We argue that this characteristic of *next* has an affinity for the dual temporal structure of the future-as-a-matter-of-course use. Consider (19):

(19) a. In the study of crime, particularly with respect to its predictability (and manipulability, which I will be looking at next), the more moderate versions of these two positions have shown some potentiality for convergence.   (BNC CRX)

    b. He'll be buying himself an island in the Bahamas next [said to someone aspiring to a life of luxury].   (Leech (2004: 68–69))

Take (19a) for example. The presence of *next* facilitates a reading in which the WBI-sentence including *will be looking at* implies the two consecutive events, i.e. looking at the predictability of crime and looking at its manipulability. The two events are likely to be interpreted as adjusting themselves to the temporal structure of the future-as-a-matter-of-course use, which includes two situations at different times. The former event is interpreted in the speaker's mind as if it were a precondition for the actualization of the latter. This phenomenon is in keeping with Hirtle's (1967: 107) observation that *next*, when co-occurring with a WBI-sentence, implies the present condition for evoking the future event as a consequence. Because the future-progressive use and the inferential present-progressive use of WBI-sentences do not include the two situations in question in their temporal structures, they are not compatible with *next*.

Thus far, we have constructed the respective temporal structures of the future-progressive use and the future-as-a-matter-of-course use, whereby we argue that WBI-sentences are semantically ambiguous between the two future reference uses (recall that in our model, uses associated with different temporal structures are semantically different). This is verified by Lakoff's (1970) ambiguity test.[14] Consider (20):

(20)   Toru will be flying to Venice at 5 p.m., and Yoko will, too.

If the first conjunct receives the future-progressive reading, then the second conjunct must receive the same reading, not the future-as-a-matter-of-course reading; if the first conjunct receives the future-as-a-matter-of-course reading, the second conjunct must also receive the same reading.

Having constructed and justified the temporal structure of the future-as-a-

---

[14] In my previous book (Wada (2001a: Ch. 8; fn.18)), I argued, following Geeraerts (1993) and Tuggy (1993), that the ambiguity test may yield indeterminate results or the ambiguity results show not only ambiguous cases but also polysemous cases (cf. Depraetere (2014: 162–163)). In the present model, the semantic uses (meanings) associated with their respective temporal structures are in a 'polyesmous' relationship and the results observed in the main text conform to this argument. In this connection, I have something to say about the results of the ambiguity test with respect to the present perfect observed in my previous book (Wada (2001a: Ch. 4)). In Chapter 4 of the present book, I argued that the four basic uses of the present perfect are semantically different because they have their respective temporal structures. Nevertheless, the test in question appeared to show the vagueness results of the present perfect (Wada (2001a: 94–95)). How can we accommodate this apparent discrepancy? I argue that this is one of the indeterminate results mentioned above and one of the reasons why the results for the present perfect are different from those for the WBI form is the degree of cohesion between the finite and non-finite parts. As we saw in note 24 of Chapter 2, the perfect *have* and the past participle make a simple phase and the degree of their cohesion is high. This is supported by the observation that the boundaries among the four basic uses of the present perfect are fuzzy (see Chapter 4 of the present book and Chapter 4 of my previous book). Due to this cohesion, the semantic uses of the present perfect are regarded as more closely related to each other than those of the WBI form and the results of the ambiguity test, e.g. the proform *do so* test, show that the two perfect forms used in this test allow "vagueness" results. For example, Bolinger (1977: 19) notes that in (i), the first perfect clause can have a "hot-news" (i.e. completive) reading and the second an experiential reading.

(i)   Max has been fired, and so has Fred.   (Bolinger (1977: 19))

However, in the present model what such results suggest is that the four uses of the present perfect are not in a vagueness relationship, but in a polysemous relationship, though the present perfect has a lower degree of polysemy than the WBI-form.

Chapter 10   The Future Progressive

matter-of-course use of WBI-sentences, I will, in what follows, explain the linguistic facts observed in Section 10.2. Let us first consider the distinctive characteristic of this use, namely that a prerequisite for the occurrence of the participial situation in the future has been met by speech time or that the pre-stage is already ongoing at speech time. Take, for example, (4a), i.e. *Your son will be staying with the other first formers in block D.* In this example, the speaker predicts that the main situation (i.e. the stay of the addressee's son) will occur after the end of the pre-stage (e.g. the preparation for what is necessary for his staying together with the other first formers) ongoing at speech time and for the pre-stage to be ongoing at speech time, its beginning part has already occurred before that time. This is in keeping with the temporal structure of the future-as-a-matter-of-course use in Figure 2 above.

Second, the observation that the future-as-a-matter-of-course use receives the "already decided" reading and the observation that this use does not convey the volition of the grammatical subject occurring at speech time are two sides of the same coin. As stated in Section 5.4.1, because volition is defined as a mental activity of making a practical decision, it involves a decision to pursue something. The idea that the pre-stage is ongoing at speech time presupposes that such a decision has already been made before that time. In other words, the prerequisite observed in the last paragraph is identified here as the decision made before speech time. In this connection, Celle and Smith (2010: 251) convincingly state that in the case of WBI-sentences, "the relation between the speaker and the predication as a whole takes precedence over the relation between the grammatical subject and the verb." The former relationship is related to a speaker's attitude toward the situation (i.e. predictive modality) described by WBI-sentences, whereas the latter is related to the volition of the grammatical subject. Seen from our perspective, this precedence is, at least in the future-as-a-matter-of-course use, due to the presence of the pre-stage ongoing at speech time in its temporal structure. Although human (controllable) activities may more or less imply volition of some sort, the presence of the pre-stage — which indicates that the decision has already been made — makes the volition of the grammatical subject at speech time "out of focus" and basically "irrelevant" to the interpretation (cf. Wekker (1976: 119)). Furthermore, in our model, the pre-stage is more closely related to the main situation than the preliminary stage (of BGT-sentences) because it is a presupposed part of the main situation. It is conceptually impossible to make a decision about the situation which has already been on the way to its actualization. For this reason, the future-as-a-matter-of-course use is not interpreted as conveying the volition of the grammatical subject at speech time.

Third, the temporal structure approach adopted in this study is useful for explaining the compatibility of the future-as-a-matter-of-course use with a future time adverb. Recall the fact that this use is compatible with a time adverb referring to the near future, as in (3a), i.e. *Professor Baxter will be giving another lecture on Roman glass-making at the same time next week*, a time adverb referring to the immediate future, as in (5b), i.e. *Miranda will be coming in in a minute*, or a time adverb referring to the somewhat distant future, as in (6c), i.e. *Without pilots gaining experience at the lowest level, we will be shaping up for another chronic pilots shortage in a few years' time*. This fact is explained in the following manner. In Figure 2, the pre-stage ongoing at speech time suggests that the beginning part of the participial situation is already "set in motion" and in the cognitive schema the end of the pre-stage is followed by the occurrence of the main part of the participial situation. This temporal-structure information implies that the main situation will come into existence in the near future, unless otherwise indicated. Hence the future-as-a-matter-of-course use typically goes with a time adverb referring to the near future, as shown in (3a) above. However, this nearness in time is not an absolute and objective notion but can be a subjective one deriving from the interaction between the temporal structure and contextual information (i.e. an implicature). It is thus possible that the pre-stage comes to an end immediately, as in (5b) above, or continues for a while, as in (6c) above.

Fourth, our temporal structure approach can explain why the use in question tends to be incompatible with situations that are abnormal or occur suddenly, illustrated in (7) above. Recall that the pre-stage, which itself is a schematic situation, must be specified in the interpretation process to indicate a precondition for the occurrence of the main situation. To do this specification smoothly, the semantic content of the pre-stage should be the one easily retrievable from our encyclopedic knowledge of the world, namely that it should be an ordinary situation in daily life, without further contextual information. Without detailed information, an extraordinary situation is usually difficult to conceptualize in our mind, so that we can hardly specify its pre-stage. Thus, the low acceptability of (7a), i.e. *Margot will be poisoning her husband when he gets home*, is based on the following reasoning: the pre-stage of this situation may be the situation of Margot's making poisonous chemicals to kill her husband, but such s scene is extraordinary in daily life and therefore difficult to regard as happening in everyday life contexts without further contextual information. However, as Leech (2004: 68–69) points out, if detailed information enables us to easily imagine the extraordinary scene described by a WBI-sentence or if a WBI-sentence is used idiomatically in an oral context,

Chapter 10   The Future Progressive

then such a WBI-sentence will be acceptable, as illustrated in (21):

(21) a.   You'll be losing your head one of these days [said to a very forgetful
          person].   (Leech (2004: 68))
     b.   He'll be buying himself an island in the Bahamas next [said to some-
          one aspiring to a life of luxury].   (=19b)

This implies that in the context where we can easily imagine the precondition
for killing someone by poison, sentence (7a) would be acceptable.

   Fifth, the temporal structure analysis adopted here can explain the fact that,
as illustrated in (8) above, the future-as-a-matter-of-course use is compatible
with purely stative verbs, state verbs which do not appear in the progressive
form reflecting progressive aspect alone. As stated in note 4 of this chapter,
purely stative verbs such as *own* or *need* cannot appear in the progressive
form in its aspectual use. This is due to the redundant marking of
unboundedness. Because the stative verbs by themselves refer to unbounded
situations, they do not need the help of the progressive form, a grammatical
means of expressing unboundedness (imperfectiveness).

   By contrast, as shown in Figure 2, the temporal structure of the future-as-a-
matter-of-course use does not reflect pure imperfectivity. What is ongoing (in
progress) is the pre-stage of the participial situation and therefore progressive
(imperfective) aspect is relevant to the pre-stage part. The main situation is
viewed in its entirety and therefore regarded as perfective. The situations described by pure stative verbs are converted to be perfective situations. As a
result, there is no such redundancy when purely stative verbs are employed in
the use under discussion. For example, (8a), i.e. *He'll be owning his own
house next*, is interpreted as depicting the main situation (i.e. owning his own
house) as a situation viewed in its entirety which comes about after the end of
the pre-stage (e.g. doing something leading to the occurrence of the main
situation). Note that this interpretation is facilitated by the presence of *next*.

   Sixth, the temporal structure of the future-as-a-matter-of-course use explains
why this use can refer to a future situation occurring as part of daily routine
activities, exemplified by (9) above. This is a less typical case, where the pre-
stage is interpreted as referring to part of the structure of the world at speech
time. Based on what constitutes part of the world structure, we can predict
that the target situation will occur as a matter of course in the world structure.
In the case of the WBI-sentence in (9a), i.e. *Bill will be driving to London tomorrow,* the speaker views Bill's habit of regularly driving to London (constituting part of the world structure) as a precondition (i.e. the pre-stage) for the
occurrence of his driving there tomorrow (i.e. the main situation). The point

here is that even this less typical case is in keeping with the temporal structure in Figure 2. As the cognitive schema part suggests, it is predicted in the conceptualization process that what constitutes part of the world structure (i.e. the pre-stage) leads to the occurrence of the main situation.

Seventh, the temporal structure in Figure 2 can account for why the future-as-a-matter-of-course use sometimes refers to natural and/or physiological phenomena, as illustrated in (10) above. In this case, the speaker assumes that the pre-stage is something related to our encyclopedic knowledge about natural and/or physiological phenomena—the semantic content of the pre-stage is specified by the interaction between that of the WBI-sentence involved and the context. The speaker predicts that the natural and/or physiological phenomenon involved (i.e. the main situation) will occur as a natural consequence of the pre-stage. For example, in (10a), i.e. *The cherry blossom will be falling in a few days*, the pre-stage may be the state of cherry blossoms being in full bloom, i.e. a precondition for the occurrence of the main situation (i.e. their falling off), and the speaker predicts that the falling off will come about in a few days because we know from encyclopedic knowledge that cherry blossoms in full bloom will fall off in a couple of days, or sooner if they are subject to wind and/or rain.

Finally, our claim that the future-progressive use and the future-as-a-matter-of-course use have different temporal structures (i.e. those in Figures 1 and 2 above) explains why and how WBI-sentences with a future time adverbial can be interpreted ambiguously, as exemplified by (11) above. In both uses, a future time adverbial refers to E_3, i.e. the event time of (the main part of) the participial situation.[15] In the future-progressive use, E_3 is the length of time corresponding to the middle part of the present participle situation and it is this length of time that is specified by the future time adverbial. In the future-as-a-matter-of-course use, by contrast, E_3 is the length of time corresponding to the main part of the present participle situation as a whole, which is specified by the future time adverbial. Consider, for example, (11a), i.e. *When the meeting ends we'll be flying to Bonn*. When it is interpreted as an instance of the future-progressive use, the *when*-clause refers to the time of the middle part of the participial situation as E_3; when it is interpreted as an instance of the future-as-a-matter-of-course use, the *when*-clause refers to the whole time of the main situation as E_3. This difference reflects whether the participial situ-

---

[15] In the case of the future-progressive use, a future time adverbial can in theory specify E^O_2. In this case, however, E^O_2 is included in E_3, as shown in Figure 1. The result is therefore the same as the case where it specifies E_3, as far as the temporal reference is concerned.

ation itself is viewed as imperfective or perfective.

10.3.3. Temporal Structure of the Inferential Present-Progressive Use

Finally, I will construct the temporal structure of the inferential present-progressive use whereby I explain the linguistic facts concerning this use observed in Section 10.2.[16] This use is employed to infer a current ongoing situation, often accompanied by a present time adverbial. The temporal structure of this use is schematically represented in Figure 3:

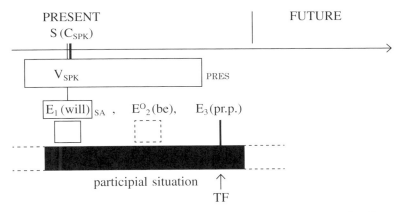

Figure 3: Temporal Structure of the Inferential Present-Progressive Use of WBI-Sentences

The *will* + infinitive part reflects the temporal structure of the predictive-present use of *will*-sentences (Figure 7 in Chapter 5). *Will* expresses predictive modality as a speaker's S-attitude, which occurs at the same time as speech time (S), and its event time (E_1) is therefore simultaneous with speech time. Since this use refers to the present, the event time of *be* is located in the present time-area. Here again, this event time is an orientational type, i.e. $E^O{}_2$, for the same reason we saw in the case of the temporal structure of the future-progressive use in Section 10.3.1. With respect to the part of *be* + present participle, it expresses progressive aspect. The participial situation is interpreted as unbounded (ongoing or in process) and there is no change in time with respect to this situation. Due to the tense-structure information of the

---

[16] I add the term *inferential* to the name of this use to distinguish it from other types of the progressive form expressing present progressive aspect (e.g. the unmodalized present progressive form) as well as to stress that inference is crucially relevant to the interpretation of this use.

present participle (i.e. simultaneity), its event time (E_3) is thus simultaneous with or including E^O_2 as the time of orientation.[17] Finally, for the same reason we saw with respect to the temporal structure of the future-progressive use in Section 10.3.1, the temporal focus (TF) is automatically directed at the event time of the present participle (E_3). We can thus justify the temporal structure of the inferential present-progressive use of WBI-sentences schematized in Figure 3.

This temporal structure straightforwardly explains why the use in question always shows the framing effect. (It seems that this point is not stressed in the literature.) Since speech time (S) is regarded as a moment on the time line, the event time (E_1) of the modality as an speaker's S-attitude — occurring at the same time as S — is also regarded as a moment. The event time of *be* (E^O_2), which is simultaneous with E_1 and S, is associated with a semantically bleached situation; its time length is flexibly adjusted and only the length of time corresponding to E_1 is regarded as E^O_2. From these observations, it follows that E_3, i.e. the event time of the participial situation expressing ongoingness and thus requiring some length of time, necessarily includes the moments S, E_1 and E^O_2. For this reason, the inferential present-progressive use always shows the framing effect.

The temporal structure in Figure 3 also accounts for why the inferential present-progressive use expresses pure imperfectivity. As shown in the cognitive schema of the temporal structure, the middle part of the participial situation (represented by the black rectangle) is foregrounded (which corresponds to E_3) and the initial and final boundaries (represented by the broken-line portions) are backgrounded. Consider, for instance, (12a), i.e. *By now they'll be eating dinner [looking at one's watch]*. Here, the speaker predicts that the situation described by the progressive form (i.e. eating dinner) is ongoing or in progress at speech time. The information about when it starts and when it ends is not guaranteed by the temporal structure of this WBI-sentence. It is therefore possible that with further contextual information, the participial situation may be interpreted as extending further into the past, as in (22a), or into the future, as in (22b).

---

[17] Because this participial situation is interpreted as ongoing at speech time, the use in question never receives a volitional reading because of the properties of volition defined in Section 5.4.1. Just as *will*-sentences with present time reference (i.e. the predictive-present use) cannot receive a volitional reading, so the inferential present-progressive use of WBI-sentences cannot, either.

Chapter 10   The Future Progressive

(22) a.   When I went to Bruce's room an hour ago, he was playing the guitar.
          I think he will still be playing it now.

     b.   By now Akane will be playing the flute in earnest, so she may not
          notice the return of her husband around ten o'clock.

Note, however, that this extension of the time range is cancellable in appropriate contexts and is thus not semantically entailed in the temporal structure of the inferential present-progressive use.

Finally, our claim that this use is different in terms of the temporal structure from the future-progressive use or the future-as-a-matter-of-course use is also justified by Lakoff's (1970) ambiguity test. Consider (23):

(23)   Hitomi will be eating dinner, and Ken will, too.

If the first conjunct receives the "present-progressive" reading, then the second conjunct cannot receive the "future-progressive" or "future-as-a-matter-of-course" reading, but must receive the "present-progressive" reading. The inferential present-progressive use is therefore semantically independent from the other two uses.

10.4.   Comparison of (the Future-as-a-Matter-of-Course Use of) WBI-Sentences with Other Future Expressions

We have shown that the temporal structures of the three uses of WBI-sentences can straightforwardly explain their temporal phenomena. To enhance the validity of the temporal structure approach, this section shows that some differences and similarities between WBI-sentences, especially WBI-sentences in their future-as-a-matter-of-course use, on the one hand, and *will*-sentences (i.e. sentences containing *will*) or PPF-sentences (i.e. sentences containing the present progressive futurate), on the other, can be explained based on their temporal structures.[18]

10.4.1.   Comparison with *Will*-Sentences

I begin by comparing WBI-sentences (in their future-as-a-matter-of-course use) with *will*-sentences (with future time reference), confirming that three major phenomena concerning the two constructions can be explained in terms

---

[18] In this section, we will be considering WBI-sentences in their future-as-a-matter-of-course use, *will*-sentences in their future reference uses, and PPF-sentences, unless otherwise indicated.

of their temporal structures.

Let us start with volitionality. *Will*-sentences tend to refer to a volitional situation when they contain animate, especially human, subjects and non-stative verbs describing controllable situations. By contrast, WBI-sentences tend to refer to a non-volitional situation under the same circumstances (Thomson and Martinet (1986), Leech (2004)). To illustrate the point, consider the following examples, cited from Leech (2004: 67):

(24) a.   I'll drive into London next week. ('I've made up my mind. That's what I've decided.')

   b.   I'll be driving into London next week. ('This will happen as a matter of course.')

The reason why the WBI-sentence in (24b) does not express volitional future is due to its temporal structure (see Figure 2 and the explanation in Section 10.3.2). The pre-stage (e.g. the speaker's schedule being already fixed) is construed as obtaining at speech time and therefore as having started or been initiated before that time, so that we interpret a precondition (associated with the pre-stage) for the actualization of the main situation in the future (i.e. the driving itself) as already under way. This implies that the volition of the grammatical subject (i.e. a decision to pursue the main situation) has already been made before the occurrence of the pre-stage and therefore cannot occur at (or just before) speech time. Hence sentence (24b) does not have a volitional reading.

On the other hand, as shown in Figure 4 in Section 5.4.1, the temporal structure of *will*-sentences in their volitional use does not include an earlier stage such as the pre-stage and thus nothing has already been set in motion. In (24a), the volition of the grammatical subject (i.e. the decision by the grammatical subject to pursue the infinitival situation) comes into play at or just before speech time, as shown in the parentheses. The *will*-sentence in (24a) can therefore receive a volitional reading. However, *will*-sentences satisfying the conditions for the volitional reading can actually have both a volitional and a non-volitional reading, depending on context.

Be that as it may, in the pair under consideration, *will*-sentences tend to be used for the volitional reading. This is due to Grice's (1975) Maxim of Manner. Given that *will*-sentences can receive both a volitional and non-volitional reading whereas WBI-sentences can only receive a non-volitional reading, we may infer that to avoid ambiguity, the speaker exclusively chooses WBI-sentences for the non-volitional reading and thus *will*-sentences for the other option, i.e. to refer to the volition of the grammatical subject made at or

Chapter 10   The Future Progressive   383

just before speech time.

We now turn to the observation that when used with non-agentive subjects, WBI-sentences do not make a striking contrast with *will*-sentences with respect to volitionality (Quirk et al. (1985: 217), Leech (2004: 68)). Compare (25a) with (25b):

(25) a.   The next train to London will be arriving at platform four.

(Quirk et al. (1985: 217))

    b.   The next train to London will arrive at platform four.

(Quirk et al. (1985: 217))

In both cases it is usually predicted that the target situation will happen on the basis of, say, an announcement or platform display which informs us about where and when the train will arrive. With respect to the WBI-sentence in (25a), the temporal structure involves the pre-stage ongoing at speech time, which leads us to regard the information about the train's arrival as a precondition for the actualization of the main situation (i.e. the train's arrival itself). On the other hand, although the *will*-sentence in (25b) does not include the pre-stage in its temporal structure, the speaker, using the same information available in this context, predicts that the target situation is highly likely to occur.

In both cases, the volition of the grammatical subject is irrelevant in interpreting the target situation. In addition, the source information for the speaker to make a prediction (i.e. an announcement or platform display which informs the speaker about the train's arrival) is highly credible. The semantic difference between the WBI-sentence and the *will*-sentence here is therefore a minimum and does not matter. Based on these observations, we conclude that as with WBI-sentences, *will*-sentences—which do not include an earlier stage like the pre-stage—can describe a situation highly likely to occur, depending on context. However, this similarity happens to occur as a result of the interaction between the semantic content of the relevant sentences and the context and does not indicate that the temporal structures of the two types of sentences are the same.

Finally, the present approach explains why *will*-sentences can pragmatically be interpreted as implying a request, command, or offer, while WBI-sentences cannot (Thomson and Martinet (1986: 192), Declerck (1991a: 166)). Compare (26) with (27):

(26) a.   Will you please bring the piano in here?   [request]

(Thomson and Martinet (1986: 192))

b. You will work in this office. [command]

(Thomson and Martinet (1986: 192))

c. Will you have some custard? [offer] (Declerck (1991a: 166))

(27) a. Will you be bringing the piano in here?

(Thomson and Martinet (1986: 192))

b. You will be working here. (Thomson and Martinet (1986: 192))

c. Will you be going to the library this afternoon?

(Declerck (1991a: 166))

First, *will*-sentences can convey these speech acts because, as discussed in Section 5.4.6, they are all construed as instances of the volitional use in the situation construal tier; the speech acts satisfy the conditions for the volitional use observed in Section 5.4.1. Note here that in interrogative sentences or sentences having an imperative nuance, the volition is attributed to a second person. The above sentences are then interpreted as conveying specific speech acts in the situation report tier, where the interpersonal-relationship information as well as the contextual information has an influence on the identification of the pragmatic meaning or interpretation involved. For example, in (26a), in the situation construal tier the speaker has in mind the question of whether or not the hearer has an intention to bring the piano in the place where he/she is. Since the relevant situation is a controllable type, this construal is possible. In the situation report tier, the question is addressed to the hearer because the sentence is an interrogative. Because the hearer's performing the action in question benefits the speaker, the addition of *please* implies that the speaker is asking the hearer to do it by asking about the latter's intention. In this way, the sentence in question is interpreted as conveying the speaker's request (which is based on the hearer's volition) as a speech act.[19] In so doing, the metonymic relationship between question and request can be in operation (Panther and Thornburg (1998, 2007)).

In contrast, by using WBI-sentences, the speaker is just making a statement or asking about the situation which will occur as a matter of course. As we have seen, WBI-sentences can hardly be viewed as expressing the subject's volition occurring at speech time. With interrogative sentences, the volition involved is the hearer's one. Thus, in (27a), the speaker cannot ask about the hearer's volition to realize the action involved, i.e. whether the hearer has an intention to bring the piano into the place where he/she is. The temporal structure of WBI-sentences does not guarantee the subject's or hearer's voli-

---

[19] I owe the discussion here to Yukio Hirose (personal communication).

Chapter 10   The Future Progressive

tion occurring at speech time and thus cannot convey speech acts, such as a request, command, or offer, i.e. pragmatic notions based on the volition of the hearer as the second-person subject.

10.4.2.   Comparison with PPF-Sentences

Let us next compare WBI-sentences (in their future-as-a-matter-of-course use) with PPF-sentences, considering four major phenomena concerning the two constructions in terms of their temporal structures.

First, it is generally said that PPF-sentences refer to more definite situations in the future because they usually make definite arrangements, deliberate actions, and scheduled events, whereas WBI-sentences refer to less definite situations in the future because they typically denote future-as-a-matter-of-course situations (i.e. arranged or "already decided" situations) which are predicted to happen as a natural progression. Compare (28) with (29):

(28)   I am seeing Tom tomorrow.   (Thomson and Martinet (1986: 191))
(29)   I'll be seeing Tom tomorrow.   (Thomson and Martinet (1986: 191))

Thomson and Martinet (1986: 191) state that the PPF-sentence in (28) refers to an arranged meeting, while the WBI-sentence in (29) indicates a future-as-a-matter-of-course situation. A deliberately arranged situation such as an arranged meeting is harder to change or halt and therefore more certain to occur than a situation simply predicted to occur as a natural progression. We usually tend not to change or halt the things that we have made efforts to produce or agreed with others to realize. For this reason, the situation described by PPF-sentences will more definitely occur than that described by WBI-sentences.

This difference can be explained by the different temporal structures of WBI-sentences and PPF-sentences. To be more specific, WBI-sentences contain the modal *will* expressing predictive modality (Figure 2 in this chapter) and thus describe a less definite situation than PPF-sentences, which are accompanied by assertive modality in the process of tense interpretation (Figure 4 in Section 7.4.1). This is because assertion is located higher on the scale of the degree of epistemicity than prediction. Assertive modality is employed to construe the situation involved as if it is a fact or absolutely certain to occur, while predictive modality is employed to construe it as if it is highly likely to occur or obtain.[20]

---

[20] The explanation here can also explain the fact that PPF-sentences when describing situations that are abnormal or occur suddenly (see Section 10.3.2) are less acceptable than their WBI-sentence counterparts. Compare (i) with (ii):

This explanation is verified by the following examples:

(30) *It is raining tomorrow.[21]   (Wekker (1976: 108))

(31)   It will be raining tomorrow.[22]   (Wekker (1976: 118))

PPF-sentences are basically interpreted as accompanied by assertive modality in main or independent clauses and therefore require controllable non-stative situations to be involved because uncontrollable non-stative situations cannot be made sure by human beings.[23] Rainfall is an uncontrollable non-stative situation and hence sentence (30) is unacceptable. On the other hand, WBI-sentences express predictive modality, which implies that the speaker of this type of sentence does not necessarily make sure the actualization of the situation involved. WBI-sentences can thus go with uncontrollable non-stative situations, such as rainfall.

Second, the temporal structure approach adopted in this book can explain why PPF-sentences denote a definite and/or near future situation by default, while WBI-sentences need not (cf. Thomson and Martinet (1986)). This is illustrated by the following contrast, cited from Thomson and Martinet (1986: 192):

(32)   I am meeting him tomorrow.

(33)   I'll be meeting him {tomorrow / next year / some time}.

    (i) ?Mary will be poisoning her husband when he gets home.

                                    (Williams (2002a: 207)) (cf. (7a))
    (ii)??Mary is poisoning her husband when he gets home.   (Williams (2002a: 207))
Although sentence (i) is judged to be worse in Leech (2004: 68), here I follow the acceptability judgments by Williams (2002a), who seems to attribute the acceptability difference to the present orientation of PPF-sentences vs. the future orientation of WBI-sentences (Williams (2002a: 208–209)). In our model, since PPF-sentences are accompanied by assertive modality, the speaker regards the situation involved as more certain to occur or obtain than the one described by WBI-sentences involving predictive modality. Usually, making an assertion about situations which are abnormal or occur suddenly is harder than making a prediction about them. Hence the lower acceptability of (ii).

[21] An anonymous reviewer of *English Language and Linguistics* regards this example as not so bad. For this reason, I put a question mark, but not an asterisk, on this example in Wada (2013b: 405). Here, I follow Wekker's acceptability judgment.

[22] Wekker (1976: 118) notes that this example is not related to volitionality and consequently the difference between this WBI-sentence and its *will*-sentence counterpart, as in (i), is neutralized.

    (i)   It will rain tomorrow.   (Wekker (1976: 118))
This phenomenon is related to the second linguistic fact observed in Section 10.4.1.

[23] Here, I am ignoring the types of situations available for the simple-future use because PPF-sentences and WBI-sentences do not have the simple-future use (see note 29 in Chapter 7 and note 10 in this chapter).

Chapter 10   The Future Progressive

Both PPF-sentences and WBI-sentences involve the pre-stage in their temporal structures, but how to construe the pre-stage and thus the main part of the participial situation differs.   In the case of PPF-sentences, the situation involved is construed with assertive modality, while in the case of WBI-sentences, it is construed with predictive modality.   For a future situation to be asserted, it must usually occur at a definite time, because if the "anchoring site" of the target situation on the time line is not clear, we usually cannot judge whether or not it is a fact.   In addition, the further future a situation is located in, the more difficult we make an assertion about it, because the further away something is, the less clear it is.   For these reasons, PPF-sentences tend to refer to a definite and/or near future situation.

By contrast, for a future situation to be predicted, it is not necessary for the situation to occur at a definite time.   An indefinite situation can be predicted, as illustrated in (34a).   Moreover, a remote future situation can be predictable, as shown in (34b).

(34) a.   One day he will happily walk along a busy road.   (BNC A17)
     b.   Often a bereaved family will return to the bones of dead elephants many years later.   (BNC G2V)

WBI-sentences can thus refer to an indefinite and/or remote future situation.

Third, the present approach also explains the fact that WBI-sentences can co-occur with expressions with a lower degree of certainty, while PPF-sentences cannot.   Compare (35) with (36), both of which are cited from Kashino (1999: 99):

(35) a.   I'll probably be spending more time here than in New York.
     b.   So I guess you'll be going to Berkeley, huh?
(36) a.   *Perhaps I am leaving for America next month.
     b.   *I expect I am leaving for America next month.

In our model, in the case of PPF-sentences, the precondition for the relevant situation as already obtaining at speech time is construed with assertive modality, i.e. a speaker's S-attitude used when the speaker intends to view it as a fact or absolutely certain to occur in his/her mind.   A kind of contradiction therefore arises when PPF-sentences co-occur with expressions with a lower degree of certainty and hence (36) is unacceptable.   By contrast, WBI-sentences involve predictive modality, i.e. a speaker's mental attitude which can express a lower degree of certainty than assertive modality.   The speaker merely predicts that the future situation will occur as a natural consequence of the present condition.   They can thus co-occur with expressions with a lower degree of certainty, as shown in (35).

Finally, I will explain, in terms of the temporal structures of the two sentences, why pure stative verbs like *own* or *need* cannot appear in the PPF form, as in (37), while they can appear in the WBI form, as we saw in (8) above.

(37) a. *Next week we're owning the house.   (Prince (1982: 455))
    b. *I'm knowing the answer tomorrow.   (Prince (1982: 455))

Recall first that PPF-sentences are basically allowed when the situation involved conveys human agency or is controllable. In addition, PPF-sentences are construed as accompanied by assertive modality in main or independent clauses. Within our framework, the speaker of PPF-sentences asserts that the main (part of the infinitival) situation will occur as a natural consequence of the present situation implied by the pre-stage, which is specified depending on the interaction between the semantic content of the rest of the sentence and the context. However, pure stative verbs refer to uncontrollable situations and we usually cannot make an arrangement or plan in advance for such situations. We may thus conclude that PPF-sentences—whose temporal structure includes the pre-stage intended to indicate an arrangement or plan—cannot go with pure stative verbs, which describe uncontrollable situations. This is a versatile approach because it has already explained the ungrammaticality of PPF-sentences which contain non-stative verbs describing uncontrollable situations, as below (see Section 7.4.1).

(38) a. *The sun is rising at 5 o'clock tomorrow.   (Leech (2004: 63))
    b. *The cherry blossom is falling in a few days.   (Sawada (2006: 471))

These uncontrollable situations do not have an affinity for PPF-sentences because their temporal structure includes the pre-stage, a portion triggering the notion of controllability.

On the other hand, WBI-sentences do not necessarily refer to highly definite situations such as fixed or arranged ones, as we saw with respect to the first phenomenon in this sub-section. Uncontrollable situations can therefore appear in the WBI form. We have already seen why WBI-sentences are compatible with pure stative verbs in Section 10.3.2.

10.5. Concluding Remarks

In this chapter, we have considered a variety of linguistic phenomena concerning the three major uses of WBI-sentences taken up in the literature, i.e.

Chapter 10   The Future Progressive

the future-progressive use, the future-as-a-matter-of-course use, and the inferential present-progressive use. As far as I know, there have been only a few detailed studies on WBI-sentences, such as Williams (2002a), Sawada (2006), and Celle and Smith (2010), and I surveyed the three studies as representatives, pointing out their problems. To not only solve the problems but also explain the linguistic phenomena of WBI-sentences systematically in a general theory of tense, I adopted a temporal structure approach that can provide a unified account of the temporal phenomena of WBI-sentences as well as those of other future expressions such as *will*-sentences and PPF-sentences.

One basic notion characterizing my analysis is compositionality. Unless a given tense form is subject to semantic bleaching or "opaquization" in the process of grammaticalization, the temporal structure of a tense form is composed of the combination of the meanings of its constituents. On this basis, we have argued that the temporal structure of the future-progressive use (of WBI-sentences) consists of the combination of those of *will*-sentences in their predictive-future use and the non-finite version of progressive sentences in their aspectual use; the temporal structure of the future-as-a-matter-of-course use consists of the combination of those of the modal *will* and the non-finite version of PPF-sentences; and the temporal structure of the inferential present-progressive use consists of the combination of those of *will*-sentences in their predictive-present use and the non-finite version of progressive sentences in their aspectual use. The characteristics of each use of WBI-sentences derive from the interaction between their temporal structure and other factors such as their semantic content and the contextual information. Because the three uses have different temporal structures, they are regarded as semantically different uses, which is justified by Lakoff's (1970) ambiguity test.

In addition, we have explained the differences between WBI-sentences and *will*-sentences, both of which are accompanied by predictive modality, on one hand, and the differences between WBI-sentences and PPF-sentences, both of which include the pre-stage in their temporal structures, on the other. By assuming that the temporal semantics of a given tense form is not an "opaque" unit but the combination of the meanings of its constituents, we can not only consider the differences among the uses of the same tense form from a general point of view, but also explain the similarities and differences between the target tense form and other related forms from a common point of view.

Chapter 11

Conclusion

In this book, I have revised and developed the theory of tense proposed in Wada (2001a) in terms of, especially, the theory of modality and speaker's mental attitudes motivated by the Three-Tier Model of Language Use (Hirose (2013, 2015, 2016a, 2016b, 2017), Ikarashi (2015), Konno (2015), Shizawa (2013, 2015), Shizawa and Hirose (2015), Wada (2013a, 2017b)) as a general theory of language use. I hope I have constructed a more comprehensive framework that can systematically deal with not only temporal and aspectual phenomena but also related issues such as modality, mental attitudes, and speech acts, in a unified way and from a wider perspective.

Let us briefly summarize what we have observed in this book. The term *tense* had been used in various ways and/or under various interpretations in the literature and so I clarified how the notion tense should be treated or what it means within my framework, raising the research questions stated in (8) in Chapter 1. To be more specific, I argued in Wada (2001a) for the necessity of distinguishing the level dealing with tense forms from that dealing with tense interpretation/temporal value calculation (concerning temporal meanings/semantics), which is also inherited in the framework developed in this book. I adopted Comrie's (1985) definition of tense (i.e. grammaticalized expression of location in time) to cover both absolute and relative tense forms, claiming that not only finite forms (verbs or predicates) but also non-finite forms (verbs or predicates) are necessarily regarded as tense forms. In English, finite forms are absolute tense forms, while non-finite forms are relative tense forms.

This was a natural consequence from the position that in English, finite forms are accompanied by an A-morpheme, i.e. a tense morpheme which changes according to person, number, and mood (i.e. grammatical categories representing deixis), whereas non-finite forms are accompanied by an R-morpheme, i.e. a tense morpheme which does not change according to such grammatical categories. An A-morpheme represents the positional relationship of a

391

time-sphere (i.e. grammatical time range) to the speaker's t(emporal)-view-point (i.e. the deictic center of grammatical time). While the present model is based on a cognitive linguistic perspective, it involves the level of the gram-maticalized information constituting part of the grammatical system of a lan-guage, where a cognitive notion like viewpoint can be grammaticalized and internalized as a tense-structure element; e.g., the speaker's t-viewpoint is a grammaticalized notion internalized in absolute tense forms. English has only two A-morphemes and thus two time-spheres, i.e. the present and past time-spheres, while French has at least one more A-morpheme and one more time-sphere, i.e. the future time-sphere.

One of the distinctive characteristics of this theory of tense was that non-fi-nite markers are also tense morphemes, though they do not involve such no-tions as the speaker's t-viewpoint or time-spheres. Instead, such tense mor-phemes, i.e. R-morphemes, represent a relative relationship between the event time associated with the verb (predicate) involved and the time of orientation for evaluating its position, which is a type of tense-structure information. In relative tense forms, the speaker's SD-viewpoint (i.e. the viewpoint from which to see or evaluate the situation involved) doubles as the viewpoint for choosing the tense form involved. The position of the speaker's SD-viewpoint depends on the environmental properties and/or contextual information as well as lexical and sentential information.

In the literature, it was usually assumed that only verb (predicate) forms representing a deictic relationship between speech time and their event time (i.e. "deictic interpretation" in my terminology) represent tenses, but such a position cannot deal with finite forms representing "relative tenses" (i.e. "non-deictic interpretation" in my terminology). Once one admits that relative tenses are also tenses, one has no reasons to exclude non-finite forms from tense forms because they represent relative time relations and satisfy the defi-nition of tense observed above. This lends support to our view that both finite and non-finite forms are tense forms.

Since the proposed model distinguishes between the levels of tense form and tense interpretation (i.e. the tense-structure level and the tense-interpreta-tion level), it systematically allows cases where absolute tense forms (e.g. English finite forms) do not establish a deictic relationship (i.e. a non-deictic interpretation) or cases where relative tense forms (e.g. English non-finite forms) establish a deictic relationship (i.e. a deictic interpretation). This mod-el, based on a cognitive linguistic perspective, presupposes that the speaker as the tense-form chooser is involved in tense interpretation. Thus, in the case of absolute tense forms, the speaker's t-viewpoint internalized in their tense structure fuses, by default, with the consciousness of the speaker at speech time—because of the default-interpretation principle in (4) in Chapter 2—on the tense-interpretation level. As a result, speech time serves as the first time of orientation for evaluating the event time(s) of absolute tense forms—this is a case of deictic interpretation.

This default operation was motivated in the following manner. The speaker is the subject of cognitive or mental activities in situation construal, including tense interpretation. The speaker's consciousness is the center of such activities (i.e. cognition) and thus fixed at speech time, i.e. the center of cognitive time. The speaker's t-viewpoint as the center of grammatical time can have an affinity for speech time as the center of cognitive time. Hence the default-interpretation principle stated above comes into operation. When the default-interpretation principle is not at work and the speaker's t-viewpoint is located at a time other than speech time, absolute tense forms allow non-deictic interpretations, such as the historical present.

The tense-interpretation level is an interface between the tense-structure information and information from other grammatical fields, especially tense-related fields such as aspect, modality, speaker's mental attitudes, and speech acts, as well as the cognitive system. At this level, the temporal structure of a given tense form is referred to and constructed (in the speaker's mind) under the influence of information from time adverbials, aspect (including Aktionsart), situation types, the linguistic environment in which it appears, the context, and the like. A temporal structure serves as a "template" triggering a tense interpretation of the tense form involved and different temporal structures are allocated to different semantic uses or functions of the tense form.

Since both finite and non-finite forms are tense forms, their verb (or predicate) stem is regarded as a part of the tense structure and associated with the event time, i.e. the time of the relevant part of the situation involved. Under this view, modals as well as aspectual auxiliaries (e.g. the progressive *be* and the perfect *have*) can describe their own situations and accordingly have their own event times. Note, however, that the situations denoted by verbs (including verbal units and auxiliaries) are not of uniform type: some describe contentful situations, others denote schematic situations, and still others indicate semantically bleached situations.

With respect to future expressions, factors such as modality and speaker's mental attitudes are inevitable for tense interpretation. However, few previous studies have shown how the two notions are defined or treated in relation to a unified model of tense and modality/mental attitudes, let alone one motivated by a general theory of language use. As far as I know, most previous studies have considered tense theories separately from theories as to modality and/or speaker's mental attitudes and have not constructively related them to the latter. In this book, therefore, I combined the theory of tense proposed in Wada (2001a) with the theory of modality and speaker's mental attitudes closely related to the semantic theory of sentential utterances and then introduced the Three-Tier Model of Language Use (i.e. a general theory of language use) to motivate the theory of modality and speaker's mental attitudes. In this model, the combination of the propositional content and a speaker's mental attitude toward the situation involved constitutes the situation construal tier and the addition of a speaker's mental attitude toward the addressee (addressee-orientedness) to the situation construal tier constitutes the situation report tier. Notions closely related to tense interpretation such as predictive and assertive modality, which are inevitable in construing absolute tense forms (especially in independent or main clauses), are considered modalities as speaker's mental attitudes toward the target situation in the situation construal tier. When the construed situation is conveyed to the addressee (i.e. in the situation report tier), addressee-oriented mental attitudes of the speaker, including speech acts, are at work.

After having constructed the present framework and confirmed its validity by considering two test cases (i.e. the simple present and present perfect), I provided a temporal structure approach to the six future expressions in English, i.e. *will*-sentences, BGT-sentences (sentences with *be going to*), present progressive sentences with future time reference, simple present sentences with future time reference, BAT-sentences (sentences with *be about to*), and WBI-sentences (sentences with *will be -ing*). In analyzing them, compositionality, comprehensiveness, systematicity, and cognitive schema served as key notions. Compositionality is used in the sense that the time information of a tense form basically consists of the combination of the temporal meanings of its constituents, unless the tense form is fully or largely subject to semantic bleaching or "opaquization" in the process of grammaticalization. In the conceptual area called *future*, where tense information interacts closely with modality and speaker's mental attitudes, we cannot decide which theory of tense is better when only looking at tense phenomena. We thus constructed a comprehensive model which can deal not only with temporal and aspectual phenomena but also with those concerning modality, speaker's mental attitudes, and speech acts. The established model is also comprehensive in that it was able to deal with uses with a high degree of grammaticalization, where the principle of compositionality can only partially work or almost cannot work. Systematicity indicates that our approach is based on "rules" such as the default-interpretation principle (which states that the speaker's t-viewpoint fuses with the speaker's consciousness at speech time) or those for determining the time of orientation under the influence of the properties of the linguistic environments involved. We found that such an approach can systematically be applied not only to tense and tense-related phenomena of future expressions in English—including both their similarities and differences—but also those of other tense forms in English (e.g. the present perfect) and future expressions in other languages (e.g. French). Cognitive schemas are reflected in the temporal structures of tense forms, schematizing cognitive information necessary for temporal calculation, i.e. the information not directly related to the time line and temporal relations. It was shown that they also play crucial roles in the tense interpretations of the future expressions.

Before closing this book, I will briefly point out some further issues to be considered within the present framework. First, to further enhance the validity of the present framework as a comprehensive model dealing with not only tense but also modality, mental attitudes, and speech acts, we need to clarify, especially, how this model analyzes future reference sentences with modals other than *will*, as in *He {may/must} come tomorrow* (cf. Werner (2005)), those in the subjunctive mood, or those in the polite form. Second, we still have some more future expressions in English to be considered, e.g. sentences containing *be to* or those containing the form of *be X to* other than BGT-sentences and BAT-sentences (e.g. *be certain to, be sure to*). Third, we have mainly considered the future expressions that appear in independent or main clauses, but not those in complement clauses, subordinate clauses other than *if*-clauses and temporal clauses, or many past contexts. Finally, to make the framework more general and explanatory, we need to extend it not only to future expressions in other Germanic languages such as German and Dutch as well as Romance languages such as French (Dahl (2000)) but also to such areas as evidentiality (Aikhenvald (2004), Murray (2017)), accounting for the similarities and differences of future expressions between those languages and English from a more comprehensive perspective (Ayoun, Celle and Lansari (2018)). I leave these remaining issues for future research.

References

Abusch, Dorit (1988) "Sequence of Tense, Intensionality and Scope," *Proceedings of the Seventh West Coast Conference on Formal Linguistics* 1–14.

Abusch, Dorit (1997) "Sequence of Tense and Temporal De Re," *Linguistics and Philosophy* 20(1), 1–50.

Aijmer, Karin (1985) "The Development of *Will*," *Historical Semantics, Historical Word-Formation*, ed. by Jacek Fisiak, 11–21, Mouton de Gruyter, Berlin.

Aikhenvald, Alexandra (2004) *Evidentiality*, Oxford University Press, Oxford.

Alexiadou, Artemis, Monika Rathert and Arnim von Stechow, eds. (2003) *Perfect Explorations*, Mouton de Gruyter, Berlin / New York.

Austin, John L. (1962) *How to Do Things with Words*, Oxford University Press, Oxford.

Ayoun, Dalila, Agnès Celle, and Laure Lansari, eds. (2018) *Tense, Aspect, Modality, and Evidentiality: Crosslinguistic Perspectives*, John Benjamins, Amsterdam / Philadelphia.

Berglund, Ylva (1997) "Future in Present-Day English: Corpus-Based Evidence on the Rivalry of Expressions," *ICAME Journal* 21, 7–20.

Berglund, Ylva (2000a) "*Gonna* and *Going To* in the Spoken Component of the British National Corpus," *Corpus Linguistics and Linguistic Theory: Papers from the Twentieth International Conference on English Language Research on Computerized Corpora* (ICAME 20), ed. by Christian Mair and Marianne Hundt, 35–49, Rodopi, Amsterdam.

Berglund, Ylva (2000b) "Utilising Present-Day English Corpora: A Case Study Concerning Expressions of Future," *ICAME Journal* 24, 25–63.

Bergs, Alexander (2010) "Expressions of Futurity in Contemporary English: A Construction Grammar Perspective," *English Language and Linguistics* 14(2), 217–238.

Binnick, Robert I. (1971) "*Will* and *Be Going To*," *CLS* 7, 40–52.

Binnick, Robert I. (1972) "*Will* and *Be Going To* II," *CLS* 8, 3–9.

Binnick, Robert I. (1991) *Time and the Verb: A Guide to Tense and Aspect*, Oxford University Press, New York / Oxford.

Binnick, Robert I. (2006) "Aspect and Aspectuality," *The Handbook of English Linguistics*, ed. by Bas Aarts and April McMahon, 244–268, Blackwell, Malden / Oxford.

Blakemore, Diane (1992) *Understanding Utterances: An Introduction to Pragmatics*, Blackwell, Oxford.

Blevins, James P. (2006) "English Inflection and Derivation," *The Handbook of English Linguistics*, ed. by Bas Aarts and April McMahon, 507–536, Blackwell, Malden / Oxford.

Bolinger, Dwight (1977) *Meaning and Form*, Longman, London.

Boogaart, Ronny (1999) *Aspect and Temporal Ordering: A Contrastive Analysis of Dutch and English*, Holland Academic Graphics, The Hague.

Boyd, Julian and J. P. Thorne (1969) "The Semantics of Modal Verbs," *Journal of Linguistics* 5, 57–74.

Brinton, Laurel J. (1988) *The Development of Aspectual Systems: Aspectualizers and Post-Verbal Particles*, Cambridge University Press, Cambridge.

Brinton, Laurel J. (1998) "Aspectuality and Countability: A Cross-Categorial Analogy," *English Language and Linguistics* 2(1), 37–63.

Brisard, Frank (1997) "The English Tense-System as an Epistemic Category: The Case of Futurity," *Lexical and Syntactical Constructions and the Construction of Meaning*, ed. by Marjolijn Verspoor, Kee Dong Lee and Eve Sweetser, 271–285, John Benjamins, Amsterdam.

Brisard, Frank (2001) "*Be Going To*: An Exercise in Grounding," *Journal of Linguistics* 37(2), 251–285.

Brisard, Frank (2002) "The English Present," *Grounding: The Epistemic Footing of Deixis and Reference*, ed. by Frank Brisard, 251–297, Mouton de Gruyter, Berlin / New York.

Brisard, Frank (2013) "An Account of English Tense and Aspect in Cognitive Grammar," *Time: Language, Cognition, & Reality*, ed. by Kasia M. Jaszczolt and Louis de Saussure, 210–235, Oxford University Press, Oxford.

Brown, Jessica and Herman Cappelen, eds. (2011) *Assertion: New Philosophical Essays*, Oxford University Press, Oxford.

Bühler, Karl (1982) "The Deictic Field of Language and Deictic Words," *Speech, Place, and Action: Studies in Deixis and Related Topics*, ed. by Robert J. Jarvella and Wolfgang Klein, 9–30, John Wiley & Sons, New York.

Bybee, Joan L. and William Pagliuca (1987) "The Evolution of Future Meaning," *Papers from the 7th International Conference on Historical Linguistics*, ed. by Anna Giacalone Ramat, Onofrio Carruba and Giuliano Bernini, 109–122, John Benjamins, Amsterdam / Philadelphia.

Bybee, Joan, Revere Perkins and William Pagliuca (1994) *The Evolution of Grammar: Tense, Aspect, and Modality in the Languages of the World*, University of Chicago Press, Chicago / London.

Calver, Edward (1946) "The Uses of the Present Tense Forms in English," *Language* 22, 317–325.

Cappelen, Herman (2011) "Against Assertion," *Assertion: New Philosophical Essays*, ed. by Jessica Brown and Herman Cappelen, 21–47, Oxford University Press, Oxford.

Cappelle, Bert and Ilse Depraetere (2016) "Short-Circuited Interpretations of Modal Verb Constructions: Some Evidence from The Simpsons," *Constructions and Frames* 8(1): *Modal Meaning in Construction Grammar*, 7–39.

Carey, Kathleen (1995) "Subjectification and the Development of the English Perfect," *Subjectivity and Subjectivisation: Linguistic Perspectives*, ed. by Dieter Stein and Susan Wright, 83–102, Cambridge University Press, Cambridge.

Celle, Agnès (1997) *Etude Contrastive du Futur Français et de Ses Realisations en Anglais*, Ophrys, Paris.

Celle, Agnès (2005) "The French Future Tense and English *Will* as Markers of Epistemic Modality," *Languages in Contrast* 5(2), 181–218.

Celle, Agnès (2008) "Tense, Modality and Commitment in Modes of Mixed Enunciation," *Commitment*, ed. by Philippe de Brabanter and Patrick Dendale, 15–36, John Benjamins, Amsterdam.

Celle, Agnès (2009) "Hearsay Adverbs and Modality," *Modality in English: Theory and Description*, ed. by Raphael Salkie, Pierre Busuttil and Johan van der Auwera, 269–293, Oxford University Press, Oxford.

Celle, Agnés and Nicholas Smith (2010) "Beyond Aspect: *Will Be -Ing* and *Shall Be -Ing*," *English Language and Linguistics* 14(2), 239–269.

Chafe, Wallance (1994) *Discourse, Consciousness, and Time: The Flow and Displacement of Conscious Experience in Speaking and Writing*, University of Chicago Press, Chicago / London.

Chilton, Paul (2013) "Frames of Reference and the Linguistic Conceptualization of Time: Present and Future," *Time: Language, Cognition, & Reality*, ed. by Kasia M. Jaszczolt and Louis de Saussure, 236–258, Oxford University Press, Oxford.

Close, Reginald A. (1977) "Some Observations on the Meaning and Function of Verb Phrases Having Future Reference," *Studies in English Usage: The Resources of a Present-Day English Corpus for Linguistic Analysis*, ed. by Wolf-Dietrich Bald and Robert Ilson, 125–156, Peter Lang, Frankfurt.

Close, Reginald A. (1981) *English as a Foreign Language: Its Constant Grammatical Problems*, 3rd. ed., George Allen & Unwin, London.

Coates, Jennifer (1983) *The Semantics of the Modal Auxiliaries*, Croom Helm, London / Canberra.

Coates, Jennifer (1995) "The Expression of Root and Epistemic Possibility in English," *Modality in Grammar and Discourse*, ed. by Joan Bybee and Suzanne Fleischman, 55–66, John Benjamins, Amsterdam / Philadelphia.

Collins, Peter (2009) *Modals and Quasi-Modals in English*, Rodopi, Amsterdam / New York.

Comrie, Bernard (1976) *Aspect*, Cambridge University Press, Cambridge.

Comrie, Bernard (1985) *Tense*, Cambridge University Press, Cambridge.

Comrie, Bernard (1989) "On Identifying Future Tenses," *Tempus-Aspekt-Modus: Die Lexikalisachen und Grammatischen Formen in den Germanischen Sprachen*, ed. by Werner Abraham and Theo Janssen, 51–63, Niemeyer, Tübingen.

Copley, Bridget (2009) *The Semantics of the Future*, Routledge, New York / London.

Copley, Bridget (2014) "Causal Chain for Futures," *Future Times, Future Tenses*, ed. by Philippe de Brabanter, Mikhail Kissine and Saghie Sharifzadeh, 72–86, Oxford University Press, Oxford.

Coulmas, Florian, ed. (1986) *Direct and Indirect Speech*, Mouton de Gruyter, Berlin / New York.

Cowper, Elizabeth (1998) "The Simple Present Tense in English: A Unified Treatment," *Studia Linguistica* 52(1), 1–18.

Culioli, Antoine (1995) *Cognition and Representation in Linguistic Theory*, John Benjamins, Amsterdam / Philadelphia.

Cutrer, Michelle (1994) *Time and Tense in Narrative and in Everyday Language*, Doctoral dissertation, US San Diego.

Dahl, Östen (1985) *Tense and Aspect Systems*, Blackwell, Oxford.

Dahl, Östen (2000) *Tense and Aspect in the Languages of Europe*, Mouton de Gruyter, Berlin / New York.

Danchev, Andrei, Anna Pavlova, Malvina Nalchadjan and Octavia Zlatareva (1965) "The Construction *Going To + inf.* in Modern English," *Zeitschrift für Anglistik und Amerikanistik* 13, 375–386.

Danchev, Andrei and Merja Kytö (1994) "The Construction *Be Going To + Infinitive* in Early Modern English," *Studies in Early Modern English*, ed. by Dieter Kastovsky, 59–77, Mouton de Gruyter, Berlin / New York.

Dancygier, Barbara (1998) *Conditionals and Prediction: Time, Knowledge and Causation in Conditional Constructions*, Cambridge University Press, Cambridge.

Dancygier, Barbara and Eve Sweetser (2005) *Mental Spaces in Grammar: Conditional Constructions*, Cambridge University Press, Cambridge.

Davidsen-Nielsen, Niels (1990) *Tense and Mood in English: A Comparison with Danish*, Mouton de Gruyter, Berlin.

De Brabanter, Philippe, Mikhail Kissine and Saghie Sharifzadeh, eds. (2014) *Future Times, Future Tenses*, Oxford University Press, Oxford.

Declerck, Renaat (1986) "From Reichenbach (1947) to Comrie (1985) and beyond: Towards a Theory of Tense," *Lingua* 70(4), 305–364.

Declerck, Renaat (1991a) *A Comprehensive Descriptive Grammar of English*, Kaitakusha, Tokyo.

Declerck, Renaat (1991b) *Tense in English: Its Structure and Use in Discourse*, Routledge, London.

Declerck, Renaat (1997) When-*Clauses and Temporal Structure*, Routledge, London / New York.

Declerck, Renaat (1999) "A Critical Evaluation of Wada's Theory of Tense in English," *English Linguistics* 16(2), 465–500.

Declerck, Renaat (2003) "How to Manipulate Tenses to Express a Character's Point of View," *Journal of Literary Semantics* 32(2), 85–112.

Declerck, Renaat [in cooperation with Susan Reed and Bert Cappelle] (2006) The Grammar of the English Verb Phrase Volume I: *The Grammar of the English Tense System: A Comprehensive Analysis*, Mouton de Gruyter, Berlin / New York.

References 401

Declerck, Renaat (2010) "Future Time Reference Expressed by *Be To* in Present-Day English," *English Language and Linguistics* 14(2), 271–291.

Declerck, Renaat and Susan Reed (2001) *Conditionals: A Comprehensive Empirical Analysis*, Mouton de Gruyter, Berlin / New York.

Del Prete, Fabio (2014) "The Interpretation of Indefinites in Future Tense Sentences: A Novel Argument for the Modality of *Will*?", *Future Times, Future Tenses*, ed. by Philippe de Brabanter, Mikhail Kissine and Saghie Sharifzadeh, 43–71, Oxford University Press, Oxford.

Depraetere, Ilse (1996) *The Tense System in English Relative Clauses: A Corpus-Based Analysis*, Mouton de Gruyter, Berlin / New York.

Depraetere, Ilse (2010) "Some Observations on the Meaning of Modals," *Distinctions in English Grammar, Offered to Renaat Declerck*, ed. by Bert Cappelle and Naoaki Wada, 72–91, Kaitakusha, Tokyo.

Depraetere, Ilse (2014) "Modals and Lexically-Regulated Saturation," *Journal of Pragmatics* 71, 160–177.

Depraetere, Ilse and Chad Langford (2012) *Advanced English Grammar: A Linguistic Approach*, Continuum, London / New York.

Depraetere, Ilse and Susan Reed (2006) "Mood and Modality in English," *The Handbook of English Linguistics*, ed. by Bas Aarts and April McMahon, 269–290, Blackwell, Oxford.

Depraetere, Ilse and Raphael Salkie, eds. (2017) *Semantics and Pragmatics: Drawing a Line*, Springer, Cham.

De Smet, Hendrik (2014) "Constrained Confusion: The Gerund/Participle Distinction in Late Modern English," *Late Modern English Syntax*, ed. by Marianne Hundt, 224–238, Cambridge University Press, Cambridge.

De Smet, Hendrik and Liesbet Heyvaert (2011) "The Meaning of the English Present Participle," *English Language and Linguistics* 15(3), 473–498.

De Wit, Astrid (2017) *The Present Perfective Paradox across Languages*, Oxford University Press, Oxford.

De Wit, Astrid and Frank Brisard (2014) "A Cognitive Grammar Account of the Semantics of the English Present Progressive," *Journal of Linguistics* 50(1), 49–90.

De Wit, Astrid, Adeline Patard and Frank Brisard (2013) "A Contrastive Analysis of the Present Progressive in French and English," *Studies in Language* 37(4), 846–879.

De Wit, Astrid and Adeline Patard (2013) "Modality, Aspect and the Progressive: The Semantics of the Present Progressive in French in Comparison with English," *Languages in Contrast* 13(1), 113–132.

Dowty, David R. (1975) "The Stative in the Progressive and Other Essence/Accident Contrasts," *Linguistic Inquiry* 6(4), 579–588.

Dowty, David R. (1977) "Toward a Semantic Analysis of Verb Aspect and the English 'Imperfective' Progressive," *Linguistics and Philosophy* 1(1), 45–77.

Duffley, Patrick (1992) *The English Infinitive*, Longman, London.

Duffley, Patrick (2000) "Gerund Versus Infinitive as Complement of Transitive Verbs in English: The Problems of 'Tense' and 'Control'," *Journal of English Linguistics*

28(3), 221–248.

Duffley, Patrick (2006) *The English Gerund-Participle: A Comparison with the Infinitive*, Peter Lang, New York.

Eckardt, Regine (2006) *Meaning Change in Grammaticalization: An Enquiry into Semantic Reanalysis*, Oxford University Press, Oxford.

Ehrlich, Susan (1990) *Point of View: A Linguistic Analysis of Literary Style*, Routledge, London.

Elsness, Johan (2009) "The Perfect and the Preterite in Australian and New Zealand English," *Comparative Studies in Australian and New Zealand English: Grammar and beyond*, ed. by Pam Peters, Peter Collins and Adam Smith, 89–114, John Benjamins, Amsterdam / Philadelphia.

Enç, Mürvet (1996) "Tense and Modality," *The Handbook of Contemporary Semantic Theory*, ed. by Shalom Lappin, 345–358, Blackwell, Oxford.

Evans, Vyvyan (2013) *Language and Time: A Cognitive Linguistics Approach*, Cambridge University Press, Cambridge.

Fabiszak, Malgorzata (2012) "Conceptual Principles and Relations," *Cognitive Pragmatics*, ed. by Hans-Jörg Schmid, 123–150, Mouton de Gruyter, Berlin / Boston.

Fleischman, Suzanne (1982) *The Future in Thought and Language: Diachronic Evidence from Romance*, Cambridge University Press, Cambridge.

Fleischman, Suzanne (1990) *Tense and Narrativity: From Medieval Performance to Modern Fiction*, The University of Texas Press, Austin.

Fludernik, Monika (2009) *An Introduction to Narratology*, Routledge, London / New York.

Geeraerts, Dirk (1993) "Vagueness's Puzzles, Polysemy's Vagaries," *Cognitive Linguistics* 4(3), 223–272.

Genette, Gérard (1980) *Narrative Discourse* [Translated by Jane E. Lewin], Basil Blackwell, Oxford.

Gesuato, Sara and Roberta Facchinetti (2011) "*GOING TO V vs GOING TO V-ing*: Two Equivalent Patterns?" *ICAME Journal* 35, 59–94.

Givón, Talmy (2005) *Context as Other Minds: The Pragmatics of Sociality, Cognition and Communication*, John Benjamins, Amsterdam / Philadelphia.

Goldsmith, John and Erich Woistschlaeger (1982) "The Logic of the English Progressive," *Linguistic Inquiry* 13(1), 79–89.

Goodman, Fred (1973) "On the Semantics of Futurate Sentences," *Ohio State University Working Paper in Linguistics* 16, 76–89.

Gotti, Maurizio (2003) "*Shall* and *Will* in Contemporary English: A Comparison with Past Uses," *Modality in Contemporary English*, ed. by Roberta Facchinetti, Frank Palmer and Manfred Krug, 267–300, Mouton de Gruyter, Berlin / New York.

Grice, Herbert Paul (1975) "Logic and Conversation," *Syntax and Semantics 3: Speech Acts*, ed. by Peter Cole and Jerry L. Morgan, 41–58, Academic Press, New York.

Groefsema, Marjolein (1995) "*Can, May, Must* and *Should*: A Relevance Theoretic Account," *Journal of Linguistics* 31(1), 53–79.

Guéron, Jacqueline and Jacqueline Lecarme, eds. (2004) *The Syntax of Time*, MIT Press, Cambridge, MA / London.

References

Haegeman, Liliane (1983) *The Semantics of* Will *in Present-Day British English: A Unified Account*, Paleis der Academiën, Brussel.

Haegeman, Liliane (1989) "*Be Going To* and *Will*: A Pragmatic Account," *Journal of Linguistics* 25(2), 291–317.

Haegeman, Liliane and Herman Chr. Wekker (1984) "The Syntax and Interpretation of Futurate Conditionals in English," *Journal of Linguistics* 20(1), 45–55.

Halliday, Michael A. K. (1970) "Functional Diversity in Language as Seen from a Consideration of Modality and Mood in English," *Foundations of Language* 6(3), 322–361.

Hamann, Cornelia (1989) "English Temporal Clauses in a Reference Frame Model," *Essays on Tensing in English* Vol.II: *Time, Text and Modality*, ed. by Alfred Schopf, 31–154, Niemeyer, Tübingen.

Harder, Peter (1996) *Functional Semantics: A Theory of Meaning, Structure and Tense in English*, Mouton de Gruyter, Berlin / New York.

Hare, Richard M. (1970) "Meaning and Speech Acts," *The Philosophical Review* 79(1), 3–24.

Hatav, Galia (2012) "Bound Tenses," *The Oxford Handbook of Tense and Aspect*, ed. by Robert I. Binnick, 611–637, Oxford University Press, Oxford.

Hayase, Naoko (2002) *Eigo Koobun no Kategorii Keesee: Nintigengogaku no Siten kara* [Categorization of Constructions in English: From a Cognitive Linguistic Perspective], Keiso Shobo, Tokyo.

Heine, Bernd, Ulrike Claudi, and Friederike Hünnermeyer (1991) *Grammaticalization: A Conceptual Framework*, University of Chicago Press, Chicago / London.

Heine, Bernd (1993) *Auxiliaries: Cognitive Forces and Grammaticalization*, Oxford University Press, New York / Oxford.

Heine, Bernd (1995) "Agent-Oriented vs. Epistemic Modality: Some Observations on German Modals," *Modality in Grammar and Discourse*, ed. by Joan Bybee and Suzanne Fleischman, 17–53, John Benjamins, Amsterdam / Philadelphia.

Helland, Hans Petter (1995) "A Compositional Analysis of the French Tense System," *Tense Systems in European Languages* II, ed. by Rolf Thieroff, 69–94, Niemeyer, Tübingen.

Higuchi, Mariko (1991) "*Will* and *Be Going To*: Present Thought and Present Reality," *Bulletin of the Faculty of Computer Science and Systems Engineering* (Human Science) 6, 53–70, Kyushu Institute of Technology.

Hilpert, Martin (2008) *Germanic Future Constructions: A Usage-based Approach to Language Change*, John Benjamins, Amsterdam / Philadelphia.

Hirose, Yukio (1995) "Direct and Indirect Speech as Quotations of Public and Private Expression," *Lingua* 95(4), 223–238.

Hirose, Yukio (1997) "Hito o Arawasu Kotoba to Syoo-oo [Words of Reference to Persons and Anaphora]," *Sizi to Syoo-oo to Hitee* [Reference, Anaphora, and Negation], ed. by Minoru Nakau, 1–89, Kenkyusha, Tokyo.

Hirose, Yukio (2000) "Public and Private Self as Two Aspects of the Speaker: A Contrastive Study of Japanese and English," *Journal of Pragmatics* 32(11), 1623–1656.

Hirose, Yukio (2002) "Viewpoint and the Nature of the Japanese Reflexive *Zibun*," *Cognitive Linguistics* 13(4), 357–401.

Hirose, Yukio (2013) "Deconstruction of the Speaker and the Three-Tier Model of Language Use," *Tsukuba English Studies* 32, 1–28.

Hirose, Yukio (2015) "An Overview of the Three-Tier Model of Language Use," *English Linguistics* 32(1), 120–138.

Hirose, Yukio (2016a) "Nitieigo niokeru Zikan no Metafaa to Syukansee [Temporal Metaphor and Subjectivity in Japanese and English]," *Gengo no Syukansee: Ninti to Poraitonesu no Setten* [Subjectivity in Language: The Interface between Cognition and Politeness], ed. by Masaki Ono and Ri Kinan, 19–34, Kurosio, Tokyo.

Hirose, Yukio (2016b) "Syukansee to Gengosiyoo no Sansoo Moderu [Subjectivity and the Three-Tier Model of Language Use]," *Langacker no (Kan)Syukansee to sono Tenkai* [Langacker's (inter)Subjectivity and Its Development], ed. by Yoshihisa Nakamura and Satoshi Uehara, 333–355, Kaitakusha, Tokyo.

Hirose, Yukio (2017) "Zibun no Gengogaku: Gengosiyoo no Sansoo Moderu ni mukete [The Linguistics of *Zibun*; Toward the Three-Tier Model of Language Use]," *Sansoo Moderu de Mietekuru Gengo no Kinoo to Sikumi* [The Functions and Mechanism of Language Revealed by the Three-Tier Model of Language Use], 2–24.

Hirose, Yukio and Yoko Hasegawa (2010) *Nihongo kara Mita Nihonzin: Syutaisee no Gengogaku* [Japanese People as Seen from the Japanese Language: Linguistics of Subjectivity]," Kaitakusha, Tokyo.

Hirtle, Walter H. (1967) *The Simple and Progressive Forms: An Analytical Approach*, Les Presses de l'Université Laval, Québec.

Hirtle, Walter H. (1995) "The Simple Form Again: An Analysis of Direction-Giving and Related Issues," *Journal of Pragmatics* 24(3), 265–281.

Hirtle, Walter H. and Violetta N. Curat (1986) "The Simple and the Progressive: 'Future' Use," *Transactions of the Philological Society* 84, 42–84.

Hoffman, T.R. (1976) "Past Tense Replacement and the Modal System," *Syntax and Semantics* 7: *Notes from the Linguistic Underground*, ed. by James D. McCawley, 85–100, Academic Press, New York.

Hooper, Joan (1975) "On Assertive Predicates," *Syntax and Semantics* 4, ed. by John P. Kimball, 91–124, Academic Press, New York.

Hopper, Paul J. and Sandra A. Thompson (1980) "Transitivity in Grammar and Discourse," *Language* 56(2), 251–299.

Hopper, Paul J. and Elizabeth C. Traugott (1993) *Grammaticalization*, Cambridge University Press, Cambridge.

Hopper, Paul J. and Elizabeth C. Traugott (2003) *Grammaticalization*, 2nd. ed., Cambridge University Press, Cambridge.

Horn, Laurence R. (1984) "Toward a Taxonomy for Pragmatic Inference: Q-Based and R-Based Implicature," *Meaning, Form, and Use in Context: Linguistic Applications*, ed. by Deborah Schffrin, 11–42, Georgetown University Press, Washington D.C.

Hornby, Albert S. (1975) *Guide to Patterns and Usage in English*, 2nd. ed., Oxford University Press, Oxford.

Hornstein, Norbert (1990) *As Time Goes By: Tense and Universal Grammar*, MIT Press, Cambridge, MA.

Hoye, Leo (1997) *Adverbs and Modality in English*, Longman, London / New York.

Huddleston, Rodney (1969) "Some Observations on Tense and Deixis in English," *Language* 45(4), 777–806.

Huddleston, Rodney (1977) "The Futurate Construction," *Linguistic Inquiry* 8(4), 730–736.

Huddleston, Rodney (1995) "The Case against a Future Tense in English," *Studies in Language* 19(2), 399–446.

Huddleston, Rodney and Geoffrey Pullum (2002) *The Cambridge Grammar of the English Language*, Cambridge University Press, Cambridge.

Hundt, Marianne (2004) "Animacy, Agentivity, and the Spread of the Progressive in Modern English," *English Language and Linguistics* 8(1), 47–69.

Iatridou, Sabine (1994) "On the Contribution of Conditional Then," *Natural Language Semantics* 2(3), 171–199.

Ikarashi, Keita (2013) "The Performative Clause *I Tell You*, Interpersonal Relationship, and Informational Superiority," *Tsukuba English Studies* 32, 111–126.

Ikarashi, Keita (2015) *A Functional Approach to English Constructions Related to Evidentiality*, Doctoral dissertation, University of Tsukuba.

Iwasaki, Sho-ichi (1993) *Subjectivity in Grammar and Discourse: Theoretical Considerations and a Case Study of Japanese Spoken Discourse*, John Benjamins, Amsterdam / Philadelphia.

Jacobsson, Bengt (1984) "Notes on Tense and Modality in Conditional *If*-Clauses," *Studia Linguistica* 38(2), 129–147.

Jackendoff, Ray (1983) *Semantics and Cognition*, MIT Press, Cambridge, MA.

Janssen, Theo, A. J. M. (1994) "Preterit and Perfect in Dutch," *Tense and Aspect in Discourse*, ed. by Co Vet and Carl Vetters, 115–146, Mouton de Gruyter, Berlin / New York.

Janssen, Theo, A. J. M. (1996) "Tense in Reported Speech and Its Frame of Reference," *Reported Speech*, ed. by Theo A. J. M. Janssen and Wim van der Wurff, 237–259, John Benjamins, Amsterdam / Philadelphia.

Janssen, Theo, A.J.M., and van der Wurff, eds. (1996) *Reported Speech*, John Benjamins, Amsterdam / Philadelphia.

Jaszczolt, Kasia M. (2009) *Representing Time: An Essay on Temporality and Modality*, Oxford University Press, Oxford.

Jespersen, Otto (1931) *A Modern English Grammar on Historical Principles IV*, George Allen and Unwin, London.

Jones, Michael Allan (1996) *Foundations of French Syntax*, Cambridge University Press, Cambridge.

Kamp, Hans and Uwe Reyle (1993) *From Discourse to Logic: Introduction to Model-theoretic Semantics of Natural Language*, Formal Logic and Discourse Representation Theory, Kluwer Academic, Dordrecht / Boston / London.

Kashino, Kenji (1993) *Imiron kara Mita Gohoo* [Usage as Seen from Semantics], Kenkyusha, Tokyo.

Kashino, Kenji (1999) *Tensu to Asupekuto no Gohoo* [Usage of Tense and Aspect], Kaitakusha, Tokyo.

Kashino, Kenji (2005) "'Be Going To' and Emotionality," *Osaka Shoo-in Josi Daigaku Eibeibungakukaisi* 41, 1–13.

Katz, Graham (2003) "On the Stativity of the English Perfect," *Perfect Explorations*, ed. by Artemis Alexiadou, Monika Rathert, and Arnim von Stechow, 205–234, Mouton de Gruyter, Berlin / New York.

Killie, Kristin (2004) "Subjectivity and the English Progressive," *English Language and Linguistics* 8(1), 25–46.

Killie, Kristin (2014) "The Development of the English BE + V-*ende* / V-*ing* Periphrasis: From Emphatic to Progressive Marker?" *English Language and Linguistics* 18(3), 361–386.

Kiparsky, Paul (2002) "Event Structure and the Perfect," *The Construction of Meaning*, ed. by David I. Beaver, Luis D. Casillas Martínez, Brady Z. Clark and Stefan Kaufmann, 113–135, Center for the Study of Language and Information, Stanford.

Kiparsky, Paul and Carol Kiparsky (1970) "Fact," *Progress in Linguistics*, ed. by Manfred Bierwisch and Karl Erich Heidolph, 143–173, Mouton, The Hague / Paris.

Kira, Fumitaka (2018) *Kotoba o Irodoru* 1: *Tensu, Asupekuto* [Coloring Language 1: Tense and Aspect], Kenkyusha, Tokyo.

Kissine, Mikhail (2008) "Why *Will* is not a Modal," *Natural Language Semantics* 16(2), 129–155.

Klein, Wolfgang (1992) "The Present Perfect Puzzle," *Language* 68(3), 525–552.

Klein, Wolfgang (1994) Time in Language, Routledge, London / New York.

Klinge, Alex (1993) "The English Modal Auxiliaries: From Lexical Semantics to Utterance Interpretation," *Journal of Linguistics* 29(2), 315–357.

Klinge, Alex (2005) "Where There is a Will, There is a Modal," *Modality: Studies in Form and Function*, ed. by Alex Klinge and Henrik Höeg Müller, 169–186, Equinox, London / Oakville.

Konno, Hiro-aki (2015) "The Grammatical Significance of Private Expression and Its Implications for the Three-Tier Model of Language Use," *English Linguistics* 32(1), 139–155.

Kortmann, Bernd (1991) "The Triad 'Tense-Aspect-Aktionsart': Problems and Possible Solutions," *Belgian Journal of Linguistics* 6, 9–30.

Kranich, Svenja (2010) *The Progressive in Modern English: A Corpus-Based Study of Grammaticalization and Related Changes*, Rodopi, Amsterdam / New York.

Krug, Manfred G. (2000) *Emerging English Modals: A Corpus-Based Study of Grammaticalization*, Mouton de Gruyter, Berlin / New York.

Kurotaki, Mariko (2005) *Deonthikku kara Episutemikku eno Fuhensee to Sootaisee: Modarithi no Nitieigo Taisyookenkyuu* [Universality and Relativeness: From Deontic to Epistemic Modality — A Contrastive Study of Modality in Japanese and English], Kurosio, Tokyo.

Kytö, Merja (1990) "*Shall* or *Will*? Choice of the Variant Form in Early Modern English, British and American," *Historical Linguistics 1987*: *Papers from the 8th International Conference on Historical Linguistics*, ed. by Henning Andersen and

Konrad Koemer, 275–288, John Benjamins, Amsterdam / Philadelphia.

Lakoff, George (1970) "A Note on Vagueness and Ambiguity," *Linguistic Inquiry* 1(3), 357–359.

Lakoff, George and Mark Johnson (1999) *Philosophy in the Flesh: The Embodied Mind and Its Challenge to Western Thought*, Basic Books, New York.

Lakoff, Robin (1970) "Tense and Its Relation to Participants," *Language* 46, 838–849.

Lakoff, Robin (1972) "The Pragmatics of Modality," *CLS* 8, 229–246.

Landman, Fred (1992) "The Progressive," *Natural Language Semantics* 1(1), 1–32.

Langacker, Ronald W. (1990) "Subjectification," *Cognitive Linguistics* 1(1), 5–38.

Langacker, Ronald W. (1991) *Foundation of Cognitive Grammar Volume II: Descriptive Application*, Stanford University Press, Stanford.

Langacker, Ronald W. (1993) "Reference-Point Constructions," *Cognitive Linguistics* 4(1), 1–38.

Langacker, Ronald W. (2001) "The English Present Tense," *English Language and Linguistics* 5(2), 251–271.

Langacker Ronald W. (2003) "Extreme Subjectification," *Motivation in Language*, ed. by Hubert Cuyckens, Thomas Berg, René Dirven and Klaus-Uwe Panther, 3–26, John Benjamins, Amsterdam / Philadelphia.

Langacker, Ronald W. (2008) *Cognitive Grammar: A Basic Introduction*, Oxford University Press, Oxford.

Langacker, Ronald W. (2011a) "The English Present: Temporal Coincidence vs. Epistemic Immediacy," *Cognitive Approaches to Tense, Aspect, and Epistemic Modality*, ed. by Adeline Patard and Frank Brisard, 45–86, John Benjamins, Amsterdam / Philadelphia.

Langacker, Ronald W. (2011b) "On the Subject of Impersonals," *Cognitive Linguistics: Convergence and Expansion*, ed. by Mario Brdar, Stefan Th. Gries and Milena Žic Fucks, 179–217, John Benjamins, Amsterdam / Philadelphia.

Lansari, Laure (2009) *Linguistique Contrastive et Traduction. Les Périphrases Verbles Aller + Infinitif et Be Going To,* Ophrys, Paris.

Larreya, Paul (2001) "Modal Verbs and the Expression of Futurity in English, French and Italian," *Modal Verbs in Germanic and Romance Languages*, ed. by Johan van der Auwera and Patrick Dendale, 115–129, John Benjamins, Amsterdam.

Leech, Geoffrey N. (1971) *Meaning and the English Verb*, Longman, London.

Leech, Geoffrey N. (1983) *Principles of Pragmatics*, Longman, London.

Leech, Geoffrey N. (1987) *Meaning and the English Verb*, 2nd. ed., Longman, London.

Leech, Geoffrey N. (2004) *Meaning and the English Verb*, 3rd. ed., Longman, London.

Leech, Geoffrey N. (2014) *The Pragmatics of Politeness*, Oxford University Press, Oxford.

Levinson, Stephen C. (1983) *Pragmatics*, Cambridge University Press, Cambridge.

Levinson, Stephen C. (2000) *Presumptive Meanings: The Theory of Generalized Conversational Implicature*, MIT Press, Cambridge, MA.

Ludlow, Peter (2013) "Tensism," *Time: Language, Cognition, & Reality*, ed. by Kasia M. Jaszczolt and Louis de Saussure, 175–192, Oxford University Press, Oxford.

Lyons, John (1977) *Semantics*, Two Volumes, Cambridge University Press, Cambridge.

Lyons, John (1995) *Linguistic Semantics: An Introduction*, Cambridge University Press, Cambridge.

McIntosh, Angus (1966) "Predictive Statements," *In Memory of J. R. Firth*, ed. by Charles E. Bazell, John C. Catford, Michael A. K. Halliday and Robert H. Robins, 303–320, Longmans, London.

Michaelis, Laura (1993) "'Continuity' within Three Scalar Models: The Polysemy of Adverbial *Still*," *Journal of Semantics* 10(3), 193–237.

Michaelis, Laura (1998) *Aspectual Grammar and Past-Time Reference*, Routledge, London / New York.

Mihara, Ken-ichi (1992) *Ziseekaisyaku to Toogogensyoo* [Interpretation of Tense and Syntactic Phenomena], Kurosio, Tokyo.

Mori, Yu-ichi (1998) "'Syutaika' o Megutte [On 'Subjectification']," *Tookyoo Daigaku Kokugo Kenkyuusitu Soosetu Hyakusyuunen Kinen Kokugo Kenkyuu Ronsyuu* [Collection of Papers on Japanese on the Occasion of the 100th Aniversary of the University of Tokyo's Department of Japanese], ed. by Tookyoo Daigaku Kokugo Kenkyuusitu Soosetu Hyakusyuunen Kinen Kokugo Kenkyuu Ronsyuu Hensyuu Iinkai, 186–198, Kyuuko Shoin, Tokyo.

Mourelatos, Alexander P. D. (1978) "Events, Processes and States," *Linguistics and Philosophy* 2(3), 415–434.

Murray, Sarah E. (2017) *The Semantics of Evidentials*, Oxford University Press, Oxford.

Nakano, Hirozo (1993) *Eigo Hoozyodoosi no Imiron* [Semantics of English Modal Auxiliaries], Eichosha, Tokyo.

Nakau, Minoru (1992) "Modality and Subjective Semantics," *Tsukuba English Studies* 11, 1–45.

Nakau, Minoru (1994) *Ninti-Imiron no Genri* [Principles of Cognitive Semantics], Taishukan, Tokyo.

Nehls, Dietrich (1988) "Modality and the Expression of Future Time in English," *International Review of Applied Linguistics in Language Teaching* 26(4), 295–307.

Nesselhauf, Nadja (2007) "The Spread of the Progressive and Its 'Future' Use," *English Language and Linguistics* 11(1), 193–209.

Nesselhauf, Nadja (2010) "The Development of Future Time Expressions in Late Modern English: Redistribution of Forms or Change in Discourse?" *English Language and Linguistics* 14(2), 163–186.

Nicolle, Steve (1997) "A Relevance-Theoretic Account of *Be Going To*," *Journal of Linguistics* 33(2), 355–377.

Nicolle, Steve (1998) "*Be Going To* and *Will*: A Monosemous Account," *English Language and Linguistics* 2(2), 223–243.

Nunburg, Geoffrey, Ivan Sag and Thomas Wasow (1994) "Idioms," *Language* 70, 491–538.

Nuyts, Jan (2001) *Epistemic Modality, Language and Conceptualization*, John Benjamins, Amsterdam / Philadelphia.

Nuyts, Jan (2005) "The Modal Confusion: On Terminology and the Concepts behind It," *Modality: Studies in Form and Function*, ed. by Alex Klinge and Henrik Höeg

Müller, 5–38, Equinox, London / Oakville.

Nuyts, Jan (2006) "Modality: Overview and Linguistic Issues," *The Expression of Modality*, ed. by William Frawley, 1–26, Mouton de Gruyter, Berlin / New York.

Nuyts, Jan and Johan van der Auwera (2016) *The Oxford Handbook of Modality and Mood*, Oxford University Press, Oxford.

Ogihara, Toshiyuki (1996) *Tense, Attitudes, and Scope*, Kluwer Academic, Dordrecht.

Ogihara, Toshiyuki (2007) "Tense and Aspect in Truth-Conditional Semantics," *Lingua* 117(2), 392–418.

Ogihara, Toshiyuki and Yael Sharvit (2012) "Embedded Tenses," *The Oxford Handbook of Tense and Aspect*, ed. by Robert I. Binnick, 638–668, Oxford University Press, Oxford.

Okada, Sadayuki (2002) *Gendaieego no Tooikoozoo: Sono Keesiki to Imi* [Coordinate Structures in Present-Day English: Its Form and Semantic Function], Oosaka-daigaku-Syuppankai, Osaka.

Okamura, Yusuke (1996) "The Grammatical Status of Pure Future 'Will' and the Category of Future Form," *Studia Linguistica* 50(1), 35–49.

Ota, Akira (1998) *Collected Writings: On the Study and Teaching of English*, Kaitaku-sha, Tokyo.

Palmer, Frank, R. (1974) *The English Verb*, Longman, London.

Palmer, Frank, R. (1979) *Modality and the English Modals*, Longman, London.

Palmer, Frank, R. (1986) *Mood and Modality*, Cambridge University Press, Cambridge.

Palmer, Frank, R. (1987) *The English Verb*, 2nd. ed., Longman, London.

Palmer, Frank, R. (1990) *Modality and the English Modals*, 2nd. ed., Longman, London.

Palmer, Frank, R. (2001) *Mood and Modality*, 2nd. ed., Cambridge University Press, Cambridge.

Palmer, Frank, R. (2003) "Modality in English: Theoretical, Descriptive and Typological Issues," *Modality in Contemporary English*, ed. by Roberta Facchinetti, Frank Palmer and Manfred Krug, 1–17, Mouton de Gruyter, Berlin / New York.

Pancheva, Roumyana, and Arnim von Stechow (2004) "On the Present Perfect Puzzle," *Proceedings of the Thirty-Forth Annual Meeting of the North East Linguistic Society*, volume 2, ed. by Keir Moulton and Matthew Wolf, 469–483, GLSA, Amherst.

Panther, Klaus-Uwe and Linda L. Thornburg (1998) "A Cognitive Approach to Inferencing in Conversation," *Journal of Pragmatics* 30(6), 755–769.

Panther, Klaus-Uwe and Linda L. Thornburg (2007) "Metonymy," *The Oxford Handbook of Cognitive Linguistics*, 236–263, Oxford University Press, Oxford.

Papafragou, Anna (1998) "Inference and Word Meaning: The Case of Modal Auxiliaries," *Lingua* 105(1), 1–47.

Papafragou, Anna (2000) "On Speech-Act Modality," *Journal of Pragmatics* 32(5), 519–538.

Papafragou, Anna (2006) "Epistemic Modality and Truth Conditions," *Lingua* 116(10), 1688–1702.

Partee, Barbara H. (1973) "Some Structural Analogies between Tenses and Pronouns in English," *The Journal of Philosophy* 70(18), 601–609.

Partee, Barbara H. (1984) "Nominal and Temporal Anaphora," *Linguistics and Philosophy* 7(3), 243–286.

Patard, Adeline and Frank Brisard, eds. (2011) *Cognitive Approaches to Tense, Aspect, and Epistemic Modality*, John Benjamins, Amsterdam / Philadelphia.

Perkins, Michael R. (1983) *Modal Expressions in English*, Frances Pinter, London.

Porter, Paul (2003) "The (Temporal) Semantics and (Modal) Pragmatics of the Perfect," *Linguistics and Philosophy* 26(4), 459–510.

Prince, Ellen F. (1982) "The Simple Futurate: Not Simply Progressive Futurate Minus Progressive," *CLS* 18, 453–465.

Quirk, Randolph, Sidney Greenbaum, Geoffrey Leech and Jan Svartvik (1985) *A Comprehensive Grammar of the English Language*, Longman, London.

Radden, Günter and René Dirven (2007) *Cognitive English Grammar*, John Benjamins, Amsterdam / Philadelphia.

Reichenbach, Hans (1947) *Elements of Symbolic Logic*, Free Press, New York.

Rescher, Nicholas (1968) *Topics in Philosophical Logic*, Reidel, Dordrecht.

Rigter, Bob (1982) "Intensional Domains and the Use of Tense, Perfect and Modals in English," *Journal of Semantics* 1(2), 95–145.

Rothstein, Björn (2008) *The Perfect Time Span: On the Present Perfect in German, Swedish and English*, John Benjamins, Amsterdam / Philadelphia.

Salkie, Raphael (2009) "Degree of Modality," *Modality in English: Theory and Description*, ed. by Raphael Salkie, Pierre Busuttil and Johan van der Auwera, 79–103, Oxford University Press, Oxford.

Salkie, Raphael (2010) "*Will*: Tense or Modal or Both?" *English Language and Linguistics* 14(2), 187–215.

Sampson, Geoffrey (1971) "Subordinate Future Deletion and Hyperclauses," *Linguistic Inquiry* 2(4), 587–589.

Sarker, Anoop (1998) "The Conflict between Future Tense and Modality: The Case of *Will* in English," *University of Pennsylvania Working Papers in Linguistics* 5(2), 91–117.

Sato, Kenji (2016) "Jookenbun no Kiketusetu niokeru Be Going To ni kansuru Kijututeki Kenkyuu [A Descriptive Study of *Be Going To* in Apodoses of Conditional Sentences]," *Eigo Gohoo Bunpoo Kenkyuu* 23, 143–159.

Sawada, Harumi (1995) *Studies in English and Japanese Auxiliaries: A Multi-Stratal Approach*, Hituzi Syobo, Tokyo.

Sawada, Harumi (2006) *Modarithi* [Modality], Kaitakusha, Tokyo.

Schachter, Paul (1972) "Constraints on Coordination," *Language* 53(1), 86–103.

Schiffrin, Deborah (1981) "Tense Variation in Narrative," *Language* 57, 45–62.

Searle, John (1969) *Speech Acts: An Essay in the Philosophy of Language*, Cambridge University Press, Cambridge.

Searle, John (1975) "Indirect Speech Acts," *Syntax and Semantics* 3: *Speech Acts*, ed. by Peter Cole and Jerry L. Morgan, 59–82, Academic Press, New York.

Searle, John (1979) *Expression and Meaning: Studies in the Theory of Speech Acts*, Cambridge University Press, Cambridge.

Shizawa, Takashi (2013) "Locative Inversion Constructions in English and Their Counterparts in Japanese: From the Viewpoint of Joint Attention and the Three-Tier Model of Language Use," *Tsukuba English Studies* 32, 91–110.

Shizawa, Takashi (2015) "The Rhetorical Effect of Locative Inversion Constructions from the Perspective of the Three-Tier Model of Language Use," *English Linguistics* 32(1), 156–176.

Smith, Aaron K. (2007) "The Development of the English Progressive," *Journal of Germanic Linguistics* 19(3), 205–241.

Smith, Carlota S. (1978) "The Syntax and Interpretation of Temporal Expressions in English," *Linguistics and Philosophy* 2(1), 43–99.

Smith, Carlota S. (1981) "The Futurate Progressive: Not Simply Future + Progressive," *CLS* 17, 369–382.

Smith, Carlota S. (1983) "A Theory of Aspectual Choice," *Language* 59(3), 479–501.

Smith, Carlota S. (1991) *The Parameter of Aspect*, Kluwer Academic, Dordrecht.

Smith, Carlota S. (1997) *The Parameter of Aspect*, 2nd. ed., Kluwer Academic, Dordrecht / Boston / London.

Smith, Carlota S. (2003) *Modes of Discourse: The Local Structure of Texts*, Cambridge University Press, Cambridge.

Smith, Carlota S. (2007) "Tense and Temporal Interpretation," *Lingua* 117(2), 419–436.

Smith, Carlota S. and Mary S. Erbaugh (2005) "Temporal Interpretation in Mandarin Chinese," *Linguistics* 43(4), 713–756.

Sperber, Dan, and Deirdre Wilson (1986) *Relevance: Communication and Cognition*, Blackwell, Oxford.

Stojanovic, Isidora (2014) "Talking about the Future: Unsettled Truth and Assertion," *Future Times, Future Tenses*, ed. by Philippe de Brabanter, Mikhail Kissine and Saghie Sharifzadeh, 26–43, Oxford University Press, Oxford.

Stowell, Tim (2007) "The Syntactic Expression of Tense," *Lingua* 117(2), 437–463.

Stowell, Tim (2012) "Syntax," *The Oxford Handbook of Tense and Aspect*, ed. by Robert I. Binnick, 184–211, Oxford University Press, Oxford.

Swan, Michael (1995) *Practical English Usage*, 2nd. ed., Oxford University Press, Oxford.

Swan, Michael (2005) *Practical English Usage*, 3rd. ed., Oxford University Press, Oxford.

Sweetser, Eve (1988) "Grammaticalization and Semantic Bleaching," *BLS* 14, 389–405.

Sweetser, Eve (1990) *From Etymology to Pragmatics: Metaphorical and Cultural Aspects of Semantic Structure*, Cambridge University Press, Cambridge.

Szmrecsanyi, Benedikt (2003) "BE GOING TO Versus WILL / SHALL: Does Syntax Matter?" *Journal of English Linguistics* 31(4), 295–323.

Tagliamonte, Sali A., Mercedes Durham, and Jennifer Smith (2014) "Grammaticalization at an Early Stage: Future *Be Going To* in Conservative British Dialects," *English Language and Linguistics* 18(1), 75–108.

Talmy, Leonard (1988) "Force Dynamics in Language and Cognition," *Cognitive Science* 12(1), 49–100.

Talmy, Leonard (2000) *Toward a Cognitive Semantics* Volume I: *Concept Structuring Systems*, MIT Press, Cambridge, MA.

Tenny, Carol (1994) *Aspectual Roles and the Syntax-Semantics Interface*, Kluwer Academic Publishers, Dordrecht.

Thompson, Ellen (2005) *Time in Natural Language: Syntactic Interfaces with Semantics and Discourse*, Mouton de Gruyter, Berlin / New York.

Thomson, Audrey J. and Agnes V. Martinet (1986) *A Practical English Grammar*, 4th ed., Oxford University Press, Oxford.

Tomozawa, Hirotaka (2003) "Aspects of the Semantics of the English Participial Construction," *English Linguistics* 20(2), 493–517.

Torres-Cacoullos, Rena and James A. Walker (2009) "The Present of the English Future: Grammatical Variation and Collocations in Discourse," *Language* 85(2), 321–354.

Traugott, Elizabeth C. (1988) "Pragmatic Strengthening and Grammaticalization," *Proceedings of the Fourteenth Annual Meeting of the Berkeley Linguistics Society*, 406–416.

Traugott, Elizabeth C. (1989) "On the Rise of Epistemic Meanings in English: An Example of Subjectification in Semantic Change," *Language* 65(1), 31–55.

Traugott, Elizabeth C. (1995) "Subjectification in Grammaticalisation," *Subjectivity and Subjectivisation: Linguistic Perspectives*, ed. by Dieter Stein and Susan Wright, 31–54, Cambridge University Press, Cambridge.

Traugott, Elizabeth C. (2006) "Historical Aspects of Modality," *The Expression of Modality*, ed. by William Frawley, 107–139, Mouton de Gruyter, Berlin / New York.

Traugott, Elizabeth C. (2010) "(Inter)Subjectivity and (Inter)Subjectification: A Reassessment," *Subjectification, Intersubjectification, and Grammaticalization*, ed. by Kristin Davidse, Lieven Vandelanotte and Hubert Cuyckens, 29–71, Mouton de Gruyter, Berlin / New York.

Traugott, Elizabeth C. and Richard B. Dasher (2002) *Regularity in Semantic Change*, Cambridge University Press, Cambridge.

Tuggy, David (1993) "Ambiguity, Polysemy, and Vagueness," *Cognitive Linguistics* 4(3), 273–290.

Tyler, Andrea, and Hana Jan (2017) "*Be Going To* and *Will*: Talking about the Future Using Embodied Experience," *Language and Cognition* 9, 412–445.

van der Auwera, Johan and Vladimir A. Plungian (1998) "Modality's Semantic Map," *Linguistic Typology* 2, 79–124.

Vandelanotte, Lieven (2009) Speech and Thought Representation in English: A Cognitive-Functional Approach, Mouton de Gruyter, Berlin / New York.

Vendler, Zeno (1967) *Linguistics in Philosophy*, Cornell University Press, Ithaca.

Verstraete, Jean-Christophe (2001) "Subjective and Objective Modality: Interpersonal and Ideational Functions in the English Modal Auxiliary System," *Journal of Pragmatics* 33(10), 1505–1528.

Vetter, David C. (1973) "Someone Solves This Problem Tomorrow," *Linguistic Inquiry* 4(1), 104–108.

von Wright, Georg H. (1951) *An Essay in Modal Logic*, North-Holland, Amsterdam.

Wada, Naoaki (1996) "Does Doc Brown Know Which Expression Takes Us Back to the Future: *Be Going To* or *Will*?" *English Linguistics* 13, 169–198.

References

Wada, Naoaki (2000) "*Be Going To* and *Be About To*: Just Because Doc Brown Was Going to Take Us Back to the Future Does Not Mean That He Was About to Do So," *English Linguistics* 17(2), 386–416.

Wada, Naoaki (2001a) *Interpreting English Tenses: A Compositional Approach*, Kaitakusha, Tokyo.

Wada, Naoaki (2001b) "The Case for the Compositional Tense Theory: A Reply to Declerck," *English Linguistics* 18(2), 428–459.

Wada, Naoaki (2001c) "Eigo no Kanryookee, Nihongo no Kanryookee Sootoohyoogen no Zikankoozoo to Teeziten Fukusirui tono Kyookisee [The (In)Compatibility of the Perfect Form with Adverbials of Definite Time Position in English and Japanese]," *Gengo Kenkyuu* 119, 77–110.

Wada, Naoaki (2006a) "Teekee Doosi Hobu ni Syooziru Hiteekee Doosi no Zisee Kaisyaku [Tense Interpretation of Non-Finite Verbs in the Complement of Finite Verbs]," *Kotoba no Kizuna* [Bonds of Language], ed. by Yuji Ushiro, Kazuaki Ota, Satoshi Ota, Naohiro Takizawa, Shin-ichi Tanaka, Ko-ichi Nishida and Eiji Yamada, 397–410, Kaitakusha, Tokyo.

Wada, Naoaki (2006b) "Kakobunsikee no Ziseekaisyaku no Mekanizumu [The Mechanism of Tense Interpretation of Past Participles]," *Bungei Gengo Kenkyuu: Gengo Hen* [Studies in Language and Literature: Language] 50, 85–128.

Wada, Naoaki (2009a) "The Present Progressive with Future Time Reference vs. *Be Going To*: Is Doc Brown Going Back to the Future Because He Is Going to Reconstruct It?" *English Linguistics* 26(1), 96–131.

Wada, Naoaki (2009b) "'Uti' no Siten / 'Soto' no Siten to Zisee Gensyoo: Nitieigo Taisyookenkyuu ['Inside' Viewpoint and 'Outside' Viewpoint and Tense Phenomena: A Contrastive Study of Japanese and English," *'Uti' to 'Soto' no Gengogaku* [The Linguistics of 'Uti' and 'Soto': Inside and Outside], ed. by Atsuro Tsubomoto, Naoko Hayase and Naoaki Wada, 249–295, Kaitakusha, Tokyo.

Wada, Naoaki (2011a) "On the Mechanism of Temporal Interpretation of *Will*-Sentences," *Tsukuba English Studies* 29, 37–61.

Wada, Naoaki (2011b) "Nitieigo Zisee Gensyoo no Taisyoo Gengogakuteki Bunseki: Jookensetu o Zireekenkyuu tosite [A Contrastive Linguistic Analysis of Tense Phenomena in Japanese and English: A Case Study of Conditional Clauses]," *Bungei Gengo Kenkyuu: Gengo Hen* [Studies in Language and Literature: Language] 60, 107–146.

Wada, Naoaki (2013a) "A Unified Model of Tense and Modality and the Three-Tier Model of Language Use," *Tsukuba English Studies* 32, 29–70.

Wada, Naoaki (2013b) "On the So-Called Future-Progressive Construction," *English Language and Linguistics* 17(3), 391–414.

Wada, Naoaki (2015a) "Eego no San-ninsyoo Syoosetu ni okeru Kakoziseekeesiki no Kaisyaku Mekanizumu [The Mechanism of Interpreting Past Tense Forms in English Third-Person Novels]," *Nintigengogakuronkoo* [Studies in Cognitive Linguistics] 12, 291–335.

Wada, Naoaki (2015b) "Eego no Tanjyungenzaikee no Bunseki Futatabi [An Analysis of the English Simple Present Form: A Revisit]," *Gengokenkyuu no Siza* [Perspectives in Linguistic Research], ed. by Chie Fukada, Ko-ichi Nishida and Toshihiro Tamura, 292–308, Kaitakusha, Tokyo.

Wada, Naoaki (2015c) "Eego no Tanjyungenzaikee no Hookatuteki Bunseki [A Comprehensive Analysis of the English Simple Present Form]," *Zisee narabini Sono Kanrenryooiki to Ninti no Mekanizumu* [Tense and Its Related Areas and the Mechanism of Cognition], ed. by Naoaki Wada and Jun-ya Watanabe, 1–45, TAME Kenkyuukai, University of Tsukuba.

Wada, Naoaki (2017a) "Eego no Miraihyoogen to Yosoku no Modarithi / Dantee no Modarithi [English Future Expressions and Predictive Modality / Assertive Modality]," *JELS* 34, 220–226.

Wada, Naoaki (2017b) "Gengo Siyoo no Sansoo Moderu to Zisee, Modarithi, Syintekitaido [The Three-Tier Model of Language Use and Tense, Modality, and Mental Attitudes]," *Sansoo Moderu de Mietekuru Gengo no Kinoo to Sikumi* [The Functions and Mechanism of Language Revealed by the Three-Tier Model of Language Use], 44–68.

Wada, Naoaki and Jun-ya Watanabe (2016) "*Be Going To* and *Aller*: A Temporal Structure-Based Analysis of 'Go'-Futures in English and French," paper presented at Chronos 12 (Université de Caen, France).

Watanabe, Jun-ya (2014) *Furansugo no Zisee to Modarithi* [Tense and Modality in French], Soobi-Syuppansya, Tokyo.

Watanabe, Takuto (2011) "On the Development of the Immediate Future Use of *Be About To* in the History of English with Special Reference to Late Modern English," *English Linguistics* 28(1), 56–90.

Wekker, Herman Chr. (1976) *The Expression of Future Time in Contemporary British English*, North-Holland, Amsterdam.

Werner, Tom (2005) "The Temporal Interpretation of Some Modal Sentences in English (Involving a Future/Epistemic Alternation)," *Crosslinguistic Views on Tense, Aspect and Modality*, ed. by Bart Hollebrandse, Angeliek van Hout and Co Vet, 247–259, Rodopi, Amsterdam / New York.

Werner, Valentin, Elena Seoane and Cristina Suárez-Gómez, ed. (2016) *Re-Assessing the Present Perfect*, Mouton de Gruyter, Berlin / Boston.

Whittaker, Sidney F. (1983) "The Future Progressive: An Experimental Approach," *International Review of Applied Linguistics in Language Teaching* 21(2), 145–154.

Williams, Christopher (2002a) *Non-Progressive and Progressive Aspect in English*, Schena Editore, Fasano.

Williams, Christopher (2002b) "Non-Progressive Aspect in English in Commentaries and Demonstrations Using the Present Tense," *Journal of Pragmatics* 34, 1235–1256.

Wolfson, Nessa (1979) "The Conversational Historical Present Alternation," *Language* 55, 168–182.

Wright, Susan (1994) "The Mystery of the Modal Progressive," *Studies in Early Modern English*, ed. by Dieter Kastovsky, 467–485, Mouton de Gruyter, Berlin / New York.

Wright, Susan (1995) "Subjectivity and Experiential Syntax," *Subjectivity and Subjecti-*

visation: Linguistic Perspectives*, ed. by Dieter Stein and Susan Wright, 151–172, Cambridge University Press, Cambridge.

Yamaguchi, Haruhiko (2009) *Meisekina In-yoo, Sinayakana In-yoo* [Explicit Quotation and Flexible Quotation], Kurosio, Tokyo.

Yamanashi, Masa-aki (1999) *Nintigengogaku Genri* [Principles of Cognitive Linguistics], Kurosio, Tokyo.

Zhu, Jing (2004) "Intention and Volition," *Canadian Journal of Philosophy* 34(2), 175–194.

Ziegeler, Debra (1996) "A Synchronic Perspective on the Grammaticalization of *Will* in Hypothetical Predicates," *Studies in Language* 20(2), 411–442.

Ziegeler, Debra (2006) "Omnitemporal *Will*," *Language Sciences* 28, 76–119.

Dictionaries

Crowther, Jonathan et al. (1995) *Oxford Advanced Learner's Dictionary*, 5th. ed., Oxford University Press, Oxford.

Sinclair, John et al. (2006) *Collins COBUILD Advanced Learner's English Dictionary*, 5th. ed., HarperCollins, Glasgow.

Index

Name Index

Binnick, R. 41, 231, 233

Boogaart, R. 9, 100, 111

Boyd, J. and J. Thorne 61, 134, 158

Brisard, F. 134–136, 202, 254

Bybee, J., R. Perkins and W. Pagliuca 61–63, 69–70, 102, 172, 197

Calver, E. 296

Celle, A. (and N. Smith) 64, 69, 140, 177, 179, 182–183, 364

Chafe, W. 28–29, 341

Close, R. 70, 129, 151, 163, 170, 302, 318

Coates, J. 46, 60, 71, 128–129, 136, 141–142, 156, 224, 363

Collins, P. 39, 125, 151, 155, 192–193, 224

Comrie, B. 1, 4, 9, 42–43

Copley, B. 12–13, 89, 111, 164, 179, 220, 235, 238, 243, 255, 281, 299–300

Cutrer, M. 13

Dancygier, B. (and E. Sweetser) 13, 90, 128–129, 164, 168–169, 237

De Brabanter, P., M,. Kissine and S.

Sharifzadeh 30, 188–189

Declerck, R. 1–5, 8–10, 14, 22, 26–27, 96, 107, 140, 151, 185, 187, 242, 271, 304–306, 320, 332, 358–359

Declerck, R. and S. Reed 164, 169–170

Depraetere, I. 97, 127, 133, 374

De Wit, A. 41–42

De Wit, A. and F. Brisard 42, 254, 260

De Wit, A. and A. Patard 261

Dowty, D. 30, 254, 263, 299

Duffley, P. 27, 131, 194, 331

Enç, M. 2

Fleischman, S. 98, 106, 148, 297, 339

Goldsmith, J. and E. Woistschlaeger 103, 254, 258

Goodman, F. 275, 280, 299–300

Grice, P. 73, 88, 181, 243, 382

Haegeman, L. 37, 59, 133–134, 136, 139, 141, 145–146, 164, 171, 191, 202

Halliday, M. 63, 65–66, 136

Heine, B. 38, 40, 60, 175
Hilpert, M. 172, 212
Hirose, Y. 17, 59, 74–79, 144, 242, 384
Hirtle, W. 31, 373
Hirtle, W. and V. Curat 314
Hopper, P. 322
Hopper, P. and E. Traugott 120, 194, 201, 214, 225
Huddleston, R. 4, 38
Huddleston, R. and G. Pullum 6, 8, 10, 27, 41, 141, 147, 328–329

Janssen, T. 4, 9
Jaszczolt, K. 13, 29–30, 69, 88, 128, 141

Kashino, K. 212, 217, 267
Killie, K. 257, 261, 357
Kranich, S. 254, 261
Kytö, M. 141, 320

Lakoff, G. 374, 381
Lakoff, R. 126, 136, 183
Langacker, R. 30, 32, 39, 55, 62, 74, 100, 104, 106, 134, 197, 243, 257, 260, 263, 330, 346, 368
Leech, G. 83, 98, 100, 125, 128, 134, 139, 141–142, 157–158, 161, 193, 209, 227, 267, 269, 277, 300, 302–303, 359, 376, 382
Lyons, J. 2, 46, 63–65, 72, 84, 91, 136, 165

Nakau, M. 3–4, 9–10, 41, 46, 62, 66, 148
Nesselhauf, N. 172, 261
Nicolle, S. 87–88

Nuyts, J. 60, 62, 67, 69, 88

Palmer, F. 47, 60–61, 64, 68, 70, 80, 134, 138, 151, 156, 158, 164
Panther, K. and L. Thornburg 225, 266, 384
Perkins, M. 60, 64, 68, 322, 325
Prince, E. 104, 263, 272, 339

Reichenbach, H. 7–9, 96

Salkie, R. 126, 141, 176, 362–364
Sato, K. 235, 239
Sawada, H. 62, 66, 134, 148, 362–364
Searle, J. 58, 67, 81, 84, 169
Smith, C. 10, 32, 41–43, 50, 177, 186, 264

Talmy, L. 244
Torres-Cacoullos, R. and J. Walker 126, 134, 267
Traugott, E. 68, 193–194, 222, 225–226, 325
Tyler, A. and H. Jan 202

Vendler, Z. 41, 372
Verstraete, J. 63–65, 67, 90

Wekker, C. 154, 227–229, 231, 238–239, 299, 314, 372, 375, 386
Williams, C. 6, 100, 111, 217, 223, 254, 264, 269, 276, 286, 293, 361–362, 372, 386

Ziegeler, D. 138, 144–145, 165, 172–173

Subject Index

about 325, 329

A(bsolute tense)-component 24–25

absolute tense form 24–25, 28–29, 48–49, 185–186, 195–196

A(bsolute tense)-morpheme 24–26, 28, 57–58, 189, 195

"already decided" reading 364–365, 371, 375, 385

anterior reading 23, 43–44

aspect 41–46
  imperfective (aspect) 7, 41–42, 100, 218, 262–264, 358, 368, 371, 377, 379
  perfective (aspect) 7, 41–44, 100, 264–265, 371, 377, 379
  situation aspect / type (Aktionsart) 41–44
  viewpoint (grammatical) aspect 13, 41

assertable time range 310, 332, 344–345

assertion (opposite notion of presupposition) / asserted part 10, 58, 90, 278, 303–305

assertion (as speech act) 49, 58, 64, 70–73, 81–82, 169–171
  restriction on assertion 49, 105, 111, 258, 296, 306, 308, 310, 312–313, 317

assertive modality 17–18, 45–49, 57–59, 69–74, 77–78, 81–82, 85–93, 105, 107, 134, 140, 143, 151–154, 158, 161, 167, 173, 180, 198–199, 203–206, 216, 224, 229, 236–240, 250, 258, 261, 266, 280. 286, 296–298, 301, 303–304, 308, 312–314, 317, 331–332, 385–388, 394

backgrounding (of the private self) 143–145, 167

bare infinitive, *see* infinitive

base point in time / base time 2–3, 7, 9, 22–23, 26–27, 29, 32–35

(be) about to 14, 64, 192, 325–329

be about to (BAT)-sentences 319–353
  basic temporal structure of, *see* temporal structure
  basic temporal structure in the past tense 333
  basic temporal structure in the present tense 330–331

be going to 13–14, 39–40, 53, 64, 125, 140, 188, 191–198, 202, 204–205, 208–210, 222–223, 226–227, 236, 244, 271, 278, 320, 325–327, 319
  inferential *be going to* 193, 226

be going to (BGT)-sentences 191–251, 265–266, 269–291, 320–338, 341–344, 348–350
  basic temporal structure of, *see* temporal structure
  basic use 198–203
  bleached-coda use 213–216, 219, 228–229, 245–246, 288, 338, 342–343, 350
  bleached-onset use 214–216, 225–226, 245
  future-condition use 236–240
  immediate-future use 193, 210–212, 225, 245, 248, 334
  inferential-present use 219, 222–224, 226
  reference to near future 207–208, 227–229
  ongoingness of, *see* ongoing(ness)
  past tense 241–249, 341–344
  predictability use 193, 219–221, 226
  predictive-future use 193, 202–210, 225
  reference to remote future 227–228

speech act use 224–225, 239
simple-future use 193, 216–219, 225–226, 228–229, 236–238, 248–249, 272, 302, 338
typical use 202–211, 224–225, 228, 230–234, 241, 247, 282–283, 325, 334, 350
volitional use 193, 202–210, 225, 229–231, 244–248

can 4, 38, 58, 60–61, 88, 363
categorical assertion 72–73
coda 197–198, 212–216, 225, 228–229, 245–247, 272, 288, 338, 342–343
cognitive linguistic approach / analysis 11, 13, 15, 120
cognitive schema 15–16, 100, 102, 115, 117–118
cognitive shift (coercion) 262–263, 267–268, 273, 345–348, 351
cognitive time (information) 3, 11, 21–24, 28–29
command (as speech act) 61, 285–286, 383–385
commitment 67–73, 85, 90–92
compositionality 15, 250, 325, 394
compositional theory of tense 16, 21–55
comprehensiveness 15–16
conditional clause 89–91, 136, 163–171
Type A conditional clause 164–168, 173, 193, 204, 234–240, 282–286, 306, 363
Type B conditional clause 164–166, 169–171, 235, 240–241
construction grammar approach / analysis 11, 13–14
conversational text(s) 323, 334, 341–351
current-relevance effect 111–112
current speaker 85–92, 138, 141–151, 161–162, 170–171, 224, 230

deictic center 2–4, 24–26, 28
deictic interpretation 34–35, 49, 178–179
deontic modality / modal 60–68, 80, 83–84, 138, 172, 224
descriptive approach / analysis 11–12, 62, 96
desire 61, 168, 172–173
director 111, 255, 276, 279–281, 290, 299–301
double-access reading 184
durative present 10, 31, 102, 104, 157, 159
dynamic modality / modal 47, 60–61, 63–68, 87–89, 138, 141, 147, 193

elliptical / ellipticality 231–233
epistemic modality / modal 60–70, 80, 83, 88, 126, 129, 134–135, 147, 155–156, 165, 170, 172, 183, 193, 362–364
epistemic will 136, 156, 223, 362
evaluation time 7–9
event time
    event-time calculation / computation / evaluation 32–33, 50
    event time (in my use) 7–10, 23–27, 30–34, 36–37, 50–51
    event time (in the sense of Reichenbach) 7–9
    orientational event time 50–51, 152–153, 216, 220, 222, 249, 258, 261, 303, 329–330, 332–333, 344–345, 368–369
evidentiality 65, 67–69, 73, 93

finite form / verb 4–6, 9–11, 14, 24–25, 48, 57–58
foregrounding (of the private self) 145, 167
formal semantic(s) approach / analysis 2, 6, 11–13, 235
framing effect 357, 369, 380
French 24–25, 112, 126–128, 176–188

Index 421

fusion of the speaker's t(emporal)-view-point and consciousness 28–32

future orientation 53, 146, 148, 174, 188, 219, 224, 227, 231, 302

trace of future orientation 213, 216–224, 226, 237

future progressive, *see* WBI (*will + be + ~ing*)-sentences and *will be ~ing*

future tense marker (auxiliary) 1, 57–58, 96, 126–129, 151, 176, 181, 183, 362, 364

future verification 183, 222, 224, 364

generative syntactic approach / analysis 12–13

generic use
 generic-present use 97, 101–103, 120, 157
 W-generic use 157–160, 172, 220–221

gerund 6, 25, 27–28, 45

grammaticalization 13, 16, 38, 54, 63, 120, 127, 168, 172–175, 194–196, 214, 218–220, 225–228, 236, 262–263, 267, 325, 338, 366, 389

grammatical time (information / value) 3, 5–6, 11, 21–22, 24–26, 28

habitual use
 habitual-present use 97, 101–104, 120, 157
 W-habitual use 157–160, 172

high probability 4, 17, 134–137, 140–141, 152, 155, 158, 188, 205, 280, 364

illocutionary point / force(s) 58, 67, 79–81, 84, 93, 144, 158

indirect speech (complement) 23, 34–36, 44, 49–50, 76–77, 81–86, 91–92, 183–187

infinitive

A-infinitive 325–333, 335, 338, 345, 347, 352

bare-infinitive 4, 6, 25, 27, 48–49, 53, 126, 130–133, 137, 139–140, 148, 186, 194–196, 218, 325

to-infinitive 6, 25, 27, 320, 325–331

in progress, *see* ongoing(ness)

insistence 128, 141–142, 144

instruction (as speech act) 129, 162–163, 224–225

intention 61, 67, 128, 138, 141–142, 146, 172, 193, 239, 242, 271, 276–279, 282, 320, 367, 384

intend 130, 209

invitation 83–84, 171

Japanese 6–7, 74–78, 83

linguistic environment(s) 5, 33–35, 48–50, 88–91, 100, 106–107, 131, 164–168, 180–181, 185–186

Maxim of Manner 382

Maxim of Quality 73

Maxim of Quantity 181, 243

may 4, 38, 58, 64, 80–82, 127, 131–132, 137, 172, 363, 395

mental space approach / analysis 13

mental world 139, 142–146, 149, 169, 231, 254, 311, 313–314

metaphorical extension 194, 197

metonymic extension 194

metonymy 194, 202, 266–268

modal adjective 68

modal adverb 47, 60, 72, 135–136, 155, 363

modal *will* 3–4, 18, 47, 50–51, 57–58, 127, 130–132

modal noun 60, 64, 68

modally unmarked form, *see* unmodalized

form

momentary present 10

monosemous approach 62, 119, 127, 146–147, 165, 175

Moore's Paradox 91

must 38, 58, 60–61, 63–64, 69, 83, 131–132, 156, 172, 362

narrative(s)

descriptive narrative part(s) 322–324, 334, 338–344, 348–351

narrative now 106, 248, 343, 348–350

scene description part(s) 340–343

third-person past-form narrative(s) 31, 106–107, 247–248 323, 338, 341–342, 344

narrator 106–107, 243, 248, 338–343, 349

non-compositional semantic approach / analysis 11, 14

non-deictic interpretation 34–35, 49

non-finite form / verb 4–6, 9–11, 25, 27, 37. 108, 110, 130, 177, 182

non-stative situation(s) 42–44, 99–100, 132, 182, 305, 310, 338, 368, 386

objective modality 63–64

objective use (of modality) 63, 84–87, 157

objectivity 59, 63–64, 68, 93

offer (as speech act) 134, 161, 179, 383–385

ongoing(ness) / in progress 104–106, 193–194, 197–198, 200–208, 228–230, 258–269, 282–284, 317, 356–357, 360–361, 365–381

onset 197–198, 214–216, 245, 330–333, 335–337, 344–351

order (as speech act) 129, 162–163, 224–225, 285–286

past context(s) 49, 243–248, 290–292, 395

past-in-the-future 31–32, 35–36, 48

past participle (marker / morpheme) 6, 9–10, 25, 27, 39, 43, 45–46, 108–118, 131, 185, 219

past progressive futurate sentences 288–291

perfect aspect / form 45, 108, 110–111, 218, 363

perfect *have* 9, 40, 45, 108–116, 126, 131, 155, 218–219, 258–259

performative sentence 7

performativity

modal performativity 64–65, 67, 88

performativity in general sense 65, 67–68, 73

perspective

of the character 340

of the narrator 323, 339–340

of the (original) speaker 34–36

polysemous approach 62, 127, 147

polysemous relationship 118–120, 133, 374

posterior reading 43–44, 49–50, 131–132

potential speaker 75–76, 84–85, 138, 142, 170–171, 183, 207, 229, 244

potential world 131

pragmatic strengthening 173, 175, 225, 291

predetermination 364–365, 368

predictability 128–129, 151, 157–160, 193, 219–221, 223, 226

prediction 47–48, 50, 58, 70–71, 81, 128–129, 134, 145–151, 157–158, 168, 172–174, 184–185, 193, 199. 203–204, 241, 245, 248–249, 300, 372, 383–386

predictive modality 17, 46–48, 69–71, 93, 126–129, 145–157, 161–168, 179–181, 184–186, 190, 204–205, 224, 232, 236, 239–240, 363–367, 375, 379, 385–388

predictive overtones / nuances 221, 224,

237–238

preliminary stage 197–216 228–241, 245–248, 265–266, 271–282, 334, 338. 342–345, 348–350

prolonged preliminary stage 228

(semantically) bleached preliminary stage 212, 217, 220–221, 236–237, 256, 282

present orientation 53, 205, 231, 386

present participle (marker / morpheme) 5–6, 25, 27, 219, 257–260, 262, 264, 266, 271, 287, 328, 366–368, 379–380

present perfect (form) 9, 98, 108–118, 374

completive use 108–110, 113–116

continuative use 43, 45, 108–110, 116–117

experiential use 108–110, 114–117

habitual use 108–110, 117–118

perfective in the criterion to subdivide the uses of 109–110, 113–115

present state 112–118

present progressive (form / sentences) 253–292, 328, 361

aspectual (normal) use 259–264, 287

basic temporal structure of, *see* temporal structure

future time reference 269–270, 282–287

tense structure 256–257

present progressive futurate sentences (PPF-sentences) 253–286, 299–301, 366, 370–372, 385–388

basic temporal structure, *see* temporal structure

future-condition use 284–286

immediate-future use 269, 274–275

speech act use / meaning 260, 285–286

typical use 274–275, 282–283, 286

present scene 311–314

pre-stage 264–286, 289–291, 369–378, 382–383, 388–389

(semantically) bleached pre-stage 283–286

presupposition / presupposed part 58, 90, 236, 266, 277–278, 282, 286, 305–306, 342, 370, 372, 375

private expression 76–81, 84–86, 170–171, 183, 186

private self 76–77, 79–80, 84–87, 141–146, 157, 161–162, 170–171, 186, 207, 229–230, 244, 304, 308, 339

private-self-centered language 76

probability 70, 82, 135–137, 141, 172, 174, 240, 271

probably 82, 135–136, 155, 271, 336, 363

proclivity 172, 174

profile shift 263, 330, 344

progressive aspect / form 42, 44, 194–195, 197, 213–214, 218, 253–254, 258, 260, 262–263, 268–269, 337–338, 356, 359, 361–363, 366–368, 371, 377, 379–380

progressive *be* 40, 50, 126, 219, 257–262, 265, 271, 287

promise (as speech act) 134, 161–162, 179

proposition (P) domain 17, 47, 65–67, 79, 87–88, 138, 140–144

prototype theory 38, 62

public expression 76–81

public self 76, 79–80, 85–86, 138, 142–143, 145, 157, 170–171, 243, 248, 304, 339

public-self-centered language 76

reference time / point of reference 7–9

refusal (as speech act) 285–286, 338

R(elative tense)-component 24–25

relative tense form 24–27

R(elative tense)-morpheme 25–27

relevance-theoretic approach / analysis 12, 15, 62, 119, 176, 242

request 62, 383–385

resultant state 45–46, 111–115

SD-viewpoint (viewpoint of situation
    description) 32–36, 48, 339–343
semantic bleaching 151, 197, 212, 214,
    285, 325, 389
semantic (de)composition of sentential
    utterances 65–68, 71, 73, 78, 165
semantic retention 54, 134, 168, 197, 226
semantic unit 195, 325, 327, 329
should 61, 126, 183
simple future (in French) 176–188, 222
    basic temporal structure 177–180
    compatibility with present time
        adverbials 181–182
    present time reference 177–179, 182–
        183
    in complement clauses 185–187
simple present (form / sentences) 96–108,
    293–318
    basic temporal structure of, *see* temporal
        structure
    either-or use 310–311, 313–314
    fixed-future use 296–301
    future-reference-in-subordinate-clause use
        303–306
    generic-present use, *see* present use
    habitual-present use, *see* habitual use
    historical-present use 31, 48, 97–98,
        105–107, 119, 315–316, 352
    immediate-future use 308–310
    instantaneous-present use 99–100
    instruction-giving use 310–312
    "note" use 307–308
    performative-present use 100, 104–105,
        107
    simple-future use 301–303
    simple present in temporal clauses 180–
        181, 305
    stage-direction use 314–317

stative-present use 99–101
structural-description use 100, 103–104
simple futurate in the present tense / simple
    present futurate (SFP-sentences) 293–
    301
simultaneous reading 23, 43, 100, 132
situation
    be going to-situation 198, 200, 202
    controllable situation 150–151, 193, 276,
        280–281, 372, 382, 388
    general (non-specific) situation 36, 102,
        104, 110, 114, 117, 158
    infinitival situation 51, 128, 132, 139–
        141, 146–158, 175, 182, 184, 193–194,
        197–249, 266, 269, 271–272, 276–277,
        282, 288, 302–306, 323–324, 329–338,
        341–351
        fulfillment of 242, 245, 247, 323–
            324, 338, 341–343, 347–350
        non-fulfillment of 241–242, 245–247,
            288, 324, 338, 341–344, 347–350
    ongoing situation 286, 356, 360, 368,
        379
    past participle situation 112–118
    present participle situation 257–267,
        269–278, 284, 288, 358 368–369, 378
schematic situation 36, 39, 50, 53, 101,
    111–112, 116, 132, 216, 225, 259, 265,
    271, 277, 328, 370, 376
    semantically bleached situation 39, 50,
        153, 201, 262, 265, 328, 331, 346,
        370, 380
    specific situation 38, 50–52, 101–102,
        104, 109, 113–116, 148, 157, 193, 257,
        259, 290, 297, 303–307, 309, 312,
        316–317, 368
    superordinate situation 102–104, 115–
        118, 157–160, 173–174, 220–222, 311–
        314
situation construal 66, 71, 74–78, 129

situation construal (SC) tier   17, 75–87, 134, 138, 140, 143, 145, 148–151, 161–163, 224, 258, 260, 286, 384

situation report (communication)   65–66, 74–81

situation report (SR) tier   17, 75–87, 90–91, 142–146, 161–163, 170–171, 224–225, 230, 243, 286, 384

sloppy simultaneity / simultaneous   5, 140, 305–306, 332–333

speaker's consciousness   28–30, 66, 98

speaker's (mental) attitude(s)   17, 58–59, 65–69

   addressee-oriented mental attitude(s) of the speaker / speaker's A-attitude(s)   17, 66–69, 79–85

   situation-oriented mental attitude(s) of the speaker / speaker's S-attitude(s)   17, 66–92

speaker's attitude (SA) domain   17, 65–73

   addressee-oriented speaker's attitude domain (ASA domain)   17, 67, 69, 73, 78–81, 90–92, 165, 169–170

   situation-oriented speaker's attitude domain (SSA domain)   17, 67, 69, 71, 73, 89–92, 169–170, 240

speaker's t(emporal)-viewpoint   26, 28–36, 98–99, 105–106

speech act(s)   11, 16–17, 48, 57–67, 71, 74, 79–84, 134, 160–163, 169–171, 179, 224–225, 239, 260, 285–286, 384–385

speech act theory   58, 62, 74, 134

speech time   2–10, 23, 28–35

state / stative verbs / predicates   10, 42–44, 100, 132, 214, 228–229, 272, 359, 377, 382, 388

stative situation(s)   26, 42–44, 132, 157, 175, 182–183, 212, 214, 218, 222, 225, 272, 305, 338

stativity   174–175, 212

still   365

structure of the world (world structure)   103–104, 258, 294–301, 316, 372, 377

   WS (world structure)-characterizing situation   297–302

subjectification   74, 168, 174

subjective modality   63–64, 85

subjectivity   12, 59–60, 63–65, 68, 82, 87

subjective use (of modality)   84–87

superordinate situation, *see* situation

systematicity   15–16

temporal clause   89–91, 167, 180–181, 303–305, 395

temporal focus (TF)   51–53, 100–102, 104, 107, 112–118, 140–142, 148–152, 155–156, 169, 174–175, 205. 209–210, 216, 223, 248–249, 260, 263, 266, 277–278, 289–291, 296, 304–307, 309, 311–314, 316, 331, 346–347, 367–368, 371, 380

   temporal focus (TF) drop   174

   temporal focus (TF) shift   174, 289–291

   temporal focus (TF) restoring   174

temporal path   194, 196–199, 202, 208–210, 212–214, 245, 302, 331, 338

temporal structure   17, 22–24, 28, 33–36, 51–55, 95–120, 127, 171–175, 295–317, 325–330, 393

   basic temporal structure   29–30, 98, 110–111, 130–133, 177–178, 192–201, 256–269, 330–333

temporal subordination   304–305

temporal value   3–6, 11, 21–24

tense

   absolute tense (in the general sense)   2

   definition of   1–2

   future tense   1

   inflection   1, 6, 24, 58, 126, 128, 177, 189, 328

   marker / auxiliary   1, 4

past tense 1

present tense 1

relative tense (in the general sense) 2

tense form choice / choice of tense form
2–3, 22–23, 32–35, 48, 50, 111

tense interpretation 11, 21–24, 26–32

tense interpretation (TI) level 21–22

tense structure 21–29, 98, 108, 130–132,
177–178, 194–196, 256–257, 296, 392–
393

tense structure (TS) level 21–22

theory of modality and the speaker's mental
attitudes 17, 65–73

theory of public / private self and public /
private expression 75

threat (as speech act) 134, 161, 237, 239

Three-Tier Model (of Language Use) 17,
57, 59, 73–78, 84, 87, 93, 339, 394

time adverbial 36–37

future time adverbial 37

past time adverbial 31

present time adverbial 37

time-area

future time-area 29–31

past time-area 29–31

present-time-area 29–31

time-gap reading 43–44

time of narration 31–32, 106–107, 243,
248–249, 339, 343, 345, 349

time of orientation 7–10, 23, 26–27, 32,
34, 42–46

potential time of orientation 26–27, 48,
110, 130, 189, 330

time schema-based semantic approach /
analysis 12, 14

time-sphere

future time-sphere 178–183

past time-sphere 26, 29, 32, 246, 311

present time-sphere 26, 31–32, 58, 105–
106, 110–111, 130, 179–180, 257–

258, 263–264, 297, 307, 311, 316,
332

to 25, 27, 194–197, 208–210, 331

to-infinitive, *see* infinitive

unmodalized clause / form / sentence 47, 49,
70–74, 78, 81, 87–92, 105, 180, 186–
187, 203, 296, 306, 308, 317, 331

verbal unit 39–40, 194–197

volition 47, 50, 54, 67, 126, 128–129, 134,
138–148, 150–151, 161, 169, 172–174,
193, 203, 209, 229–231, 241–245, 249,
276, 358, 367, 375, 382–386

volitional nuances / overtones 144–148, 150,
167–168, 207, 210, 241, 246, 248

volitional reading 146–147, 156, 163–168,
173–174, 207, 229–230, 367, 380, 382

want 141, 209

WBI (*will* + *be* + ~*ing*)-sentences 355–389

future-as-a-matter-of-course use 356–
366, 368–378, 381, 385

future-progressive use 356–361, 364–
369, 373–374, 378, 380–381

inferential present-progressive use 356,
360–362, 366, 373–374, 379–381

will 3–4, 53–54, 58, 125–190, 355–389

future *will*, *see* future tense marker (auxiliary)

omnitemporal *will* 172

volitional *will* 87, 129, 138, 140, 165–
168

will be ~*ing* 14, 219, 287, 355

will-sentences 125–190, 227–249, 381–
385

basic temporal structure of, *see* temporal
structure

bleached situation of 152–153

characteristic-behavior use 157–158,

172–174

future time reference use   129, 133, 139, 148, 178, 188, 381–385

immediate-future use   179, 181–182, 210–212

past tense   241–249

predictive-future use   128, 145–150, 152, 154–155, 162–163, 167–168, 172–175, 229, 232, 238, 240, 248, 362, 367

predictive-present use   128, 154–157, 173, 175

P-volitional use   167–169, 173

simple-future use   128, 147, 149, 151–154, 172–175, 225–226, 228–229, 248–249, 302–303

speech act use   134, 160–163, 169–170, 179

volitional use   128, 138–149, 151, 161, 167, 202–204, 207, 229, 244, 382–384

will-sentences in indirect speech complements, *see* indirect speech (complement)

willingness   67, 141–142, 172–173

would   4, 130, 193, 242

The Grammar of Future Expressions in English

著作者　和田尚明
発行者　武村哲司
印刷所　日之出印刷株式会社

2019 年 11 月 27 日　第 1 版第 1 刷発行

発行所　株式会社　開拓社

〒 113-0023 東京都文京区向丘 1-5-2
電話　（03）5842-8900（代表）
振替　00160-8-39587
http://www.kaitakusha.co.jp

ISBN978-4-7589-2275-3　C3082

JCOPY ＜出版者著作権管理機構 委託出版物＞

本書の無断複製は，著作権法上での例外を除き禁じられています．複製される場合は，そのつど事前に，出版者著作権管理機構（電話 03-3513-6969, FAX 03-3513-6979, e-mail: info@jcopy.or.jp）の許諾を得てください．